Walt Disney's

UNCLE $CROOGE

by Carl Barks

Publisher and Executive Editor: GARY GROTH
Senior Editor: J. MICHAEL CATRON
Color Editor: JASON T. MILES
Colorist: RICH TOMMASO
Series Design: JACOB COVEY
Volume Design: KEELI McCARTHY
Production: PAUL BARESH
Editorial Consultant: DAVID GERSTEIN
Associate Publisher: ERIC REYNOLDS

- - - - - - - - - - - - - - - - - - - -

Fantagraphics Books, Inc.
7563 Lake City Way NE
Seattle WA 98115
(800) 657-1100

Visit us at fantagraphics.com. Follow us on Twitter at @fantagraphics
and on Facebook at facebook.com/fantagraphics.

Special thanks to Thomas Jensen, Kim Weston, Peter Barks Kylling, and Pedro Peirano Olate.

First printing, July 2017
ISBN 978-1-68396-013-3

Printed in Korea
Library of Congress Control Number: 2016961043

Now available in this series:
Walt Disney's Donald Duck: "Christmas on Bear Mountain" (Vol. 5)
Walt Disney's Donald Duck: "The Old Castle's Secret" (Vol. 6)
Walt Disney's Donald Duck: "Lost in the Andes" (Vol. 7)
Walt Disney's Donald Duck: "Trail of the Unicorn" (Vol. 8)
Walt Disney's Donald Duck: "The Pixilated Parrot" (Vol. 9)
Walt Disney's Donald Duck: "Terror of the Beagle Boys" (Vol. 10)
Walt Disney's Donald Duck: "A Christmas for Shacktown" (Vol. 11)
Walt Disney's Uncle Scrooge: "Only a Poor Old Man" (Vol. 12)
Walt Disney's Donald Duck: "Trick or Treat" (Vol. 13)
Walt Disney's Uncle Scrooge: "The Seven Cities of Gold" (Vol. 14)
Walt Disney's Donald Duck: "The Ghost Sheriff of Last Gasp" (Vol. 15)
Walt Disney's Uncle Scrooge: "The Lost Crown of Genghis Khan" (Vol. 16)

WALT DISNEP'S

UNCLE $CROOGE

"The Lost Crown of Genghis Khan"

----

by Carl Barks

FANTAGRAPHICS BOOKS
SEATTLE

Contents

All comics stories written and drawn by Carl Barks.

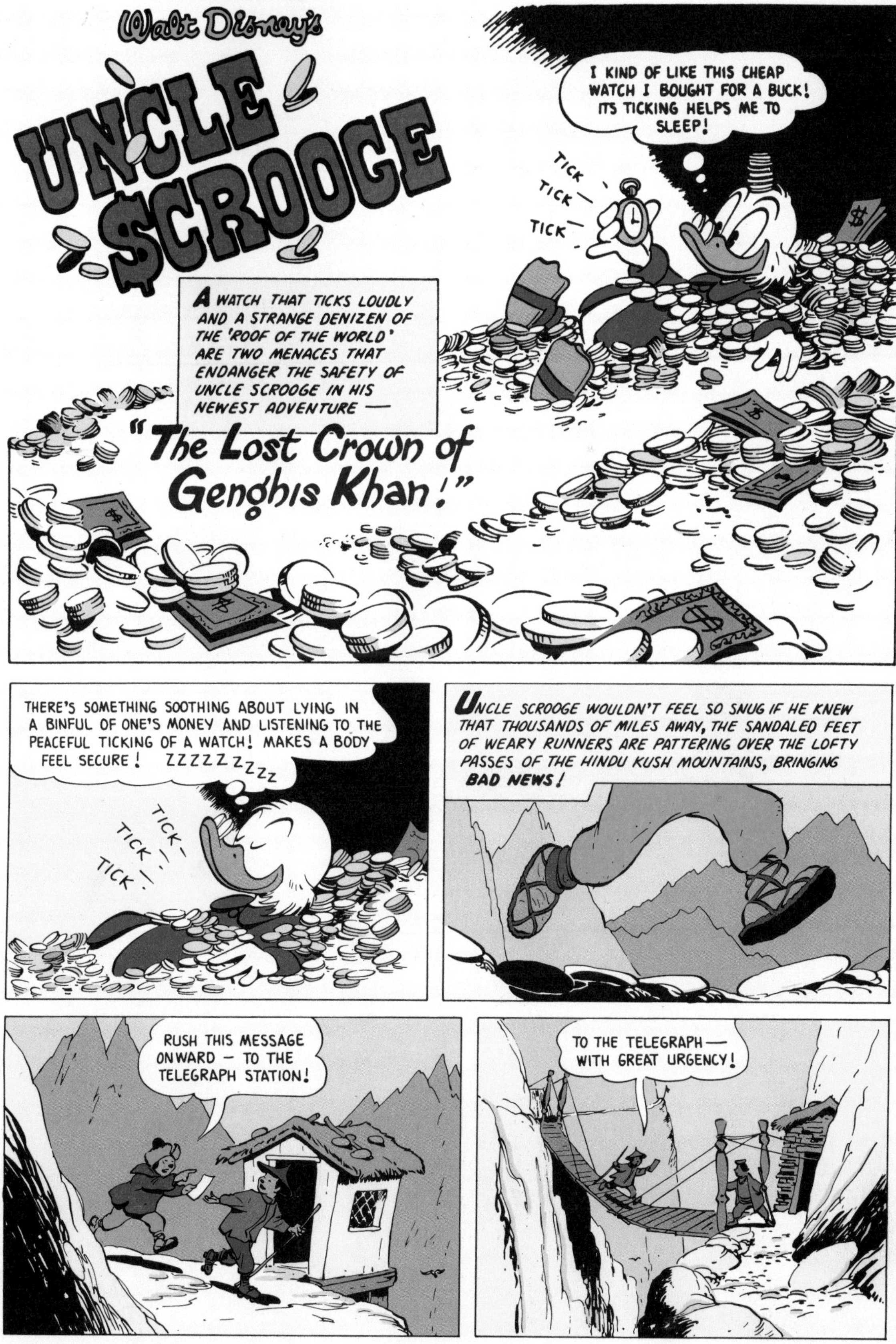
Walt Disney's
UNCLE $CROOGE
I KIND OF LIKE THIS CHEAP WATCH I BOUGHT FOR A BUCK! ITS TICKING HELPS ME TO SLEEP!
TICK TICK TICK
A WATCH THAT TICKS LOUDLY AND A STRANGE DENIZEN OF THE 'ROOF OF THE WORLD' ARE TWO MENACES THAT ENDANGER THE SAFETY OF UNCLE SCROOGE IN HIS NEWEST ADVENTURE —
"The Lost Crown of Genghis Khan!"
THERE'S SOMETHING SOOTHING ABOUT LYING IN A BINFUL OF ONE'S MONEY AND LISTENING TO THE PEACEFUL TICKING OF A WATCH! MAKES A BODY FEEL SECURE! ZZZZZZZZZ
TICK TICK TICK
UNCLE SCROOGE WOULDN'T FEEL SO SNUG IF HE KNEW THAT THOUSANDS OF MILES AWAY, THE SANDALED FEET OF WEARY RUNNERS ARE PATTERING OVER THE LOFTY PASSES OF THE HINDU KUSH MOUNTAINS, BRINGING BAD NEWS!
RUSH THIS MESSAGE ONWARD — TO THE TELEGRAPH STATION!
TO THE TELEGRAPH — WITH GREAT URGENCY!

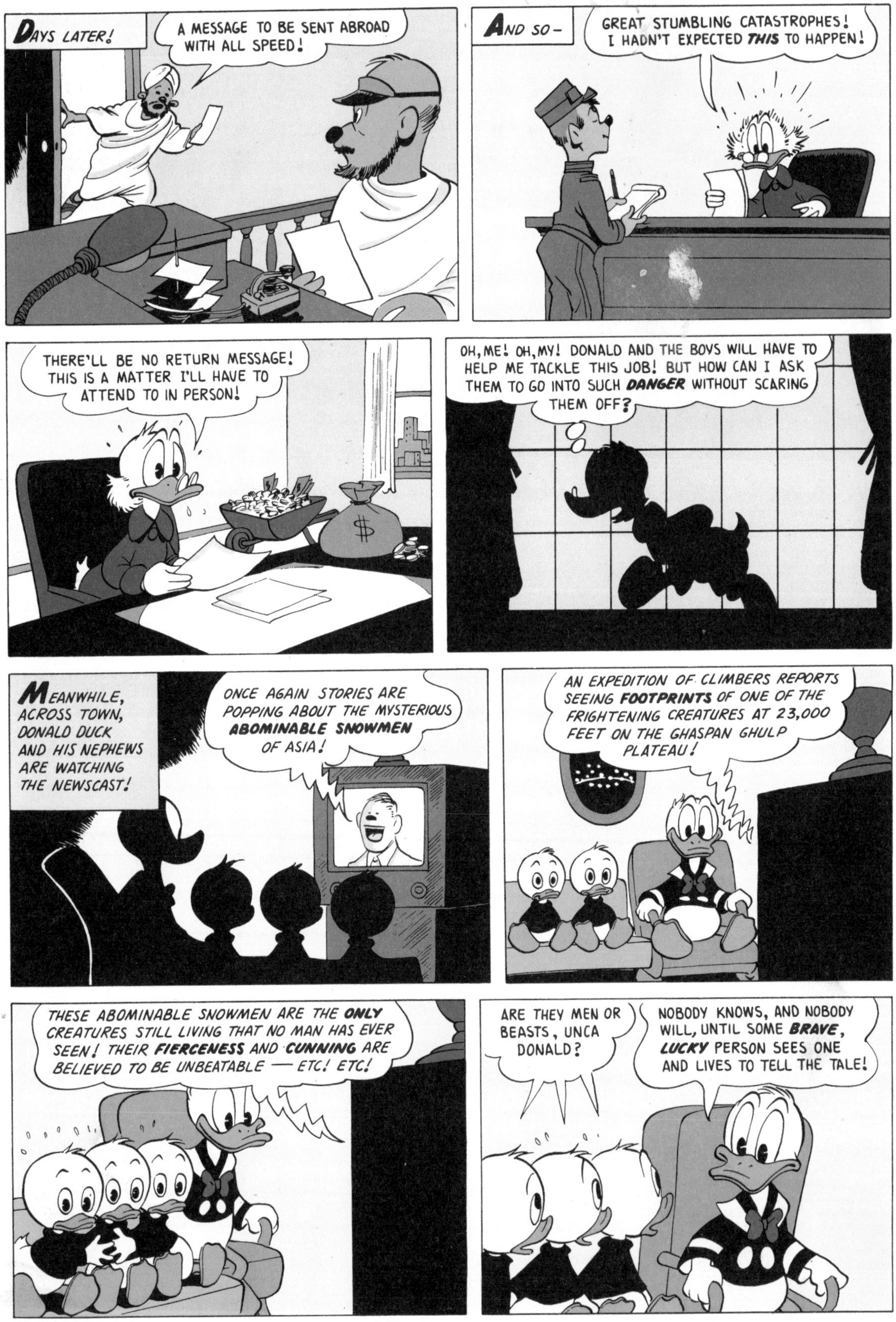
DAYS LATER!
A MESSAGE TO BE SENT ABROAD WITH ALL SPEED!
AND SO—
GREAT STUMBLING CATASTROPHES! I HADN'T EXPECTED THIS TO HAPPEN!
THERE'LL BE NO RETURN MESSAGE! THIS IS A MATTER I'LL HAVE TO ATTEND TO IN PERSON!
OH, ME! OH, MY! DONALD AND THE BOYS WILL HAVE TO HELP ME TACKLE THIS JOB! BUT HOW CAN I ASK THEM TO GO INTO SUCH DANGER WITHOUT SCARING THEM OFF?
MEANWHILE, ACROSS TOWN, DONALD DUCK AND HIS NEPHEWS ARE WATCHING THE NEWSCAST!
ONCE AGAIN STORIES ARE POPPING ABOUT THE MYSTERIOUS ABOMINABLE SNOWMEN OF ASIA!
AN EXPEDITION OF CLIMBERS REPORTS SEEING FOOTPRINTS OF ONE OF THE FRIGHTENING CREATURES AT 23,000 FEET ON THE GHASPAN GHULP PLATEAU!
THESE ABOMINABLE SNOWMEN ARE THE ONLY CREATURES STILL LIVING THAT NO MAN HAS EVER SEEN! THEIR FIERCENESS AND CUNNING ARE BELIEVED TO BE UNBEATABLE — ETC! ETC!
ARE THEY MEN OR BEASTS, UNCA DONALD?
NOBODY KNOWS, AND NOBODY WILL, UNTIL SOME BRAVE, LUCKY PERSON SEES ONE AND LIVES TO TELL THE TALE!

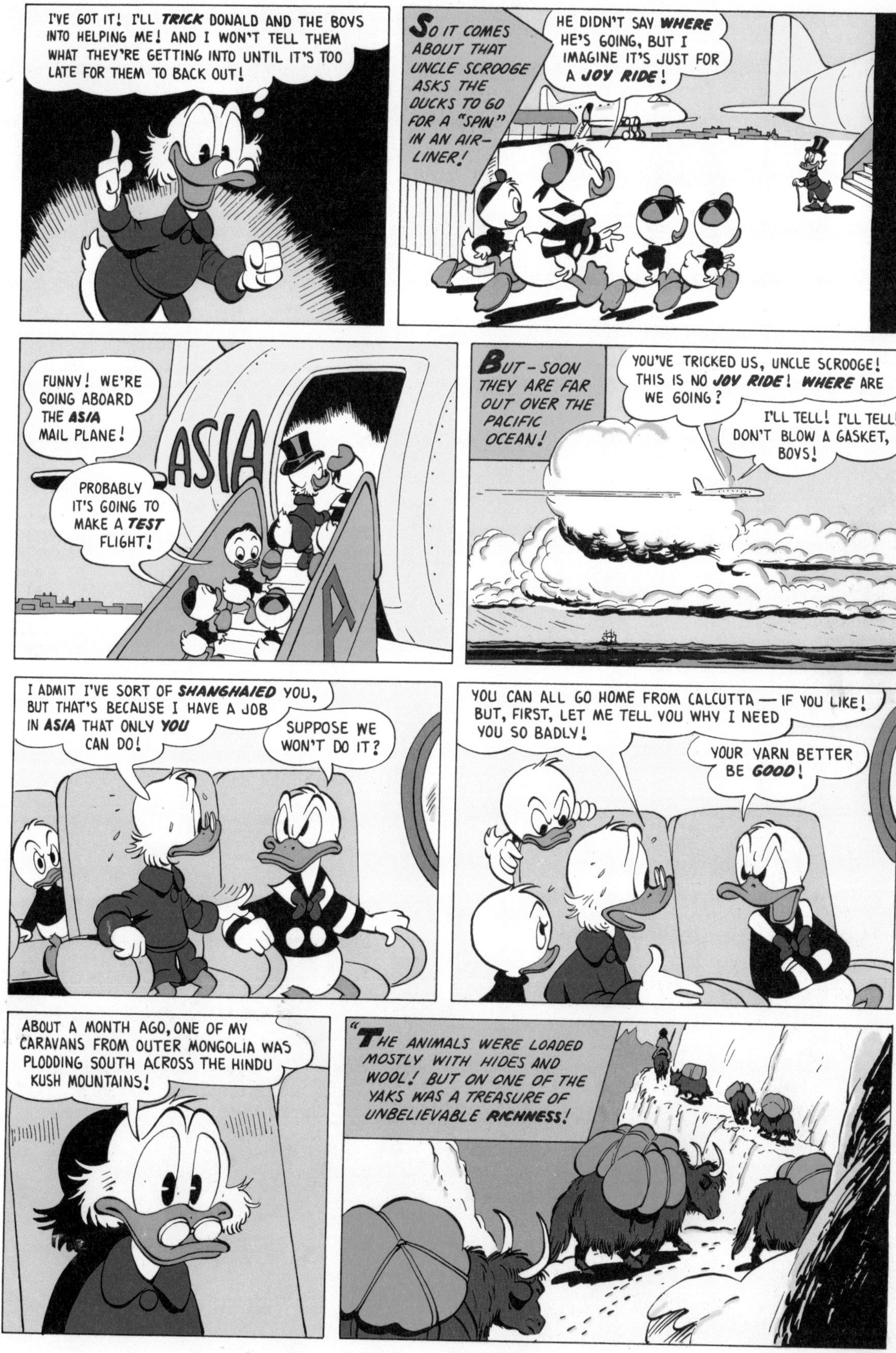
I'VE GOT IT! I'LL TRICK DONALD AND THE BOYS INTO HELPING ME! AND I WON'T TELL THEM WHAT THEY'RE GETTING INTO UNTIL IT'S TOO LATE FOR THEM TO BACK OUT!
SO IT COMES ABOUT THAT UNCLE SCROOGE ASKS THE DUCKS TO GO FOR A "SPIN" IN AN AIR-LINER!
HE DIDN'T SAY WHERE HE'S GOING, BUT I IMAGINE IT'S JUST FOR A JOY RIDE!
FUNNY! WE'RE GOING ABOARD THE ASIA MAIL PLANE!
ASIA
PROBABLY IT'S GOING TO MAKE A TEST FLIGHT!
BUT—SOON THEY ARE FAR OUT OVER THE PACIFIC OCEAN!
YOU'VE TRICKED US, UNCLE SCROOGE! THIS IS NO JOY RIDE! WHERE ARE WE GOING?
I'LL TELL! I'LL TELL! DON'T BLOW A GASKET, BOYS!
I ADMIT I'VE SORT OF SHANGHAIED YOU, BUT THAT'S BECAUSE I HAVE A JOB IN ASIA THAT ONLY YOU CAN DO!
SUPPOSE WE WON'T DO IT?
YOU CAN ALL GO HOME FROM CALCUTTA — IF YOU LIKE! BUT, FIRST, LET ME TELL YOU WHY I NEED YOU SO BADLY!
YOUR YARN BETTER BE GOOD!
ABOUT A MONTH AGO, ONE OF MY CARAVANS FROM OUTER MONGOLIA WAS PLODDING SOUTH ACROSS THE HINDU KUSH MOUNTAINS!
"THE ANIMALS WERE LOADED MOSTLY WITH HIDES AND WOOL! BUT ON ONE OF THE YAKS WAS A TREASURE OF UNBELIEVABLE RICHNESS!

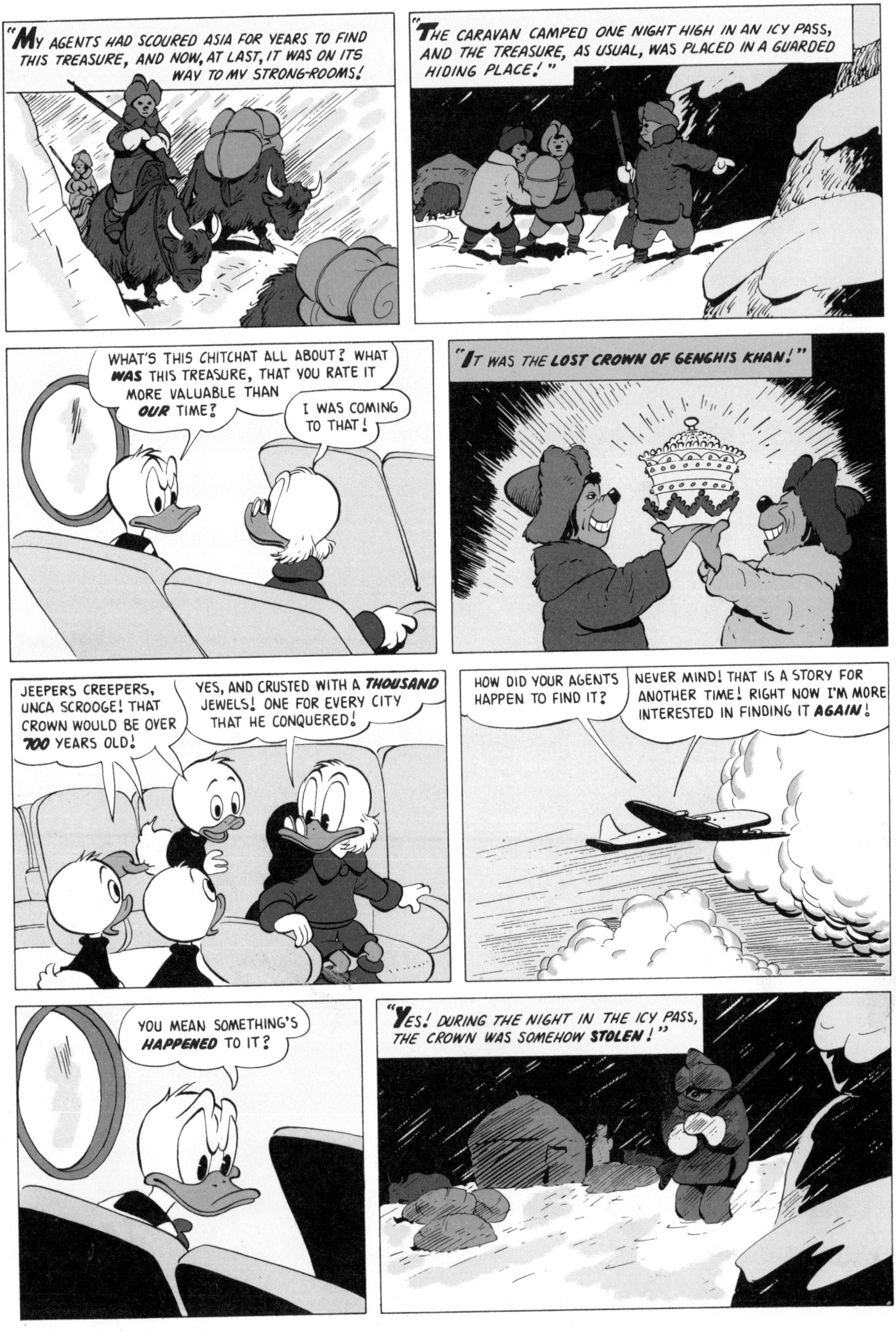
"MY AGENTS HAD SCOURED ASIA FOR YEARS TO FIND THIS TREASURE, AND NOW, AT LAST, IT WAS ON ITS WAY TO MY STRONG-ROOMS!
"THE CARAVAN CAMPED ONE NIGHT HIGH IN AN ICY PASS, AND THE TREASURE, AS USUAL, WAS PLACED IN A GUARDED HIDING PLACE!"
WHAT'S THIS CHITCHAT ALL ABOUT? WHAT WAS THIS TREASURE, THAT YOU RATE IT MORE VALUABLE THAN OUR TIME?
I WAS COMING TO THAT!
"IT WAS THE LOST CROWN OF GENGHIS KHAN!"
JEEPERS CREEPERS, UNCA SCROOGE! THAT CROWN WOULD BE OVER 700 YEARS OLD!
YES, AND CRUSTED WITH A THOUSAND JEWELS! ONE FOR EVERY CITY THAT HE CONQUERED!
HOW DID YOUR AGENTS HAPPEN TO FIND IT?
NEVER MIND! THAT IS A STORY FOR ANOTHER TIME! RIGHT NOW I'M MORE INTERESTED IN FINDING IT AGAIN!
YOU MEAN SOMETHING'S HAPPENED TO IT?
"YES! DURING THE NIGHT IN THE ICY PASS, THE CROWN WAS SOMEHOW STOLEN!"

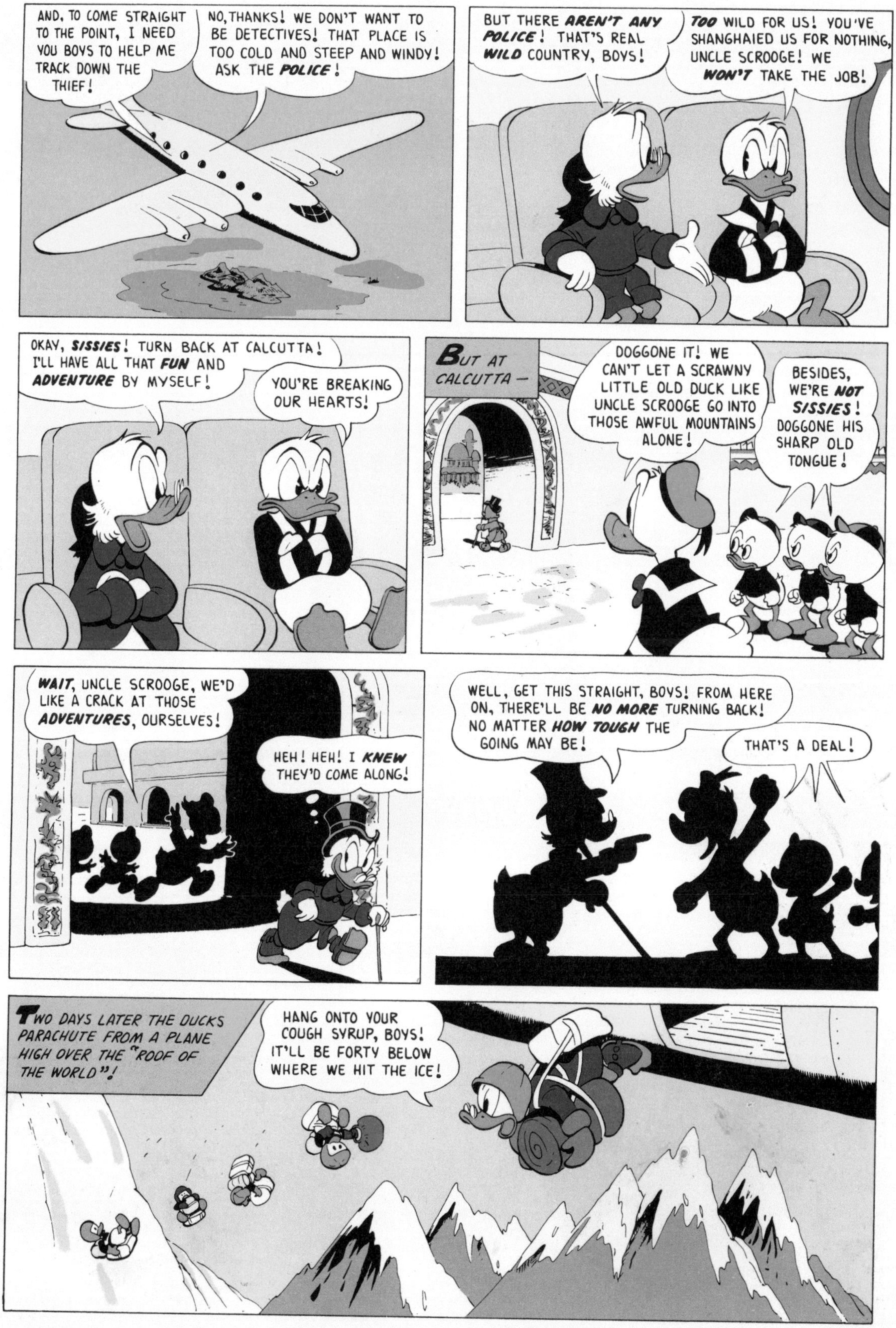

AND, TO COME STRAIGHT TO THE POINT, I NEED YOU BOYS TO HELP ME TRACK DOWN THE THIEF!
NO, THANKS! WE DON'T WANT TO BE DETECTIVES! THAT PLACE IS TOO COLD AND STEEP AND WINDY! ASK THE POLICE!
BUT THERE AREN'T ANY POLICE! THAT'S REAL WILD COUNTRY, BOYS!
TOO WILD FOR US! YOU'VE SHANGHAIED US FOR NOTHING, UNCLE SCROOGE! WE WON'T TAKE THE JOB!
OKAY, SISSIES! TURN BACK AT CALCUTTA! I'LL HAVE ALL THAT FUN AND ADVENTURE BY MYSELF!
YOU'RE BREAKING OUR HEARTS!
BUT AT CALCUTTA—
DOGGONE IT! WE CAN'T LET A SCRAWNY LITTLE OLD DUCK LIKE UNCLE SCROOGE GO INTO THOSE AWFUL MOUNTAINS ALONE!
BESIDES, WE'RE NOT SISSIES! DOGGONE HIS SHARP OLD TONGUE!
WAIT, UNCLE SCROOGE, WE'D LIKE A CRACK AT THOSE ADVENTURES, OURSELVES!
HEH! HEH! I KNEW THEY'D COME ALONG!
WELL, GET THIS STRAIGHT, BOYS! FROM HERE ON, THERE'LL BE NO MORE TURNING BACK! NO MATTER HOW TOUGH THE GOING MAY BE!
THAT'S A DEAL!
TWO DAYS LATER THE DUCKS PARACHUTE FROM A PLANE HIGH OVER THE "ROOF OF THE WORLD"!
HANG ONTO YOUR COUGH SYRUP, BOYS! IT'LL BE FORTY BELOW WHERE WE HIT THE ICE!

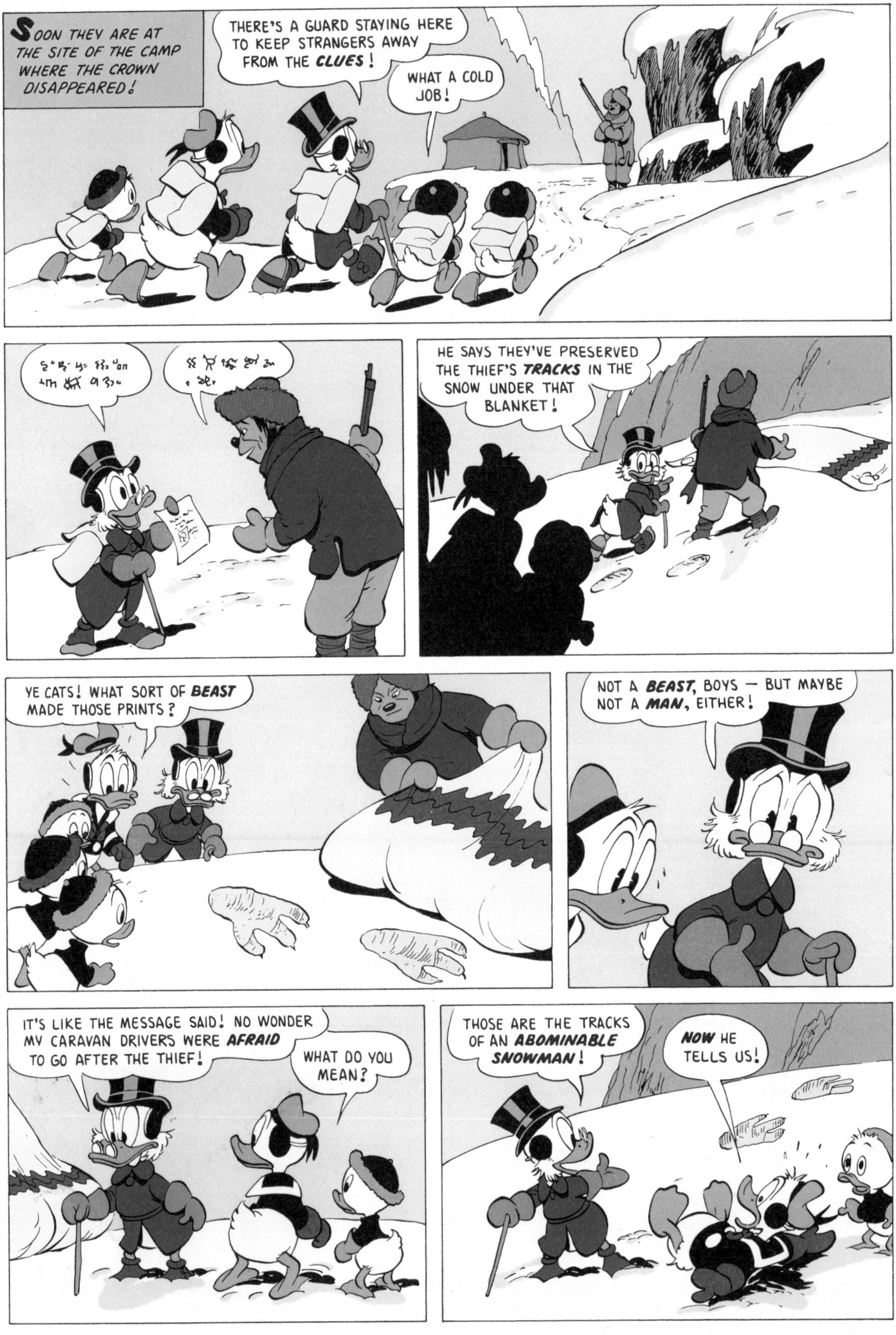
SOON THEY ARE AT THE SITE OF THE CAMP WHERE THE CROWN DISAPPEARED!
THERE'S A GUARD STAYING HERE TO KEEP STRANGERS AWAY FROM THE **CLUES**!
WHAT A COLD JOB!
HE SAYS THEY'VE PRESERVED THE THIEF'S **TRACKS** IN THE SNOW UNDER THAT BLANKET!
YE CATS! WHAT SORT OF **BEAST** MADE THOSE PRINTS?
NOT A **BEAST**, BOYS — BUT MAYBE NOT A **MAN**, EITHER!
IT'S LIKE THE MESSAGE SAID! NO WONDER MY CARAVAN DRIVERS WERE **AFRAID** TO GO AFTER THE THIEF!
WHAT DO YOU MEAN?
THOSE ARE THE TRACKS OF AN **ABOMINABLE SNOWMAN**!
NOW HE TELLS US!

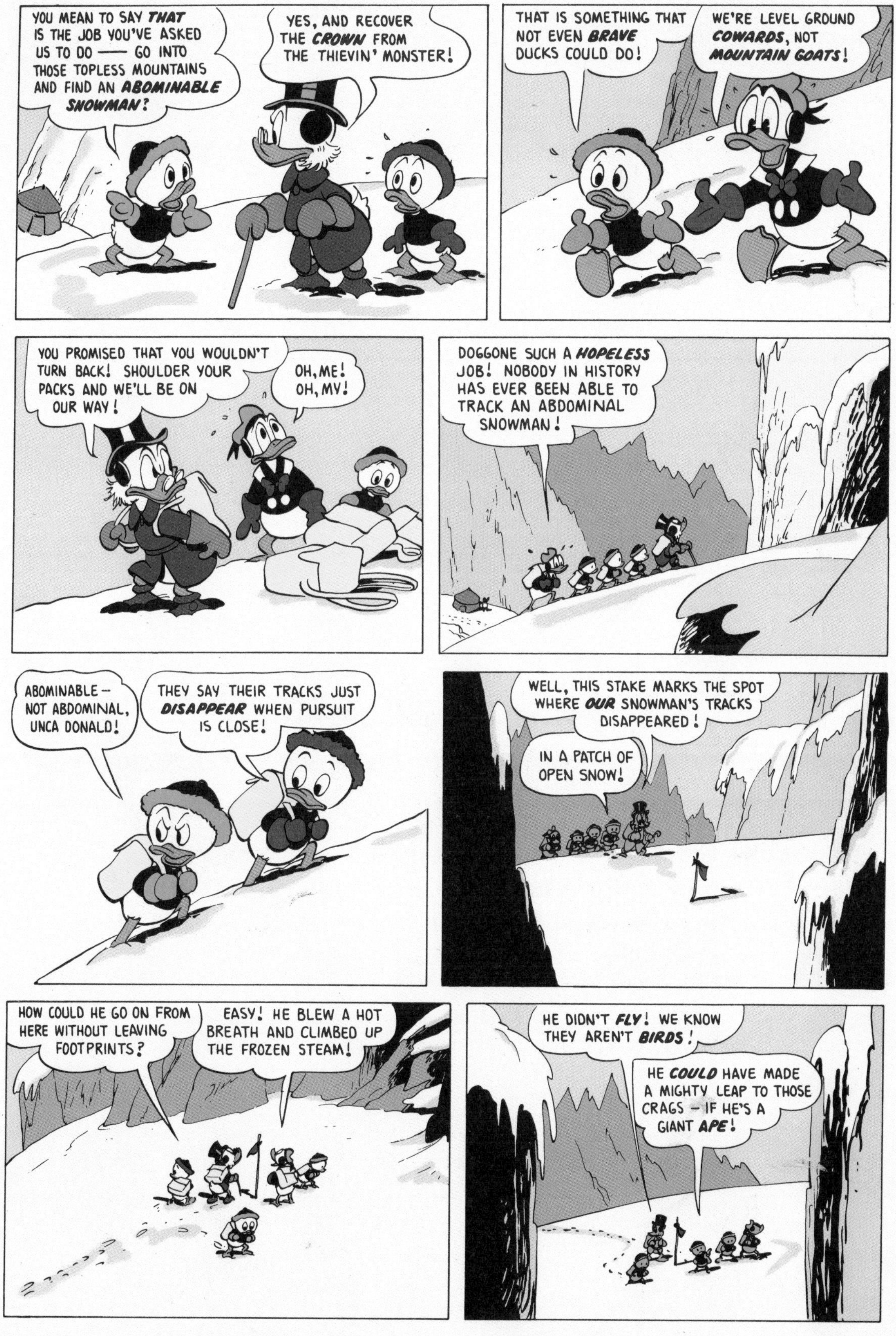
YOU MEAN TO SAY THAT IS THE JOB YOU'VE ASKED US TO DO —— GO INTO THOSE TOPLESS MOUNTAINS AND FIND AN ABOMINABLE SNOWMAN?
YES, AND RECOVER THE CROWN FROM THE THIEVIN' MONSTER!
THAT IS SOMETHING THAT NOT EVEN BRAVE DUCKS COULD DO!
WE'RE LEVEL GROUND COWARDS, NOT MOUNTAIN GOATS!
YOU PROMISED THAT YOU WOULDN'T TURN BACK! SHOULDER YOUR PACKS AND WE'LL BE ON OUR WAY!
OH, ME! OH, MY!
DOGGONE SUCH A HOPELESS JOB! NOBODY IN HISTORY HAS EVER BEEN ABLE TO TRACK AN ABDOMINAL SNOWMAN!
ABOMINABLE — NOT ABDOMINAL, UNCA DONALD!
THEY SAY THEIR TRACKS JUST DISAPPEAR WHEN PURSUIT IS CLOSE!
WELL, THIS STAKE MARKS THE SPOT WHERE OUR SNOWMAN'S TRACKS DISAPPEARED!
IN A PATCH OF OPEN SNOW!
HOW COULD HE GO ON FROM HERE WITHOUT LEAVING FOOTPRINTS?
EASY! HE BLEW A HOT BREATH AND CLIMBED UP THE FROZEN STEAM!
HE DIDN'T FLY! WE KNOW THEY AREN'T BIRDS!
HE COULD HAVE MADE A MIGHTY LEAP TO THOSE CRAGS — IF HE'S A GIANT APE!

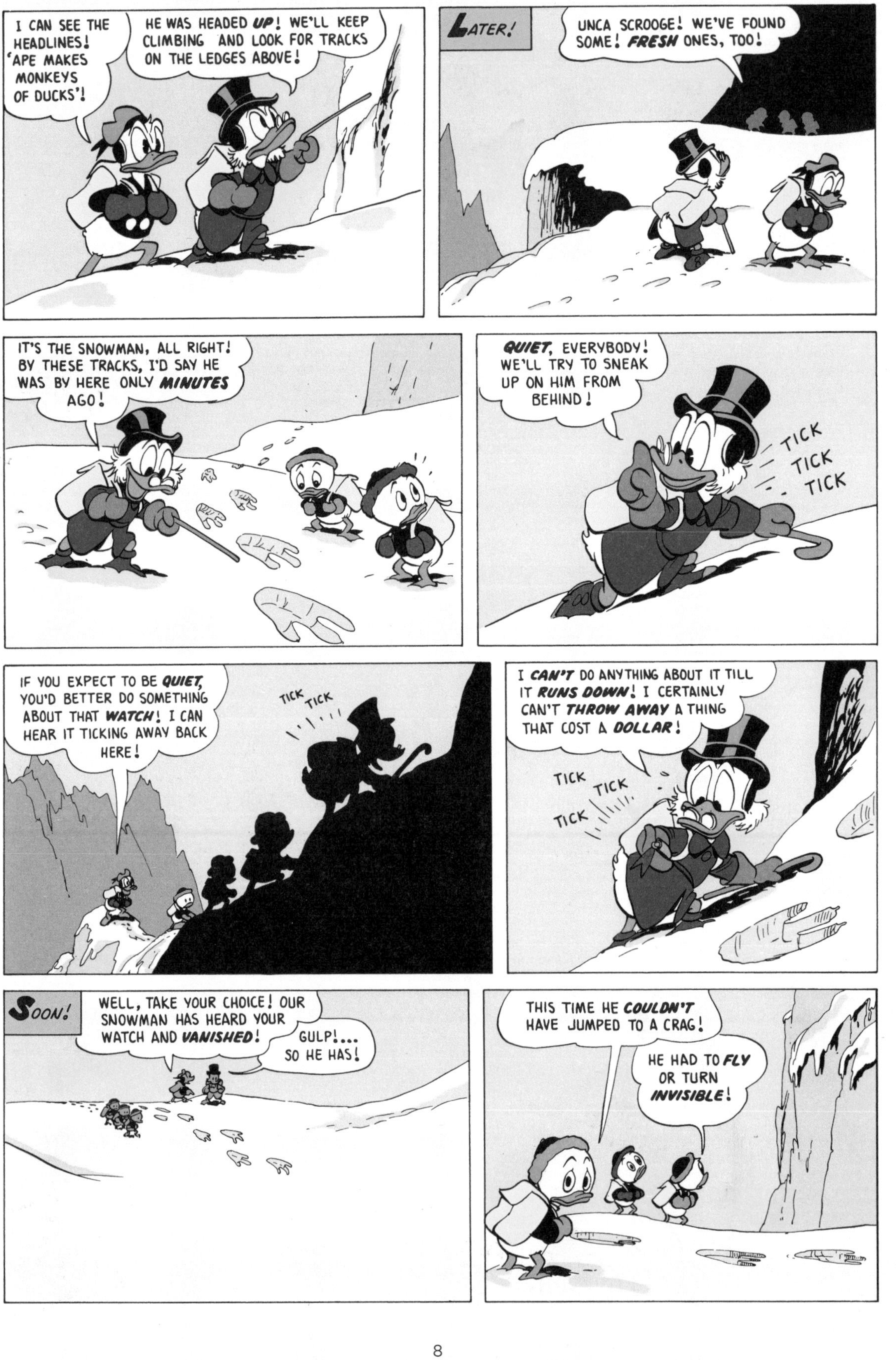
I CAN SEE THE HEADLINES! 'APE MAKES MONKEYS OF DUCKS'!
HE WAS HEADED UP! WE'LL KEEP CLIMBING AND LOOK FOR TRACKS ON THE LEDGES ABOVE!
LATER!
UNCA SCROOGE! WE'VE FOUND SOME! FRESH ONES, TOO!
IT'S THE SNOWMAN, ALL RIGHT! BY THESE TRACKS, I'D SAY HE WAS BY HERE ONLY MINUTES AGO!
QUIET, EVERYBODY! WE'LL TRY TO SNEAK UP ON HIM FROM BEHIND!
TICK TICK TICK
IF YOU EXPECT TO BE QUIET, YOU'D BETTER DO SOMETHING ABOUT THAT WATCH! I CAN HEAR IT TICKING AWAY BACK HERE!
TICK TICK
I CAN'T DO ANYTHING ABOUT IT TILL IT RUNS DOWN! I CERTAINLY CAN'T THROW AWAY A THING THAT COST A DOLLAR!
TICK TICK TICK
SOON!
WELL, TAKE YOUR CHOICE! OUR SNOWMAN HAS HEARD YOUR WATCH AND VANISHED!
GULP!... SO HE HAS!
THIS TIME HE COULDN'T HAVE JUMPED TO A CRAG!
HE HAD TO FLY OR TURN INVISIBLE!

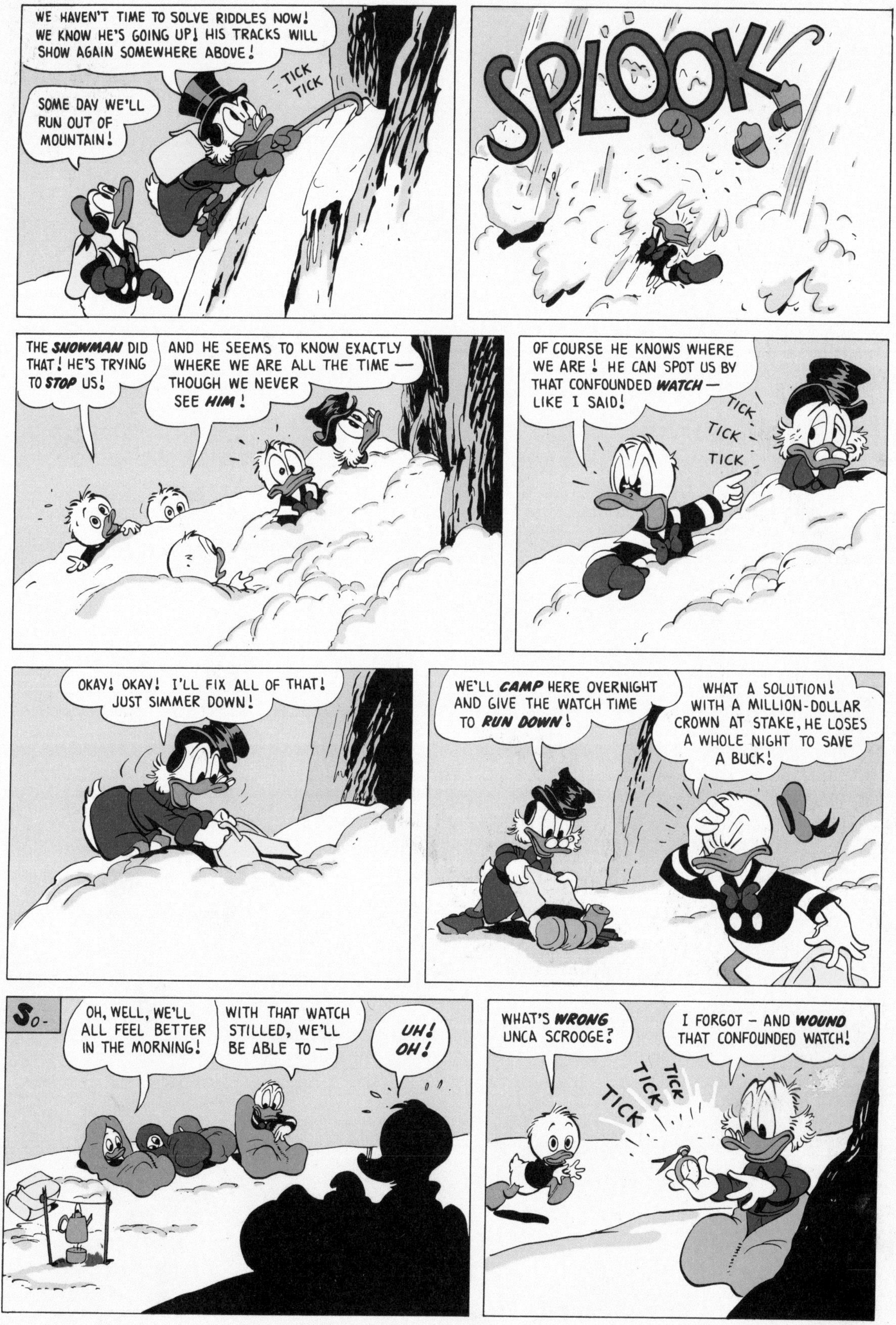
WE HAVEN'T TIME TO SOLVE RIDDLES NOW! WE KNOW HE'S GOING UP! HIS TRACKS WILL SHOW AGAIN SOMEWHERE ABOVE!
SOME DAY WE'LL RUN OUT OF MOUNTAIN!
TICK TICK
SPLOOK
THE SNOWMAN DID THAT! HE'S TRYING TO STOP US!
AND HE SEEMS TO KNOW EXACTLY WHERE WE ARE ALL THE TIME — THOUGH WE NEVER SEE HIM!
OF COURSE HE KNOWS WHERE WE ARE! HE CAN SPOT US BY THAT CONFOUNDED WATCH — LIKE I SAID!
TICK TICK TICK
OKAY! OKAY! I'LL FIX ALL OF THAT! JUST SIMMER DOWN!
WE'LL CAMP HERE OVERNIGHT AND GIVE THE WATCH TIME TO RUN DOWN!
WHAT A SOLUTION! WITH A MILLION-DOLLAR CROWN AT STAKE, HE LOSES A WHOLE NIGHT TO SAVE A BUCK!
So-
OH, WELL, WE'LL ALL FEEL BETTER IN THE MORNING!
WITH THAT WATCH STILLED, WE'LL BE ABLE TO—
UH! OH!
WHAT'S WRONG UNCA SCROOGE?
I FORGOT – AND WOUND THAT CONFOUNDED WATCH!
TICK TICK TICK

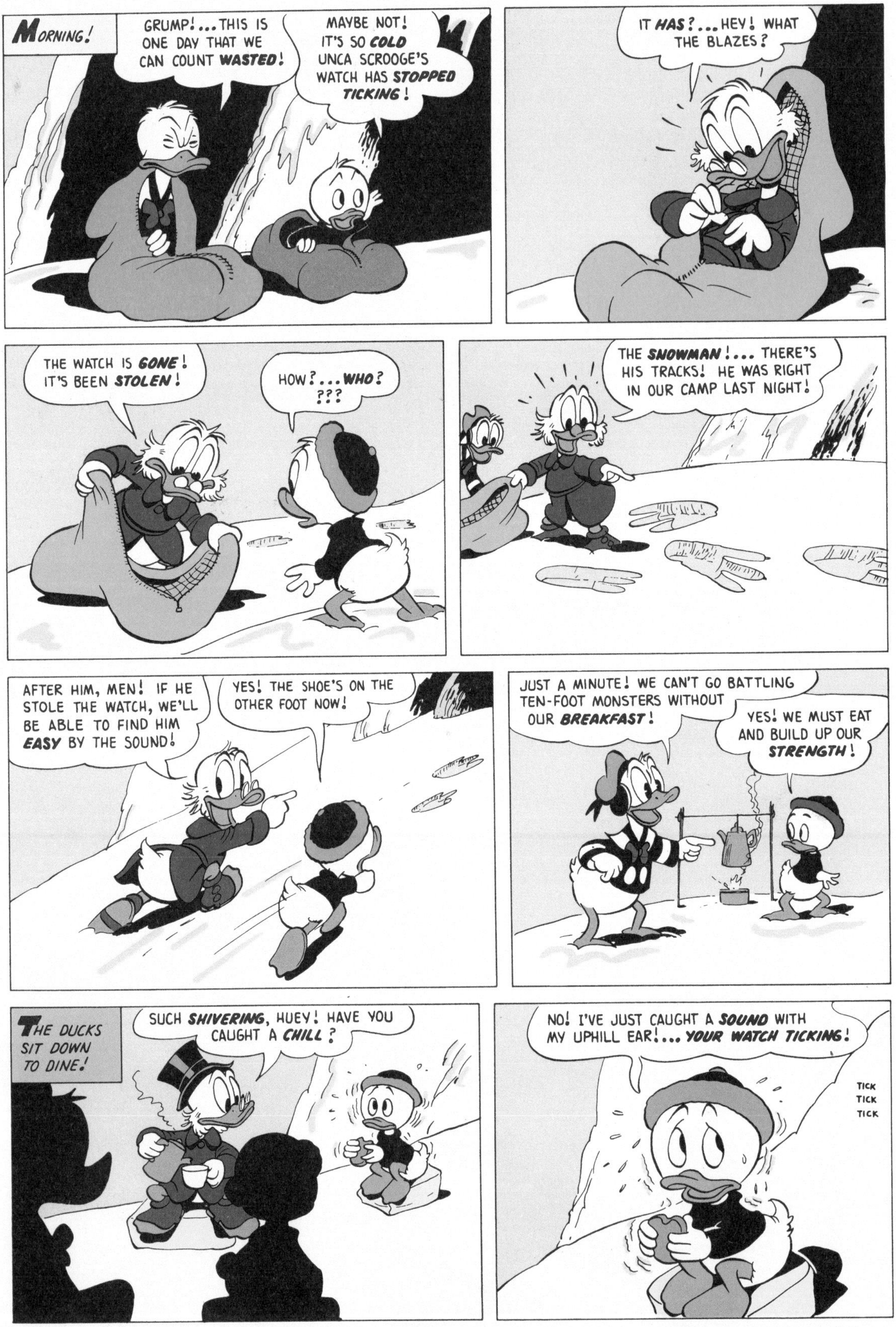
MORNING!
GRUMP! ... THIS IS ONE DAY THAT WE CAN COUNT WASTED!
MAYBE NOT! IT'S SO COLD UNCA SCROOGE'S WATCH HAS STOPPED TICKING!
IT HAS? ... HEY! WHAT THE BLAZES?
THE WATCH IS GONE! IT'S BEEN STOLEN!
HOW? ... WHO? ???
THE SNOWMAN! ... THERE'S HIS TRACKS! HE WAS RIGHT IN OUR CAMP LAST NIGHT!
AFTER HIM, MEN! IF HE STOLE THE WATCH, WE'LL BE ABLE TO FIND HIM EASY BY THE SOUND!
YES! THE SHOE'S ON THE OTHER FOOT NOW!
JUST A MINUTE! WE CAN'T GO BATTLING TEN-FOOT MONSTERS WITHOUT OUR BREAKFAST!
YES! WE MUST EAT AND BUILD UP OUR STRENGTH!
THE DUCKS SIT DOWN TO DINE!
SUCH SHIVERING, HUEY! HAVE YOU CAUGHT A CHILL?
NO! I'VE JUST CAUGHT A SOUND WITH MY UPHILL EAR! ... YOUR WATCH TICKING!
TICK
TICK
TICK

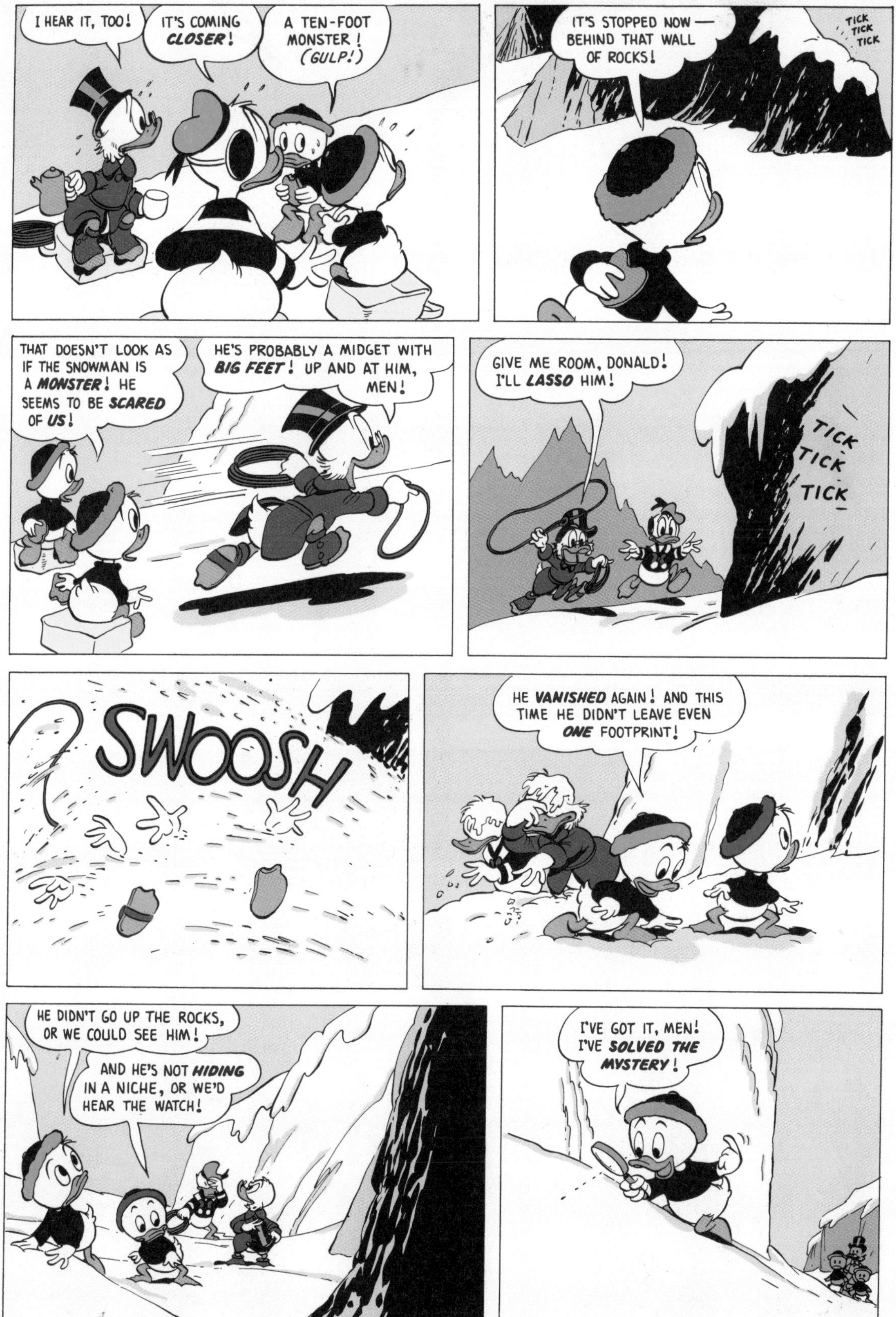
I HEAR IT, TOO!
IT'S COMING CLOSER!
A TEN-FOOT MONSTER! (GULP!)
IT'S STOPPED NOW — BEHIND THAT WALL OF ROCKS!
TICK TICK TICK
THAT DOESN'T LOOK AS IF THE SNOWMAN IS A MONSTER! HE SEEMS TO BE SCARED OF US!
HE'S PROBABLY A MIDGET WITH BIG FEET! UP AND AT HIM, MEN!
GIVE ME ROOM, DONALD! I'LL LASSO HIM!
TICK TICK TICK
SWOOSH
HE VANISHED AGAIN! AND THIS TIME HE DIDN'T LEAVE EVEN ONE FOOTPRINT!
HE DIDN'T GO UP THE ROCKS, OR WE COULD SEE HIM!
AND HE'S NOT HIDING IN A NICHE, OR WE'D HEAR THE WATCH!
I'VE GOT IT, MEN! I'VE SOLVED THE MYSTERY!

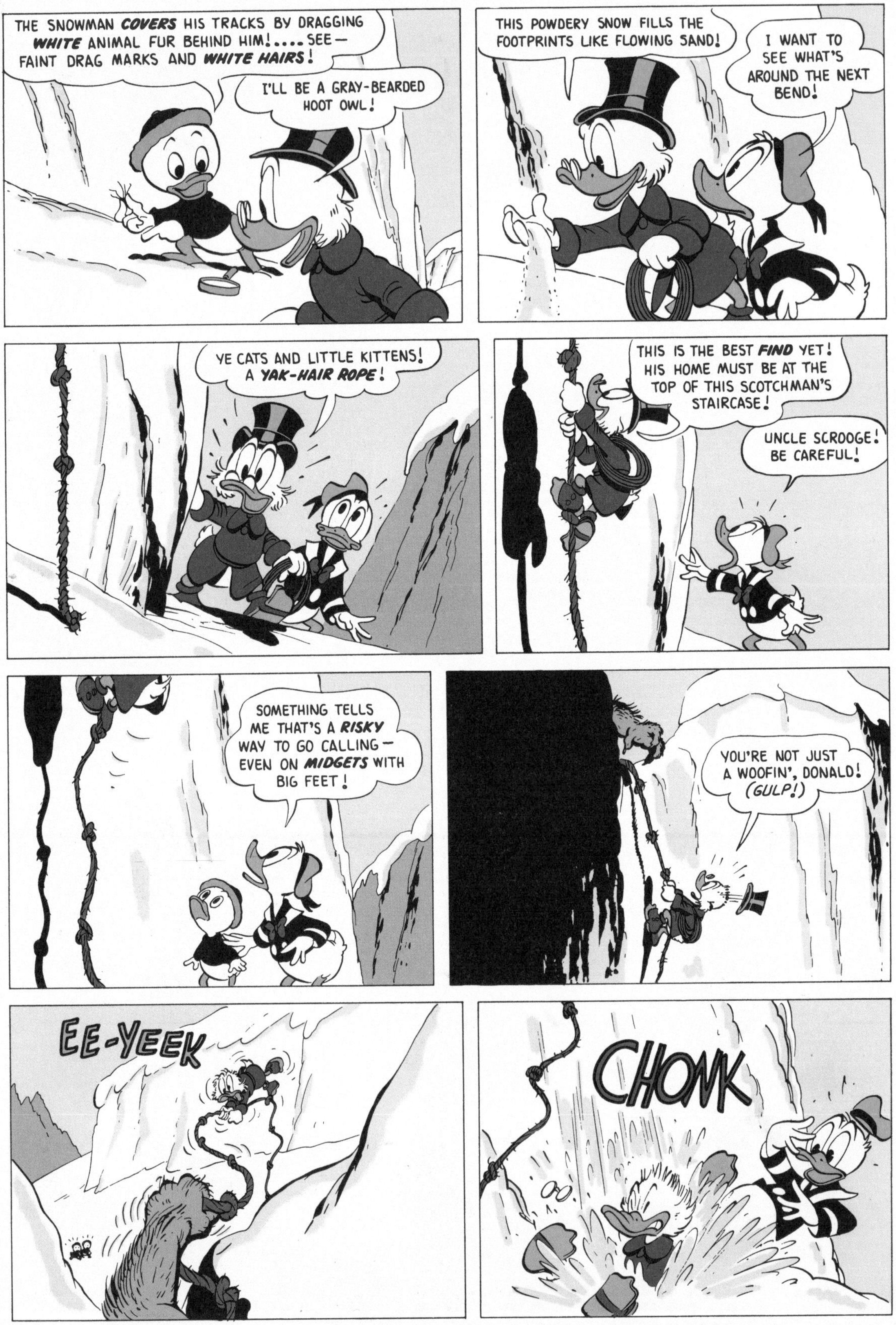
THE SNOWMAN COVERS HIS TRACKS BY DRAGGING WHITE ANIMAL FUR BEHIND HIM! .... SEE— FAINT DRAG MARKS AND WHITE HAIRS!
I'LL BE A GRAY-BEARDED HOOT OWL!
THIS POWDERY SNOW FILLS THE FOOTPRINTS LIKE FLOWING SAND!
I WANT TO SEE WHAT'S AROUND THE NEXT BEND!
YE CATS AND LITTLE KITTENS! A YAK-HAIR ROPE!
THIS IS THE BEST FIND YET! HIS HOME MUST BE AT THE TOP OF THIS SCOTCHMAN'S STAIRCASE!
UNCLE SCROOGE! BE CAREFUL!
SOMETHING TELLS ME THAT'S A RISKY WAY TO GO CALLING— EVEN ON MIDGETS WITH BIG FEET!
YOU'RE NOT JUST A WOOFIN', DONALD! (GULP!)
EE-YEEK
CHONK

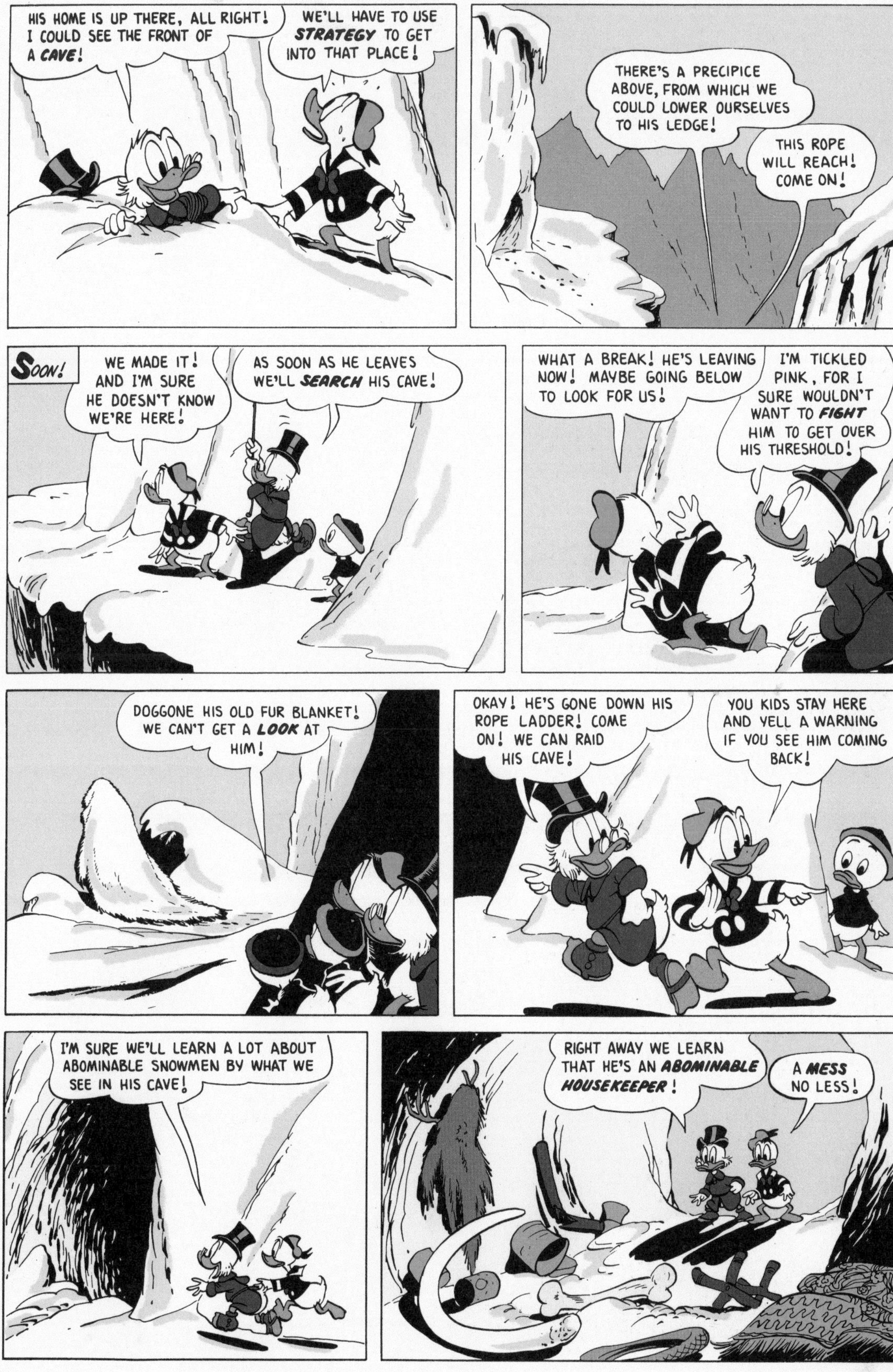
HIS HOME IS UP THERE, ALL RIGHT! I COULD SEE THE FRONT OF A CAVE!
WE'LL HAVE TO USE STRATEGY TO GET INTO THAT PLACE!
THERE'S A PRECIPICE ABOVE, FROM WHICH WE COULD LOWER OURSELVES TO HIS LEDGE!
THIS ROPE WILL REACH! COME ON!
SOON!
WE MADE IT! AND I'M SURE HE DOESN'T KNOW WE'RE HERE!
AS SOON AS HE LEAVES WE'LL SEARCH HIS CAVE!
WHAT A BREAK! HE'S LEAVING NOW! MAYBE GOING BELOW TO LOOK FOR US!
I'M TICKLED PINK, FOR I SURE WOULDN'T WANT TO FIGHT HIM TO GET OVER HIS THRESHOLD!
DOGGONE HIS OLD FUR BLANKET! WE CAN'T GET A LOOK AT HIM!
OKAY! HE'S GONE DOWN HIS ROPE LADDER! COME ON! WE CAN RAID HIS CAVE!
YOU KIDS STAY HERE AND YELL A WARNING IF YOU SEE HIM COMING BACK!
I'M SURE WE'LL LEARN A LOT ABOUT ABOMINABLE SNOWMEN BY WHAT WE SEE IN HIS CAVE!
RIGHT AWAY WE LEARN THAT HE'S AN ABOMINABLE HOUSEKEEPER!
A MESS NO LESS!

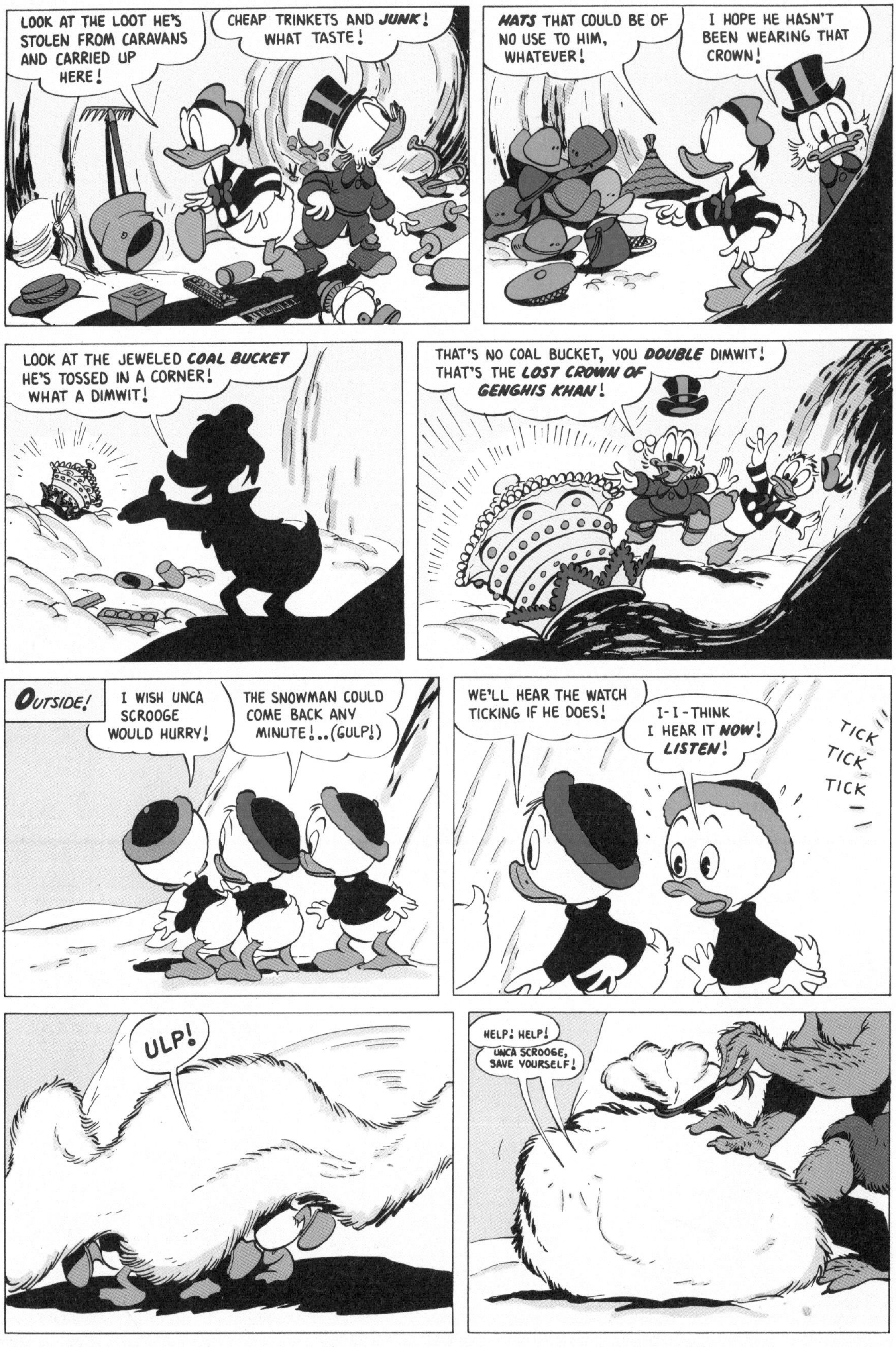
LOOK AT THE LOOT HE'S STOLEN FROM CARAVANS AND CARRIED UP HERE!
CHEAP TRINKETS AND JUNK! WHAT TASTE!
HATS THAT COULD BE OF NO USE TO HIM, WHATEVER!
I HOPE HE HASN'T BEEN WEARING THAT CROWN!
LOOK AT THE JEWELED COAL BUCKET HE'S TOSSED IN A CORNER! WHAT A DIMWIT!
THAT'S NO COAL BUCKET, YOU DOUBLE DIMWIT! THAT'S THE LOST CROWN OF GENGHIS KHAN!
OUTSIDE!
I WISH UNCA SCROOGE WOULD HURRY!
THE SNOWMAN COULD COME BACK ANY MINUTE!..(GULP!)
WE'LL HEAR THE WATCH TICKING IF HE DOES!
I-I-THINK I HEAR IT NOW! LISTEN!
TICK TICK TICK
ULP!
HELP! HELP!
UNCA SCROOGE, SAVE YOURSELF!

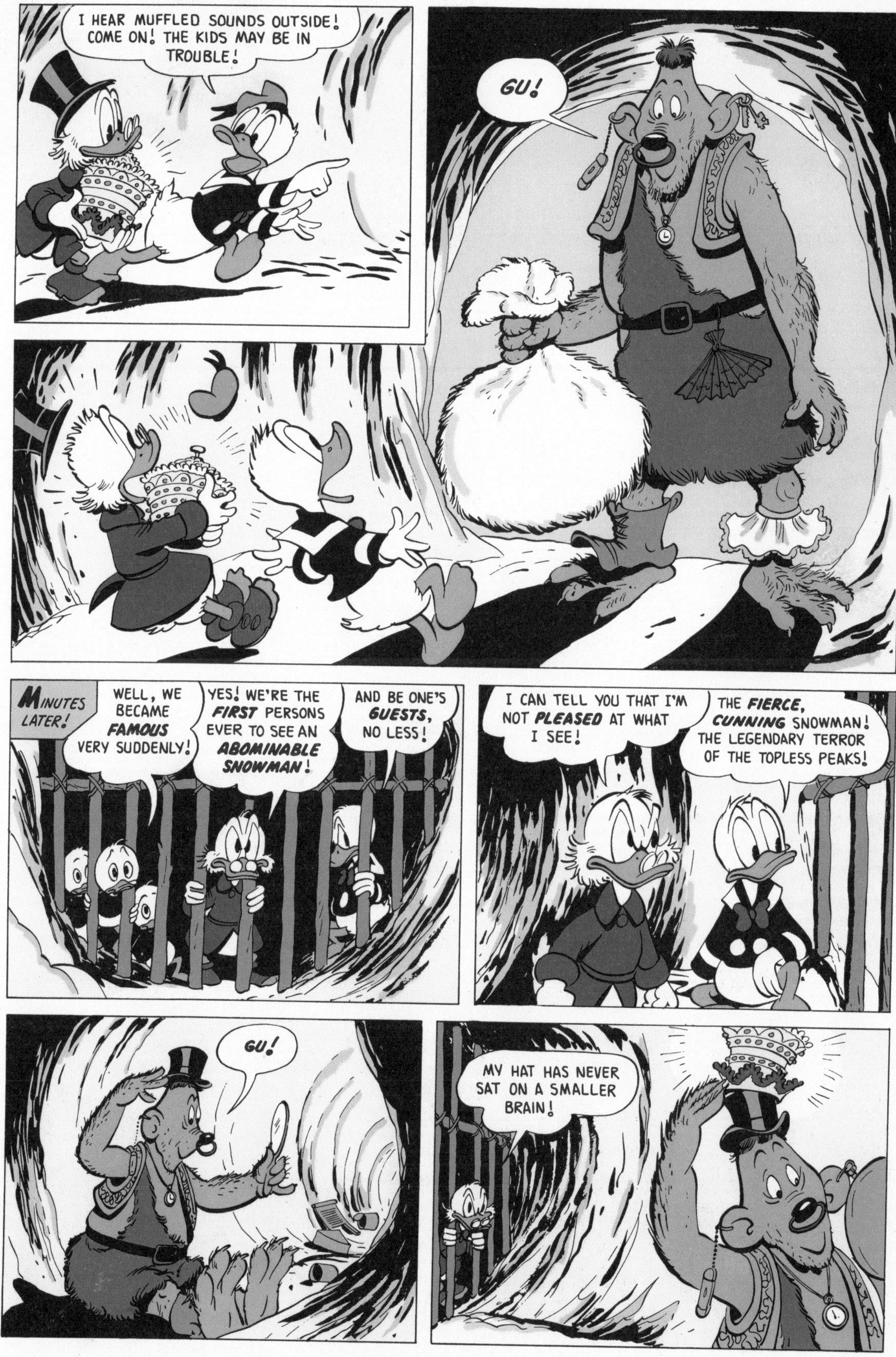

I HEAR MUFFLED SOUNDS OUTSIDE! COME ON! THE KIDS MAY BE IN TROUBLE!
GU!
MINUTES LATER!
WELL, WE BECAME FAMOUS VERY SUDDENLY!
YES! WE'RE THE FIRST PERSONS EVER TO SEE AN ABOMINABLE SNOWMAN!
AND BE ONE'S GUESTS, NO LESS!
I CAN TELL YOU THAT I'M NOT PLEASED AT WHAT I SEE!
THE FIERCE, CUNNING SNOWMAN! THE LEGENDARY TERROR OF THE TOPLESS PEAKS!
GU!
MY HAT HAS NEVER SAT ON A SMALLER BRAIN!

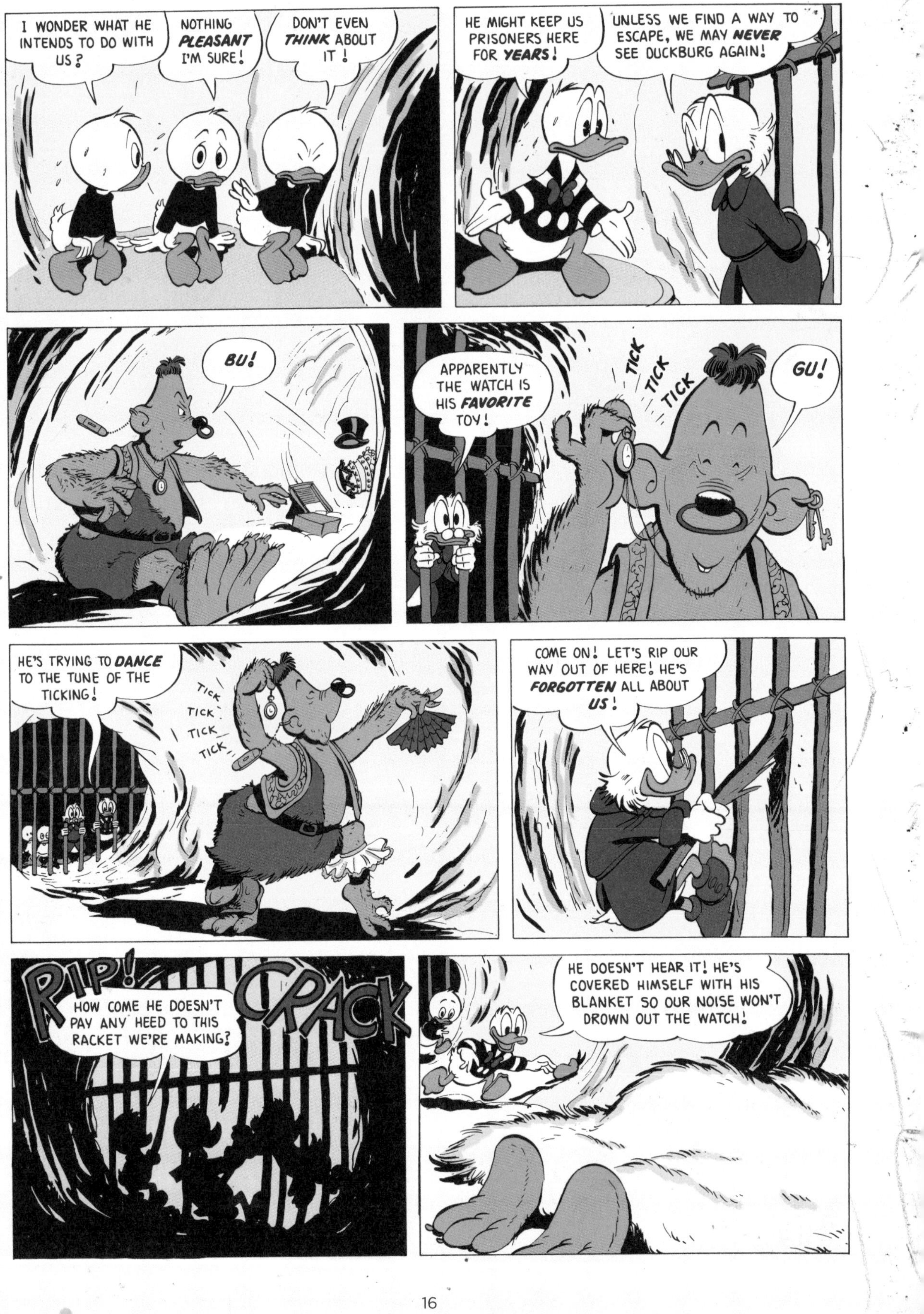
I WONDER WHAT HE INTENDS TO DO WITH US?
NOTHING PLEASANT I'M SURE!
DON'T EVEN THINK ABOUT IT!
HE MIGHT KEEP US PRISONERS HERE FOR YEARS!
UNLESS WE FIND A WAY TO ESCAPE, WE MAY NEVER SEE DUCKBURG AGAIN!
BU!
APPARENTLY THE WATCH IS HIS FAVORITE TOY!
TICK
TICK
TICK
GU!
HE'S TRYING TO DANCE TO THE TUNE OF THE TICKING!
TICK
TICK
TICK
TICK
COME ON! LET'S RIP OUR WAY OUT OF HERE! HE'S FORGOTTEN ALL ABOUT US!
RIP!
CRACK
HOW COME HE DOESN'T PAY ANY HEED TO THIS RACKET WE'RE MAKING?
HE DOESN'T HEAR IT! HE'S COVERED HIMSELF WITH HIS BLANKET SO OUR NOISE WON'T DROWN OUT THE WATCH!

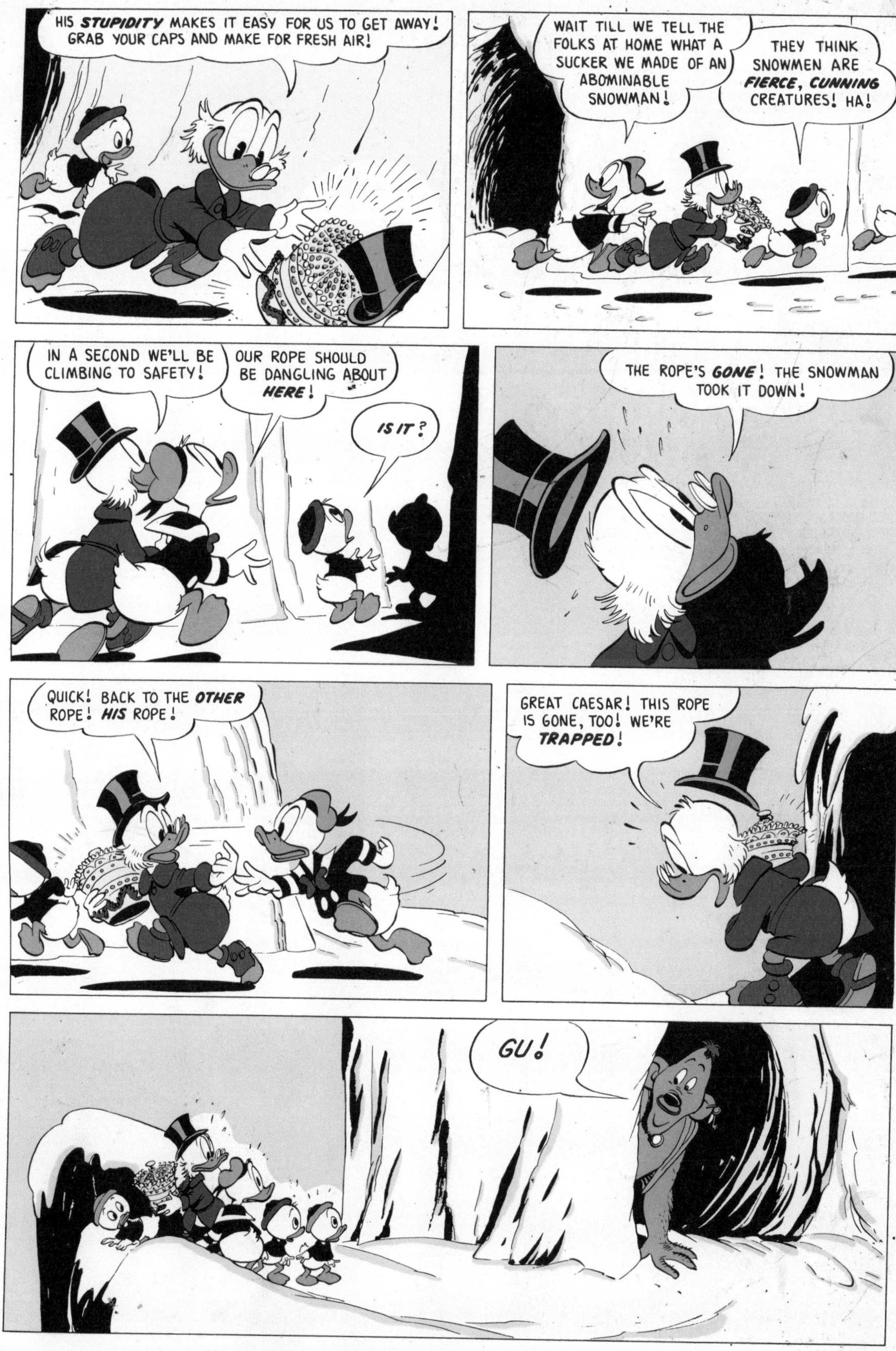
HIS STUPIDITY MAKES IT EASY FOR US TO GET AWAY! GRAB YOUR CAPS AND MAKE FOR FRESH AIR!
WAIT TILL WE TELL THE FOLKS AT HOME WHAT A SUCKER WE MADE OF AN ABOMINABLE SNOWMAN!
THEY THINK SNOWMEN ARE FIERCE, CUNNING CREATURES! HA!
IN A SECOND WE'LL BE CLIMBING TO SAFETY!
OUR ROPE SHOULD BE DANGLING ABOUT HERE!
IS IT?
THE ROPE'S GONE! THE SNOWMAN TOOK IT DOWN!
QUICK! BACK TO THE OTHER ROPE! HIS ROPE!
GREAT CAESAR! THIS ROPE IS GONE, TOO! WE'RE TRAPPED!
GU!

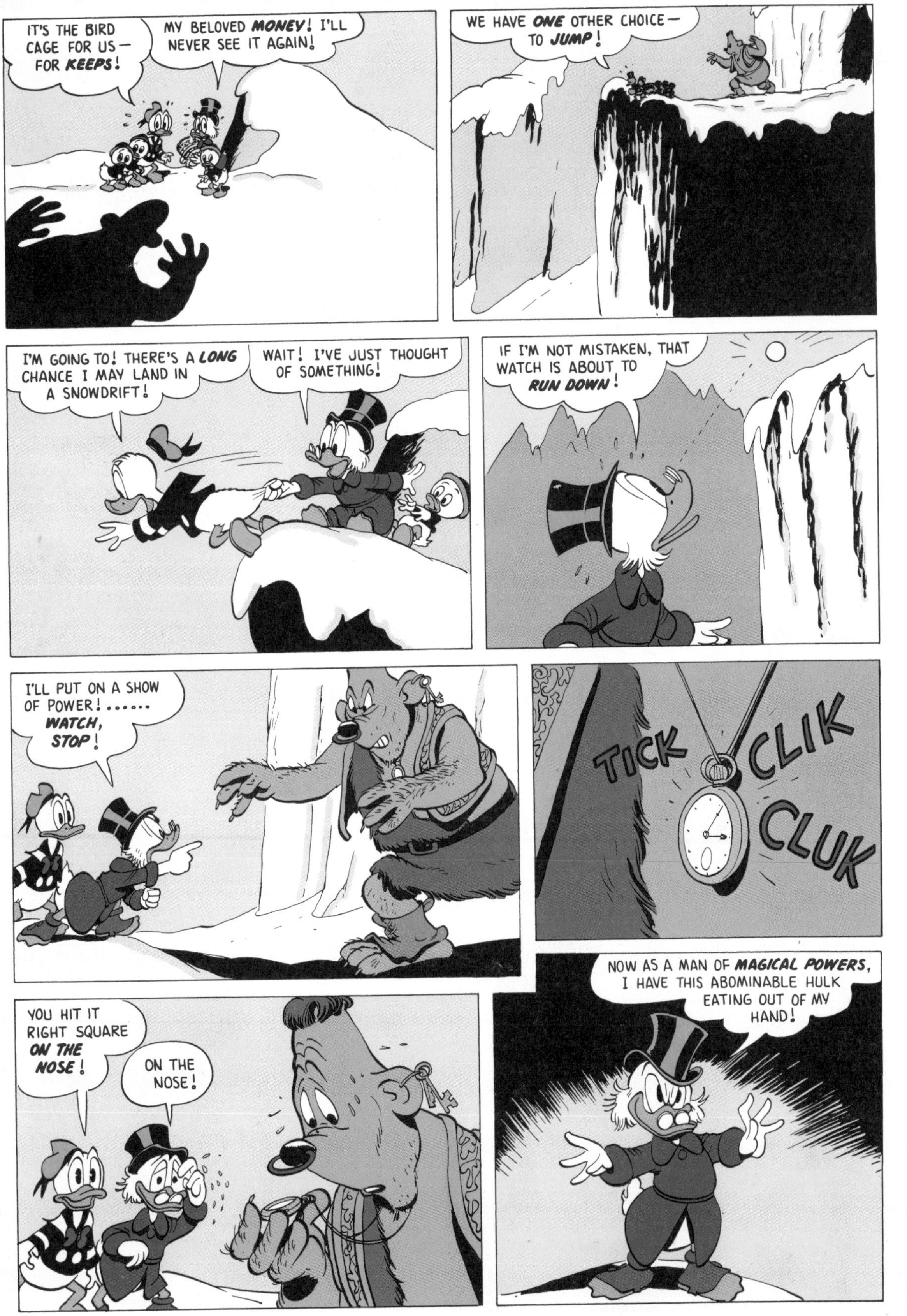
IT'S THE BIRD CAGE FOR US— FOR KEEPS!
MY BELOVED MONEY! I'LL NEVER SEE IT AGAIN!
WE HAVE ONE OTHER CHOICE— TO JUMP!
I'M GOING TO! THERE'S A LONG CHANCE I MAY LAND IN A SNOWDRIFT!
WAIT! I'VE JUST THOUGHT OF SOMETHING!
IF I'M NOT MISTAKEN, THAT WATCH IS ABOUT TO RUN DOWN!
I'LL PUT ON A SHOW OF POWER! ...... WATCH, STOP!
TICK
CLIK
CLUK
YOU HIT IT RIGHT SQUARE ON THE NOSE!
ON THE NOSE!
NOW AS A MAN OF MAGICAL POWERS, I HAVE THIS ABOMINABLE HULK EATING OUT OF MY HAND!

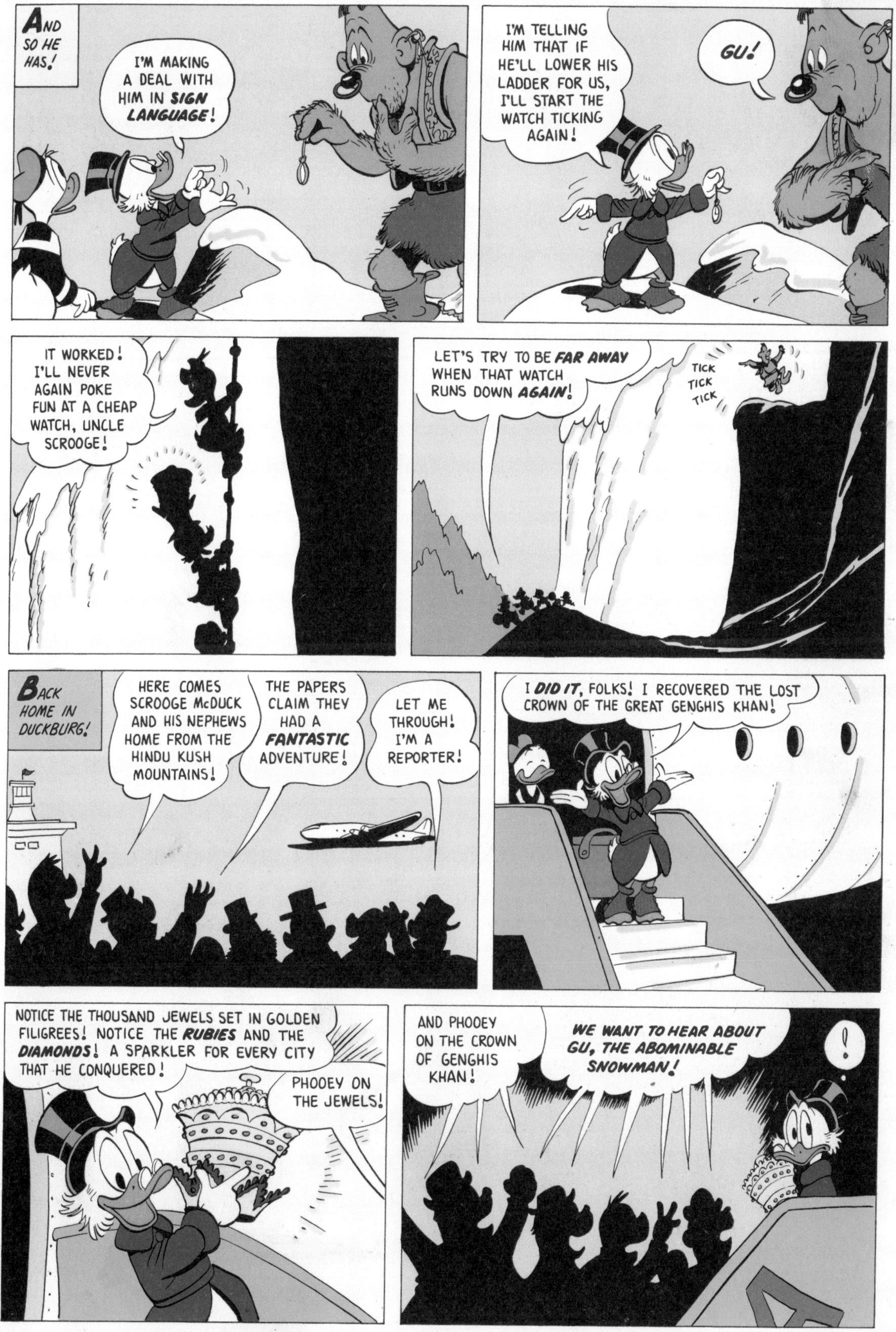
AND SO HE HAS!
I'M MAKING A DEAL WITH HIM IN SIGN LANGUAGE!
I'M TELLING HIM THAT IF HE'LL LOWER HIS LADDER FOR US, I'LL START THE WATCH TICKING AGAIN!
GU!
IT WORKED! I'LL NEVER AGAIN POKE FUN AT A CHEAP WATCH, UNCLE SCROOGE!
LET'S TRY TO BE FAR AWAY WHEN THAT WATCH RUNS DOWN AGAIN!
TICK TICK TICK
BACK HOME IN DUCKBURG!
HERE COMES SCROOGE McDUCK AND HIS NEPHEWS HOME FROM THE HINDU KUSH MOUNTAINS!
THE PAPERS CLAIM THEY HAD A FANTASTIC ADVENTURE!
LET ME THROUGH! I'M A REPORTER!
I DID IT, FOLKS! I RECOVERED THE LOST CROWN OF THE GREAT GENGHIS KHAN!
NOTICE THE THOUSAND JEWELS SET IN GOLDEN FILIGREES! NOTICE THE RUBIES AND THE DIAMONDS! A SPARKLER FOR EVERY CITY THAT HE CONQUERED!
PHOOEY ON THE JEWELS!
AND PHOOEY ON THE CROWN OF GENGHIS KHAN!
WE WANT TO HEAR ABOUT GU, THE ABOMINABLE SNOWMAN!
!

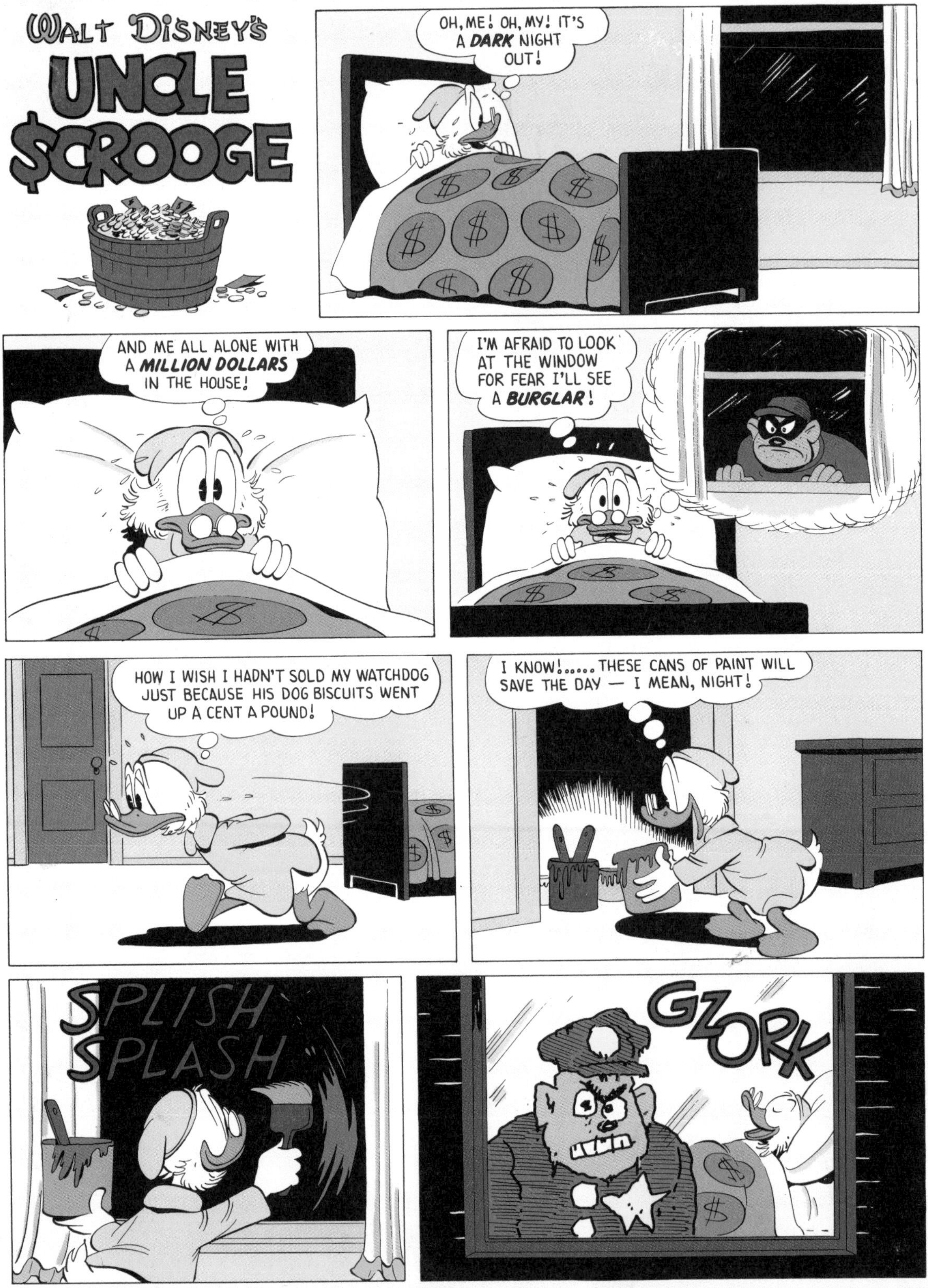
WALT DISNEY'S
UNCLE $CROOGE
OH, ME! OH, MY! IT'S A DARK NIGHT OUT!
AND ME ALL ALONE WITH A MILLION DOLLARS IN THE HOUSE!
I'M AFRAID TO LOOK AT THE WINDOW FOR FEAR I'LL SEE A BURGLAR!
HOW I WISH I HADN'T SOLD MY WATCHDOG JUST BECAUSE HIS DOG BISCUITS WENT UP A CENT A POUND!
I KNOW!...... THESE CANS OF PAINT WILL SAVE THE DAY — I MEAN, NIGHT!
SPLISH SPLASH
GZORK

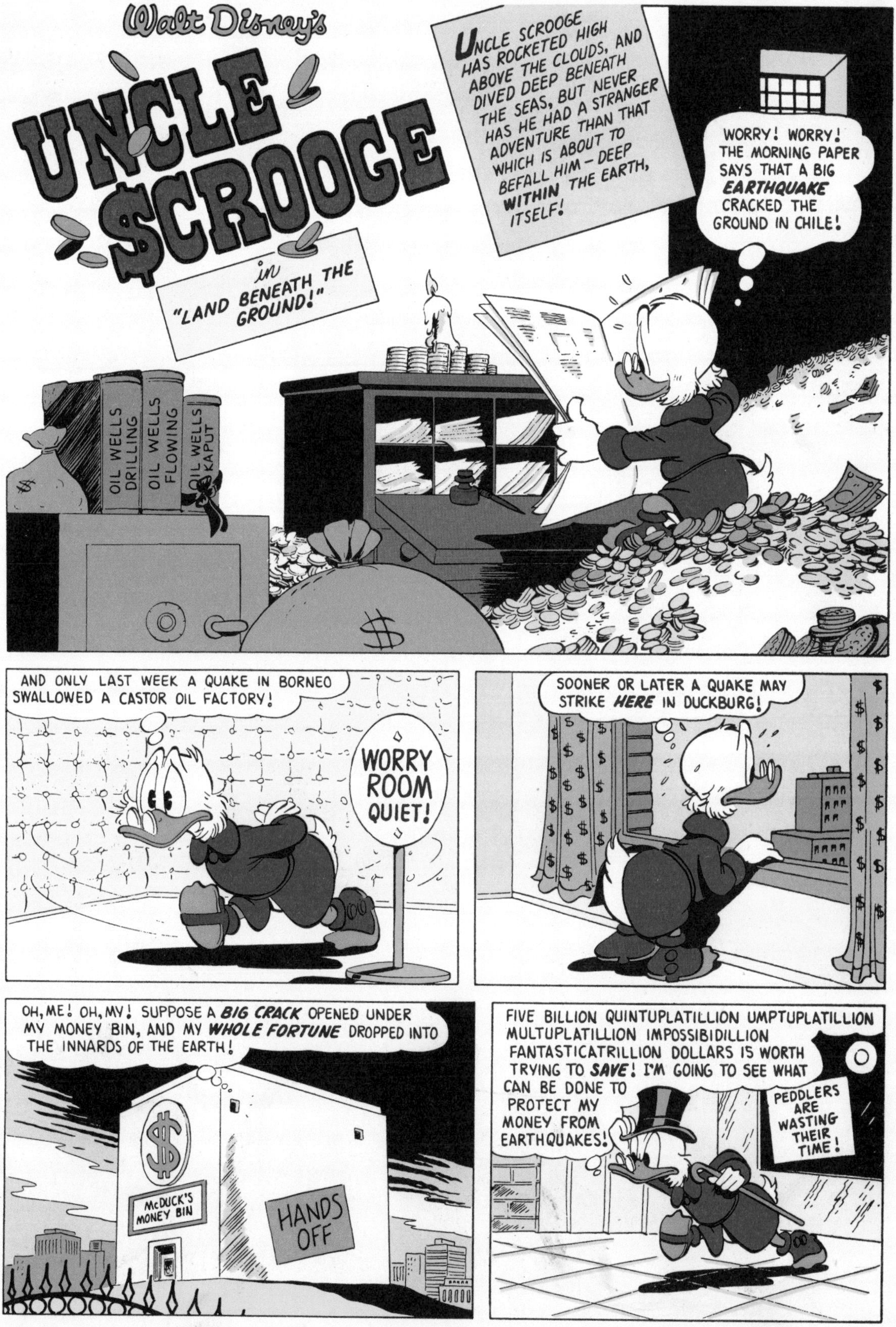
Walt Disney's
UNCLE $CROOGE
in "LAND BENEATH THE GROUND!"
UNCLE SCROOGE HAS ROCKETED HIGH ABOVE THE CLOUDS, AND DIVED DEEP BENEATH THE SEAS, BUT NEVER HAS HE HAD A STRANGER ADVENTURE THAN THAT WHICH IS ABOUT TO BEFALL HIM – DEEP WITHIN THE EARTH, ITSELF!
WORRY! WORRY! THE MORNING PAPER SAYS THAT A BIG EARTHQUAKE CRACKED THE GROUND IN CHILE!
OIL WELLS DRILLING
OIL WELLS FLOWING
OIL WELLS KAPUT
AND ONLY LAST WEEK A QUAKE IN BORNEO SWALLOWED A CASTOR OIL FACTORY!
WORRY ROOM QUIET!
SOONER OR LATER A QUAKE MAY STRIKE HERE IN DUCKBURG!
OH, ME! OH, MY! SUPPOSE A BIG CRACK OPENED UNDER MY MONEY BIN, AND MY WHOLE FORTUNE DROPPED INTO THE INNARDS OF THE EARTH!
McDUCK'S MONEY BIN
HANDS OFF
FIVE BILLION QUINTUPLATILLION UMPTUPLATILLION MULTUPLATILLION IMPOSSIBIDILLION FANTASTICATRILLION DOLLARS IS WORTH TRYING TO SAVE! I'M GOING TO SEE WHAT CAN BE DONE TO PROTECT MY MONEY FROM EARTHQUAKES!
PEDDLERS ARE WASTING THEIR TIME!

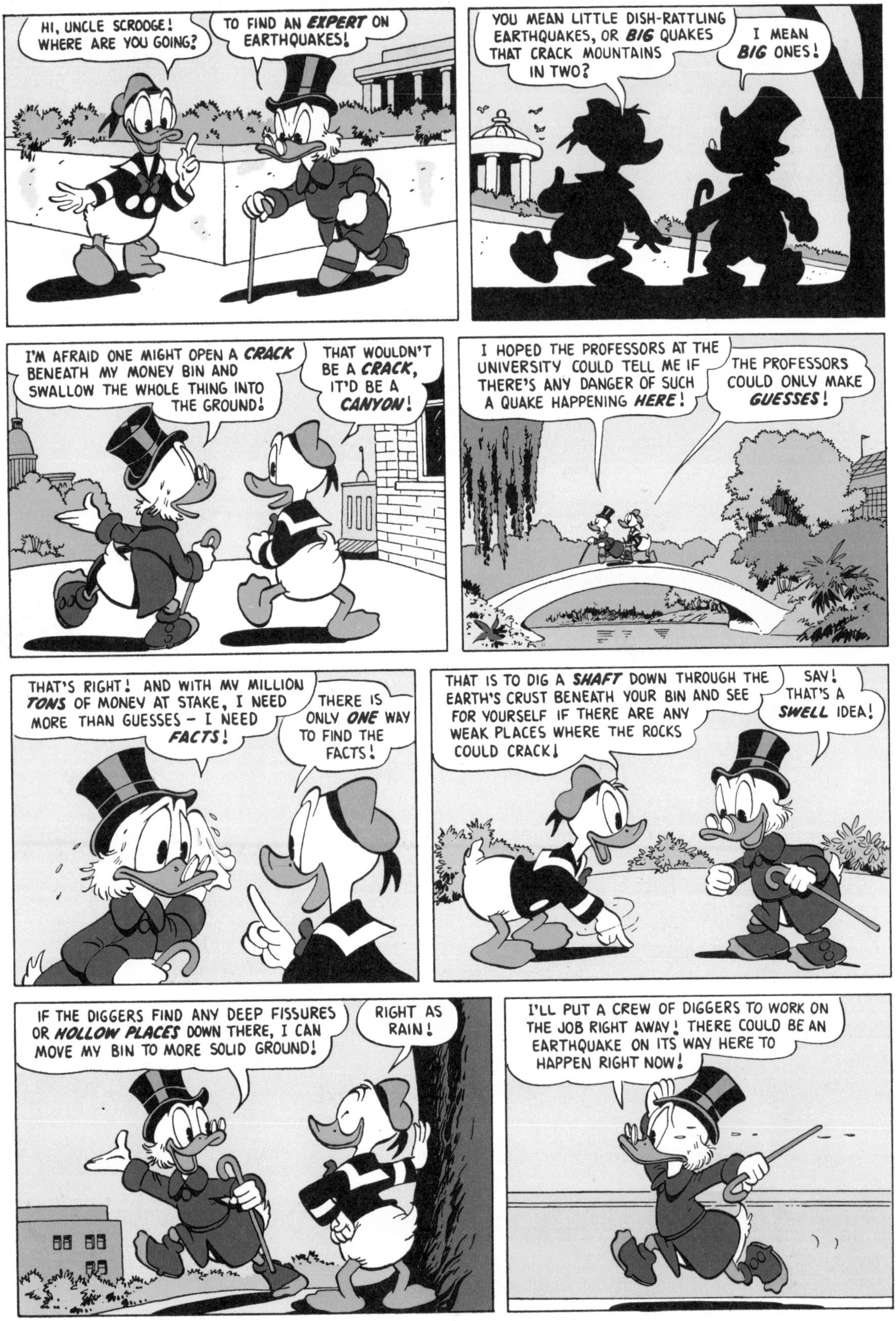
HI, UNCLE SCROOGE! WHERE ARE YOU GOING?
TO FIND AN EXPERT ON EARTHQUAKES!
YOU MEAN LITTLE DISH-RATTLING EARTHQUAKES, OR BIG QUAKES THAT CRACK MOUNTAINS IN TWO?
I MEAN BIG ONES!
I'M AFRAID ONE MIGHT OPEN A CRACK BENEATH MY MONEY BIN AND SWALLOW THE WHOLE THING INTO THE GROUND!
THAT WOULDN'T BE A CRACK, IT'D BE A CANYON!
I HOPED THE PROFESSORS AT THE UNIVERSITY COULD TELL ME IF THERE'S ANY DANGER OF SUCH A QUAKE HAPPENING HERE!
THE PROFESSORS COULD ONLY MAKE GUESSES!
THAT'S RIGHT! AND WITH MY MILLION TONS OF MONEY AT STAKE, I NEED MORE THAN GUESSES – I NEED FACTS!
THERE IS ONLY ONE WAY TO FIND THE FACTS!
THAT IS TO DIG A SHAFT DOWN THROUGH THE EARTH'S CRUST BENEATH YOUR BIN AND SEE FOR YOURSELF IF THERE ARE ANY WEAK PLACES WHERE THE ROCKS COULD CRACK!
SAY! THAT'S A SWELL IDEA!
IF THE DIGGERS FIND ANY DEEP FISSURES OR HOLLOW PLACES DOWN THERE, I CAN MOVE MY BIN TO MORE SOLID GROUND!
RIGHT AS RAIN!
I'LL PUT A CREW OF DIGGERS TO WORK ON THE JOB RIGHT AWAY! THERE COULD BE AN EARTHQUAKE ON ITS WAY HERE TO HAPPEN RIGHT NOW!

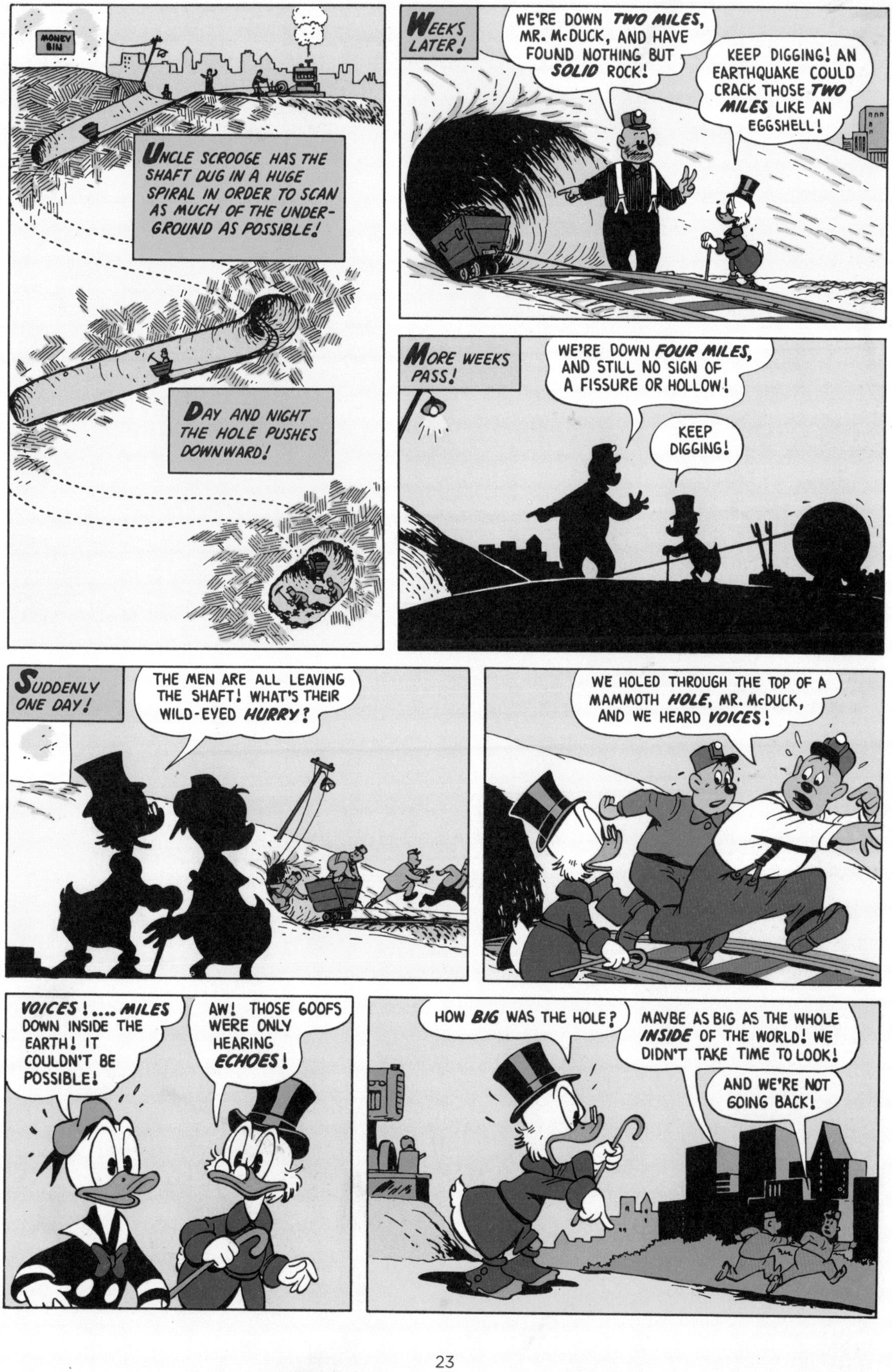
MONEY BIN
UNCLE SCROOGE HAS THE SHAFT DUG IN A HUGE SPIRAL IN ORDER TO SCAN AS MUCH OF THE UNDERGROUND AS POSSIBLE!
DAY AND NIGHT THE HOLE PUSHES DOWNWARD!
WEEKS LATER!
WE'RE DOWN TWO MILES, MR. McDUCK, AND HAVE FOUND NOTHING BUT SOLID ROCK!
KEEP DIGGING! AN EARTHQUAKE COULD CRACK THOSE TWO MILES LIKE AN EGGSHELL!
MORE WEEKS PASS!
WE'RE DOWN FOUR MILES, AND STILL NO SIGN OF A FISSURE OR HOLLOW!
KEEP DIGGING!
SUDDENLY ONE DAY!
THE MEN ARE ALL LEAVING THE SHAFT! WHAT'S THEIR WILD-EYED HURRY?
WE HOLED THROUGH THE TOP OF A MAMMOTH HOLE, MR. McDUCK, AND WE HEARD VOICES!
VOICES!.... MILES DOWN INSIDE THE EARTH! IT COULDN'T BE POSSIBLE!
AW! THOSE GOOFS WERE ONLY HEARING ECHOES!
HOW BIG WAS THE HOLE?
MAYBE AS BIG AS THE WHOLE INSIDE OF THE WORLD! WE DIDN'T TAKE TIME TO LOOK!
AND WE'RE NOT GOING BACK!

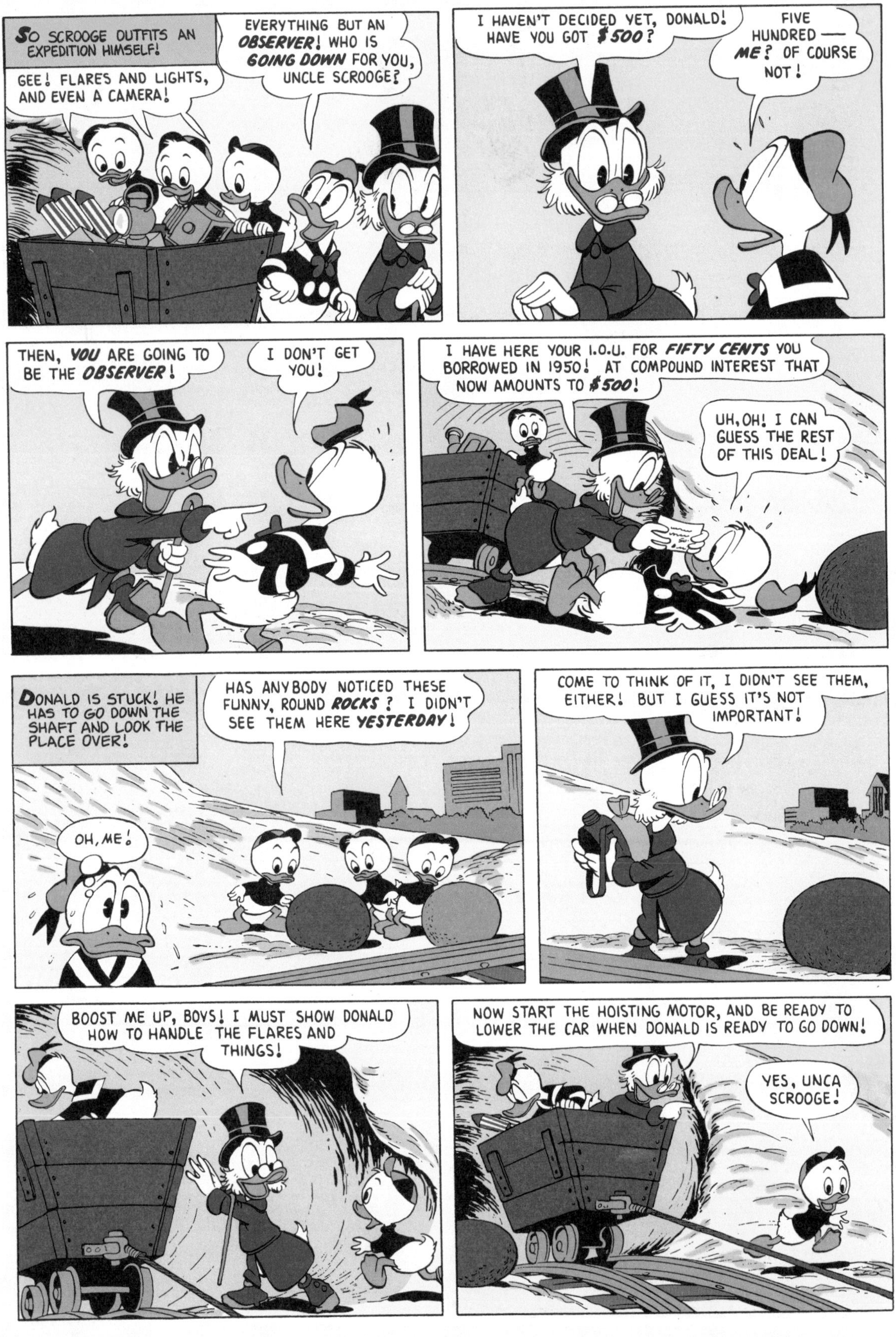

SO SCROOGE OUTFITS AN EXPEDITION HIMSELF!
GEE! FLARES AND LIGHTS, AND EVEN A CAMERA!
EVERYTHING BUT AN OBSERVER! WHO IS GOING DOWN FOR YOU, UNCLE SCROOGE?
I HAVEN'T DECIDED YET, DONALD! HAVE YOU GOT $500?
FIVE HUNDRED — ME? OF COURSE NOT!
THEN, YOU ARE GOING TO BE THE OBSERVER!
I DON'T GET YOU!
I HAVE HERE YOUR I.O.U. FOR FIFTY CENTS YOU BORROWED IN 1950! AT COMPOUND INTEREST THAT NOW AMOUNTS TO $500!
UH, OH! I CAN GUESS THE REST OF THIS DEAL!
DONALD IS STUCK! HE HAS TO GO DOWN THE SHAFT AND LOOK THE PLACE OVER!
HAS ANYBODY NOTICED THESE FUNNY, ROUND ROCKS? I DIDN'T SEE THEM HERE YESTERDAY!
OH, ME!
COME TO THINK OF IT, I DIDN'T SEE THEM, EITHER! BUT I GUESS IT'S NOT IMPORTANT!
BOOST ME UP, BOYS! I MUST SHOW DONALD HOW TO HANDLE THE FLARES AND THINGS!
NOW START THE HOISTING MOTOR, AND BE READY TO LOWER THE CAR WHEN DONALD IS READY TO GO DOWN!
YES, UNCA SCROOGE!

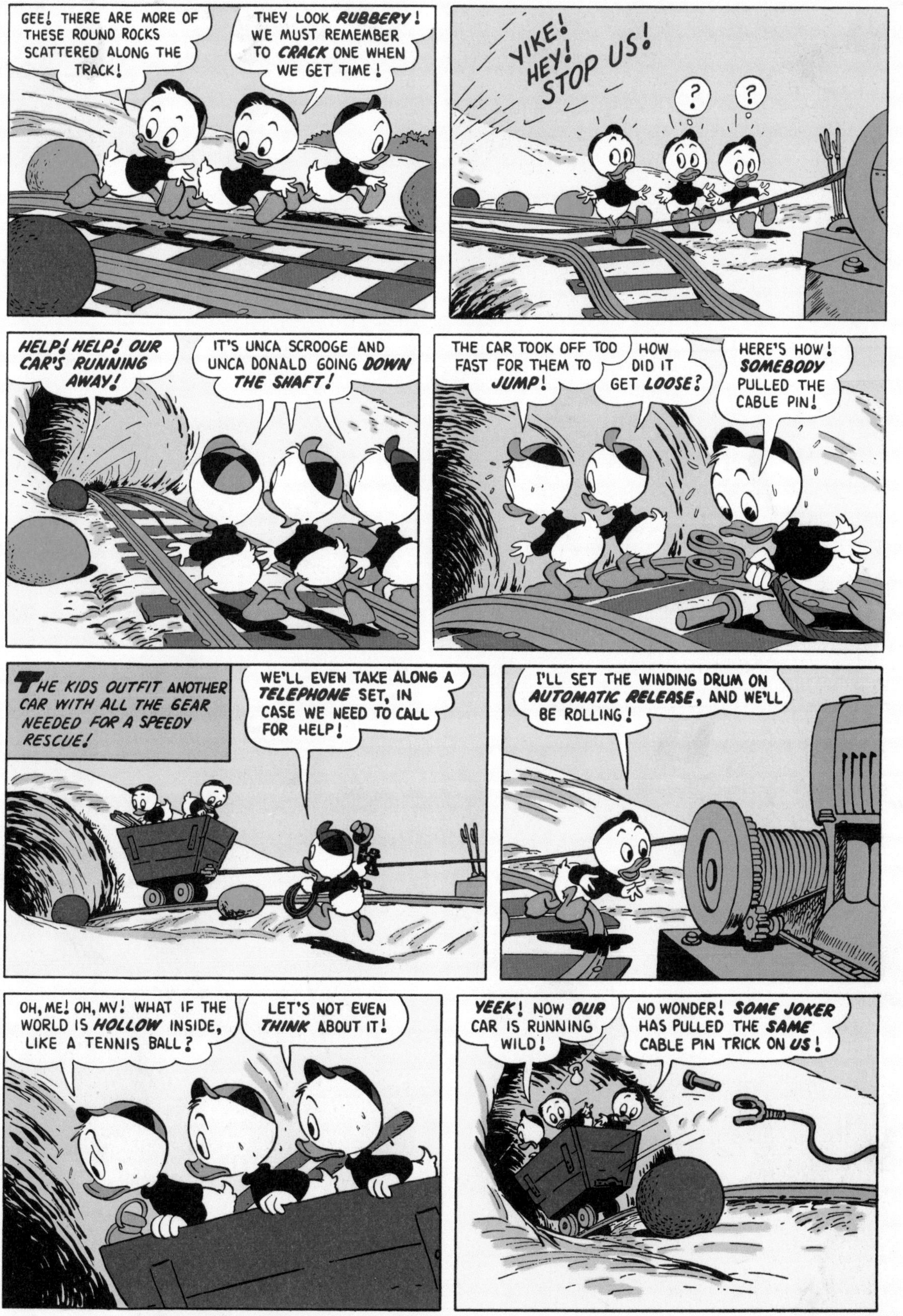

GEE! THERE ARE MORE OF THESE ROUND ROCKS SCATTERED ALONG THE TRACK!
THEY LOOK **RUBBERY**! WE MUST REMEMBER TO **CRACK** ONE WHEN WE GET TIME!
YIKE! HEY! STOP US!
?
?
HELP! HELP! OUR CAR'S RUNNING AWAY!
IT'S UNCA SCROOGE AND UNCA DONALD GOING **DOWN THE SHAFT**!
THE CAR TOOK OFF TOO FAST FOR THEM TO **JUMP**!
HOW DID IT GET **LOOSE**?
HERE'S HOW! **SOMEBODY** PULLED THE CABLE PIN!
THE KIDS OUTFIT ANOTHER CAR WITH ALL THE GEAR NEEDED FOR A SPEEDY RESCUE!
WE'LL EVEN TAKE ALONG A **TELEPHONE** SET, IN CASE WE NEED TO CALL FOR HELP!
I'LL SET THE WINDING DRUM ON **AUTOMATIC RELEASE**, AND WE'LL BE ROLLING!
OH, ME! OH, MY! WHAT IF THE WORLD IS **HOLLOW** INSIDE, LIKE A TENNIS BALL?
LET'S NOT EVEN **THINK** ABOUT IT!
YEEK! NOW **OUR** CAR IS RUNNING WILD!
NO WONDER! **SOME JOKER** HAS PULLED THE **SAME** CABLE PIN TRICK ON **US**!

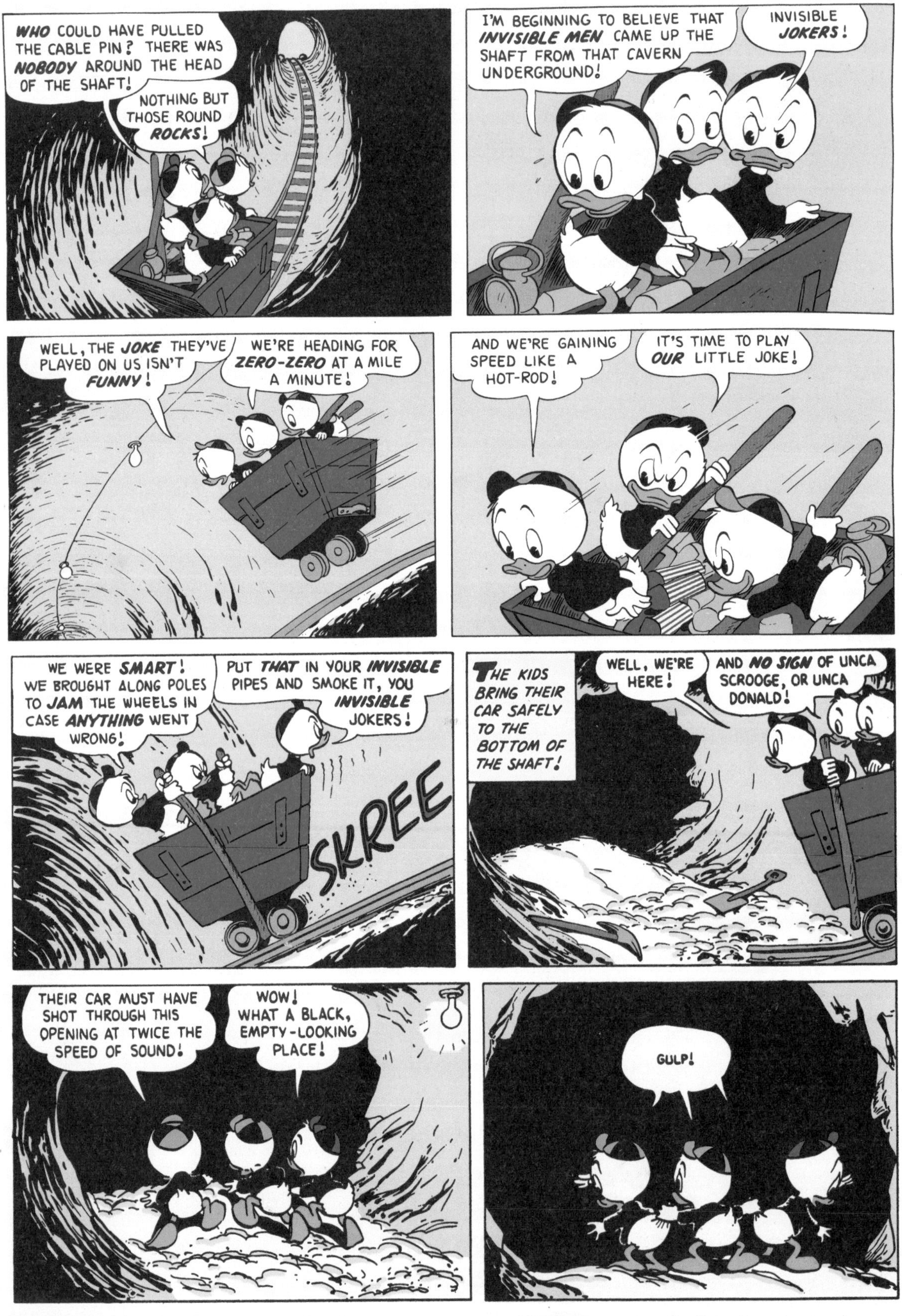
WHO COULD HAVE PULLED THE CABLE PIN? THERE WAS NOBODY AROUND THE HEAD OF THE SHAFT!
NOTHING BUT THOSE ROUND ROCKS!
I'M BEGINNING TO BELIEVE THAT INVISIBLE MEN CAME UP THE SHAFT FROM THAT CAVERN UNDERGROUND!
INVISIBLE JOKERS!
WELL, THE JOKE THEY'VE PLAYED ON US ISN'T FUNNY!
WE'RE HEADING FOR ZERO-ZERO AT A MILE A MINUTE!
AND WE'RE GAINING SPEED LIKE A HOT-ROD!
IT'S TIME TO PLAY OUR LITTLE JOKE!
WE WERE SMART! WE BROUGHT ALONG POLES TO JAM THE WHEELS IN CASE ANYTHING WENT WRONG!
PUT THAT IN YOUR INVISIBLE PIPES AND SMOKE IT, YOU INVISIBLE JOKERS!
SKREE
THE KIDS BRING THEIR CAR SAFELY TO THE BOTTOM OF THE SHAFT!
WELL, WE'RE HERE!
AND NO SIGN OF UNCA SCROOGE, OR UNCA DONALD!
THEIR CAR MUST HAVE SHOT THROUGH THIS OPENING AT TWICE THE SPEED OF SOUND!
WOW! WHAT A BLACK, EMPTY-LOOKING PLACE!
GULP!

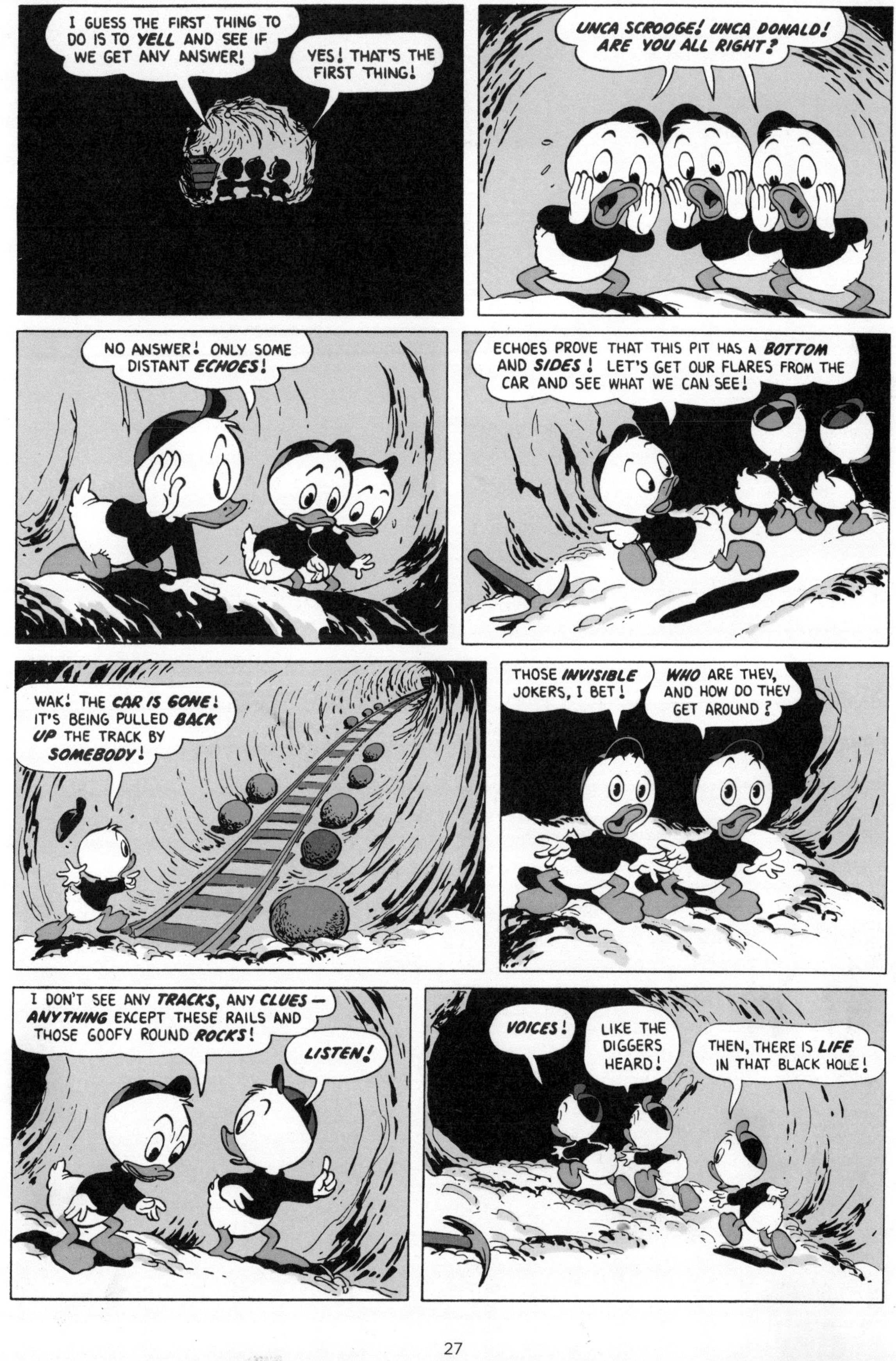
I GUESS THE FIRST THING TO DO IS TO YELL AND SEE IF WE GET ANY ANSWER!
YES! THAT'S THE FIRST THING!
UNCA SCROOGE! UNCA DONALD! ARE YOU ALL RIGHT?
NO ANSWER! ONLY SOME DISTANT ECHOES!
ECHOES PROVE THAT THIS PIT HAS A BOTTOM AND SIDES! LET'S GET OUR FLARES FROM THE CAR AND SEE WHAT WE CAN SEE!
WAK! THE CAR IS GONE! IT'S BEING PULLED BACK UP THE TRACK BY SOMEBODY!
THOSE INVISIBLE JOKERS, I BET!
WHO ARE THEY, AND HOW DO THEY GET AROUND?
I DON'T SEE ANY TRACKS, ANY CLUES — ANYTHING EXCEPT THESE RAILS AND THOSE GOOFY ROUND ROCKS!
LISTEN!
VOICES!
LIKE THE DIGGERS HEARD!
THEN, THERE IS LIFE IN THAT BLACK HOLE!

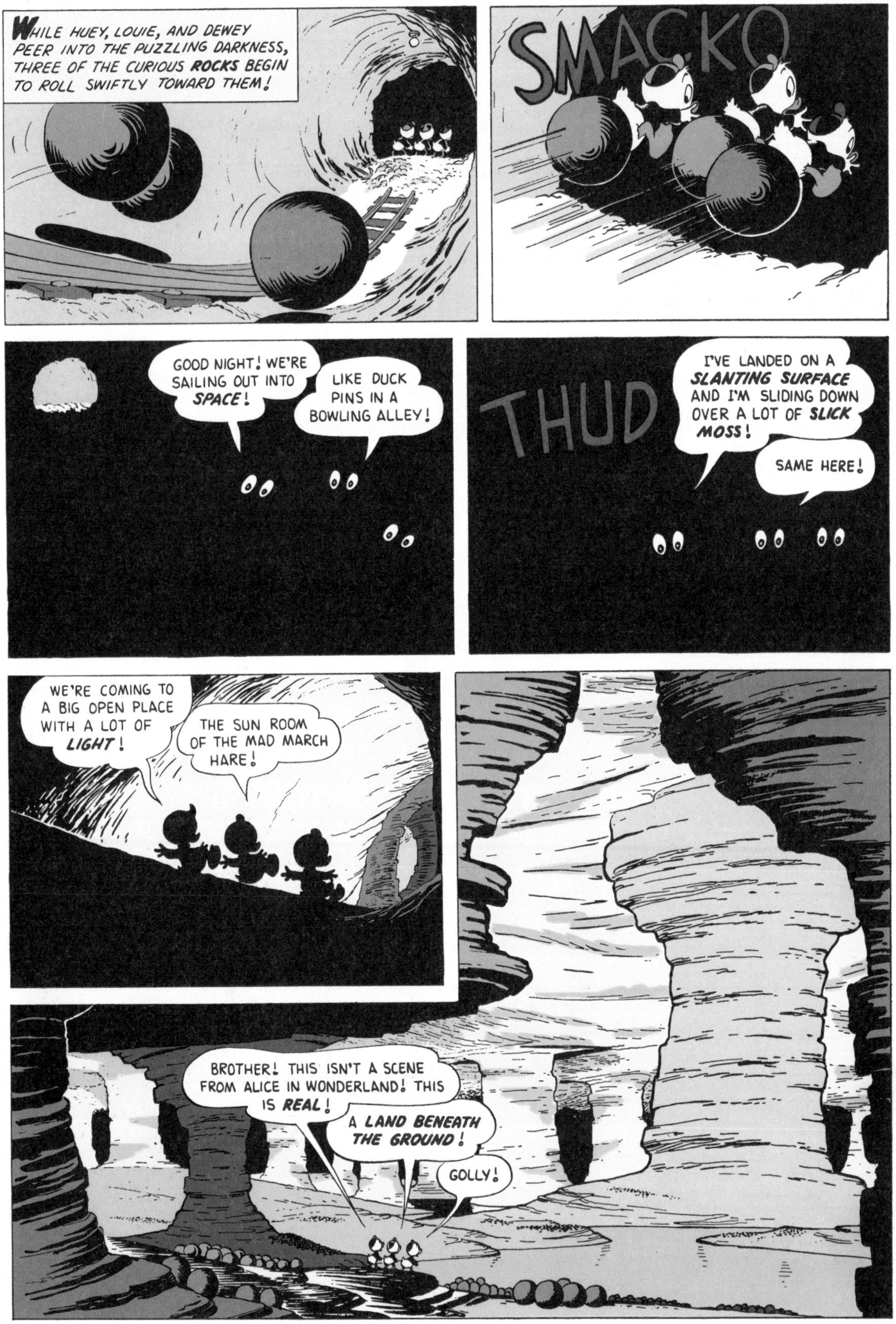

WHILE HUEY, LOUIE, AND DEWEY PEER INTO THE PUZZLING DARKNESS, THREE OF THE CURIOUS ROCKS BEGIN TO ROLL SWIFTLY TOWARD THEM!
SMACKO
GOOD NIGHT! WE'RE SAILING OUT INTO SPACE!
LIKE DUCK PINS IN A BOWLING ALLEY!
THUD
I'VE LANDED ON A SLANTING SURFACE AND I'M SLIDING DOWN OVER A LOT OF SLICK MOSS!
SAME HERE!
WE'RE COMING TO A BIG OPEN PLACE WITH A LOT OF LIGHT!
THE SUN ROOM OF THE MAD MARCH HARE!
BROTHER! THIS ISN'T A SCENE FROM ALICE IN WONDERLAND! THIS IS REAL!
A LAND BENEATH THE GROUND!
GOLLY!

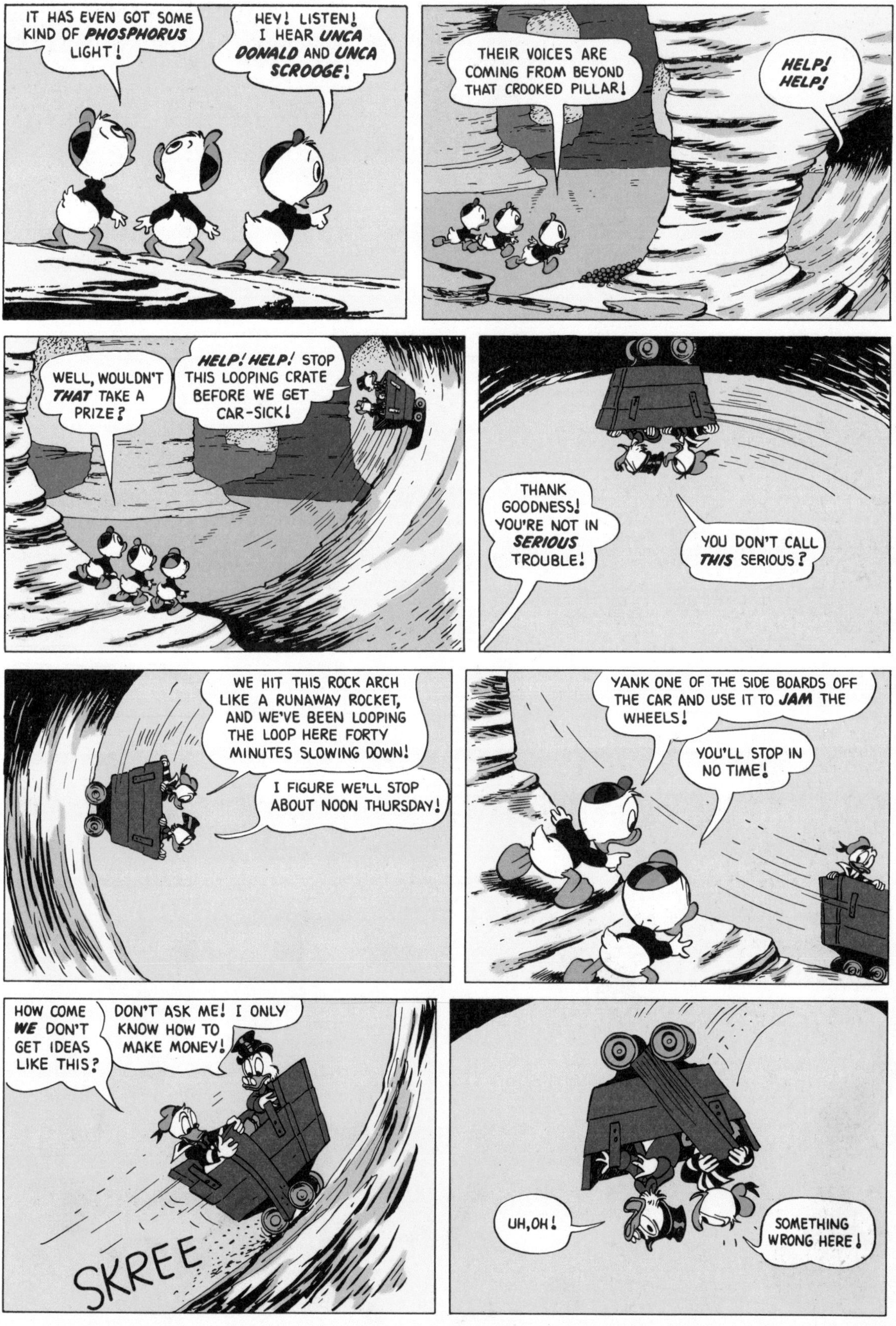
IT HAS EVEN GOT SOME KIND OF PHOSPHORUS LIGHT!
HEY! LISTEN! I HEAR UNCA DONALD AND UNCA SCROOGE!
THEIR VOICES ARE COMING FROM BEYOND THAT CROOKED PILLAR!
HELP! HELP!
WELL, WOULDN'T THAT TAKE A PRIZE?
HELP! HELP! STOP THIS LOOPING CRATE BEFORE WE GET CAR-SICK!
THANK GOODNESS! YOU'RE NOT IN SERIOUS TROUBLE!
YOU DON'T CALL THIS SERIOUS?
WE HIT THIS ROCK ARCH LIKE A RUNAWAY ROCKET, AND WE'VE BEEN LOOPING THE LOOP HERE FORTY MINUTES SLOWING DOWN!
I FIGURE WE'LL STOP ABOUT NOON THURSDAY!
YANK ONE OF THE SIDE BOARDS OFF THE CAR AND USE IT TO JAM THE WHEELS!
YOU'LL STOP IN NO TIME!
HOW COME WE DON'T GET IDEAS LIKE THIS?
DON'T ASK ME! I ONLY KNOW HOW TO MAKE MONEY!
SKREE
UH, OH!
SOMETHING WRONG HERE!

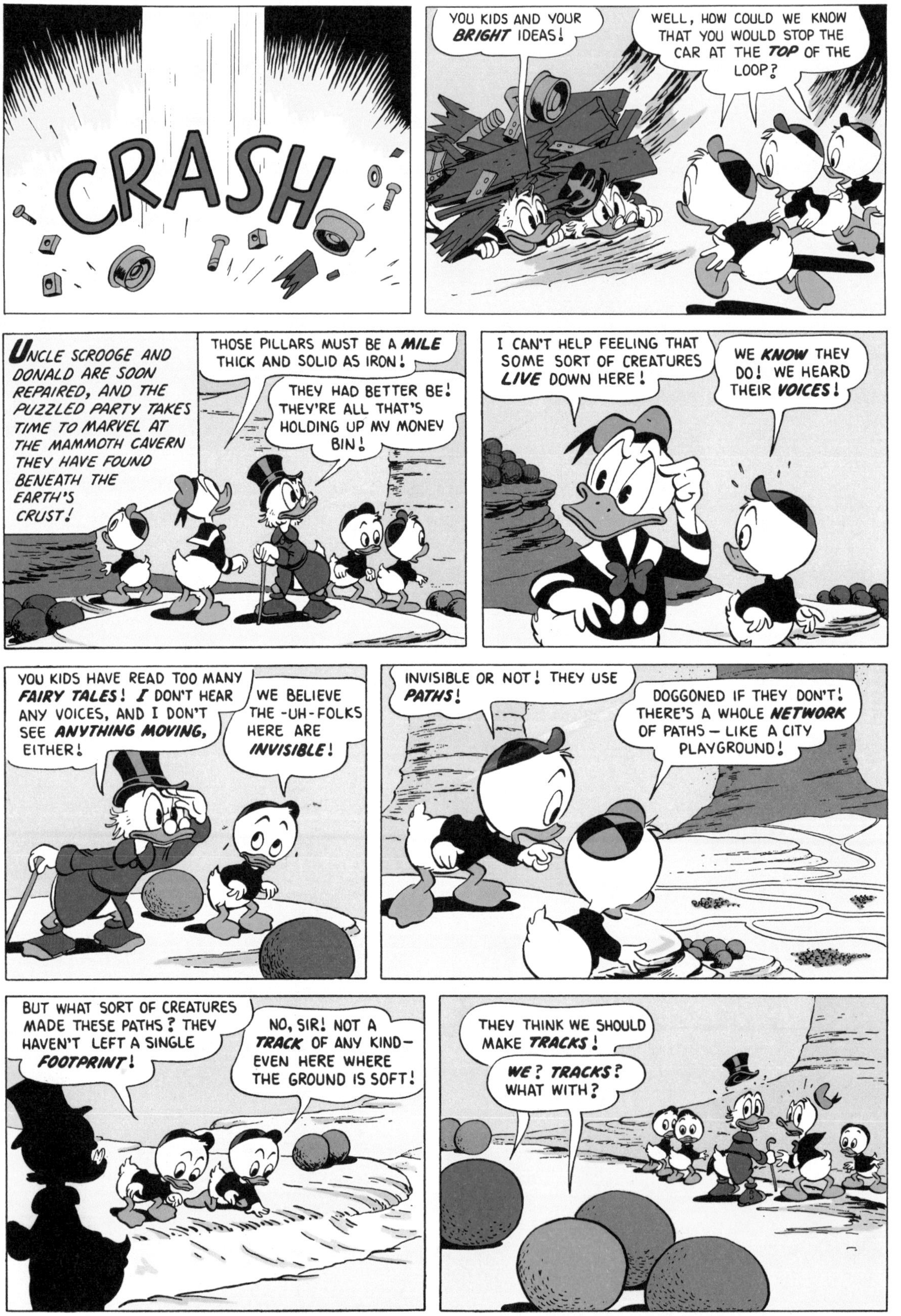
CRASH
YOU KIDS AND YOUR BRIGHT IDEAS!
WELL, HOW COULD WE KNOW THAT YOU WOULD STOP THE CAR AT THE TOP OF THE LOOP?
UNCLE SCROOGE AND DONALD ARE SOON REPAIRED, AND THE PUZZLED PARTY TAKES TIME TO MARVEL AT THE MAMMOTH CAVERN THEY HAVE FOUND BENEATH THE EARTH'S CRUST!
THOSE PILLARS MUST BE A MILE THICK AND SOLID AS IRON!
THEY HAD BETTER BE! THEY'RE ALL THAT'S HOLDING UP MY MONEY BIN!
I CAN'T HELP FEELING THAT SOME SORT OF CREATURES LIVE DOWN HERE!
WE KNOW THEY DO! WE HEARD THEIR VOICES!
YOU KIDS HAVE READ TOO MANY FAIRY TALES! I DON'T HEAR ANY VOICES, AND I DON'T SEE ANYTHING MOVING, EITHER!
WE BELIEVE THE -UH-FOLKS HERE ARE INVISIBLE!
INVISIBLE OR NOT! THEY USE PATHS!
DOGGONED IF THEY DON'T! THERE'S A WHOLE NETWORK OF PATHS — LIKE A CITY PLAYGROUND!
BUT WHAT SORT OF CREATURES MADE THESE PATHS? THEY HAVEN'T LEFT A SINGLE FOOTPRINT!
NO, SIR! NOT A TRACK OF ANY KIND— EVEN HERE WHERE THE GROUND IS SOFT!
THEY THINK WE SHOULD MAKE TRACKS!
WE? TRACKS? WHAT WITH?

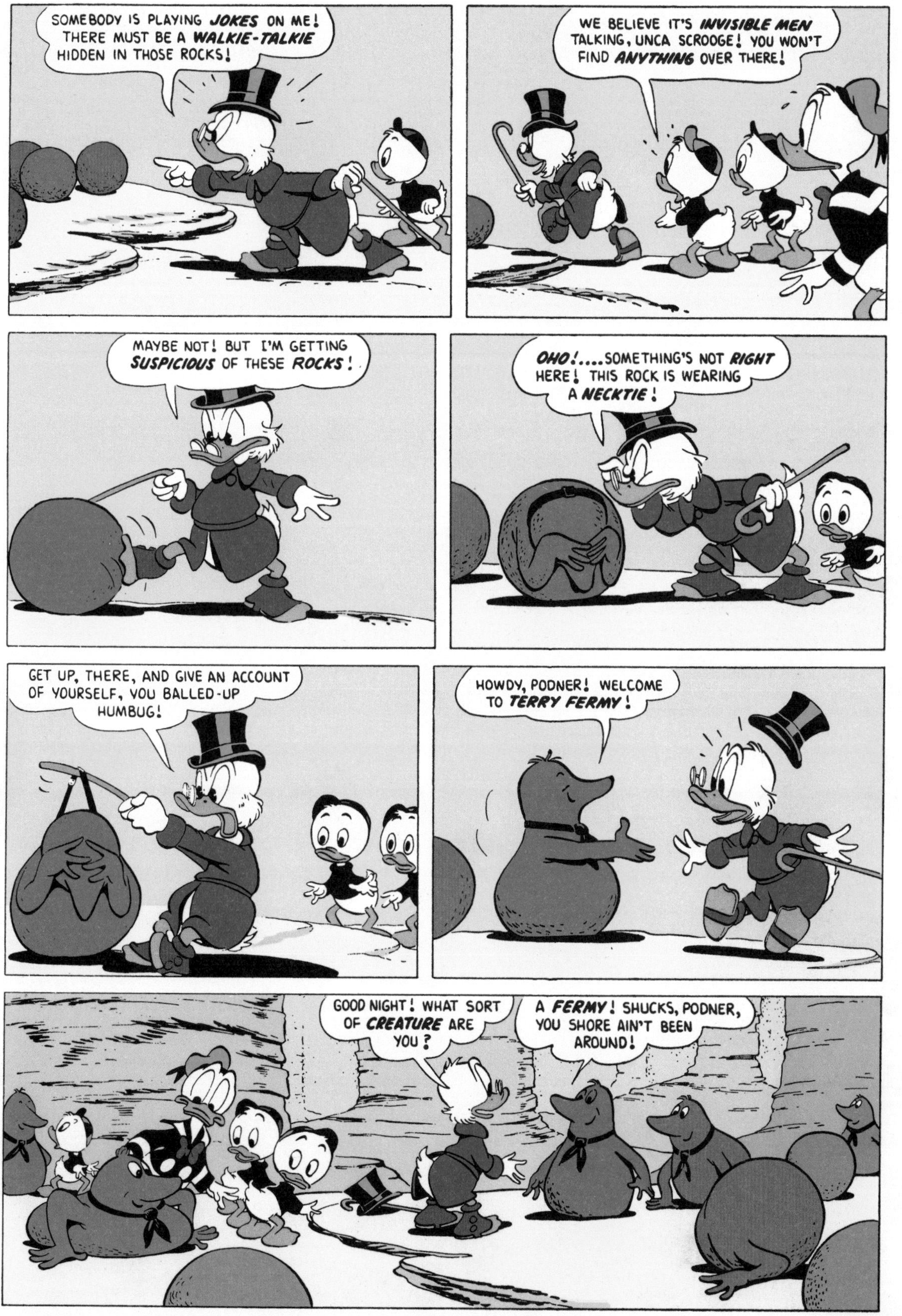
SOMEBODY IS PLAYING JOKES ON ME! THERE MUST BE A WALKIE-TALKIE HIDDEN IN THOSE ROCKS!
WE BELIEVE IT'S INVISIBLE MEN TALKING, UNCA SCROOGE! YOU WON'T FIND ANYTHING OVER THERE!
MAYBE NOT! BUT I'M GETTING SUSPICIOUS OF THESE ROCKS!
OHO!....SOMETHING'S NOT RIGHT HERE! THIS ROCK IS WEARING A NECKTIE!
GET UP, THERE, AND GIVE AN ACCOUNT OF YOURSELF, YOU BALLED-UP HUMBUG!
HOWDY, PODNER! WELCOME TO TERRY FERMY!
GOOD NIGHT! WHAT SORT OF CREATURE ARE YOU?
A FERMY! SHUCKS, PODNER, YOU SHORE AIN'T BEEN AROUND!

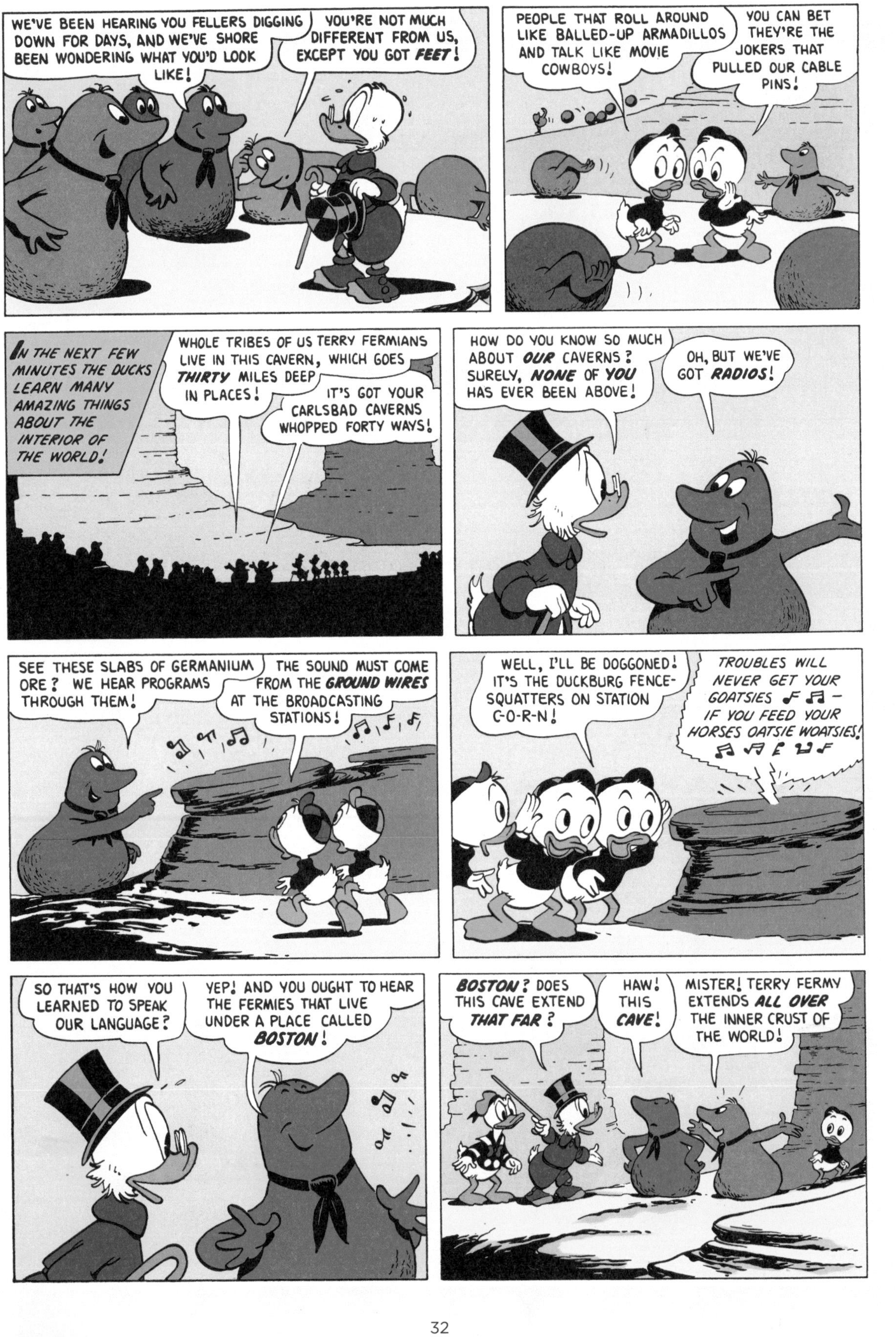

WE'VE BEEN HEARING YOU FELLERS DIGGING DOWN FOR DAYS, AND WE'VE SHORE BEEN WONDERING WHAT YOU'D LOOK LIKE!
YOU'RE NOT MUCH DIFFERENT FROM US, EXCEPT YOU GOT FEET!
PEOPLE THAT ROLL AROUND LIKE BALLED-UP ARMADILLOS AND TALK LIKE MOVIE COWBOYS!
YOU CAN BET THEY'RE THE JOKERS THAT PULLED OUR CABLE PINS!
IN THE NEXT FEW MINUTES THE DUCKS LEARN MANY AMAZING THINGS ABOUT THE INTERIOR OF THE WORLD!
WHOLE TRIBES OF US TERRY FERMIANS LIVE IN THIS CAVERN, WHICH GOES THIRTY MILES DEEP IN PLACES!
IT'S GOT YOUR CARLSBAD CAVERNS WHOPPED FORTY WAYS!
HOW DO YOU KNOW SO MUCH ABOUT OUR CAVERNS? SURELY, NONE OF YOU HAS EVER BEEN ABOVE!
OH, BUT WE'VE GOT RADIOS!
SEE THESE SLABS OF GERMANIUM ORE? WE HEAR PROGRAMS THROUGH THEM!
THE SOUND MUST COME FROM THE GROUND WIRES AT THE BROADCASTING STATIONS!
WELL, I'LL BE DOGGONED! IT'S THE DUCKBURG FENCE-SQUATTERS ON STATION C-O-R-N!
TROUBLES WILL NEVER GET YOUR GOATSIES — IF YOU FEED YOUR HORSES OATSIE WOATSIES!
SO THAT'S HOW YOU LEARNED TO SPEAK OUR LANGUAGE?
YEP! AND YOU OUGHT TO HEAR THE FERMIES THAT LIVE UNDER A PLACE CALLED BOSTON!
BOSTON? DOES THIS CAVE EXTEND THAT FAR?
HAW! THIS CAVE!
MISTER! TERRY FERMY EXTENDS ALL OVER THE INNER CRUST OF THE WORLD!

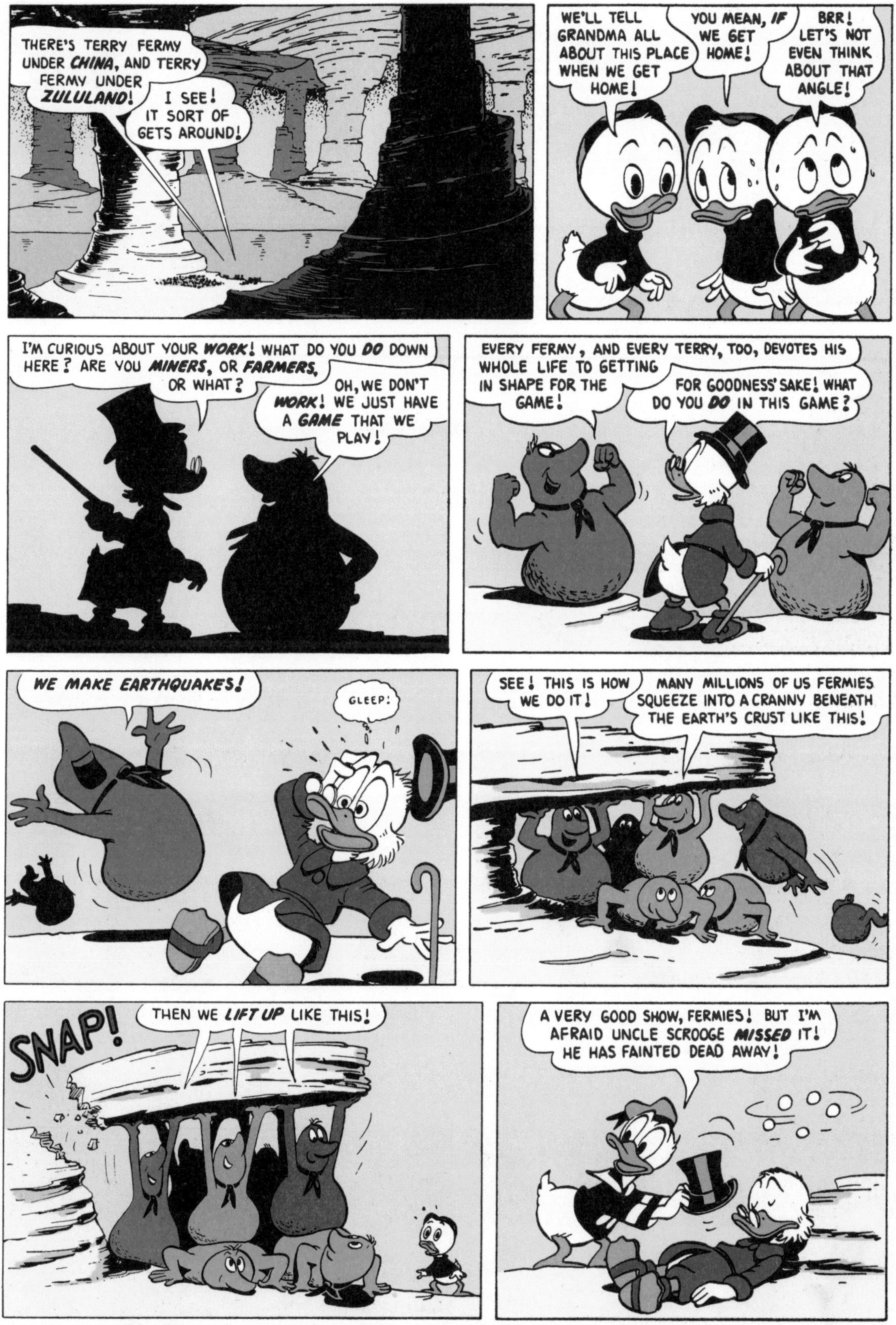
THERE'S TERRY FERMY UNDER CHINA, AND TERRY FERMY UNDER ZULULAND!
I SEE! IT SORT OF GETS AROUND!
WE'LL TELL GRANDMA ALL ABOUT THIS PLACE WHEN WE GET HOME!
YOU MEAN, IF WE GET HOME!
BRR! LET'S NOT EVEN THINK ABOUT THAT ANGLE!
I'M CURIOUS ABOUT YOUR WORK! WHAT DO YOU DO DOWN HERE? ARE YOU MINERS, OR FARMERS, OR WHAT?
OH, WE DON'T WORK! WE JUST HAVE A GAME THAT WE PLAY!
EVERY FERMY, AND EVERY TERRY, TOO, DEVOTES HIS WHOLE LIFE TO GETTING IN SHAPE FOR THE GAME!
FOR GOODNESS' SAKE! WHAT DO YOU DO IN THIS GAME?
WE MAKE EARTHQUAKES!
GLEEP!
SEE! THIS IS HOW WE DO IT!
MANY MILLIONS OF US FERMIES SQUEEZE INTO A CRANNY BENEATH THE EARTH'S CRUST LIKE THIS!
SNAP!
THEN WE LIFT UP LIKE THIS!
A VERY GOOD SHOW, FERMIES! BUT I'M AFRAID UNCLE SCROOGE MISSED IT! HE HAS FAINTED DEAD AWAY!

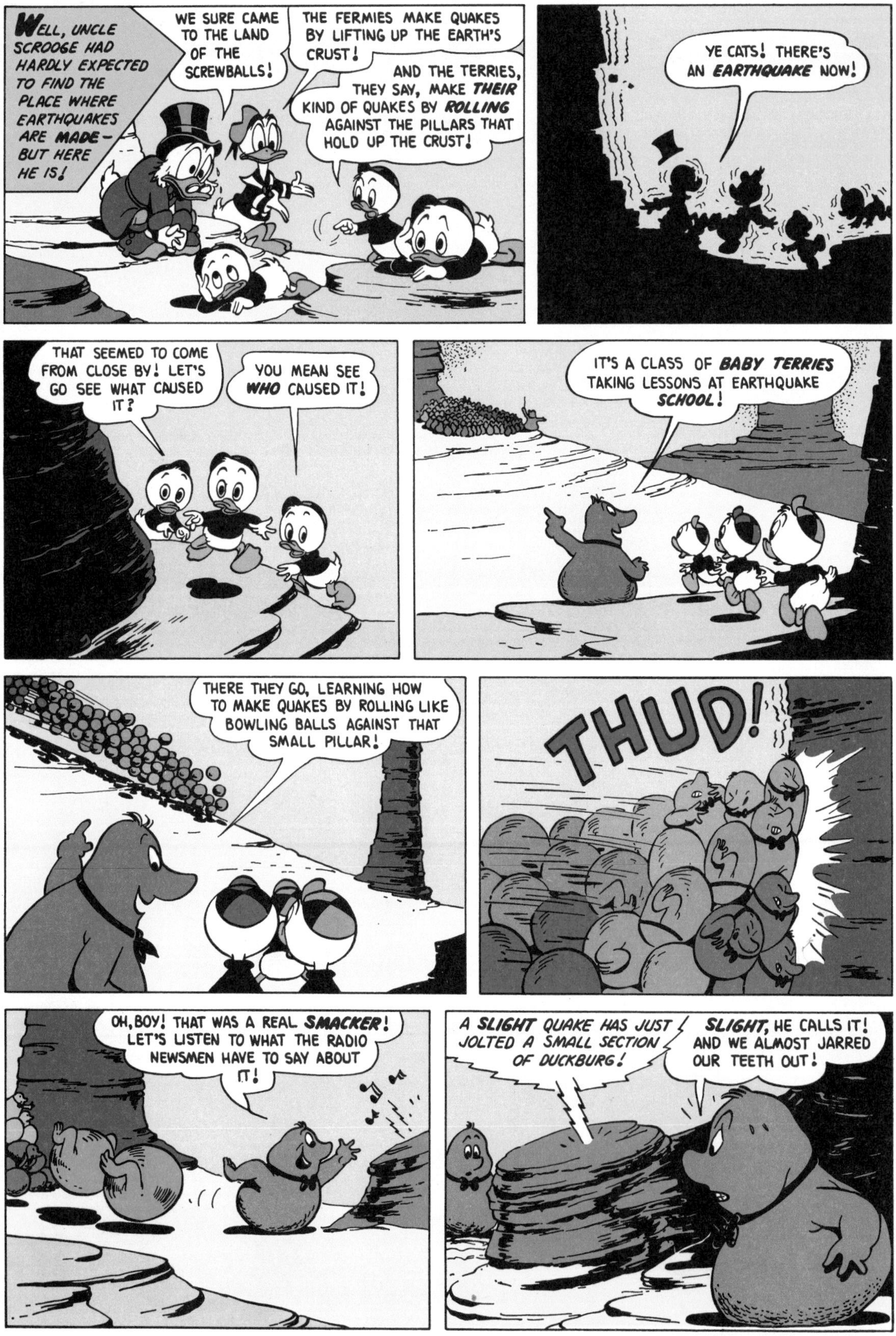
WELL, UNCLE SCROOGE HAD HARDLY EXPECTED TO FIND THE PLACE WHERE EARTHQUAKES ARE MADE— BUT HERE HE IS!
WE SURE CAME TO THE LAND OF THE SCREWBALLS!
THE FERMIES MAKE QUAKES BY LIFTING UP THE EARTH'S CRUST!
AND THE TERRIES, THEY SAY, MAKE THEIR KIND OF QUAKES BY ROLLING AGAINST THE PILLARS THAT HOLD UP THE CRUST!
YE CATS! THERE'S AN EARTHQUAKE NOW!
THAT SEEMED TO COME FROM CLOSE BY! LET'S GO SEE WHAT CAUSED IT?
YOU MEAN SEE WHO CAUSED IT!
IT'S A CLASS OF BABY TERRIES TAKING LESSONS AT EARTHQUAKE SCHOOL!
THERE THEY GO, LEARNING HOW TO MAKE QUAKES BY ROLLING LIKE BOWLING BALLS AGAINST THAT SMALL PILLAR!
THUD!
OH, BOY! THAT WAS A REAL SMACKER! LET'S LISTEN TO WHAT THE RADIO NEWSMEN HAVE TO SAY ABOUT IT!
A SLIGHT QUAKE HAS JUST JOLTED A SMALL SECTION OF DUCKBURG!
SLIGHT, HE CALLS IT! AND WE ALMOST JARRED OUR TEETH OUT!

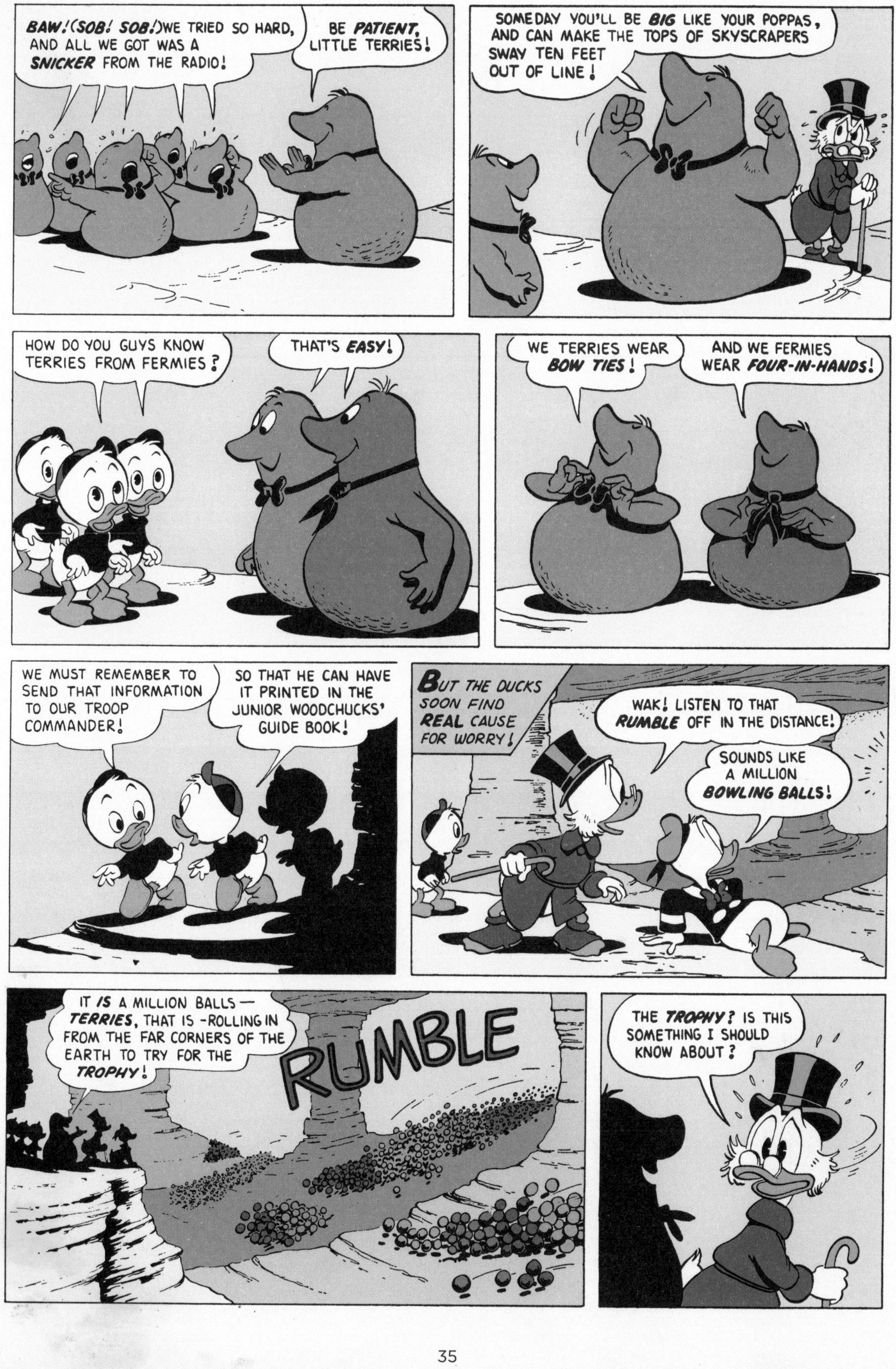
BAW! (SOB! SOB!) WE TRIED SO HARD, AND ALL WE GOT WAS A SNICKER FROM THE RADIO!
BE PATIENT, LITTLE TERRIES!
SOMEDAY YOU'LL BE BIG LIKE YOUR POPPAS, AND CAN MAKE THE TOPS OF SKYSCRAPERS SWAY TEN FEET OUT OF LINE!
HOW DO YOU GUYS KNOW TERRIES FROM FERMIES?
THAT'S EASY!
WE TERRIES WEAR BOW TIES!
AND WE FERMIES WEAR FOUR-IN-HANDS!
WE MUST REMEMBER TO SEND THAT INFORMATION TO OUR TROOP COMMANDER!
SO THAT HE CAN HAVE IT PRINTED IN THE JUNIOR WOODCHUCKS' GUIDE BOOK!
BUT THE DUCKS SOON FIND REAL CAUSE FOR WORRY!
WAK! LISTEN TO THAT RUMBLE OFF IN THE DISTANCE!
SOUNDS LIKE A MILLION BOWLING BALLS!
IT IS A MILLION BALLS— TERRIES, THAT IS -ROLLING IN FROM THE FAR CORNERS OF THE EARTH TO TRY FOR THE TROPHY!
RUMBLE
THE TROPHY? IS THIS SOMETHING I SHOULD KNOW ABOUT?

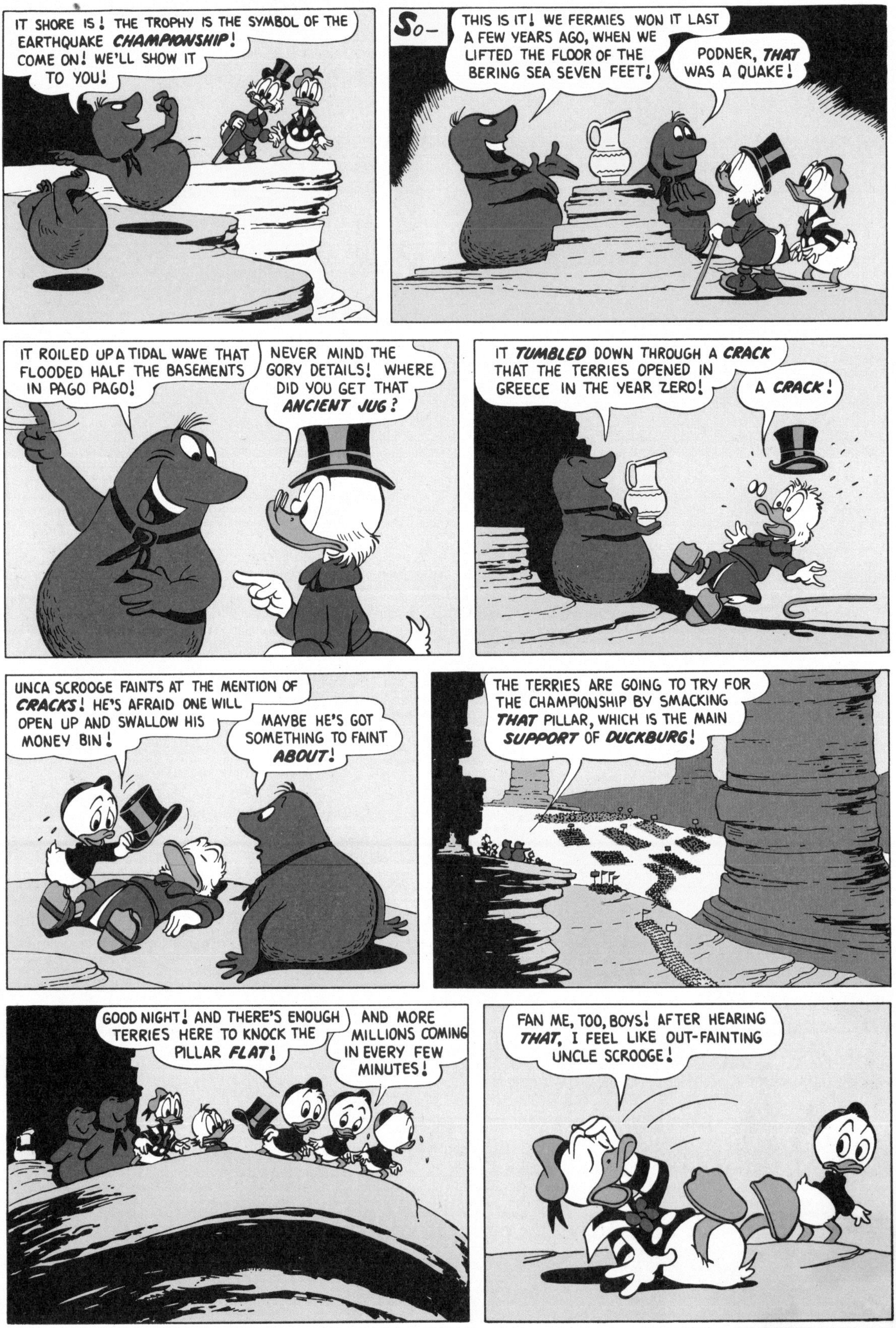
IT SHORE IS! THE TROPHY IS THE SYMBOL OF THE EARTHQUAKE CHAMPIONSHIP! COME ON! WE'LL SHOW IT TO YOU!
SO—
THIS IS IT! WE FERMIES WON IT LAST A FEW YEARS AGO, WHEN WE LIFTED THE FLOOR OF THE BERING SEA SEVEN FEET!
PODNER, THAT WAS A QUAKE!
IT ROILED UP A TIDAL WAVE THAT FLOODED HALF THE BASEMENTS IN PAGO PAGO!
NEVER MIND THE GORY DETAILS! WHERE DID YOU GET THAT ANCIENT JUG?
IT TUMBLED DOWN THROUGH A CRACK THAT THE TERRIES OPENED IN GREECE IN THE YEAR ZERO!
A CRACK!
UNCA SCROOGE FAINTS AT THE MENTION OF CRACKS! HE'S AFRAID ONE WILL OPEN UP AND SWALLOW HIS MONEY BIN!
MAYBE HE'S GOT SOMETHING TO FAINT ABOUT!
THE TERRIES ARE GOING TO TRY FOR THE CHAMPIONSHIP BY SMACKING THAT PILLAR, WHICH IS THE MAIN SUPPORT OF DUCKBURG!
GOOD NIGHT! AND THERE'S ENOUGH TERRIES HERE TO KNOCK THE PILLAR FLAT!
AND MORE MILLIONS COMING IN EVERY FEW MINUTES!
FAN ME, TOO, BOYS! AFTER HEARING THAT, I FEEL LIKE OUT-FAINTING UNCLE SCROOGE!

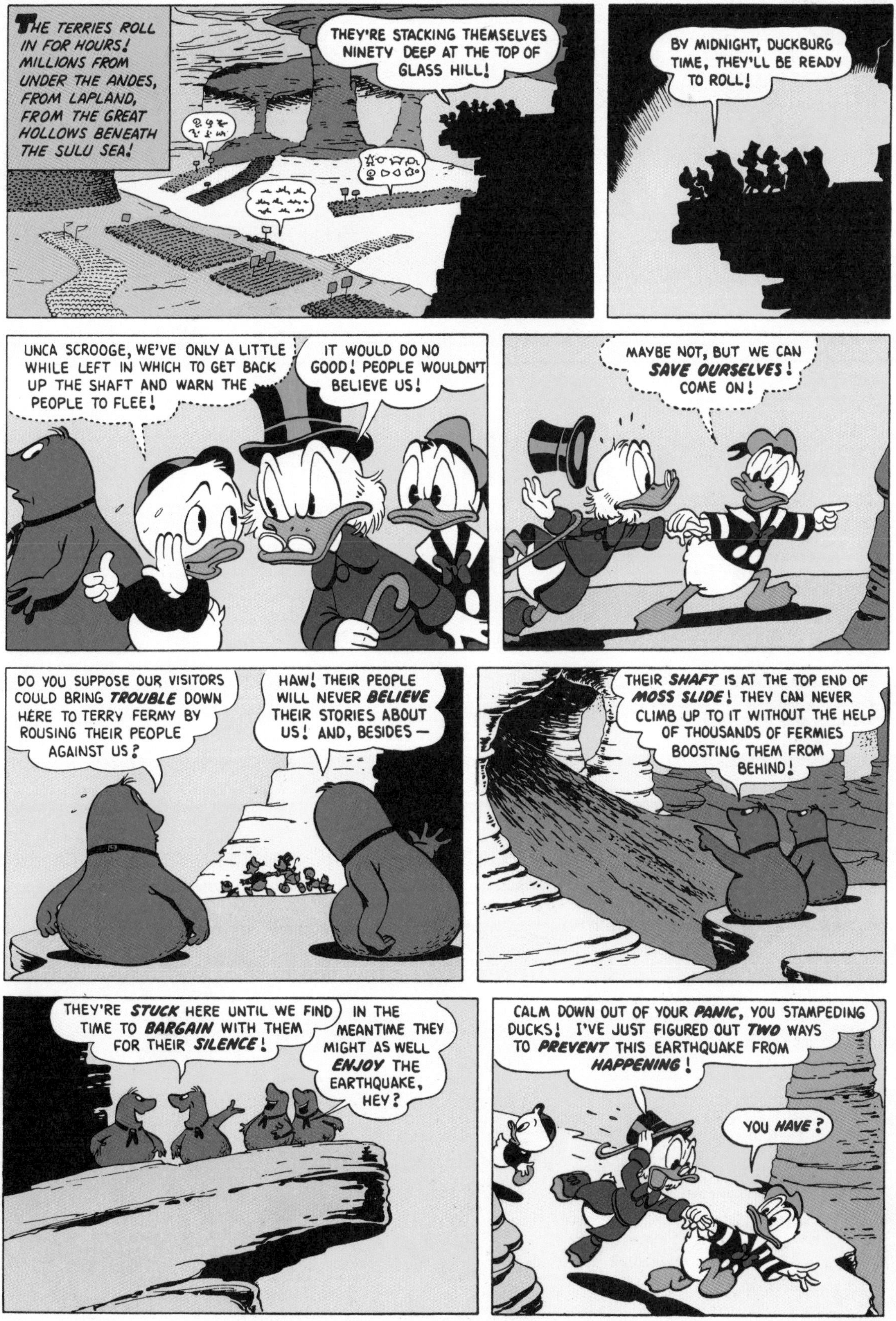
THE TERRIES ROLL IN FOR HOURS! MILLIONS FROM UNDER THE ANDES, FROM LAPLAND, FROM THE GREAT HOLLOWS BENEATH THE SULU SEA!
THEY'RE STACKING THEMSELVES NINETY DEEP AT THE TOP OF GLASS HILL!
BY MIDNIGHT, DUCKBURG TIME, THEY'LL BE READY TO ROLL!
UNCA SCROOGE, WE'VE ONLY A LITTLE WHILE LEFT IN WHICH TO GET BACK UP THE SHAFT AND WARN THE PEOPLE TO FLEE!
IT WOULD DO NO GOOD! PEOPLE WOULDN'T BELIEVE US!
MAYBE NOT, BUT WE CAN SAVE OURSELVES! COME ON!
DO YOU SUPPOSE OUR VISITORS COULD BRING TROUBLE DOWN HERE TO TERRY FERMY BY ROUSING THEIR PEOPLE AGAINST US?
HAW! THEIR PEOPLE WILL NEVER BELIEVE THEIR STORIES ABOUT US! AND, BESIDES—
THEIR SHAFT IS AT THE TOP END OF MOSS SLIDE! THEY CAN NEVER CLIMB UP TO IT WITHOUT THE HELP OF THOUSANDS OF FERMIES BOOSTING THEM FROM BEHIND!
THEY'RE STUCK HERE UNTIL WE FIND TIME TO BARGAIN WITH THEM FOR THEIR SILENCE!
IN THE MEANTIME THEY MIGHT AS WELL ENJOY THE EARTHQUAKE, HEY?
CALM DOWN OUT OF YOUR PANIC, YOU STAMPEDING DUCKS! I'VE JUST FIGURED OUT TWO WAYS TO PREVENT THIS EARTHQUAKE FROM HAPPENING!
YOU HAVE?

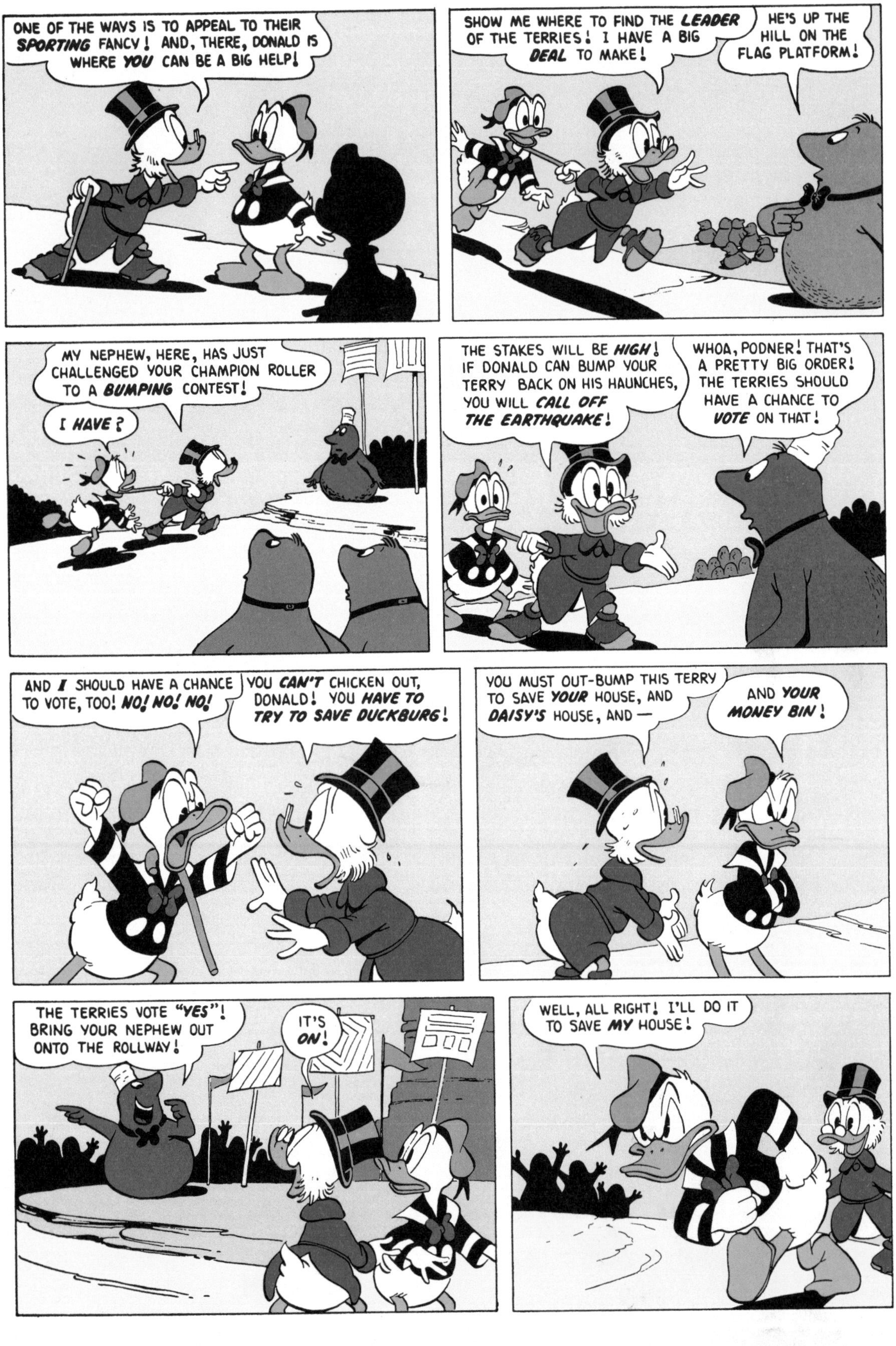
ONE OF THE WAYS IS TO APPEAL TO THEIR SPORTING FANCY! AND, THERE, DONALD IS WHERE YOU CAN BE A BIG HELP!
SHOW ME WHERE TO FIND THE LEADER OF THE TERRIES! I HAVE A BIG DEAL TO MAKE!
HE'S UP THE HILL ON THE FLAG PLATFORM!
MY NEPHEW, HERE, HAS JUST CHALLENGED YOUR CHAMPION ROLLER TO A BUMPING CONTEST!
I HAVE?
THE STAKES WILL BE HIGH! IF DONALD CAN BUMP YOUR TERRY BACK ON HIS HAUNCHES, YOU WILL CALL OFF THE EARTHQUAKE!
WHOA, PODNER! THAT'S A PRETTY BIG ORDER! THE TERRIES SHOULD HAVE A CHANCE TO VOTE ON THAT!
AND I SHOULD HAVE A CHANCE TO VOTE, TOO! NO! NO! NO!
YOU CAN'T CHICKEN OUT, DONALD! YOU HAVE TO TRY TO SAVE DUCKBURG!
YOU MUST OUT-BUMP THIS TERRY TO SAVE YOUR HOUSE, AND DAISY'S HOUSE, AND —
AND YOUR MONEY BIN!
THE TERRIES VOTE "YES"! BRING YOUR NEPHEW OUT ONTO THE ROLLWAY!
IT'S ON!
WELL, ALL RIGHT! I'LL DO IT TO SAVE MY HOUSE!

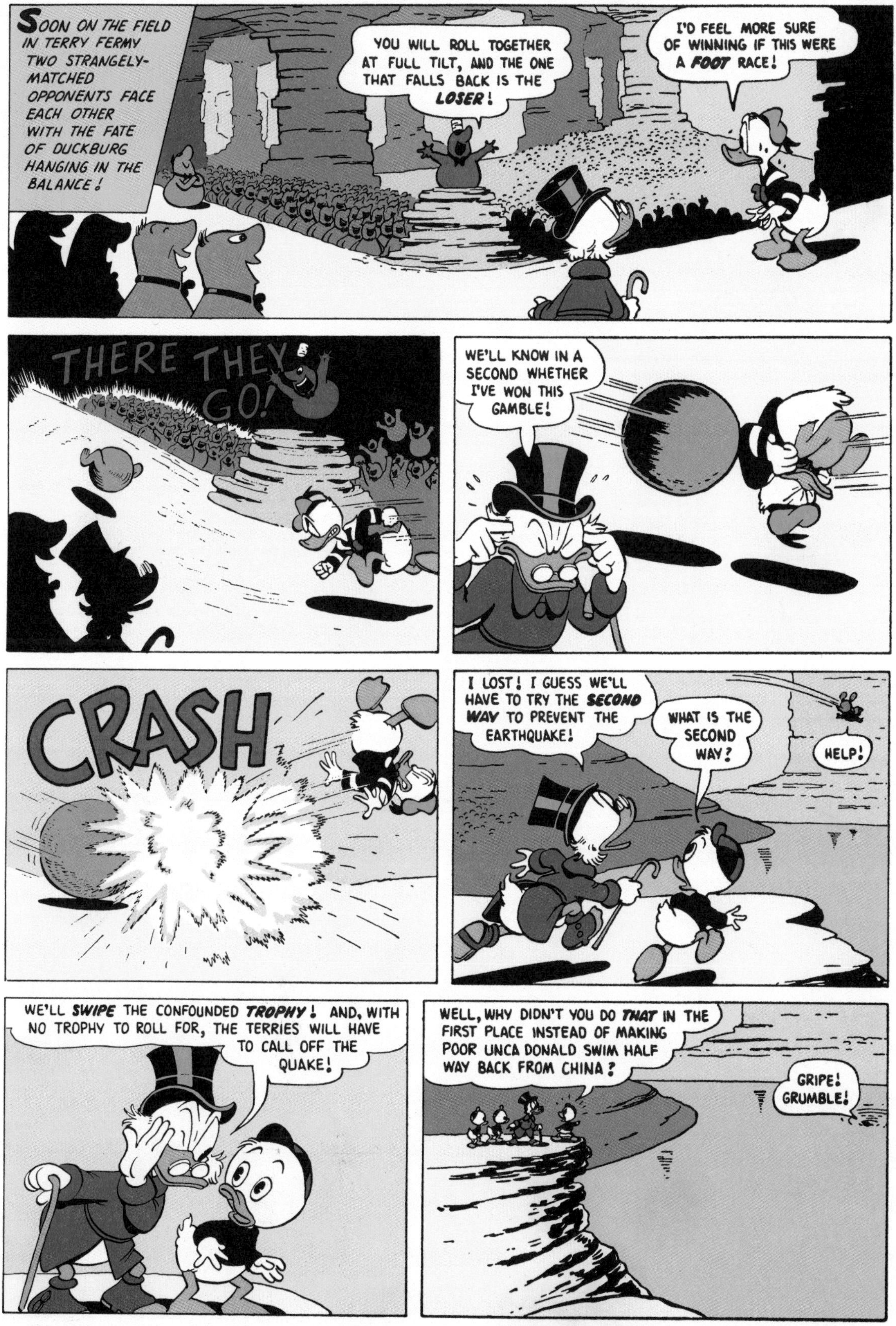
SOON ON THE FIELD IN TERRY FERMY TWO STRANGELY-MATCHED OPPONENTS FACE EACH OTHER WITH THE FATE OF DUCKBURG HANGING IN THE BALANCE!
YOU WILL ROLL TOGETHER AT FULL TILT, AND THE ONE THAT FALLS BACK IS THE LOSER!
I'D FEEL MORE SURE OF WINNING IF THIS WERE A FOOT RACE!
THERE THEY GO!
WE'LL KNOW IN A SECOND WHETHER I'VE WON THIS GAMBLE!
CRASH
I LOST! I GUESS WE'LL HAVE TO TRY THE SECOND WAY TO PREVENT THE EARTHQUAKE!
WHAT IS THE SECOND WAY?
HELP!
WE'LL SWIPE THE CONFOUNDED TROPHY! AND, WITH NO TROPHY TO ROLL FOR, THE TERRIES WILL HAVE TO CALL OFF THE QUAKE!
WELL, WHY DIDN'T YOU DO THAT IN THE FIRST PLACE INSTEAD OF MAKING POOR UNCA DONALD SWIM HALF WAY BACK FROM CHINA?
GRIPE! GRUMBLE!

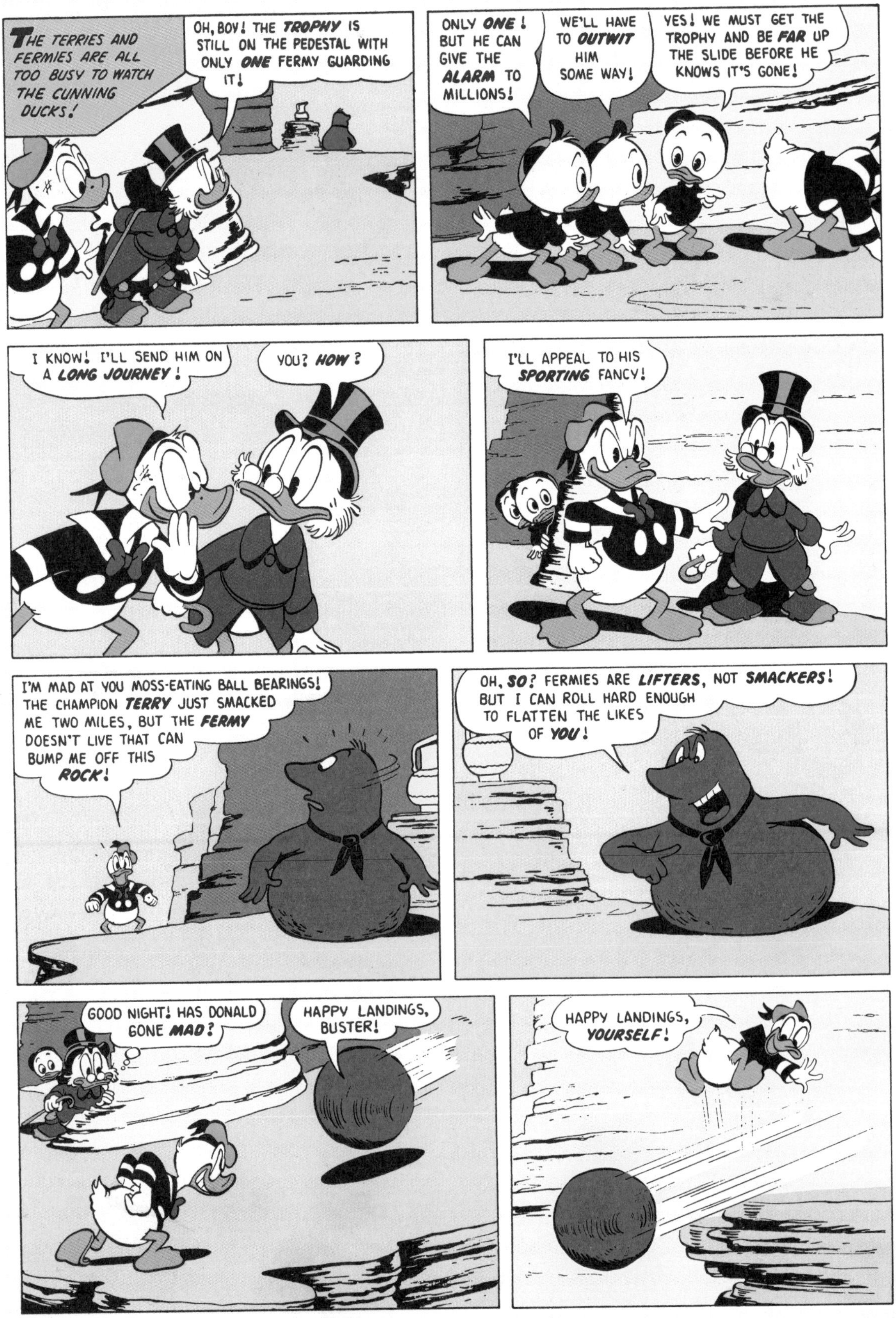
THE TERRIES AND FERMIES ARE ALL TOO BUSY TO WATCH THE CUNNING DUCKS!
OH, BOY! THE TROPHY IS STILL ON THE PEDESTAL WITH ONLY ONE FERMY GUARDING IT!
ONLY ONE! BUT HE CAN GIVE THE ALARM TO MILLIONS!
WE'LL HAVE TO OUTWIT HIM SOME WAY!
YES! WE MUST GET THE TROPHY AND BE FAR UP THE SLIDE BEFORE HE KNOWS IT'S GONE!
I KNOW! I'LL SEND HIM ON A LONG JOURNEY!
YOU? HOW?
I'LL APPEAL TO HIS SPORTING FANCY!
I'M MAD AT YOU MOSS-EATING BALL BEARINGS! THE CHAMPION TERRY JUST SMACKED ME TWO MILES, BUT THE FERMY DOESN'T LIVE THAT CAN BUMP ME OFF THIS ROCK!
OH, SO? FERMIES ARE LIFTERS, NOT SMACKERS! BUT I CAN ROLL HARD ENOUGH TO FLATTEN THE LIKES OF YOU!
GOOD NIGHT! HAS DONALD GONE MAD?
HAPPY LANDINGS, BUSTER!
HAPPY LANDINGS, YOURSELF!

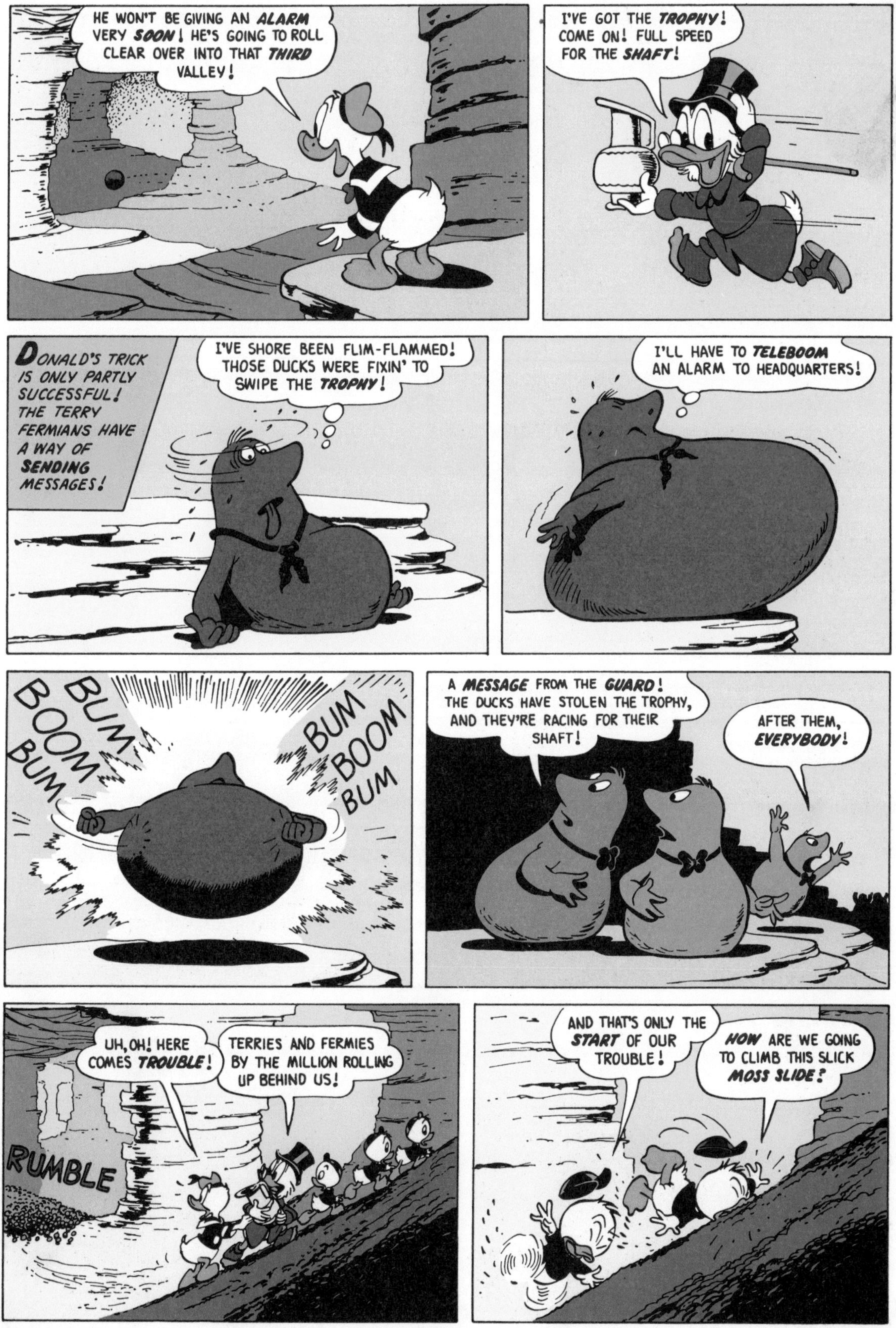
HE WON'T BE GIVING AN ALARM VERY SOON! HE'S GOING TO ROLL CLEAR OVER INTO THAT THIRD VALLEY!
I'VE GOT THE TROPHY! COME ON! FULL SPEED FOR THE SHAFT!
DONALD'S TRICK IS ONLY PARTLY SUCCESSFUL! THE TERRY FERMIANS HAVE A WAY OF SENDING MESSAGES!
I'VE SHORE BEEN FLIM-FLAMMED! THOSE DUCKS WERE FIXIN' TO SWIPE THE TROPHY!
I'LL HAVE TO TELEBOOM AN ALARM TO HEADQUARTERS!
BUM BOOM BUM
BUM BOOM BUM
A MESSAGE FROM THE GUARD! THE DUCKS HAVE STOLEN THE TROPHY, AND THEY'RE RACING FOR THEIR SHAFT!
AFTER THEM, EVERYBODY!
UH, OH! HERE COMES TROUBLE!
TERRIES AND FERMIES BY THE MILLION ROLLING UP BEHIND US!
RUMBLE
AND THAT'S ONLY THE START OF OUR TROUBLE!
HOW ARE WE GOING TO CLIMB THIS SLICK MOSS SLIDE?

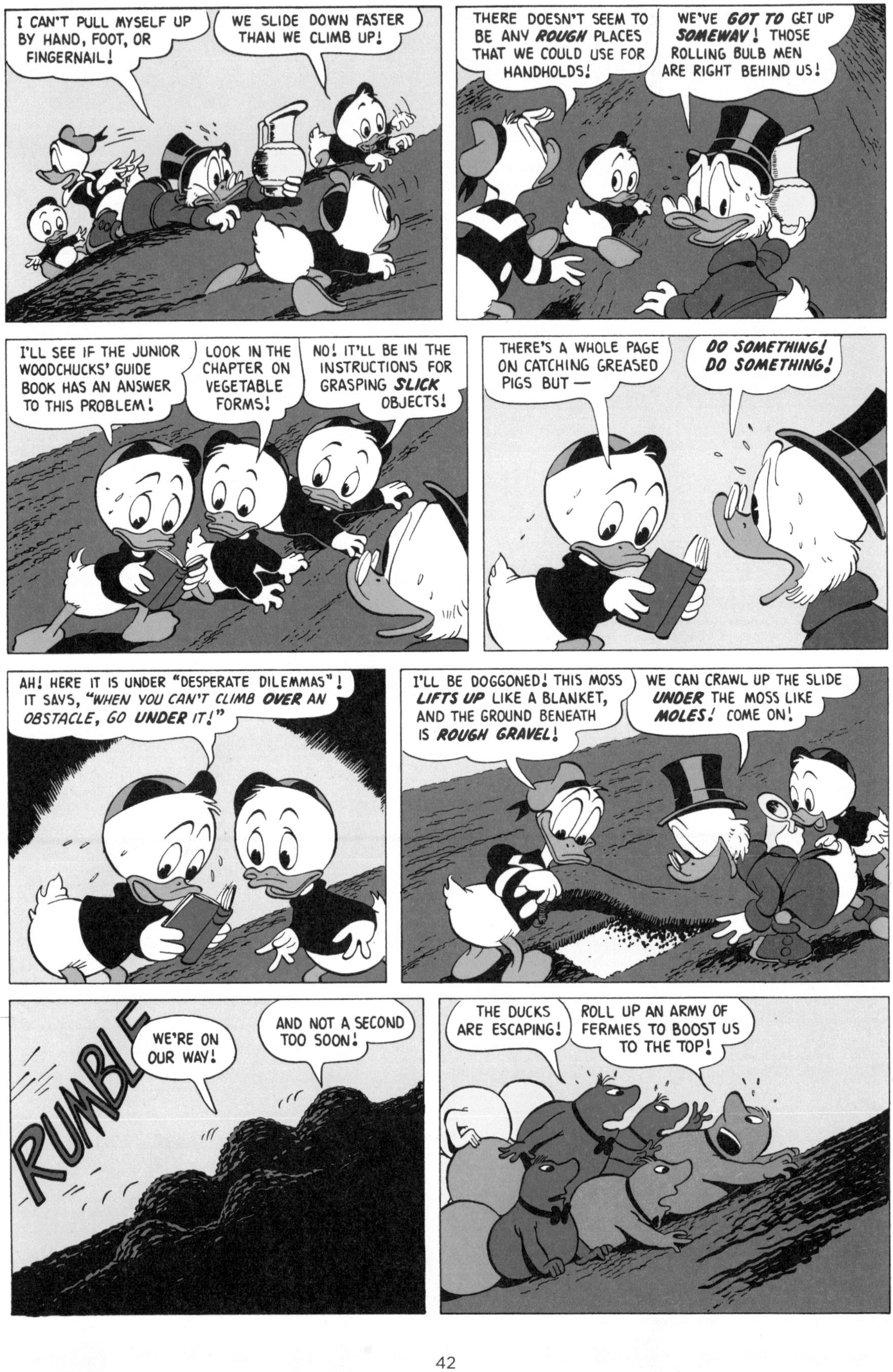

I CAN'T PULL MYSELF UP BY HAND, FOOT, OR FINGERNAIL!
WE SLIDE DOWN FASTER THAN WE CLIMB UP!
THERE DOESN'T SEEM TO BE ANY ROUGH PLACES THAT WE COULD USE FOR HANDHOLDS!
WE'VE GOT TO GET UP SOMEWAY! THOSE ROLLING BULB MEN ARE RIGHT BEHIND US!
I'LL SEE IF THE JUNIOR WOODCHUCKS' GUIDE BOOK HAS AN ANSWER TO THIS PROBLEM!
LOOK IN THE CHAPTER ON VEGETABLE FORMS!
NO! IT'LL BE IN THE INSTRUCTIONS FOR GRASPING SLICK OBJECTS!
THERE'S A WHOLE PAGE ON CATCHING GREASED PIGS BUT —
DO SOMETHING! DO SOMETHING!
AH! HERE IT IS UNDER "DESPERATE DILEMMAS"! IT SAYS, "WHEN YOU CAN'T CLIMB OVER AN OBSTACLE, GO UNDER IT!"
I'LL BE DOGGONED! THIS MOSS LIFTS UP LIKE A BLANKET, AND THE GROUND BENEATH IS ROUGH GRAVEL!
WE CAN CRAWL UP THE SLIDE UNDER THE MOSS LIKE MOLES! COME ON!
RUMBLE
WE'RE ON OUR WAY!
AND NOT A SECOND TOO SOON!
THE DUCKS ARE ESCAPING!
ROLL UP AN ARMY OF FERMIES TO BOOST US TO THE TOP!

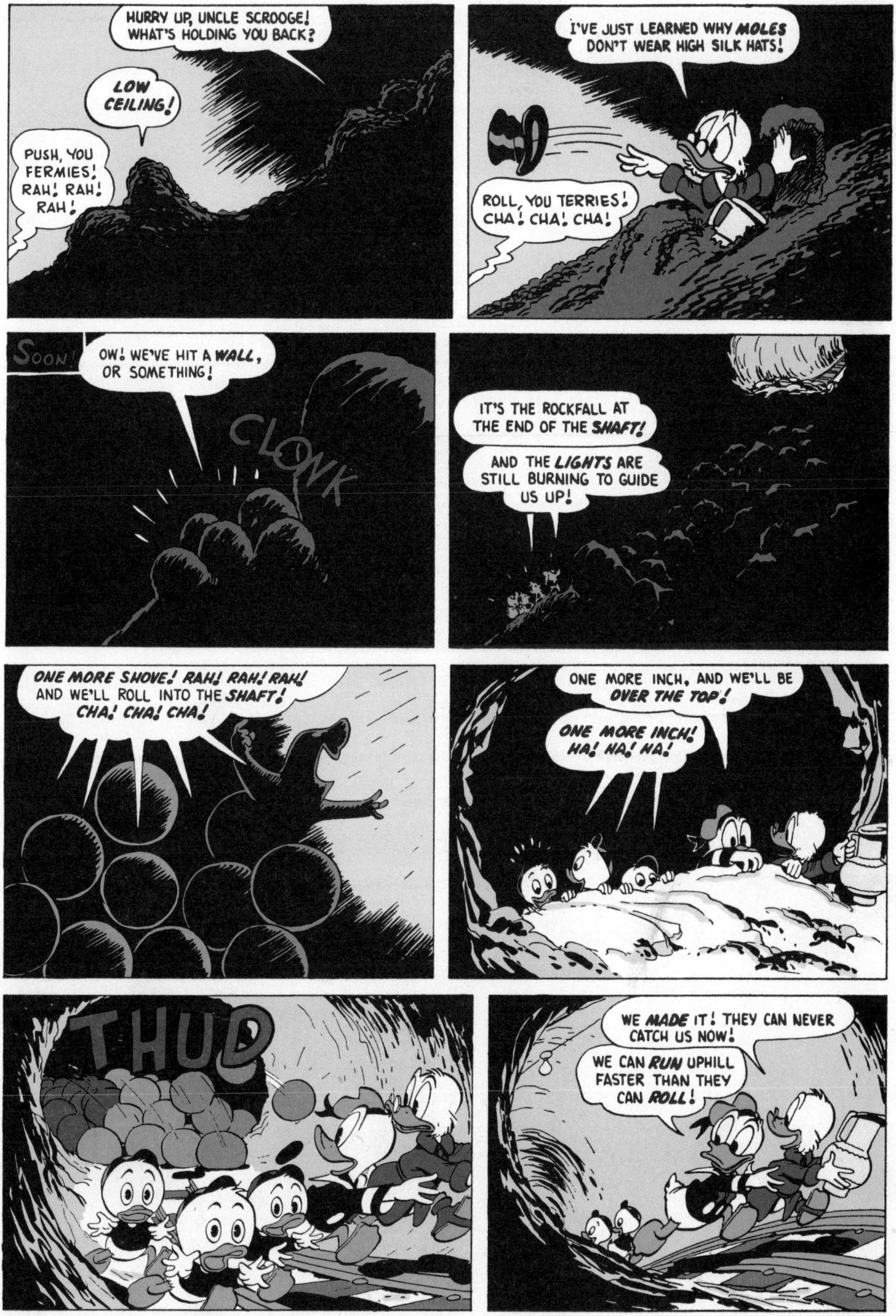

HURRY UP, UNCLE SCROOGE! WHAT'S HOLDING YOU BACK?
LOW CEILING!
PUSH, YOU FERMIES! RAH! RAH! RAH!
I'VE JUST LEARNED WHY MOLES DON'T WEAR HIGH SILK HATS!
ROLL, YOU TERRIES! CHA! CHA! CHA!
SOON!
OW! WE'VE HIT A WALL, OR SOMETHING!
CLONK
IT'S THE ROCKFALL AT THE END OF THE SHAFT!
AND THE LIGHTS ARE STILL BURNING TO GUIDE US UP!
ONE MORE SHOVE! RAH! RAH! RAH! AND WE'LL ROLL INTO THE SHAFT! CHA! CHA! CHA!
ONE MORE INCH, AND WE'LL BE OVER THE TOP!
ONE MORE INCH! HA! HA! HA!
THUD
WE MADE IT! THEY CAN NEVER CATCH US NOW!
WE CAN RUN UPHILL FASTER THAN THEY CAN ROLL!

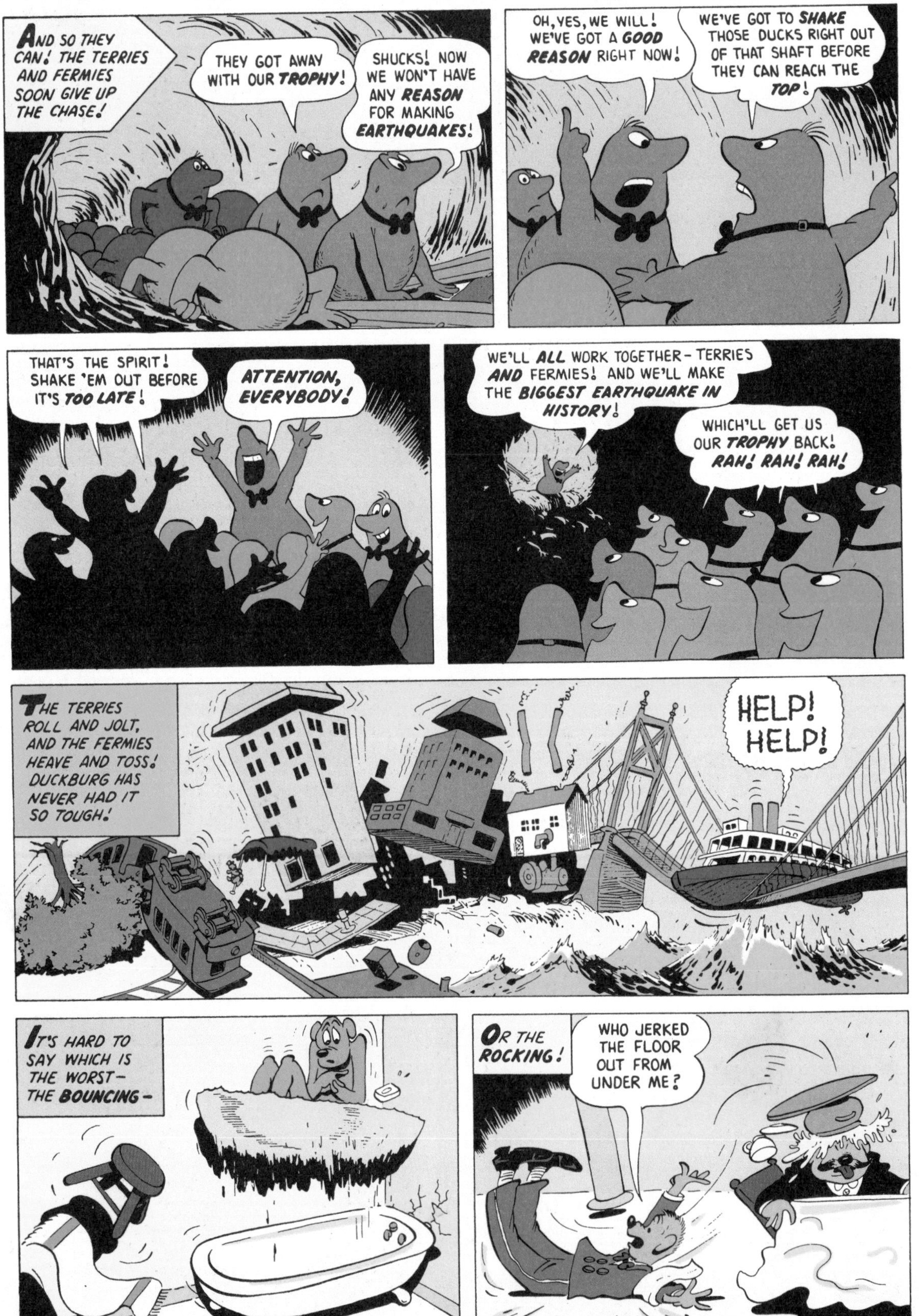
AND SO THEY CAN! THE TERRIES AND FERMIES SOON GIVE UP THE CHASE!
THEY GOT AWAY WITH OUR TROPHY!
SHUCKS! NOW WE WON'T HAVE ANY REASON FOR MAKING EARTHQUAKES!
OH, YES, WE WILL! WE'VE GOT A GOOD REASON RIGHT NOW!
WE'VE GOT TO SHAKE THOSE DUCKS RIGHT OUT OF THAT SHAFT BEFORE THEY CAN REACH THE TOP!
THAT'S THE SPIRIT! SHAKE 'EM OUT BEFORE IT'S TOO LATE!
ATTENTION, EVERYBODY!
WE'LL ALL WORK TOGETHER - TERRIES AND FERMIES! AND WE'LL MAKE THE BIGGEST EARTHQUAKE IN HISTORY!
WHICH'LL GET US OUR TROPHY BACK! RAH! RAH! RAH!
THE TERRIES ROLL AND JOLT, AND THE FERMIES HEAVE AND TOSS! DUCKBURG HAS NEVER HAD IT SO TOUGH!
HELP! HELP!
IT'S HARD TO SAY WHICH IS THE WORST— THE BOUNCING—
OR THE ROCKING!
WHO JERKED THE FLOOR OUT FROM UNDER ME?

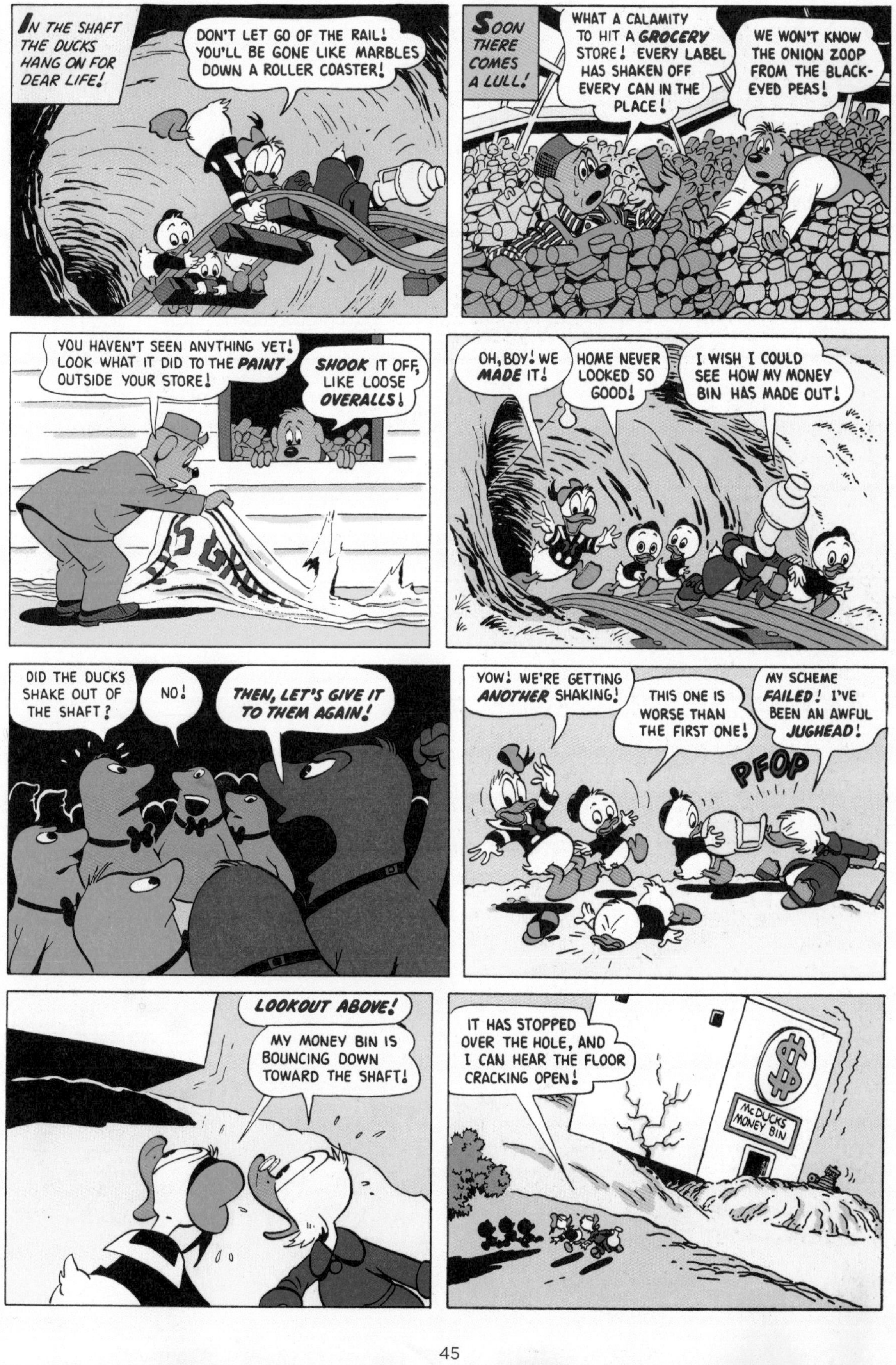
IN THE SHAFT THE DUCKS HANG ON FOR DEAR LIFE!
DON'T LET GO OF THE RAIL! YOU'LL BE GONE LIKE MARBLES DOWN A ROLLER COASTER!
SOON THERE COMES A LULL!
WHAT A CALAMITY TO HIT A GROCERY STORE! EVERY LABEL HAS SHAKEN OFF EVERY CAN IN THE PLACE!
WE WON'T KNOW THE ONION ZOOP FROM THE BLACK-EYED PEAS!
YOU HAVEN'T SEEN ANYTHING YET! LOOK WHAT IT DID TO THE PAINT OUTSIDE YOUR STORE!
SHOOK IT OFF, LIKE LOOSE OVERALLS!
OH, BOY! WE MADE IT!
HOME NEVER LOOKED SO GOOD!
I WISH I COULD SEE HOW MY MONEY BIN HAS MADE OUT!
DID THE DUCKS SHAKE OUT OF THE SHAFT?
NO!
THEN, LET'S GIVE IT TO THEM AGAIN!
YOW! WE'RE GETTING ANOTHER SHAKING!
THIS ONE IS WORSE THAN THE FIRST ONE!
MY SCHEME FAILED! I'VE BEEN AN AWFUL JUGHEAD!
PFOP
LOOKOUT ABOVE!
MY MONEY BIN IS BOUNCING DOWN TOWARD THE SHAFT!
IT HAS STOPPED OVER THE HOLE, AND I CAN HEAR THE FLOOR CRACKING OPEN!
McDUCKS MONEY BIN

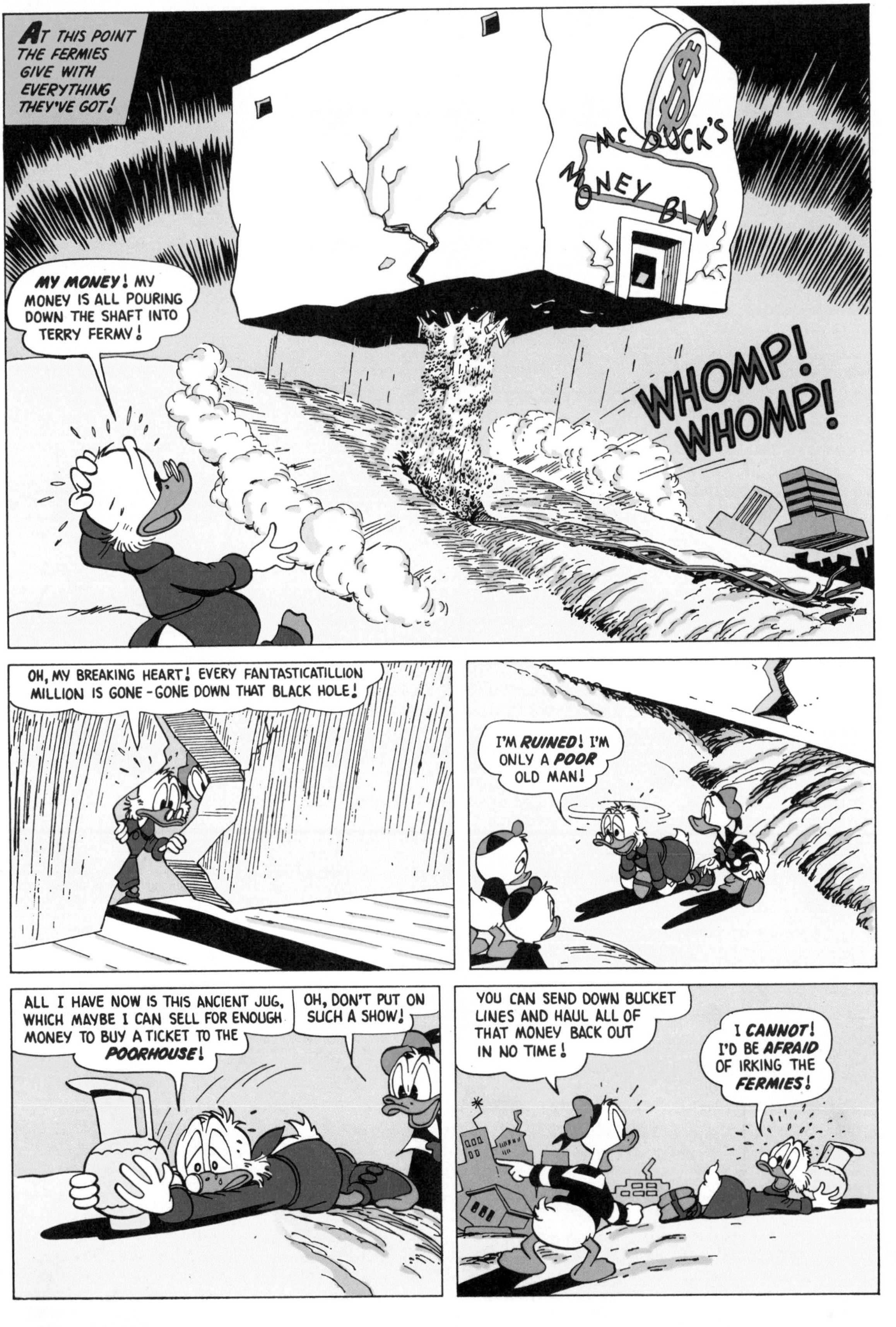

AT THIS POINT THE FERMIES GIVE WITH EVERYTHING THEY'VE GOT!
McDUCK'S MONEY BIN
MY MONEY! MY MONEY IS ALL POURING DOWN THE SHAFT INTO TERRY FERMY!
WHOMP! WHOMP!
OH, MY BREAKING HEART! EVERY FANTASTICATILLION MILLION IS GONE-GONE DOWN THAT BLACK HOLE!
I'M RUINED! I'M ONLY A POOR OLD MAN!
ALL I HAVE NOW IS THIS ANCIENT JUG, WHICH MAYBE I CAN SELL FOR ENOUGH MONEY TO BUY A TICKET TO THE POORHOUSE!
OH, DON'T PUT ON SUCH A SHOW!
YOU CAN SEND DOWN BUCKET LINES AND HAUL ALL OF THAT MONEY BACK OUT IN NO TIME!
I CANNOT! I'D BE AFRAID OF IRKING THE FERMIES!

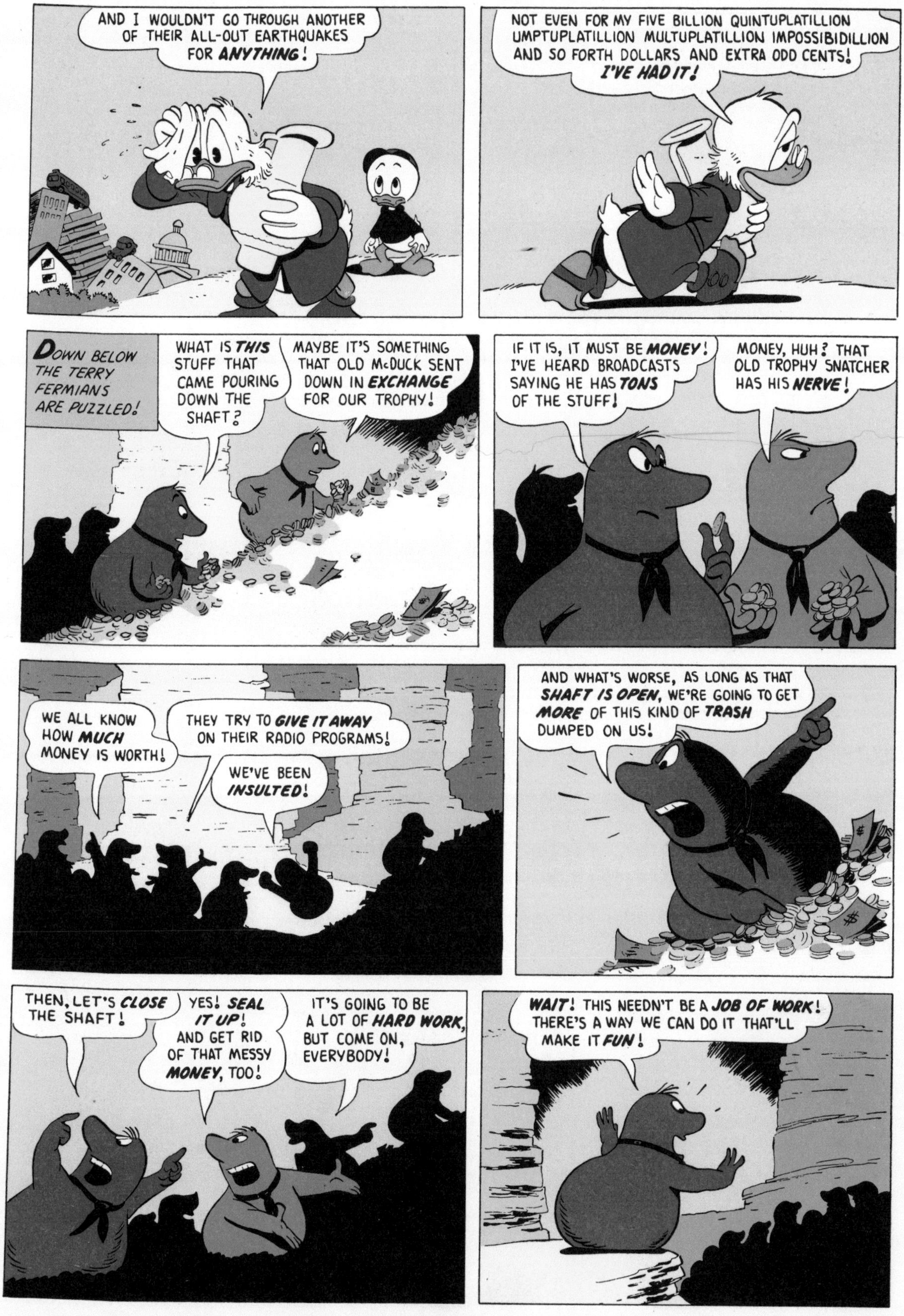
AND I WOULDN'T GO THROUGH ANOTHER OF THEIR ALL-OUT EARTHQUAKES FOR ANYTHING!
NOT EVEN FOR MY FIVE BILLION QUINTUPLATILLION UMPTUPLATILLION MULTUPLATILLION IMPOSSIBIDILLION AND SO FORTH DOLLARS AND EXTRA ODD CENTS! I'VE HAD IT!
DOWN BELOW THE TERRY FERMIANS ARE PUZZLED!
WHAT IS THIS STUFF THAT CAME POURING DOWN THE SHAFT?
MAYBE IT'S SOMETHING THAT OLD McDUCK SENT DOWN IN EXCHANGE FOR OUR TROPHY!
IF IT IS, IT MUST BE MONEY! I'VE HEARD BROADCASTS SAYING HE HAS TONS OF THE STUFF!
MONEY, HUH? THAT OLD TROPHY SNATCHER HAS HIS NERVE!
WE ALL KNOW HOW MUCH MONEY IS WORTH!
THEY TRY TO GIVE IT AWAY ON THEIR RADIO PROGRAMS!
WE'VE BEEN INSULTED!
AND WHAT'S WORSE, AS LONG AS THAT SHAFT IS OPEN, WE'RE GOING TO GET MORE OF THIS KIND OF TRASH DUMPED ON US!
THEN, LET'S CLOSE THE SHAFT!
YES! SEAL IT UP! AND GET RID OF THAT MESSY MONEY, TOO!
IT'S GOING TO BE A LOT OF HARD WORK, BUT COME ON, EVERYBODY!
WAIT! THIS NEEDN'T BE A JOB OF WORK! THERE'S A WAY WE CAN DO IT THAT'LL MAKE IT FUN!

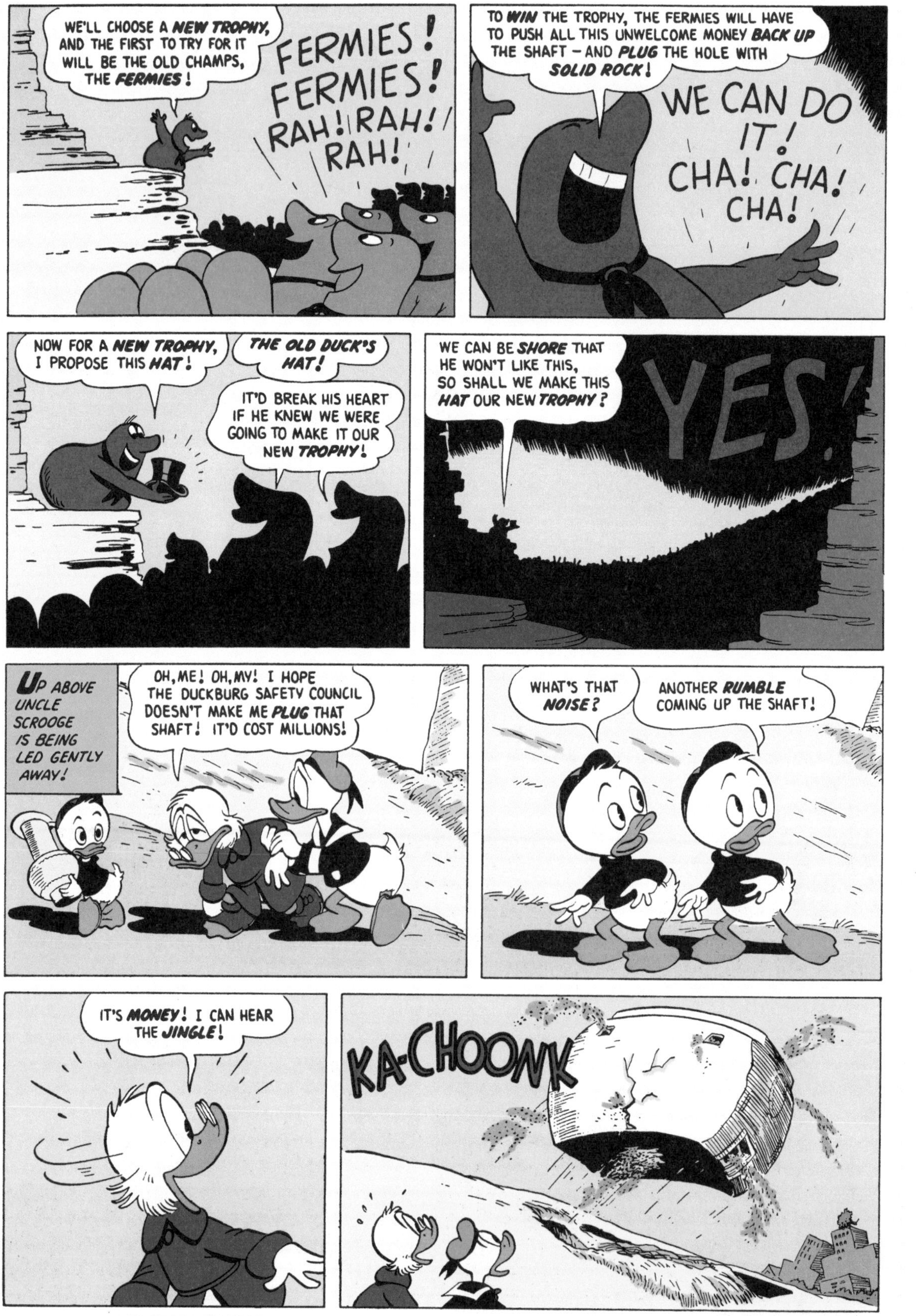
WE'LL CHOOSE A NEW TROPHY, AND THE FIRST TO TRY FOR IT WILL BE THE OLD CHAMPS, THE FERMIES!
FERMIES! FERMIES! RAH! RAH! RAH!
TO WIN THE TROPHY, THE FERMIES WILL HAVE TO PUSH ALL THIS UNWELCOME MONEY BACK UP THE SHAFT – AND PLUG THE HOLE WITH SOLID ROCK!
WE CAN DO IT! CHA! CHA! CHA!
NOW FOR A NEW TROPHY, I PROPOSE THIS HAT!
THE OLD DUCK'S HAT!
IT'D BREAK HIS HEART IF HE KNEW WE WERE GOING TO MAKE IT OUR NEW TROPHY!
WE CAN BE SHORE THAT HE WON'T LIKE THIS, SO SHALL WE MAKE THIS HAT OUR NEW TROPHY?
YES!
UP ABOVE UNCLE SCROOGE IS BEING LED GENTLY AWAY!
OH, ME! OH, MY! I HOPE THE DUCKBURG SAFETY COUNCIL DOESN'T MAKE ME PLUG THAT SHAFT! IT'D COST MILLIONS!
WHAT'S THAT NOISE?
ANOTHER RUMBLE COMING UP THE SHAFT!
IT'S MONEY! I CAN HEAR THE JINGLE!
KA-CHOONK

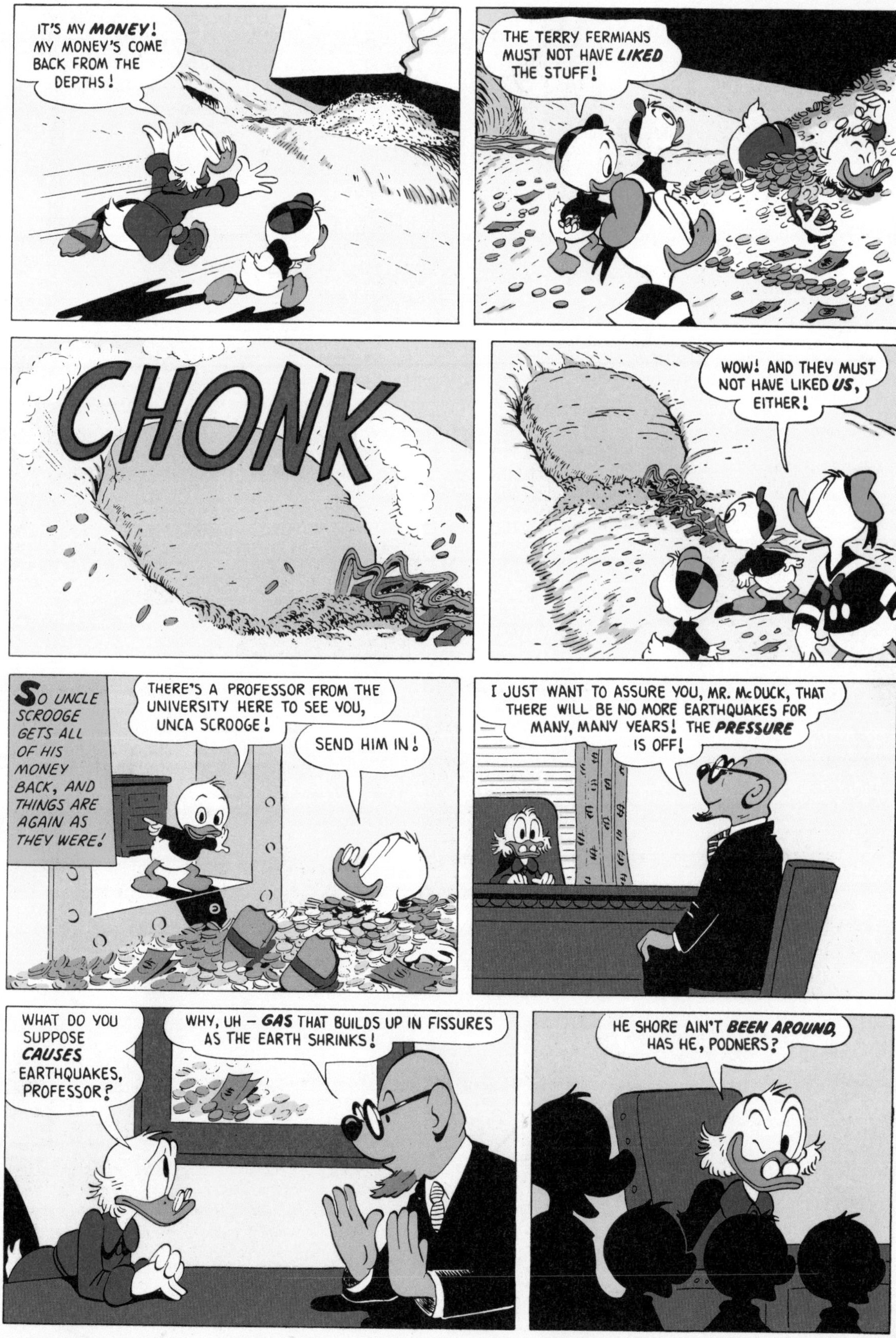
IT'S MY **MONEY**! MY MONEY'S COME BACK FROM THE DEPTHS!
THE TERRY FERMIANS MUST NOT HAVE **LIKED** THE STUFF!
CHONK
WOW! AND THEY MUST NOT HAVE LIKED **US**, EITHER!
SO UNCLE SCROOGE GETS ALL OF HIS MONEY BACK, AND THINGS ARE AGAIN AS THEY WERE!
THERE'S A PROFESSOR FROM THE UNIVERSITY HERE TO SEE YOU, UNCA SCROOGE!
SEND HIM IN!
I JUST WANT TO ASSURE YOU, MR. McDUCK, THAT THERE WILL BE NO MORE EARTHQUAKES FOR MANY, MANY YEARS! THE **PRESSURE** IS OFF!
WHAT DO YOU SUPPOSE **CAUSES** EARTHQUAKES, PROFESSOR?
WHY, UH — **GAS** THAT BUILDS UP IN FISSURES AS THE EARTH SHRINKS!
HE SHORE AIN'T **BEEN AROUND**, HAS HE, PODNERS?

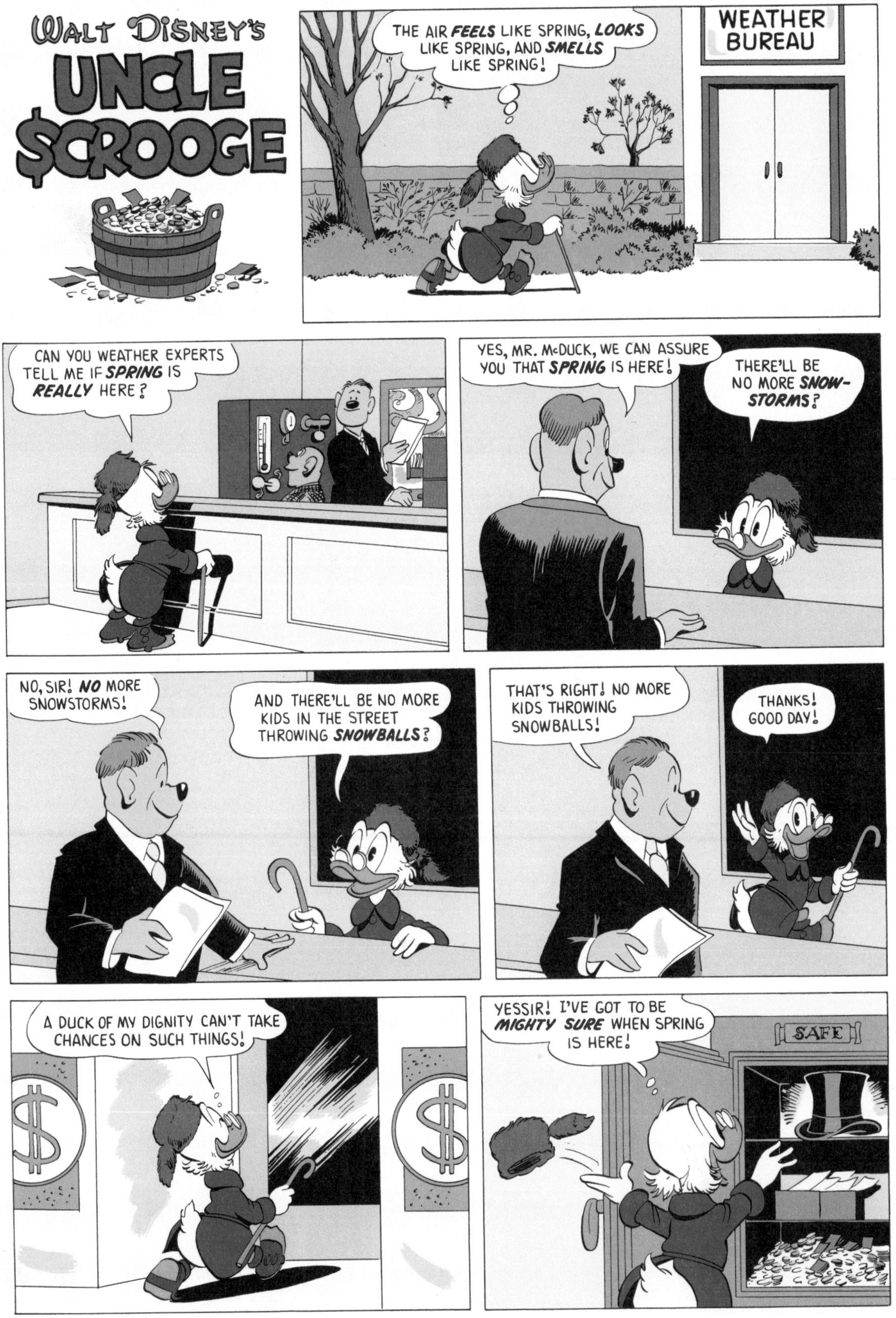
WALT DISNEY'S
UNCLE $CROOGE
THE AIR FEELS LIKE SPRING, LOOKS LIKE SPRING, AND SMELLS LIKE SPRING!
WEATHER BUREAU
CAN YOU WEATHER EXPERTS TELL ME IF SPRING IS REALLY HERE?
YES, MR. McDUCK, WE CAN ASSURE YOU THAT SPRING IS HERE!
THERE'LL BE NO MORE SNOW-STORMS?
NO, SIR! NO MORE SNOWSTORMS!
AND THERE'LL BE NO MORE KIDS IN THE STREET THROWING SNOWBALLS?
THAT'S RIGHT! NO MORE KIDS THROWING SNOWBALLS!
THANKS! GOOD DAY!
A DUCK OF MY DIGNITY CAN'T TAKE CHANCES ON SUCH THINGS!
YESSIR! I'VE GOT TO BE MIGHTY SURE WHEN SPRING IS HERE!
SAFE

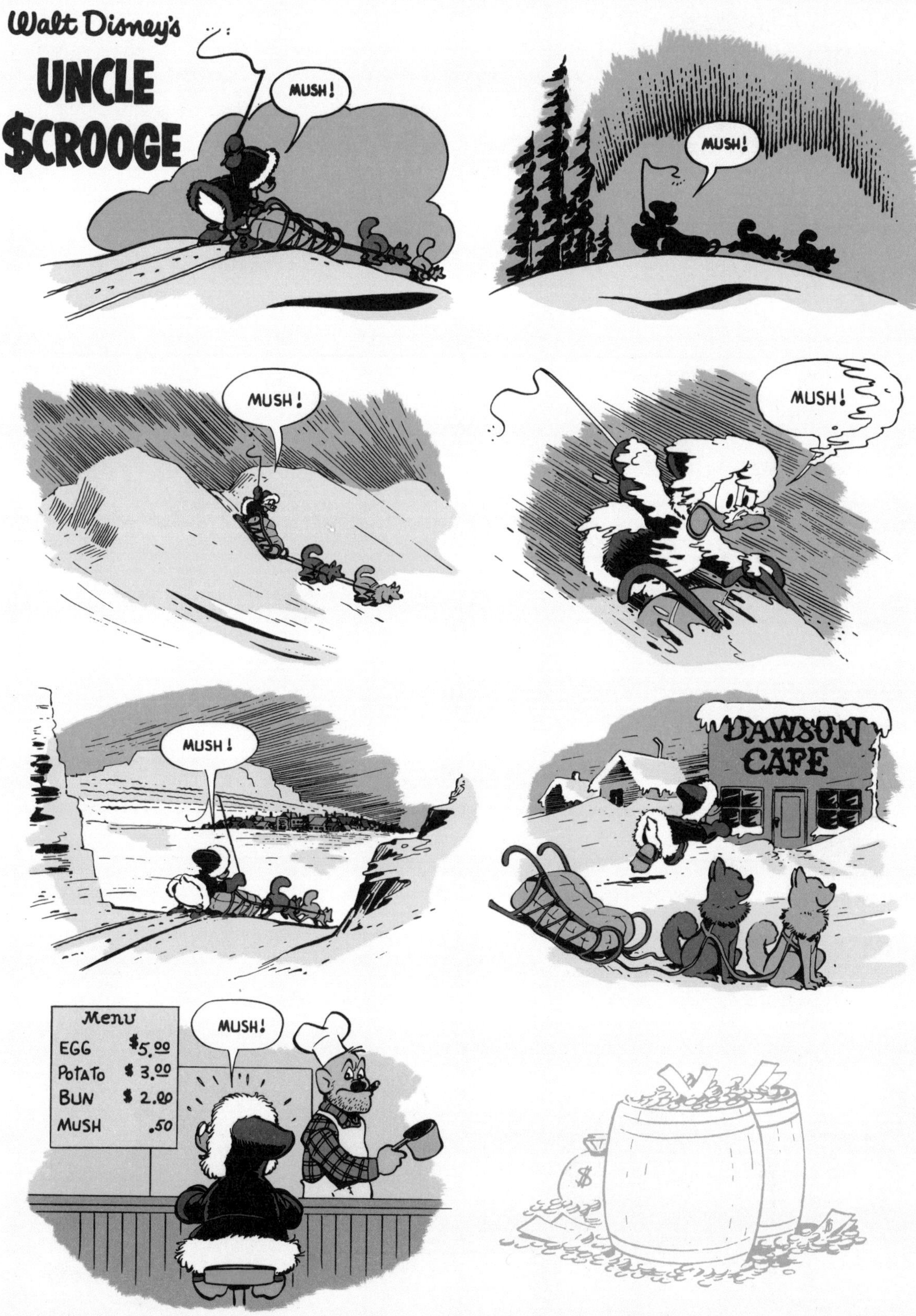

Walt Disney's
UNCLE $CROOGE
MUSH!
MUSH!
MUSH!
MUSH!
MUSH!
DAWSON CAFE
Menu
EGG $5.00
POTATO $3.00
BUN $2.00
MUSH .50
MUSH!

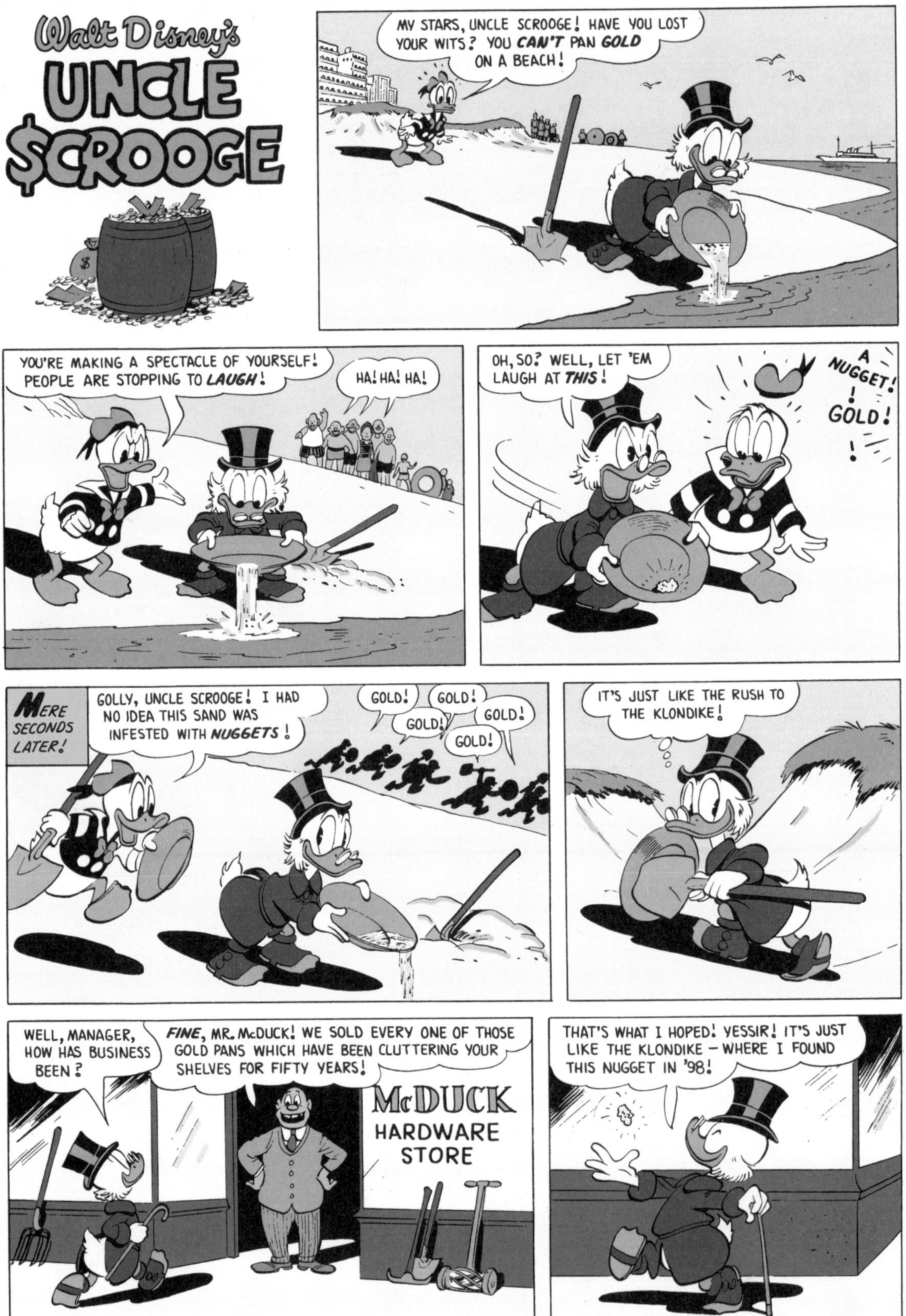
Walt Disney's
UNCLE $CROOGE
MY STARS, UNCLE SCROOGE! HAVE YOU LOST YOUR WITS? YOU CAN'T PAN GOLD ON A BEACH!
YOU'RE MAKING A SPECTACLE OF YOURSELF! PEOPLE ARE STOPPING TO LAUGH!
HA! HA! HA!
OH, SO? WELL, LET 'EM LAUGH AT THIS!
A NUGGET! ! GOLD! !
MERE SECONDS LATER!
GOLLY, UNCLE SCROOGE! I HAD NO IDEA THIS SAND WAS INFESTED WITH NUGGETS!
GOLD!
GOLD!
GOLD!
GOLD!
GOLD!
IT'S JUST LIKE THE RUSH TO THE KLONDIKE!
WELL, MANAGER, HOW HAS BUSINESS BEEN?
FINE, MR. McDUCK! WE SOLD EVERY ONE OF THOSE GOLD PANS WHICH HAVE BEEN CLUTTERING YOUR SHELVES FOR FIFTY YEARS!
McDUCK HARDWARE STORE
THAT'S WHAT I HOPED! YESSIR! IT'S JUST LIKE THE KLONDIKE – WHERE I FOUND THIS NUGGET IN '98!

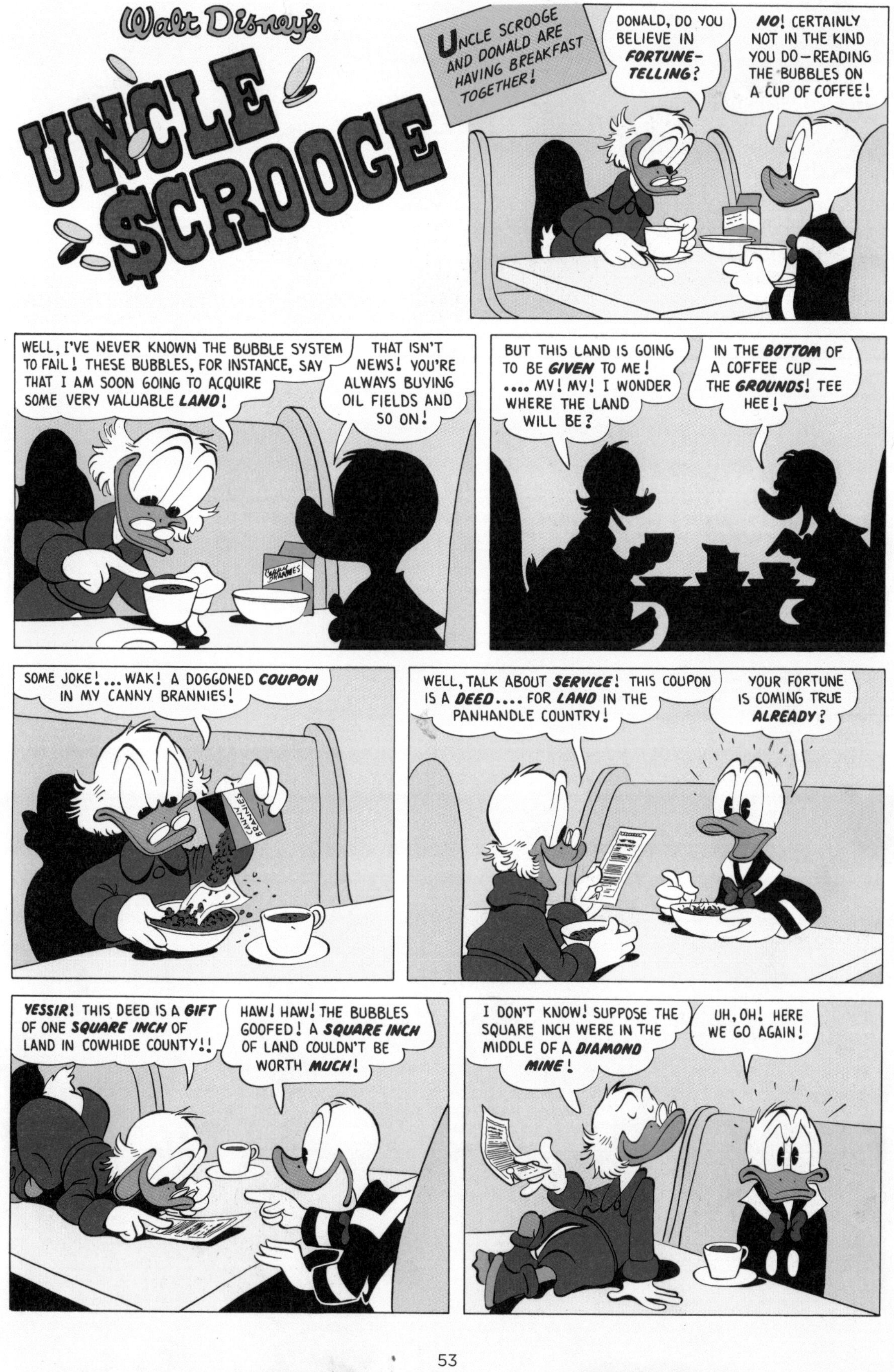
Walt Disney's
UNCLE $CROOGE
UNCLE SCROOGE AND DONALD ARE HAVING BREAKFAST TOGETHER!
DONALD, DO YOU BELIEVE IN FORTUNE-TELLING?
NO! CERTAINLY NOT IN THE KIND YOU DO—READING THE BUBBLES ON A CUP OF COFFEE!
WELL, I'VE NEVER KNOWN THE BUBBLE SYSTEM TO FAIL! THESE BUBBLES, FOR INSTANCE, SAY THAT I AM SOON GOING TO ACQUIRE SOME VERY VALUABLE LAND!
THAT ISN'T NEWS! YOU'RE ALWAYS BUYING OIL FIELDS AND SO ON!
BUT THIS LAND IS GOING TO BE GIVEN TO ME! .... MY! MY! I WONDER WHERE THE LAND WILL BE?
IN THE BOTTOM OF A COFFEE CUP — THE GROUNDS! TEE HEE!
SOME JOKE! ... WAK! A DOGGONED COUPON IN MY CANNY BRANNIES!
CANNY BRANNIES
WELL, TALK ABOUT SERVICE! THIS COUPON IS A DEED .... FOR LAND IN THE PANHANDLE COUNTRY!
YOUR FORTUNE IS COMING TRUE ALREADY?
YESSIR! THIS DEED IS A GIFT OF ONE SQUARE INCH OF LAND IN COWHIDE COUNTY!!
HAW! HAW! THE BUBBLES GOOFED! A SQUARE INCH OF LAND COULDN'T BE WORTH MUCH!
I DON'T KNOW! SUPPOSE THE SQUARE INCH WERE IN THE MIDDLE OF A DIAMOND MINE!
UH, OH! HERE WE GO AGAIN!

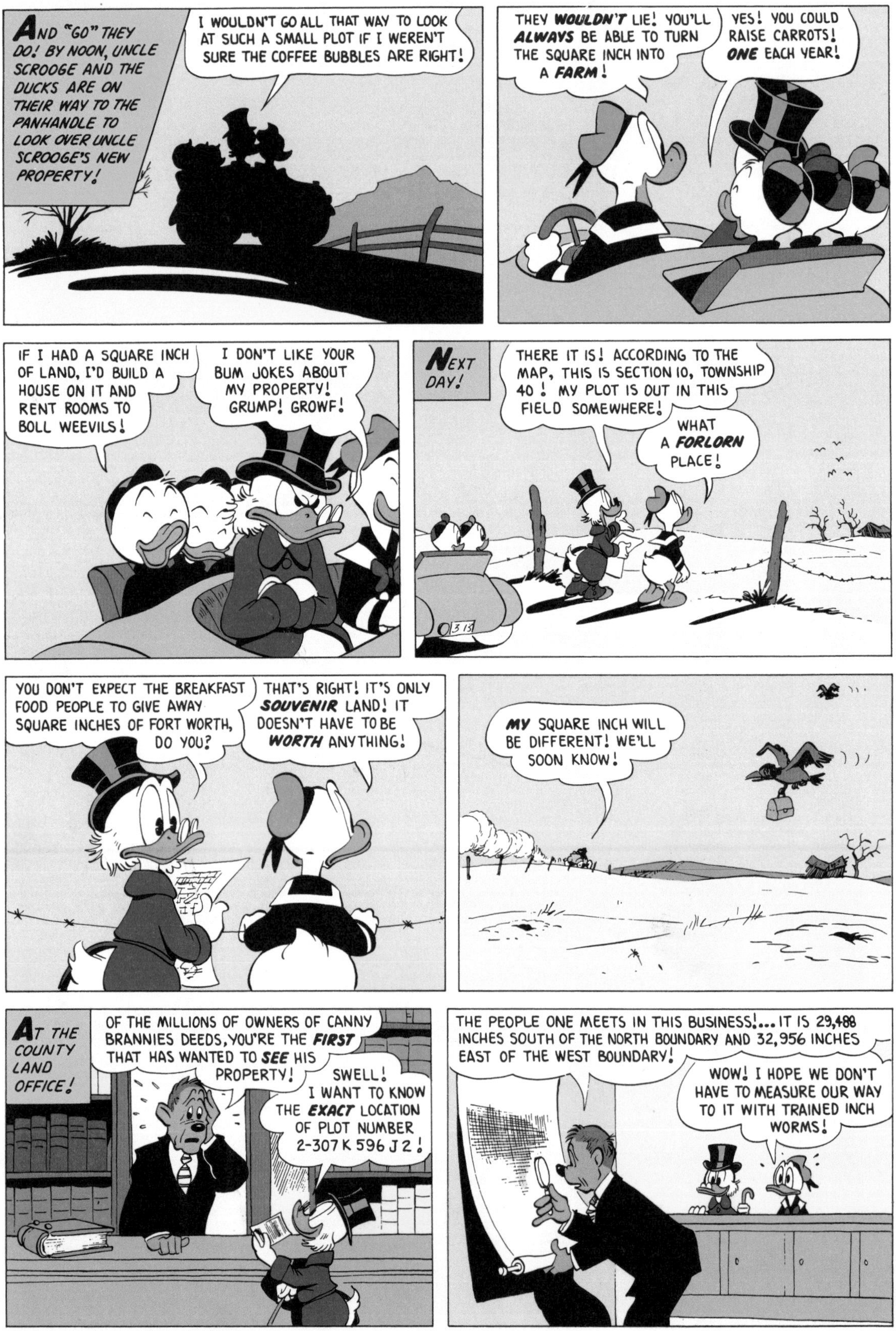
AND "GO" THEY DO! BY NOON, UNCLE SCROOGE AND THE DUCKS ARE ON THEIR WAY TO THE PANHANDLE TO LOOK OVER UNCLE SCROOGE'S NEW PROPERTY!
I WOULDN'T GO ALL THAT WAY TO LOOK AT SUCH A SMALL PLOT IF I WEREN'T SURE THE COFFEE BUBBLES ARE RIGHT!
THEY WOULDN'T LIE! YOU'LL ALWAYS BE ABLE TO TURN THE SQUARE INCH INTO A FARM!
YES! YOU COULD RAISE CARROTS! ONE EACH YEAR!
IF I HAD A SQUARE INCH OF LAND, I'D BUILD A HOUSE ON IT AND RENT ROOMS TO BOLL WEEVILS!
I DON'T LIKE YOUR BUM JOKES ABOUT MY PROPERTY! GRUMP! GROWF!
NEXT DAY!
THERE IT IS! ACCORDING TO THE MAP, THIS IS SECTION 10, TOWNSHIP 40! MY PLOT IS OUT IN THIS FIELD SOMEWHERE!
WHAT A FORLORN PLACE!
313
YOU DON'T EXPECT THE BREAKFAST FOOD PEOPLE TO GIVE AWAY SQUARE INCHES OF FORT WORTH, DO YOU?
THAT'S RIGHT! IT'S ONLY SOUVENIR LAND! IT DOESN'T HAVE TO BE WORTH ANYTHING!
MY SQUARE INCH WILL BE DIFFERENT! WE'LL SOON KNOW!
AT THE COUNTY LAND OFFICE!
OF THE MILLIONS OF OWNERS OF CANNY BRANNIES DEEDS, YOU'RE THE FIRST THAT HAS WANTED TO SEE HIS PROPERTY!
SWELL! I WANT TO KNOW THE EXACT LOCATION OF PLOT NUMBER 2-307 K 596 J 2!
THE PEOPLE ONE MEETS IN THIS BUSINESS!... IT IS 29,488 INCHES SOUTH OF THE NORTH BOUNDARY AND 32,956 INCHES EAST OF THE WEST BOUNDARY!
WOW! I HOPE WE DON'T HAVE TO MEASURE OUR WAY TO IT WITH TRAINED INCH WORMS!

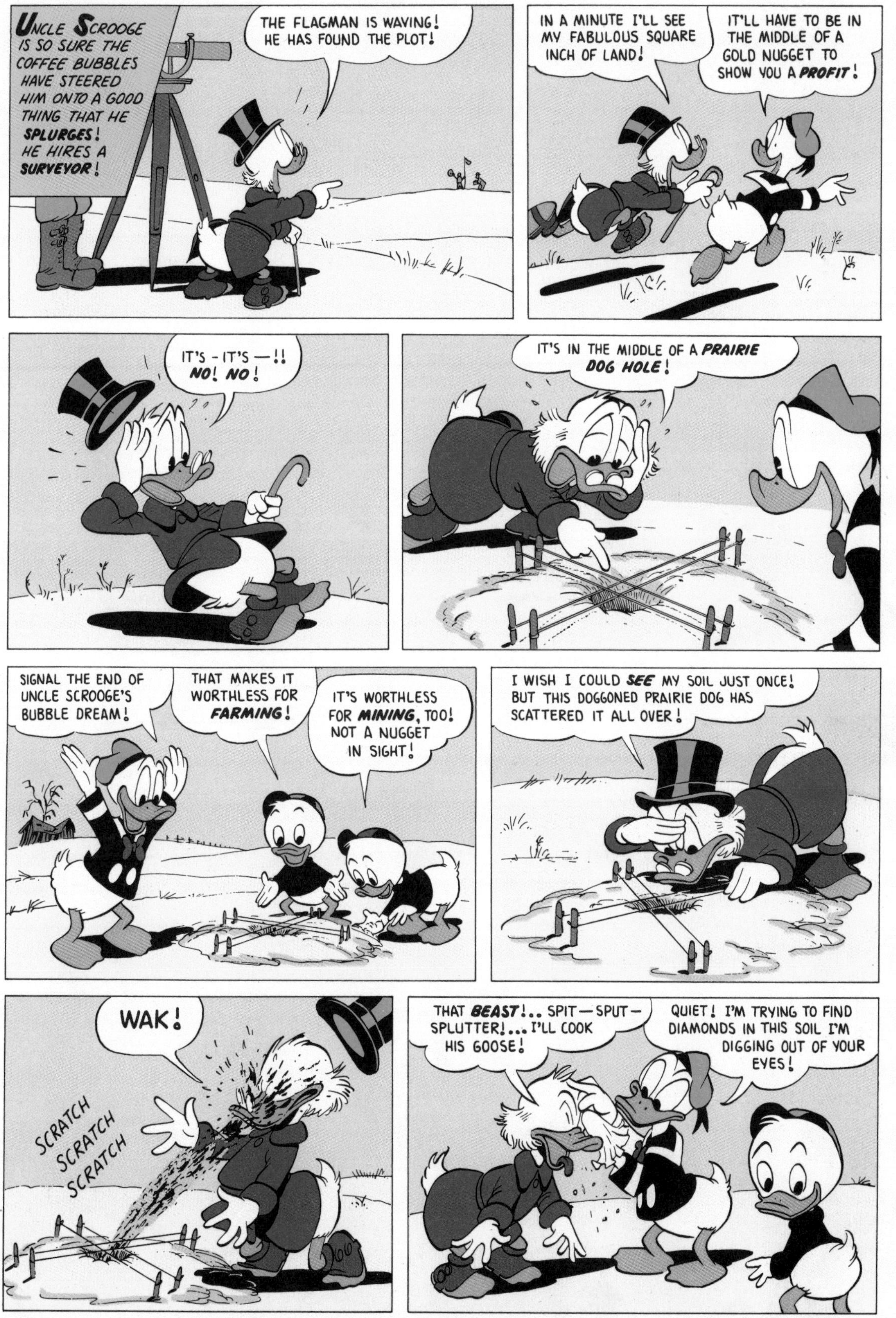
UNCLE SCROOGE IS SO SURE THE COFFEE BUBBLES HAVE STEERED HIM ONTO A GOOD THING THAT HE SPLURGES! HE HIRES A SURVEYOR!
THE FLAGMAN IS WAVING! HE HAS FOUND THE PLOT!
IN A MINUTE I'LL SEE MY FABULOUS SQUARE INCH OF LAND!
IT'LL HAVE TO BE IN THE MIDDLE OF A GOLD NUGGET TO SHOW YOU A PROFIT!
IT'S - IT'S —!! NO! NO!
IT'S IN THE MIDDLE OF A PRAIRIE DOG HOLE!
SIGNAL THE END OF UNCLE SCROOGE'S BUBBLE DREAM!
THAT MAKES IT WORTHLESS FOR FARMING!
IT'S WORTHLESS FOR MINING, TOO! NOT A NUGGET IN SIGHT!
I WISH I COULD SEE MY SOIL JUST ONCE! BUT THIS DOGGONED PRAIRIE DOG HAS SCATTERED IT ALL OVER!
WAK!
SCRATCH SCRATCH SCRATCH
THAT BEAST!.. SPIT—SPUT—SPLUTTER!... I'LL COOK HIS GOOSE!
QUIET! I'M TRYING TO FIND DIAMONDS IN THIS SOIL I'M DIGGING OUT OF YOUR EYES!

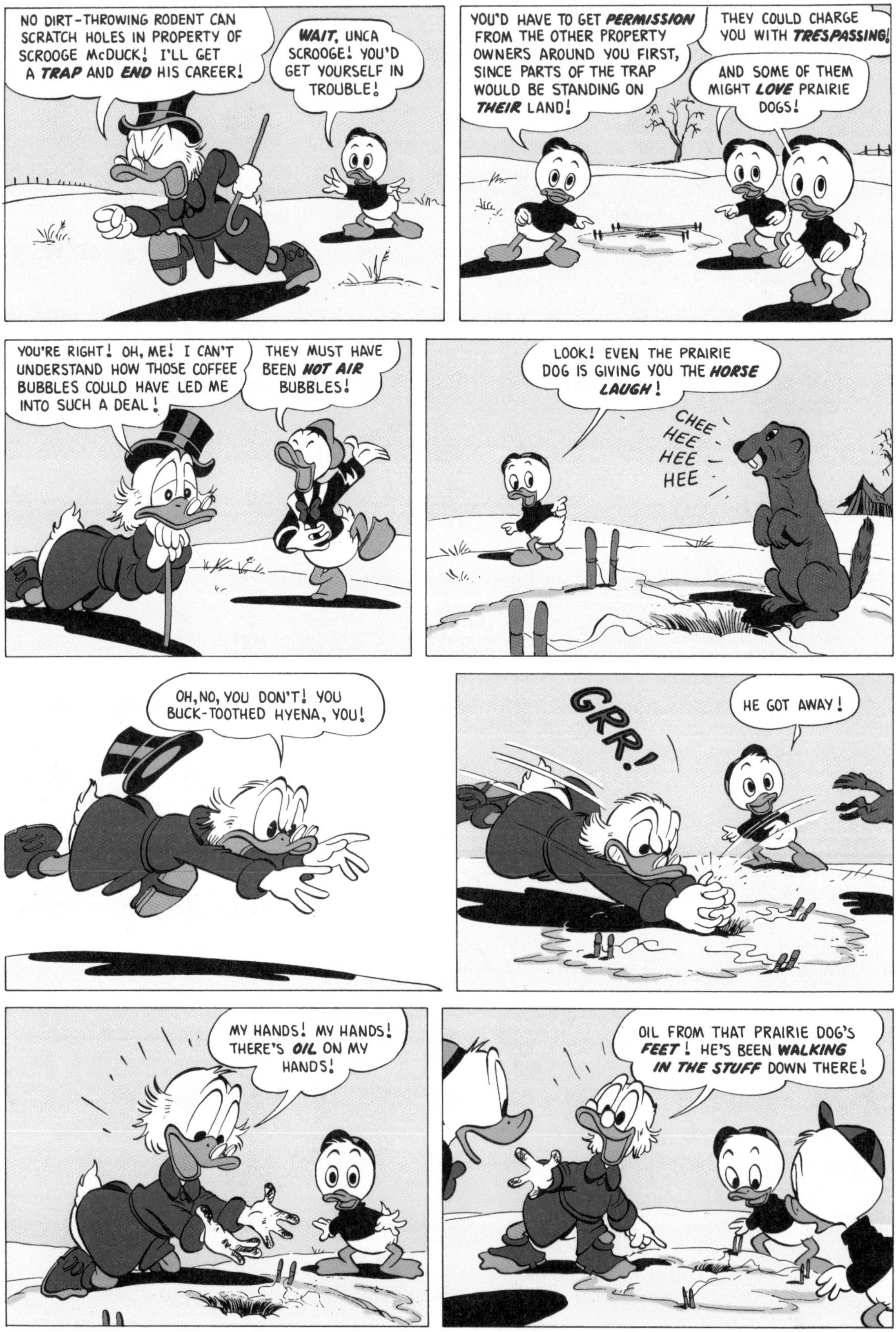
NO DIRT-THROWING RODENT CAN SCRATCH HOLES IN PROPERTY OF SCROOGE McDUCK! I'LL GET A TRAP AND END HIS CAREER!
WAIT, UNCA SCROOGE! YOU'D GET YOURSELF IN TROUBLE!
YOU'D HAVE TO GET PERMISSION FROM THE OTHER PROPERTY OWNERS AROUND YOU FIRST, SINCE PARTS OF THE TRAP WOULD BE STANDING ON THEIR LAND!
THEY COULD CHARGE YOU WITH TRESPASSING!
AND SOME OF THEM MIGHT LOVE PRAIRIE DOGS!
YOU'RE RIGHT! OH, ME! I CAN'T UNDERSTAND HOW THOSE COFFEE BUBBLES COULD HAVE LED ME INTO SUCH A DEAL!
THEY MUST HAVE BEEN HOT AIR BUBBLES!
LOOK! EVEN THE PRAIRIE DOG IS GIVING YOU THE HORSE LAUGH!
CHEE HEE HEE HEE
OH, NO, YOU DON'T! YOU BUCK-TOOTHED HYENA, YOU!
GRR!
HE GOT AWAY!
MY HANDS! MY HANDS! THERE'S OIL ON MY HANDS!
OIL FROM THAT PRAIRIE DOG'S FEET! HE'S BEEN WALKING IN THE STUFF DOWN THERE!

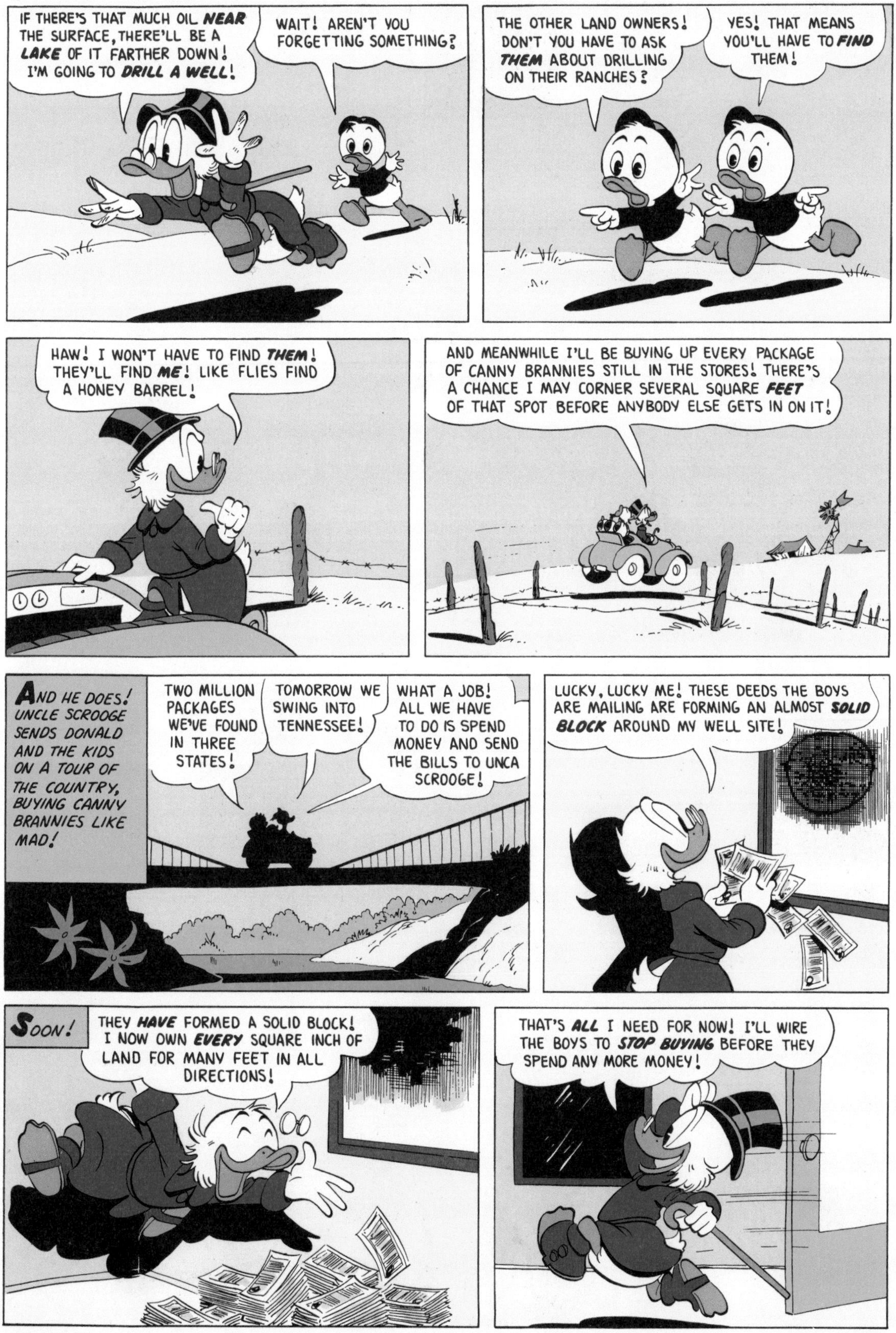
IF THERE'S THAT MUCH OIL NEAR THE SURFACE, THERE'LL BE A LAKE OF IT FARTHER DOWN! I'M GOING TO DRILL A WELL!
WAIT! AREN'T YOU FORGETTING SOMETHING?
THE OTHER LAND OWNERS! DON'T YOU HAVE TO ASK THEM ABOUT DRILLING ON THEIR RANCHES?
YES! THAT MEANS YOU'LL HAVE TO FIND THEM!
HAW! I WON'T HAVE TO FIND THEM! THEY'LL FIND ME! LIKE FLIES FIND A HONEY BARREL!
AND MEANWHILE I'LL BE BUYING UP EVERY PACKAGE OF CANNY BRANNIES STILL IN THE STORES! THERE'S A CHANCE I MAY CORNER SEVERAL SQUARE FEET OF THAT SPOT BEFORE ANYBODY ELSE GETS IN ON IT!
AND HE DOES! UNCLE SCROOGE SENDS DONALD AND THE KIDS ON A TOUR OF THE COUNTRY, BUYING CANNY BRANNIES LIKE MAD!
TWO MILLION PACKAGES WE'VE FOUND IN THREE STATES!
TOMORROW WE SWING INTO TENNESSEE!
WHAT A JOB! ALL WE HAVE TO DO IS SPEND MONEY AND SEND THE BILLS TO UNCA SCROOGE!
LUCKY, LUCKY ME! THESE DEEDS THE BOYS ARE MAILING ARE FORMING AN ALMOST SOLID BLOCK AROUND MY WELL SITE!
SOON!
THEY HAVE FORMED A SOLID BLOCK! I NOW OWN EVERY SQUARE INCH OF LAND FOR MANY FEET IN ALL DIRECTIONS!
THAT'S ALL I NEED FOR NOW! I'LL WIRE THE BOYS TO STOP BUYING BEFORE THEY SPEND ANY MORE MONEY!

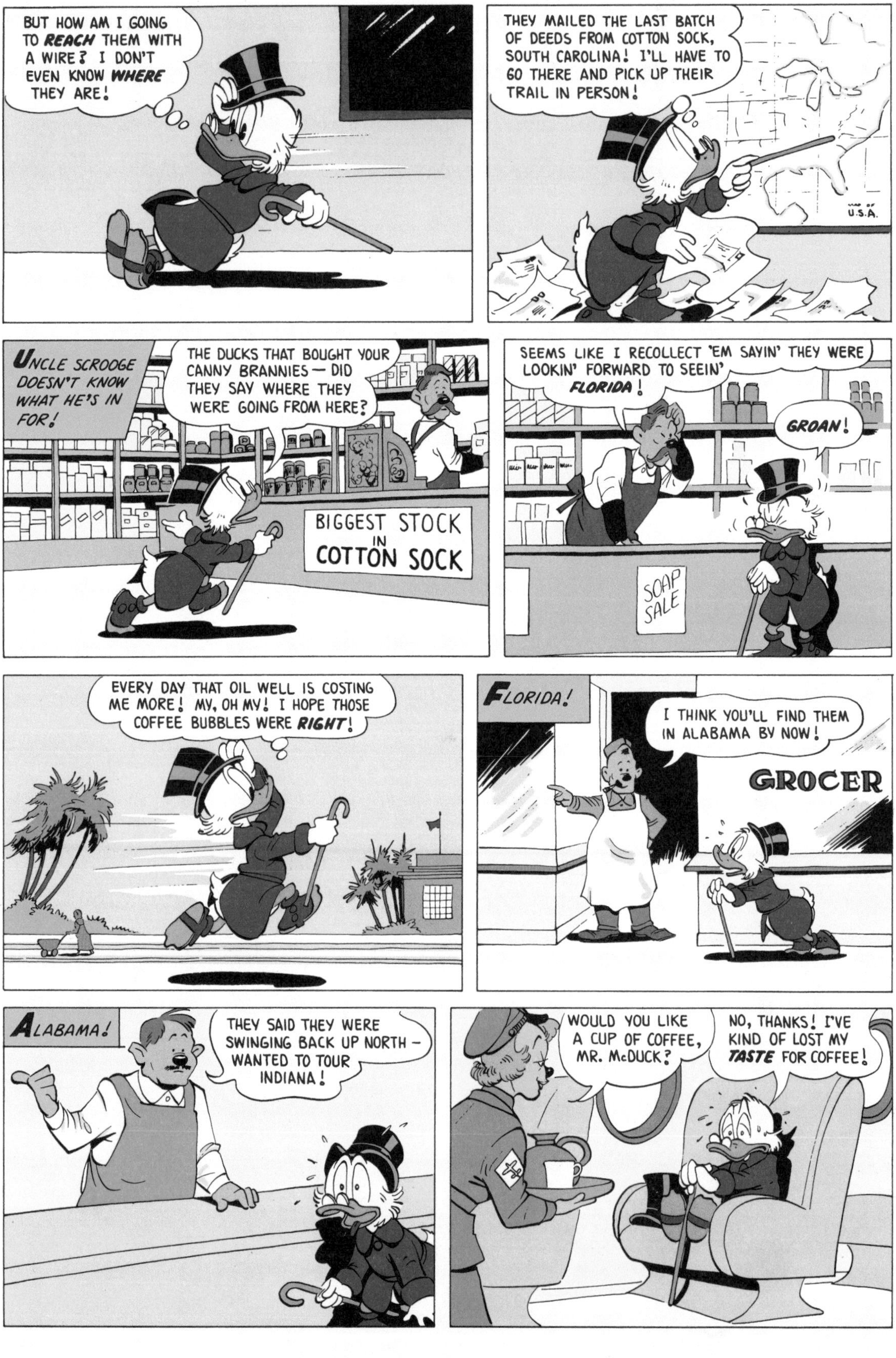
BUT HOW AM I GOING TO **REACH** THEM WITH A WIRE? I DON'T EVEN KNOW **WHERE** THEY ARE!
THEY MAILED THE LAST BATCH OF DEEDS FROM COTTON SOCK, SOUTH CAROLINA! I'LL HAVE TO GO THERE AND PICK UP THEIR TRAIL IN PERSON!
U.S.A.
UNCLE SCROOGE DOESN'T KNOW WHAT HE'S IN FOR!
THE DUCKS THAT BOUGHT YOUR CANNY BRANNIES — DID THEY SAY WHERE THEY WERE GOING FROM HERE?
BIGGEST STOCK IN COTTON SOCK
SEEMS LIKE I RECOLLECT 'EM SAYIN' THEY WERE LOOKIN' FORWARD TO SEEIN' **FLORIDA**!
GROAN!
SOAP SALE
EVERY DAY THAT OIL WELL IS COSTING ME MORE! MY, OH MY! I HOPE THOSE COFFEE BUBBLES WERE **RIGHT**!
FLORIDA!
I THINK YOU'LL FIND THEM IN ALABAMA BY NOW!
GROCER
ALABAMA!
THEY SAID THEY WERE SWINGING BACK UP NORTH — WANTED TO TOUR INDIANA!
WOULD YOU LIKE A CUP OF COFFEE, MR. McDUCK?
NO, THANKS! I'VE KIND OF LOST MY **TASTE** FOR COFFEE!

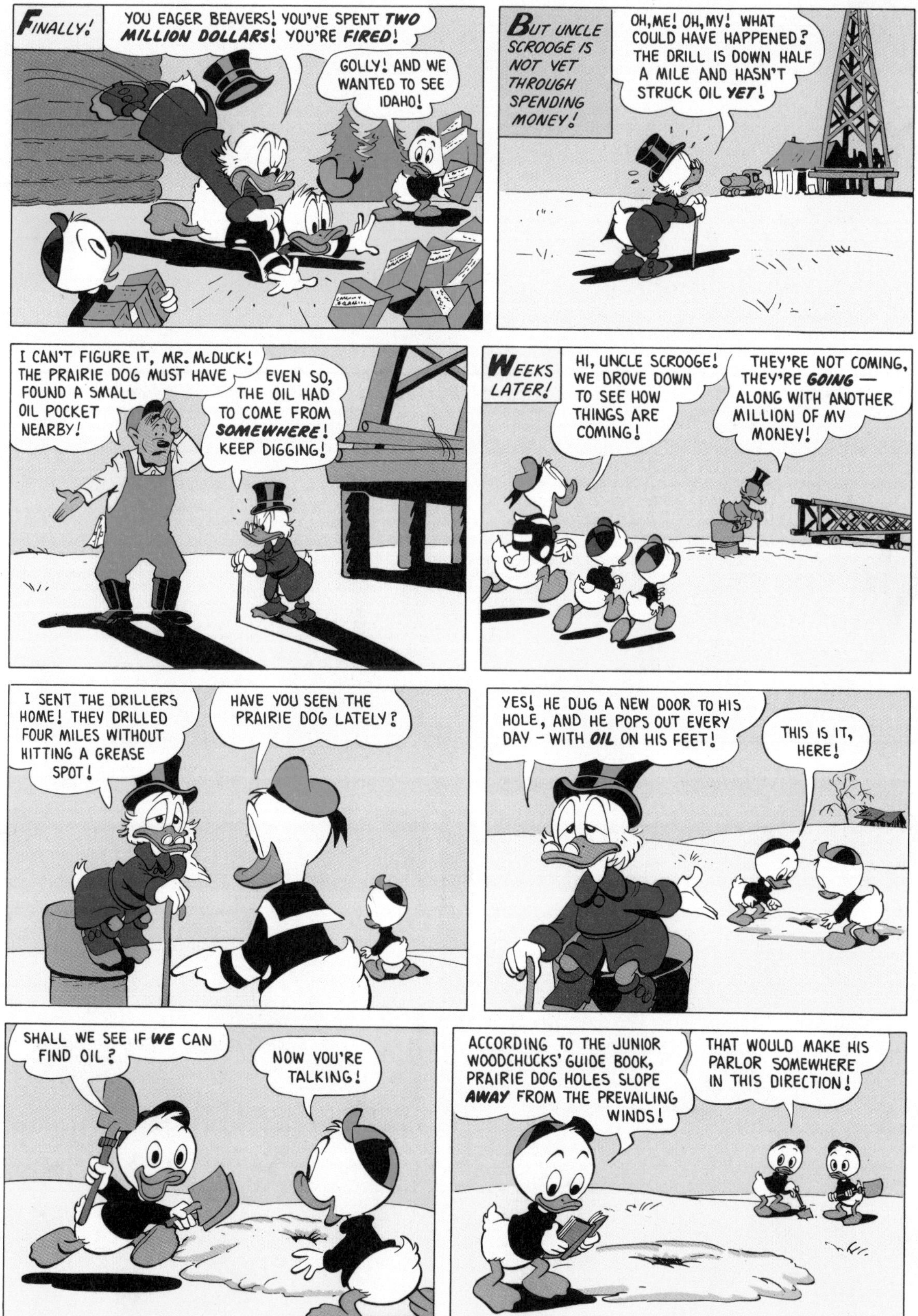
FINALLY!
YOU EAGER BEAVERS! YOU'VE SPENT TWO MILLION DOLLARS! YOU'RE FIRED!
GOLLY! AND WE WANTED TO SEE IDAHO!
BUT UNCLE SCROOGE IS NOT YET THROUGH SPENDING MONEY!
OH, ME! OH, MY! WHAT COULD HAVE HAPPENED? THE DRILL IS DOWN HALF A MILE AND HASN'T STRUCK OIL YET!
I CAN'T FIGURE IT, MR. McDUCK! THE PRAIRIE DOG MUST HAVE FOUND A SMALL OIL POCKET NEARBY!
EVEN SO, THE OIL HAD TO COME FROM SOMEWHERE! KEEP DIGGING!
WEEKS LATER!
HI, UNCLE SCROOGE! WE DROVE DOWN TO SEE HOW THINGS ARE COMING!
THEY'RE NOT COMING, THEY'RE GOING — ALONG WITH ANOTHER MILLION OF MY MONEY!
I SENT THE DRILLERS HOME! THEY DRILLED FOUR MILES WITHOUT HITTING A GREASE SPOT!
HAVE YOU SEEN THE PRAIRIE DOG LATELY?
YES! HE DUG A NEW DOOR TO HIS HOLE, AND HE POPS OUT EVERY DAY – WITH OIL ON HIS FEET!
THIS IS IT, HERE!
SHALL WE SEE IF WE CAN FIND OIL?
NOW YOU'RE TALKING!
ACCORDING TO THE JUNIOR WOODCHUCKS' GUIDE BOOK, PRAIRIE DOG HOLES SLOPE AWAY FROM THE PREVAILING WINDS!
THAT WOULD MAKE HIS PARLOR SOMEWHERE IN THIS DIRECTION!

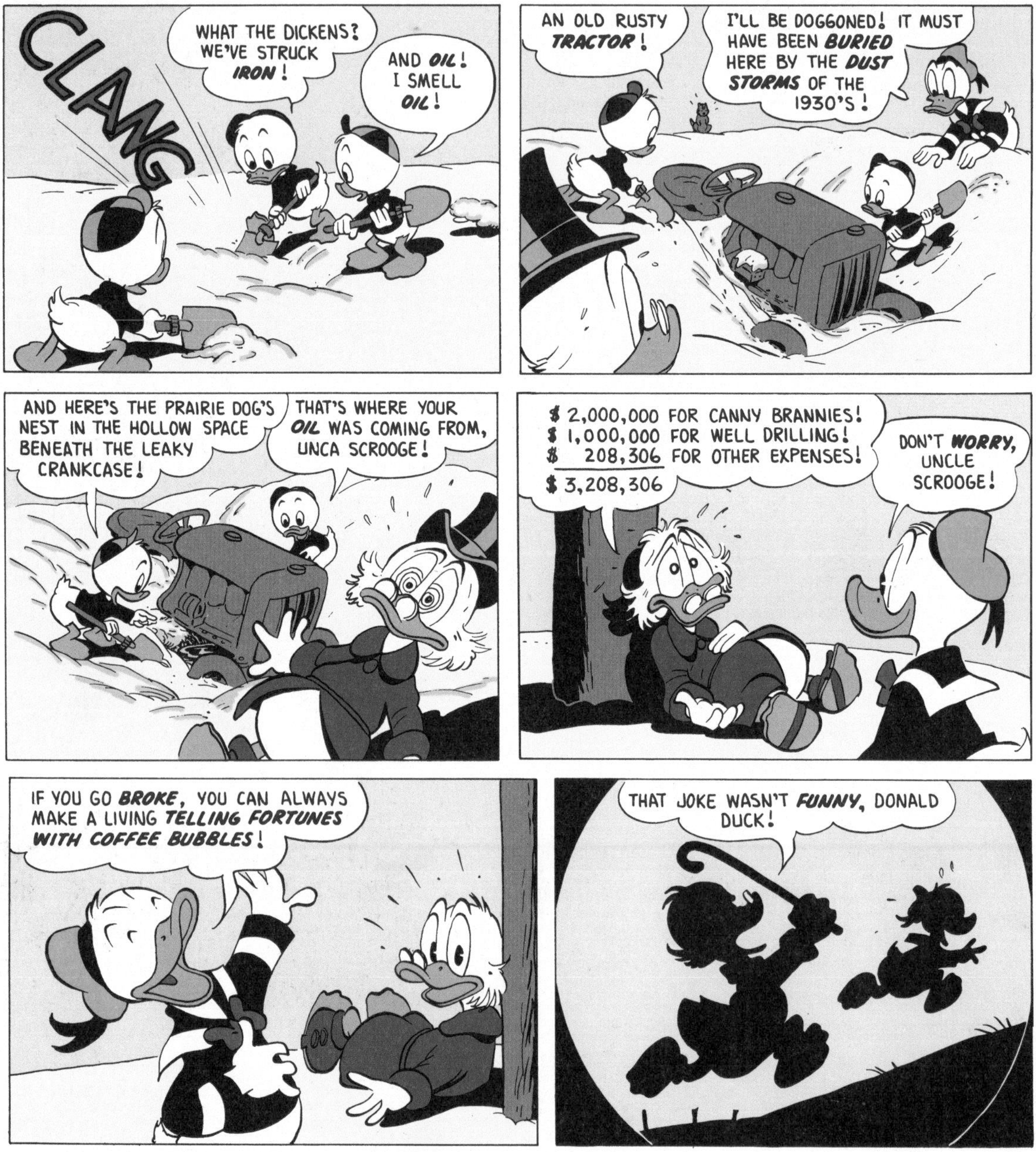
CLANG
WHAT THE DICKENS? WE'VE STRUCK IRON!
AND OIL! I SMELL OIL!
AN OLD RUSTY TRACTOR!
I'LL BE DOGGONED! IT MUST HAVE BEEN BURIED HERE BY THE DUST STORMS OF THE 1930'S!
AND HERE'S THE PRAIRIE DOG'S NEST IN THE HOLLOW SPACE BENEATH THE LEAKY CRANKCASE!
THAT'S WHERE YOUR OIL WAS COMING FROM, UNCA SCROOGE!
$ 2,000,000 FOR CANNY BRANNIES!
$ 1,000,000 FOR WELL DRILLING!
$ 208,306 FOR OTHER EXPENSES!
$ 3,208,306
DON'T WORRY, UNCLE SCROOGE!
IF YOU GO BROKE, YOU CAN ALWAYS MAKE A LIVING TELLING FORTUNES WITH COFFEE BUBBLES!
THAT JOKE WASN'T FUNNY, DONALD DUCK!

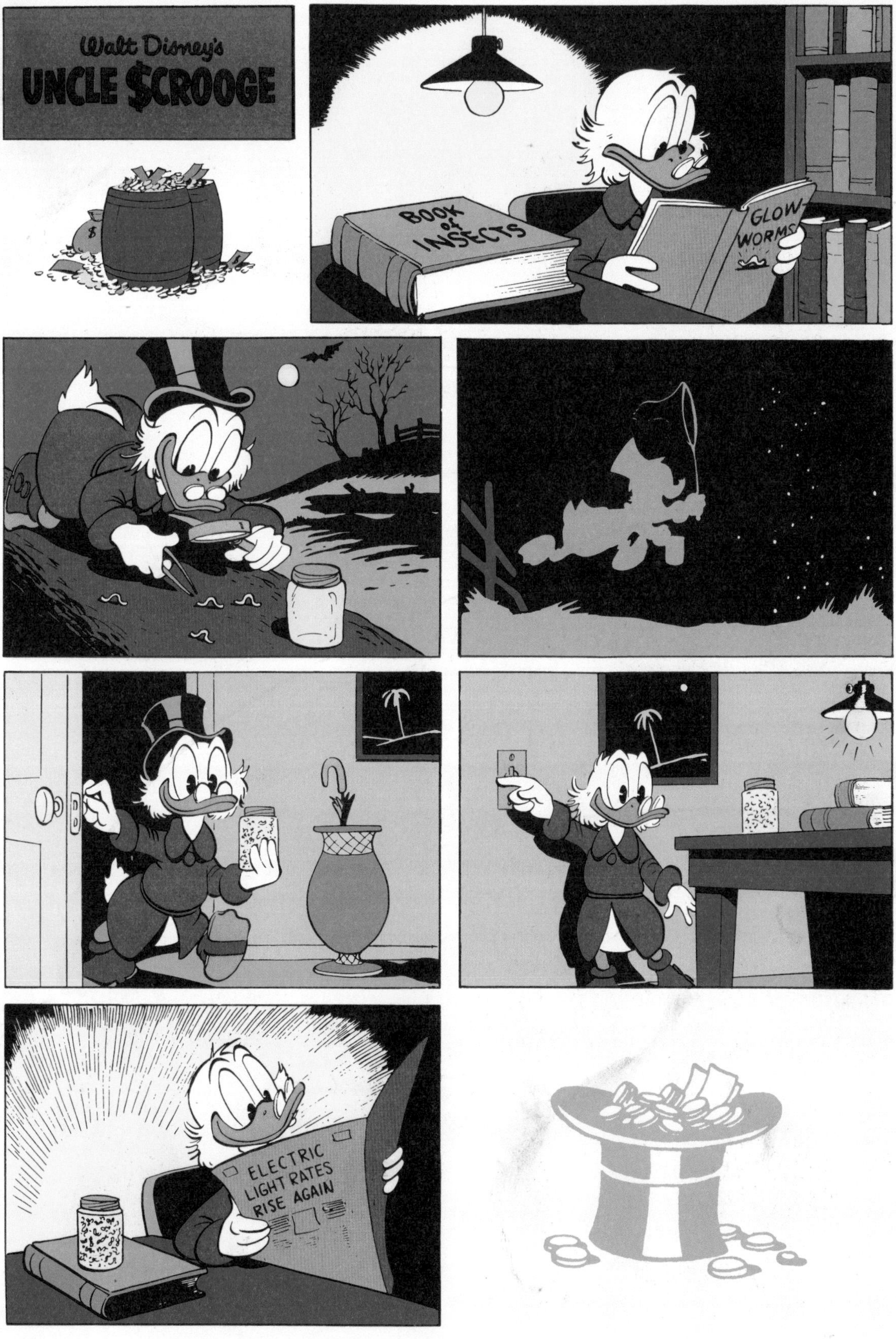
Walt Disney's
UNCLE $CROOGE
BOOK of INSECTS
GLOW-WORMS
ELECTRIC LIGHT RATES RISE AGAIN

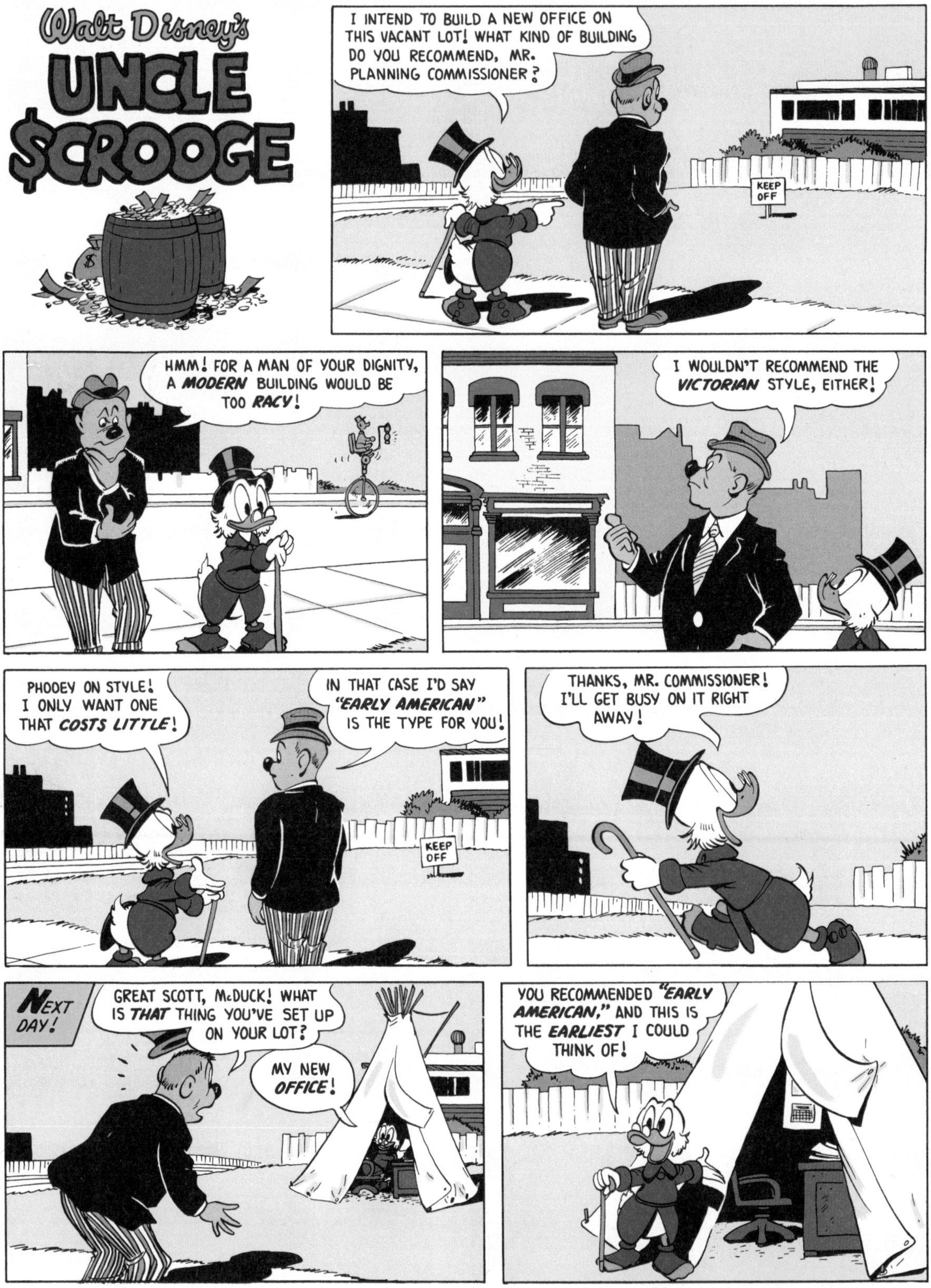
Walt Disney's
UNCLE $CROOGE
KEEP OFF
I INTEND TO BUILD A NEW OFFICE ON THIS VACANT LOT! WHAT KIND OF BUILDING DO YOU RECOMMEND, MR. PLANNING COMMISSIONER?
HMM! FOR A MAN OF YOUR DIGNITY, A MODERN BUILDING WOULD BE TOO RACY!
I WOULDN'T RECOMMEND THE VICTORIAN STYLE, EITHER!
PHOOEY ON STYLE! I ONLY WANT ONE THAT COSTS LITTLE!
IN THAT CASE I'D SAY "EARLY AMERICAN" IS THE TYPE FOR YOU!
KEEP OFF
THANKS, MR. COMMISSIONER! I'LL GET BUSY ON IT RIGHT AWAY!
NEXT DAY!
GREAT SCOTT, McDUCK! WHAT IS THAT THING YOU'VE SET UP ON YOUR LOT?
MY NEW OFFICE!
YOU RECOMMENDED "EARLY AMERICAN," AND THIS IS THE EARLIEST I COULD THINK OF!

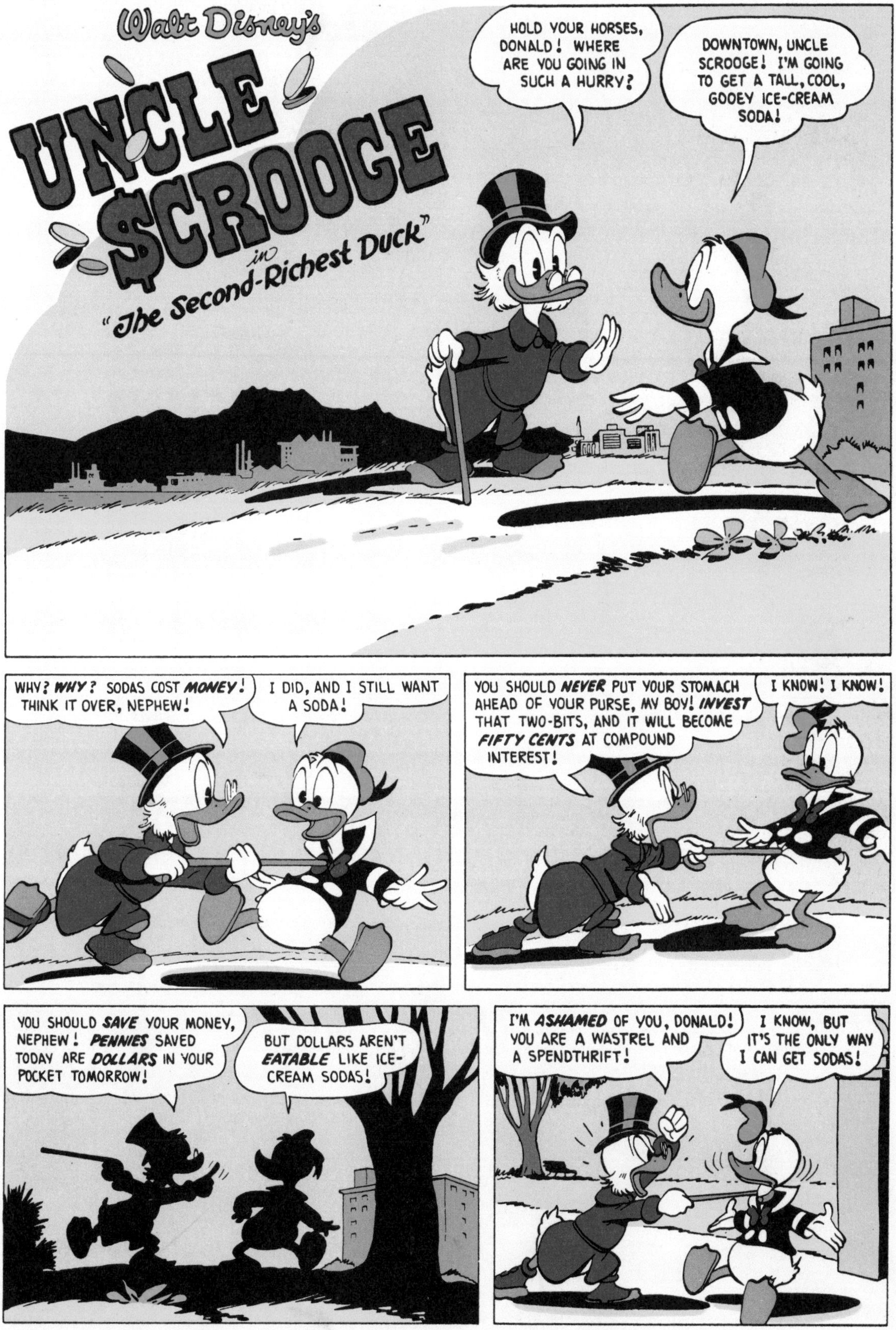

Walt Disney's
UNCLE $CROOGE
in
"The Second-Richest Duck"
HOLD YOUR HORSES, DONALD! WHERE ARE YOU GOING IN SUCH A HURRY?
DOWNTOWN, UNCLE SCROOGE! I'M GOING TO GET A TALL, COOL, GOOEY ICE-CREAM SODA!
WHY? WHY? SODAS COST MONEY! THINK IT OVER, NEPHEW!
I DID, AND I STILL WANT A SODA!
YOU SHOULD NEVER PUT YOUR STOMACH AHEAD OF YOUR PURSE, MY BOY! INVEST THAT TWO-BITS, AND IT WILL BECOME FIFTY CENTS AT COMPOUND INTEREST!
I KNOW! I KNOW!
YOU SHOULD SAVE YOUR MONEY, NEPHEW! PENNIES SAVED TODAY ARE DOLLARS IN YOUR POCKET TOMORROW!
BUT DOLLARS AREN'T EATABLE LIKE ICE-CREAM SODAS!
I'M ASHAMED OF YOU, DONALD! YOU ARE A WASTREL AND A SPENDTHRIFT!
I KNOW, BUT IT'S THE ONLY WAY I CAN GET SODAS!

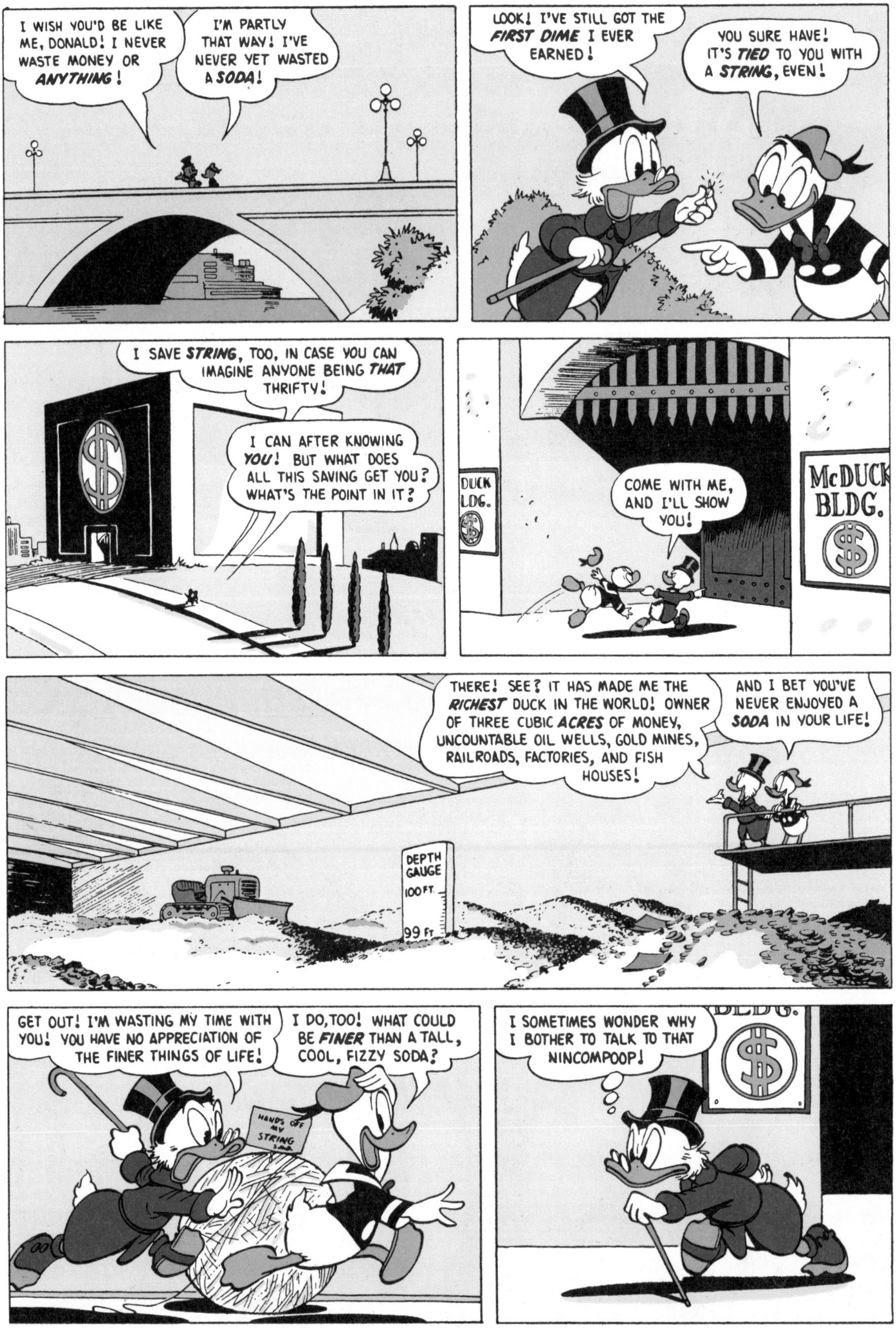
I WISH YOU'D BE LIKE ME, DONALD! I NEVER WASTE MONEY OR ANYTHING!
I'M PARTLY THAT WAY! I'VE NEVER YET WASTED A SODA!
LOOK! I'VE STILL GOT THE FIRST DIME I EVER EARNED!
YOU SURE HAVE! IT'S TIED TO YOU WITH A STRING, EVEN!
I SAVE STRING, TOO, IN CASE YOU CAN IMAGINE ANYONE BEING THAT THRIFTY!
I CAN AFTER KNOWING YOU! BUT WHAT DOES ALL THIS SAVING GET YOU? WHAT'S THE POINT IN IT?
DUCK BLDG.
COME WITH ME, AND I'LL SHOW YOU!
McDUCK BLDG.
THERE! SEE? IT HAS MADE ME THE RICHEST DUCK IN THE WORLD! OWNER OF THREE CUBIC ACRES OF MONEY, UNCOUNTABLE OIL WELLS, GOLD MINES, RAILROADS, FACTORIES, AND FISH HOUSES!
AND I BET YOU'VE NEVER ENJOYED A SODA IN YOUR LIFE!
DEPTH GAUGE
100 FT.
99 FT.
GET OUT! I'M WASTING MY TIME WITH YOU! YOU HAVE NO APPRECIATION OF THE FINER THINGS OF LIFE!
I DO, TOO! WHAT COULD BE FINER THAN A TALL, COOL, FIZZY SODA?
HANDS OFF MY STRING
I SOMETIMES WONDER WHY I BOTHER TO TALK TO THAT NINCOMPOOP!

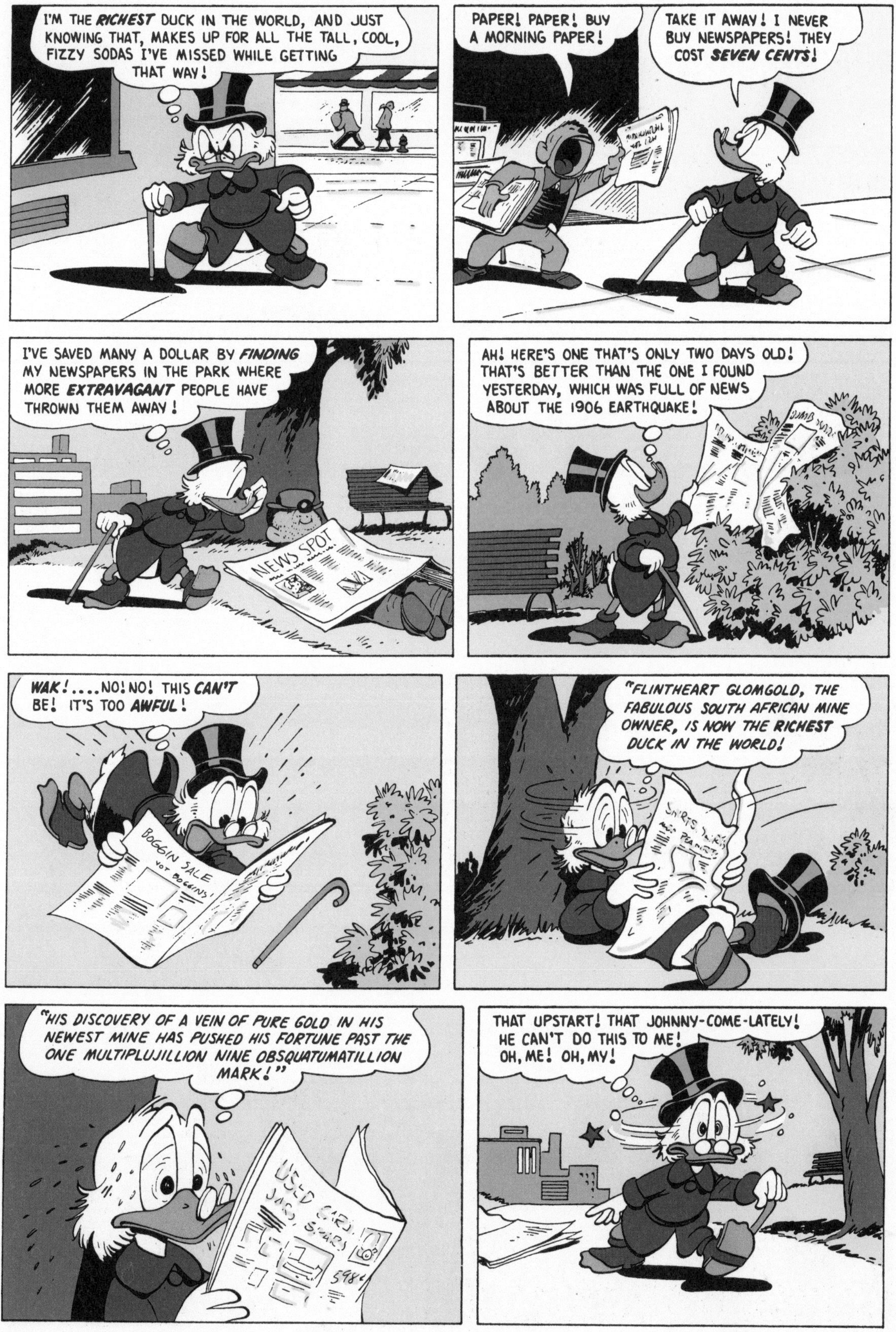
I'M THE RICHEST DUCK IN THE WORLD, AND JUST KNOWING THAT, MAKES UP FOR ALL THE TALL, COOL, FIZZY SODAS I'VE MISSED WHILE GETTING THAT WAY!
PAPER! PAPER! BUY A MORNING PAPER!
TAKE IT AWAY! I NEVER BUY NEWSPAPERS! THEY COST SEVEN CENTS!
I'VE SAVED MANY A DOLLAR BY FINDING MY NEWSPAPERS IN THE PARK WHERE MORE EXTRAVAGANT PEOPLE HAVE THROWN THEM AWAY!
NEWS SPOT
AH! HERE'S ONE THAT'S ONLY TWO DAYS OLD! THAT'S BETTER THAN THE ONE I FOUND YESTERDAY, WHICH WAS FULL OF NEWS ABOUT THE 1906 EARTHQUAKE!
WAK!....NO! NO! THIS CAN'T BE! IT'S TOO AWFUL!
BOGGIN SALE
VOT BOGGINS!
"FLINTHEART GLOMGOLD, THE FABULOUS SOUTH AFRICAN MINE OWNER, IS NOW THE RICHEST DUCK IN THE WORLD!
"HIS DISCOVERY OF A VEIN OF PURE GOLD IN HIS NEWEST MINE HAS PUSHED HIS FORTUNE PAST THE ONE MULTIPLUJILLION NINE OBSQUATUMATILLION MARK!"
USED CARS
THAT UPSTART! THAT JOHNNY-COME-LATELY! HE CAN'T DO THIS TO ME! OH, ME! OH, MY!

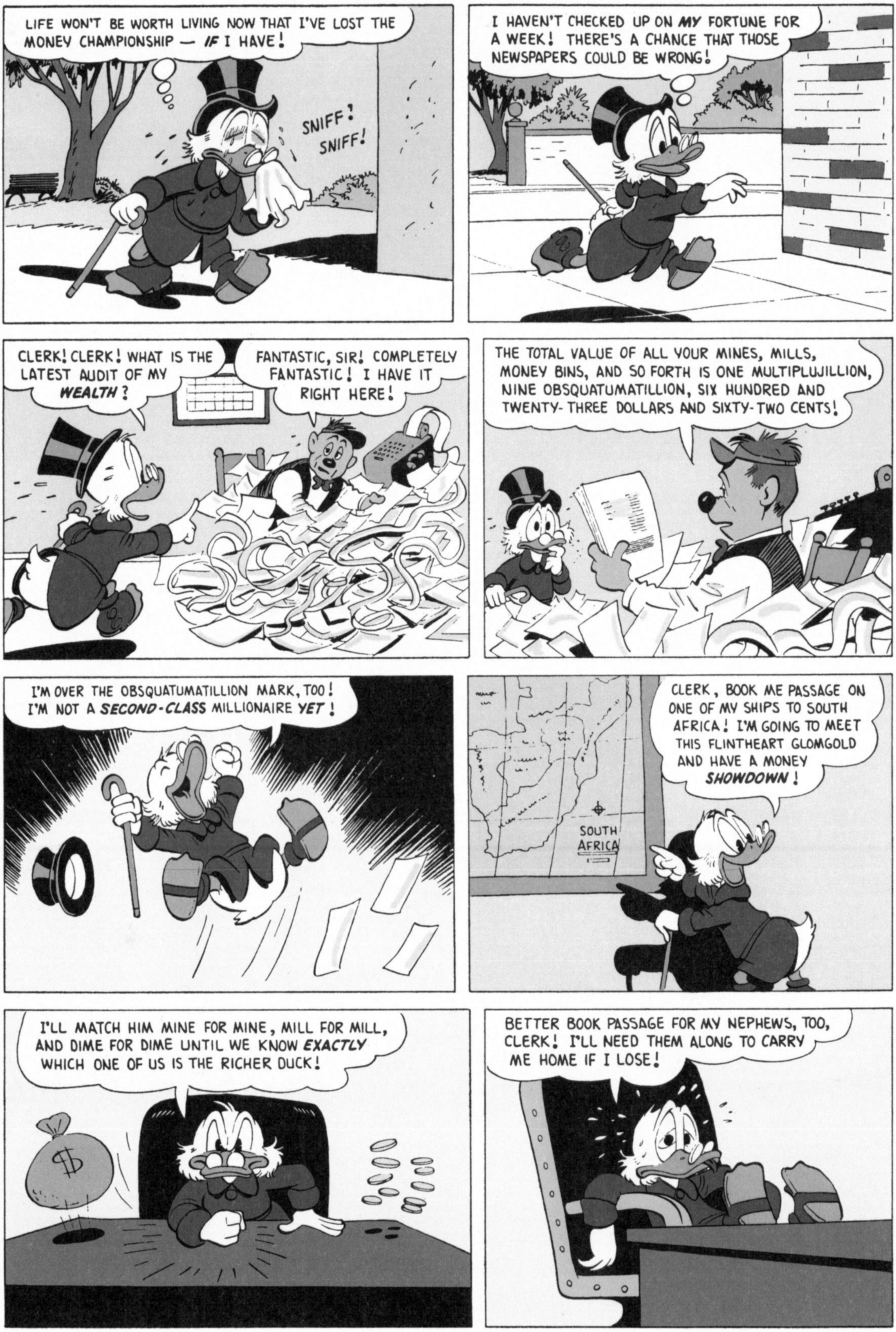

LIFE WON'T BE WORTH LIVING NOW THAT I'VE LOST THE MONEY CHAMPIONSHIP — *IF* I HAVE!
SNIFF! SNIFF!
I HAVEN'T CHECKED UP ON *MY* FORTUNE FOR A WEEK! THERE'S A CHANCE THAT THOSE NEWSPAPERS COULD BE WRONG!
CLERK! CLERK! WHAT IS THE LATEST AUDIT OF MY *WEALTH*?
FANTASTIC, SIR! COMPLETELY FANTASTIC! I HAVE IT RIGHT HERE!
THE TOTAL VALUE OF ALL YOUR MINES, MILLS, MONEY BINS, AND SO FORTH IS ONE MULTIPLUJILLION, NINE OBSQUATUMATILLION, SIX HUNDRED AND TWENTY-THREE DOLLARS AND SIXTY-TWO CENTS!
I'M OVER THE OBSQUATUMATILLION MARK, TOO! I'M NOT A *SECOND-CLASS* MILLIONAIRE *YET*!
CLERK, BOOK ME PASSAGE ON ONE OF MY SHIPS TO SOUTH AFRICA! I'M GOING TO MEET THIS FLINTHEART GLOMGOLD AND HAVE A MONEY *SHOWDOWN*!
SOUTH AFRICA
I'LL MATCH HIM MINE FOR MINE, MILL FOR MILL, AND DIME FOR DIME UNTIL WE KNOW *EXACTLY* WHICH ONE OF US IS THE RICHER DUCK!
BETTER BOOK PASSAGE FOR MY NEPHEWS, TOO, CLERK! I'LL NEED THEM ALONG TO CARRY ME HOME IF I LOSE!

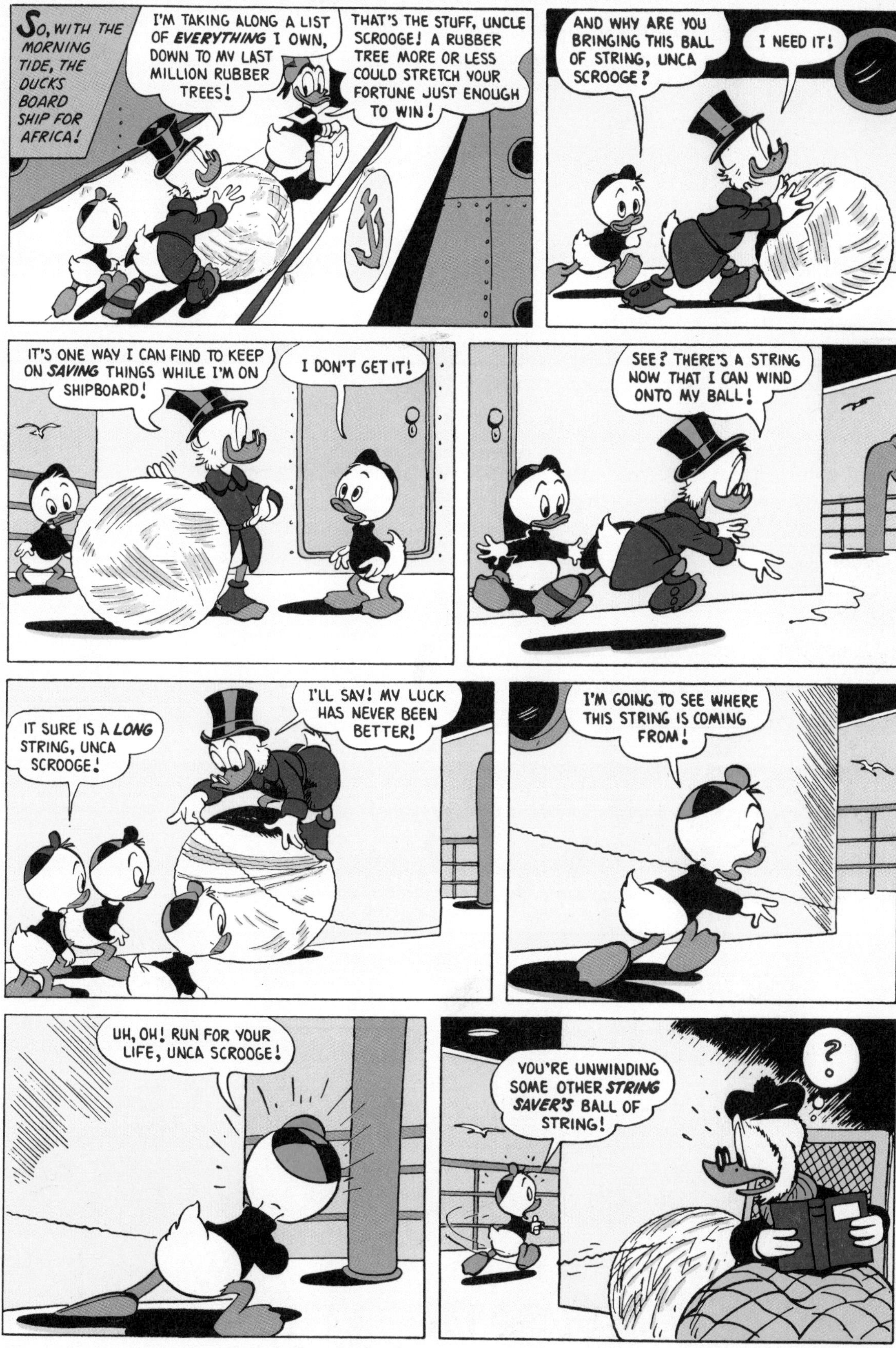
SO, WITH THE MORNING TIDE, THE DUCKS BOARD SHIP FOR AFRICA!
I'M TAKING ALONG A LIST OF EVERYTHING I OWN, DOWN TO MY LAST MILLION RUBBER TREES!
THAT'S THE STUFF, UNCLE SCROOGE! A RUBBER TREE MORE OR LESS COULD STRETCH YOUR FORTUNE JUST ENOUGH TO WIN!
AND WHY ARE YOU BRINGING THIS BALL OF STRING, UNCA SCROOGE?
I NEED IT!
IT'S ONE WAY I CAN FIND TO KEEP ON SAVING THINGS WHILE I'M ON SHIPBOARD!
I DON'T GET IT!
SEE? THERE'S A STRING NOW THAT I CAN WIND ONTO MY BALL!
IT SURE IS A LONG STRING, UNCA SCROOGE!
I'LL SAY! MY LUCK HAS NEVER BEEN BETTER!
I'M GOING TO SEE WHERE THIS STRING IS COMING FROM!
UH, OH! RUN FOR YOUR LIFE, UNCA SCROOGE!
YOU'RE UNWINDING SOME OTHER STRING SAVER'S BALL OF STRING!
?

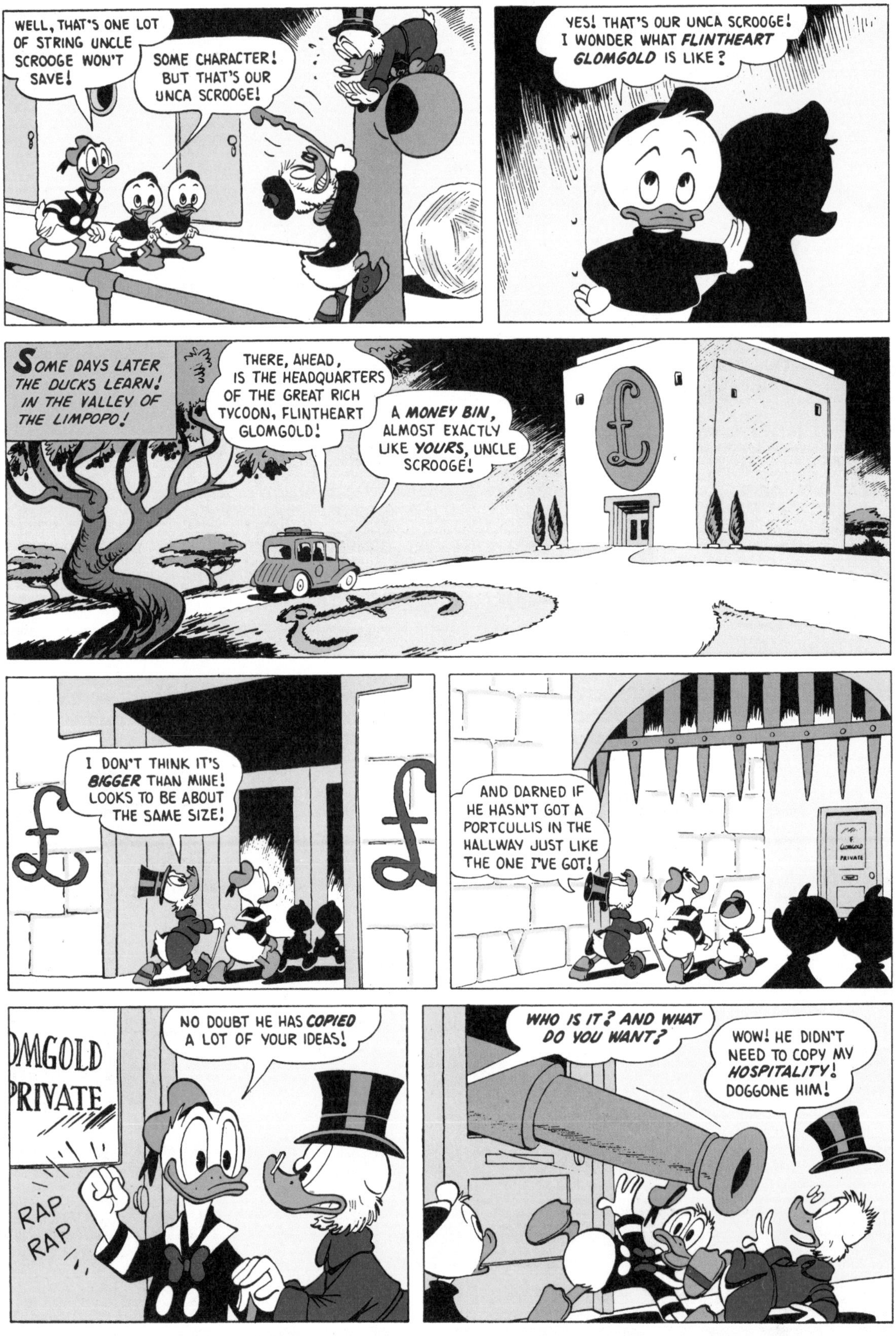
WELL, THAT'S ONE LOT OF STRING UNCLE SCROOGE WON'T SAVE!
SOME CHARACTER! BUT THAT'S OUR UNCA SCROOGE!
YES! THAT'S OUR UNCA SCROOGE! I WONDER WHAT FLINTHEART GLOMGOLD IS LIKE?
SOME DAYS LATER THE DUCKS LEARN! IN THE VALLEY OF THE LIMPOPO!
THERE, AHEAD, IS THE HEADQUARTERS OF THE GREAT RICH TYCOON, FLINTHEART GLOMGOLD!
A MONEY BIN, ALMOST EXACTLY LIKE YOURS, UNCLE SCROOGE!
I DON'T THINK IT'S BIGGER THAN MINE! LOOKS TO BE ABOUT THE SAME SIZE!
AND DARNED IF HE HASN'T GOT A PORTCULLIS IN THE HALLWAY JUST LIKE THE ONE I'VE GOT!
MGOLD PRIVATE
RAP RAP
NO DOUBT HE HAS COPIED A LOT OF YOUR IDEAS!
WHO IS IT? AND WHAT DO YOU WANT?
WOW! HE DIDN'T NEED TO COPY MY HOSPITALITY! DOGGONE HIM!

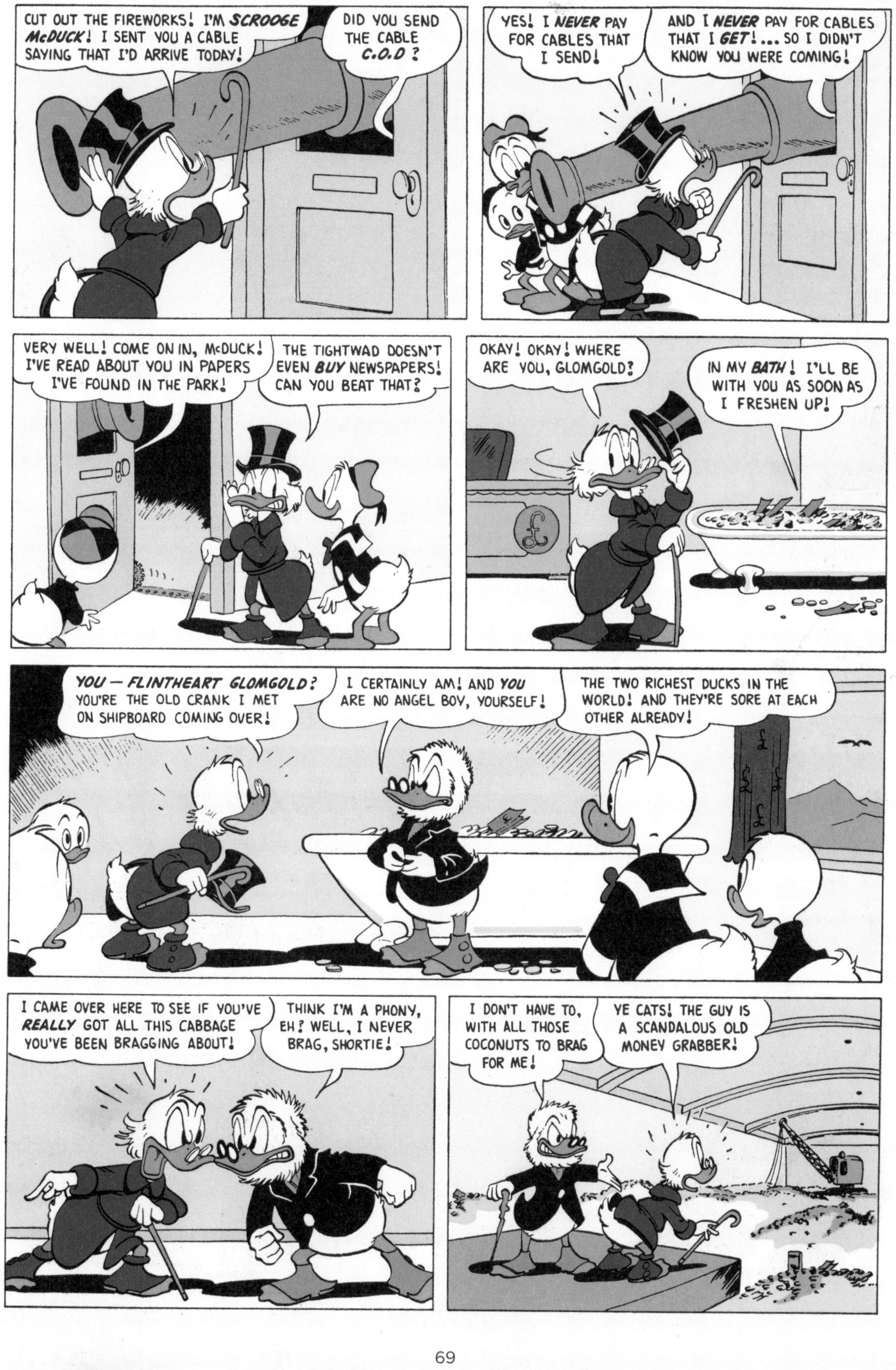
CUT OUT THE FIREWORKS! I'M SCROOGE McDUCK! I SENT YOU A CABLE SAYING THAT I'D ARRIVE TODAY!
DID YOU SEND THE CABLE C.O.D?
YES! I NEVER PAY FOR CABLES THAT I SEND!
AND I NEVER PAY FOR CABLES THAT I GET!... SO I DIDN'T KNOW YOU WERE COMING!
VERY WELL! COME ON IN, McDUCK! I'VE READ ABOUT YOU IN PAPERS I'VE FOUND IN THE PARK!
THE TIGHTWAD DOESN'T EVEN BUY NEWSPAPERS! CAN YOU BEAT THAT?
OKAY! OKAY! WHERE ARE YOU, GLOMGOLD?
IN MY BATH! I'LL BE WITH YOU AS SOON AS I FRESHEN UP!
YOU — FLINTHEART GLOMGOLD? YOU'RE THE OLD CRANK I MET ON SHIPBOARD COMING OVER!
I CERTAINLY AM! AND YOU ARE NO ANGEL BOY, YOURSELF!
THE TWO RICHEST DUCKS IN THE WORLD! AND THEY'RE SORE AT EACH OTHER ALREADY!
I CAME OVER HERE TO SEE IF YOU'VE REALLY GOT ALL THIS CABBAGE YOU'VE BEEN BRAGGING ABOUT!
THINK I'M A PHONY, EH? WELL, I NEVER BRAG, SHORTIE!
I DON'T HAVE TO, WITH ALL THOSE COCONUTS TO BRAG FOR ME!
YE CATS! THE GUY IS A SCANDALOUS OLD MONEY GRABBER!

I'M NO *PAUPER*, MYSELF, GLOMGOLD! I HAVE *THREE CUBIC ACRES* OF MONEY IN *MY* MONEY BIN!

(ULP!) HOW MUCH IS THAT IN *POUNDS* AND *SHILLINGS*?

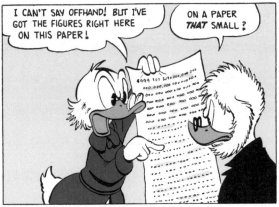

I CAN'T SAY OFFHAND! BUT I'VE GOT THE FIGURES RIGHT HERE ON THIS PAPER!

ON A PAPER *THAT* SMALL?

HMM! YOU SEEM TO HAVE ABOUT THE SAME AMOUNT OF *CASH* AS I HAVE! QUITE A SHOWING FOR THE *SECOND-RICHEST* DUCK!

YOU BETTER NOT CALL ME *THAT* UNTIL YOU CAN *PROVE* IT!

OF COURSE YOU DON'T KNOW THAT THE *BOTTOM FOUR FEET* OF *MY* MONEY BIN IS FULL OF *DIAMONDS*!

PLAN OF MONEY BIN

I'M NOT IMPRESSED! THE BOTTOM FOUR FEET OF *MY* BIN IS FULL OF *STAR SAPPHIRES*!

I'VE ALSO GOT *TWELVE TONS* OF *RUBIES*!

I'VE GOT TWELVE TONS, TOO! *LONG* TONS, SHORTIE!

I'VE GOT ONE THOUSAND AND TWO OIL WELLS!

I'VE GOT ONE THOUSAND AND TWO, TOO, AND *TWO* DIGGING!

I ALSO OWN *FARMS*! I'VE GOT SIX HUNDRED ACRES OF PUMPKINS!

NEVER MIND THE ACRES! HOW *MANY* PUMPKINS?

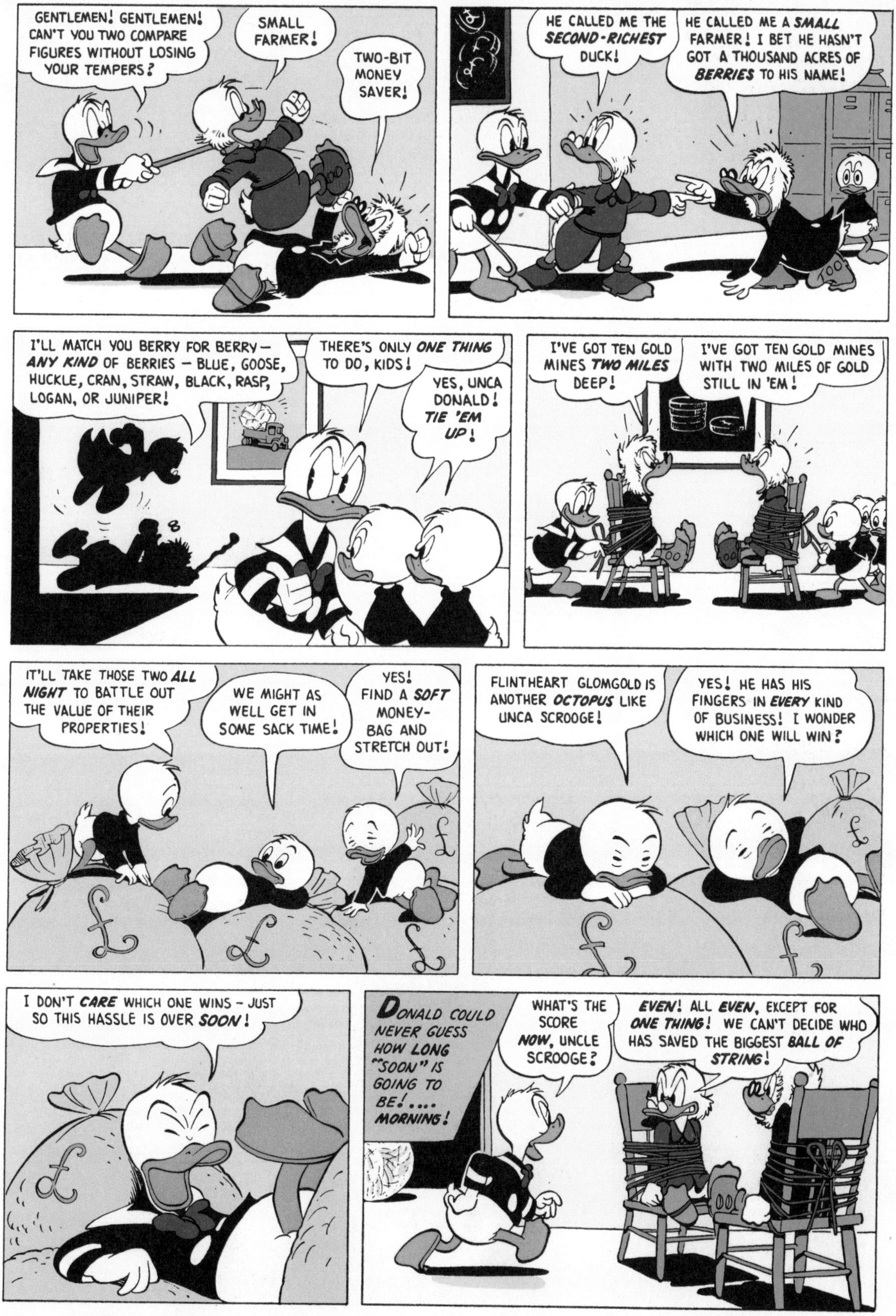

GENTLEMEN! GENTLEMEN! CAN'T YOU TWO COMPARE FIGURES WITHOUT LOSING YOUR TEMPERS?
SMALL FARMER!
TWO-BIT MONEY SAVER!
HE CALLED ME THE SECOND-RICHEST DUCK!
HE CALLED ME A SMALL FARMER! I BET HE HASN'T GOT A THOUSAND ACRES OF BERRIES TO HIS NAME!
I'LL MATCH YOU BERRY FOR BERRY— ANY KIND OF BERRIES — BLUE, GOOSE, HUCKLE, CRAN, STRAW, BLACK, RASP, LOGAN, OR JUNIPER!
THERE'S ONLY ONE THING TO DO, KIDS!
YES, UNCA DONALD! TIE 'EM UP!
I'VE GOT TEN GOLD MINES TWO MILES DEEP!
I'VE GOT TEN GOLD MINES WITH TWO MILES OF GOLD STILL IN 'EM!
IT'LL TAKE THOSE TWO ALL NIGHT TO BATTLE OUT THE VALUE OF THEIR PROPERTIES!
WE MIGHT AS WELL GET IN SOME SACK TIME!
YES! FIND A SOFT MONEY-BAG AND STRETCH OUT!
FLINTHEART GLOMGOLD IS ANOTHER OCTOPUS LIKE UNCA SCROOGE!
YES! HE HAS HIS FINGERS IN EVERY KIND OF BUSINESS! I WONDER WHICH ONE WILL WIN?
I DON'T CARE WHICH ONE WINS - JUST SO THIS HASSLE IS OVER SOON!
DONALD COULD NEVER GUESS HOW LONG "SOON" IS GOING TO BE!.... MORNING!
WHAT'S THE SCORE NOW, UNCLE SCROOGE?
EVEN! ALL EVEN, EXCEPT FOR ONE THING! WE CAN'T DECIDE WHO HAS SAVED THE BIGGEST BALL OF STRING!

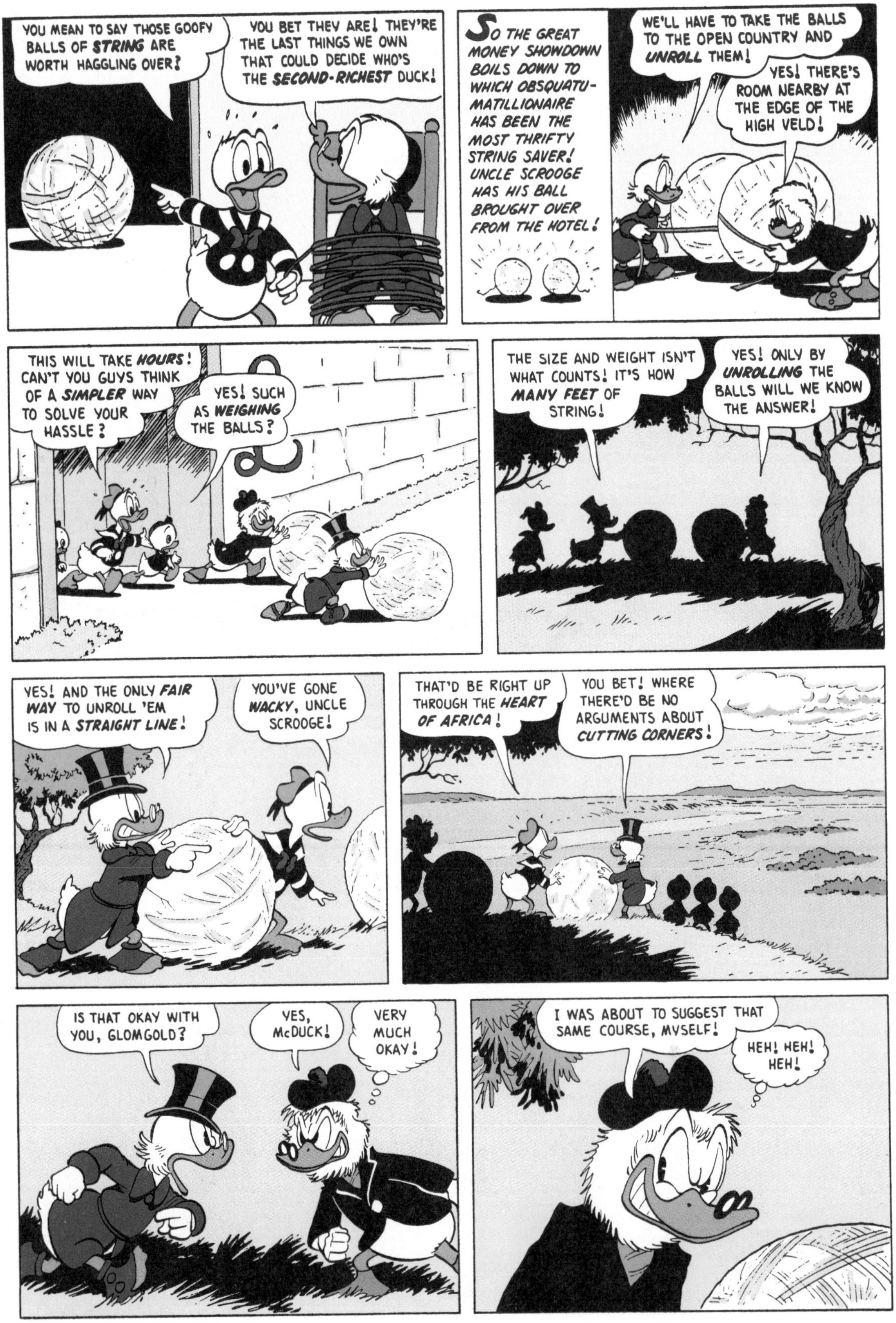
YOU MEAN TO SAY THOSE GOOFY BALLS OF STRING ARE WORTH HAGGLING OVER?
YOU BET THEY ARE! THEY'RE THE LAST THINGS WE OWN THAT COULD DECIDE WHO'S THE SECOND-RICHEST DUCK!
SO THE GREAT MONEY SHOWDOWN BOILS DOWN TO WHICH OBSQUATU-MATILLIONAIRE HAS BEEN THE MOST THRIFTY STRING SAVER! UNCLE SCROOGE HAS HIS BALL BROUGHT OVER FROM THE HOTEL!
WE'LL HAVE TO TAKE THE BALLS TO THE OPEN COUNTRY AND UNROLL THEM!
YES! THERE'S ROOM NEARBY AT THE EDGE OF THE HIGH VELD!
THIS WILL TAKE HOURS! CAN'T YOU GUYS THINK OF A SIMPLER WAY TO SOLVE YOUR HASSLE?
YES! SUCH AS WEIGHING THE BALLS?
THE SIZE AND WEIGHT ISN'T WHAT COUNTS! IT'S HOW MANY FEET OF STRING!
YES! ONLY BY UNROLLING THE BALLS WILL WE KNOW THE ANSWER!
YES! AND THE ONLY FAIR WAY TO UNROLL 'EM IS IN A STRAIGHT LINE!
YOU'VE GONE WACKY, UNCLE SCROOGE!
THAT'D BE RIGHT UP THROUGH THE HEART OF AFRICA!
YOU BET! WHERE THERE'D BE NO ARGUMENTS ABOUT CUTTING CORNERS!
IS THAT OKAY WITH YOU, GLOMGOLD?
YES, McDUCK!
VERY MUCH OKAY!
I WAS ABOUT TO SUGGEST THAT SAME COURSE, MYSELF!
HEH! HEH! HEH!

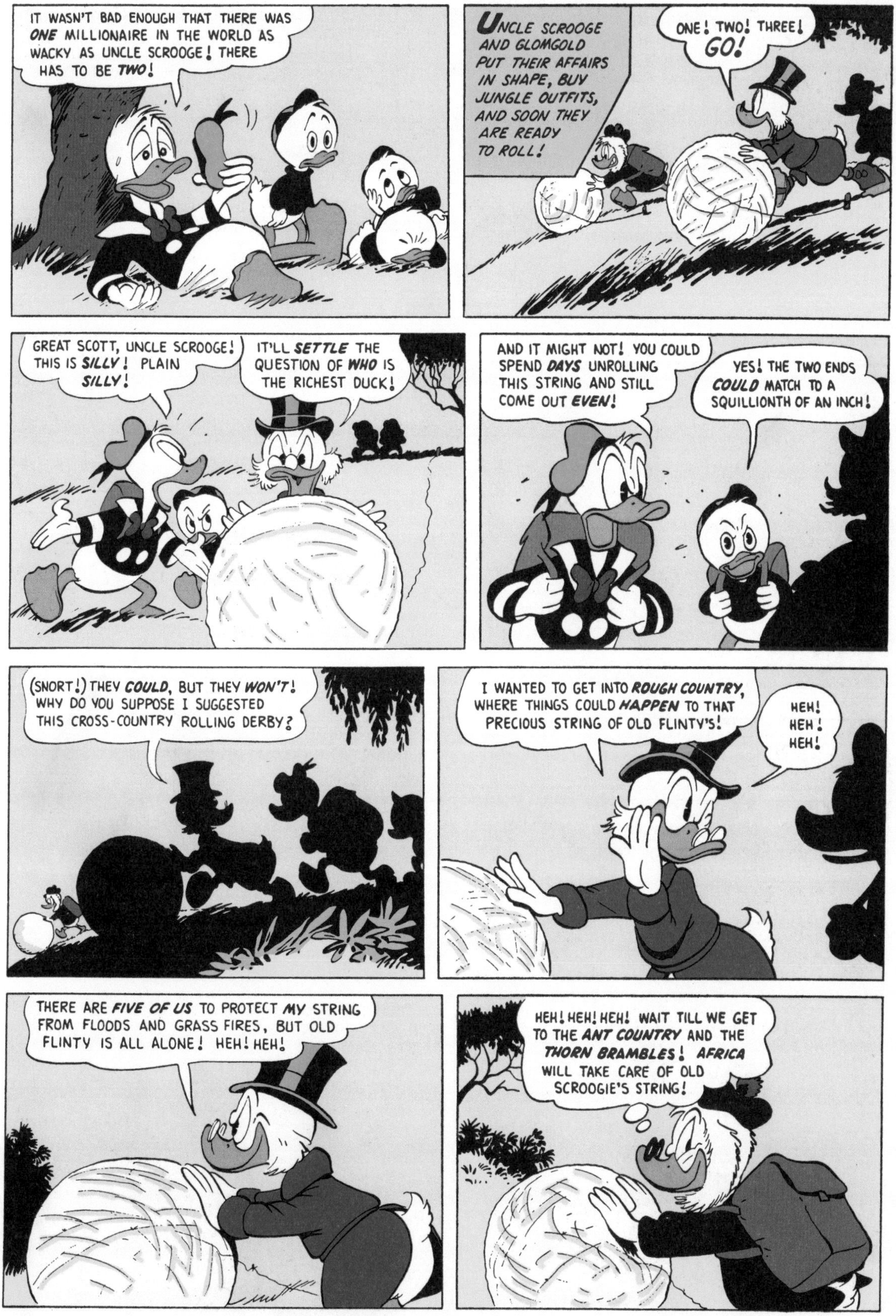
IT WASN'T BAD ENOUGH THAT THERE WAS ONE MILLIONAIRE IN THE WORLD AS WACKY AS UNCLE SCROOGE! THERE HAS TO BE TWO!
UNCLE SCROOGE AND GLOMGOLD PUT THEIR AFFAIRS IN SHAPE, BUY JUNGLE OUTFITS, AND SOON THEY ARE READY TO ROLL!
ONE! TWO! THREE! GO!
GREAT SCOTT, UNCLE SCROOGE! THIS IS SILLY! PLAIN SILLY!
IT'LL SETTLE THE QUESTION OF WHO IS THE RICHEST DUCK!
AND IT MIGHT NOT! YOU COULD SPEND DAYS UNROLLING THIS STRING AND STILL COME OUT EVEN!
YES! THE TWO ENDS COULD MATCH TO A SQUILLIONTH OF AN INCH!
(SNORT!) THEY COULD, BUT THEY WON'T! WHY DO YOU SUPPOSE I SUGGESTED THIS CROSS-COUNTRY ROLLING DERBY?
I WANTED TO GET INTO ROUGH COUNTRY, WHERE THINGS COULD HAPPEN TO THAT PRECIOUS STRING OF OLD FLINTY'S!
HEH! HEH! HEH!
THERE ARE FIVE OF US TO PROTECT MY STRING FROM FLOODS AND GRASS FIRES, BUT OLD FLINTY IS ALL ALONE! HEH! HEH!
HEH! HEH! HEH! WAIT TILL WE GET TO THE ANT COUNTRY AND THE THORN BRAMBLES! AFRICA WILL TAKE CARE OF OLD SCROOGIE'S STRING!

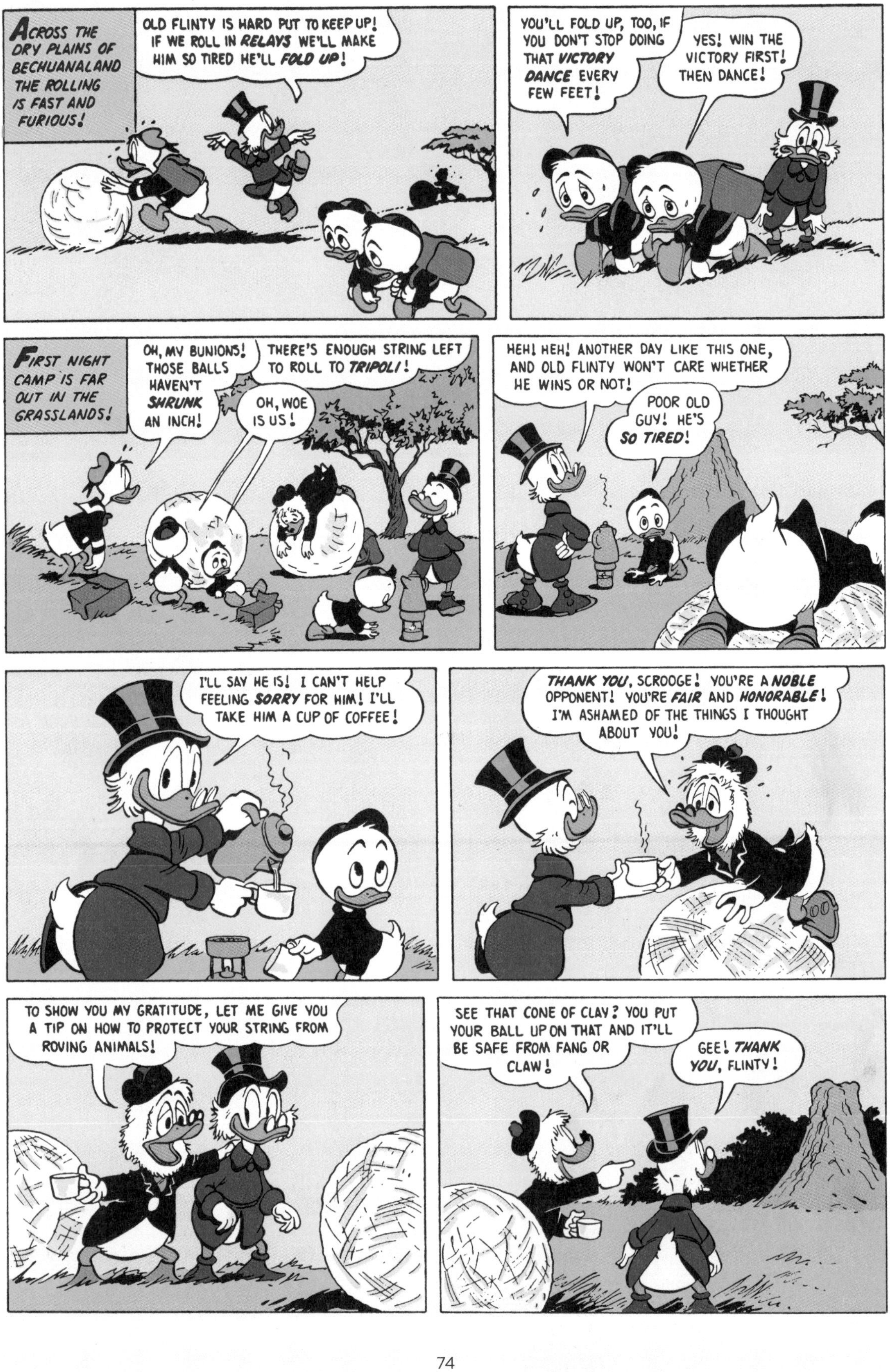
ACROSS THE DRY PLAINS OF BECHUANALAND THE ROLLING IS FAST AND FURIOUS!
OLD FLINTY IS HARD PUT TO KEEP UP! IF WE ROLL IN RELAYS WE'LL MAKE HIM SO TIRED HE'LL FOLD UP!
YOU'LL FOLD UP, TOO, IF YOU DON'T STOP DOING THAT VICTORY DANCE EVERY FEW FEET!
YES! WIN THE VICTORY FIRST! THEN DANCE!
FIRST NIGHT CAMP IS FAR OUT IN THE GRASSLANDS!
OH, MY BUNIONS! THOSE BALLS HAVEN'T SHRUNK AN INCH!
THERE'S ENOUGH STRING LEFT TO ROLL TO TRIPOLI!
OH, WOE IS US!
HEH! HEH! ANOTHER DAY LIKE THIS ONE, AND OLD FLINTY WON'T CARE WHETHER HE WINS OR NOT!
POOR OLD GUY! HE'S SO TIRED!
I'LL SAY HE IS! I CAN'T HELP FEELING SORRY FOR HIM! I'LL TAKE HIM A CUP OF COFFEE!
THANK YOU, SCROOGE! YOU'RE A NOBLE OPPONENT! YOU'RE FAIR AND HONORABLE! I'M ASHAMED OF THE THINGS I THOUGHT ABOUT YOU!
TO SHOW YOU MY GRATITUDE, LET ME GIVE YOU A TIP ON HOW TO PROTECT YOUR STRING FROM ROVING ANIMALS!
SEE THAT CONE OF CLAY? YOU PUT YOUR BALL UP ON THAT AND IT'LL BE SAFE FROM FANG OR CLAW!
GEE! THANK YOU, FLINTY!

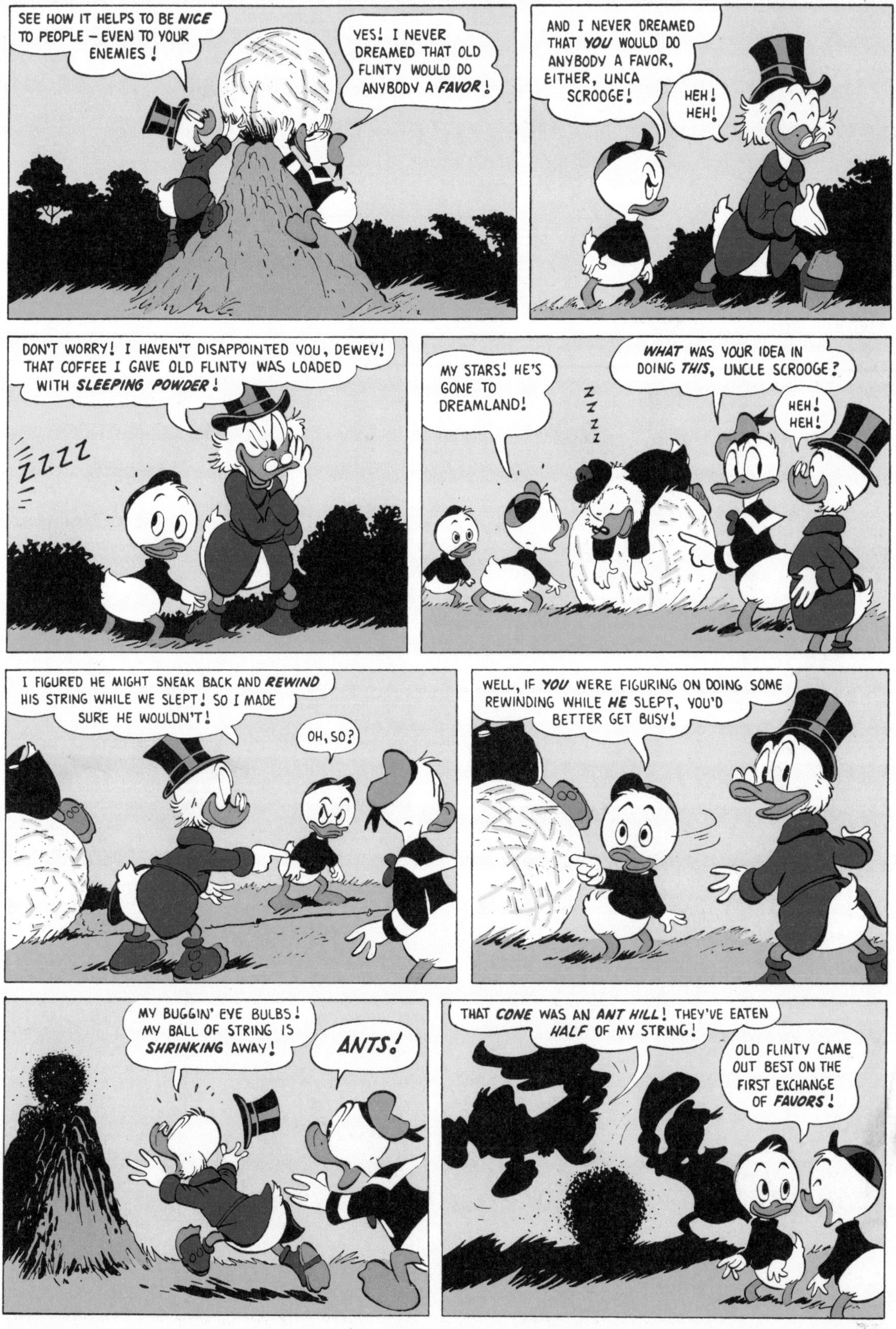
SEE HOW IT HELPS TO BE NICE TO PEOPLE – EVEN TO YOUR ENEMIES!
YES! I NEVER DREAMED THAT OLD FLINTY WOULD DO ANYBODY A FAVOR!
AND I NEVER DREAMED THAT YOU WOULD DO ANYBODY A FAVOR, EITHER, UNCA SCROOGE!
HEH! HEH!
DON'T WORRY! I HAVEN'T DISAPPOINTED YOU, DEWEY! THAT COFFEE I GAVE OLD FLINTY WAS LOADED WITH SLEEPING POWDER!
ZZZZ
MY STARS! HE'S GONE TO DREAMLAND!
WHAT WAS YOUR IDEA IN DOING THIS, UNCLE SCROOGE?
HEH! HEH!
ZZZZ
I FIGURED HE MIGHT SNEAK BACK AND REWIND HIS STRING WHILE WE SLEPT! SO I MADE SURE HE WOULDN'T!
OH, SO?
WELL, IF YOU WERE FIGURING ON DOING SOME REWINDING WHILE HE SLEPT, YOU'D BETTER GET BUSY!
MY BUGGIN' EYE BULBS! MY BALL OF STRING IS SHRINKING AWAY!
ANTS!
THAT CONE WAS AN ANT HILL! THEY'VE EATEN HALF OF MY STRING!
OLD FLINTY CAME OUT BEST ON THE FIRST EXCHANGE OF FAVORS!

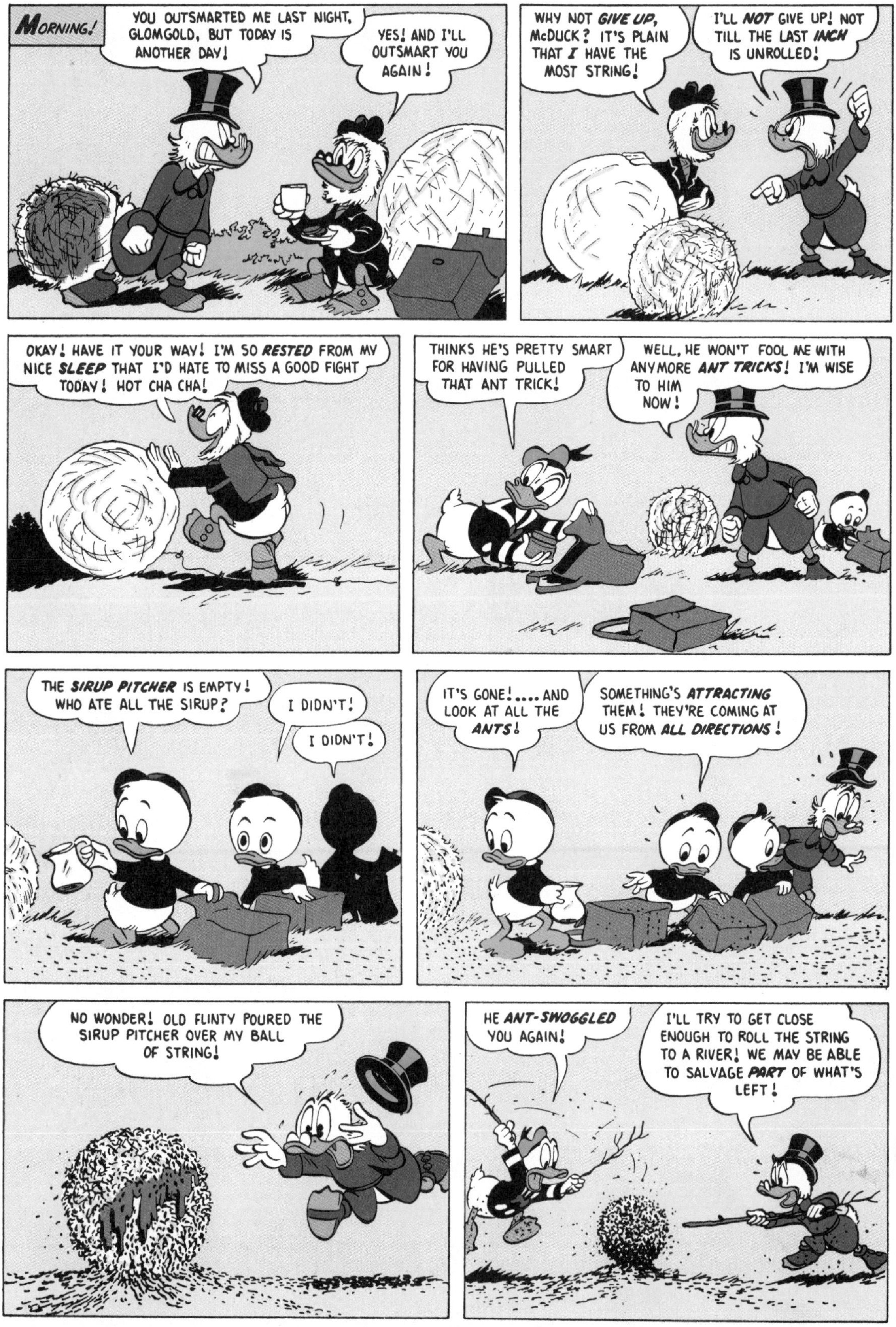
MORNING!
YOU OUTSMARTED ME LAST NIGHT, GLOMGOLD, BUT TODAY IS ANOTHER DAY!
YES! AND I'LL OUTSMART YOU AGAIN!
WHY NOT GIVE UP, McDUCK? IT'S PLAIN THAT I HAVE THE MOST STRING!
I'LL NOT GIVE UP! NOT TILL THE LAST INCH IS UNROLLED!
OKAY! HAVE IT YOUR WAY! I'M SO RESTED FROM MY NICE SLEEP THAT I'D HATE TO MISS A GOOD FIGHT TODAY! HOT CHA CHA!
THINKS HE'S PRETTY SMART FOR HAVING PULLED THAT ANT TRICK!
WELL, HE WON'T FOOL ME WITH ANYMORE ANT TRICKS! I'M WISE TO HIM NOW!
THE SIRUP PITCHER IS EMPTY! WHO ATE ALL THE SIRUP?
I DIDN'T!
I DIDN'T!
IT'S GONE!.... AND LOOK AT ALL THE ANTS!
SOMETHING'S ATTRACTING THEM! THEY'RE COMING AT US FROM ALL DIRECTIONS!
NO WONDER! OLD FLINTY POURED THE SIRUP PITCHER OVER MY BALL OF STRING!
HE ANT-SWOGGLED YOU AGAIN!
I'LL TRY TO GET CLOSE ENOUGH TO ROLL THE STRING TO A RIVER! WE MAY BE ABLE TO SALVAGE PART OF WHAT'S LEFT!

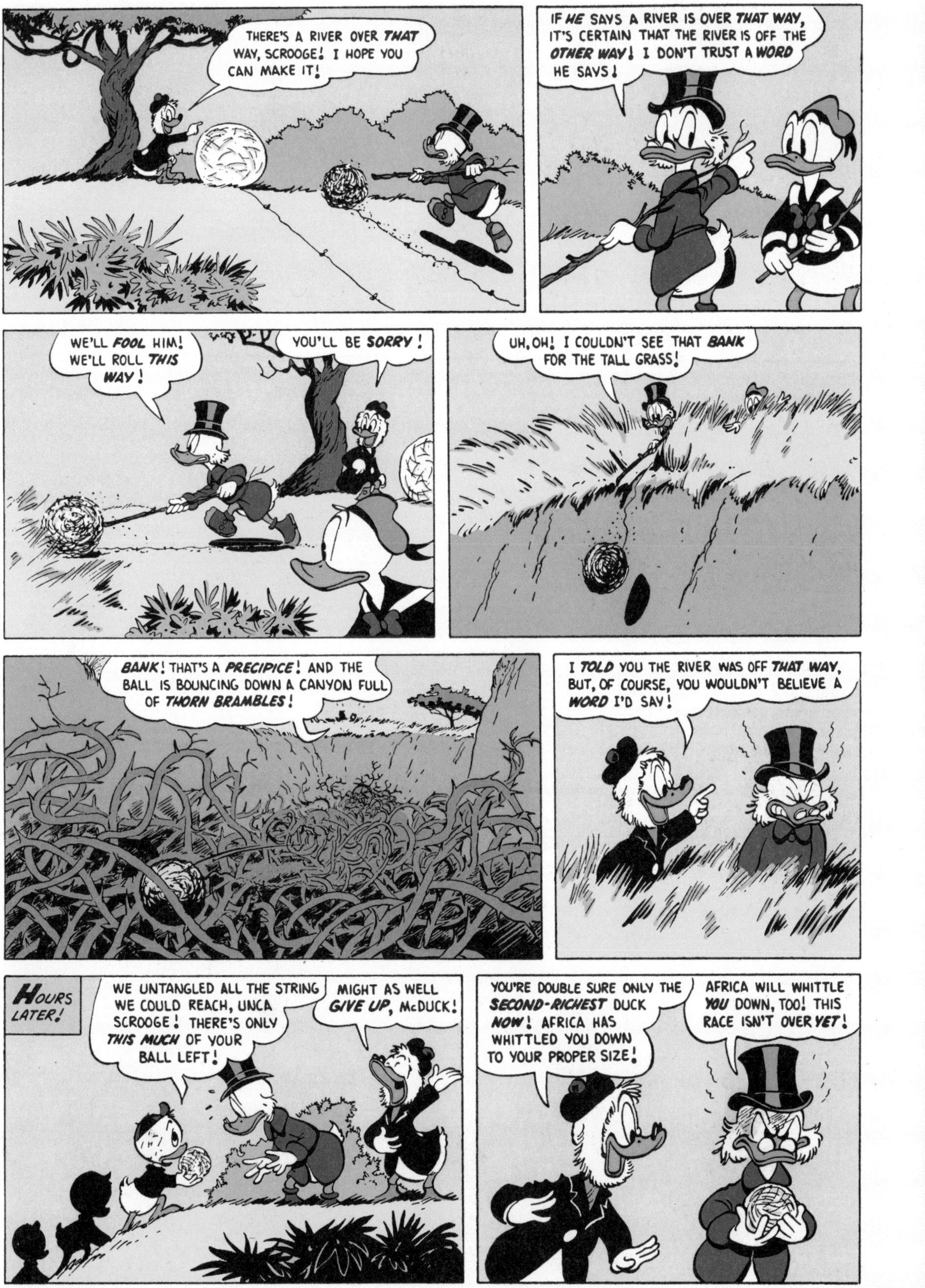
THERE'S A RIVER OVER THAT WAY, SCROOGE! I HOPE YOU CAN MAKE IT!
IF HE SAYS A RIVER IS OVER THAT WAY, IT'S CERTAIN THAT THE RIVER IS OFF THE OTHER WAY! I DON'T TRUST A WORD HE SAYS!
WE'LL FOOL HIM! WE'LL ROLL THIS WAY!
YOU'LL BE SORRY!
UH, OH! I COULDN'T SEE THAT BANK FOR THE TALL GRASS!
BANK! THAT'S A PRECIPICE! AND THE BALL IS BOUNCING DOWN A CANYON FULL OF THORN BRAMBLES!
I TOLD YOU THE RIVER WAS OFF THAT WAY, BUT, OF COURSE, YOU WOULDN'T BELIEVE A WORD I'D SAY!
HOURS LATER!
WE UNTANGLED ALL THE STRING WE COULD REACH, UNCA SCROOGE! THERE'S ONLY THIS MUCH OF YOUR BALL LEFT!
MIGHT AS WELL GIVE UP, McDUCK!
YOU'RE DOUBLE SURE ONLY THE SECOND-RICHEST DUCK NOW! AFRICA HAS WHITTLED YOU DOWN TO YOUR PROPER SIZE!
AFRICA WILL WHITTLE YOU DOWN, TOO! THIS RACE ISN'T OVER YET!

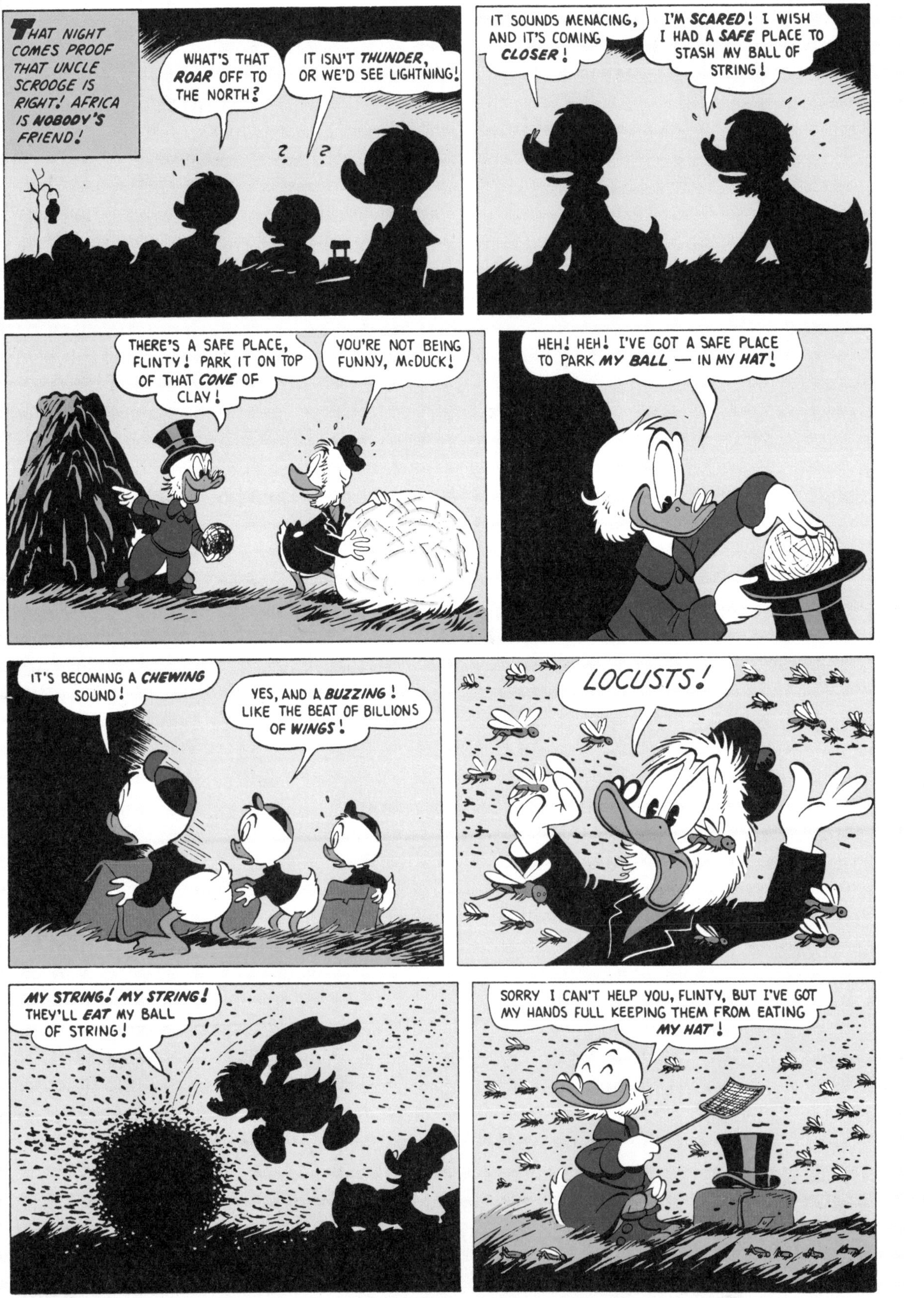
THAT NIGHT COMES PROOF THAT UNCLE SCROOGE IS RIGHT! AFRICA IS NOBODY'S FRIEND!
WHAT'S THAT ROAR OFF TO THE NORTH?
IT ISN'T THUNDER, OR WE'D SEE LIGHTNING!
IT SOUNDS MENACING, AND IT'S COMING CLOSER!
I'M SCARED! I WISH I HAD A SAFE PLACE TO STASH MY BALL OF STRING!
THERE'S A SAFE PLACE, FLINTY! PARK IT ON TOP OF THAT CONE OF CLAY!
YOU'RE NOT BEING FUNNY, McDUCK!
HEH! HEH! I'VE GOT A SAFE PLACE TO PARK MY BALL — IN MY HAT!
IT'S BECOMING A CHEWING SOUND!
YES, AND A BUZZING! LIKE THE BEAT OF BILLIONS OF WINGS!
LOCUSTS!
MY STRING! MY STRING! THEY'LL EAT MY BALL OF STRING!
SORRY I CAN'T HELP YOU, FLINTY, BUT I'VE GOT MY HANDS FULL KEEPING THEM FROM EATING MY HAT!

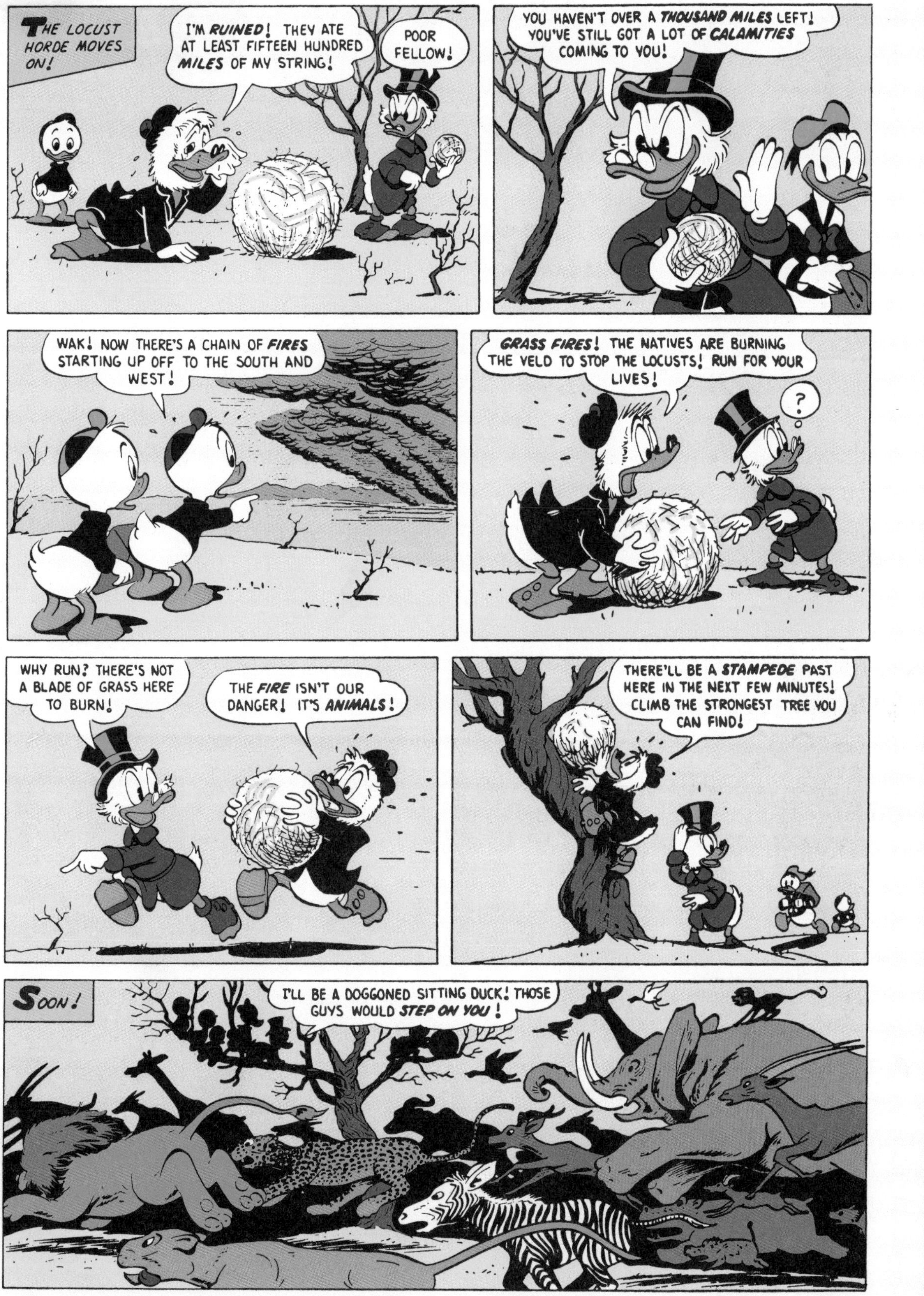
THE LOCUST HORDE MOVES ON!
I'M RUINED! THEY ATE AT LEAST FIFTEEN HUNDRED MILES OF MY STRING!
POOR FELLOW!
YOU HAVEN'T OVER A THOUSAND MILES LEFT! YOU'VE STILL GOT A LOT OF CALAMITIES COMING TO YOU!
WAK! NOW THERE'S A CHAIN OF FIRES STARTING UP OFF TO THE SOUTH AND WEST!
GRASS FIRES! THE NATIVES ARE BURNING THE VELD TO STOP THE LOCUSTS! RUN FOR YOUR LIVES!
?
WHY RUN? THERE'S NOT A BLADE OF GRASS HERE TO BURN!
THE FIRE ISN'T OUR DANGER! IT'S ANIMALS!
THERE'LL BE A STAMPEDE PAST HERE IN THE NEXT FEW MINUTES! CLIMB THE STRONGEST TREE YOU CAN FIND!
SOON!
I'LL BE A DOGGONED SITTING DUCK! THOSE GUYS WOULD STEP ON YOU!

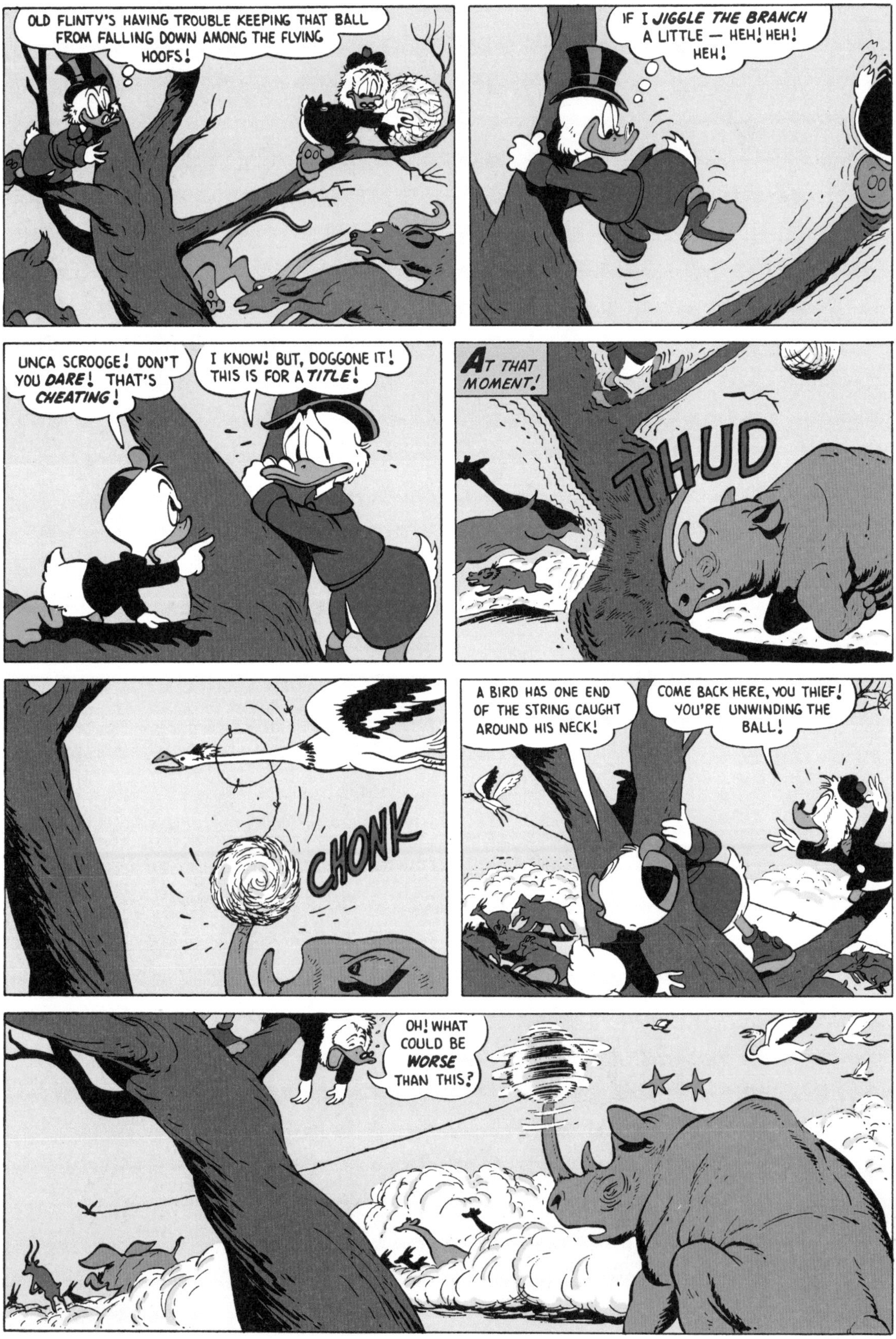
OLD FLINTY'S HAVING TROUBLE KEEPING THAT BALL FROM FALLING DOWN AMONG THE FLYING HOOFS!
IF I JIGGLE THE BRANCH A LITTLE — HEH! HEH! HEH!
UNCA SCROOGE! DON'T YOU DARE! THAT'S CHEATING!
I KNOW! BUT, DOGGONE IT! THIS IS FOR A TITLE!
AT THAT MOMENT!
THUD
CHONK
A BIRD HAS ONE END OF THE STRING CAUGHT AROUND HIS NECK!
COME BACK HERE, YOU THIEF! YOU'RE UNWINDING THE BALL!
OH! WHAT COULD BE WORSE THAN THIS?

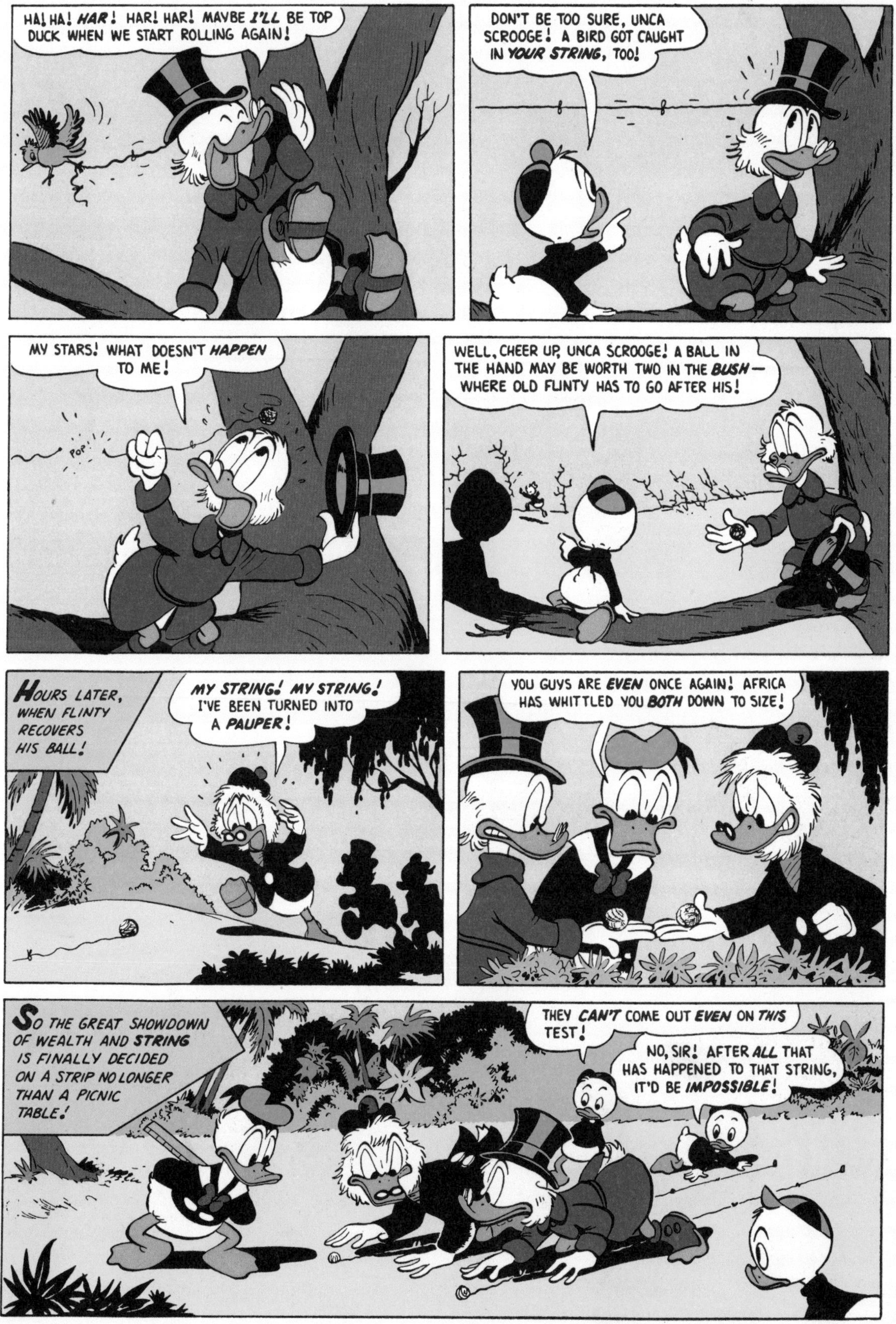
HA! HA! HAR! HAR! HAR! MAYBE I'LL BE TOP DUCK WHEN WE START ROLLING AGAIN!
DON'T BE TOO SURE, UNCA SCROOGE! A BIRD GOT CAUGHT IN YOUR STRING, TOO!
MY STARS! WHAT DOESN'T HAPPEN TO ME!
POP!
WELL, CHEER UP, UNCA SCROOGE! A BALL IN THE HAND MAY BE WORTH TWO IN THE BUSH— WHERE OLD FLINTY HAS TO GO AFTER HIS!
HOURS LATER, WHEN FLINTY RECOVERS HIS BALL!
MY STRING! MY STRING! I'VE BEEN TURNED INTO A PAUPER!
YOU GUYS ARE EVEN ONCE AGAIN! AFRICA HAS WHITTLED YOU BOTH DOWN TO SIZE!
SO THE GREAT SHOWDOWN OF WEALTH AND STRING IS FINALLY DECIDED ON A STRIP NO LONGER THAN A PICNIC TABLE!
THEY CAN'T COME OUT EVEN ON THIS TEST!
NO, SIR! AFTER ALL THAT HAS HAPPENED TO THAT STRING, IT'D BE IMPOSSIBLE!

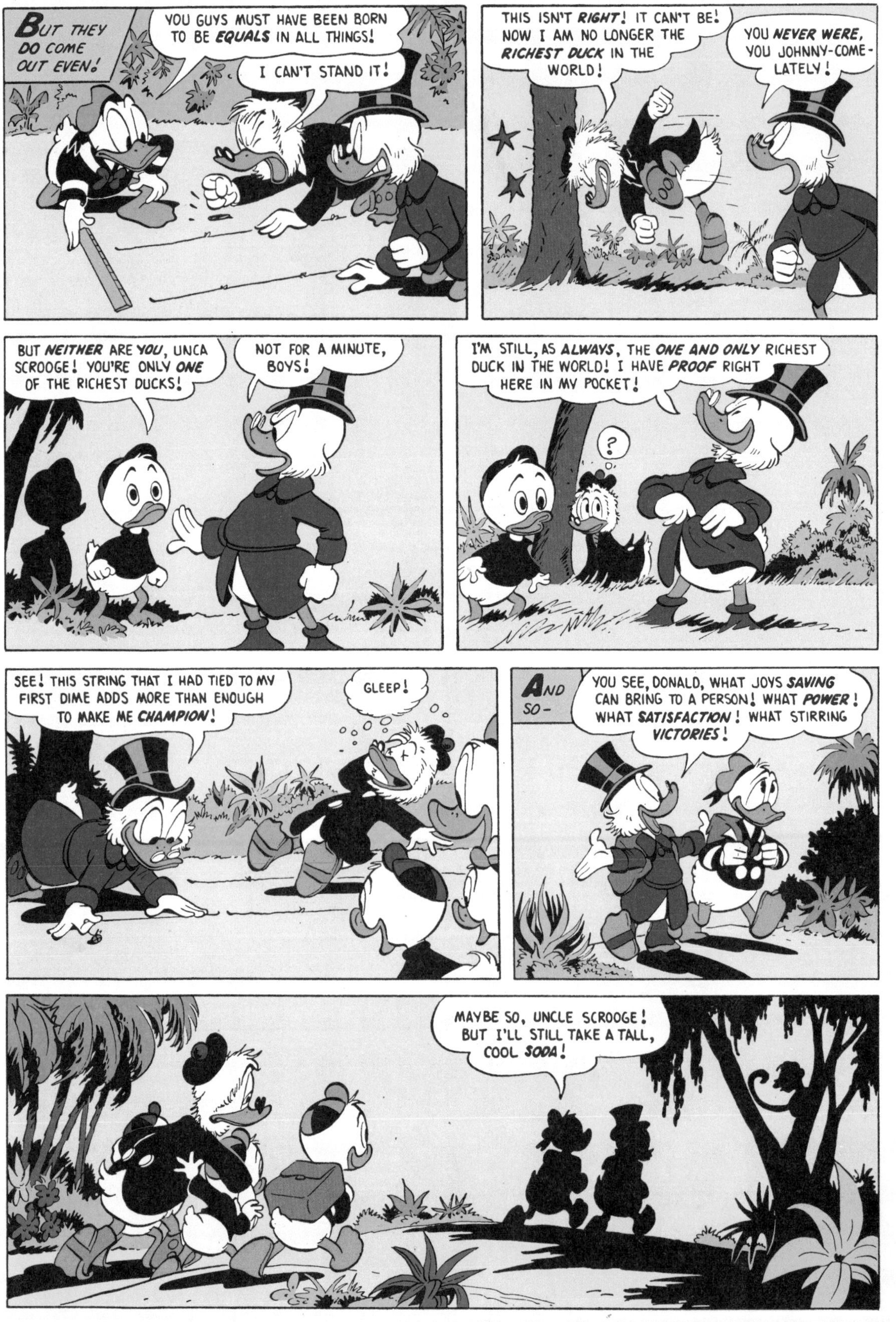
BUT THEY DO COME OUT EVEN!
YOU GUYS MUST HAVE BEEN BORN TO BE EQUALS IN ALL THINGS!
I CAN'T STAND IT!
THIS ISN'T RIGHT! IT CAN'T BE! NOW I AM NO LONGER THE RICHEST DUCK IN THE WORLD!
YOU NEVER WERE, YOU JOHNNY-COME-LATELY!
BUT NEITHER ARE YOU, UNCA SCROOGE! YOU'RE ONLY ONE OF THE RICHEST DUCKS!
NOT FOR A MINUTE, BOYS!
I'M STILL, AS ALWAYS, THE ONE AND ONLY RICHEST DUCK IN THE WORLD! I HAVE PROOF RIGHT HERE IN MY POCKET!
?
SEE! THIS STRING THAT I HAD TIED TO MY FIRST DIME ADDS MORE THAN ENOUGH TO MAKE ME CHAMPION!
GLEEP!
AND SO-
YOU SEE, DONALD, WHAT JOYS SAVING CAN BRING TO A PERSON! WHAT POWER! WHAT SATISFACTION! WHAT STIRRING VICTORIES!
MAYBE SO, UNCLE SCROOGE! BUT I'LL STILL TAKE A TALL, COOL SODA!

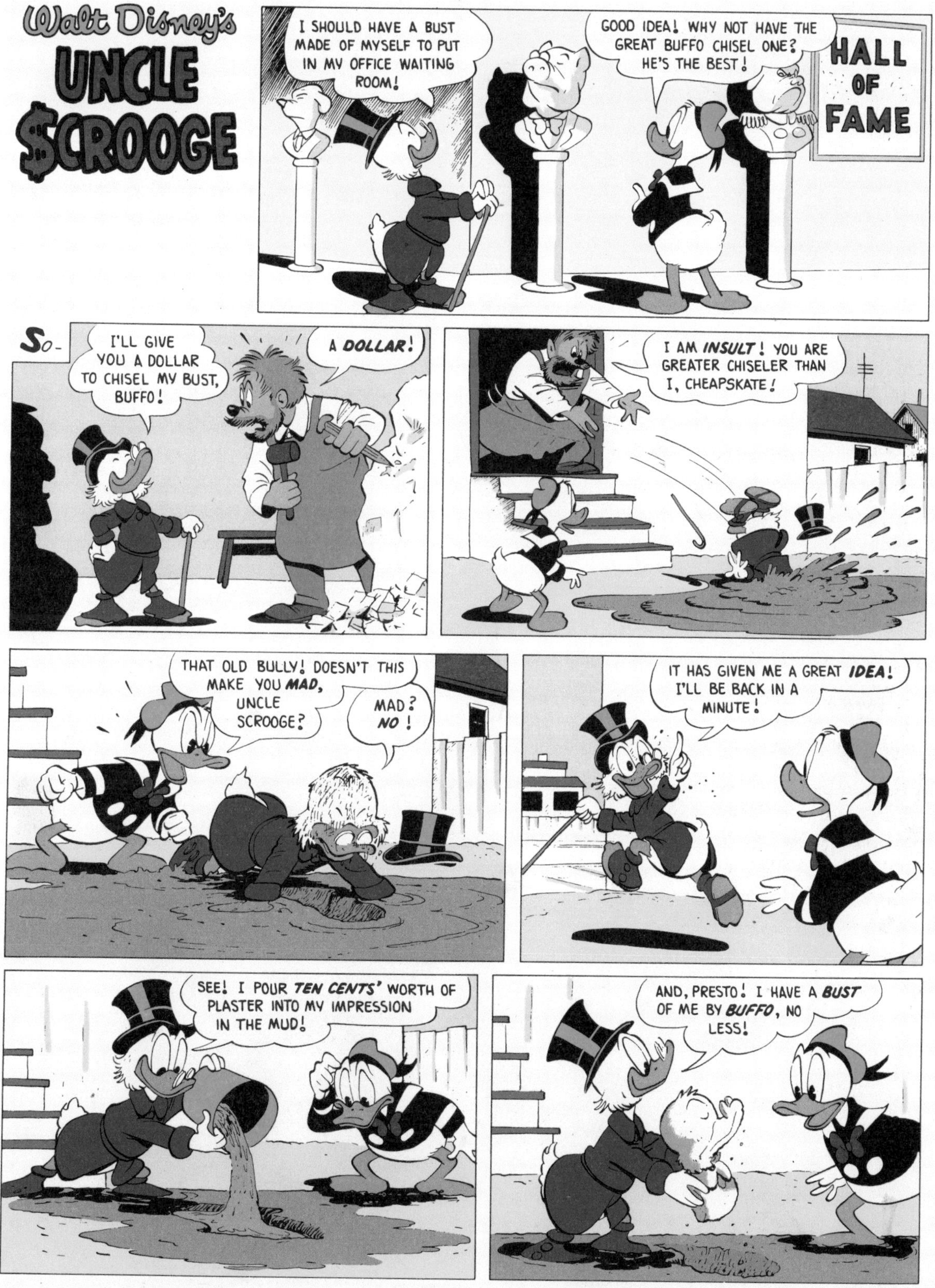
Walt Disney's
UNCLE $CROOGE
I SHOULD HAVE A BUST MADE OF MYSELF TO PUT IN MY OFFICE WAITING ROOM!
GOOD IDEA! WHY NOT HAVE THE GREAT BUFFO CHISEL ONE? HE'S THE BEST!
HALL OF FAME
SO-
I'LL GIVE YOU A DOLLAR TO CHISEL MY BUST, BUFFO!
A DOLLAR!
I AM INSULT! YOU ARE GREATER CHISELER THAN I, CHEAPSKATE!
THAT OLD BULLY! DOESN'T THIS MAKE YOU MAD, UNCLE SCROOGE?
MAD? NO!
IT HAS GIVEN ME A GREAT IDEA! I'LL BE BACK IN A MINUTE!
SEE! I POUR TEN CENTS' WORTH OF PLASTER INTO MY IMPRESSION IN THE MUD!
AND, PRESTO! I HAVE A BUST OF ME BY BUFFO, NO LESS!

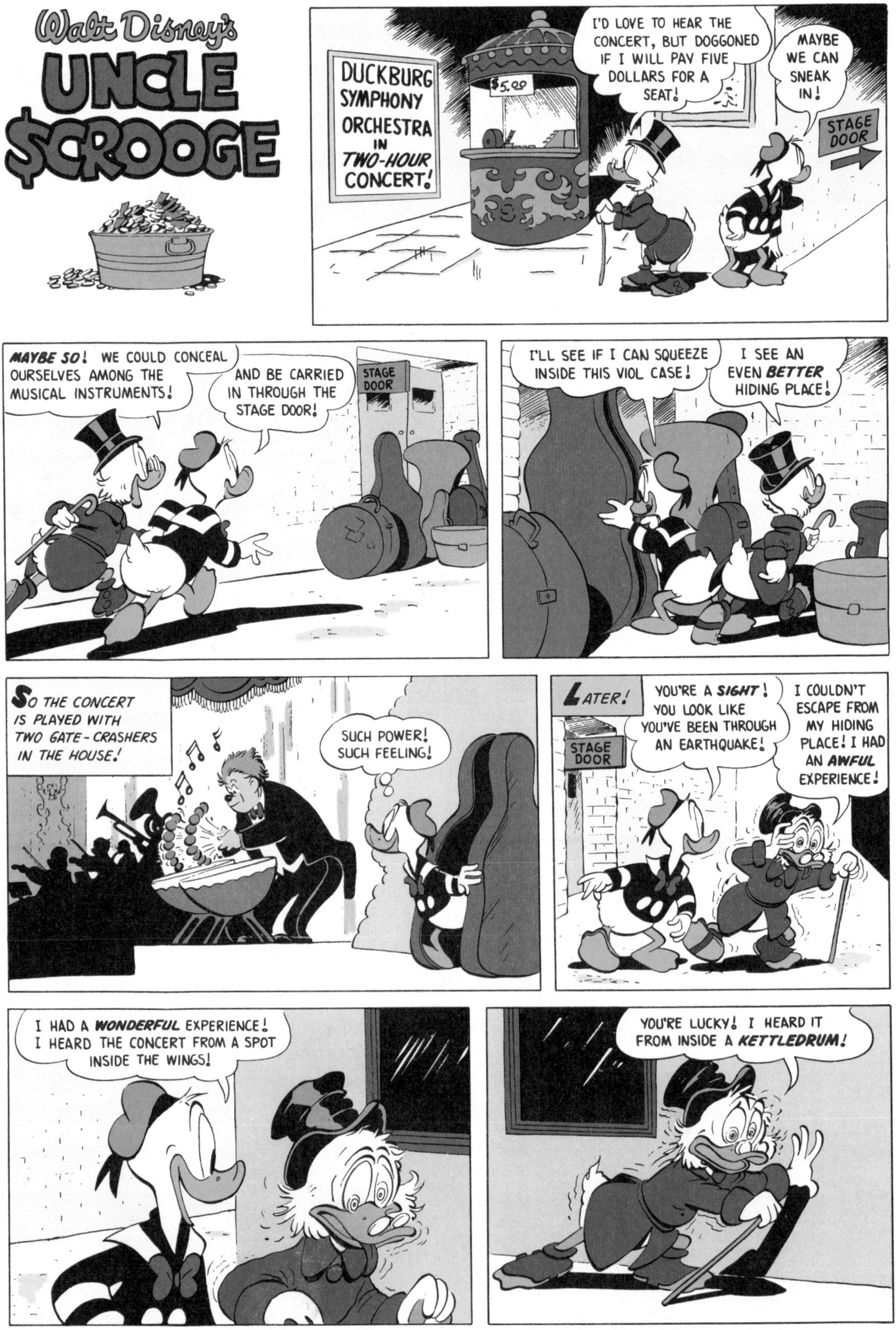
Walt Disney's
UNCLE $CROOGE
DUCKBURG SYMPHONY ORCHESTRA IN TWO-HOUR CONCERT!
$5.00
I'D LOVE TO HEAR THE CONCERT, BUT DOGGONED IF I WILL PAY FIVE DOLLARS FOR A SEAT!
MAYBE WE CAN SNEAK IN!
STAGE DOOR
MAYBE SO! WE COULD CONCEAL OURSELVES AMONG THE MUSICAL INSTRUMENTS!
AND BE CARRIED IN THROUGH THE STAGE DOOR!
STAGE DOOR
I'LL SEE IF I CAN SQUEEZE INSIDE THIS VIOL CASE!
I SEE AN EVEN BETTER HIDING PLACE!
SO THE CONCERT IS PLAYED WITH TWO GATE-CRASHERS IN THE HOUSE!
SUCH POWER! SUCH FEELING!
LATER!
STAGE DOOR
YOU'RE A SIGHT! YOU LOOK LIKE YOU'VE BEEN THROUGH AN EARTHQUAKE!
I COULDN'T ESCAPE FROM MY HIDING PLACE! I HAD AN AWFUL EXPERIENCE!
I HAD A WONDERFUL EXPERIENCE! I HEARD THE CONCERT FROM A SPOT INSIDE THE WINGS!
YOU'RE LUCKY! I HEARD IT FROM INSIDE A KETTLEDRUM!

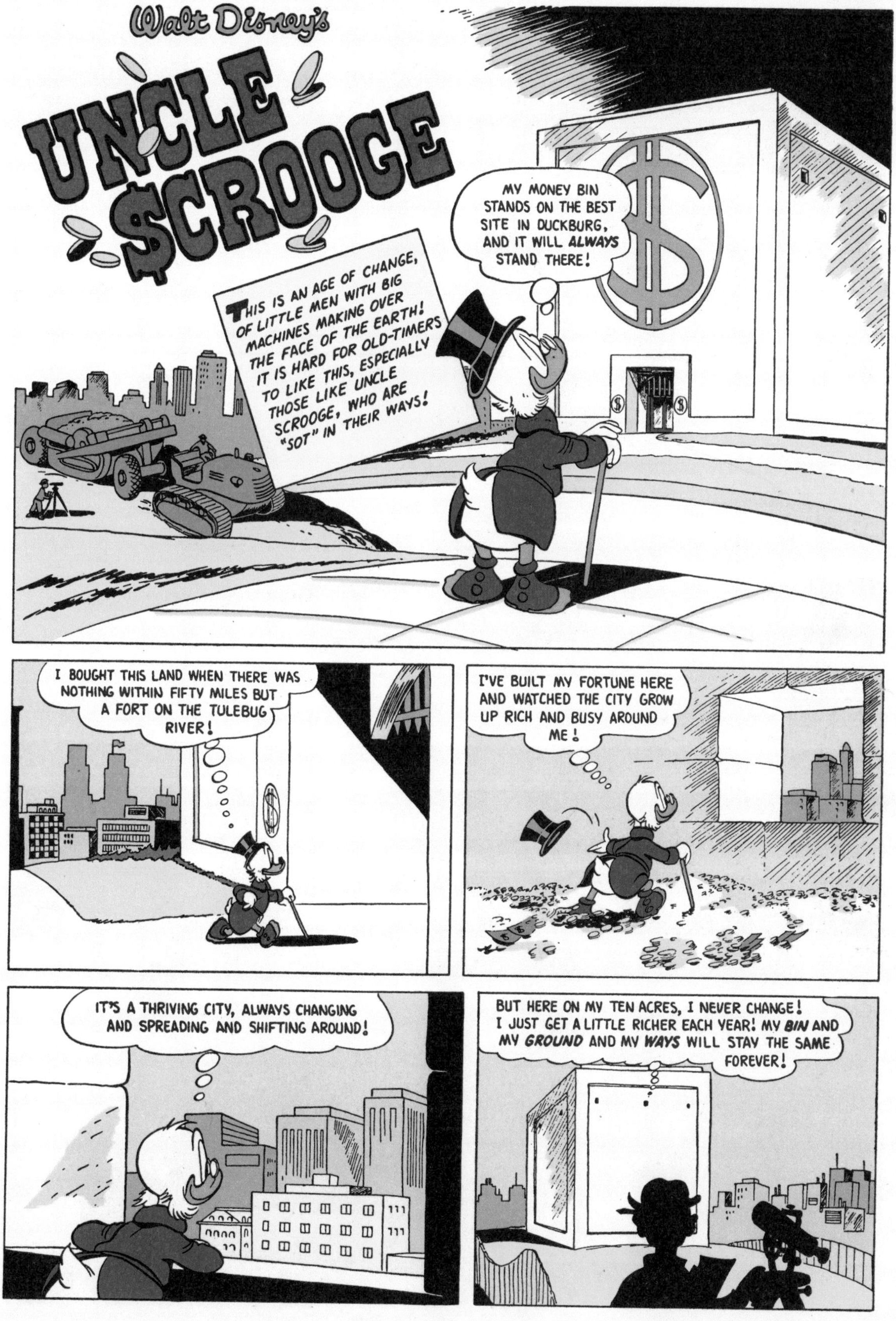
Walt Disney's
UNCLE $CROOGE
THIS IS AN AGE OF CHANGE, OF LITTLE MEN WITH BIG MACHINES MAKING OVER THE FACE OF THE EARTH! IT IS HARD FOR OLD-TIMERS TO LIKE THIS, ESPECIALLY THOSE LIKE UNCLE SCROOGE, WHO ARE "SOT" IN THEIR WAYS!
MY MONEY BIN STANDS ON THE BEST SITE IN DUCKBURG, AND IT WILL ALWAYS STAND THERE!
I BOUGHT THIS LAND WHEN THERE WAS NOTHING WITHIN FIFTY MILES BUT A FORT ON THE TULEBUG RIVER!
I'VE BUILT MY FORTUNE HERE AND WATCHED THE CITY GROW UP RICH AND BUSY AROUND ME!
IT'S A THRIVING CITY, ALWAYS CHANGING AND SPREADING AND SHIFTING AROUND!
BUT HERE ON MY TEN ACRES, I NEVER CHANGE! I JUST GET A LITTLE RICHER EACH YEAR! MY BIN AND MY GROUND AND MY WAYS WILL STAY THE SAME FOREVER!

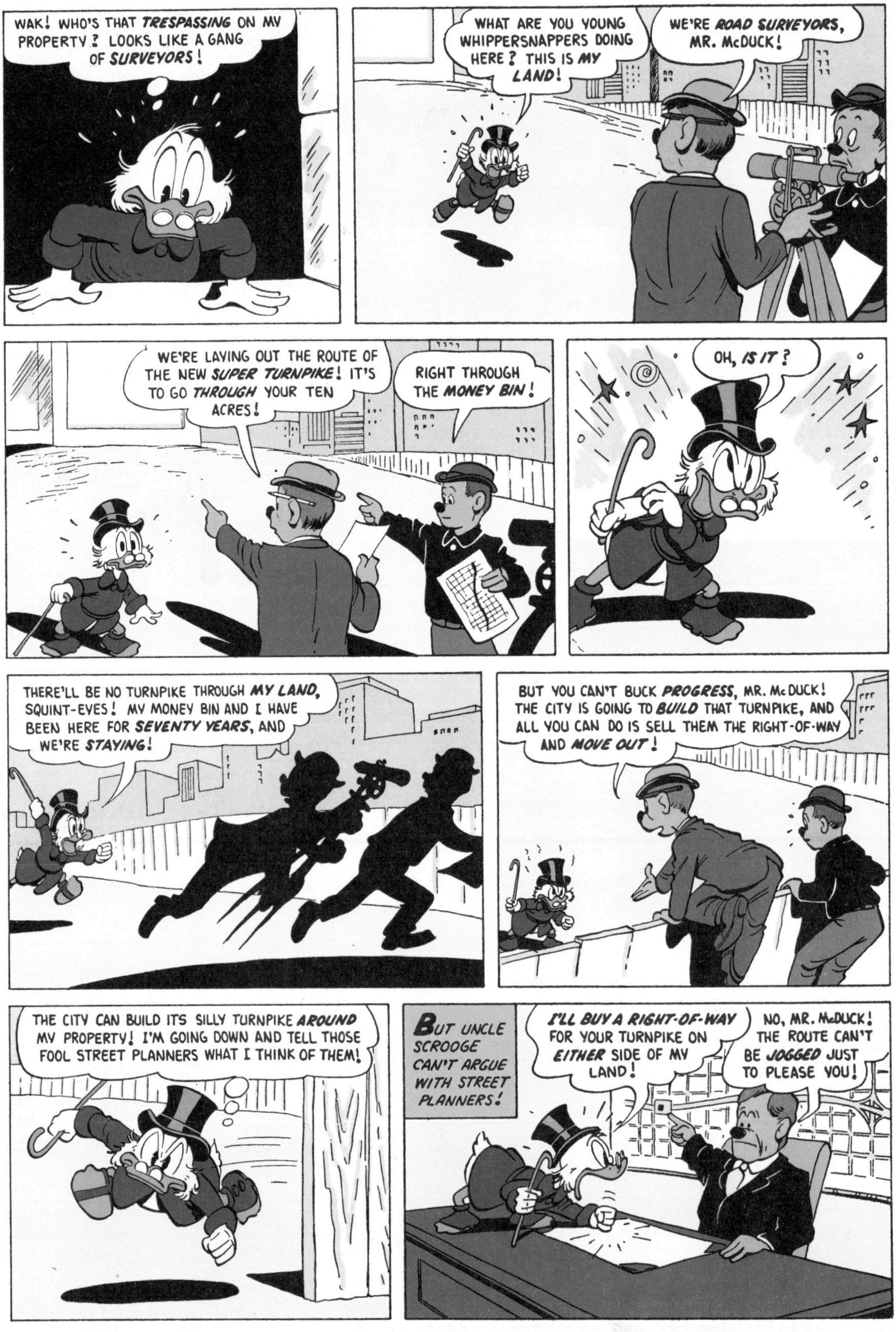
WAK! WHO'S THAT TRESPASSING ON MY PROPERTY? LOOKS LIKE A GANG OF SURVEYORS!
WHAT ARE YOU YOUNG WHIPPERSNAPPERS DOING HERE? THIS IS MY LAND!
WE'RE ROAD SURVEYORS, MR. McDUCK!
WE'RE LAYING OUT THE ROUTE OF THE NEW SUPER TURNPIKE! IT'S TO GO THROUGH YOUR TEN ACRES!
RIGHT THROUGH THE MONEY BIN!
OH, IS IT?
THERE'LL BE NO TURNPIKE THROUGH MY LAND, SQUINT-EYES! MY MONEY BIN AND I HAVE BEEN HERE FOR SEVENTY YEARS, AND WE'RE STAYING!
BUT YOU CAN'T BUCK PROGRESS, MR. McDUCK! THE CITY IS GOING TO BUILD THAT TURNPIKE, AND ALL YOU CAN DO IS SELL THEM THE RIGHT-OF-WAY AND MOVE OUT!
THE CITY CAN BUILD ITS SILLY TURNPIKE AROUND MY PROPERTY! I'M GOING DOWN AND TELL THOSE FOOL STREET PLANNERS WHAT I THINK OF THEM!
BUT UNCLE SCROOGE CAN'T ARGUE WITH STREET PLANNERS!
I'LL BUY A RIGHT-OF-WAY FOR YOUR TURNPIKE ON EITHER SIDE OF MY LAND!
NO, MR. McDUCK! THE ROUTE CAN'T BE JOGGED JUST TO PLEASE YOU!

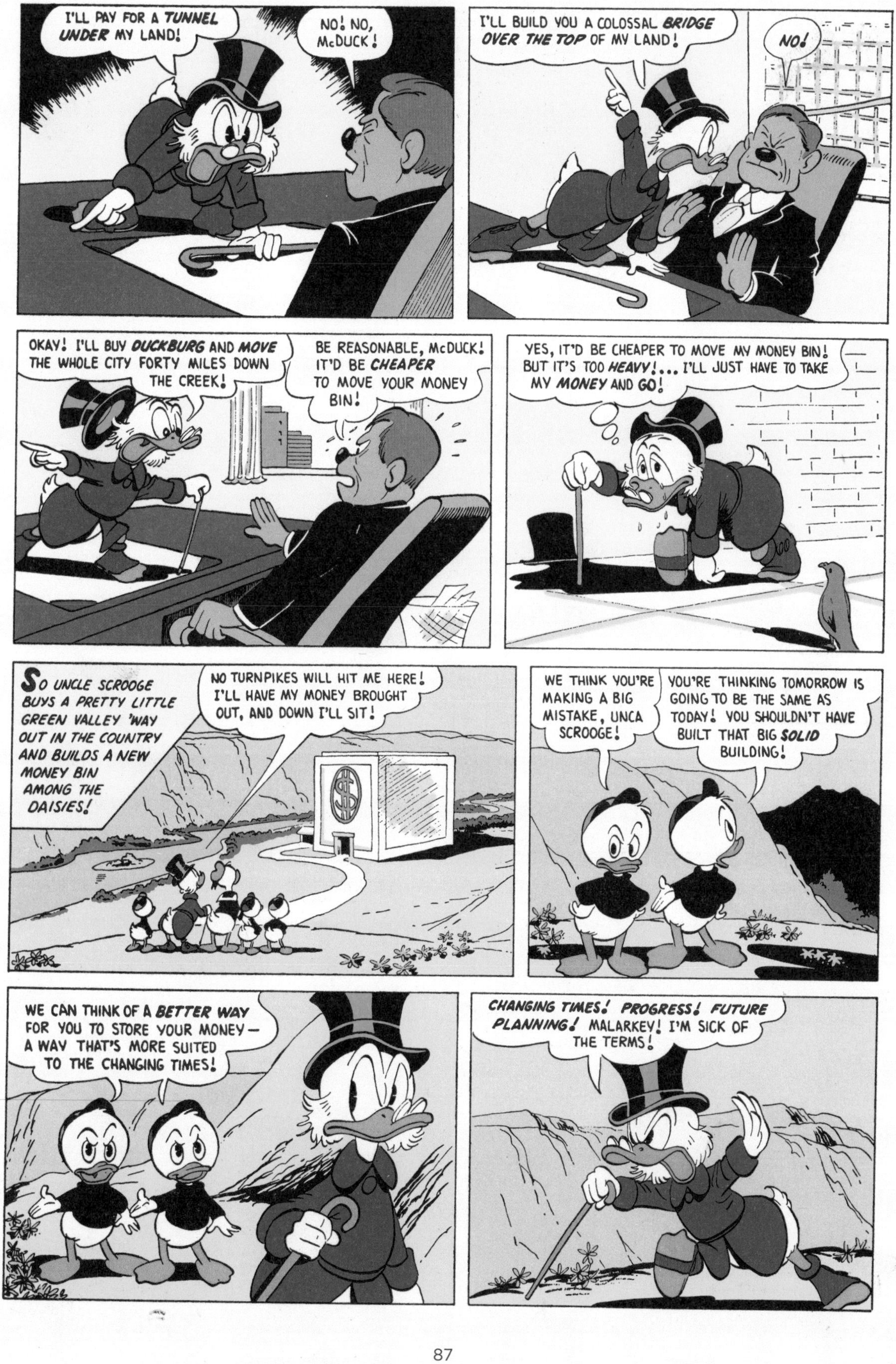
I'LL PAY FOR A TUNNEL UNDER MY LAND!
NO! NO, McDUCK!
I'LL BUILD YOU A COLOSSAL BRIDGE OVER THE TOP OF MY LAND!
NO!
OKAY! I'LL BUY DUCKBURG AND MOVE THE WHOLE CITY FORTY MILES DOWN THE CREEK!
BE REASONABLE, McDUCK! IT'D BE CHEAPER TO MOVE YOUR MONEY BIN!
YES, IT'D BE CHEAPER TO MOVE MY MONEY BIN! BUT IT'S TOO HEAVY!... I'LL JUST HAVE TO TAKE MY MONEY AND GO!
SO UNCLE SCROOGE BUYS A PRETTY LITTLE GREEN VALLEY 'WAY OUT IN THE COUNTRY AND BUILDS A NEW MONEY BIN AMONG THE DAISIES!
NO TURNPIKES WILL HIT ME HERE! I'LL HAVE MY MONEY BROUGHT OUT, AND DOWN I'LL SIT!
WE THINK YOU'RE MAKING A BIG MISTAKE, UNCA SCROOGE!
YOU'RE THINKING TOMORROW IS GOING TO BE THE SAME AS TODAY! YOU SHOULDN'T HAVE BUILT THAT BIG SOLID BUILDING!
WE CAN THINK OF A BETTER WAY FOR YOU TO STORE YOUR MONEY— A WAY THAT'S MORE SUITED TO THE CHANGING TIMES!
CHANGING TIMES! PROGRESS! FUTURE PLANNING! MALARKEY! I'M SICK OF THE TERMS!

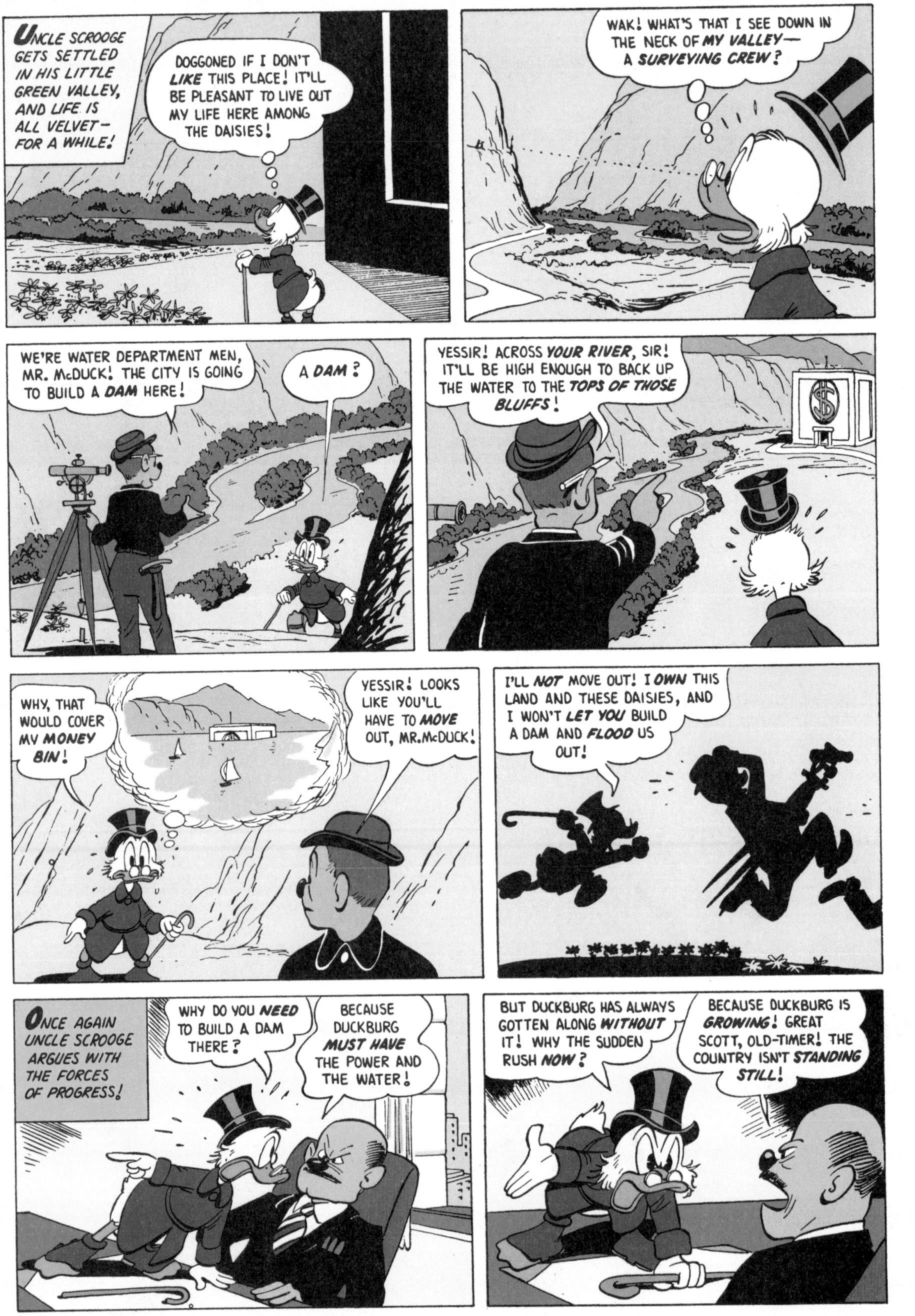
UNCLE SCROOGE GETS SETTLED IN HIS LITTLE GREEN VALLEY, AND LIFE IS ALL VELVET— FOR A WHILE!
DOGGONED IF I DON'T LIKE THIS PLACE! IT'LL BE PLEASANT TO LIVE OUT MY LIFE HERE AMONG THE DAISIES!
WAK! WHAT'S THAT I SEE DOWN IN THE NECK OF MY VALLEY— A SURVEYING CREW?
WE'RE WATER DEPARTMENT MEN, MR. McDUCK! THE CITY IS GOING TO BUILD A DAM HERE!
A DAM?
YESSIR! ACROSS YOUR RIVER, SIR! IT'LL BE HIGH ENOUGH TO BACK UP THE WATER TO THE TOPS OF THOSE BLUFFS!
WHY, THAT WOULD COVER MY MONEY BIN!
YESSIR! LOOKS LIKE YOU'LL HAVE TO MOVE OUT, MR. McDUCK!
I'LL NOT MOVE OUT! I OWN THIS LAND AND THESE DAISIES, AND I WON'T LET YOU BUILD A DAM AND FLOOD US OUT!
ONCE AGAIN UNCLE SCROOGE ARGUES WITH THE FORCES OF PROGRESS!
WHY DO YOU NEED TO BUILD A DAM THERE?
BECAUSE DUCKBURG MUST HAVE THE POWER AND THE WATER!
BUT DUCKBURG HAS ALWAYS GOTTEN ALONG WITHOUT IT! WHY THE SUDDEN RUSH NOW?
BECAUSE DUCKBURG IS GROWING! GREAT SCOTT, OLD-TIMER! THE COUNTRY ISN'T STANDING STILL!

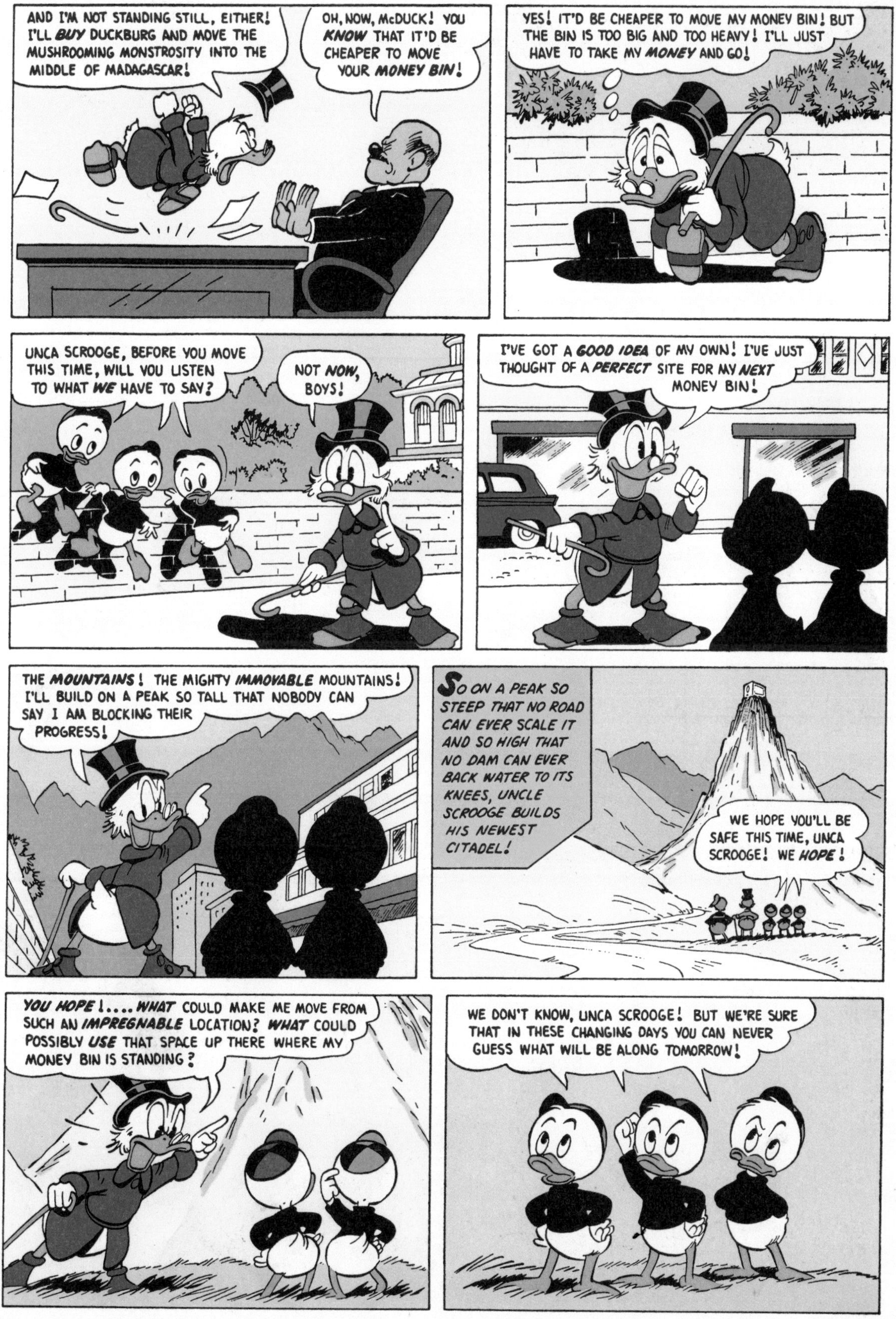
AND I'M NOT STANDING STILL, EITHER! I'LL BUY DUCKBURG AND MOVE THE MUSHROOMING MONSTROSITY INTO THE MIDDLE OF MADAGASCAR!
OH, NOW, McDUCK! YOU KNOW THAT IT'D BE CHEAPER TO MOVE YOUR MONEY BIN!
YES! IT'D BE CHEAPER TO MOVE MY MONEY BIN! BUT THE BIN IS TOO BIG AND TOO HEAVY! I'LL JUST HAVE TO TAKE MY MONEY AND GO!
UNCA SCROOGE, BEFORE YOU MOVE THIS TIME, WILL YOU LISTEN TO WHAT WE HAVE TO SAY?
NOT NOW, BOYS!
I'VE GOT A GOOD IDEA OF MY OWN! I'VE JUST THOUGHT OF A PERFECT SITE FOR MY NEXT MONEY BIN!
THE MOUNTAINS! THE MIGHTY IMMOVABLE MOUNTAINS! I'LL BUILD ON A PEAK SO TALL THAT NOBODY CAN SAY I AM BLOCKING THEIR PROGRESS!
SO ON A PEAK SO STEEP THAT NO ROAD CAN EVER SCALE IT AND SO HIGH THAT NO DAM CAN EVER BACK WATER TO ITS KNEES, UNCLE SCROOGE BUILDS HIS NEWEST CITADEL!
WE HOPE YOU'LL BE SAFE THIS TIME, UNCA SCROOGE! WE HOPE!
YOU HOPE!.... WHAT COULD MAKE ME MOVE FROM SUCH AN IMPREGNABLE LOCATION? WHAT COULD POSSIBLY USE THAT SPACE UP THERE WHERE MY MONEY BIN IS STANDING?
WE DON'T KNOW, UNCA SCROOGE! BUT WE'RE SURE THAT IN THESE CHANGING DAYS YOU CAN NEVER GUESS WHAT WILL BE ALONG TOMORROW!

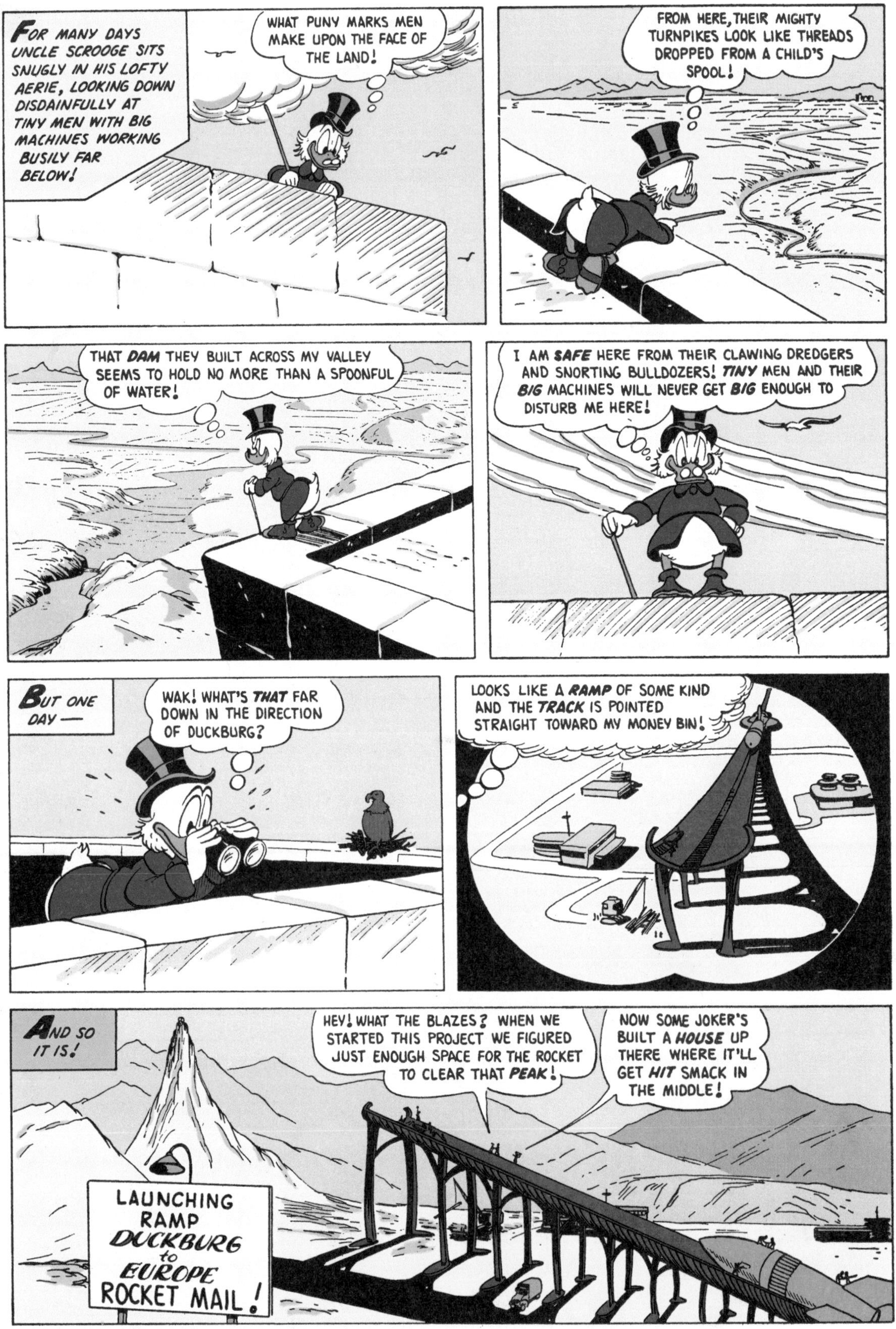
FOR MANY DAYS UNCLE SCROOGE SITS SNUGLY IN HIS LOFTY AERIE, LOOKING DOWN DISDAINFULLY AT TINY MEN WITH BIG MACHINES WORKING BUSILY FAR BELOW!
WHAT PUNY MARKS MEN MAKE UPON THE FACE OF THE LAND!
FROM HERE, THEIR MIGHTY TURNPIKES LOOK LIKE THREADS DROPPED FROM A CHILD'S SPOOL!
THAT DAM THEY BUILT ACROSS MY VALLEY SEEMS TO HOLD NO MORE THAN A SPOONFUL OF WATER!
I AM SAFE HERE FROM THEIR CLAWING DREDGERS AND SNORTING BULLDOZERS! TINY MEN AND THEIR BIG MACHINES WILL NEVER GET BIG ENOUGH TO DISTURB ME HERE!
BUT ONE DAY —
WAK! WHAT'S THAT FAR DOWN IN THE DIRECTION OF DUCKBURG?
LOOKS LIKE A RAMP OF SOME KIND AND THE TRACK IS POINTED STRAIGHT TOWARD MY MONEY BIN!
AND SO IT IS!
HEY! WHAT THE BLAZES? WHEN WE STARTED THIS PROJECT WE FIGURED JUST ENOUGH SPACE FOR THE ROCKET TO CLEAR THAT PEAK!
NOW SOME JOKER'S BUILT A HOUSE UP THERE WHERE IT'LL GET HIT SMACK IN THE MIDDLE!
LAUNCHING RAMP DUCKBURG to EUROPE ROCKET MAIL!

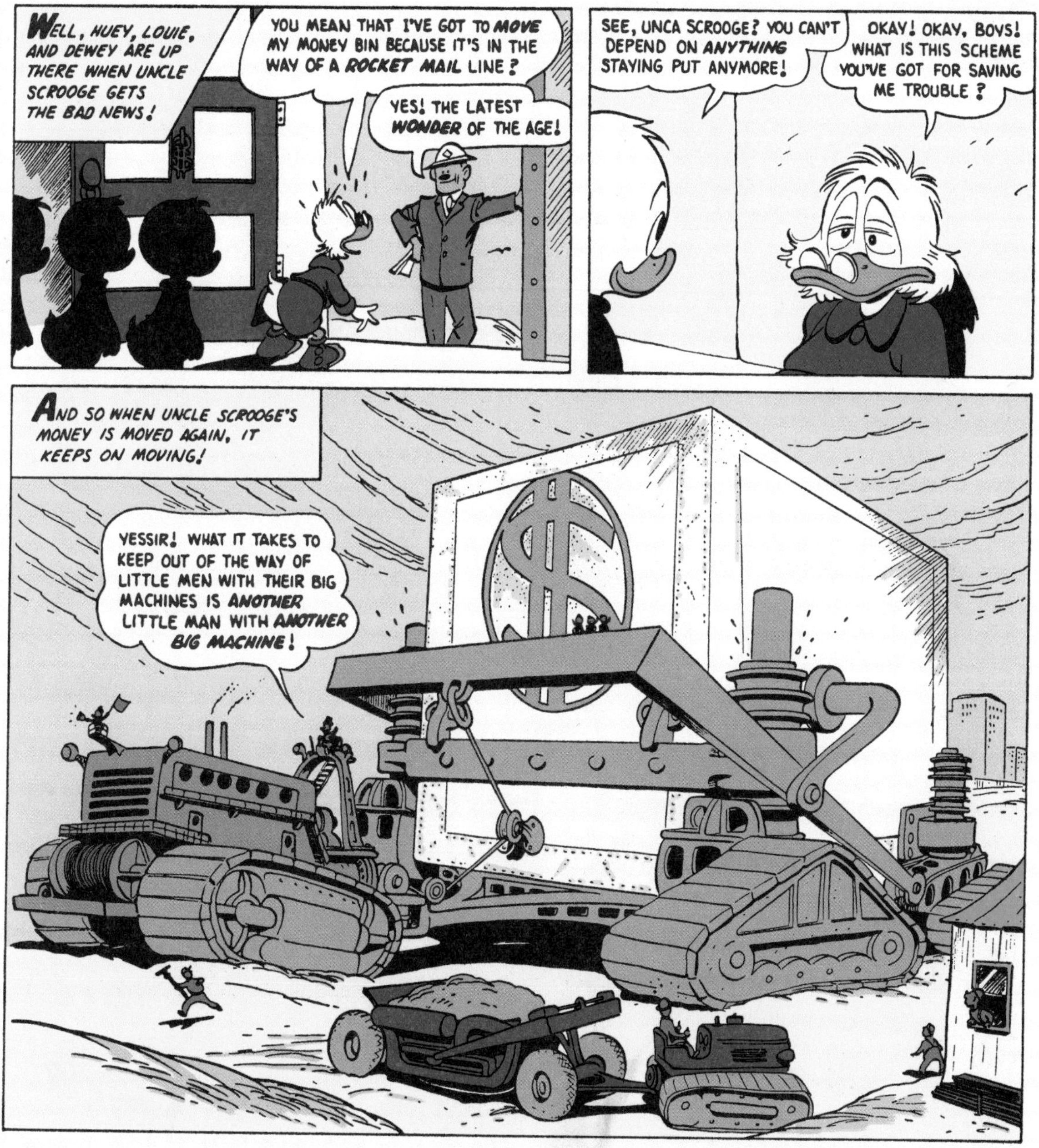
WELL, HUEY, LOUIE, AND DEWEY ARE UP THERE WHEN UNCLE SCROOGE GETS THE BAD NEWS!
YOU MEAN THAT I'VE GOT TO MOVE MY MONEY BIN BECAUSE IT'S IN THE WAY OF A ROCKET MAIL LINE?
YES! THE LATEST WONDER OF THE AGE!
SEE, UNCA SCROOGE? YOU CAN'T DEPEND ON ANYTHING STAYING PUT ANYMORE!
OKAY! OKAY, BOYS! WHAT IS THIS SCHEME YOU'VE GOT FOR SAVING ME TROUBLE?
AND SO WHEN UNCLE SCROOGE'S MONEY IS MOVED AGAIN, IT KEEPS ON MOVING!
YESSIR! WHAT IT TAKES TO KEEP OUT OF THE WAY OF LITTLE MEN WITH THEIR BIG MACHINES IS ANOTHER LITTLE MAN WITH ANOTHER BIG MACHINE!

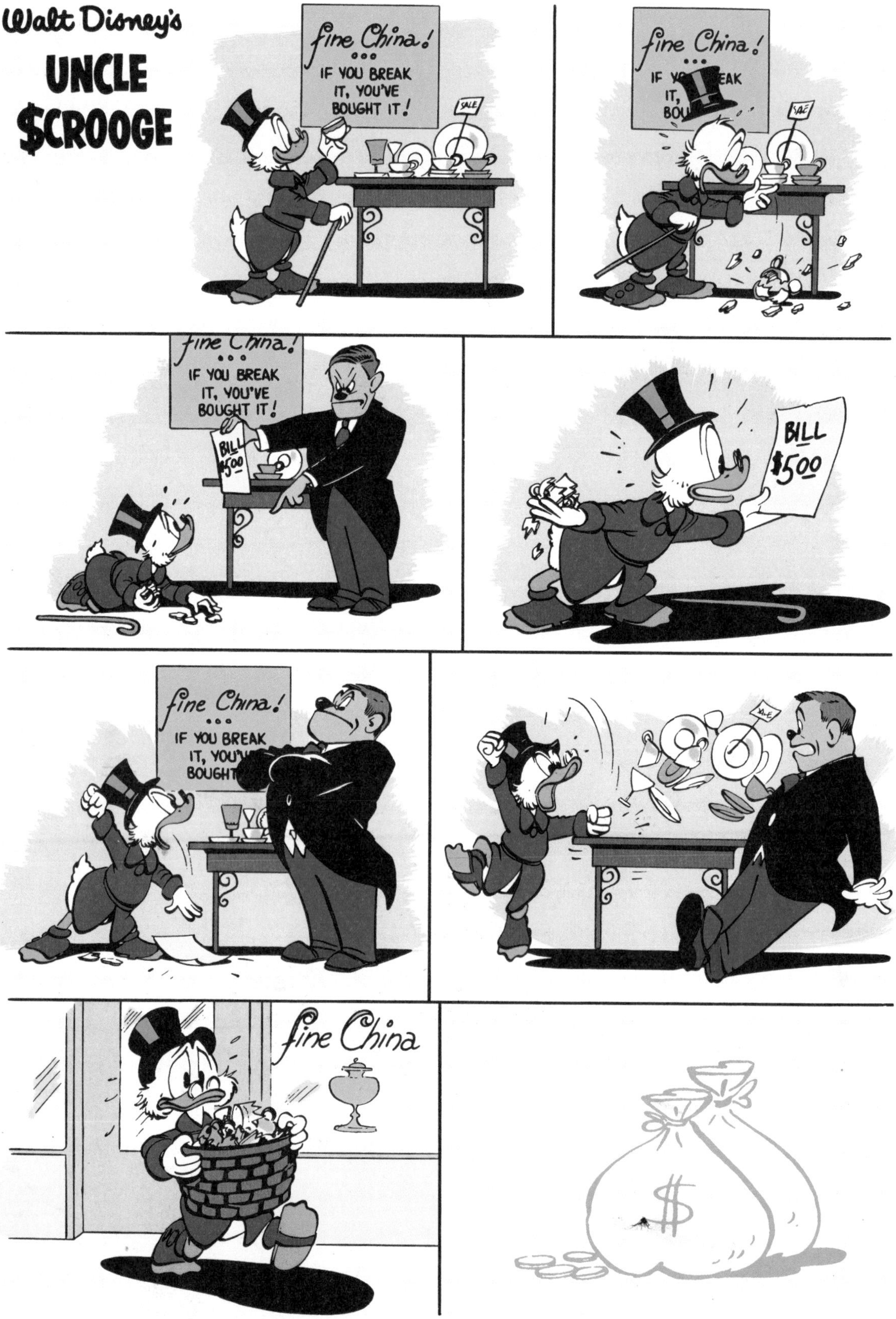

Walt Disney's
UNCLE $CROOGE
fine China! ... IF YOU BREAK IT, YOU'VE BOUGHT IT!
SALE
BILL $5.00
BILL $5.00
fine China

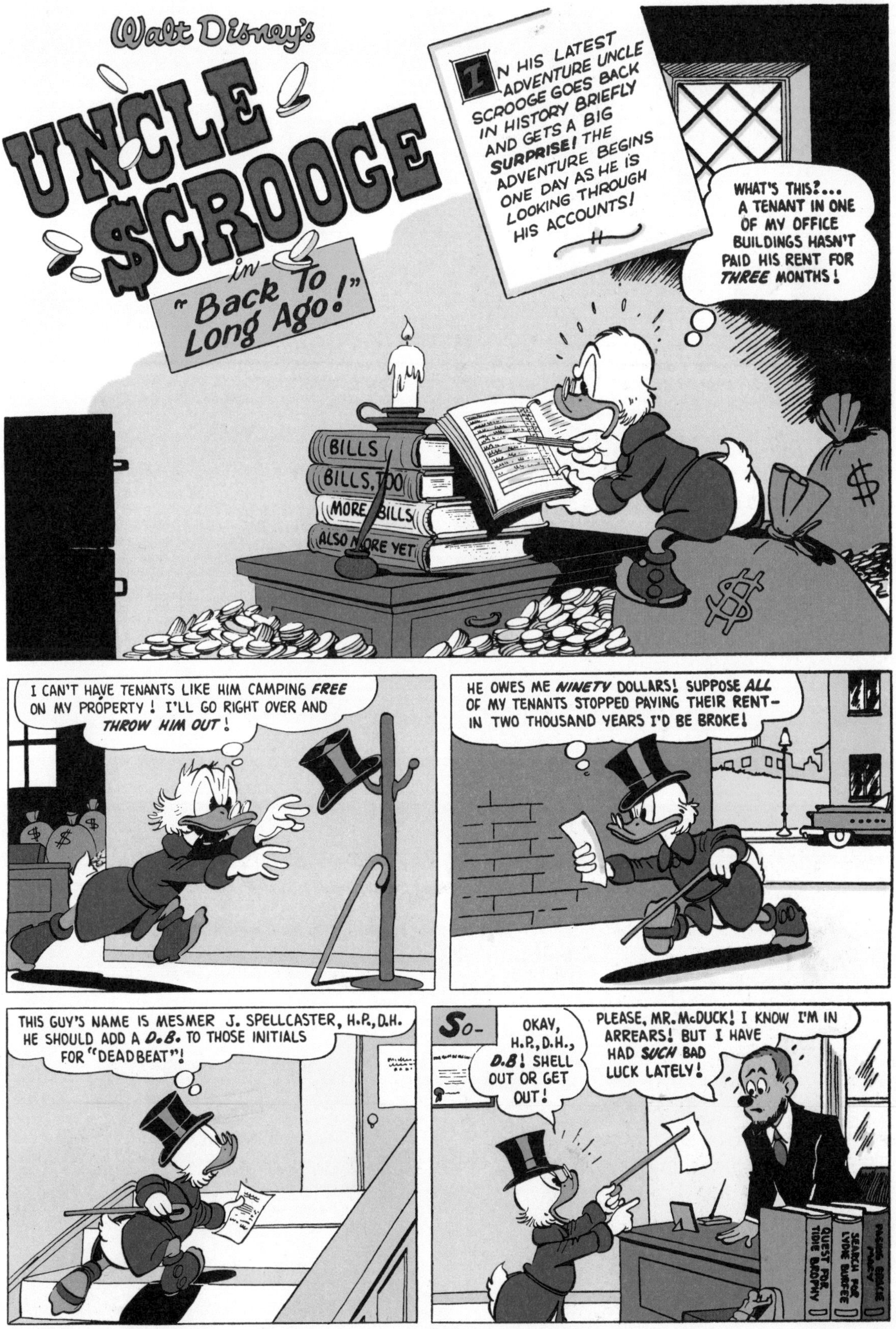
Walt Disney's
UNCLE $CROOGE
in
"Back To Long Ago!"
IN HIS LATEST ADVENTURE UNCLE SCROOGE GOES BACK IN HISTORY BRIEFLY AND GETS A BIG SURPRISE! THE ADVENTURE BEGINS ONE DAY AS HE IS LOOKING THROUGH HIS ACCOUNTS!
WHAT'S THIS?... A TENANT IN ONE OF MY OFFICE BUILDINGS HASN'T PAID HIS RENT FOR THREE MONTHS!
BILLS
BILLS, TOO
MORE BILLS
ALSO MORE YET
I CAN'T HAVE TENANTS LIKE HIM CAMPING FREE ON MY PROPERTY! I'LL GO RIGHT OVER AND THROW HIM OUT!
HE OWES ME NINETY DOLLARS! SUPPOSE ALL OF MY TENANTS STOPPED PAYING THEIR RENT—IN TWO THOUSAND YEARS I'D BE BROKE!
THIS GUY'S NAME IS MESMER J. SPELLCASTER, H.P., D.H. HE SHOULD ADD A D.B. TO THOSE INITIALS FOR "DEADBEAT"!
SO-
OKAY, H.P., D.H., D.B! SHELL OUT OR GET OUT!
PLEASE, MR. McDUCK! I KNOW I'M IN ARREARS! BUT I HAVE HAD SUCH BAD LUCK LATELY!

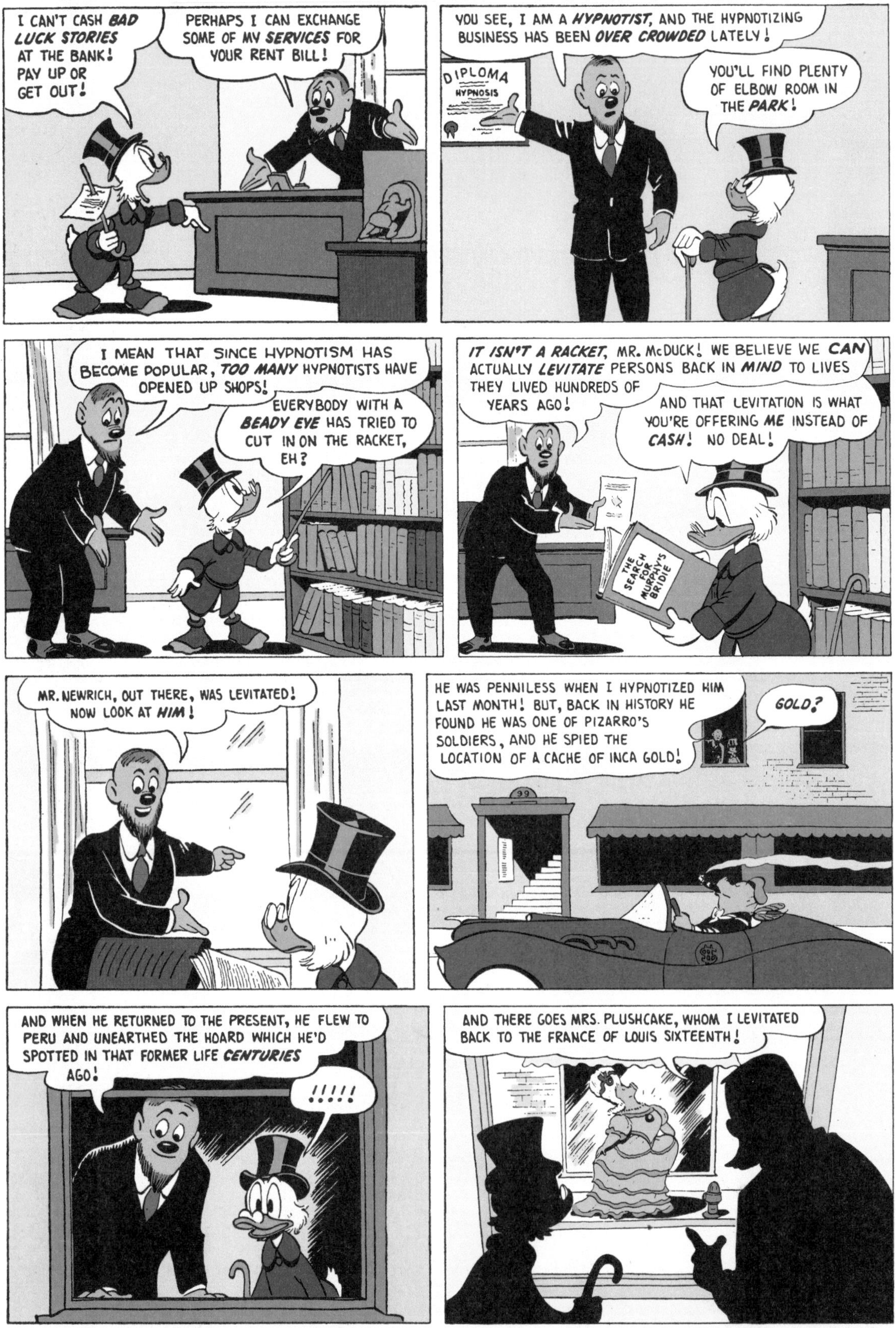
I CAN'T CASH BAD LUCK STORIES AT THE BANK! PAY UP OR GET OUT!
PERHAPS I CAN EXCHANGE SOME OF MY SERVICES FOR YOUR RENT BILL!
YOU SEE, I AM A HYPNOTIST, AND THE HYPNOTIZING BUSINESS HAS BEEN OVER CROWDED LATELY!
DIPLOMA
HYPNOSIS
YOU'LL FIND PLENTY OF ELBOW ROOM IN THE PARK!
I MEAN THAT SINCE HYPNOTISM HAS BECOME POPULAR, TOO MANY HYPNOTISTS HAVE OPENED UP SHOPS!
EVERYBODY WITH A BEADY EYE HAS TRIED TO CUT IN ON THE RACKET, EH?
IT ISN'T A RACKET, MR. McDUCK! WE BELIEVE WE CAN ACTUALLY LEVITATE PERSONS BACK IN MIND TO LIVES THEY LIVED HUNDREDS OF YEARS AGO!
AND THAT LEVITATION IS WHAT YOU'RE OFFERING ME INSTEAD OF CASH! NO DEAL!
THE SEARCH FOR MURPHY'S BRIDIE
MR. NEWRICH, OUT THERE, WAS LEVITATED! NOW LOOK AT HIM!
HE WAS PENNILESS WHEN I HYPNOTIZED HIM LAST MONTH! BUT, BACK IN HISTORY HE FOUND HE WAS ONE OF PIZARRO'S SOLDIERS, AND HE SPIED THE LOCATION OF A CACHE OF INCA GOLD!
GOLD?
99
AND WHEN HE RETURNED TO THE PRESENT, HE FLEW TO PERU AND UNEARTHED THE HOARD WHICH HE'D SPOTTED IN THAT FORMER LIFE CENTURIES AGO!
!!!!!
AND THERE GOES MRS. PLUSHCAKE, WHOM I LEVITATED BACK TO THE FRANCE OF LOUIS SIXTEENTH!

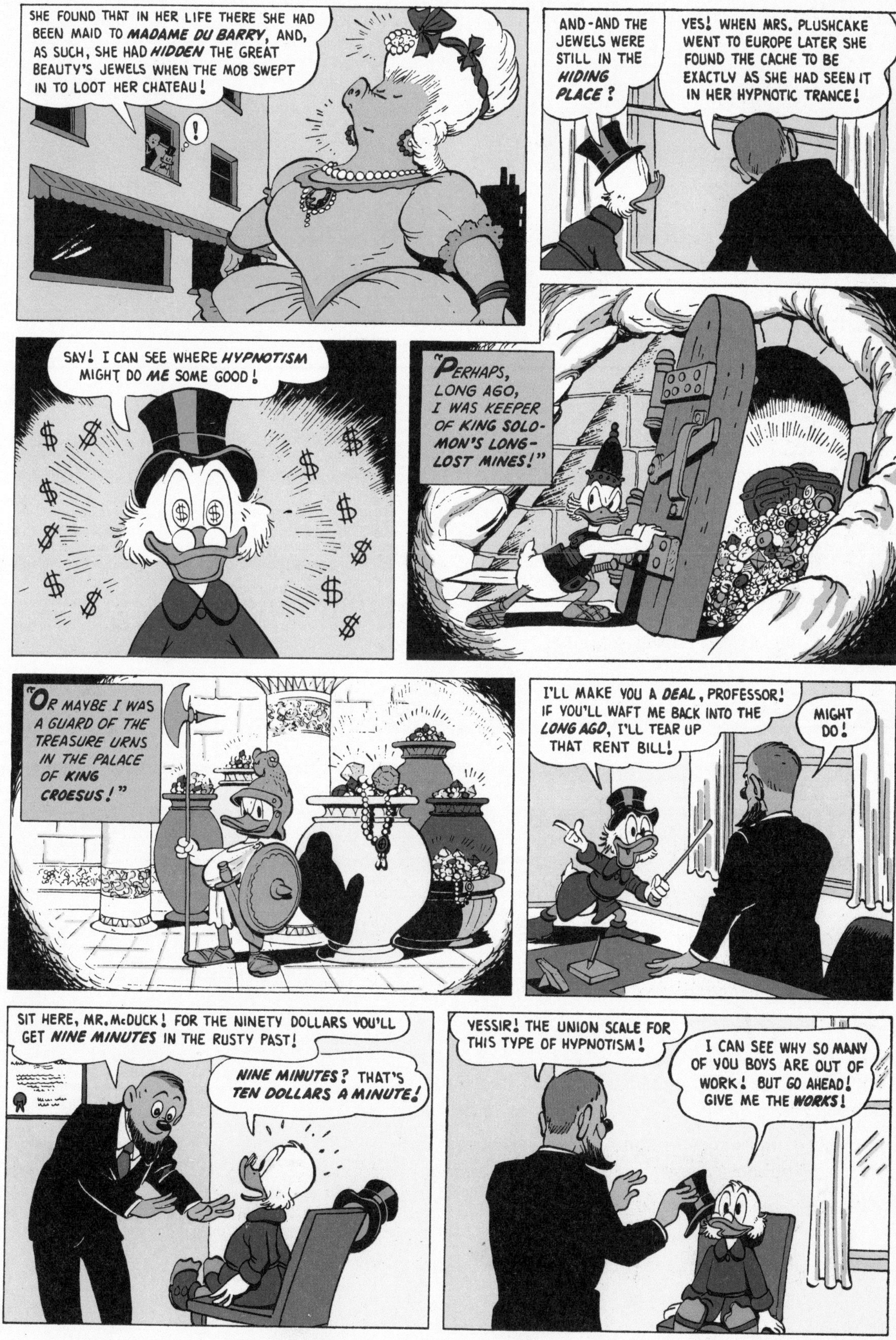
SHE FOUND THAT IN HER LIFE THERE SHE HAD BEEN MAID TO MADAME DU BARRY, AND, AS SUCH, SHE HAD HIDDEN THE GREAT BEAUTY'S JEWELS WHEN THE MOB SWEPT IN TO LOOT HER CHATEAU!
!
AND-AND THE JEWELS WERE STILL IN THE HIDING PLACE?
YES! WHEN MRS. PLUSHCAKE WENT TO EUROPE LATER SHE FOUND THE CACHE TO BE EXACTLY AS SHE HAD SEEN IT IN HER HYPNOTIC TRANCE!
SAY! I CAN SEE WHERE HYPNOTISM MIGHT DO ME SOME GOOD!
"PERHAPS, LONG AGO, I WAS KEEPER OF KING SOLOMON'S LONG-LOST MINES!"
"OR MAYBE I WAS A GUARD OF THE TREASURE URNS IN THE PALACE OF KING CROESUS!"
I'LL MAKE YOU A DEAL, PROFESSOR! IF YOU'LL WAFT ME BACK INTO THE LONG AGO, I'LL TEAR UP THAT RENT BILL!
MIGHT DO!
SIT HERE, MR. McDUCK! FOR THE NINETY DOLLARS YOU'LL GET NINE MINUTES IN THE RUSTY PAST!
NINE MINUTES? THAT'S TEN DOLLARS A MINUTE!
VESSIR! THE UNION SCALE FOR THIS TYPE OF HYPNOTISM!
I CAN SEE WHY SO MANY OF YOU BOYS ARE OUT OF WORK! BUT GO AHEAD! GIVE ME THE WORKS!

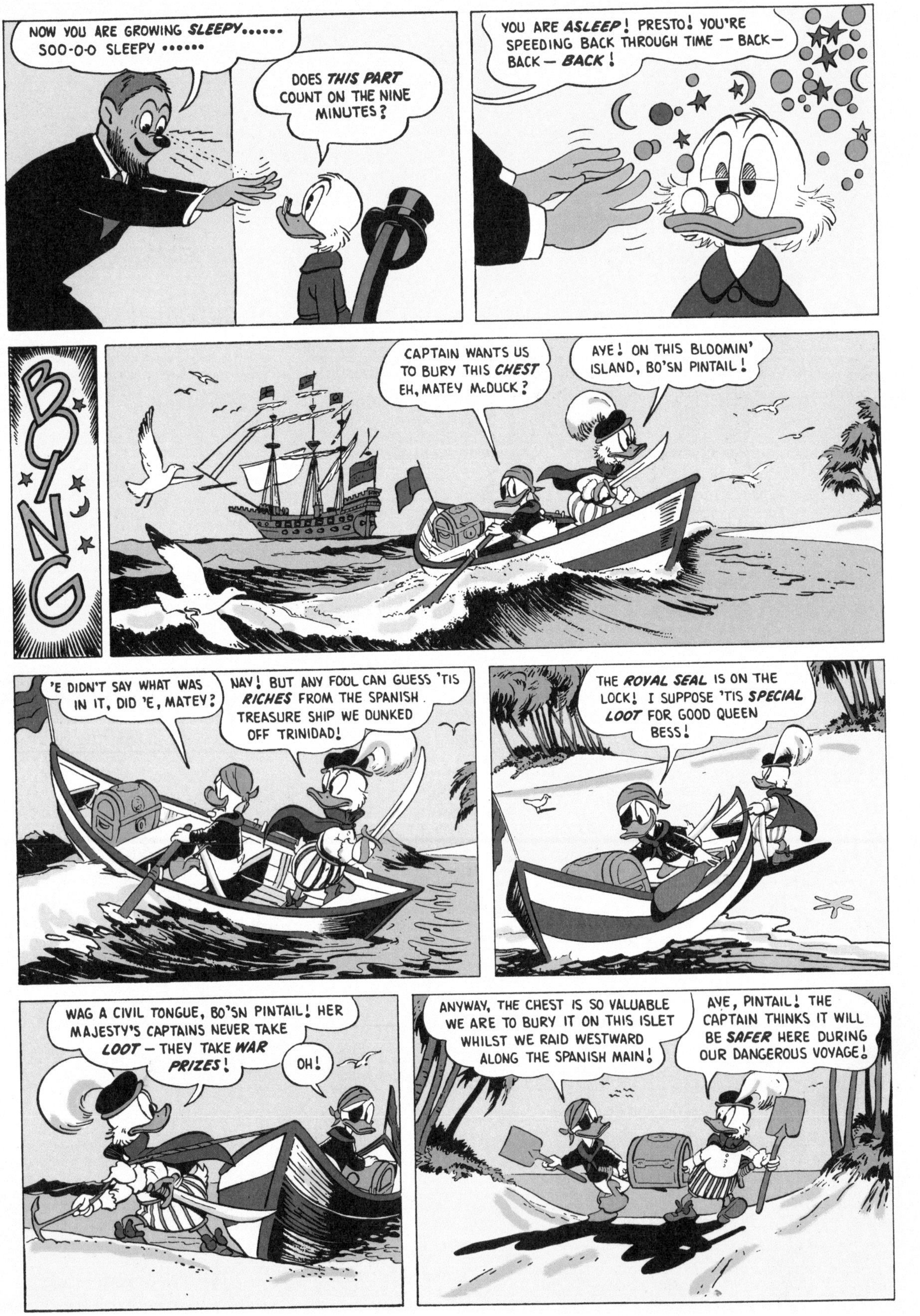
NOW YOU ARE GROWING SLEEPY...... SOO-O-O SLEEPY ......
DOES THIS PART COUNT ON THE NINE MINUTES?
YOU ARE ASLEEP! PRESTO! YOU'RE SPEEDING BACK THROUGH TIME — BACK— BACK— BACK!
BOING
CAPTAIN WANTS US TO BURY THIS CHEST EH, MATEY McDUCK?
AYE! ON THIS BLOOMIN' ISLAND, BO'SN PINTAIL!
'E DIDN'T SAY WHAT WAS IN IT, DID 'E, MATEY?
NAY! BUT ANY FOOL CAN GUESS 'TIS RICHES FROM THE SPANISH TREASURE SHIP WE DUNKED OFF TRINIDAD!
THE ROYAL SEAL IS ON THE LOCK! I SUPPOSE 'TIS SPECIAL LOOT FOR GOOD QUEEN BESS!
WAG A CIVIL TONGUE, BO'SN PINTAIL! HER MAJESTY'S CAPTAINS NEVER TAKE LOOT — THEY TAKE WAR PRIZES!
OH!
ANYWAY, THE CHEST IS SO VALUABLE WE ARE TO BURY IT ON THIS ISLET WHILST WE RAID WESTWARD ALONG THE SPANISH MAIN!
AYE, PINTAIL! THE CAPTAIN THINKS IT WILL BE SAFER HERE DURING OUR DANGEROUS VOYAGE!

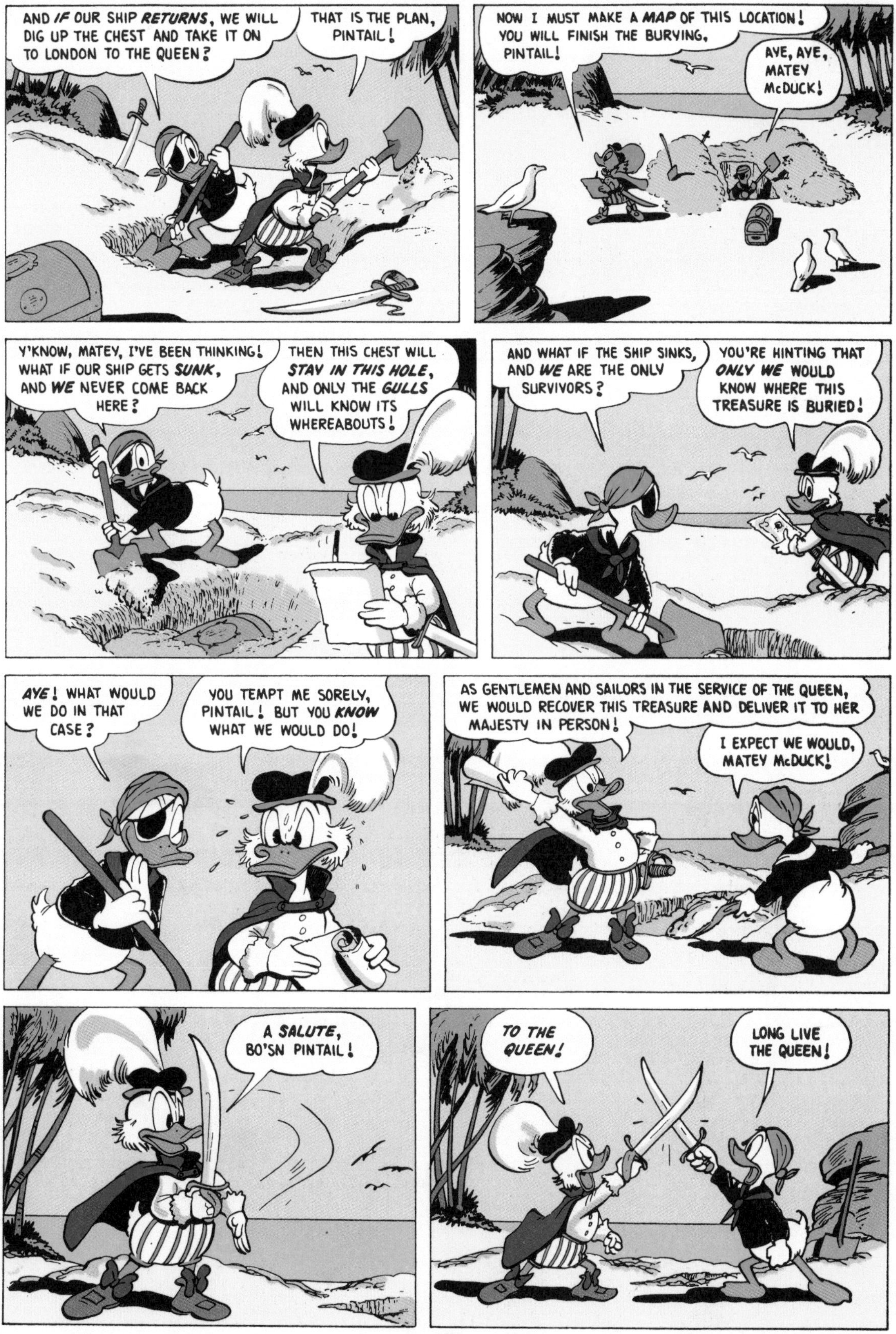
AND *IF* OUR SHIP *RETURNS*, WE WILL DIG UP THE CHEST AND TAKE IT ON TO LONDON TO THE QUEEN?
THAT IS THE PLAN, PINTAIL!
NOW I MUST MAKE A *MAP* OF THIS LOCATION! YOU WILL FINISH THE BURYING, PINTAIL!
AYE, AYE, MATEY McDUCK!
Y'KNOW, MATEY, I'VE BEEN THINKING! WHAT IF OUR SHIP GETS *SUNK*, AND *WE* NEVER COME BACK HERE?
THEN THIS CHEST WILL *STAY IN THIS HOLE*, AND ONLY THE *GULLS* WILL KNOW ITS WHEREABOUTS!
AND WHAT IF THE SHIP SINKS, AND *WE* ARE THE ONLY SURVIVORS?
YOU'RE HINTING THAT *ONLY WE* WOULD KNOW WHERE THIS TREASURE IS BURIED!
AYE! WHAT WOULD WE DO IN THAT CASE?
YOU TEMPT ME SORELY, PINTAIL! BUT YOU *KNOW* WHAT WE WOULD DO!
AS GENTLEMEN AND SAILORS IN THE SERVICE OF THE QUEEN, WE WOULD RECOVER THIS TREASURE AND DELIVER IT TO HER MAJESTY IN PERSON!
I EXPECT WE WOULD, MATEY McDUCK!
A *SALUTE*, BO'SN PINTAIL!
TO THE QUEEN!
LONG LIVE THE QUEEN!

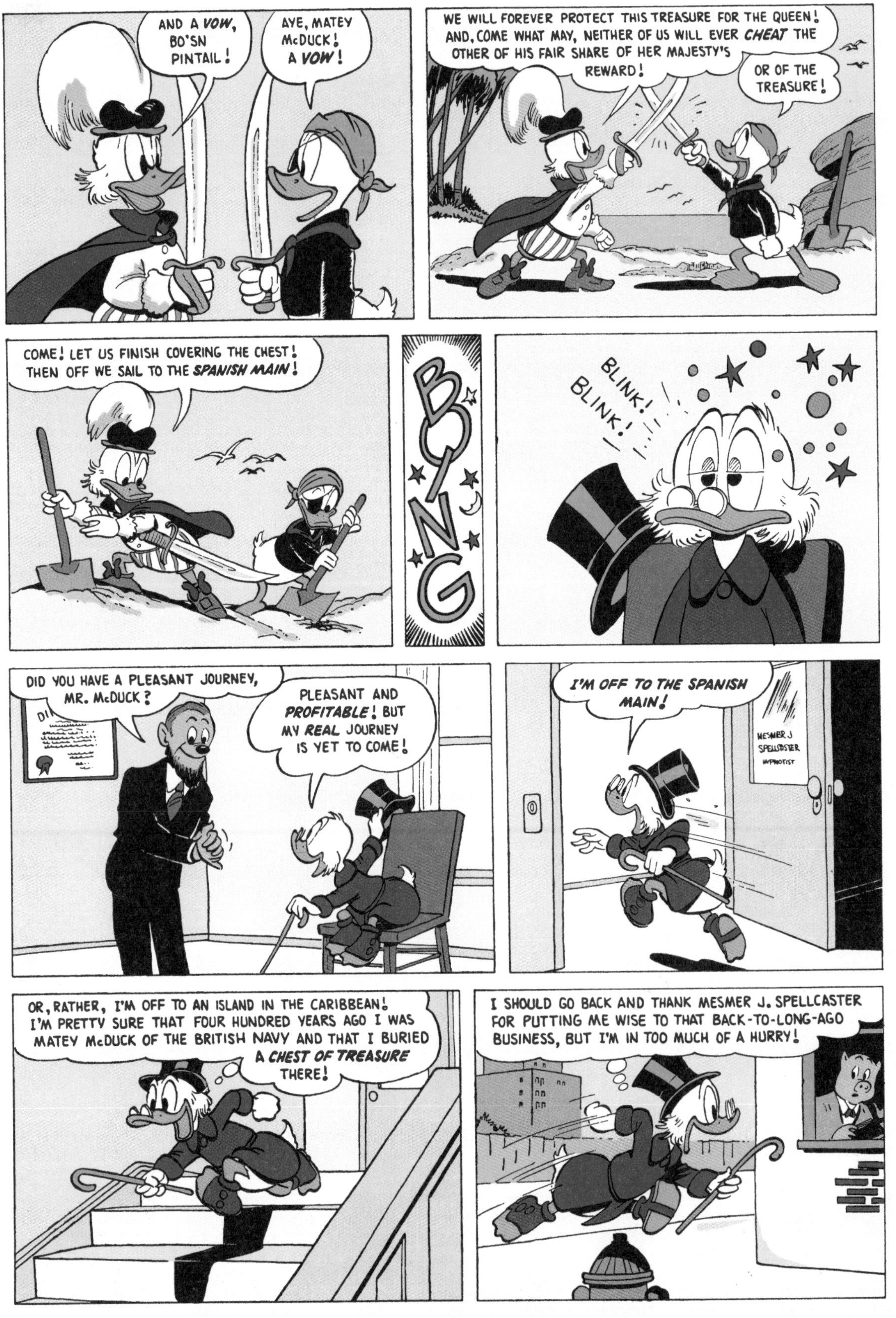
AND A VOW, BO'SN PINTAIL!
AYE, MATEY McDUCK! A VOW!
WE WILL FOREVER PROTECT THIS TREASURE FOR THE QUEEN! AND, COME WHAT MAY, NEITHER OF US WILL EVER CHEAT THE OTHER OF HIS FAIR SHARE OF HER MAJESTY'S REWARD!
OR OF THE TREASURE!
COME! LET US FINISH COVERING THE CHEST! THEN OFF WE SAIL TO THE SPANISH MAIN!
BOING
BLINK! BLINK!
DID YOU HAVE A PLEASANT JOURNEY, MR. McDUCK?
PLEASANT AND PROFITABLE! BUT MY REAL JOURNEY IS YET TO COME!
I'M OFF TO THE SPANISH MAIN!
MESMER J. SPELLCASTER HYPNOTIST
OR, RATHER, I'M OFF TO AN ISLAND IN THE CARIBBEAN! I'M PRETTY SURE THAT FOUR HUNDRED YEARS AGO I WAS MATEY McDUCK OF THE BRITISH NAVY AND THAT I BURIED A CHEST OF TREASURE THERE!
I SHOULD GO BACK AND THANK MESMER J. SPELLCASTER FOR PUTTING ME WISE TO THAT BACK-TO-LONG-AGO BUSINESS, BUT I'M IN TOO MUCH OF A HURRY!

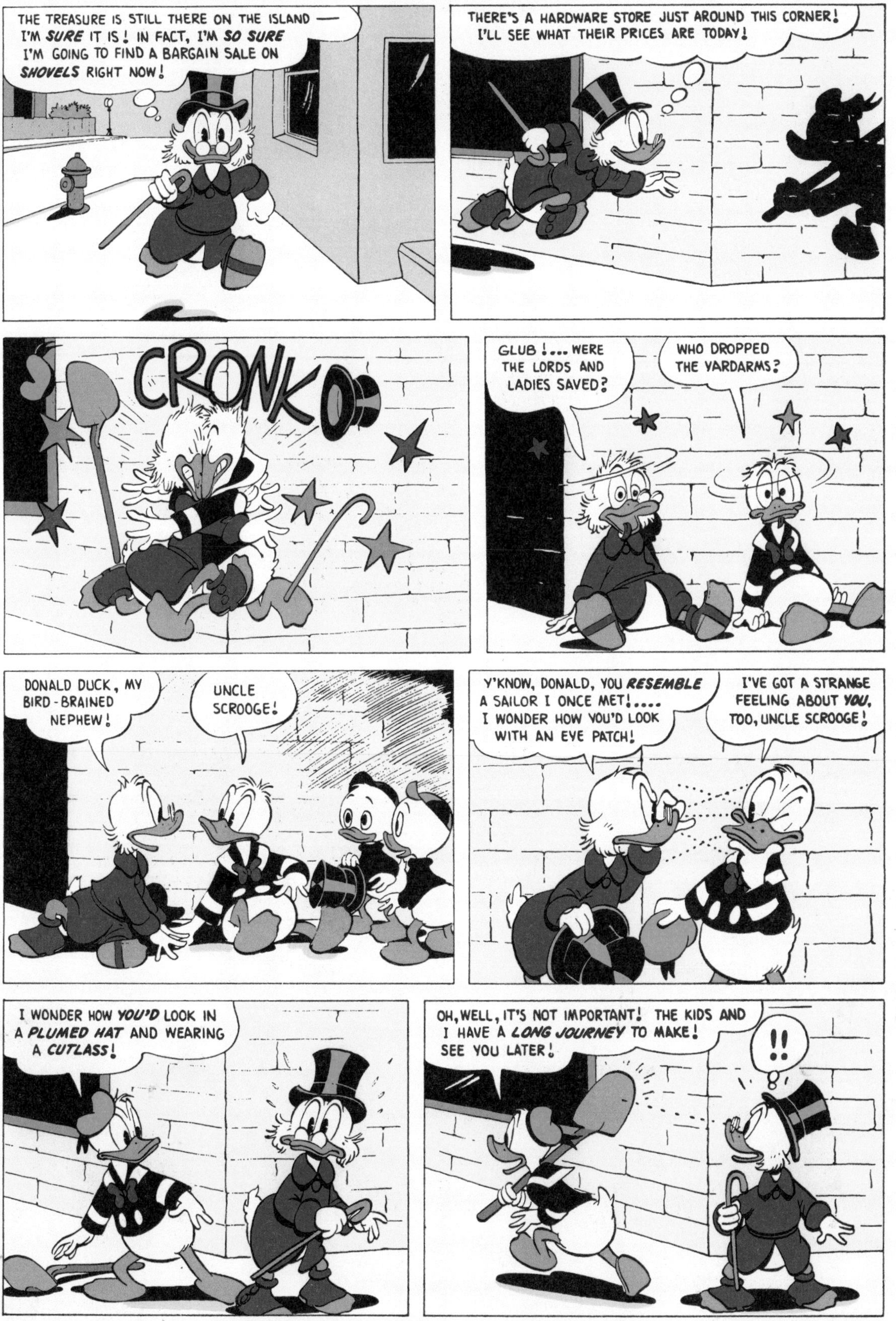
THE TREASURE IS STILL THERE ON THE ISLAND — I'M SURE IT IS! IN FACT, I'M SO SURE I'M GOING TO FIND A BARGAIN SALE ON SHOVELS RIGHT NOW!
THERE'S A HARDWARE STORE JUST AROUND THIS CORNER! I'LL SEE WHAT THEIR PRICES ARE TODAY!
CRONK
GLUB!... WERE THE LORDS AND LADIES SAVED?
WHO DROPPED THE YARDARMS?
DONALD DUCK, MY BIRD-BRAINED NEPHEW!
UNCLE SCROOGE!
Y'KNOW, DONALD, YOU RESEMBLE A SAILOR I ONCE MET!.... I WONDER HOW YOU'D LOOK WITH AN EYE PATCH!
I'VE GOT A STRANGE FEELING ABOUT YOU, TOO, UNCLE SCROOGE!
I WONDER HOW YOU'D LOOK IN A PLUMED HAT AND WEARING A CUTLASS!
OH, WELL, IT'S NOT IMPORTANT! THE KIDS AND I HAVE A LONG JOURNEY TO MAKE! SEE YOU LATER!
!!

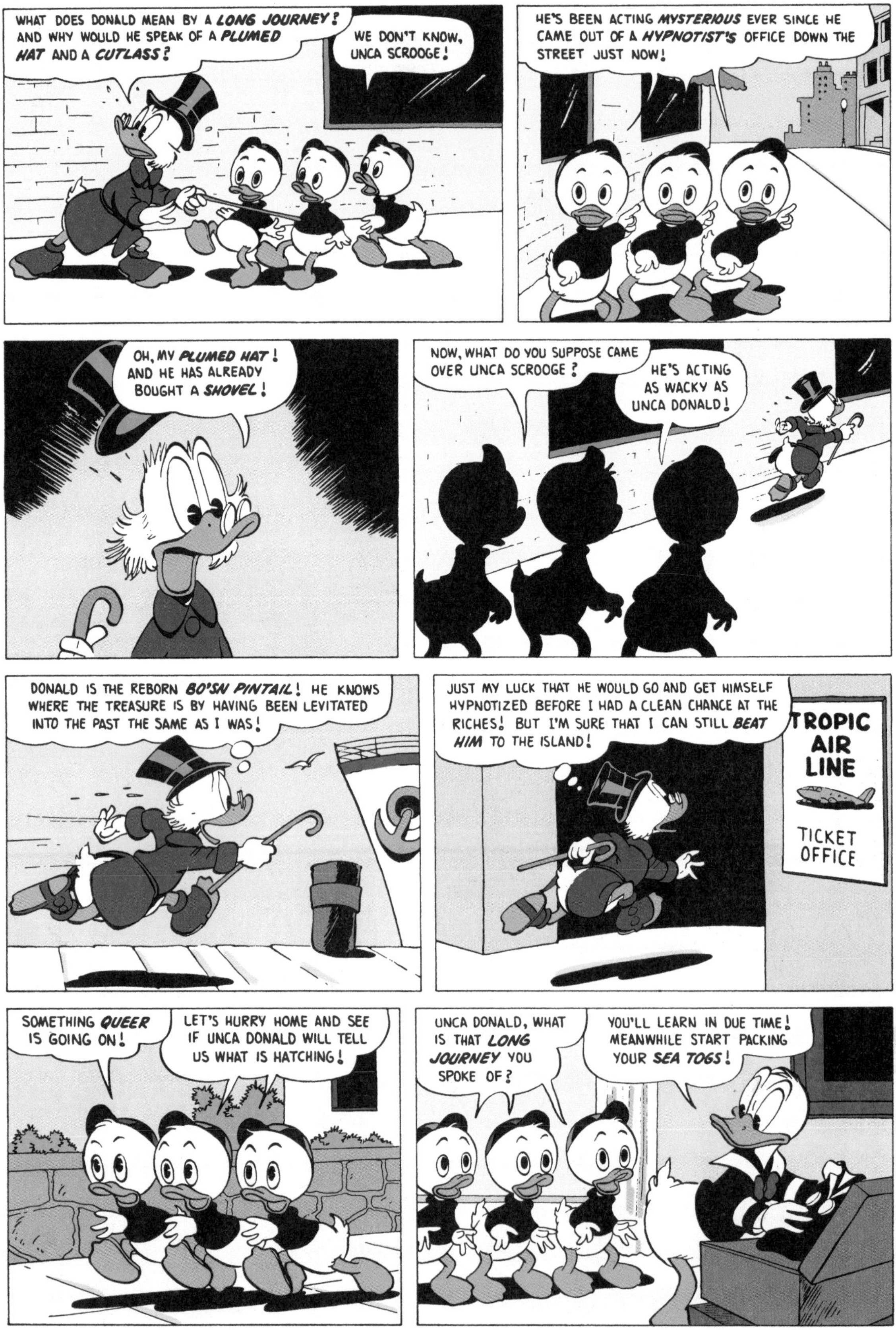

WHAT DOES DONALD MEAN BY A LONG JOURNEY? AND WHY WOULD HE SPEAK OF A PLUMED HAT AND A CUTLASS?
WE DON'T KNOW, UNCA SCROOGE!
HE'S BEEN ACTING MYSTERIOUS EVER SINCE HE CAME OUT OF A HYPNOTIST'S OFFICE DOWN THE STREET JUST NOW!
OH, MY PLUMED HAT! AND HE HAS ALREADY BOUGHT A SHOVEL!
NOW, WHAT DO YOU SUPPOSE CAME OVER UNCA SCROOGE?
HE'S ACTING AS WACKY AS UNCA DONALD!
DONALD IS THE REBORN BO'SN PINTAIL! HE KNOWS WHERE THE TREASURE IS BY HAVING BEEN LEVITATED INTO THE PAST THE SAME AS I WAS!
JUST MY LUCK THAT HE WOULD GO AND GET HIMSELF HYPNOTIZED BEFORE I HAD A CLEAN CHANCE AT THE RICHES! BUT I'M SURE THAT I CAN STILL BEAT HIM TO THE ISLAND!
TROPIC AIR LINE
TICKET OFFICE
SOMETHING QUEER IS GOING ON!
LET'S HURRY HOME AND SEE IF UNCA DONALD WILL TELL US WHAT IS HATCHING!
UNCA DONALD, WHAT IS THAT LONG JOURNEY YOU SPOKE OF?
YOU'LL LEARN IN DUE TIME! MEANWHILE START PACKING YOUR SEA TOGS!

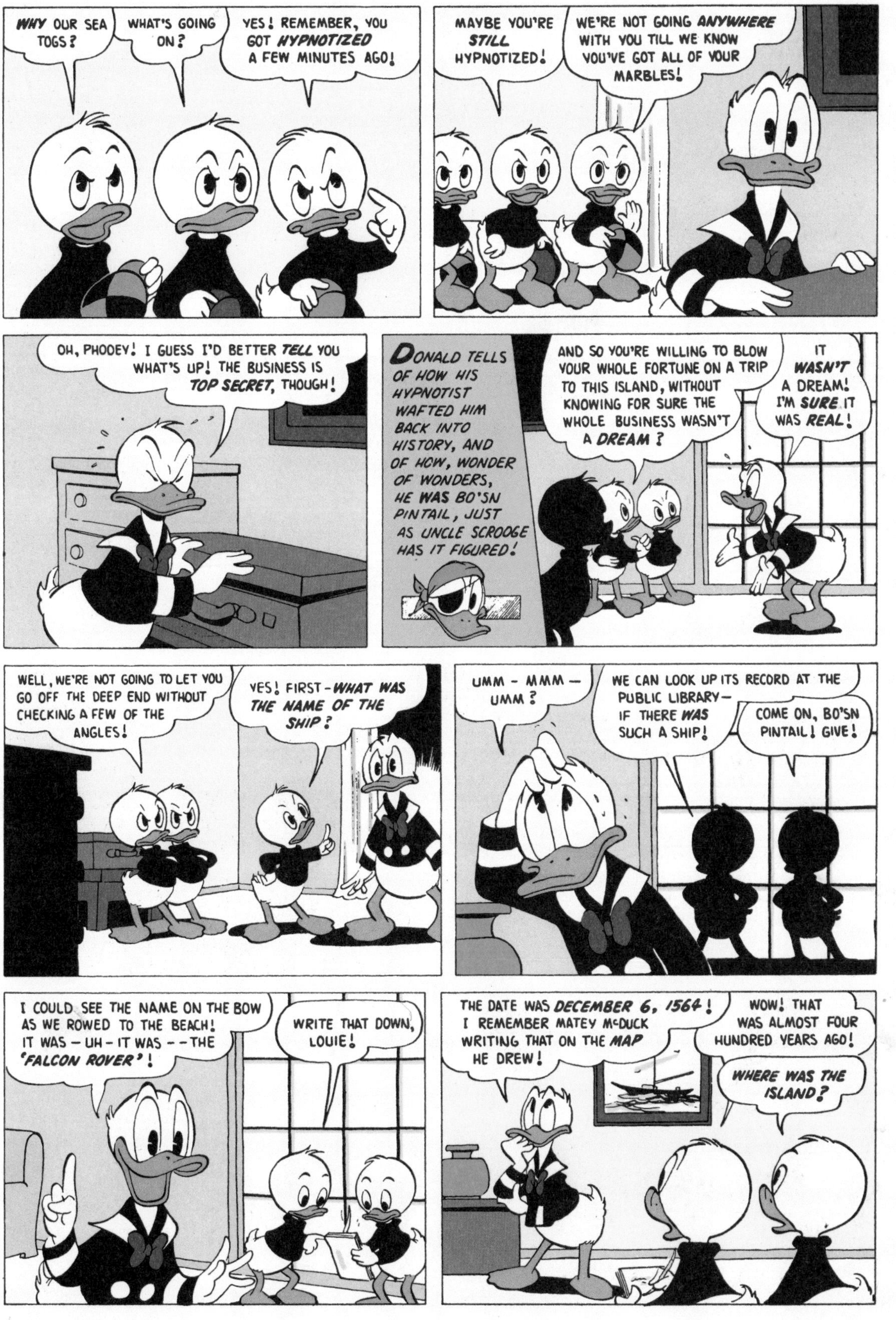

WHY OUR SEA TOGS?
WHAT'S GOING ON?
YES! REMEMBER, YOU GOT HYPNOTIZED A FEW MINUTES AGO!
MAYBE YOU'RE STILL HYPNOTIZED!
WE'RE NOT GOING ANYWHERE WITH YOU TILL WE KNOW YOU'VE GOT ALL OF YOUR MARBLES!
OH, PHOOEY! I GUESS I'D BETTER TELL YOU WHAT'S UP! THE BUSINESS IS TOP SECRET, THOUGH!
DONALD TELLS OF HOW HIS HYPNOTIST WAFTED HIM BACK INTO HISTORY, AND OF HOW, WONDER OF WONDERS, HE WAS BO'SN PINTAIL, JUST AS UNCLE SCROOGE HAS IT FIGURED!
AND SO YOU'RE WILLING TO BLOW YOUR WHOLE FORTUNE ON A TRIP TO THIS ISLAND, WITHOUT KNOWING FOR SURE THE WHOLE BUSINESS WASN'T A DREAM?
IT WASN'T A DREAM! I'M SURE IT WAS REAL!
WELL, WE'RE NOT GOING TO LET YOU GO OFF THE DEEP END WITHOUT CHECKING A FEW OF THE ANGLES!
YES! FIRST–WHAT WAS THE NAME OF THE SHIP?
UMM – MMM – UMM?
WE CAN LOOK UP ITS RECORD AT THE PUBLIC LIBRARY– IF THERE WAS SUCH A SHIP!
COME ON, BO'SN PINTAIL! GIVE!
I COULD SEE THE NAME ON THE BOW AS WE ROWED TO THE BEACH! IT WAS – UH – IT WAS – – THE 'FALCON ROVER'!
WRITE THAT DOWN, LOUIE!
THE DATE WAS DECEMBER 6, 1564! I REMEMBER MATEY McDUCK WRITING THAT ON THE MAP HE DREW!
WOW! THAT WAS ALMOST FOUR HUNDRED YEARS AGO!
WHERE WAS THE ISLAND?

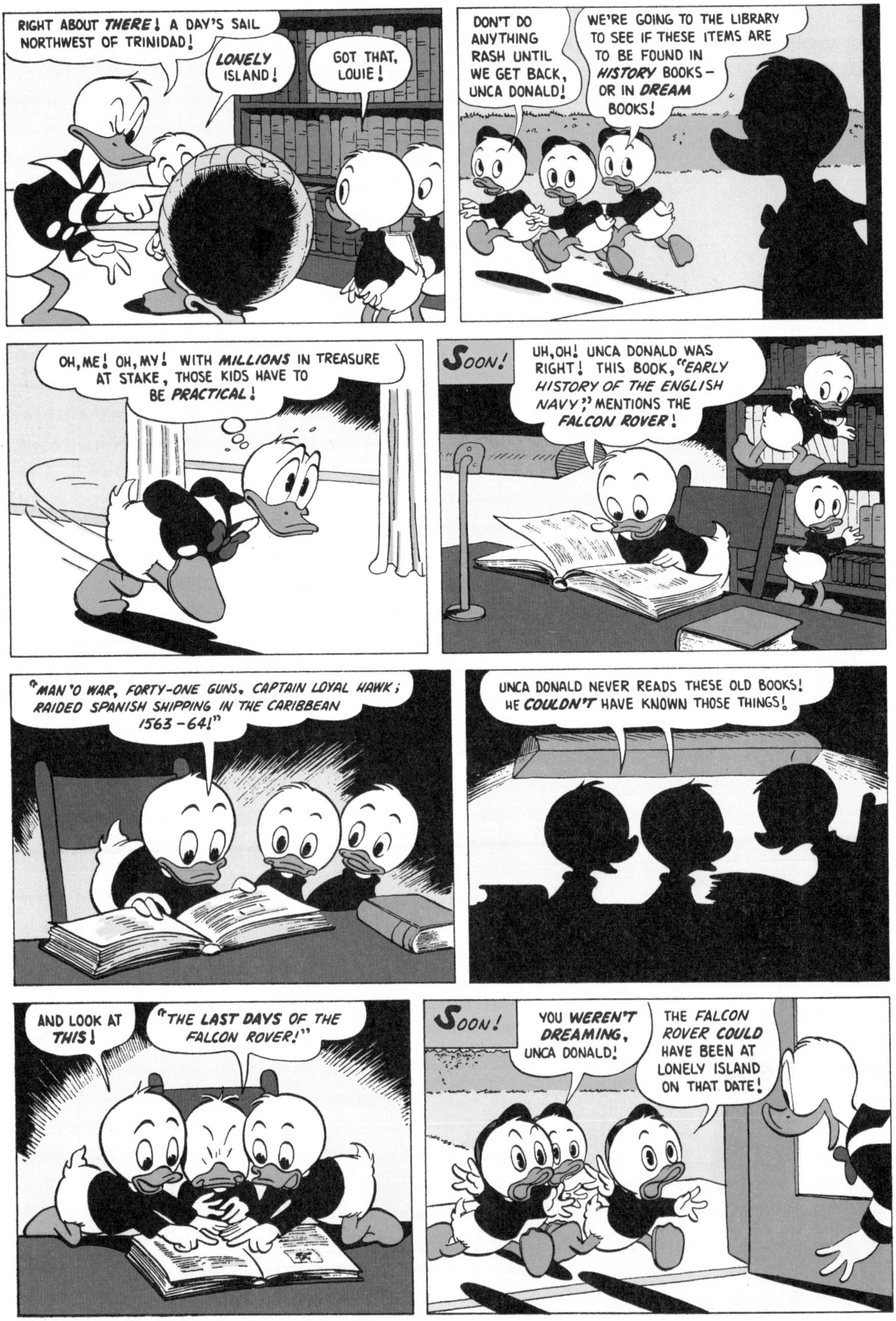

RIGHT ABOUT THERE! A DAY'S SAIL NORTHWEST OF TRINIDAD!
LONELY ISLAND!
GOT THAT, LOUIE!
DON'T DO ANYTHING RASH UNTIL WE GET BACK, UNCA DONALD!
WE'RE GOING TO THE LIBRARY TO SEE IF THESE ITEMS ARE TO BE FOUND IN HISTORY BOOKS— OR IN DREAM BOOKS!
OH, ME! OH, MY! WITH MILLIONS IN TREASURE AT STAKE, THOSE KIDS HAVE TO BE PRACTICAL!
SOON!
UH, OH! UNCA DONALD WAS RIGHT! THIS BOOK, "EARLY HISTORY OF THE ENGLISH NAVY," MENTIONS THE FALCON ROVER!
"MAN 'O WAR, FORTY-ONE GUNS, CAPTAIN LOYAL HAWK; RAIDED SPANISH SHIPPING IN THE CARIBBEAN 1563-64!"
UNCA DONALD NEVER READS THESE OLD BOOKS! HE COULDN'T HAVE KNOWN THOSE THINGS!
AND LOOK AT THIS!
"THE LAST DAYS OF THE FALCON ROVER!"
SOON!
YOU WEREN'T DREAMING, UNCA DONALD!
THE FALCON ROVER COULD HAVE BEEN AT LONELY ISLAND ON THAT DATE!

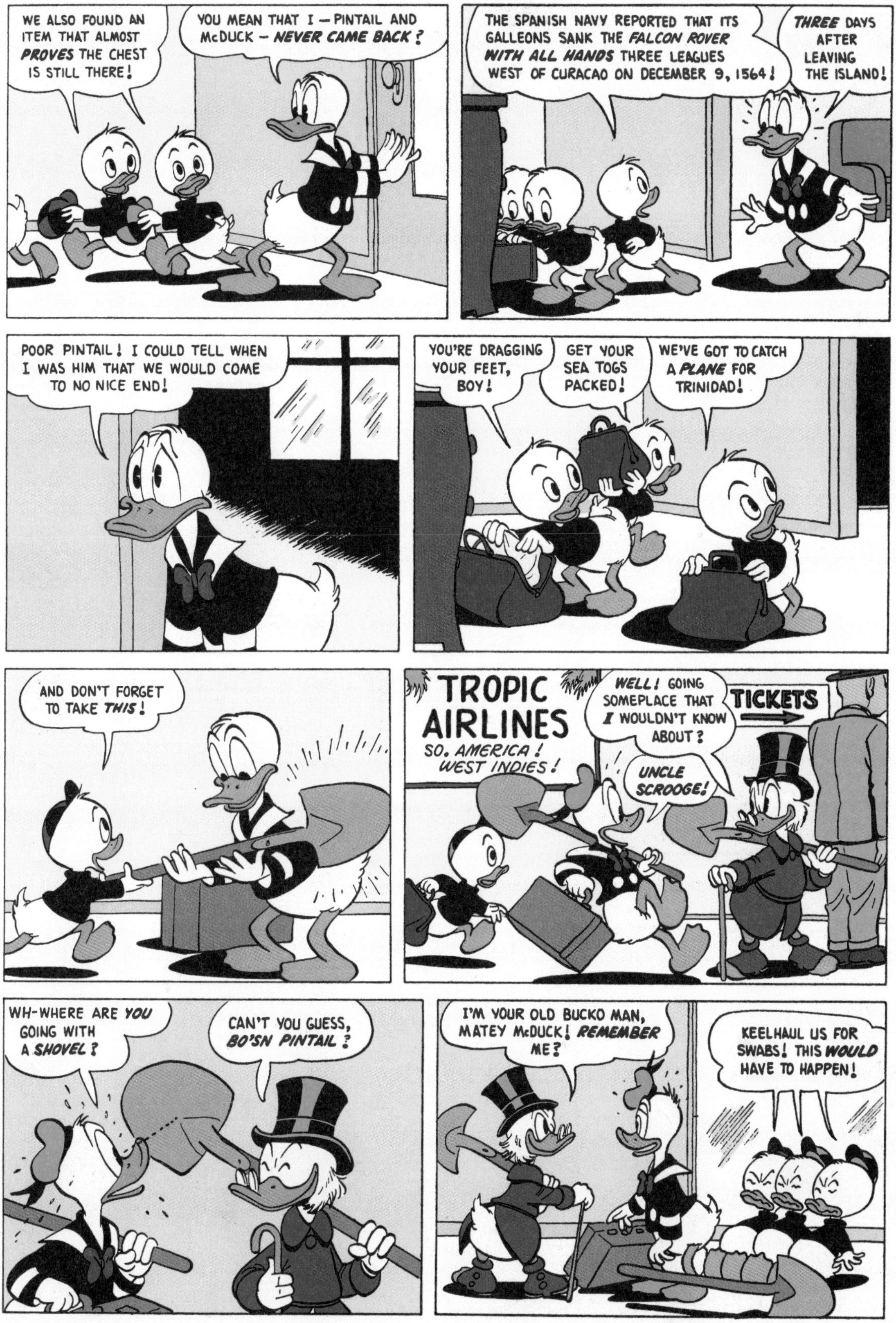

WE ALSO FOUND AN ITEM THAT ALMOST PROVES THE CHEST IS STILL THERE!
YOU MEAN THAT I — PINTAIL AND McDUCK — NEVER CAME BACK?
THE SPANISH NAVY REPORTED THAT ITS GALLEONS SANK THE FALCON ROVER WITH ALL HANDS THREE LEAGUES WEST OF CURACAO ON DECEMBER 9, 1564!
THREE DAYS AFTER LEAVING THE ISLAND!
POOR PINTAIL! I COULD TELL WHEN I WAS HIM THAT WE WOULD COME TO NO NICE END!
YOU'RE DRAGGING YOUR FEET, BOY!
GET YOUR SEA TOGS PACKED!
WE'VE GOT TO CATCH A PLANE FOR TRINIDAD!
AND DON'T FORGET TO TAKE THIS!
TROPIC AIRLINES
SO. AMERICA! WEST INDIES!
TICKETS
WELL! GOING SOMEPLACE THAT I WOULDN'T KNOW ABOUT?
UNCLE SCROOGE!
WH-WHERE ARE YOU GOING WITH A SHOVEL?
CAN'T YOU GUESS, BO'SN PINTAIL?
I'M YOUR OLD BUCKO MAN, MATEY McDUCK! REMEMBER ME?
KEELHAUL US FOR SWABS! THIS WOULD HAVE TO HAPPEN!

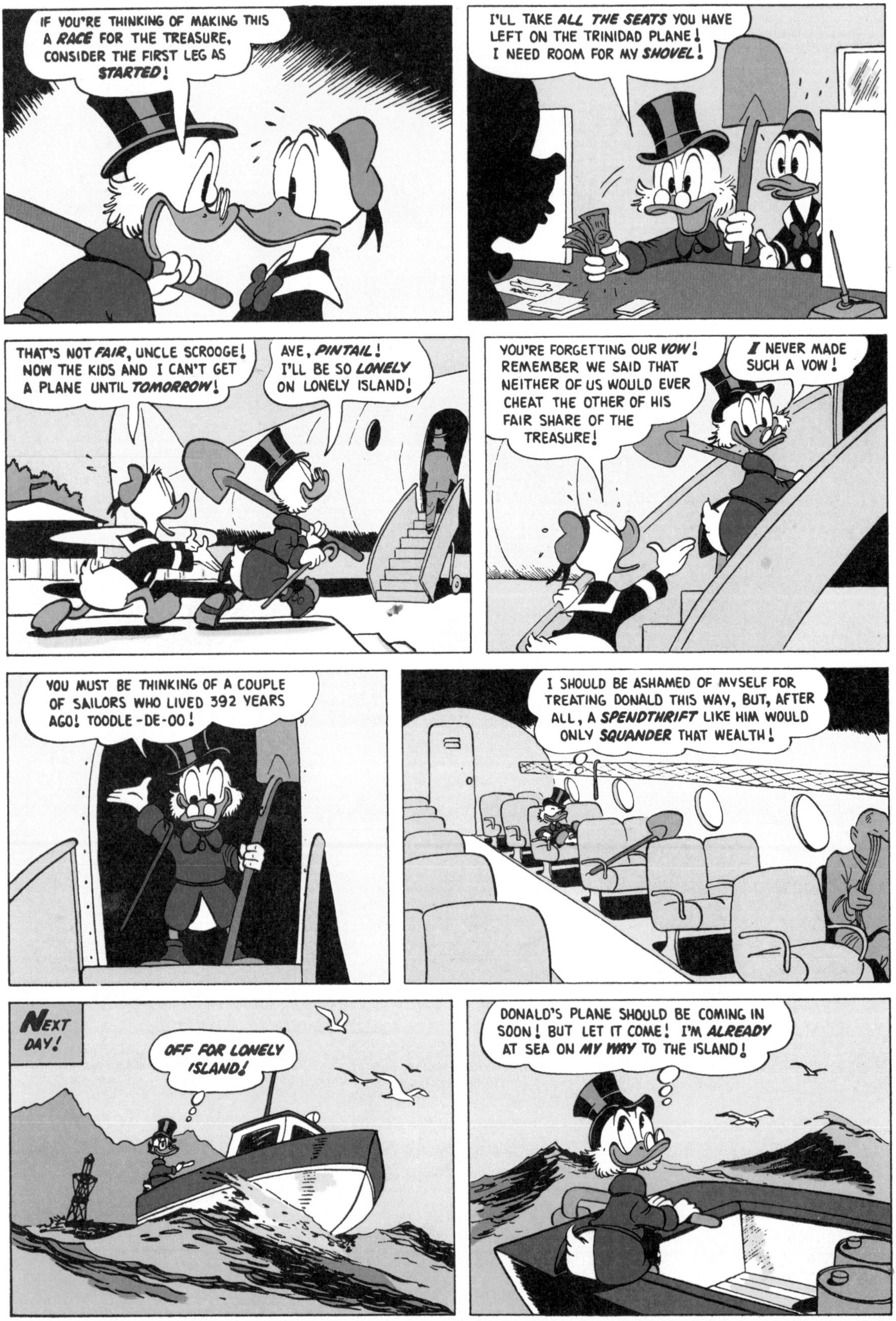
IF YOU'RE THINKING OF MAKING THIS A RACE FOR THE TREASURE, CONSIDER THE FIRST LEG AS STARTED!
I'LL TAKE ALL THE SEATS YOU HAVE LEFT ON THE TRINIDAD PLANE! I NEED ROOM FOR MY SHOVEL!
THAT'S NOT FAIR, UNCLE SCROOGE! NOW THE KIDS AND I CAN'T GET A PLANE UNTIL TOMORROW!
AYE, PINTAIL! I'LL BE SO LONELY ON LONELY ISLAND!
YOU'RE FORGETTING OUR VOW! REMEMBER WE SAID THAT NEITHER OF US WOULD EVER CHEAT THE OTHER OF HIS FAIR SHARE OF THE TREASURE!
I NEVER MADE SUCH A VOW!
YOU MUST BE THINKING OF A COUPLE OF SAILORS WHO LIVED 392 YEARS AGO! TOODLE-DE-OO!
I SHOULD BE ASHAMED OF MYSELF FOR TREATING DONALD THIS WAY, BUT, AFTER ALL, A SPENDTHRIFT LIKE HIM WOULD ONLY SQUANDER THAT WEALTH!
NEXT DAY!
OFF FOR LONELY ISLAND!
DONALD'S PLANE SHOULD BE COMING IN SOON! BUT LET IT COME! I'M ALREADY AT SEA ON MY WAY TO THE ISLAND!

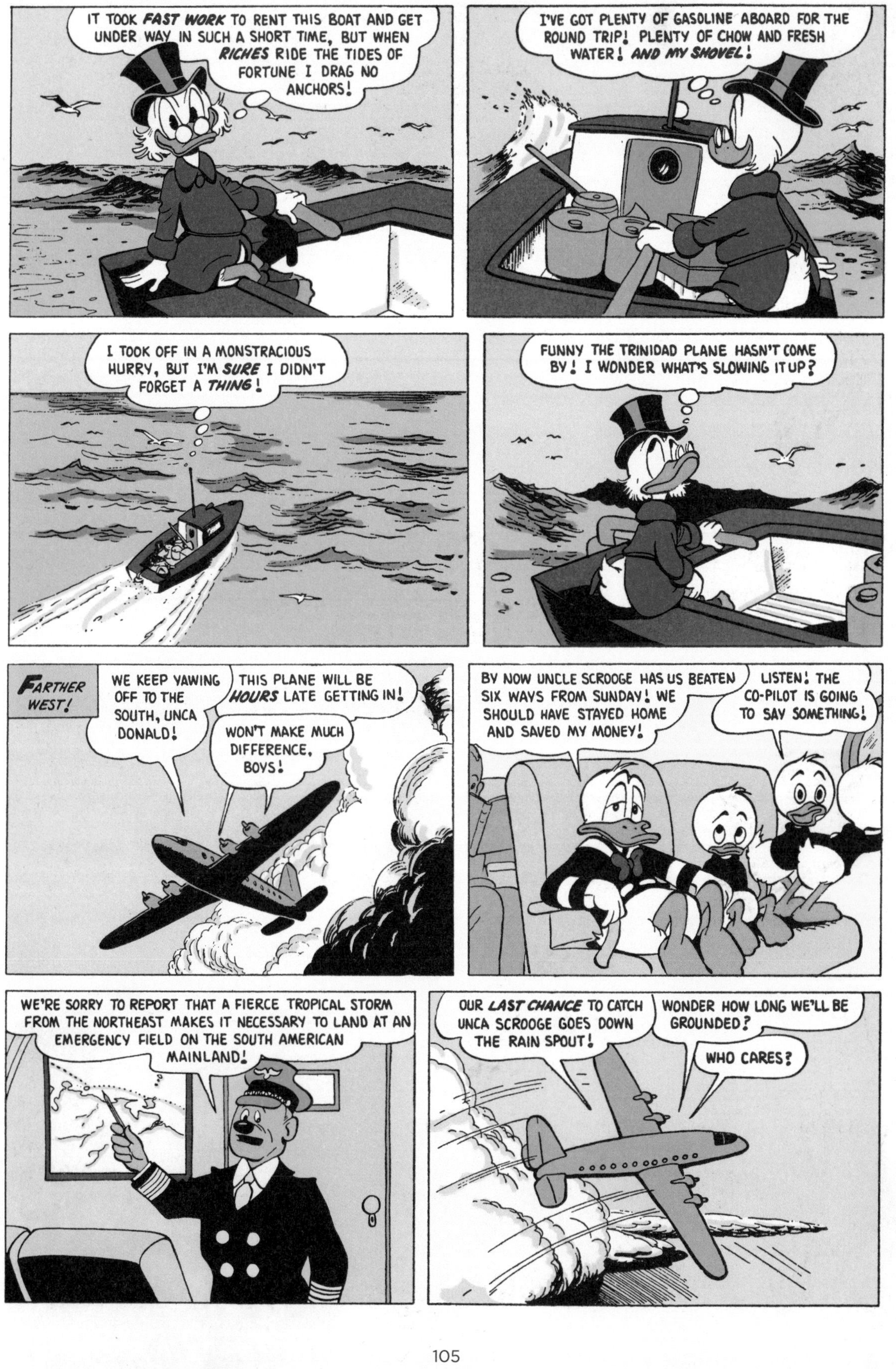
IT TOOK FAST WORK TO RENT THIS BOAT AND GET UNDER WAY IN SUCH A SHORT TIME, BUT WHEN RICHES RIDE THE TIDES OF FORTUNE I DRAG NO ANCHORS!
I'VE GOT PLENTY OF GASOLINE ABOARD FOR THE ROUND TRIP! PLENTY OF CHOW AND FRESH WATER! AND MY SHOVEL!
I TOOK OFF IN A MONSTRACIOUS HURRY, BUT I'M SURE I DIDN'T FORGET A THING!
FUNNY THE TRINIDAD PLANE HASN'T COME BY! I WONDER WHAT'S SLOWING IT UP?
FARTHER WEST!
WE KEEP YAWING OFF TO THE SOUTH, UNCA DONALD!
THIS PLANE WILL BE HOURS LATE GETTING IN!
WON'T MAKE MUCH DIFFERENCE, BOYS!
BY NOW UNCLE SCROOGE HAS US BEATEN SIX WAYS FROM SUNDAY! WE SHOULD HAVE STAYED HOME AND SAVED MY MONEY!
LISTEN! THE CO-PILOT IS GOING TO SAY SOMETHING!
WE'RE SORRY TO REPORT THAT A FIERCE TROPICAL STORM FROM THE NORTHEAST MAKES IT NECESSARY TO LAND AT AN EMERGENCY FIELD ON THE SOUTH AMERICAN MAINLAND!
OUR LAST CHANCE TO CATCH UNCA SCROOGE GOES DOWN THE RAIN SPOUT!
WONDER HOW LONG WE'LL BE GROUNDED?
WHO CARES?

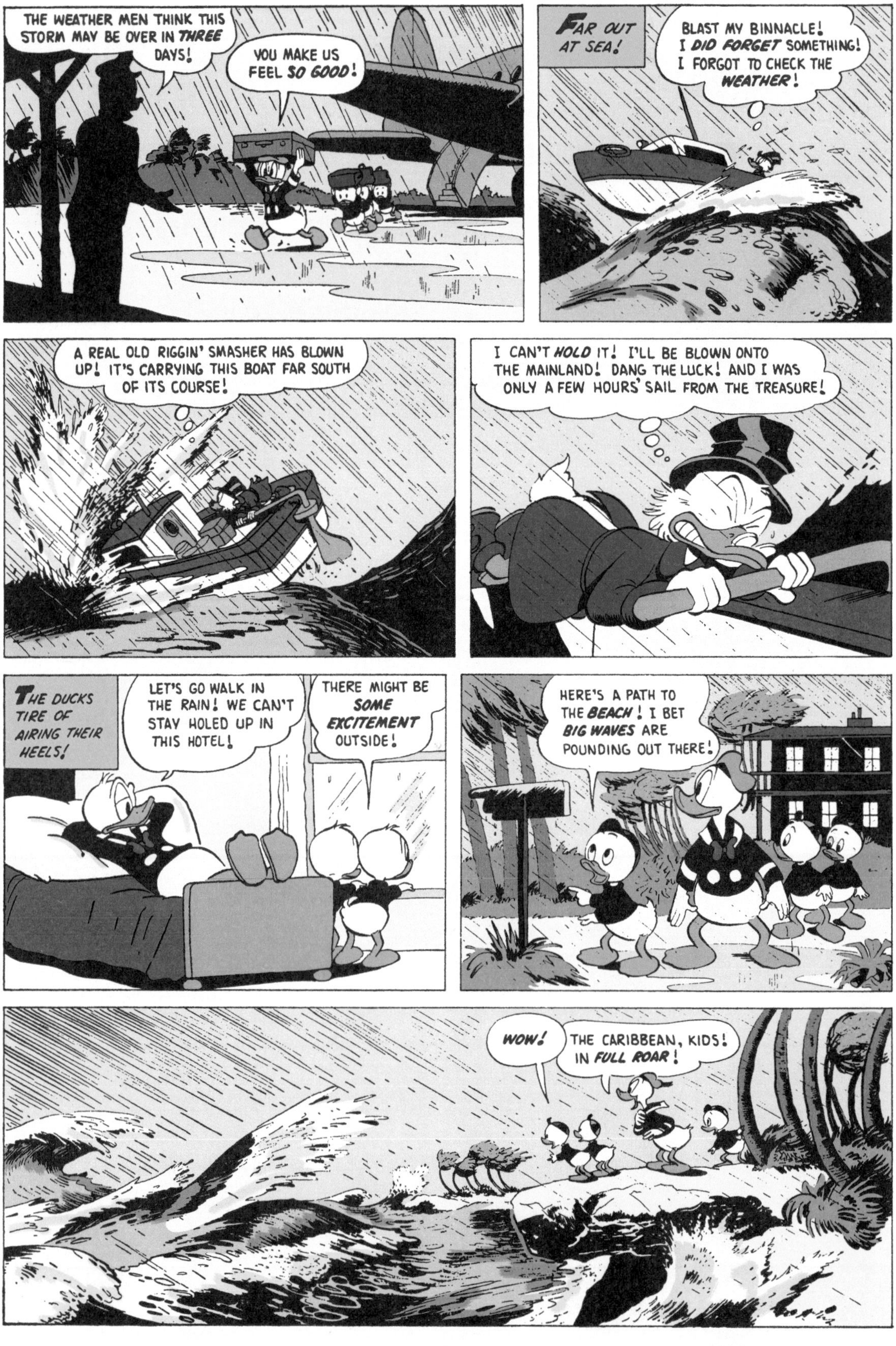
THE WEATHER MEN THINK THIS STORM MAY BE OVER IN THREE DAYS!
YOU MAKE US FEEL SO GOOD!
FAR OUT AT SEA!
BLAST MY BINNACLE! I DID FORGET SOMETHING! I FORGOT TO CHECK THE WEATHER!
A REAL OLD RIGGIN' SMASHER HAS BLOWN UP! IT'S CARRYING THIS BOAT FAR SOUTH OF ITS COURSE!
I CAN'T HOLD IT! I'LL BE BLOWN ONTO THE MAINLAND! DANG THE LUCK! AND I WAS ONLY A FEW HOURS' SAIL FROM THE TREASURE!
THE DUCKS TIRE OF AIRING THEIR HEELS!
LET'S GO WALK IN THE RAIN! WE CAN'T STAY HOLED UP IN THIS HOTEL!
THERE MIGHT BE SOME EXCITEMENT OUTSIDE!
HERE'S A PATH TO THE BEACH! I BET BIG WAVES ARE POUNDING OUT THERE!
WOW!
THE CARIBBEAN, KIDS! IN FULL ROAR!

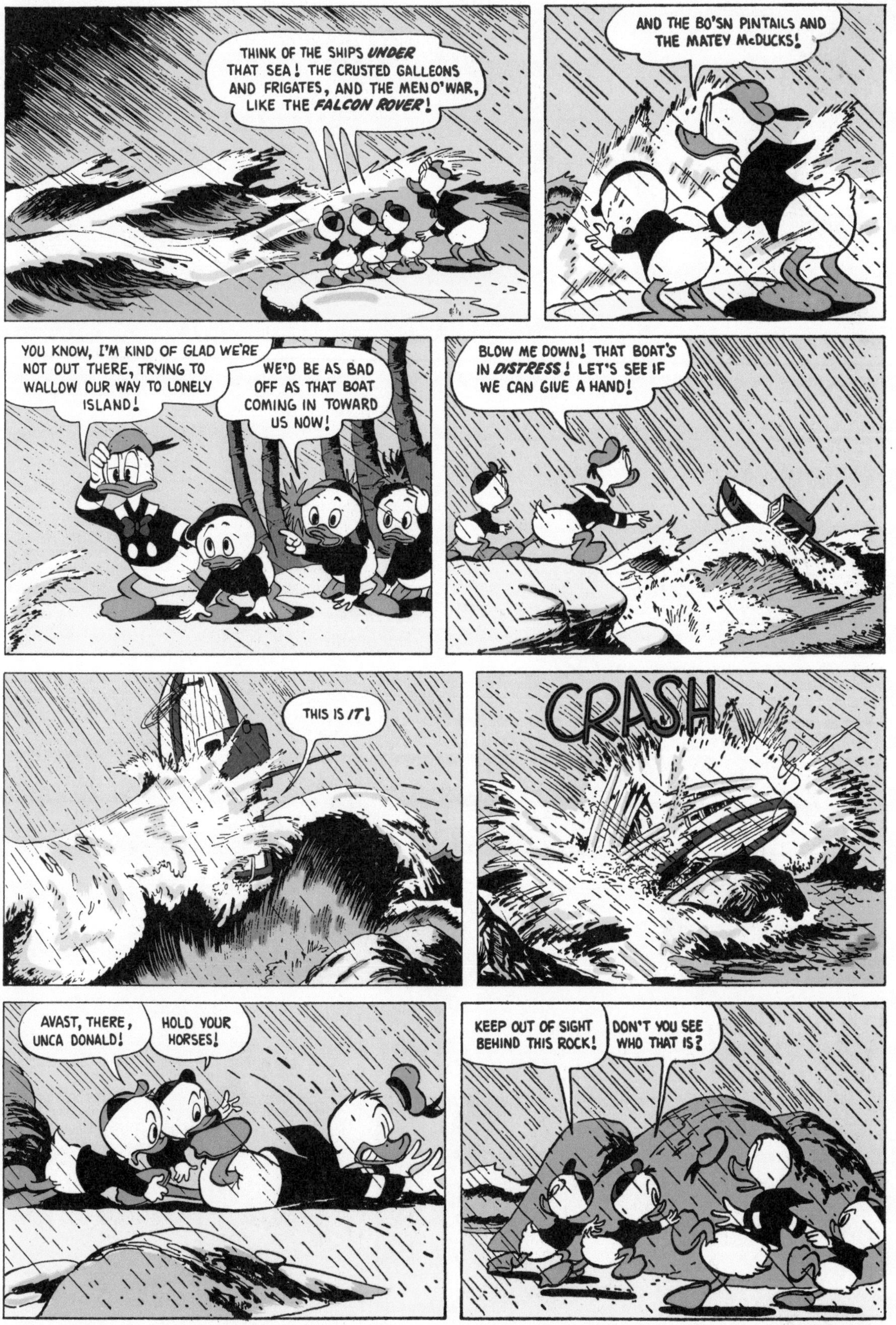

THINK OF THE SHIPS *UNDER* THAT SEA! THE CRUSTED GALLEONS AND FRIGATES, AND THE MEN O'WAR, LIKE THE *FALCON ROVER*!
AND THE BO'SN PINTAILS AND THE MATEY McDUCKS!
YOU KNOW, I'M KIND OF GLAD WE'RE NOT OUT THERE, TRYING TO WALLOW OUR WAY TO LONELY ISLAND!
WE'D BE AS BAD OFF AS THAT BOAT COMING IN TOWARD US NOW!
BLOW ME DOWN! THAT BOAT'S IN *DISTRESS*! LET'S SEE IF WE CAN GIVE A HAND!
THIS IS *IT*!
CRASH
AVAST, THERE, UNCA DONALD!
HOLD YOUR HORSES!
KEEP OUT OF SIGHT BEHIND THIS ROCK!
DON'T YOU SEE WHO THAT IS?

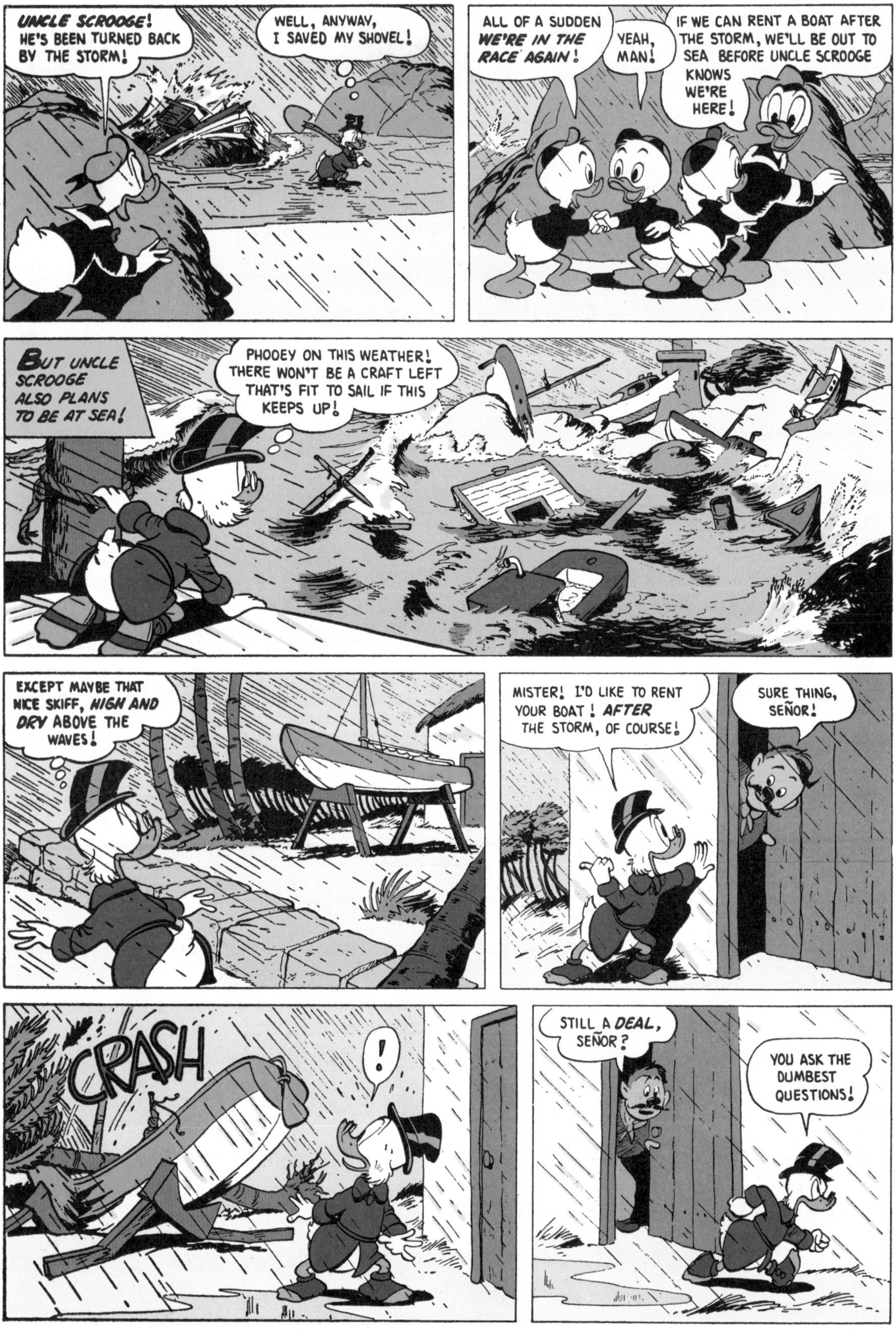
UNCLE SCROOGE! HE'S BEEN TURNED BACK BY THE STORM!
WELL, ANYWAY, I SAVED MY SHOVEL!
ALL OF A SUDDEN WE'RE IN THE RACE AGAIN!
YEAH, MAN!
IF WE CAN RENT A BOAT AFTER THE STORM, WE'LL BE OUT TO SEA BEFORE UNCLE SCROOGE KNOWS WE'RE HERE!
BUT UNCLE SCROOGE ALSO PLANS TO BE AT SEA!
PHOOEY ON THIS WEATHER! THERE WON'T BE A CRAFT LEFT THAT'S FIT TO SAIL IF THIS KEEPS UP!
EXCEPT MAYBE THAT NICE SKIFF, HIGH AND DRY ABOVE THE WAVES!
MISTER! I'D LIKE TO RENT YOUR BOAT! AFTER THE STORM, OF COURSE!
SURE THING, SEÑOR!
CRASH
!
STILL A DEAL, SEÑOR?
YOU ASK THE DUMBEST QUESTIONS!

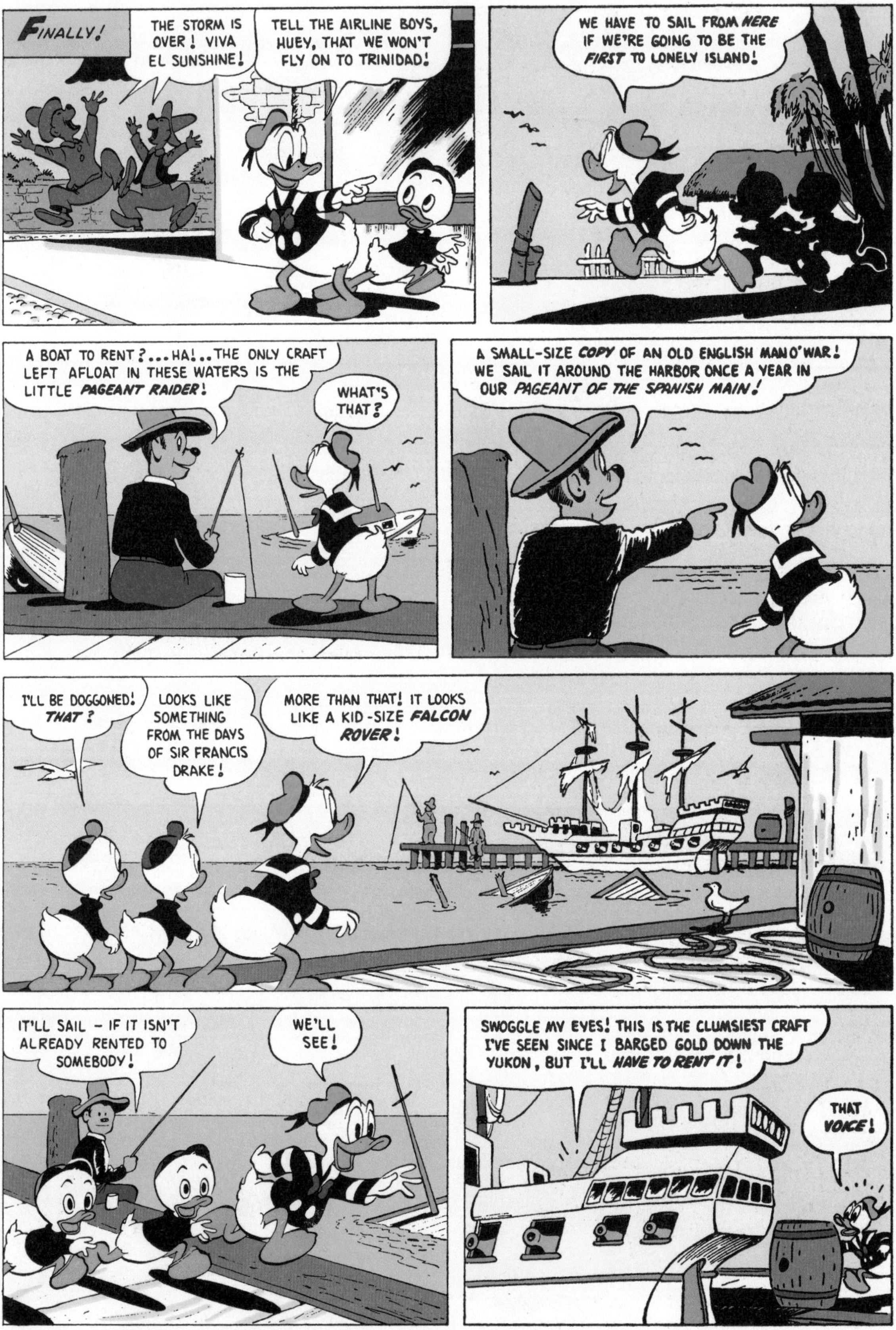
FINALLY!
THE STORM IS OVER! VIVA EL SUNSHINE!
TELL THE AIRLINE BOYS, HUEY, THAT WE WON'T FLY ON TO TRINIDAD!
WE HAVE TO SAIL FROM HERE IF WE'RE GOING TO BE THE FIRST TO LONELY ISLAND!
A BOAT TO RENT?...HA!..THE ONLY CRAFT LEFT AFLOAT IN THESE WATERS IS THE LITTLE PAGEANT RAIDER!
WHAT'S THAT?
A SMALL-SIZE COPY OF AN OLD ENGLISH MAN O'WAR! WE SAIL IT AROUND THE HARBOR ONCE A YEAR IN OUR PAGEANT OF THE SPANISH MAIN!
I'LL BE DOGGONED! THAT?
LOOKS LIKE SOMETHING FROM THE DAYS OF SIR FRANCIS DRAKE!
MORE THAN THAT! IT LOOKS LIKE A KID-SIZE FALCON ROVER!
IT'LL SAIL - IF IT ISN'T ALREADY RENTED TO SOMEBODY!
WE'LL SEE!
SWOGGLE MY EYES! THIS IS THE CLUMSIEST CRAFT I'VE SEEN SINCE I BARGED GOLD DOWN THE YUKON, BUT I'LL HAVE TO RENT IT!
THAT VOICE!

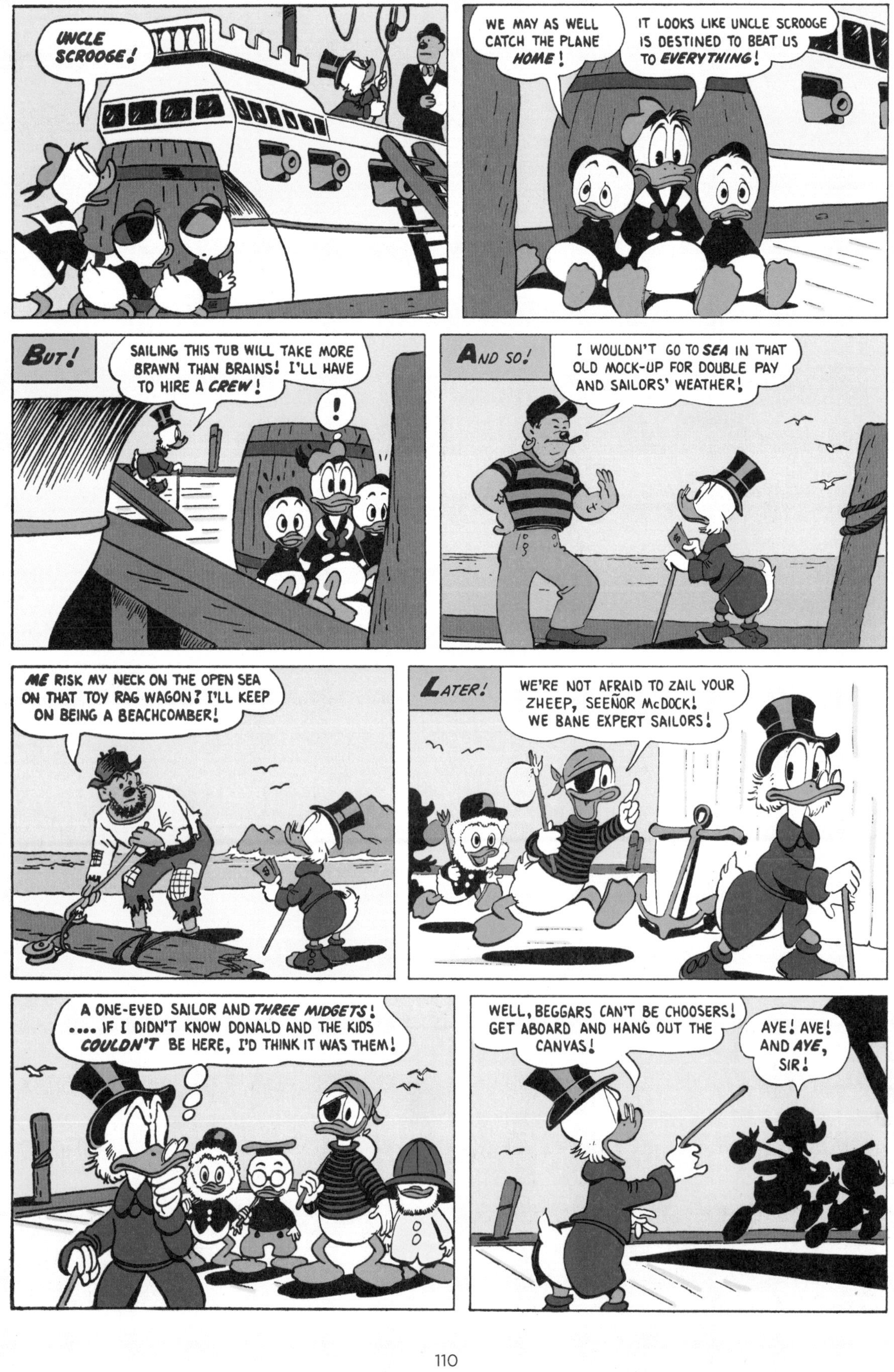
UNCLE SCROOGE!
WE MAY AS WELL CATCH THE PLANE HOME!
IT LOOKS LIKE UNCLE SCROOGE IS DESTINED TO BEAT US TO EVERYTHING!
BUT!
SAILING THIS TUB WILL TAKE MORE BRAWN THAN BRAINS! I'LL HAVE TO HIRE A CREW!
!
AND SO!
I WOULDN'T GO TO SEA IN THAT OLD MOCK-UP FOR DOUBLE PAY AND SAILORS' WEATHER!
ME RISK MY NECK ON THE OPEN SEA ON THAT TOY RAG WAGON? I'LL KEEP ON BEING A BEACHCOMBER!
LATER!
WE'RE NOT AFRAID TO ZAIL YOUR ZHEEP, SEEÑOR McDOCK! WE BANE EXPERT SAILORS!
A ONE-EYED SAILOR AND THREE MIDGETS! .... IF I DIDN'T KNOW DONALD AND THE KIDS COULDN'T BE HERE, I'D THINK IT WAS THEM!
WELL, BEGGARS CAN'T BE CHOOSERS! GET ABOARD AND HANG OUT THE CANVAS!
AYE! AYE! AND AYE, SIR!

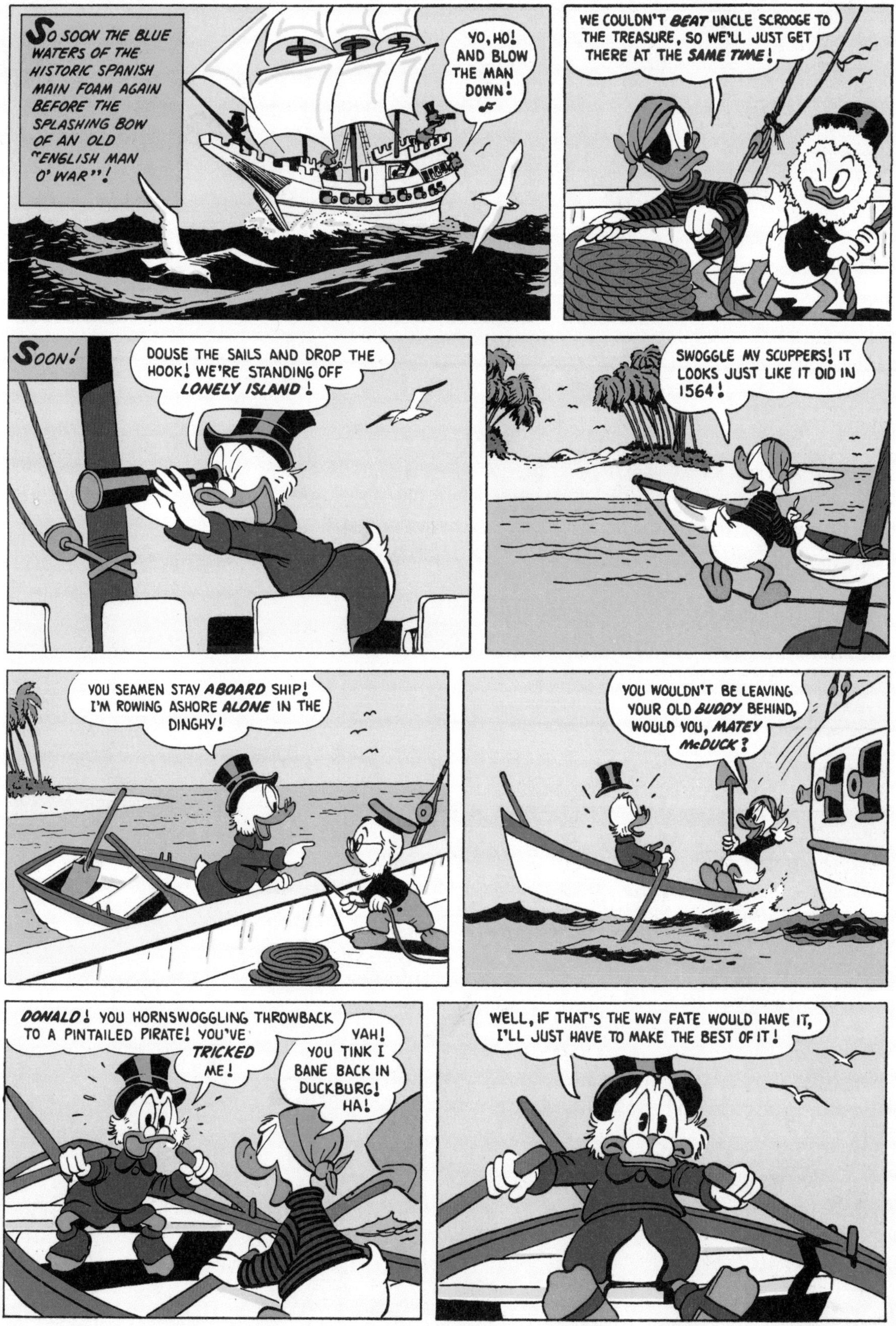
SO SOON THE BLUE WATERS OF THE HISTORIC SPANISH MAIN FOAM AGAIN BEFORE THE SPLASHING BOW OF AN OLD "ENGLISH MAN O' WAR"!
YO, HO! AND BLOW THE MAN DOWN!
WE COULDN'T BEAT UNCLE SCROOGE TO THE TREASURE, SO WE'LL JUST GET THERE AT THE SAME TIME!
SOON!
DOUSE THE SAILS AND DROP THE HOOK! WE'RE STANDING OFF LONELY ISLAND!
SWOGGLE MY SCUPPERS! IT LOOKS JUST LIKE IT DID IN 1564!
YOU SEAMEN STAY ABOARD SHIP! I'M ROWING ASHORE ALONE IN THE DINGHY!
YOU WOULDN'T BE LEAVING YOUR OLD BUDDY BEHIND, WOULD YOU, MATEY McDUCK?
DONALD! YOU HORNSWOGGLING THROWBACK TO A PINTAILED PIRATE! YOU'VE TRICKED ME!
YAH! YOU TINK I BANE BACK IN DUCKBURG! HA!
WELL, IF THAT'S THE WAY FATE WOULD HAVE IT, I'LL JUST HAVE TO MAKE THE BEST OF IT!

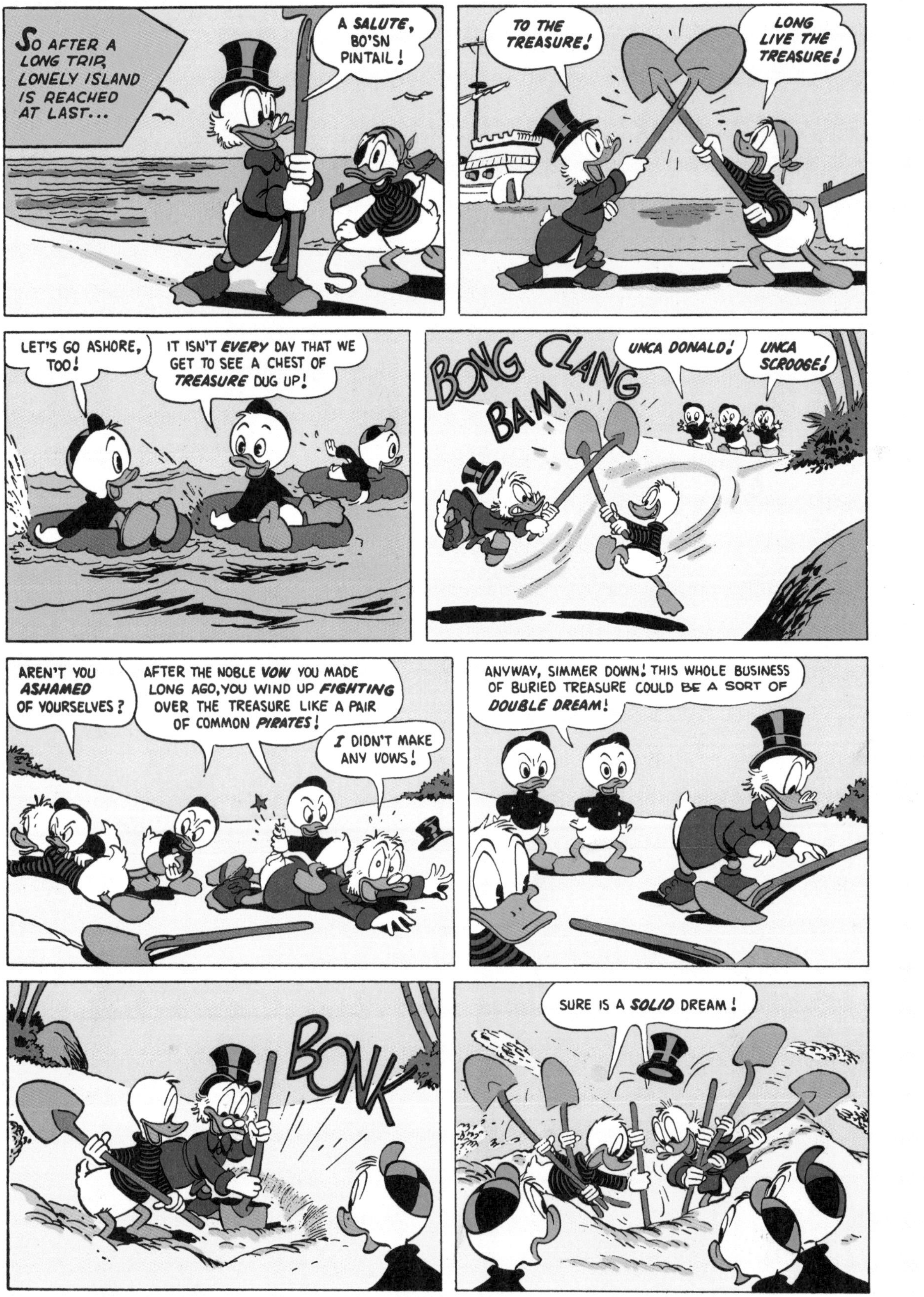

SO AFTER A LONG TRIP, LONELY ISLAND IS REACHED AT LAST...
A SALUTE, BO'SN PINTAIL!
TO THE TREASURE!
LONG LIVE THE TREASURE!
LET'S GO ASHORE, TOO!
IT ISN'T EVERY DAY THAT WE GET TO SEE A CHEST OF TREASURE DUG UP!
BONG CLANG BAM
UNCA DONALD!
UNCA SCROOGE!
AREN'T YOU ASHAMED OF YOURSELVES?
AFTER THE NOBLE VOW YOU MADE LONG AGO, YOU WIND UP FIGHTING OVER THE TREASURE LIKE A PAIR OF COMMON PIRATES!
I DIDN'T MAKE ANY VOWS!
ANYWAY, SIMMER DOWN! THIS WHOLE BUSINESS OF BURIED TREASURE COULD BE A SORT OF DOUBLE DREAM!
BONK
SURE IS A SOLID DREAM!

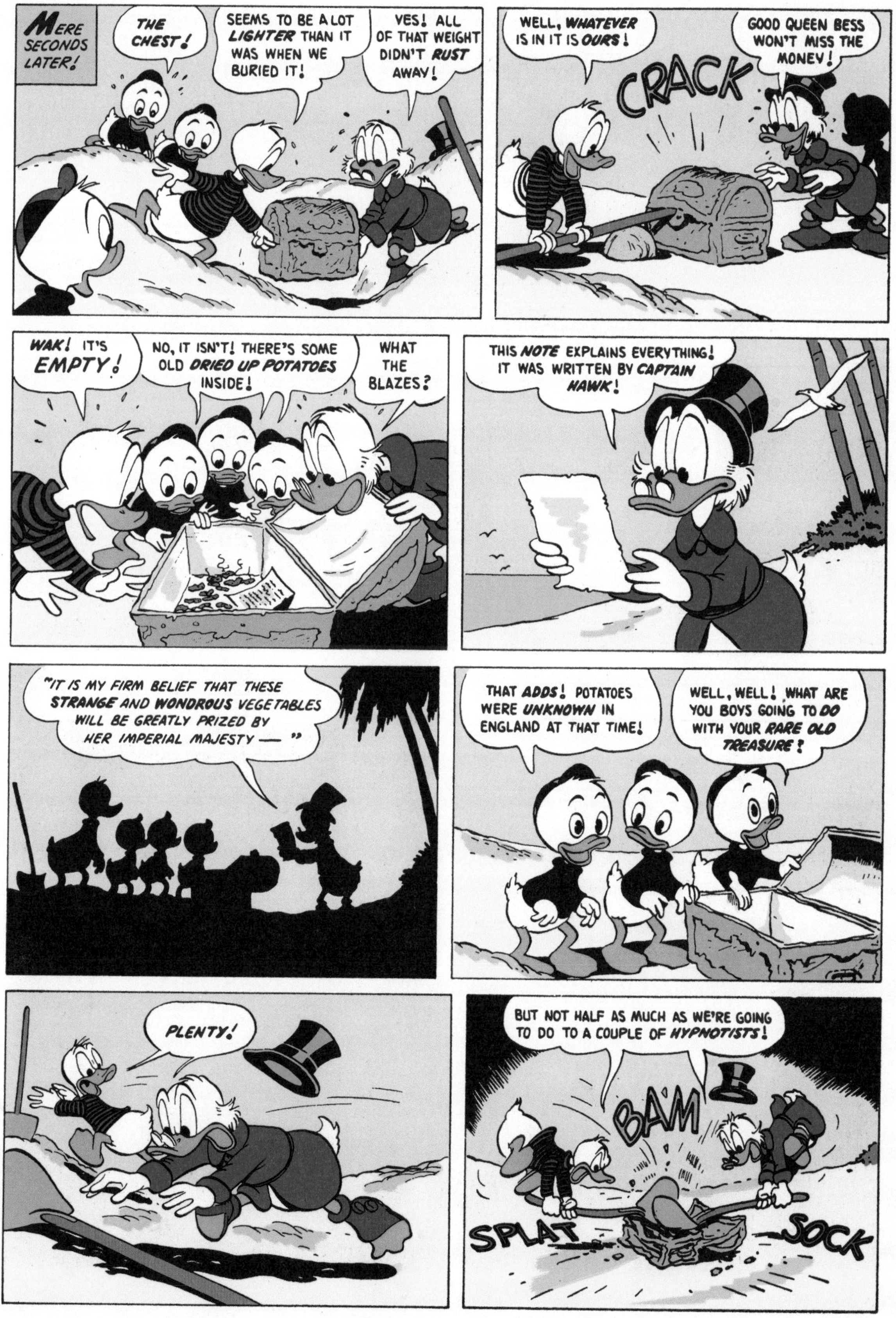
MERE SECONDS LATER!
THE CHEST!
SEEMS TO BE A LOT LIGHTER THAN IT WAS WHEN WE BURIED IT!
YES! ALL OF THAT WEIGHT DIDN'T RUST AWAY!
WELL, WHATEVER IS IN IT IS OURS!
GOOD QUEEN BESS WON'T MISS THE MONEY!
CRACK
WAK! IT'S EMPTY!
NO, IT ISN'T! THERE'S SOME OLD DRIED UP POTATOES INSIDE!
WHAT THE BLAZES?
THIS NOTE EXPLAINS EVERYTHING! IT WAS WRITTEN BY CAPTAIN HAWK!
"IT IS MY FIRM BELIEF THAT THESE STRANGE AND WONDROUS VEGETABLES WILL BE GREATLY PRIZED BY HER IMPERIAL MAJESTY — "
THAT ADDS! POTATOES WERE UNKNOWN IN ENGLAND AT THAT TIME!
WELL, WELL! WHAT ARE YOU BOYS GOING TO DO WITH YOUR RARE OLD TREASURE?
PLENTY!
BUT NOT HALF AS MUCH AS WE'RE GOING TO DO TO A COUPLE OF HYPNOTISTS!
BAM
SPLAT
SOCK

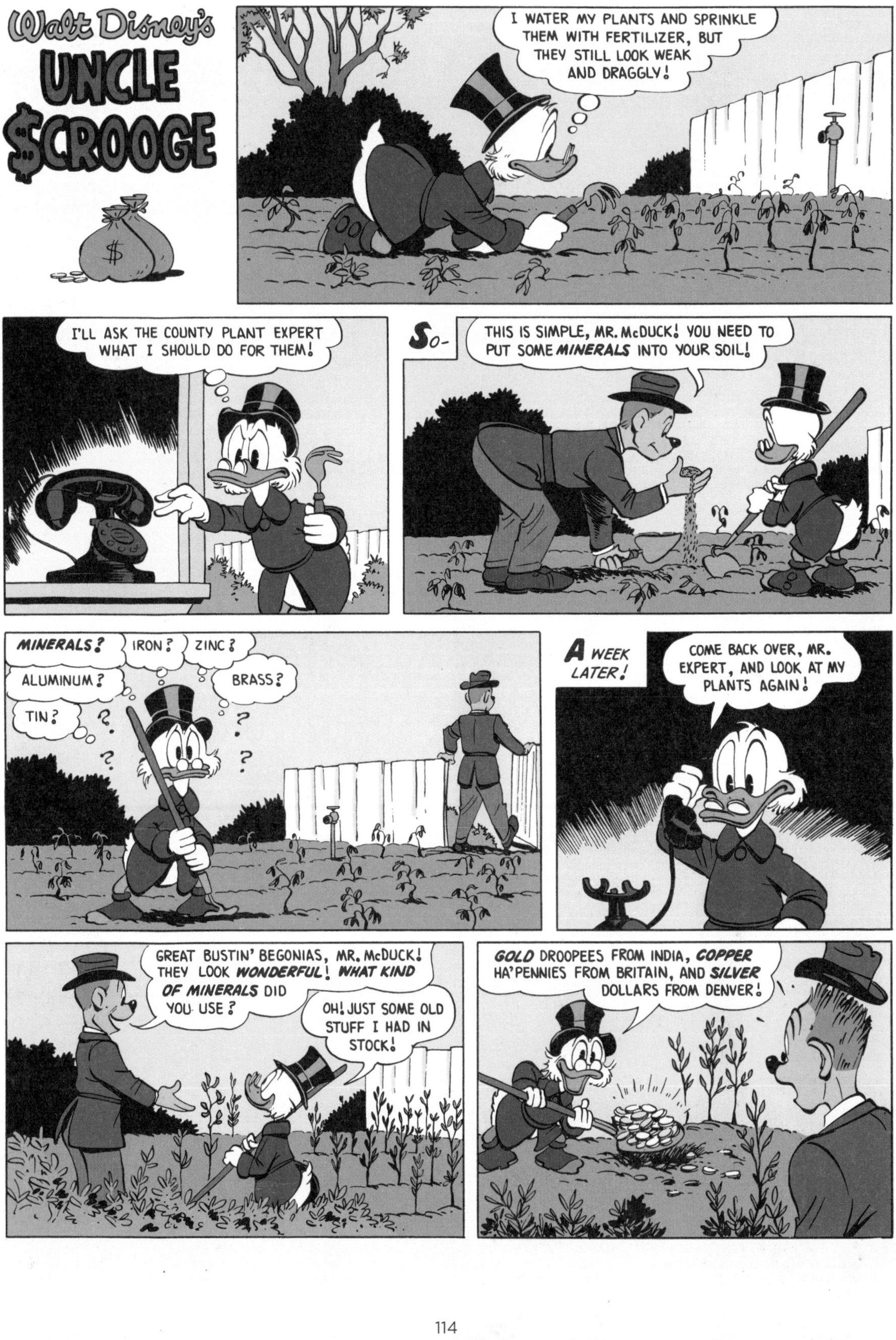
Walt Disney's
UNCLE $CROOGE
I WATER MY PLANTS AND SPRINKLE THEM WITH FERTILIZER, BUT THEY STILL LOOK WEAK AND DRAGGLY!
I'LL ASK THE COUNTY PLANT EXPERT WHAT I SHOULD DO FOR THEM!
SO-
THIS IS SIMPLE, MR. McDUCK! YOU NEED TO PUT SOME MINERALS INTO YOUR SOIL!
MINERALS?
IRON?
ZINC?
ALUMINUM?
BRASS?
TIN?
A WEEK LATER!
COME BACK OVER, MR. EXPERT, AND LOOK AT MY PLANTS AGAIN!
GREAT BUSTIN' BEGONIAS, MR. McDUCK! THEY LOOK WONDERFUL! WHAT KIND OF MINERALS DID YOU USE?
OH! JUST SOME OLD STUFF I HAD IN STOCK!
GOLD DROOPEES FROM INDIA, COPPER HA'PENNIES FROM BRITAIN, AND SILVER DOLLARS FROM DENVER!

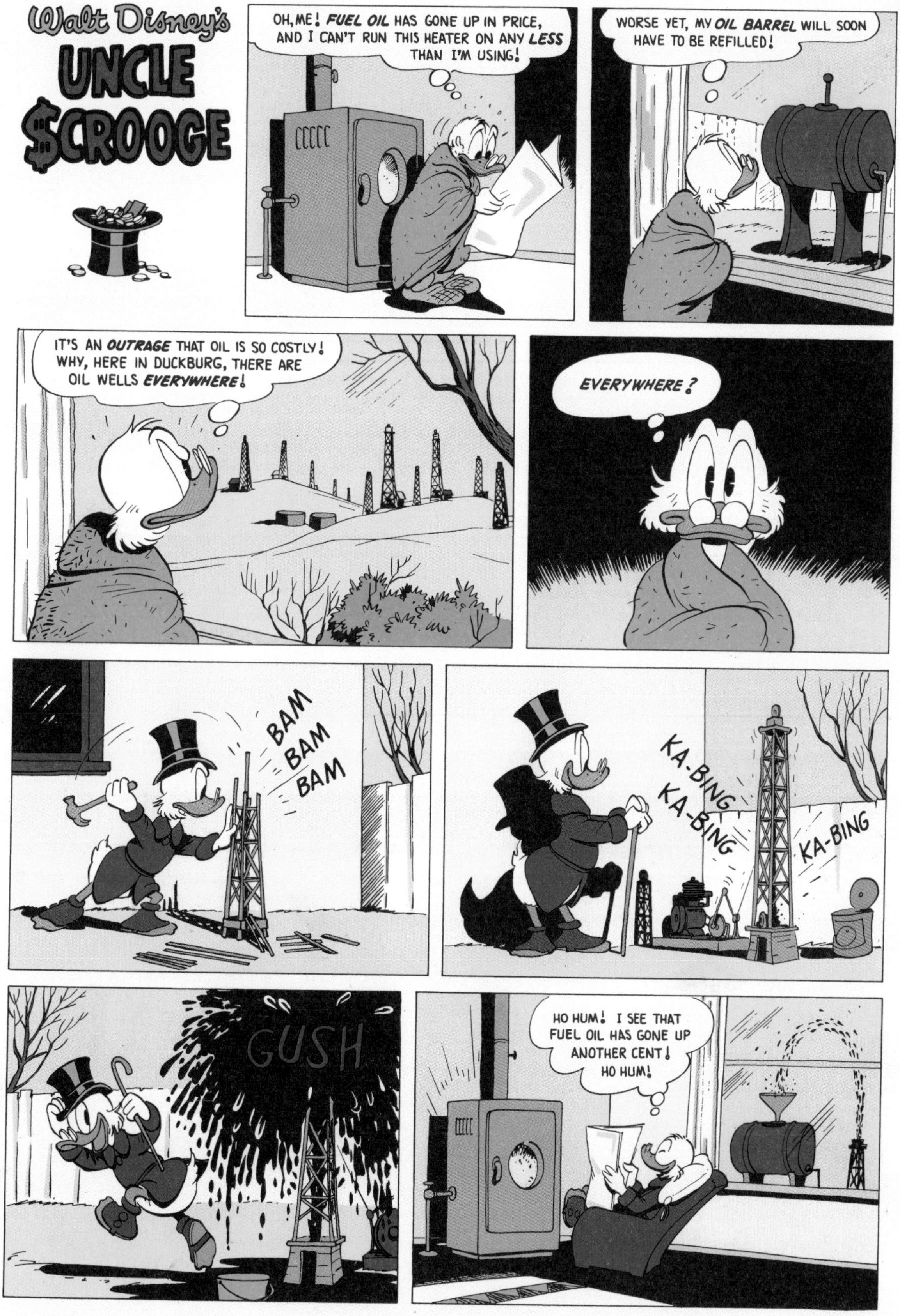
Walt Disney's
UNCLE $CROOGE
OH, ME! FUEL OIL HAS GONE UP IN PRICE, AND I CAN'T RUN THIS HEATER ON ANY LESS THAN I'M USING!
WORSE YET, MY OIL BARREL WILL SOON HAVE TO BE REFILLED!
IT'S AN OUTRAGE THAT OIL IS SO COSTLY! WHY, HERE IN DUCKBURG, THERE ARE OIL WELLS EVERYWHERE!
EVERYWHERE?
BAM BAM BAM
KA-BING KA-BING
KA-BING
GUSH
HO HUM! I SEE THAT FUEL OIL HAS GONE UP ANOTHER CENT! HO HUM!

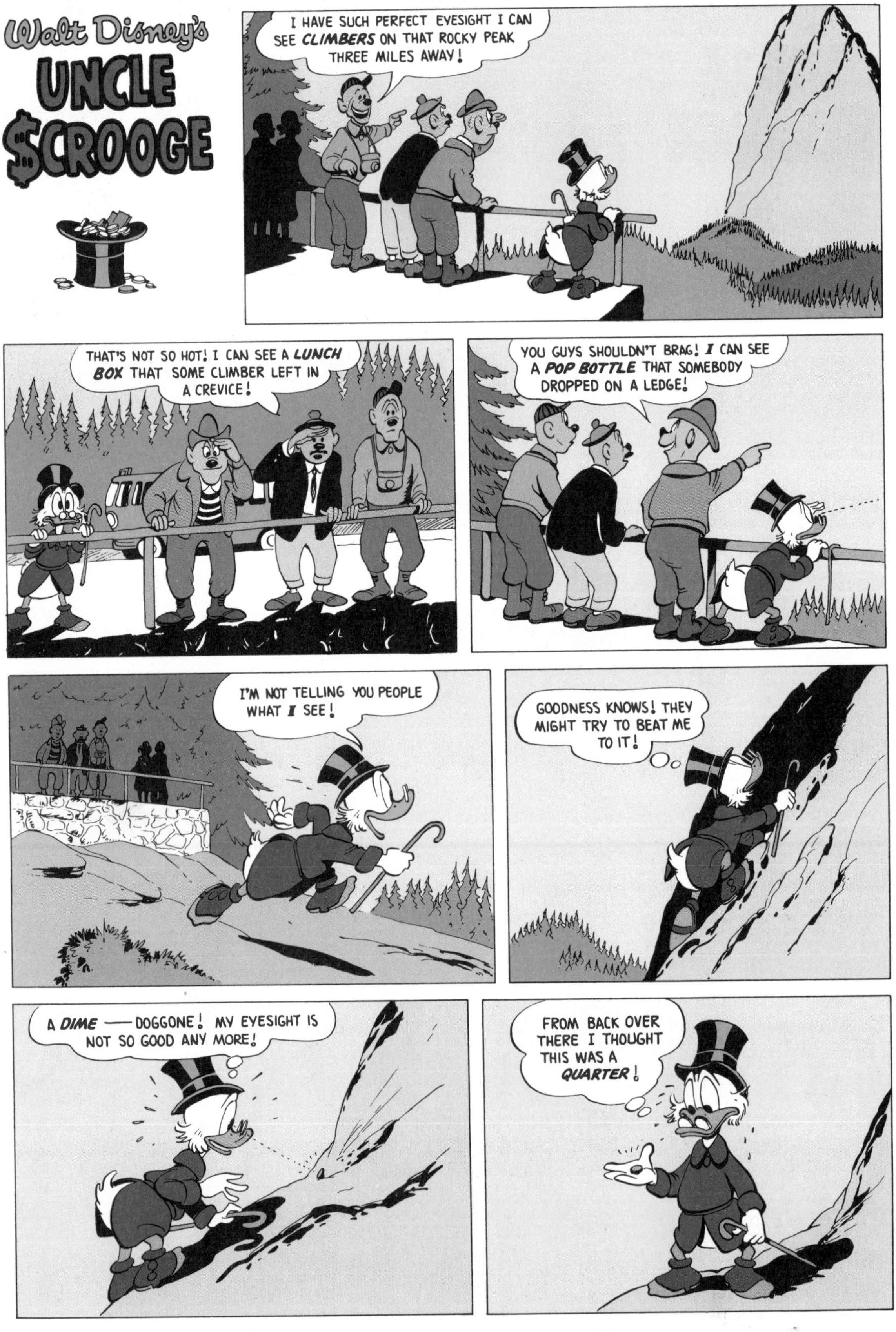
Walt Disney's
UNCLE $CROOGE
I HAVE SUCH PERFECT EYESIGHT I CAN SEE CLIMBERS ON THAT ROCKY PEAK THREE MILES AWAY!
THAT'S NOT SO HOT! I CAN SEE A LUNCH BOX THAT SOME CLIMBER LEFT IN A CREVICE!
YOU GUYS SHOULDN'T BRAG! I CAN SEE A POP BOTTLE THAT SOMEBODY DROPPED ON A LEDGE!
I'M NOT TELLING YOU PEOPLE WHAT I SEE!
GOODNESS KNOWS! THEY MIGHT TRY TO BEAT ME TO IT!
A DIME — DOGGONE! MY EYESIGHT IS NOT SO GOOD ANY MORE!
FROM BACK OVER THERE I THOUGHT THIS WAS A QUARTER!

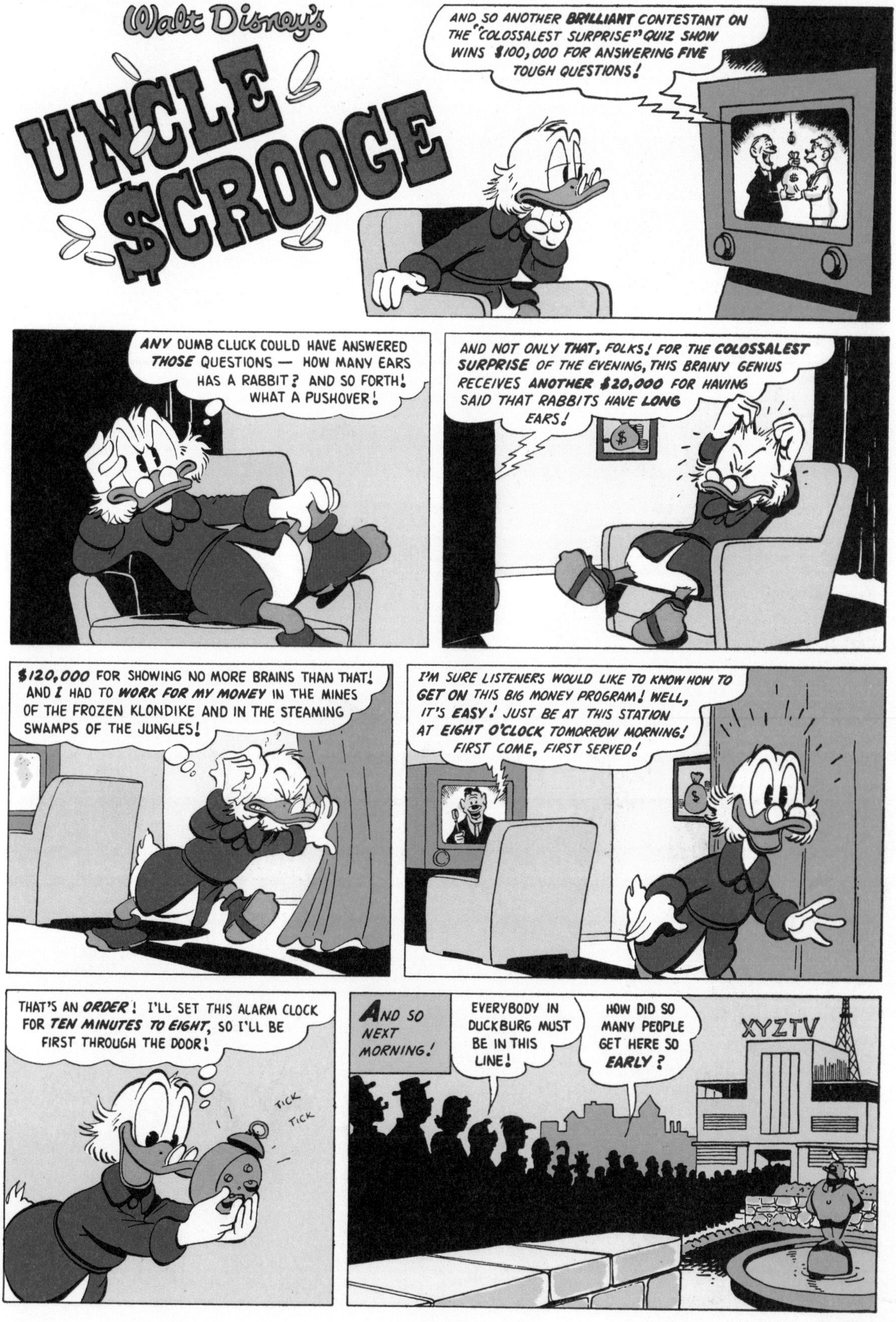
Walt Disney's
UNCLE $CROOGE
AND SO ANOTHER BRILLIANT CONTESTANT ON THE "COLOSSALEST SURPRISE" QUIZ SHOW WINS $100,000 FOR ANSWERING FIVE TOUGH QUESTIONS!
ANY DUMB CLUCK COULD HAVE ANSWERED THOSE QUESTIONS — HOW MANY EARS HAS A RABBIT? AND SO FORTH! WHAT A PUSHOVER!
AND NOT ONLY THAT, FOLKS! FOR THE COLOSSALEST SURPRISE OF THE EVENING, THIS BRAINY GENIUS RECEIVES ANOTHER $20,000 FOR HAVING SAID THAT RABBITS HAVE LONG EARS!
$120,000 FOR SHOWING NO MORE BRAINS THAN THAT! AND I HAD TO WORK FOR MY MONEY IN THE MINES OF THE FROZEN KLONDIKE AND IN THE STEAMING SWAMPS OF THE JUNGLES!
I'M SURE LISTENERS WOULD LIKE TO KNOW HOW TO GET ON THIS BIG MONEY PROGRAM! WELL, IT'S EASY! JUST BE AT THIS STATION AT EIGHT O'CLOCK TOMORROW MORNING! FIRST COME, FIRST SERVED!
THAT'S AN ORDER! I'LL SET THIS ALARM CLOCK FOR TEN MINUTES TO EIGHT, SO I'LL BE FIRST THROUGH THE DOOR!
TICK
TICK
AND SO NEXT MORNING!
EVERYBODY IN DUCKBURG MUST BE IN THIS LINE!
HOW DID SO MANY PEOPLE GET HERE SO EARLY?
XYZTV

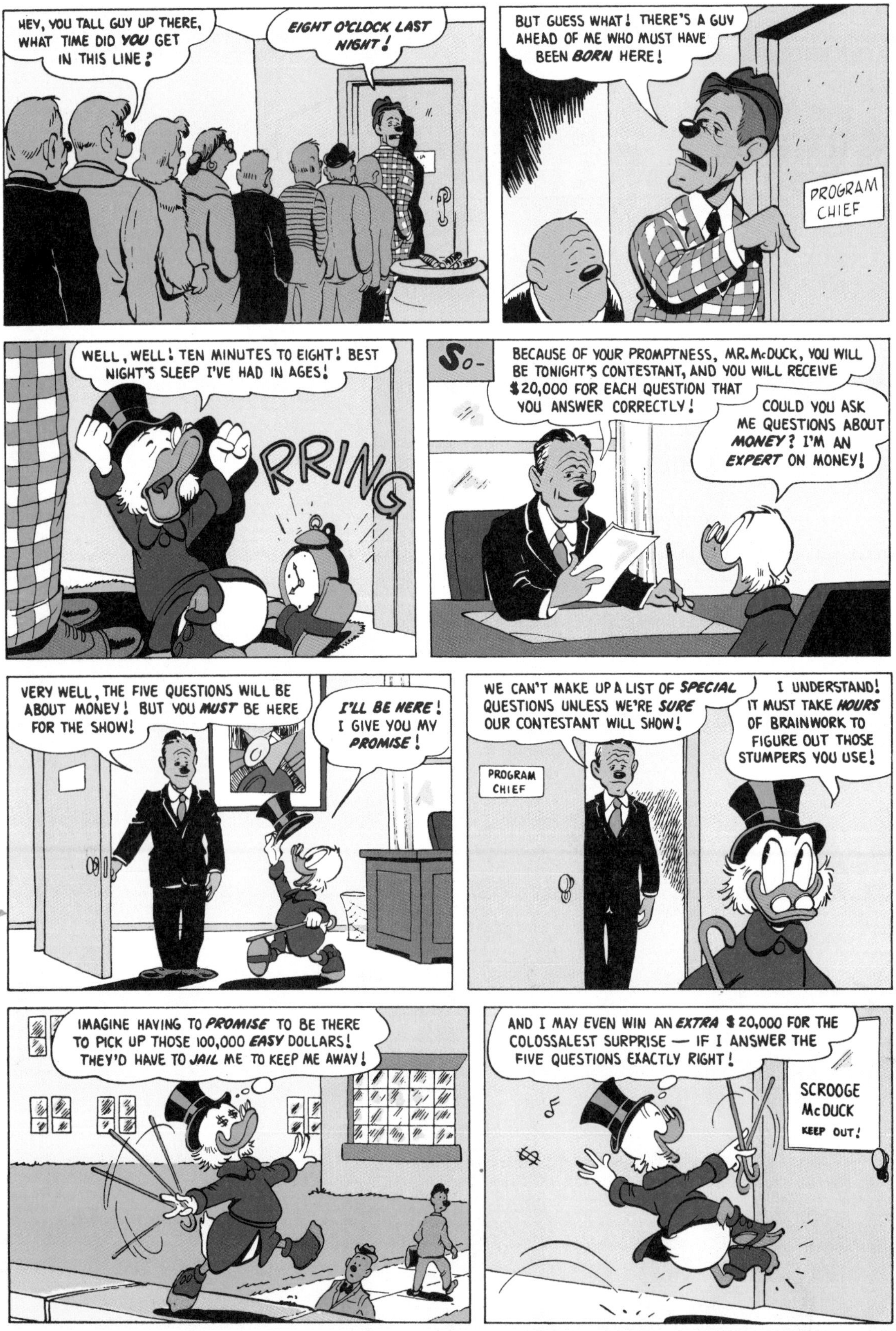
HEY, YOU TALL GUY UP THERE, WHAT TIME DID YOU GET IN THIS LINE?
EIGHT O'CLOCK LAST NIGHT!
BUT GUESS WHAT! THERE'S A GUY AHEAD OF ME WHO MUST HAVE BEEN BORN HERE!
PROGRAM CHIEF
WELL, WELL! TEN MINUTES TO EIGHT! BEST NIGHT'S SLEEP I'VE HAD IN AGES!
RRING
SO-
BECAUSE OF YOUR PROMPTNESS, MR. McDUCK, YOU WILL BE TONIGHT'S CONTESTANT, AND YOU WILL RECEIVE $20,000 FOR EACH QUESTION THAT YOU ANSWER CORRECTLY!
COULD YOU ASK ME QUESTIONS ABOUT MONEY? I'M AN EXPERT ON MONEY!
VERY WELL, THE FIVE QUESTIONS WILL BE ABOUT MONEY! BUT YOU MUST BE HERE FOR THE SHOW!
I'LL BE HERE! I GIVE YOU MY PROMISE!
WE CAN'T MAKE UP A LIST OF SPECIAL QUESTIONS UNLESS WE'RE SURE OUR CONTESTANT WILL SHOW!
I UNDERSTAND! IT MUST TAKE HOURS OF BRAINWORK TO FIGURE OUT THOSE STUMPERS YOU USE!
PROGRAM CHIEF
IMAGINE HAVING TO PROMISE TO BE THERE TO PICK UP THOSE 100,000 EASY DOLLARS! THEY'D HAVE TO JAIL ME TO KEEP ME AWAY!
AND I MAY EVEN WIN AN EXTRA $20,000 FOR THE COLOSSALEST SURPRISE — IF I ANSWER THE FIVE QUESTIONS EXACTLY RIGHT!
SCROOGE McDUCK KEEP OUT!

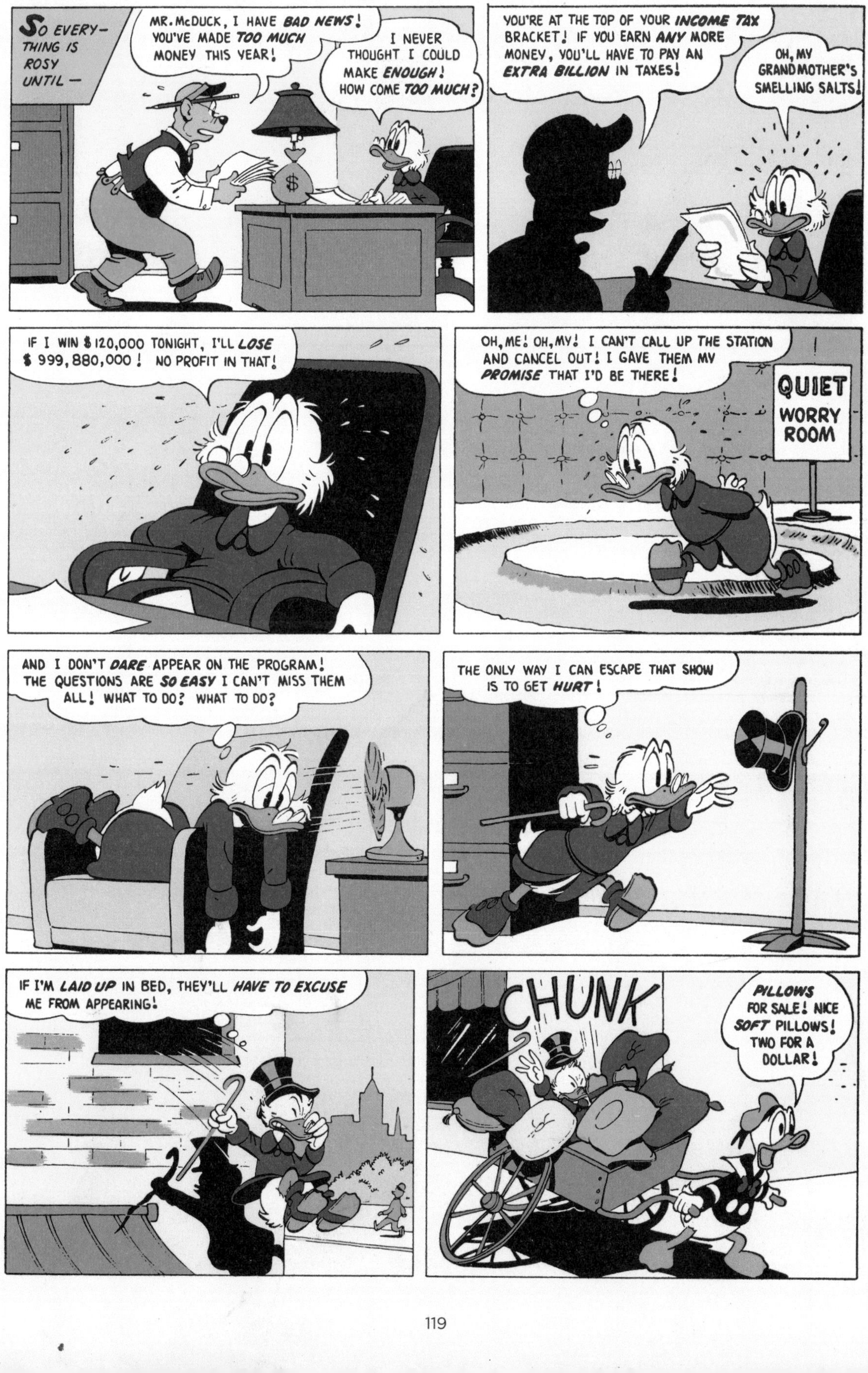
SO EVERY-THING IS ROSY UNTIL —
MR. McDUCK, I HAVE BAD NEWS! YOU'VE MADE TOO MUCH MONEY THIS YEAR!
I NEVER THOUGHT I COULD MAKE ENOUGH! HOW COME TOO MUCH?
YOU'RE AT THE TOP OF YOUR INCOME TAX BRACKET! IF YOU EARN ANY MORE MONEY, YOU'LL HAVE TO PAY AN EXTRA BILLION IN TAXES!
OH, MY GRANDMOTHER'S SMELLING SALTS!
IF I WIN $120,000 TONIGHT, I'LL LOSE $999,880,000! NO PROFIT IN THAT!
OH, ME! OH, MY! I CAN'T CALL UP THE STATION AND CANCEL OUT! I GAVE THEM MY PROMISE THAT I'D BE THERE!
QUIET WORRY ROOM
AND I DON'T DARE APPEAR ON THE PROGRAM! THE QUESTIONS ARE SO EASY I CAN'T MISS THEM ALL! WHAT TO DO? WHAT TO DO?
THE ONLY WAY I CAN ESCAPE THAT SHOW IS TO GET HURT!
IF I'M LAID UP IN BED, THEY'LL HAVE TO EXCUSE ME FROM APPEARING!
CHUNK
PILLOWS FOR SALE! NICE SOFT PILLOWS! TWO FOR A DOLLAR!

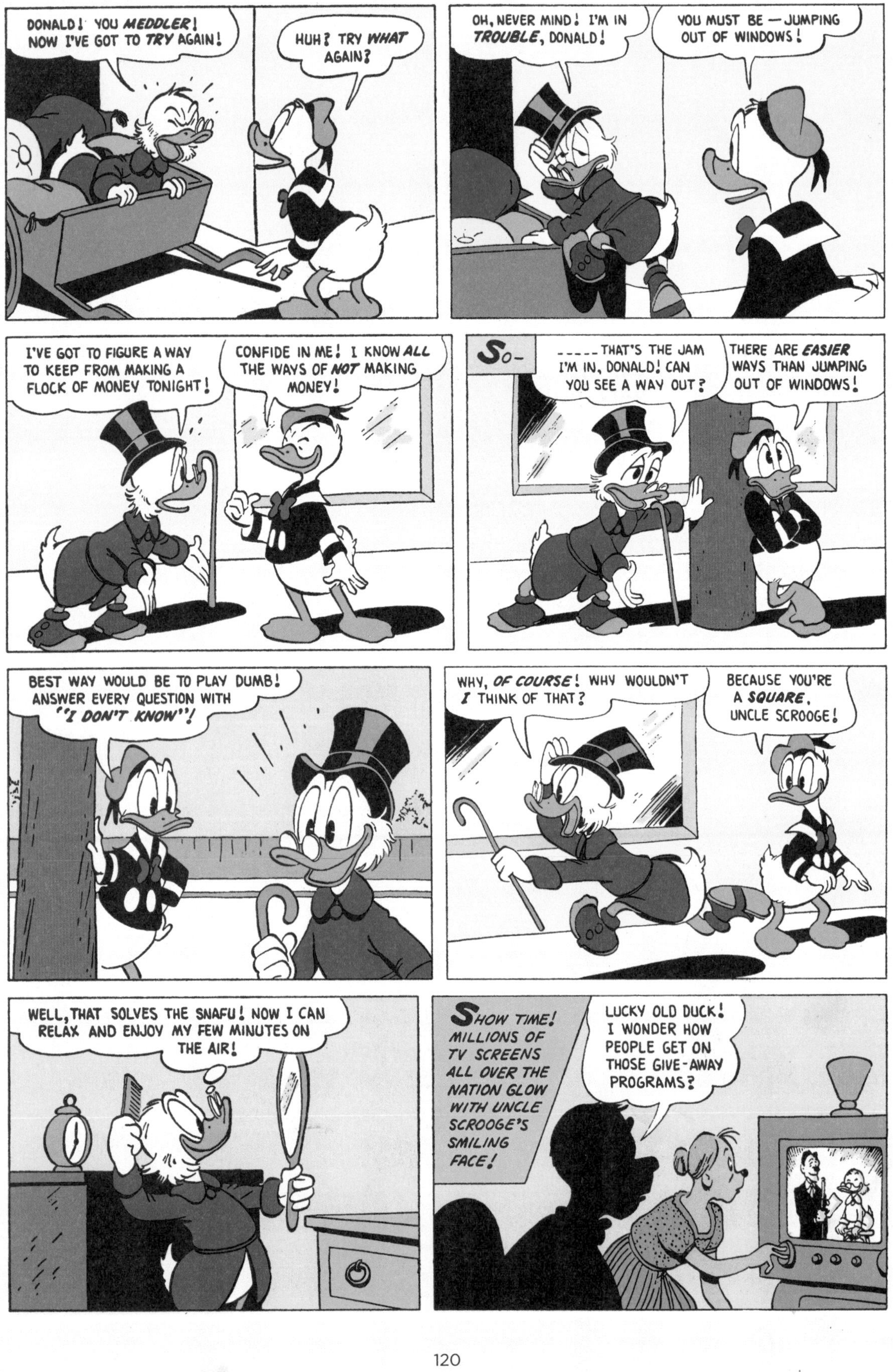
DONALD! YOU MEDDLER! NOW I'VE GOT TO TRY AGAIN!
HUH? TRY WHAT AGAIN?
OH, NEVER MIND! I'M IN TROUBLE, DONALD!
YOU MUST BE — JUMPING OUT OF WINDOWS!
I'VE GOT TO FIGURE A WAY TO KEEP FROM MAKING A FLOCK OF MONEY TONIGHT!
CONFIDE IN ME! I KNOW ALL THE WAYS OF NOT MAKING MONEY!
SO-
-----THAT'S THE JAM I'M IN, DONALD! CAN YOU SEE A WAY OUT?
THERE ARE EASIER WAYS THAN JUMPING OUT OF WINDOWS!
BEST WAY WOULD BE TO PLAY DUMB! ANSWER EVERY QUESTION WITH "I DON'T KNOW"!
WHY, OF COURSE! WHY WOULDN'T I THINK OF THAT?
BECAUSE YOU'RE A SQUARE, UNCLE SCROOGE!
WELL, THAT SOLVES THE SNAFU! NOW I CAN RELAX AND ENJOY MY FEW MINUTES ON THE AIR!
SHOW TIME! MILLIONS OF TV SCREENS ALL OVER THE NATION GLOW WITH UNCLE SCROOGE'S SMILING FACE!
LUCKY OLD DUCK! I WONDER HOW PEOPLE GET ON THOSE GIVE-AWAY PROGRAMS?

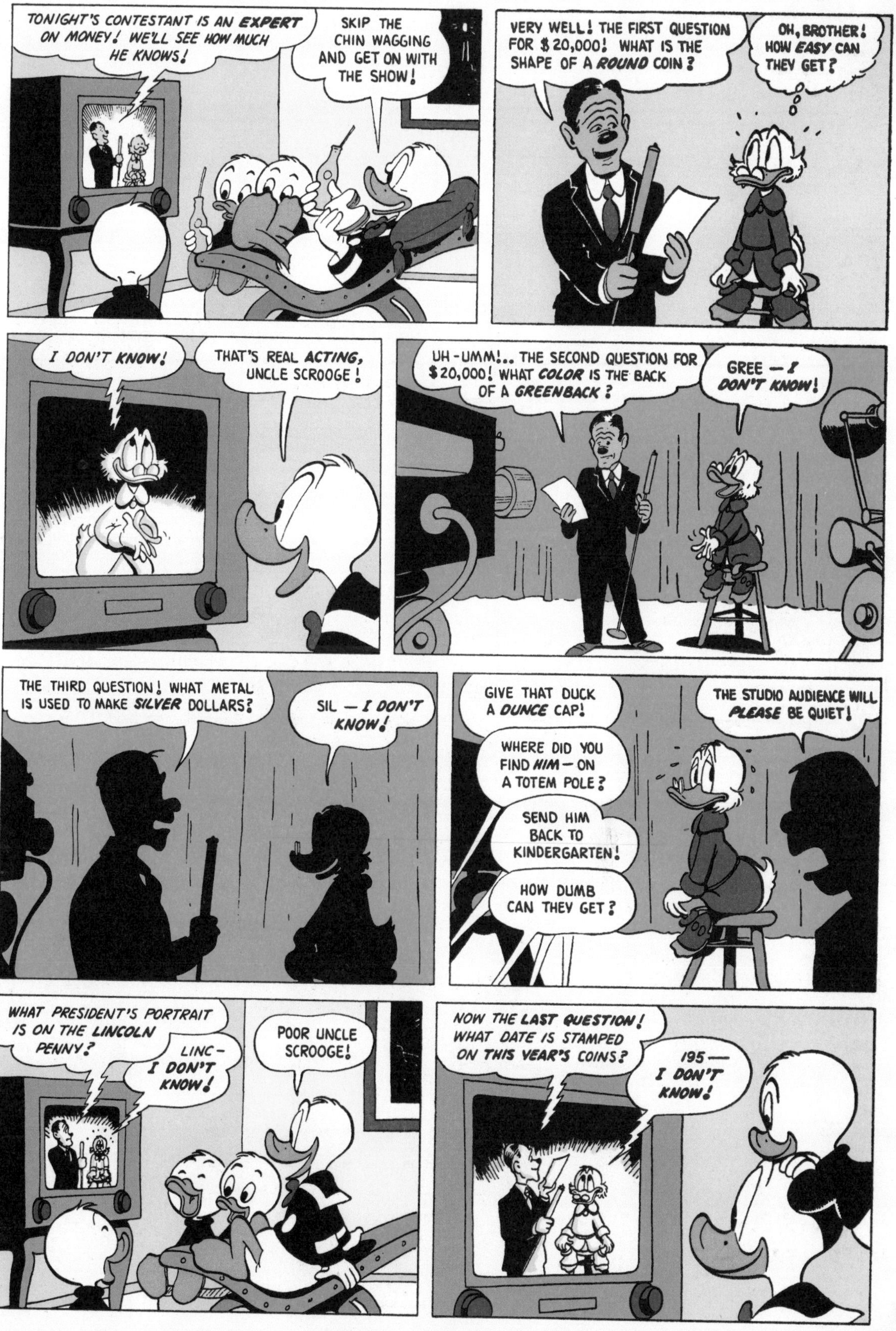

TONIGHT'S CONTESTANT IS AN EXPERT ON MONEY! WE'LL SEE HOW MUCH HE KNOWS!
SKIP THE CHIN WAGGING AND GET ON WITH THE SHOW!
VERY WELL! THE FIRST QUESTION FOR $20,000! WHAT IS THE SHAPE OF A ROUND COIN?
OH, BROTHER! HOW EASY CAN THEY GET?
I DON'T KNOW!
THAT'S REAL ACTING, UNCLE SCROOGE!
UH-UMM!.. THE SECOND QUESTION FOR $20,000! WHAT COLOR IS THE BACK OF A GREENBACK?
GREE — I DON'T KNOW!
THE THIRD QUESTION! WHAT METAL IS USED TO MAKE SILVER DOLLARS?
SIL — I DON'T KNOW!
GIVE THAT DUCK A DUNCE CAP!
THE STUDIO AUDIENCE WILL PLEASE BE QUIET!
WHERE DID YOU FIND HIM — ON A TOTEM POLE?
SEND HIM BACK TO KINDERGARTEN!
HOW DUMB CAN THEY GET?
WHAT PRESIDENT'S PORTRAIT IS ON THE LINCOLN PENNY?
LINC— I DON'T KNOW!
POOR UNCLE SCROOGE!
NOW THE LAST QUESTION! WHAT DATE IS STAMPED ON THIS YEAR'S COINS?
195 — I DON'T KNOW!

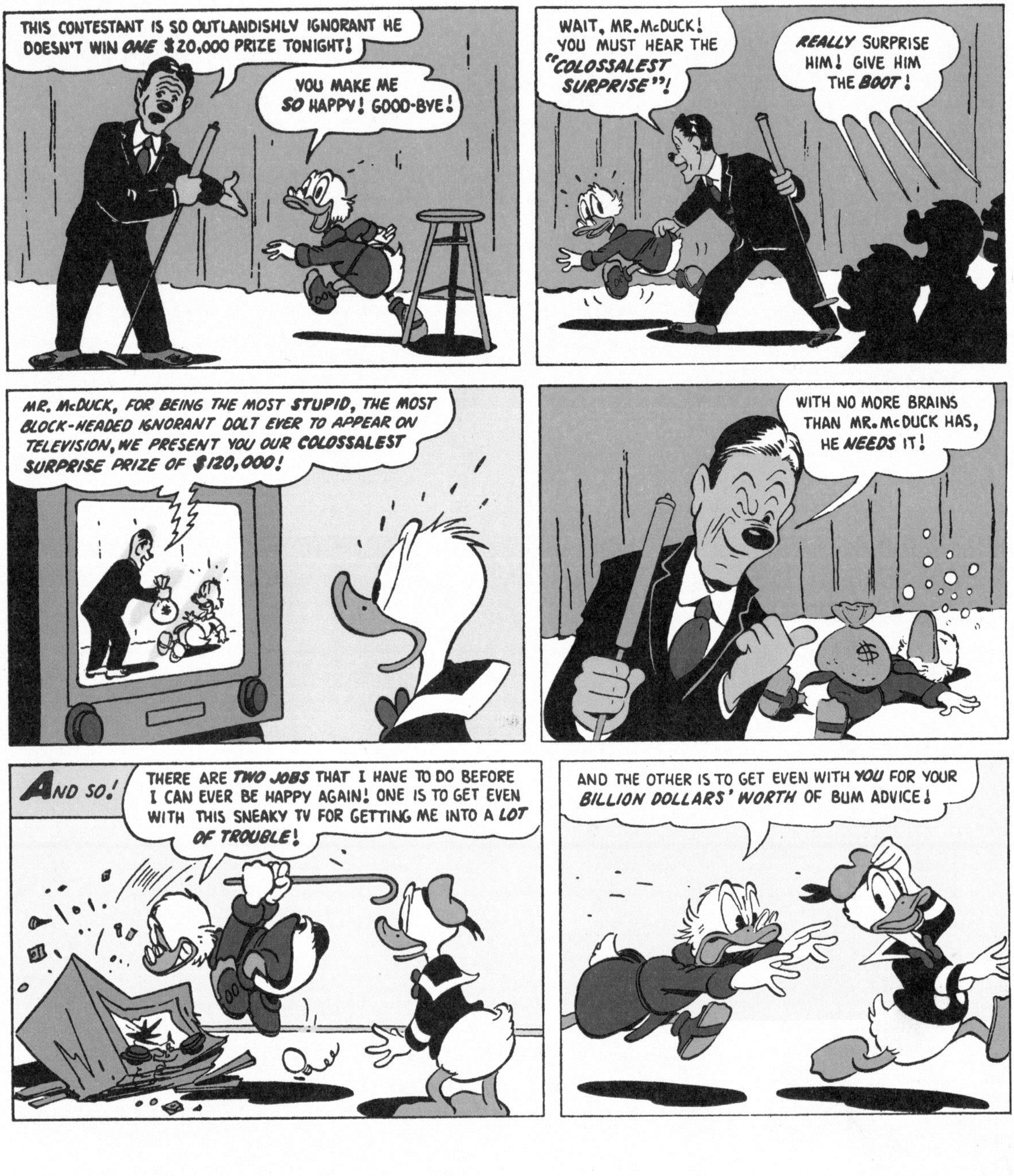

THIS CONTESTANT IS SO OUTLANDISHLY IGNORANT HE DOESN'T WIN ONE $20,000 PRIZE TONIGHT!
YOU MAKE ME SO HAPPY! GOOD-BYE!
WAIT, MR. McDUCK! YOU MUST HEAR THE "COLOSSALEST SURPRISE"!
REALLY SURPRISE HIM! GIVE HIM THE BOOT!
MR. McDUCK, FOR BEING THE MOST STUPID, THE MOST BLOCK-HEADED IGNORANT DOLT EVER TO APPEAR ON TELEVISION, WE PRESENT YOU OUR COLOSSALEST SURPRISE PRIZE OF $120,000!
WITH NO MORE BRAINS THAN MR. McDUCK HAS, HE NEEDS IT!
AND SO!
THERE ARE TWO JOBS THAT I HAVE TO DO BEFORE I CAN EVER BE HAPPY AGAIN! ONE IS TO GET EVEN WITH THIS SNEAKY TV FOR GETTING ME INTO A LOT OF TROUBLE!
AND THE OTHER IS TO GET EVEN WITH YOU FOR YOUR BILLION DOLLARS' WORTH OF BUM ADVICE!

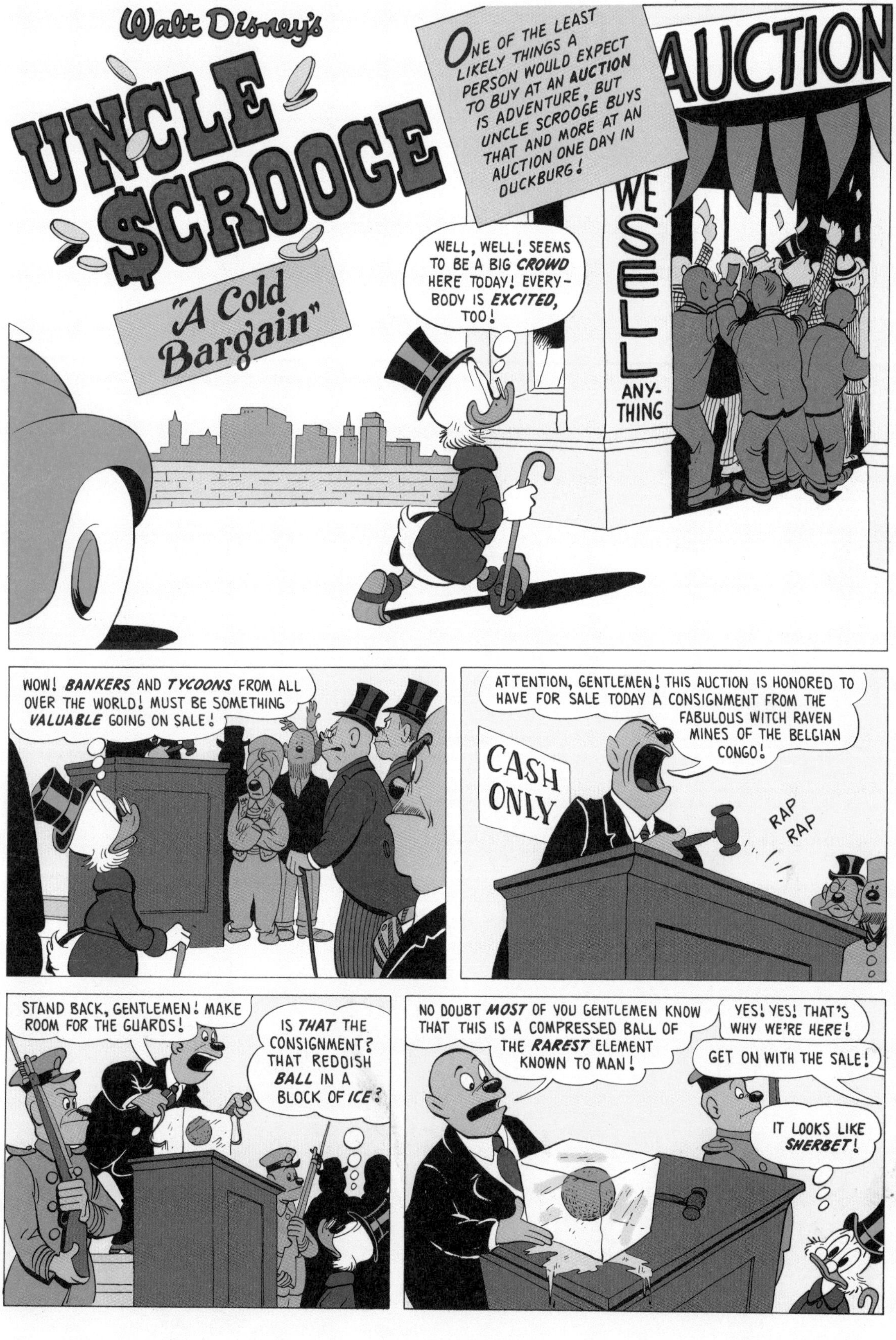
Walt Disney's
UNCLE $CROOGE
"A Cold Bargain"
ONE OF THE LEAST LIKELY THINGS A PERSON WOULD EXPECT TO BUY AT AN AUCTION IS ADVENTURE, BUT UNCLE SCROOGE BUYS THAT AND MORE AT AN AUCTION ONE DAY IN DUCKBURG!
AUCTION
WE SELL ANY-THING
WELL, WELL! SEEMS TO BE A BIG CROWD HERE TODAY! EVERY-BODY IS EXCITED, TOO!
WOW! BANKERS AND TYCOONS FROM ALL OVER THE WORLD! MUST BE SOMETHING VALUABLE GOING ON SALE!
ATTENTION, GENTLEMEN! THIS AUCTION IS HONORED TO HAVE FOR SALE TODAY A CONSIGNMENT FROM THE FABULOUS WITCH RAVEN MINES OF THE BELGIAN CONGO!
CASH ONLY
RAP RAP
STAND BACK, GENTLEMEN! MAKE ROOM FOR THE GUARDS!
IS THAT THE CONSIGNMENT? THAT REDDISH BALL IN A BLOCK OF ICE?
NO DOUBT MOST OF YOU GENTLEMEN KNOW THAT THIS IS A COMPRESSED BALL OF THE RAREST ELEMENT KNOWN TO MAN!
YES! YES! THAT'S WHY WE'RE HERE!
GET ON WITH THE SALE!
IT LOOKS LIKE SHERBET!

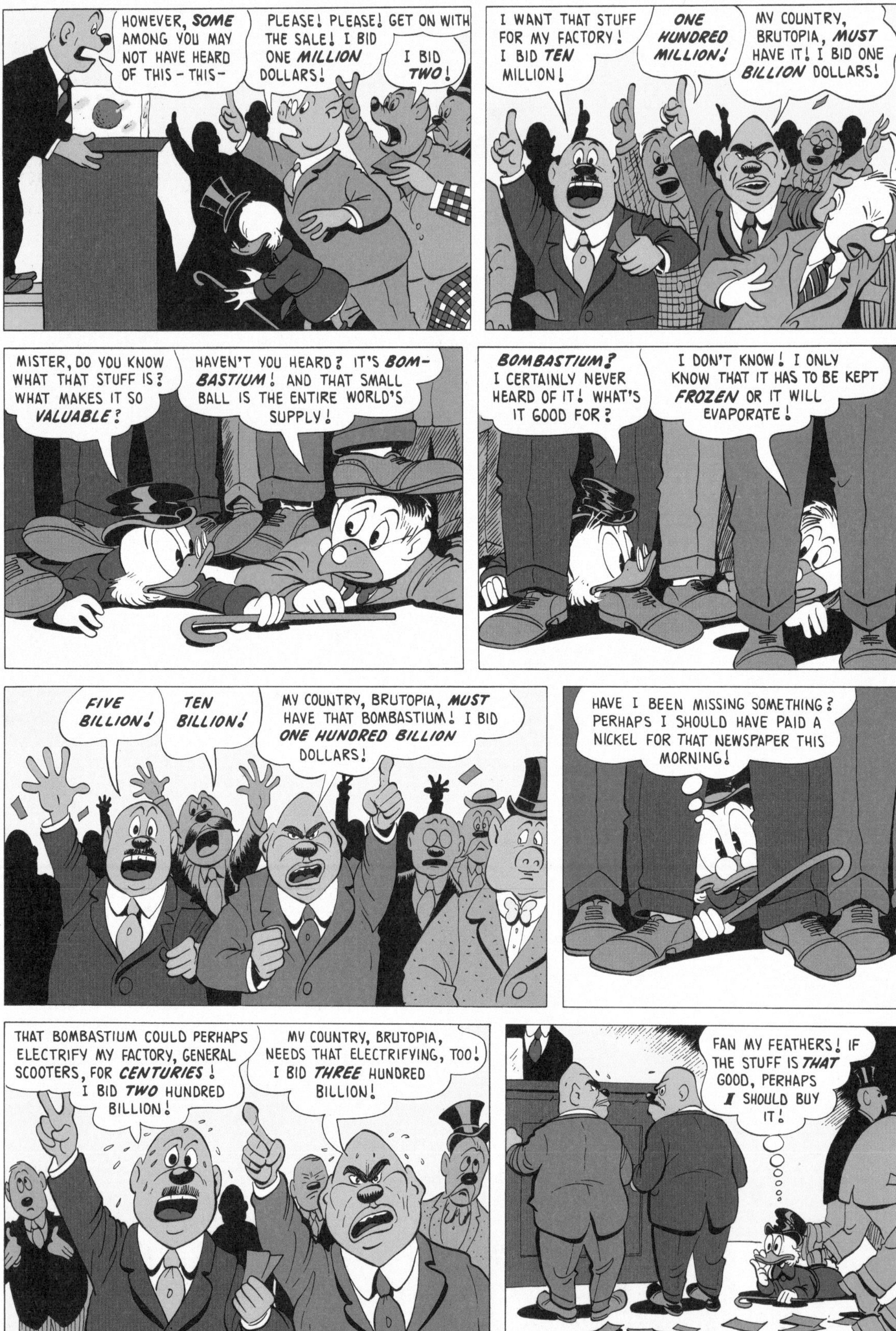
HOWEVER, SOME AMONG YOU MAY NOT HAVE HEARD OF THIS - THIS-
PLEASE! PLEASE! GET ON WITH THE SALE! I BID ONE MILLION DOLLARS!
I BID TWO!
I WANT THAT STUFF FOR MY FACTORY! I BID TEN MILLION!
ONE HUNDRED MILLION!
MY COUNTRY, BRUTOPIA, MUST HAVE IT! I BID ONE BILLION DOLLARS!
MISTER, DO YOU KNOW WHAT THAT STUFF IS? WHAT MAKES IT SO VALUABLE?
HAVEN'T YOU HEARD? IT'S BOMBASTIUM! AND THAT SMALL BALL IS THE ENTIRE WORLD'S SUPPLY!
BOMBASTIUM? I CERTAINLY NEVER HEARD OF IT! WHAT'S IT GOOD FOR?
I DON'T KNOW! I ONLY KNOW THAT IT HAS TO BE KEPT FROZEN OR IT WILL EVAPORATE!
FIVE BILLION!
TEN BILLION!
MY COUNTRY, BRUTOPIA, MUST HAVE THAT BOMBASTIUM! I BID ONE HUNDRED BILLION DOLLARS!
HAVE I BEEN MISSING SOMETHING? PERHAPS I SHOULD HAVE PAID A NICKEL FOR THAT NEWSPAPER THIS MORNING!
THAT BOMBASTIUM COULD PERHAPS ELECTRIFY MY FACTORY, GENERAL SCOOTERS, FOR CENTURIES! I BID TWO HUNDRED BILLION!
MY COUNTRY, BRUTOPIA, NEEDS THAT ELECTRIFYING, TOO! I BID THREE HUNDRED BILLION!
FAN MY FEATHERS! IF THE STUFF IS THAT GOOD, PERHAPS I SHOULD BUY IT!

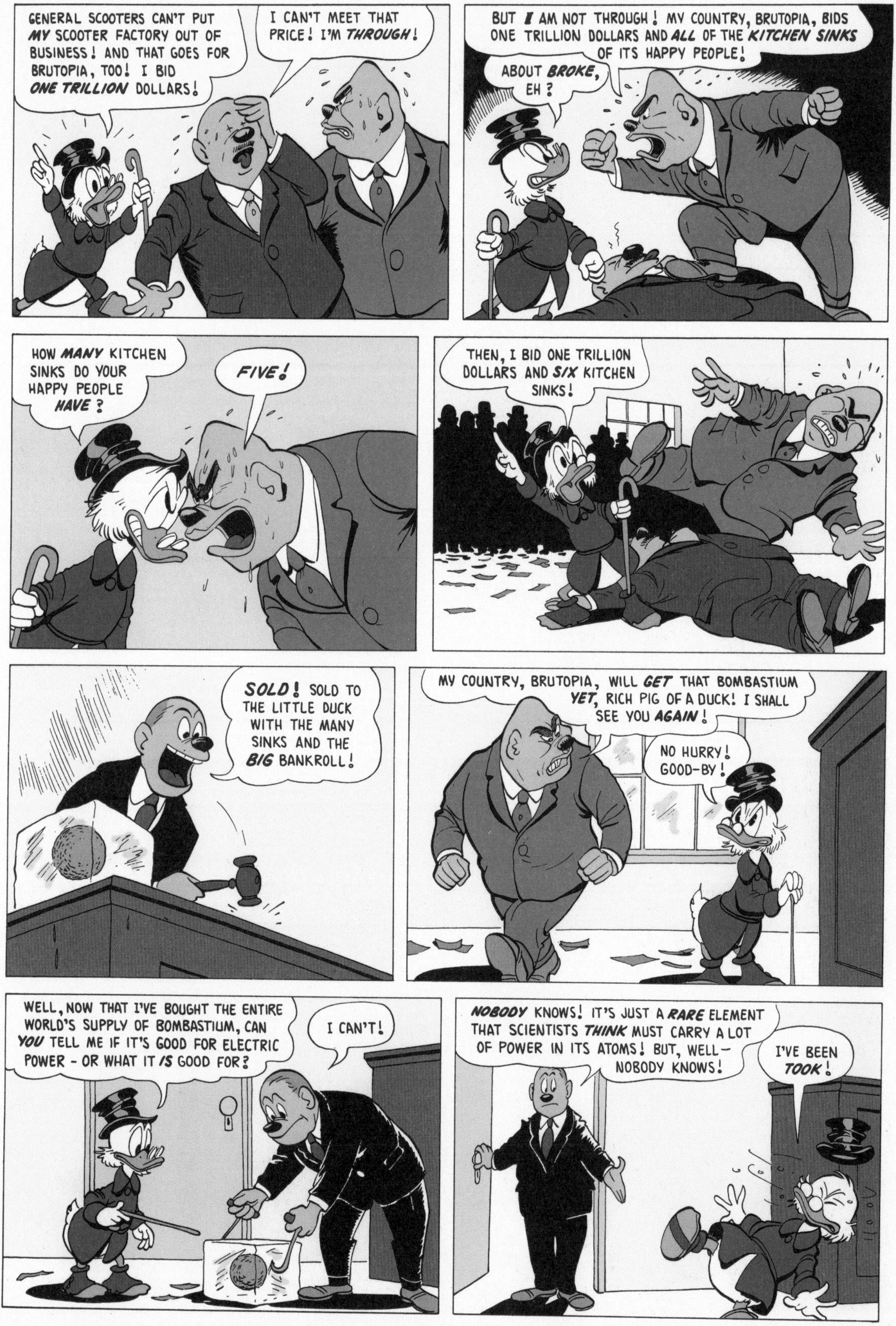
GENERAL SCOOTERS CAN'T PUT MY SCOOTER FACTORY OUT OF BUSINESS! AND THAT GOES FOR BRUTOPIA, TOO! I BID ONE TRILLION DOLLARS!
I CAN'T MEET THAT PRICE! I'M THROUGH!
BUT I AM NOT THROUGH! MY COUNTRY, BRUTOPIA, BIDS ONE TRILLION DOLLARS AND ALL OF THE KITCHEN SINKS OF ITS HAPPY PEOPLE!
ABOUT BROKE, EH?
HOW MANY KITCHEN SINKS DO YOUR HAPPY PEOPLE HAVE?
FIVE!
THEN, I BID ONE TRILLION DOLLARS AND SIX KITCHEN SINKS!
SOLD! SOLD TO THE LITTLE DUCK WITH THE MANY SINKS AND THE BIG BANKROLL!
MY COUNTRY, BRUTOPIA, WILL GET THAT BOMBASTIUM YET, RICH PIG OF A DUCK! I SHALL SEE YOU AGAIN!
NO HURRY! GOOD-BY!
WELL, NOW THAT I'VE BOUGHT THE ENTIRE WORLD'S SUPPLY OF BOMBASTIUM, CAN YOU TELL ME IF IT'S GOOD FOR ELECTRIC POWER - OR WHAT IT IS GOOD FOR?
I CAN'T!
NOBODY KNOWS! IT'S JUST A RARE ELEMENT THAT SCIENTISTS THINK MUST CARRY A LOT OF POWER IN ITS ATOMS! BUT, WELL-NOBODY KNOWS!
I'VE BEEN TOOK!

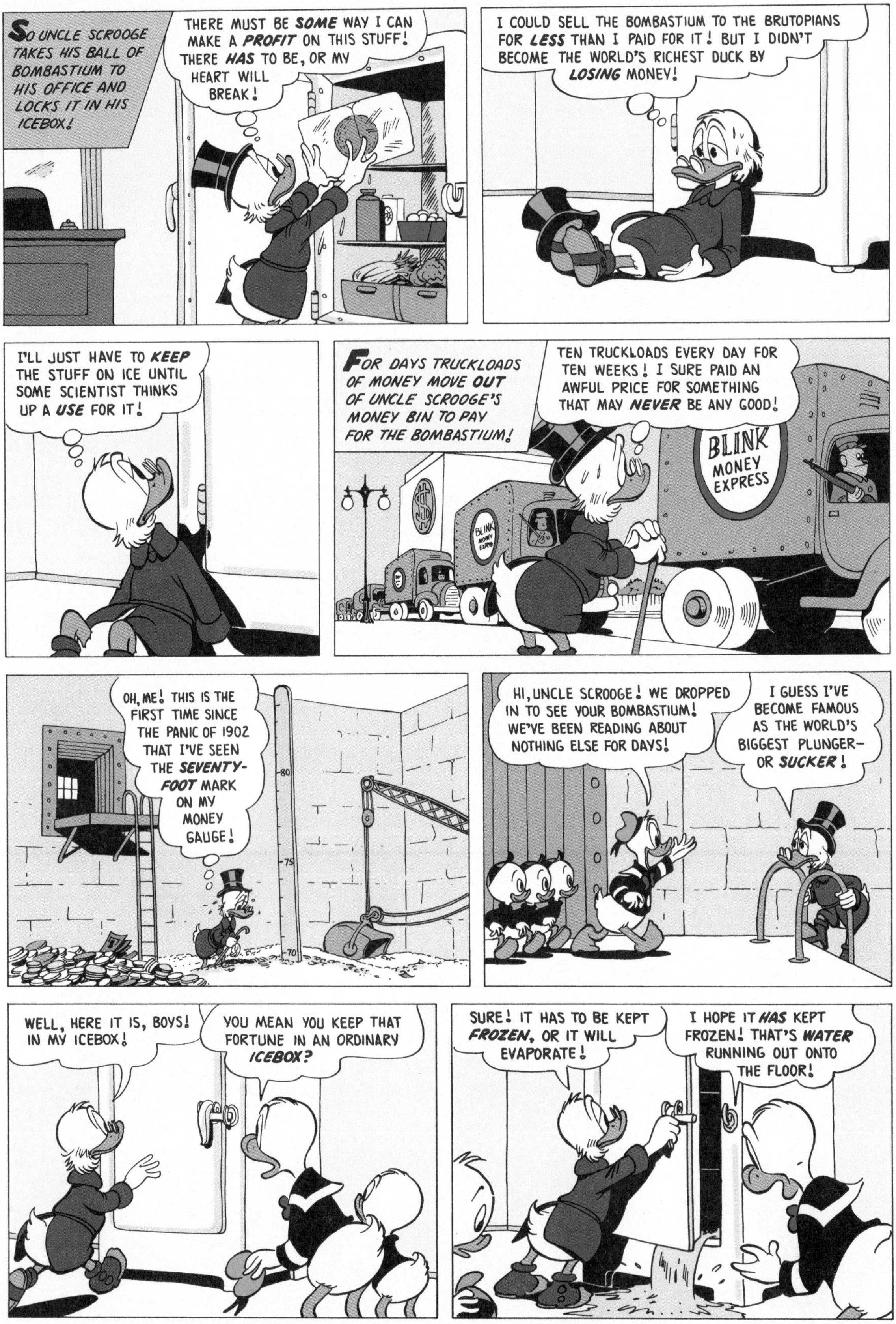

SO UNCLE SCROOGE TAKES HIS BALL OF BOMBASTIUM TO HIS OFFICE AND LOCKS IT IN HIS ICEBOX!
THERE MUST BE SOME WAY I CAN MAKE A PROFIT ON THIS STUFF! THERE HAS TO BE, OR MY HEART WILL BREAK!
I COULD SELL THE BOMBASTIUM TO THE BRUTOPIANS FOR LESS THAN I PAID FOR IT! BUT I DIDN'T BECOME THE WORLD'S RICHEST DUCK BY LOSING MONEY!
I'LL JUST HAVE TO KEEP THE STUFF ON ICE UNTIL SOME SCIENTIST THINKS UP A USE FOR IT!
FOR DAYS TRUCKLOADS OF MONEY MOVE OUT OF UNCLE SCROOGE'S MONEY BIN TO PAY FOR THE BOMBASTIUM!
TEN TRUCKLOADS EVERY DAY FOR TEN WEEKS! I SURE PAID AN AWFUL PRICE FOR SOMETHING THAT MAY NEVER BE ANY GOOD!
BLINK MONEY EXPRESS
OH, ME! THIS IS THE FIRST TIME SINCE THE PANIC OF 1902 THAT I'VE SEEN THE SEVENTY-FOOT MARK ON MY MONEY GAUGE!
80
75
70
HI, UNCLE SCROOGE! WE DROPPED IN TO SEE YOUR BOMBASTIUM! WE'VE BEEN READING ABOUT NOTHING ELSE FOR DAYS!
I GUESS I'VE BECOME FAMOUS AS THE WORLD'S BIGGEST PLUNGER— OR SUCKER!
WELL, HERE IT IS, BOYS! IN MY ICEBOX!
YOU MEAN YOU KEEP THAT FORTUNE IN AN ORDINARY ICEBOX?
SURE! IT HAS TO BE KEPT FROZEN, OR IT WILL EVAPORATE!
I HOPE IT HAS KEPT FROZEN! THAT'S WATER RUNNING OUT ONTO THE FLOOR!

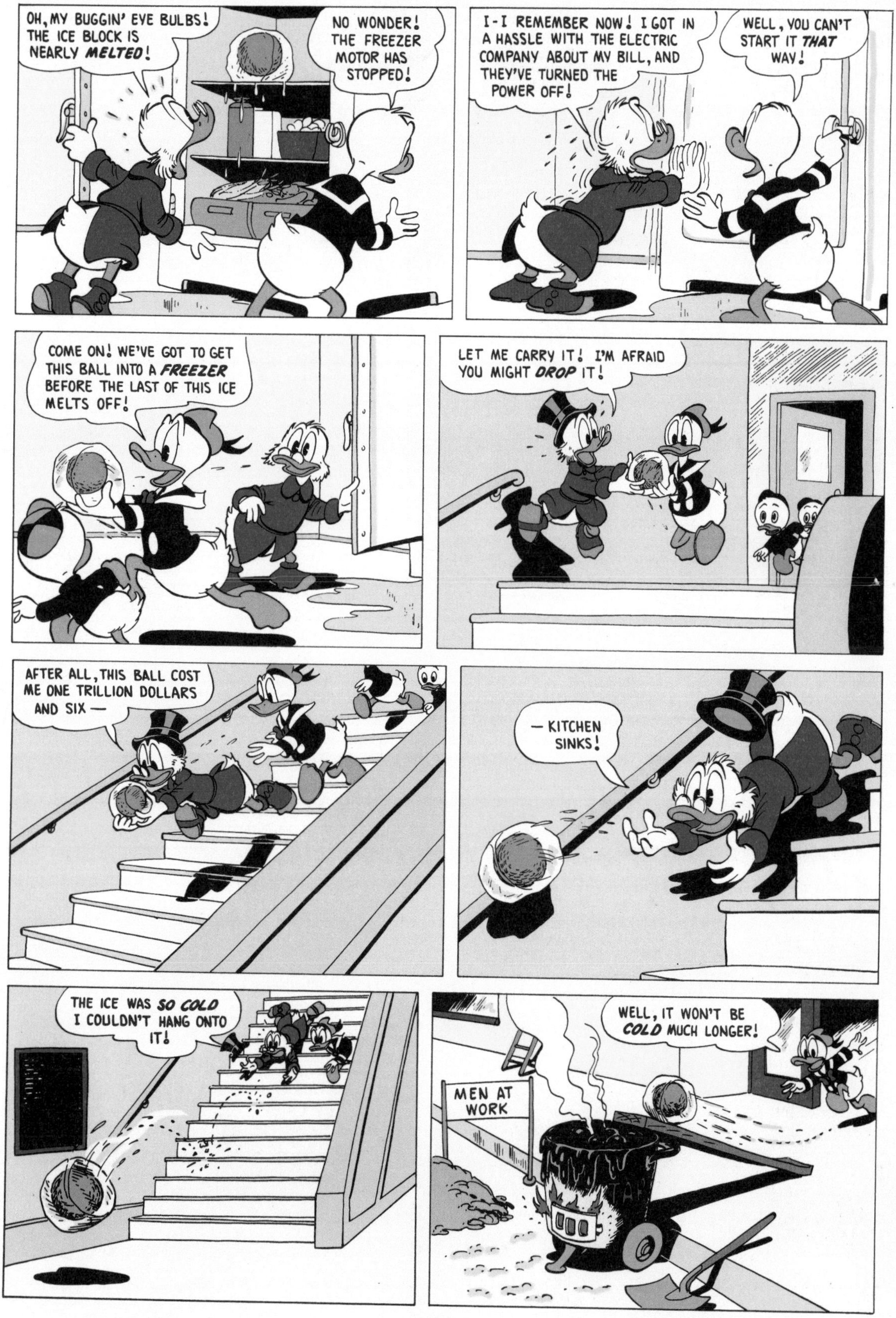
OH, MY BUGGIN' EYE BULBS! THE ICE BLOCK IS NEARLY MELTED!
NO WONDER! THE FREEZER MOTOR HAS STOPPED!
I-I REMEMBER NOW! I GOT IN A HASSLE WITH THE ELECTRIC COMPANY ABOUT MY BILL, AND THEY'VE TURNED THE POWER OFF!
WELL, YOU CAN'T START IT THAT WAY!
COME ON! WE'VE GOT TO GET THIS BALL INTO A FREEZER BEFORE THE LAST OF THIS ICE MELTS OFF!
LET ME CARRY IT! I'M AFRAID YOU MIGHT DROP IT!
AFTER ALL, THIS BALL COST ME ONE TRILLION DOLLARS AND SIX —
— KITCHEN SINKS!
THE ICE WAS SO COLD I COULDN'T HANG ONTO IT!
WELL, IT WON'T BE COLD MUCH LONGER!
MEN AT WORK

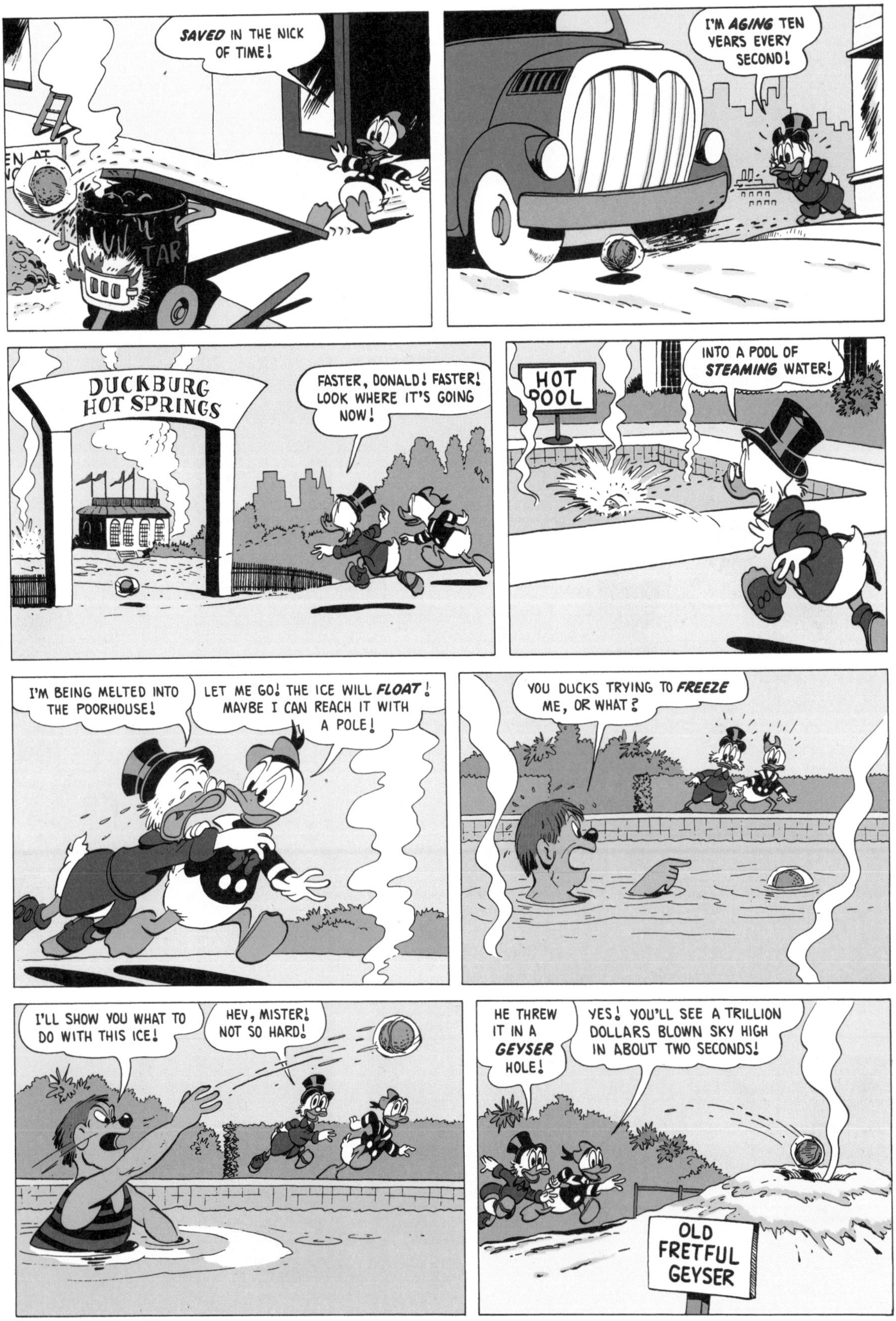
SAVED IN THE NICK OF TIME!
TAR
I'M AGING TEN YEARS EVERY SECOND!
DUCKBURG HOT SPRINGS
FASTER, DONALD! FASTER! LOOK WHERE IT'S GOING NOW!
HOT POOL
INTO A POOL OF STEAMING WATER!
I'M BEING MELTED INTO THE POORHOUSE!
LET ME GO! THE ICE WILL FLOAT! MAYBE I CAN REACH IT WITH A POLE!
YOU DUCKS TRYING TO FREEZE ME, OR WHAT?
I'LL SHOW YOU WHAT TO DO WITH THIS ICE!
HEY, MISTER! NOT SO HARD!
HE THREW IT IN A GEYSER HOLE!
YES! YOU'LL SEE A TRILLION DOLLARS BLOWN SKY HIGH IN ABOUT TWO SECONDS!
OLD FRETFUL GEYSER

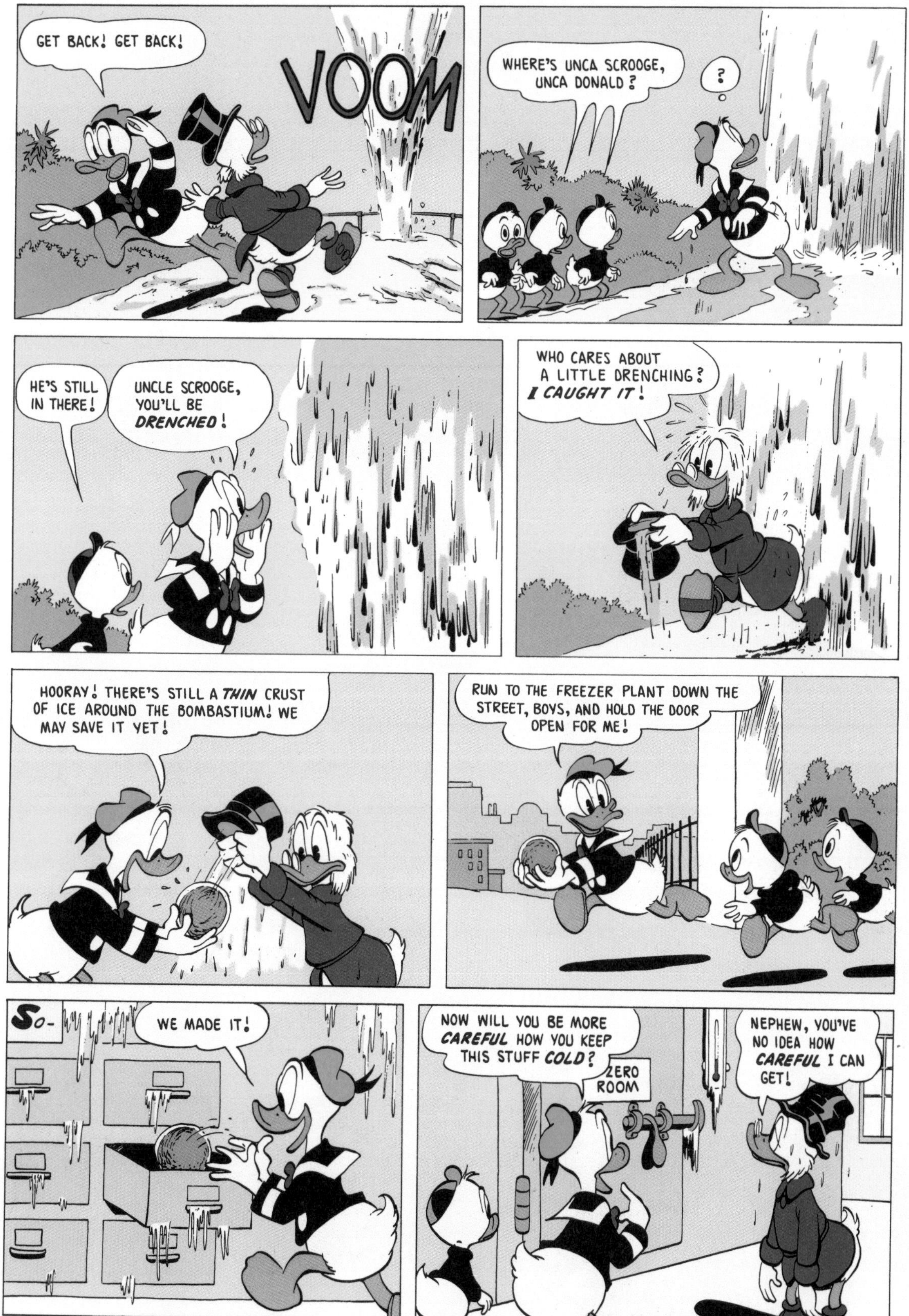
GET BACK! GET BACK!
VOOM
WHERE'S UNCA SCROOGE, UNCA DONALD?
?
HE'S STILL IN THERE!
UNCLE SCROOGE, YOU'LL BE *DRENCHED*!
WHO CARES ABOUT A LITTLE DRENCHING? *I CAUGHT IT*!
HOORAY! THERE'S STILL A *THIN* CRUST OF ICE AROUND THE BOMBASTIUM! WE MAY SAVE IT YET!
RUN TO THE FREEZER PLANT DOWN THE STREET, BOYS, AND HOLD THE DOOR OPEN FOR ME!
SO-
WE MADE IT!
NOW WILL YOU BE MORE *CAREFUL* HOW YOU KEEP THIS STUFF *COLD*?
ZERO ROOM
NEPHEW, YOU'VE NO IDEA HOW *CAREFUL* I CAN GET!

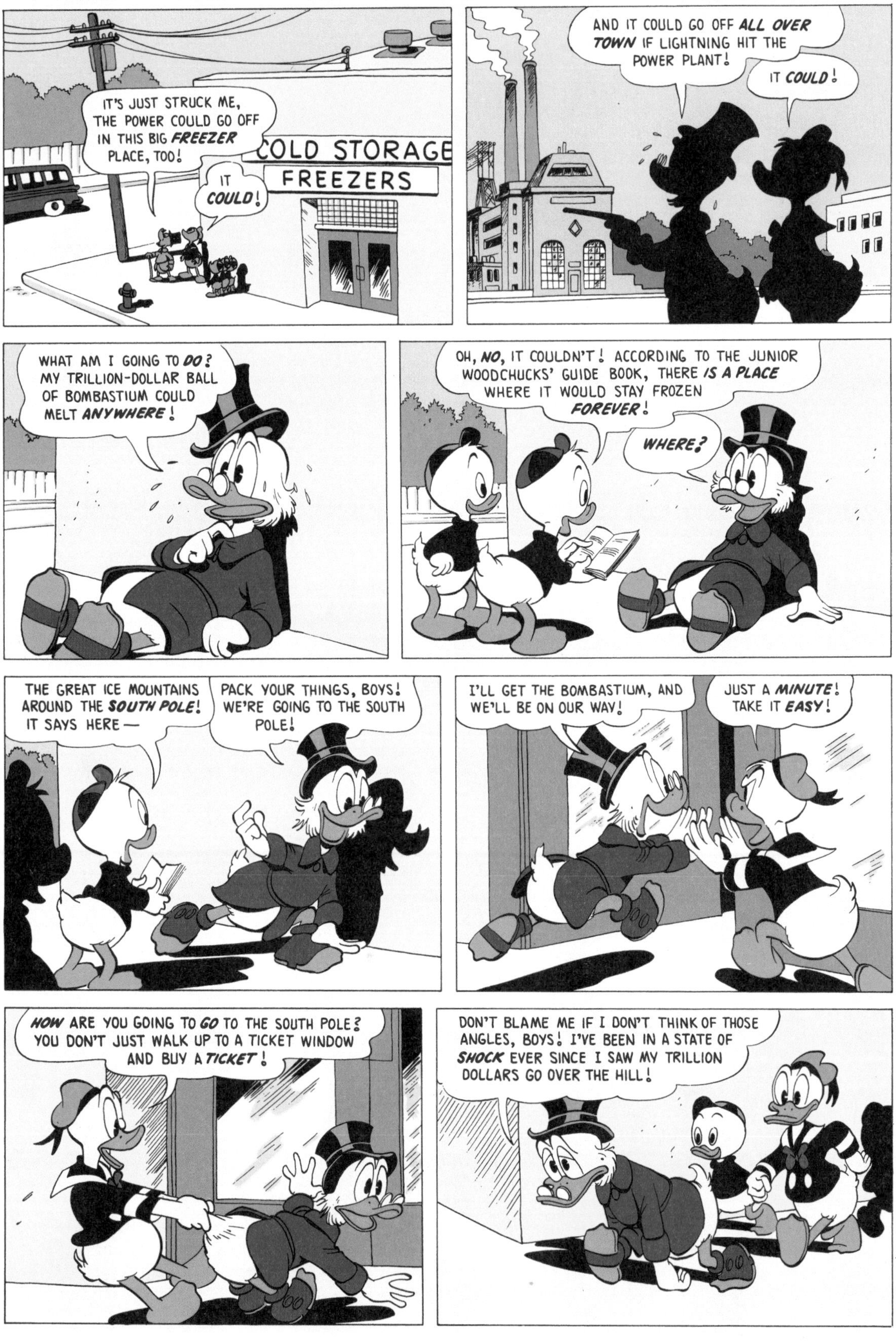

IT'S JUST STRUCK ME, THE POWER COULD GO OFF IN THIS BIG FREEZER PLACE, TOO!
IT COULD!
COLD STORAGE
FREEZERS
AND IT COULD GO OFF ALL OVER TOWN IF LIGHTNING HIT THE POWER PLANT!
IT COULD!
WHAT AM I GOING TO DO? MY TRILLION-DOLLAR BALL OF BOMBASTIUM COULD MELT ANYWHERE!
OH, NO, IT COULDN'T! ACCORDING TO THE JUNIOR WOODCHUCKS' GUIDE BOOK, THERE IS A PLACE WHERE IT WOULD STAY FROZEN FOREVER!
WHERE?
THE GREAT ICE MOUNTAINS AROUND THE SOUTH POLE! IT SAYS HERE—
PACK YOUR THINGS, BOYS! WE'RE GOING TO THE SOUTH POLE!
I'LL GET THE BOMBASTIUM, AND WE'LL BE ON OUR WAY!
JUST A MINUTE! TAKE IT EASY!
HOW ARE YOU GOING TO GO TO THE SOUTH POLE? YOU DON'T JUST WALK UP TO A TICKET WINDOW AND BUY A TICKET!
DON'T BLAME ME IF I DON'T THINK OF THOSE ANGLES, BOYS! I'VE BEEN IN A STATE OF SHOCK EVER SINCE I SAW MY TRILLION DOLLARS GO OVER THE HILL!

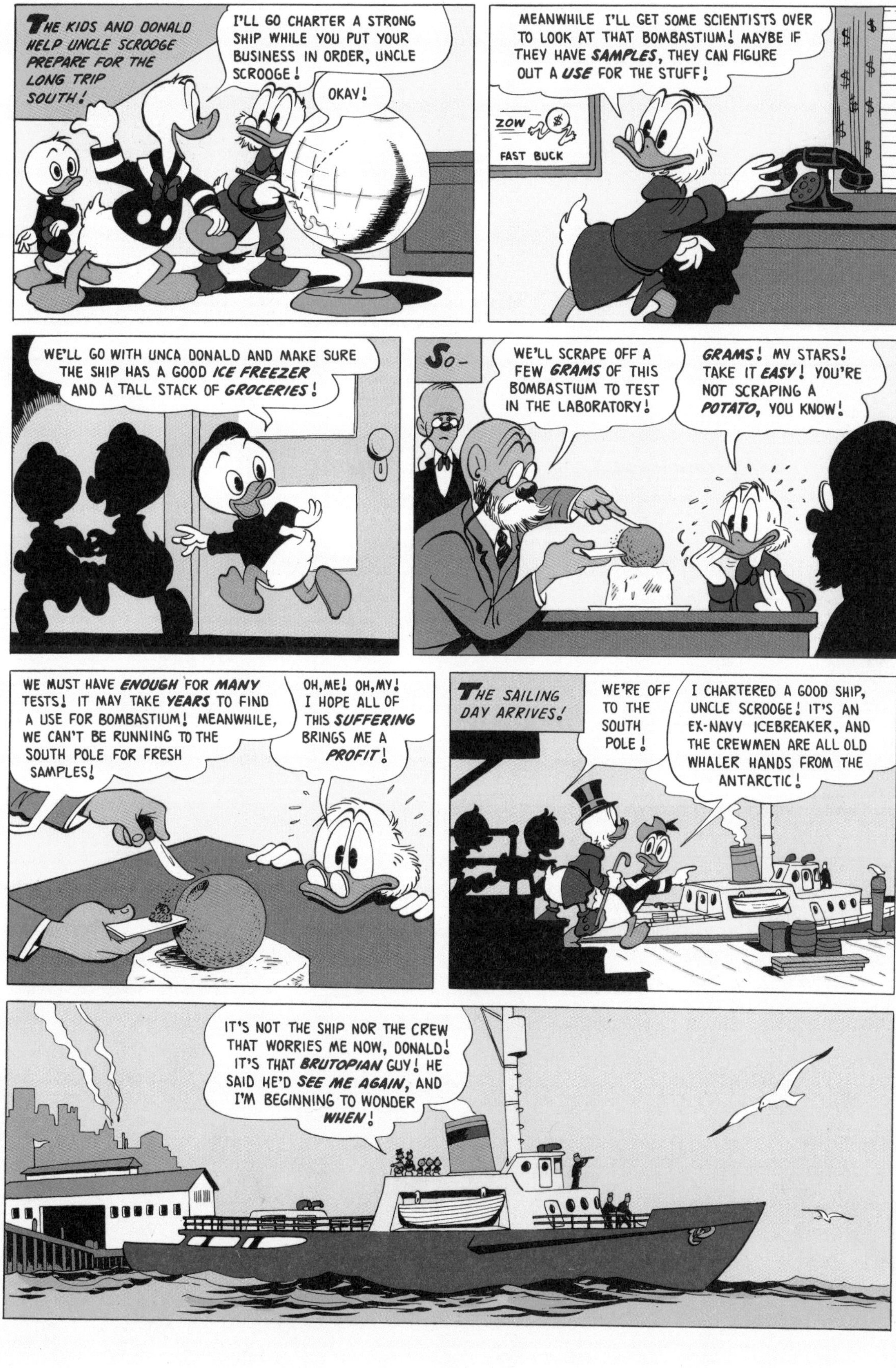
THE KIDS AND DONALD HELP UNCLE SCROOGE PREPARE FOR THE LONG TRIP SOUTH!
I'LL GO CHARTER A STRONG SHIP WHILE YOU PUT YOUR BUSINESS IN ORDER, UNCLE SCROOGE!
OKAY!
MEANWHILE I'LL GET SOME SCIENTISTS OVER TO LOOK AT THAT BOMBASTIUM! MAYBE IF THEY HAVE SAMPLES, THEY CAN FIGURE OUT A USE FOR THE STUFF!
ZOW
FAST BUCK
WE'LL GO WITH UNCA DONALD AND MAKE SURE THE SHIP HAS A GOOD ICE FREEZER AND A TALL STACK OF GROCERIES!
SO-
WE'LL SCRAPE OFF A FEW GRAMS OF THIS BOMBASTIUM TO TEST IN THE LABORATORY!
GRAMS! MY STARS! TAKE IT EASY! YOU'RE NOT SCRAPING A POTATO, YOU KNOW!
WE MUST HAVE ENOUGH FOR MANY TESTS! IT MAY TAKE YEARS TO FIND A USE FOR BOMBASTIUM! MEANWHILE, WE CAN'T BE RUNNING TO THE SOUTH POLE FOR FRESH SAMPLES!
OH, ME! OH, MY! I HOPE ALL OF THIS SUFFERING BRINGS ME A PROFIT!
THE SAILING DAY ARRIVES!
WE'RE OFF TO THE SOUTH POLE!
I CHARTERED A GOOD SHIP, UNCLE SCROOGE! IT'S AN EX-NAVY ICEBREAKER, AND THE CREWMEN ARE ALL OLD WHALER HANDS FROM THE ANTARCTIC!
IT'S NOT THE SHIP NOR THE CREW THAT WORRIES ME NOW, DONALD! IT'S THAT BRUTOPIAN GUY! HE SAID HE'D SEE ME AGAIN, AND I'M BEGINNING TO WONDER WHEN!

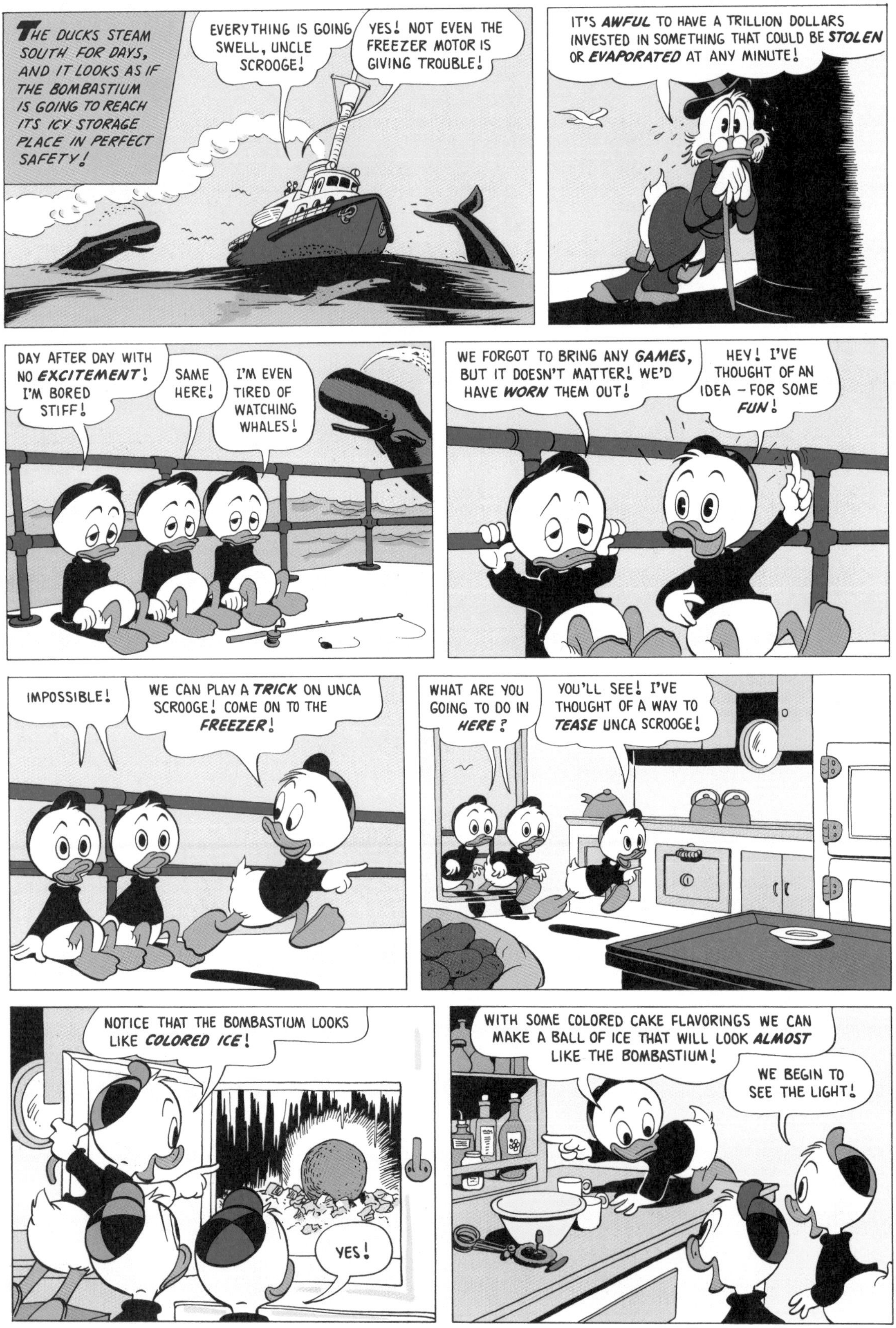
THE DUCKS STEAM SOUTH FOR DAYS, AND IT LOOKS AS IF THE BOMBASTIUM IS GOING TO REACH ITS ICY STORAGE PLACE IN PERFECT SAFETY!
EVERYTHING IS GOING SWELL, UNCLE SCROOGE!
YES! NOT EVEN THE FREEZER MOTOR IS GIVING TROUBLE!
IT'S AWFUL TO HAVE A TRILLION DOLLARS INVESTED IN SOMETHING THAT COULD BE STOLEN OR EVAPORATED AT ANY MINUTE!
DAY AFTER DAY WITH NO EXCITEMENT! I'M BORED STIFF!
SAME HERE!
I'M EVEN TIRED OF WATCHING WHALES!
WE FORGOT TO BRING ANY GAMES, BUT IT DOESN'T MATTER! WE'D HAVE WORN THEM OUT!
HEY! I'VE THOUGHT OF AN IDEA – FOR SOME FUN!
IMPOSSIBLE!
WE CAN PLAY A TRICK ON UNCA SCROOGE! COME ON TO THE FREEZER!
WHAT ARE YOU GOING TO DO IN HERE?
YOU'LL SEE! I'VE THOUGHT OF A WAY TO TEASE UNCA SCROOGE!
NOTICE THAT THE BOMBASTIUM LOOKS LIKE COLORED ICE!
YES!
WITH SOME COLORED CAKE FLAVORINGS WE CAN MAKE A BALL OF ICE THAT WILL LOOK ALMOST LIKE THE BOMBASTIUM!
WE BEGIN TO SEE THE LIGHT!

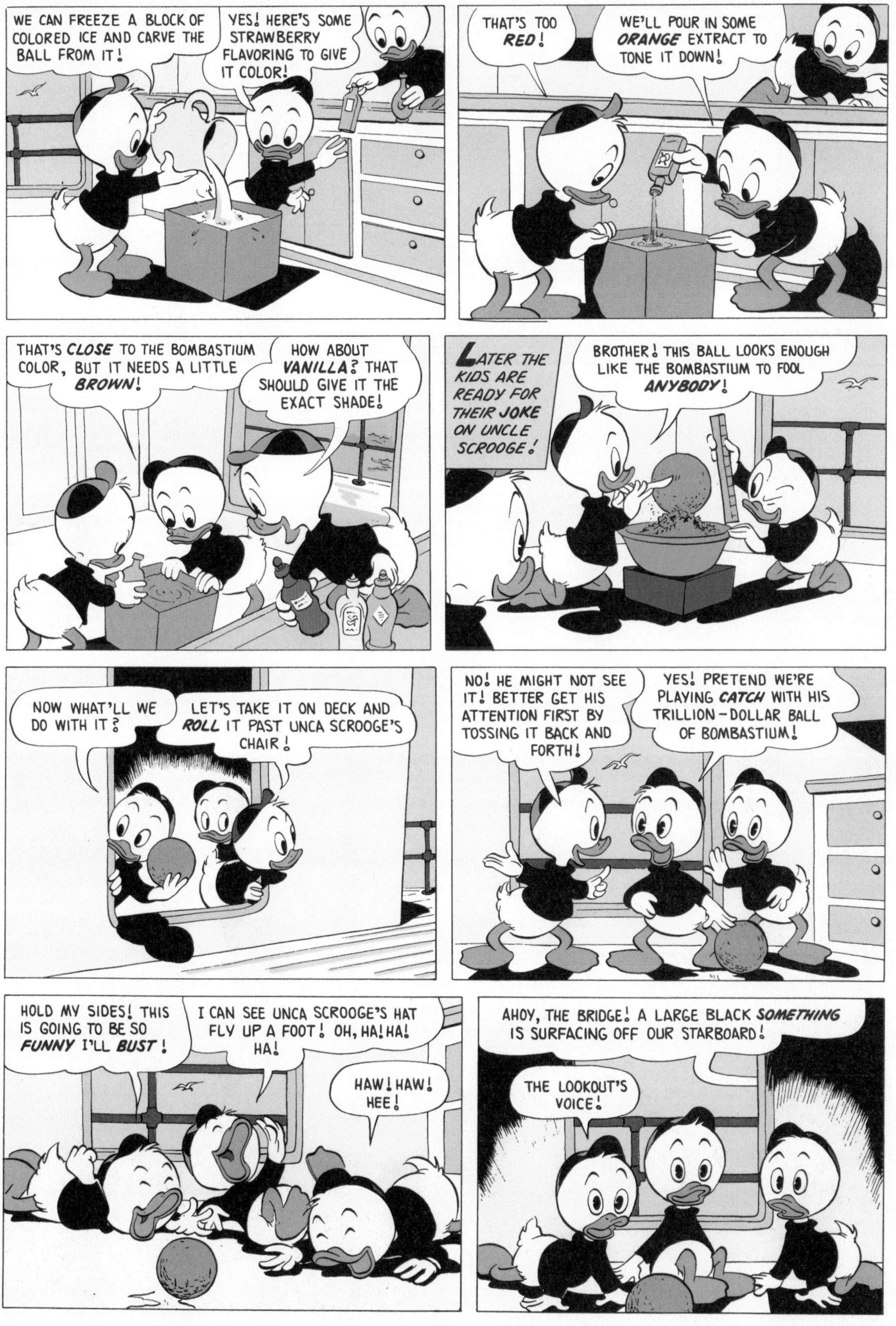
WE CAN FREEZE A BLOCK OF COLORED ICE AND CARVE THE BALL FROM IT!
YES! HERE'S SOME STRAWBERRY FLAVORING TO GIVE IT COLOR!
THAT'S TOO RED!
WE'LL POUR IN SOME ORANGE EXTRACT TO TONE IT DOWN!
THAT'S CLOSE TO THE BOMBASTIUM COLOR, BUT IT NEEDS A LITTLE BROWN!
HOW ABOUT VANILLA? THAT SHOULD GIVE IT THE EXACT SHADE!
LATER THE KIDS ARE READY FOR THEIR JOKE ON UNCLE SCROOGE!
BROTHER! THIS BALL LOOKS ENOUGH LIKE THE BOMBASTIUM TO FOOL ANYBODY!
NOW WHAT'LL WE DO WITH IT?
LET'S TAKE IT ON DECK AND ROLL IT PAST UNCA SCROOGE'S CHAIR!
NO! HE MIGHT NOT SEE IT! BETTER GET HIS ATTENTION FIRST BY TOSSING IT BACK AND FORTH!
YES! PRETEND WE'RE PLAYING CATCH WITH HIS TRILLION-DOLLAR BALL OF BOMBASTIUM!
HOLD MY SIDES! THIS IS GOING TO BE SO FUNNY I'LL BUST!
I CAN SEE UNCA SCROOGE'S HAT FLY UP A FOOT! OH, HA! HA! HA!
HAW! HAW! HEE!
AHOY, THE BRIDGE! A LARGE BLACK SOMETHING IS SURFACING OFF OUR STARBOARD!
THE LOOKOUT'S VOICE!

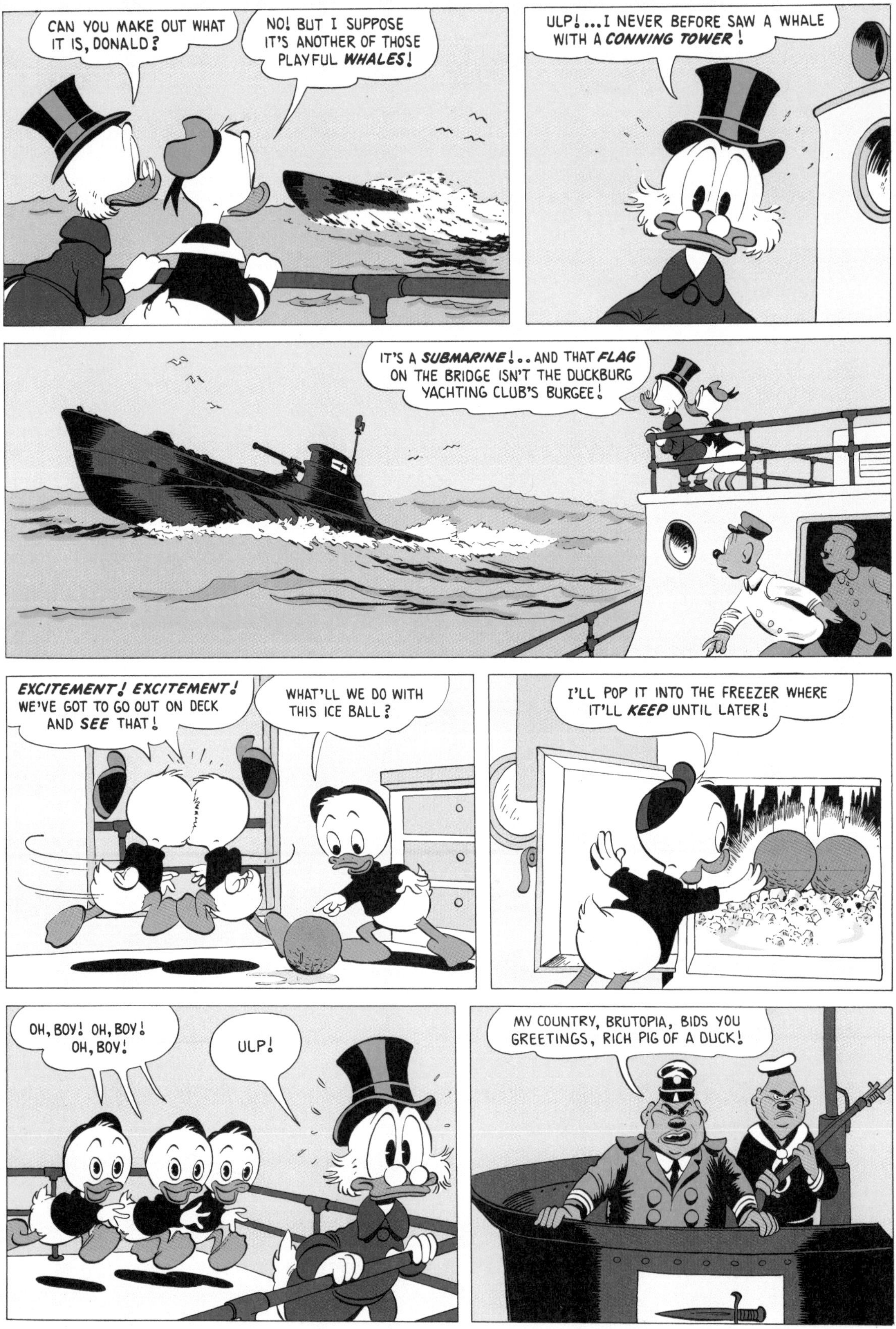
CAN YOU MAKE OUT WHAT IT IS, DONALD?
NO! BUT I SUPPOSE IT'S ANOTHER OF THOSE PLAYFUL WHALES!
ULP! ...I NEVER BEFORE SAW A WHALE WITH A CONNING TOWER!
IT'S A SUBMARINE! .. AND THAT FLAG ON THE BRIDGE ISN'T THE DUCKBURG YACHTING CLUB'S BURGEE!
EXCITEMENT! EXCITEMENT! WE'VE GOT TO GO OUT ON DECK AND SEE THAT!
WHAT'LL WE DO WITH THIS ICE BALL?
I'LL POP IT INTO THE FREEZER WHERE IT'LL KEEP UNTIL LATER!
OH, BOY! OH, BOY! OH, BOY!
ULP!
MY COUNTRY, BRUTOPIA, BIDS YOU GREETINGS, RICH PIG OF A DUCK!

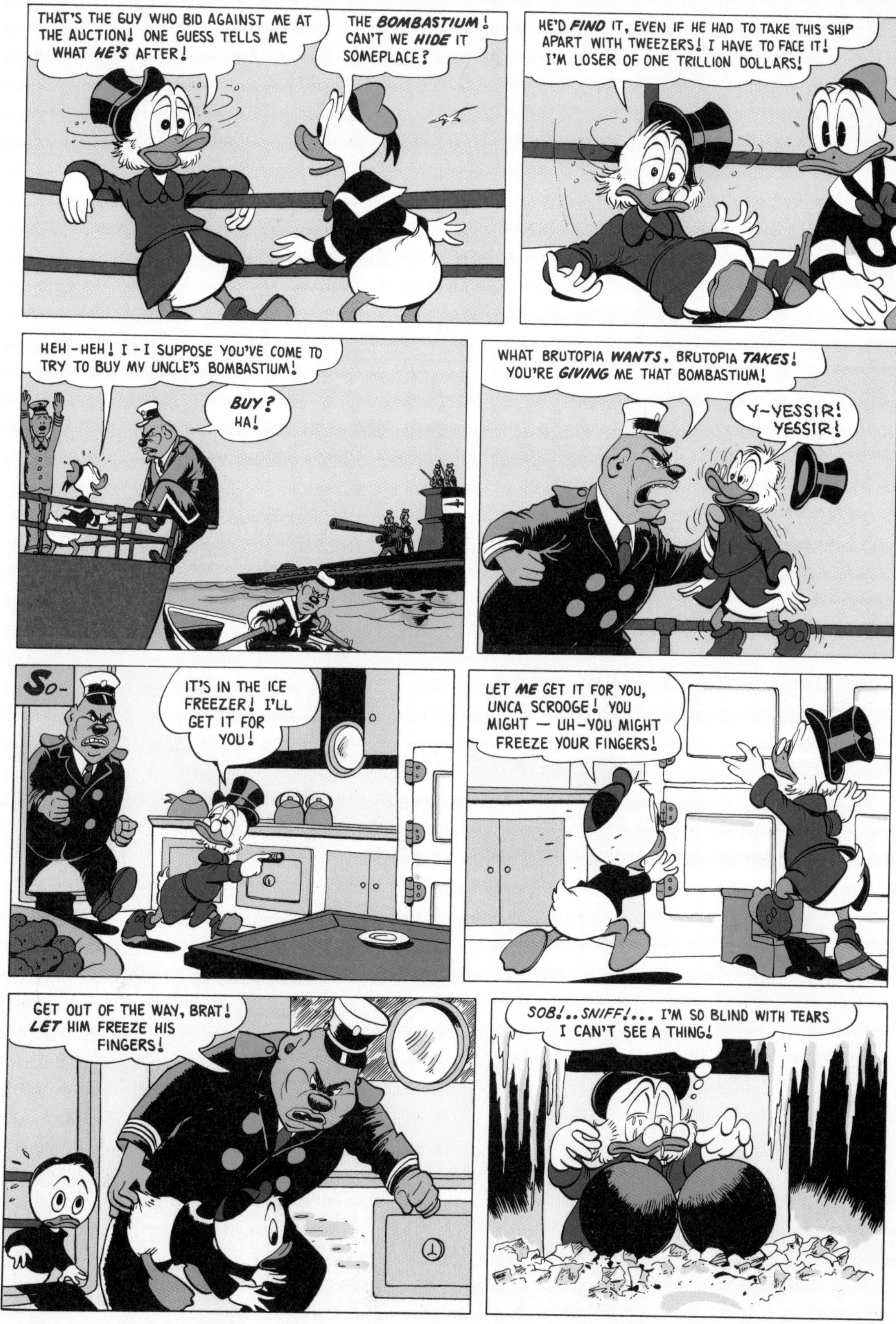
THAT'S THE GUY WHO BID AGAINST ME AT THE AUCTION! ONE GUESS TELLS ME WHAT HE'S AFTER!
THE BOMBASTIUM! CAN'T WE HIDE IT SOMEPLACE?
HE'D FIND IT, EVEN IF HE HAD TO TAKE THIS SHIP APART WITH TWEEZERS! I HAVE TO FACE IT! I'M LOSER OF ONE TRILLION DOLLARS!
HEH-HEH! I-I SUPPOSE YOU'VE COME TO TRY TO BUY MY UNCLE'S BOMBASTIUM!
BUY? HA!
WHAT BRUTOPIA WANTS, BRUTOPIA TAKES! YOU'RE GIVING ME THAT BOMBASTIUM!
Y-YESSIR! YESSIR!
SO-
IT'S IN THE ICE FREEZER! I'LL GET IT FOR YOU!
LET ME GET IT FOR YOU, UNCA SCROOGE! YOU MIGHT — UH-YOU MIGHT FREEZE YOUR FINGERS!
GET OUT OF THE WAY, BRAT! LET HIM FREEZE HIS FINGERS!
SOB!..SNIFF!... I'M SO BLIND WITH TEARS I CAN'T SEE A THING!

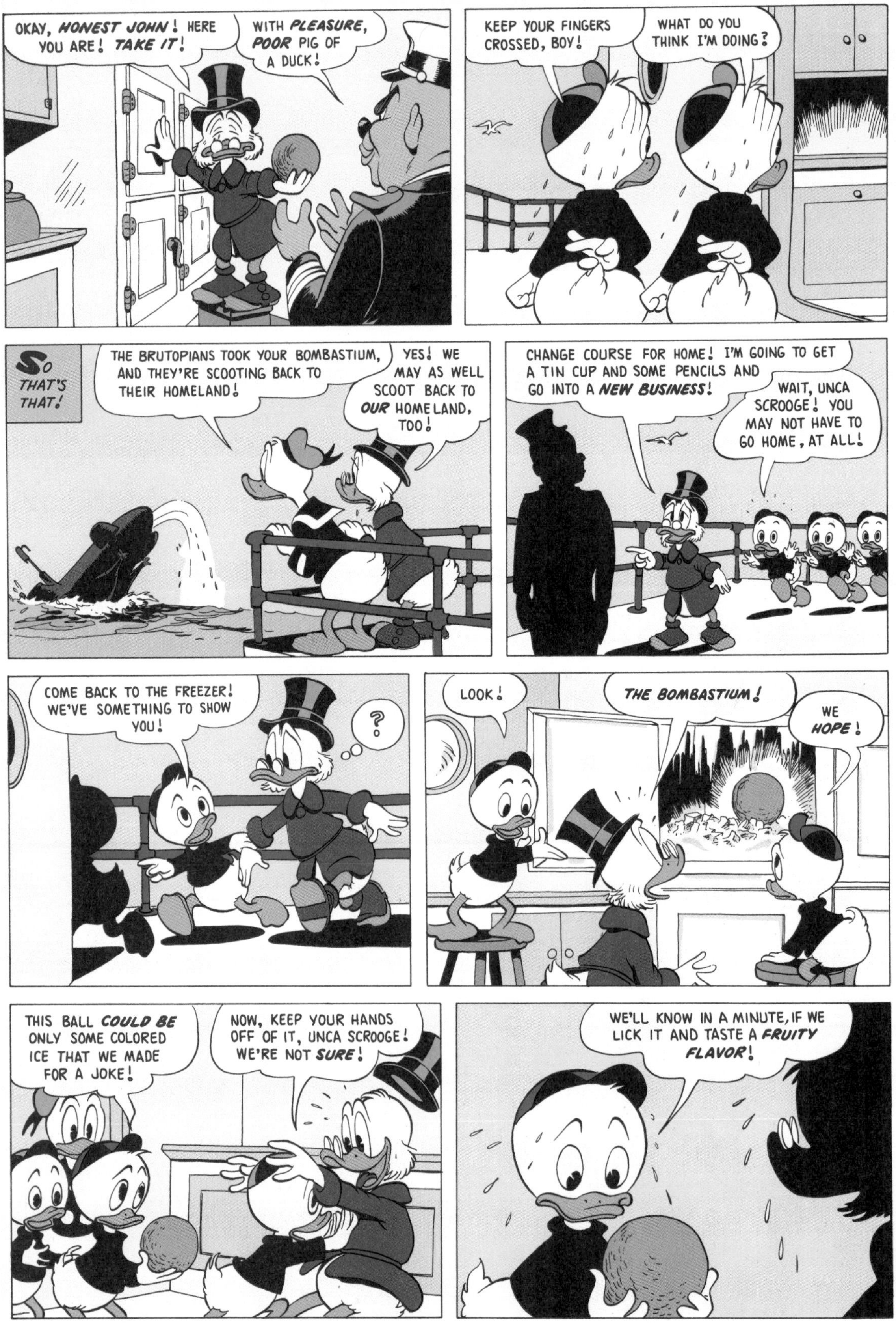
OKAY, HONEST JOHN! HERE YOU ARE! TAKE IT!
WITH PLEASURE, POOR PIG OF A DUCK!
KEEP YOUR FINGERS CROSSED, BOY!
WHAT DO YOU THINK I'M DOING?
SO THAT'S THAT!
THE BRUTOPIANS TOOK YOUR BOMBASTIUM, AND THEY'RE SCOOTING BACK TO THEIR HOMELAND!
YES! WE MAY AS WELL SCOOT BACK TO OUR HOME LAND, TOO!
CHANGE COURSE FOR HOME! I'M GOING TO GET A TIN CUP AND SOME PENCILS AND GO INTO A NEW BUSINESS!
WAIT, UNCA SCROOGE! YOU MAY NOT HAVE TO GO HOME, AT ALL!
COME BACK TO THE FREEZER! WE'VE SOMETHING TO SHOW YOU!
?
LOOK!
THE BOMBASTIUM!
WE HOPE!
THIS BALL COULD BE ONLY SOME COLORED ICE THAT WE MADE FOR A JOKE!
NOW, KEEP YOUR HANDS OFF OF IT, UNCA SCROOGE! WE'RE NOT SURE!
WE'LL KNOW IN A MINUTE, IF WE LICK IT AND TASTE A FRUITY FLAVOR!

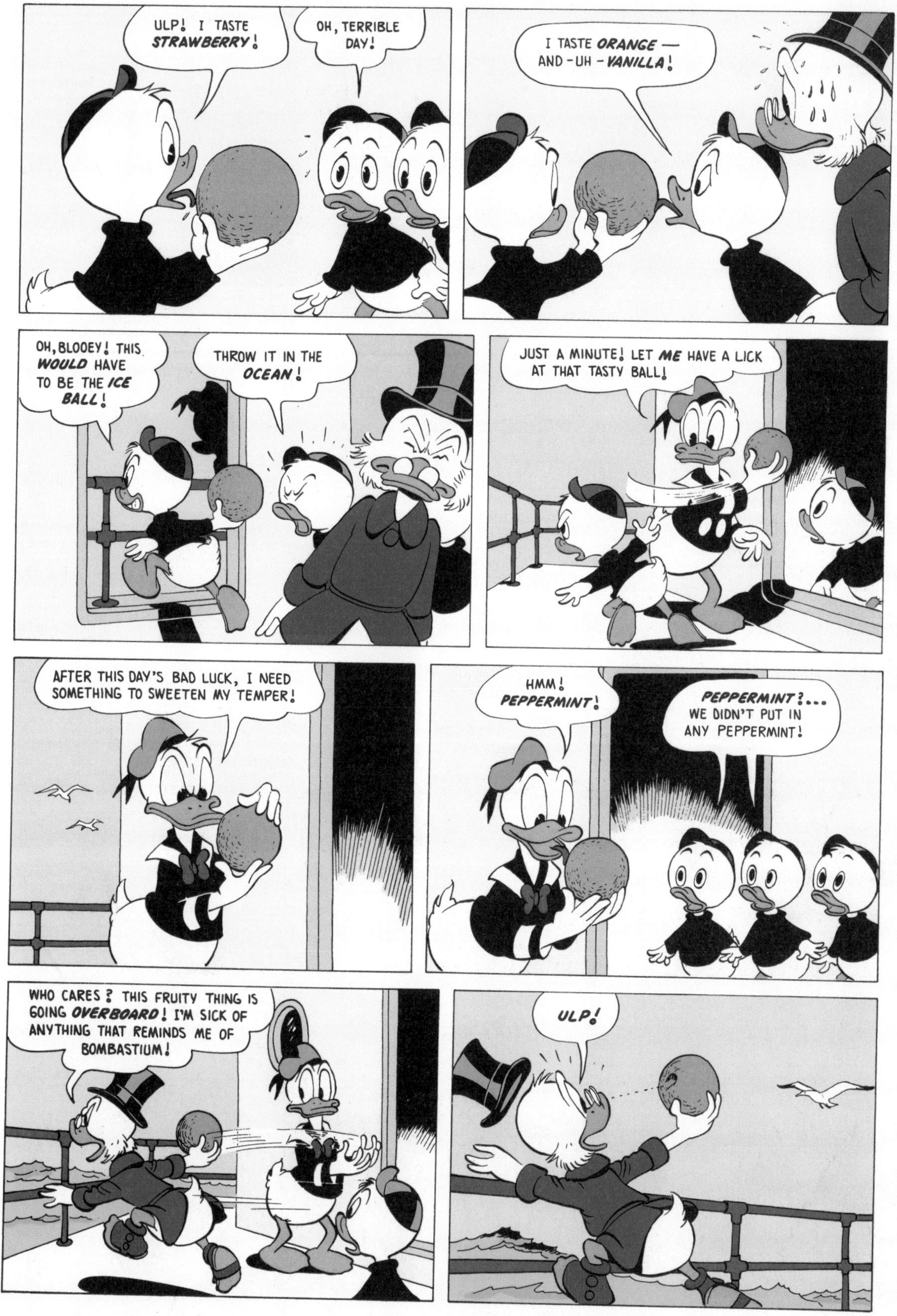
ULP! I TASTE STRAWBERRY!
OH, TERRIBLE DAY!
I TASTE ORANGE — AND-UH-VANILLA!
OH, BLOOEY! THIS WOULD HAVE TO BE THE ICE BALL!
THROW IT IN THE OCEAN!
JUST A MINUTE! LET ME HAVE A LICK AT THAT TASTY BALL!
AFTER THIS DAY'S BAD LUCK, I NEED SOMETHING TO SWEETEN MY TEMPER!
HMM! PEPPERMINT!
PEPPERMINT?... WE DIDN'T PUT IN ANY PEPPERMINT!
WHO CARES? THIS FRUITY THING IS GOING OVERBOARD! I'M SICK OF ANYTHING THAT REMINDS ME OF BOMBASTIUM!
ULP!

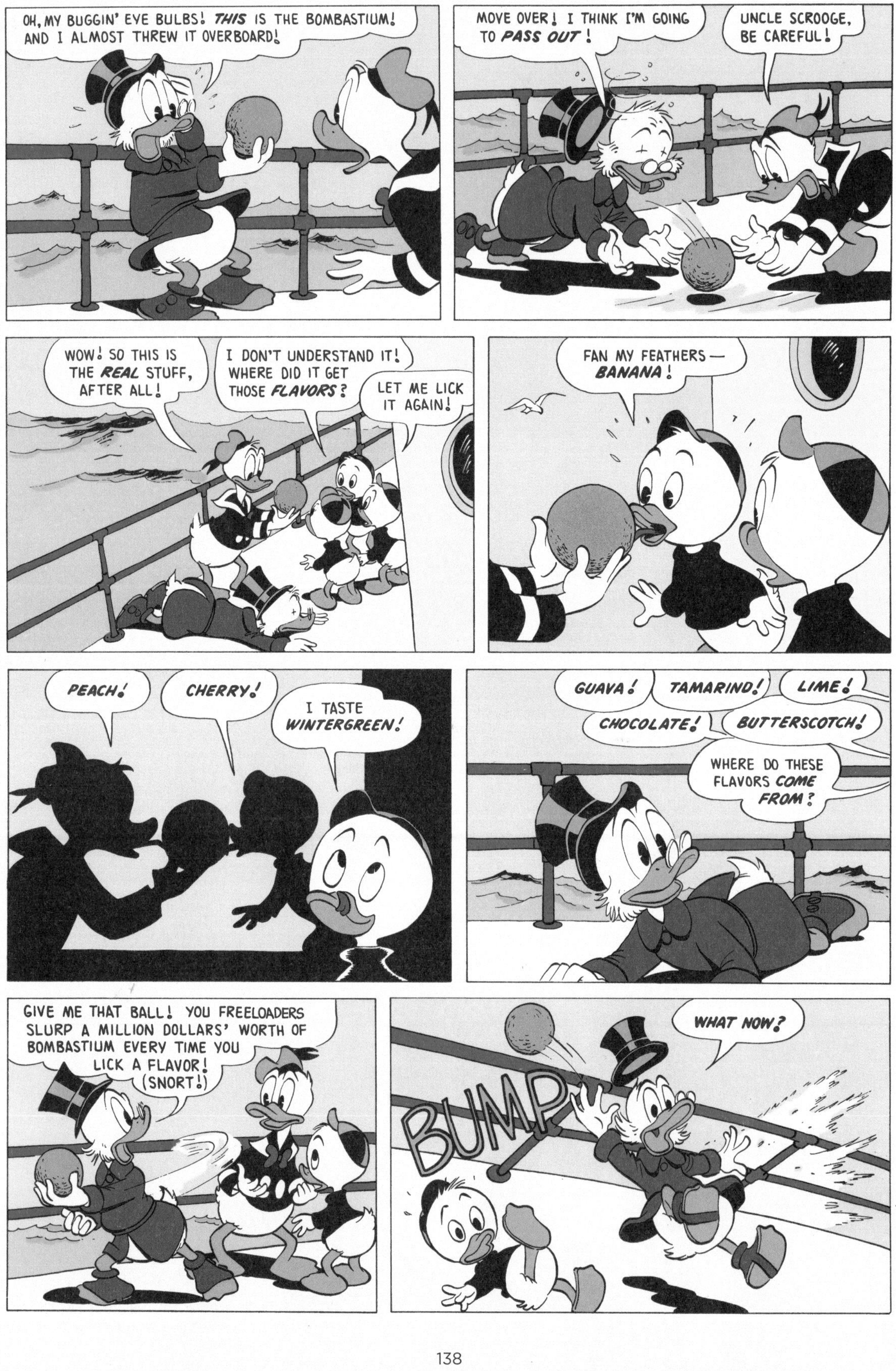
OH, MY BUGGIN' EYE BULBS! THIS IS THE BOMBASTIUM! AND I ALMOST THREW IT OVERBOARD!
MOVE OVER! I THINK I'M GOING TO PASS OUT!
UNCLE SCROOGE, BE CAREFUL!
WOW! SO THIS IS THE REAL STUFF, AFTER ALL!
I DON'T UNDERSTAND IT! WHERE DID IT GET THOSE FLAVORS?
LET ME LICK IT AGAIN!
FAN MY FEATHERS— BANANA!
PEACH!
CHERRY!
I TASTE WINTERGREEN!
GUAVA!
TAMARIND!
LIME!
CHOCOLATE!
BUTTERSCOTCH!
WHERE DO THESE FLAVORS COME FROM?
GIVE ME THAT BALL! YOU FREELOADERS SLURP A MILLION DOLLARS' WORTH OF BOMBASTIUM EVERY TIME YOU LICK A FLAVOR! (SNORT!)
WHAT NOW?
BUMP

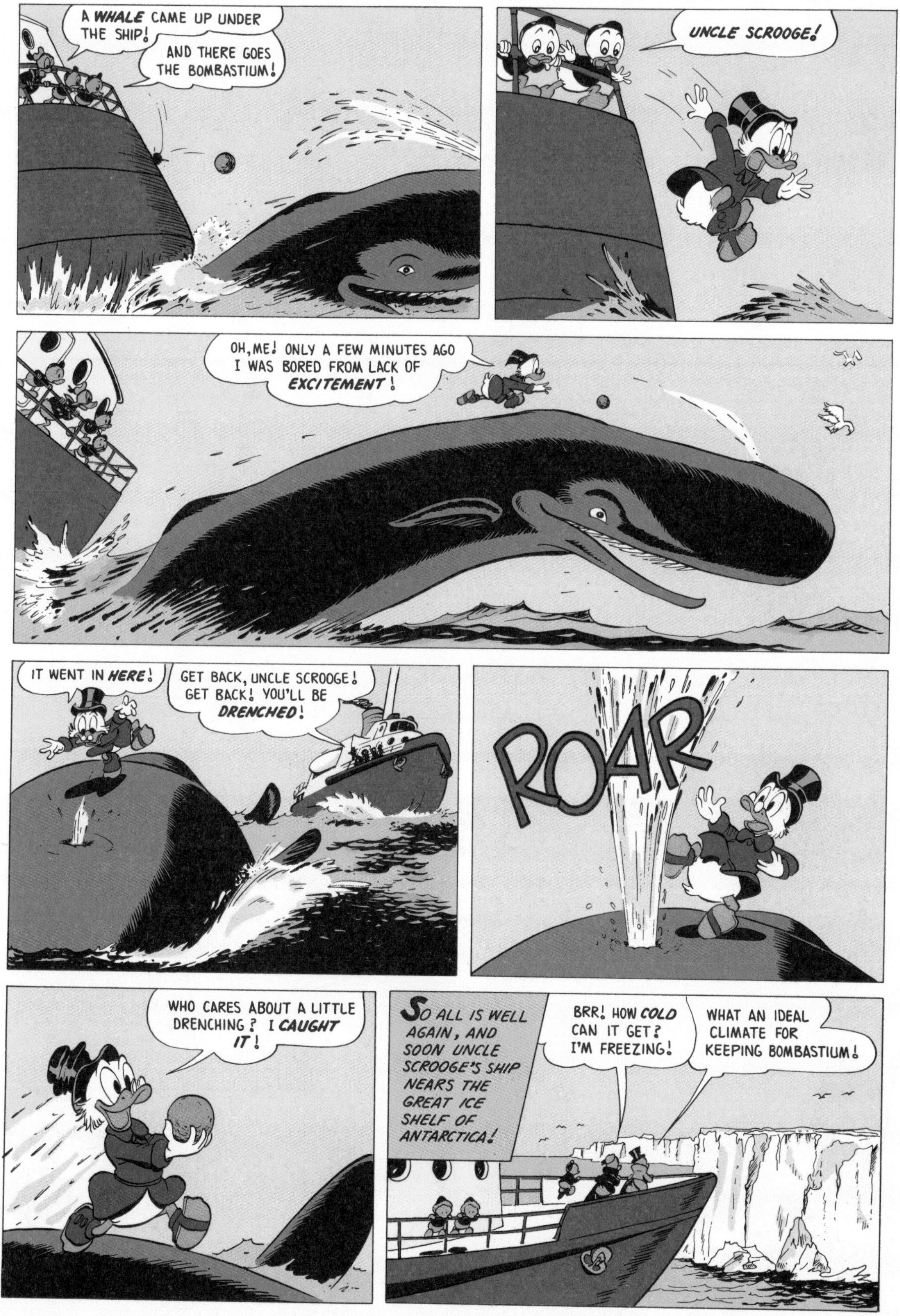
A WHALE CAME UP UNDER THE SHIP!
AND THERE GOES THE BOMBASTIUM!
UNCLE SCROOGE!
OH, ME! ONLY A FEW MINUTES AGO I WAS BORED FROM LACK OF EXCITEMENT!
IT WENT IN HERE!
GET BACK, UNCLE SCROOGE! GET BACK! YOU'LL BE DRENCHED!
ROAR
WHO CARES ABOUT A LITTLE DRENCHING? I CAUGHT IT!
SO ALL IS WELL AGAIN, AND SOON UNCLE SCROOGE'S SHIP NEARS THE GREAT ICE SHELF OF ANTARCTICA!
BRR! HOW COLD CAN IT GET? I'M FREEZING!
WHAT AN IDEAL CLIMATE FOR KEEPING BOMBASTIUM!

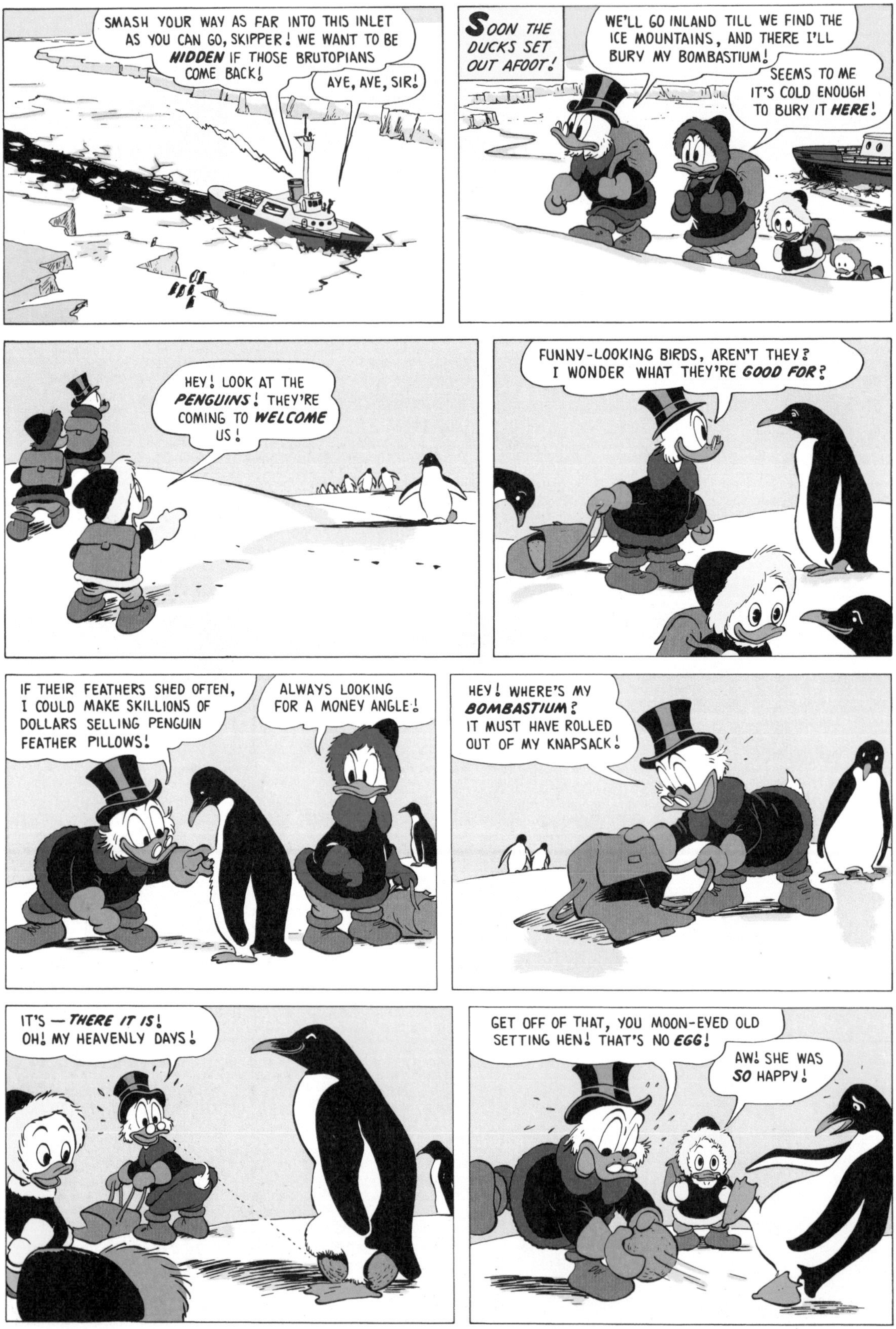
SMASH YOUR WAY AS FAR INTO THIS INLET AS YOU CAN GO, SKIPPER! WE WANT TO BE HIDDEN IF THOSE BRUTOPIANS COME BACK!
AYE, AYE, SIR!
SOON THE DUCKS SET OUT AFOOT!
WE'LL GO INLAND TILL WE FIND THE ICE MOUNTAINS, AND THERE I'LL BURY MY BOMBASTIUM!
SEEMS TO ME IT'S COLD ENOUGH TO BURY IT HERE!
HEY! LOOK AT THE PENGUINS! THEY'RE COMING TO WELCOME US!
FUNNY-LOOKING BIRDS, AREN'T THEY? I WONDER WHAT THEY'RE GOOD FOR?
IF THEIR FEATHERS SHED OFTEN, I COULD MAKE SKILLIONS OF DOLLARS SELLING PENGUIN FEATHER PILLOWS!
ALWAYS LOOKING FOR A MONEY ANGLE!
HEY! WHERE'S MY BOMBASTIUM? IT MUST HAVE ROLLED OUT OF MY KNAPSACK!
IT'S — THERE IT IS! OH! MY HEAVENLY DAYS!
GET OFF OF THAT, YOU MOON-EYED OLD SETTING HEN! THAT'S NO EGG!
AW! SHE WAS SO HAPPY!

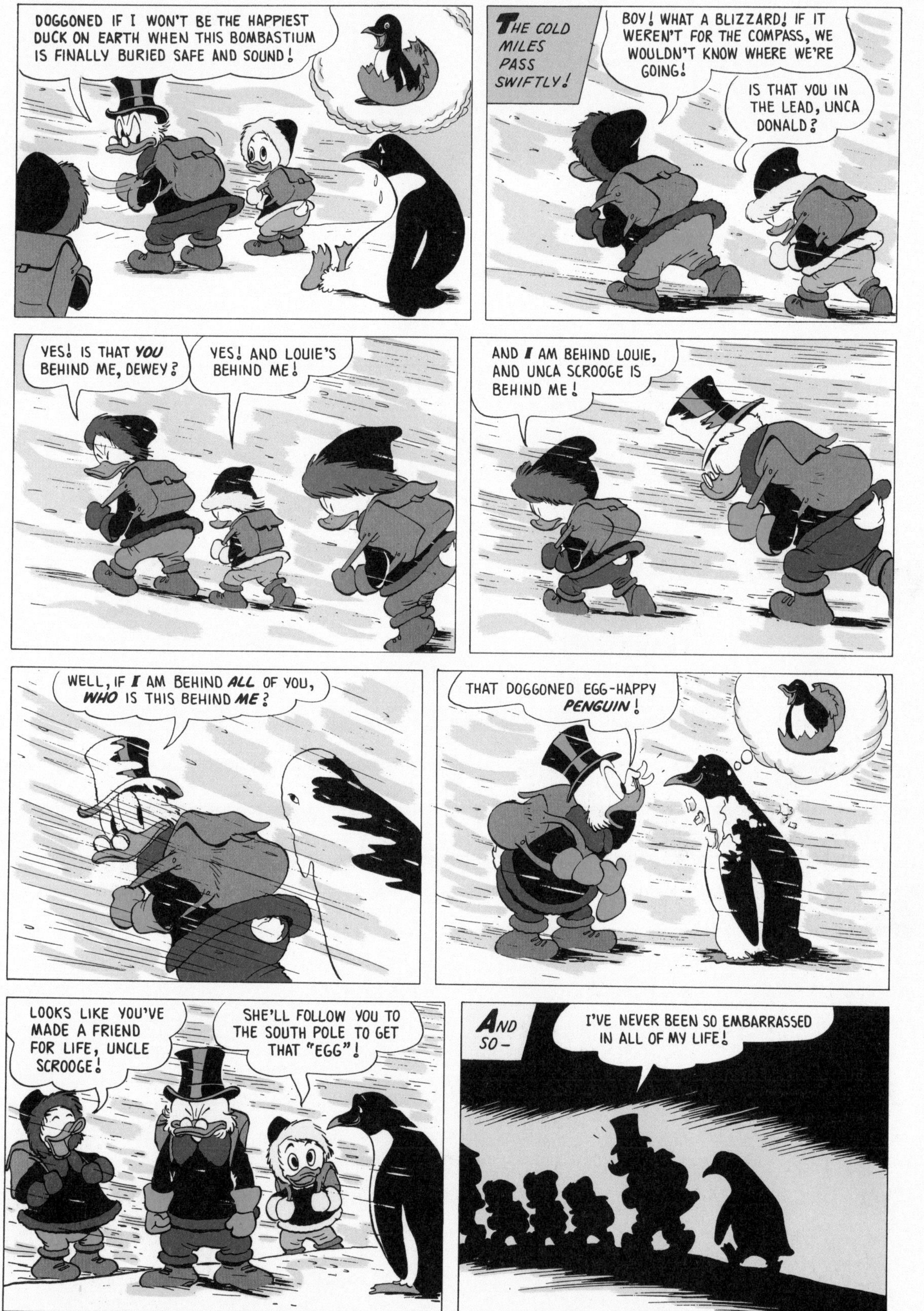
DOGGONED IF I WON'T BE THE HAPPIEST DUCK ON EARTH WHEN THIS BOMBASTIUM IS FINALLY BURIED SAFE AND SOUND!
THE COLD MILES PASS SWIFTLY!
BOY! WHAT A BLIZZARD! IF IT WEREN'T FOR THE COMPASS, WE WOULDN'T KNOW WHERE WE'RE GOING!
IS THAT YOU IN THE LEAD, UNCA DONALD?
YES! IS THAT YOU BEHIND ME, DEWEY?
YES! AND LOUIE'S BEHIND ME!
AND I AM BEHIND LOUIE, AND UNCA SCROOGE IS BEHIND ME!
WELL, IF I AM BEHIND ALL OF YOU, WHO IS THIS BEHIND ME?
THAT DOGGONED EGG-HAPPY PENGUIN!
LOOKS LIKE YOU'VE MADE A FRIEND FOR LIFE, UNCLE SCROOGE!
SHE'LL FOLLOW YOU TO THE SOUTH POLE TO GET THAT "EGG"!
AND SO—
I'VE NEVER BEEN SO EMBARRASSED IN ALL OF MY LIFE!

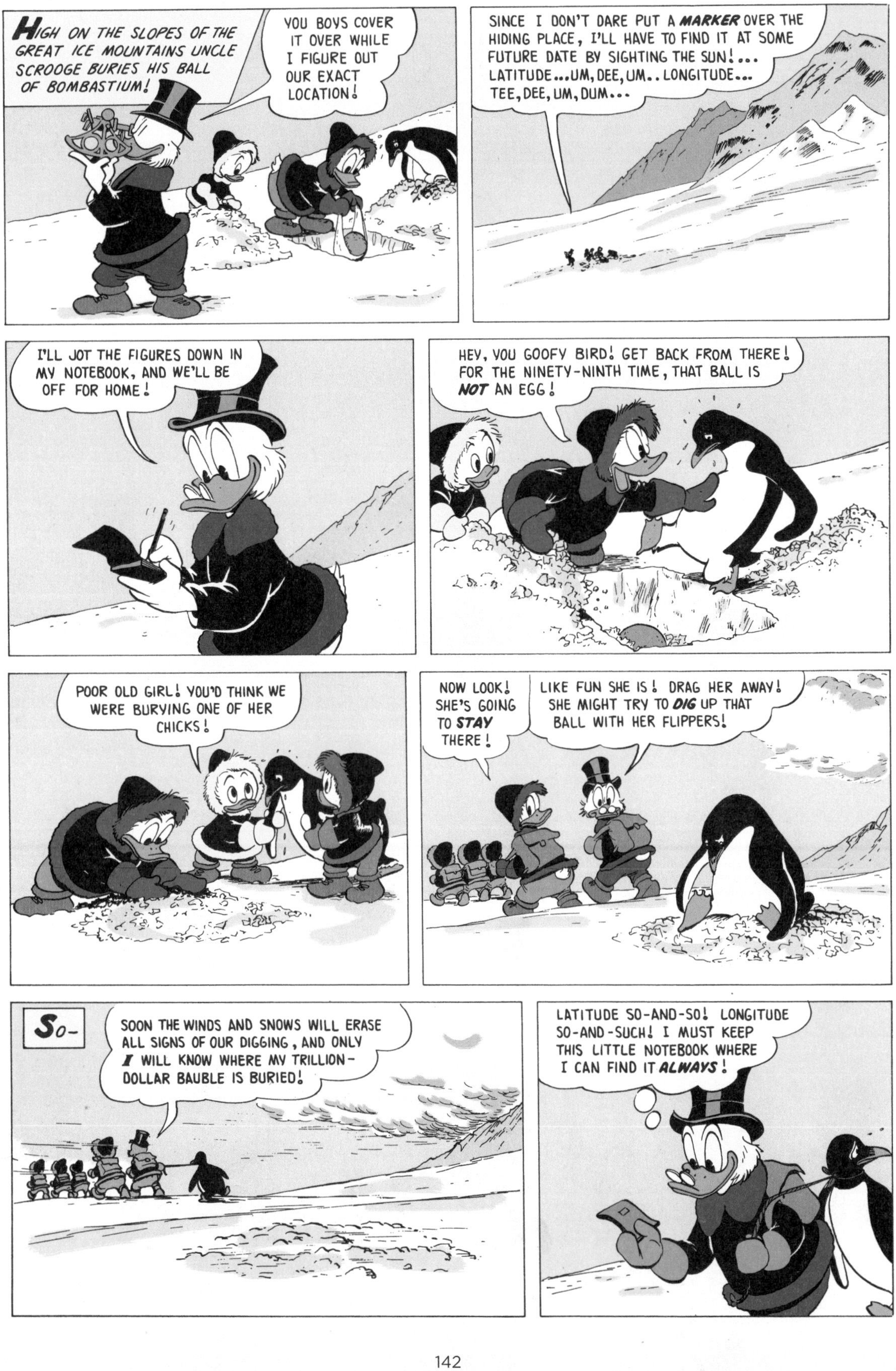
HIGH ON THE SLOPES OF THE GREAT ICE MOUNTAINS UNCLE SCROOGE BURIES HIS BALL OF BOMBASTIUM!
YOU BOYS COVER IT OVER WHILE I FIGURE OUT OUR EXACT LOCATION!
SINCE I DON'T DARE PUT A MARKER OVER THE HIDING PLACE, I'LL HAVE TO FIND IT AT SOME FUTURE DATE BY SIGHTING THE SUN!... LATITUDE...UM, DEE, UM.. LONGITUDE... TEE, DEE, UM, DUM...
I'LL JOT THE FIGURES DOWN IN MY NOTEBOOK, AND WE'LL BE OFF FOR HOME!
HEY, YOU GOOFY BIRD! GET BACK FROM THERE! FOR THE NINETY-NINTH TIME, THAT BALL IS NOT AN EGG!
POOR OLD GIRL! YOU'D THINK WE WERE BURYING ONE OF HER CHICKS!
NOW LOOK! SHE'S GOING TO STAY THERE!
LIKE FUN SHE IS! DRAG HER AWAY! SHE MIGHT TRY TO DIG UP THAT BALL WITH HER FLIPPERS!
SO-
SOON THE WINDS AND SNOWS WILL ERASE ALL SIGNS OF OUR DIGGING, AND ONLY I WILL KNOW WHERE MY TRILLION-DOLLAR BAUBLE IS BURIED!
LATITUDE SO-AND-SO! LONGITUDE SO-AND-SUCH! I MUST KEEP THIS LITTLE NOTEBOOK WHERE I CAN FIND IT ALWAYS!

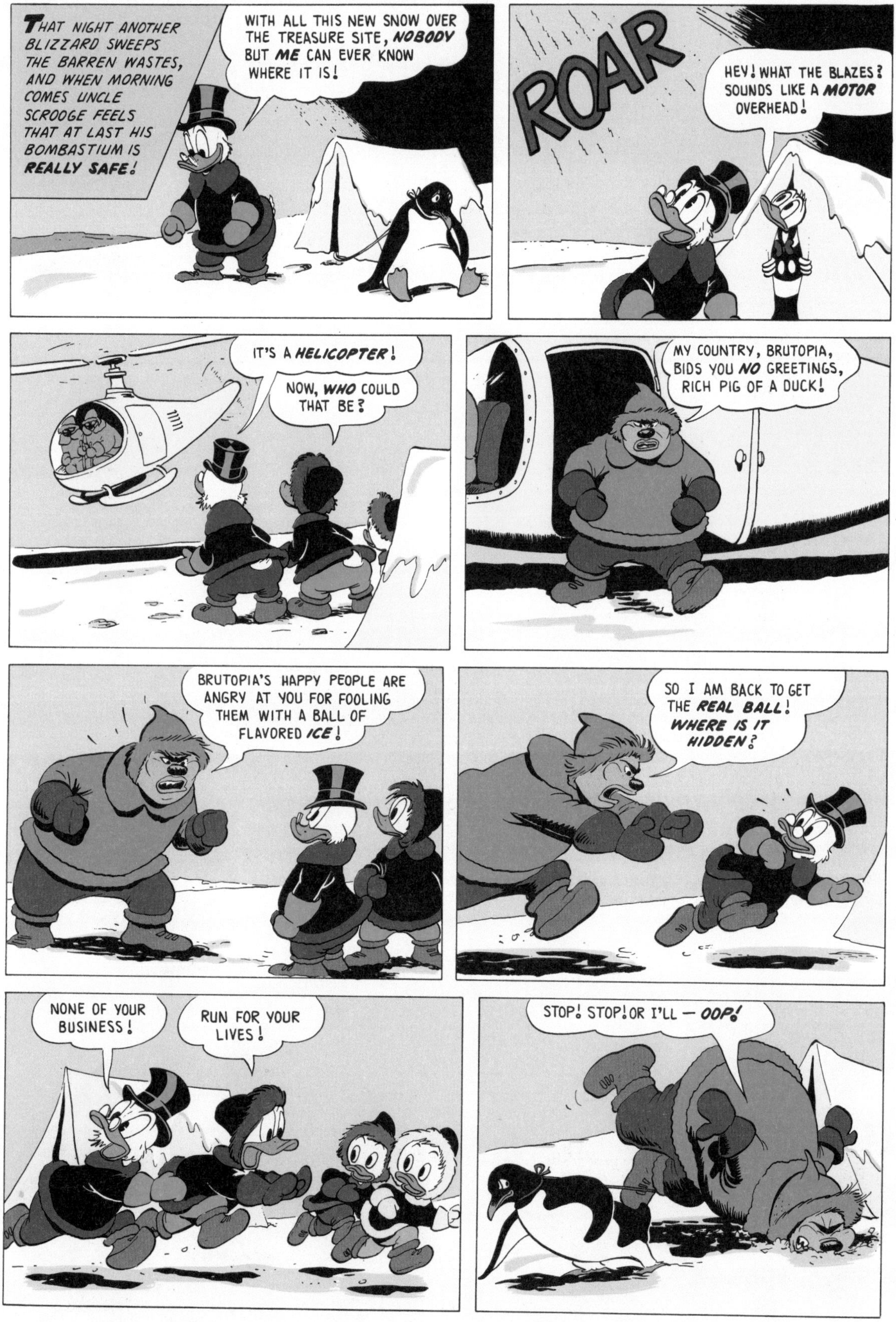
THAT NIGHT ANOTHER BLIZZARD SWEEPS THE BARREN WASTES, AND WHEN MORNING COMES UNCLE SCROOGE FEELS THAT AT LAST HIS BOMBASTIUM IS REALLY SAFE!
WITH ALL THIS NEW SNOW OVER THE TREASURE SITE, NOBODY BUT ME CAN EVER KNOW WHERE IT IS!
ROAR
HEY! WHAT THE BLAZES? SOUNDS LIKE A MOTOR OVERHEAD!
IT'S A HELICOPTER!
NOW, WHO COULD THAT BE?
MY COUNTRY, BRUTOPIA, BIDS YOU NO GREETINGS, RICH PIG OF A DUCK!
BRUTOPIA'S HAPPY PEOPLE ARE ANGRY AT YOU FOR FOOLING THEM WITH A BALL OF FLAVORED ICE!
SO I AM BACK TO GET THE REAL BALL! WHERE IS IT HIDDEN?
NONE OF YOUR BUSINESS!
RUN FOR YOUR LIVES!
STOP! STOP! OR I'LL — OOP!

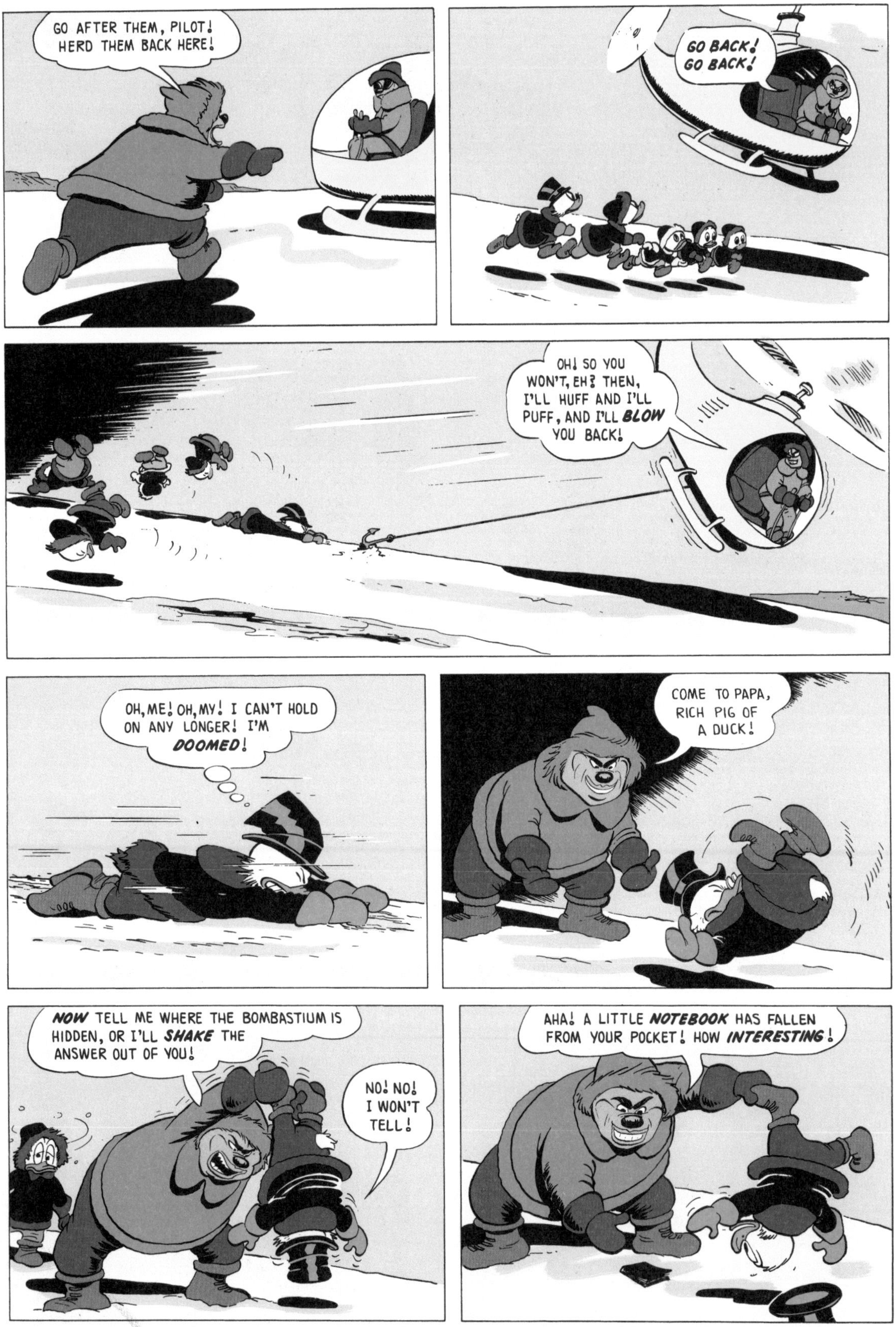
GO AFTER THEM, PILOT! HERD THEM BACK HERE!
GO BACK! GO BACK!
OH! SO YOU WON'T, EH? THEN, I'LL HUFF AND I'LL PUFF, AND I'LL BLOW YOU BACK!
OH, ME! OH, MY! I CAN'T HOLD ON ANY LONGER! I'M DOOMED!
COME TO PAPA, RICH PIG OF A DUCK!
NOW TELL ME WHERE THE BOMBASTIUM IS HIDDEN, OR I'LL SHAKE THE ANSWER OUT OF YOU!
NO! NO! I WON'T TELL!
AHA! A LITTLE NOTEBOOK HAS FALLEN FROM YOUR POCKET! HOW INTERESTING!

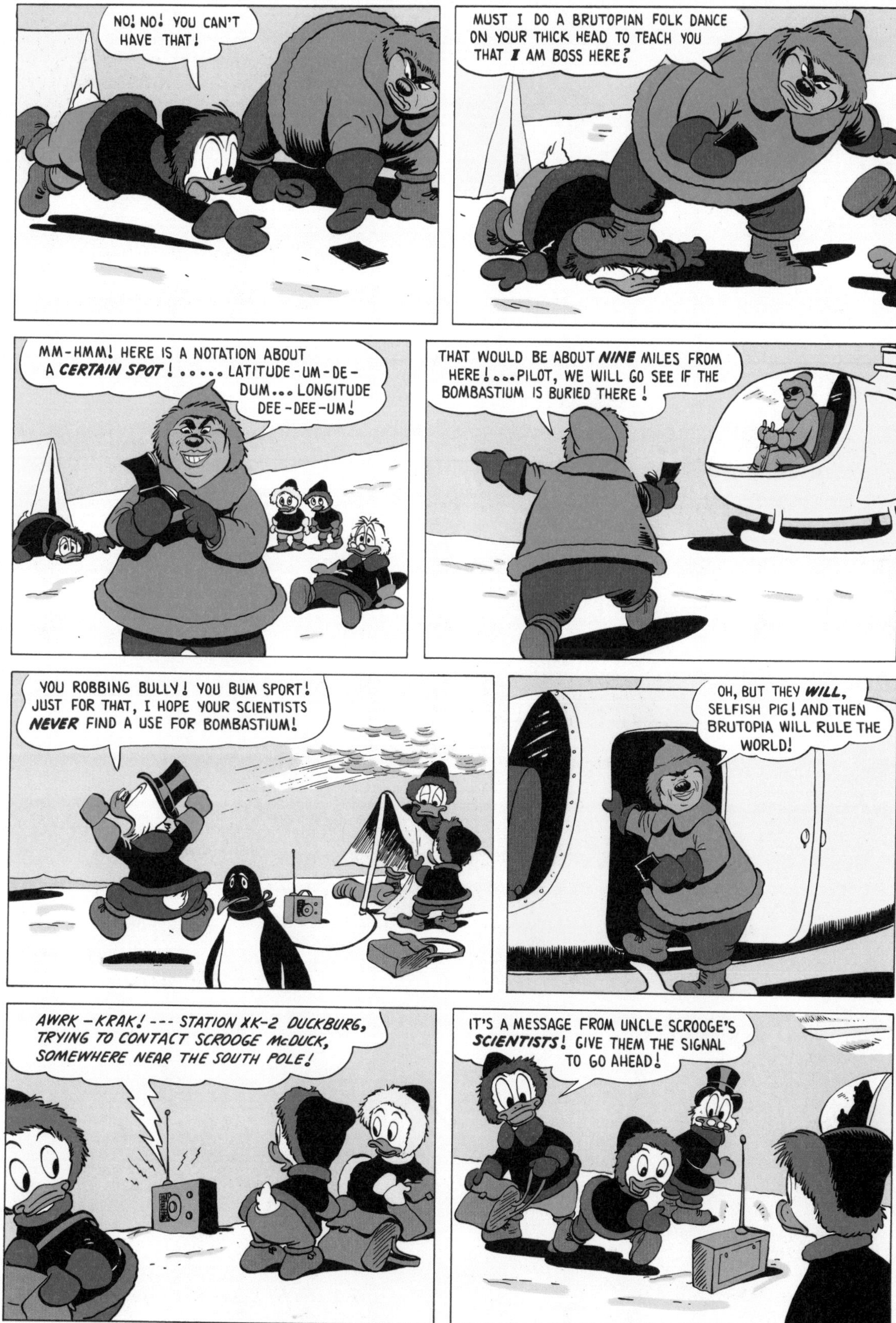
NO! NO! YOU CAN'T HAVE THAT!
MUST I DO A BRUTOPIAN FOLK DANCE ON YOUR THICK HEAD TO TEACH YOU THAT I AM BOSS HERE?
MM-HMM! HERE IS A NOTATION ABOUT A CERTAIN SPOT! ..... LATITUDE-UM-DE-DUM... LONGITUDE DEE-DEE-UM!
THAT WOULD BE ABOUT NINE MILES FROM HERE!...PILOT, WE WILL GO SEE IF THE BOMBASTIUM IS BURIED THERE!
YOU ROBBING BULLY! YOU BUM SPORT! JUST FOR THAT, I HOPE YOUR SCIENTISTS NEVER FIND A USE FOR BOMBASTIUM!
OH, BUT THEY WILL, SELFISH PIG! AND THEN BRUTOPIA WILL RULE THE WORLD!
AWRK-KRAK! --- STATION XK-2 DUCKBURG, TRYING TO CONTACT SCROOGE McDUCK, SOMEWHERE NEAR THE SOUTH POLE!
IT'S A MESSAGE FROM UNCLE SCROOGE'S SCIENTISTS! GIVE THEM THE SIGNAL TO GO AHEAD!

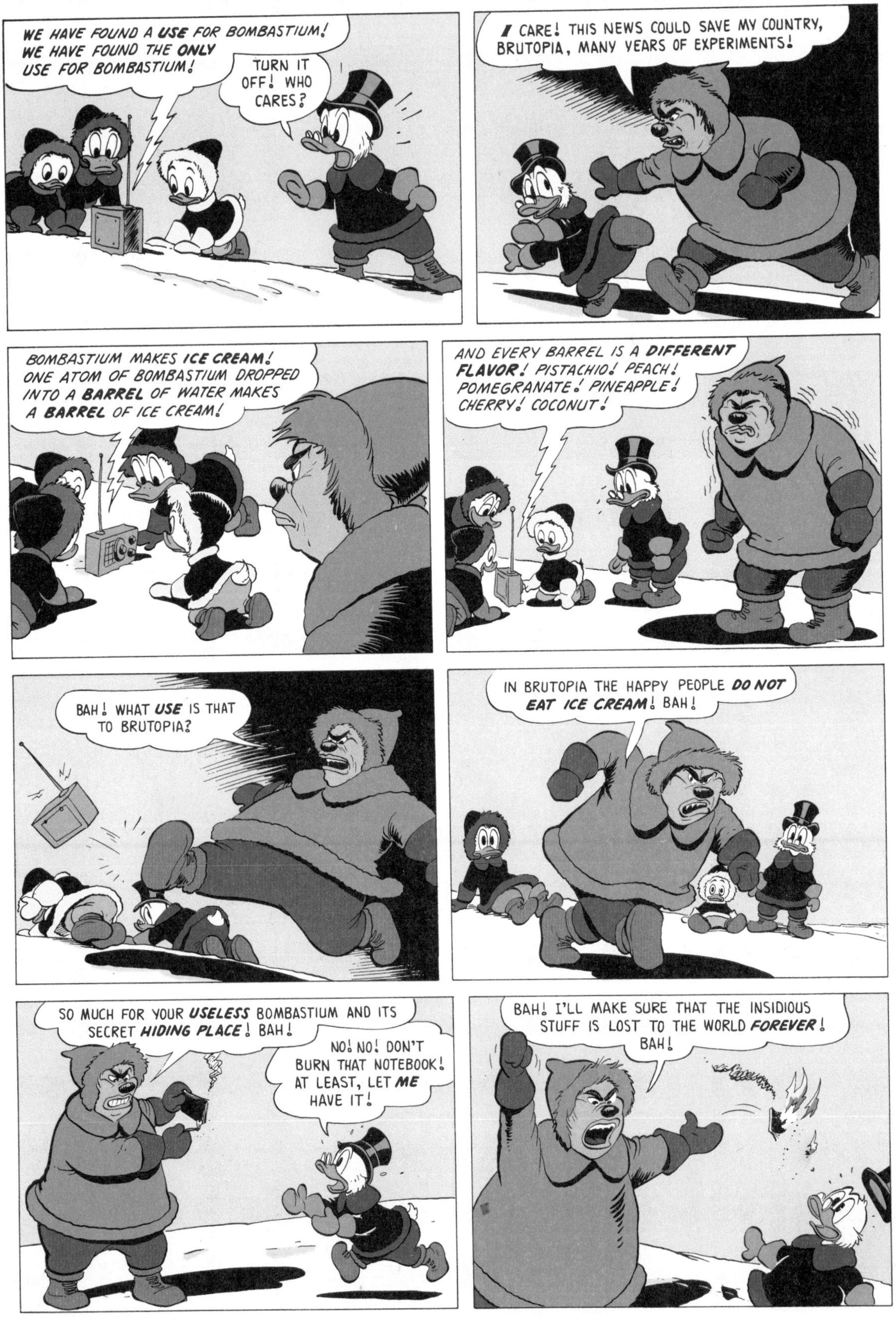
WE HAVE FOUND A USE FOR BOMBASTIUM! WE HAVE FOUND THE ONLY USE FOR BOMBASTIUM!
TURN IT OFF! WHO CARES?
I CARE! THIS NEWS COULD SAVE MY COUNTRY, BRUTOPIA, MANY YEARS OF EXPERIMENTS!
BOMBASTIUM MAKES ICE CREAM! ONE ATOM OF BOMBASTIUM DROPPED INTO A BARREL OF WATER MAKES A BARREL OF ICE CREAM!
AND EVERY BARREL IS A DIFFERENT FLAVOR! PISTACHIO! PEACH! POMEGRANATE! PINEAPPLE! CHERRY! COCONUT!
BAH! WHAT USE IS THAT TO BRUTOPIA?
IN BRUTOPIA THE HAPPY PEOPLE DO NOT EAT ICE CREAM! BAH!
SO MUCH FOR YOUR USELESS BOMBASTIUM AND ITS SECRET HIDING PLACE! BAH!
NO! NO! DON'T BURN THAT NOTEBOOK! AT LEAST, LET ME HAVE IT!
BAH! I'LL MAKE SURE THAT THE INSIDIOUS STUFF IS LOST TO THE WORLD FOREVER! BAH!

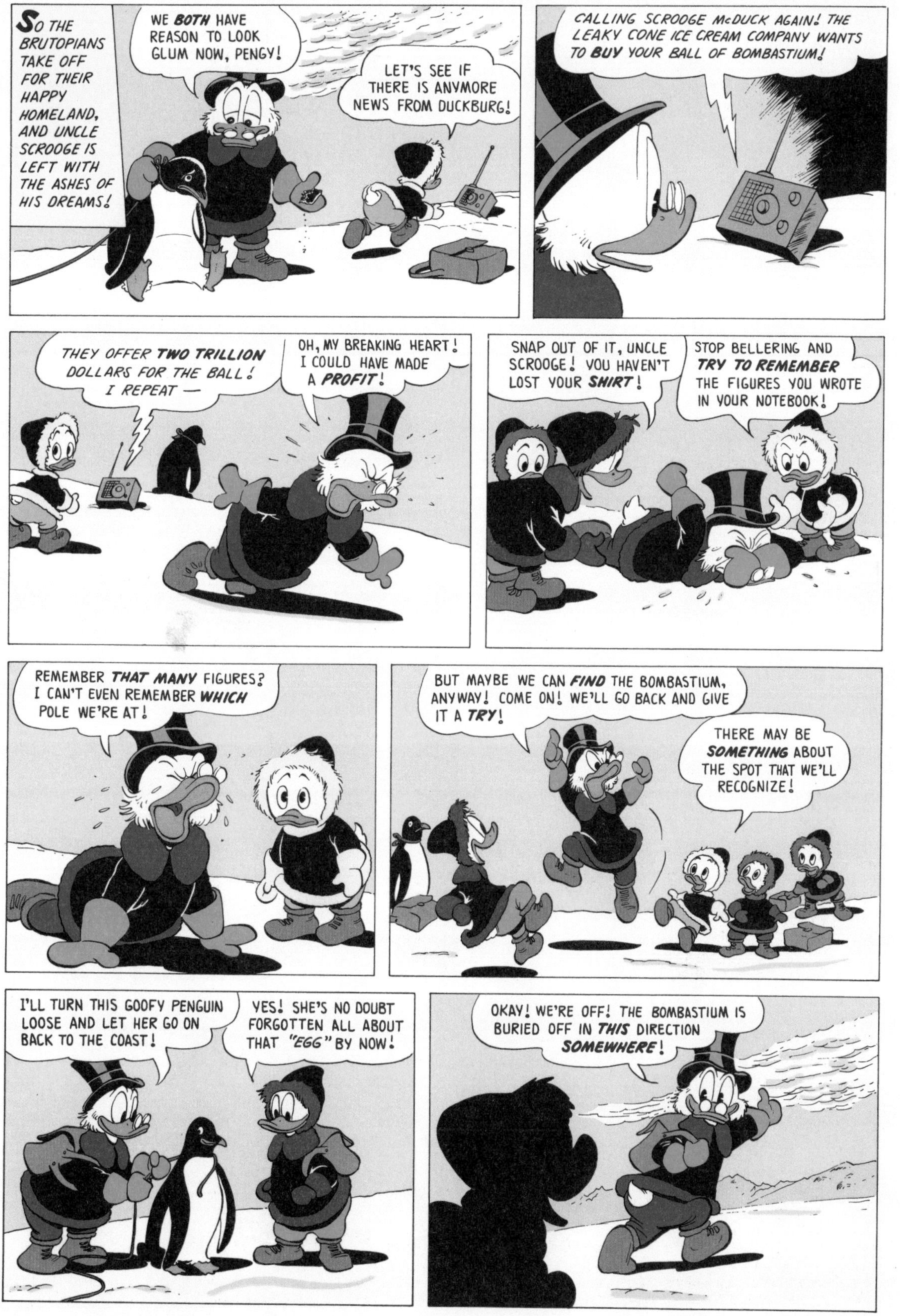
SO THE BRUTOPIANS TAKE OFF FOR THEIR HAPPY HOMELAND, AND UNCLE SCROOGE IS LEFT WITH THE ASHES OF HIS DREAMS!
WE BOTH HAVE REASON TO LOOK GLUM NOW, PENGY!
LET'S SEE IF THERE IS ANYMORE NEWS FROM DUCKBURG!
CALLING SCROOGE McDUCK AGAIN! THE LEAKY CONE ICE CREAM COMPANY WANTS TO BUY YOUR BALL OF BOMBASTIUM!
THEY OFFER TWO TRILLION DOLLARS FOR THE BALL! I REPEAT —
OH, MY BREAKING HEART! I COULD HAVE MADE A PROFIT!
SNAP OUT OF IT, UNCLE SCROOGE! YOU HAVEN'T LOST YOUR SHIRT!
STOP BELLERING AND TRY TO REMEMBER THE FIGURES YOU WROTE IN YOUR NOTEBOOK!
REMEMBER THAT MANY FIGURES? I CAN'T EVEN REMEMBER WHICH POLE WE'RE AT!
BUT MAYBE WE CAN FIND THE BOMBASTIUM, ANYWAY! COME ON! WE'LL GO BACK AND GIVE IT A TRY!
THERE MAY BE SOMETHING ABOUT THE SPOT THAT WE'LL RECOGNIZE!
I'LL TURN THIS GOOFY PENGUIN LOOSE AND LET HER GO ON BACK TO THE COAST!
YES! SHE'S NO DOUBT FORGOTTEN ALL ABOUT THAT "EGG" BY NOW!
OKAY! WE'RE OFF! THE BOMBASTIUM IS BURIED OFF IN THIS DIRECTION SOMEWHERE!

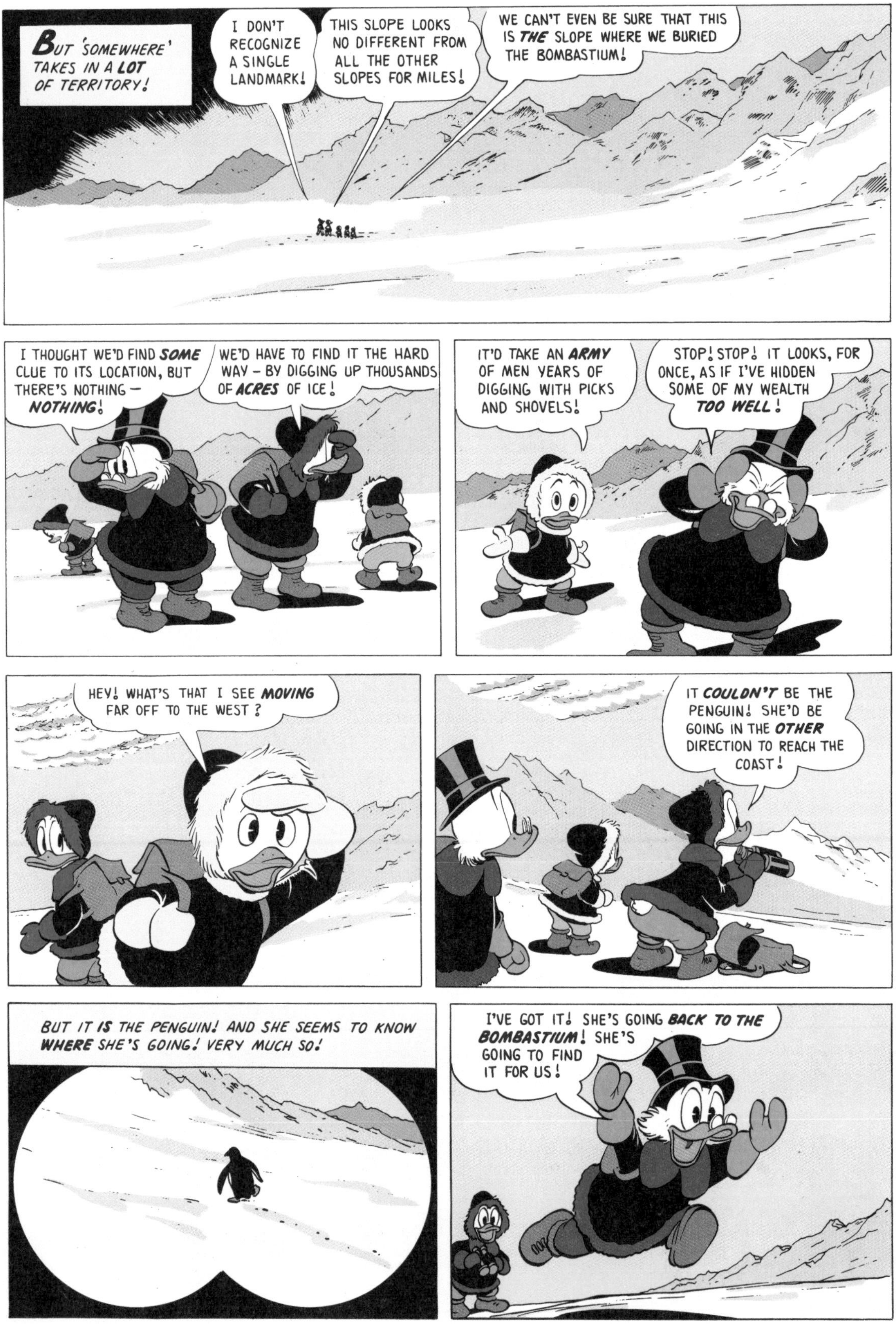
BUT 'SOMEWHERE' TAKES IN A LOT OF TERRITORY!
I DON'T RECOGNIZE A SINGLE LANDMARK!
THIS SLOPE LOOKS NO DIFFERENT FROM ALL THE OTHER SLOPES FOR MILES!
WE CAN'T EVEN BE SURE THAT THIS IS THE SLOPE WHERE WE BURIED THE BOMBASTIUM!
I THOUGHT WE'D FIND SOME CLUE TO ITS LOCATION, BUT THERE'S NOTHING — NOTHING!
WE'D HAVE TO FIND IT THE HARD WAY – BY DIGGING UP THOUSANDS OF ACRES OF ICE!
IT'D TAKE AN ARMY OF MEN YEARS OF DIGGING WITH PICKS AND SHOVELS!
STOP! STOP! IT LOOKS, FOR ONCE, AS IF I'VE HIDDEN SOME OF MY WEALTH TOO WELL!
HEY! WHAT'S THAT I SEE MOVING FAR OFF TO THE WEST?
IT COULDN'T BE THE PENGUIN! SHE'D BE GOING IN THE OTHER DIRECTION TO REACH THE COAST!
BUT IT IS THE PENGUIN! AND SHE SEEMS TO KNOW WHERE SHE'S GOING! VERY MUCH SO!
I'VE GOT IT! SHE'S GOING BACK TO THE BOMBASTIUM! SHE'S GOING TO FIND IT FOR US!

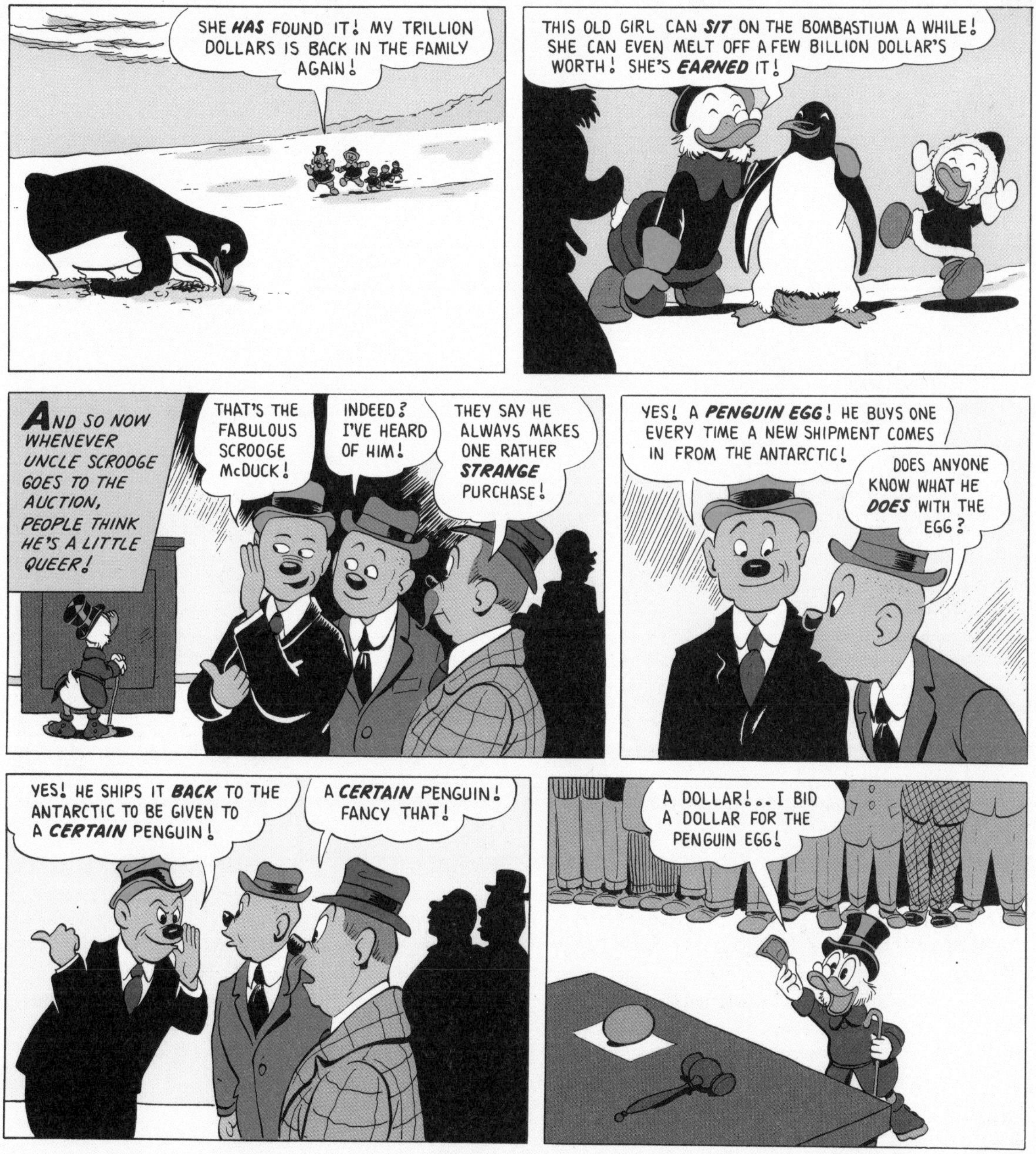
SHE HAS FOUND IT! MY TRILLION DOLLARS IS BACK IN THE FAMILY AGAIN!
THIS OLD GIRL CAN SIT ON THE BOMBASTIUM A WHILE! SHE CAN EVEN MELT OFF A FEW BILLION DOLLAR'S WORTH! SHE'S EARNED IT!
AND SO NOW WHENEVER UNCLE SCROOGE GOES TO THE AUCTION, PEOPLE THINK HE'S A LITTLE QUEER!
THAT'S THE FABULOUS SCROOGE McDUCK!
INDEED? I'VE HEARD OF HIM!
THEY SAY HE ALWAYS MAKES ONE RATHER STRANGE PURCHASE!
YES! A PENGUIN EGG! HE BUYS ONE EVERY TIME A NEW SHIPMENT COMES IN FROM THE ANTARCTIC!
DOES ANYONE KNOW WHAT HE DOES WITH THE EGG?
YES! HE SHIPS IT BACK TO THE ANTARCTIC TO BE GIVEN TO A CERTAIN PENGUIN!
A CERTAIN PENGUIN! FANCY THAT!
A DOLLAR!.. I BID A DOLLAR FOR THE PENGUIN EGG!

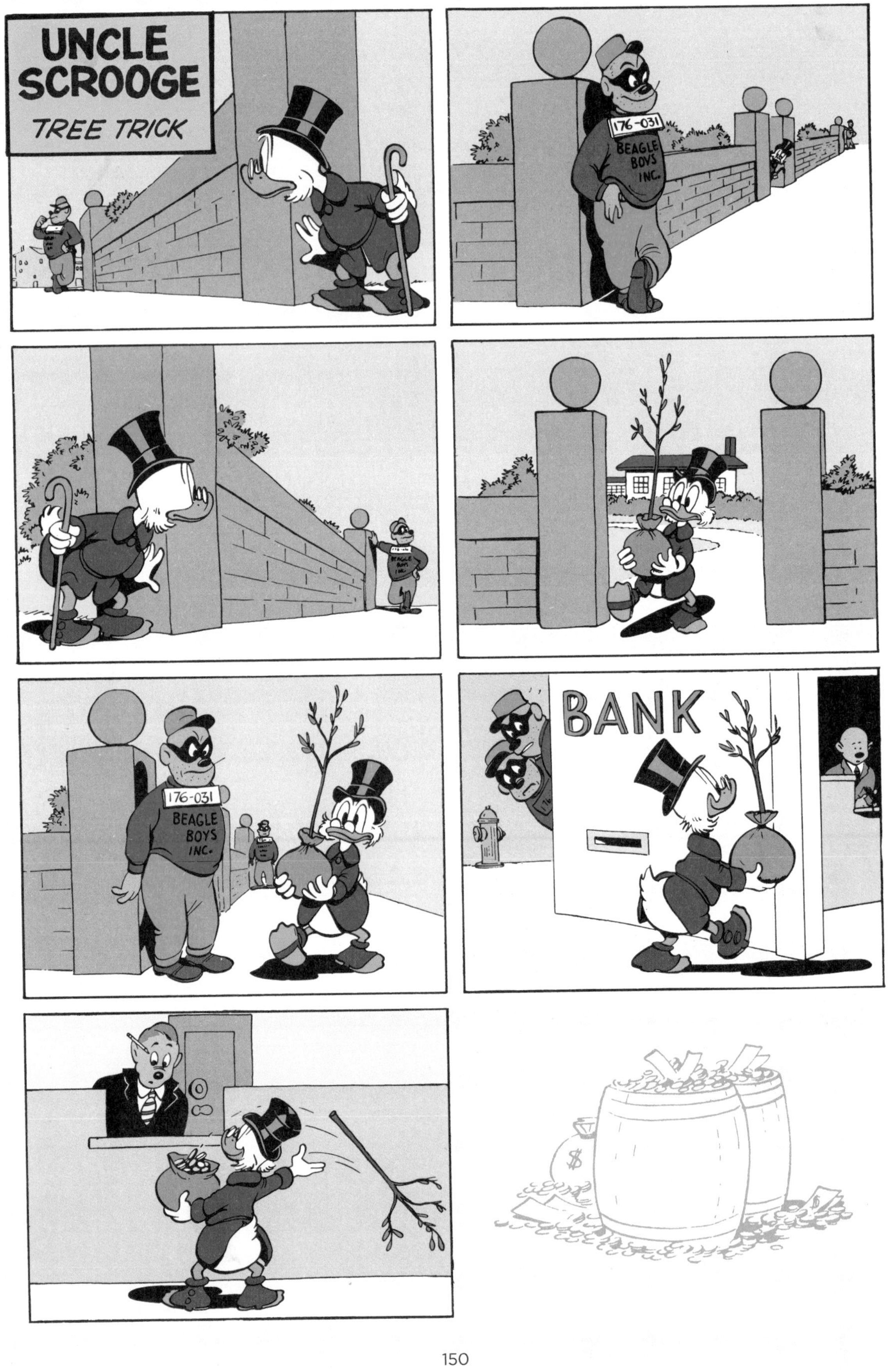
UNCLE SCROOGE
TREE TRICK
176-031
BEAGLE BOYS INC.
176-031
BEAGLE BOYS INC.
BANK

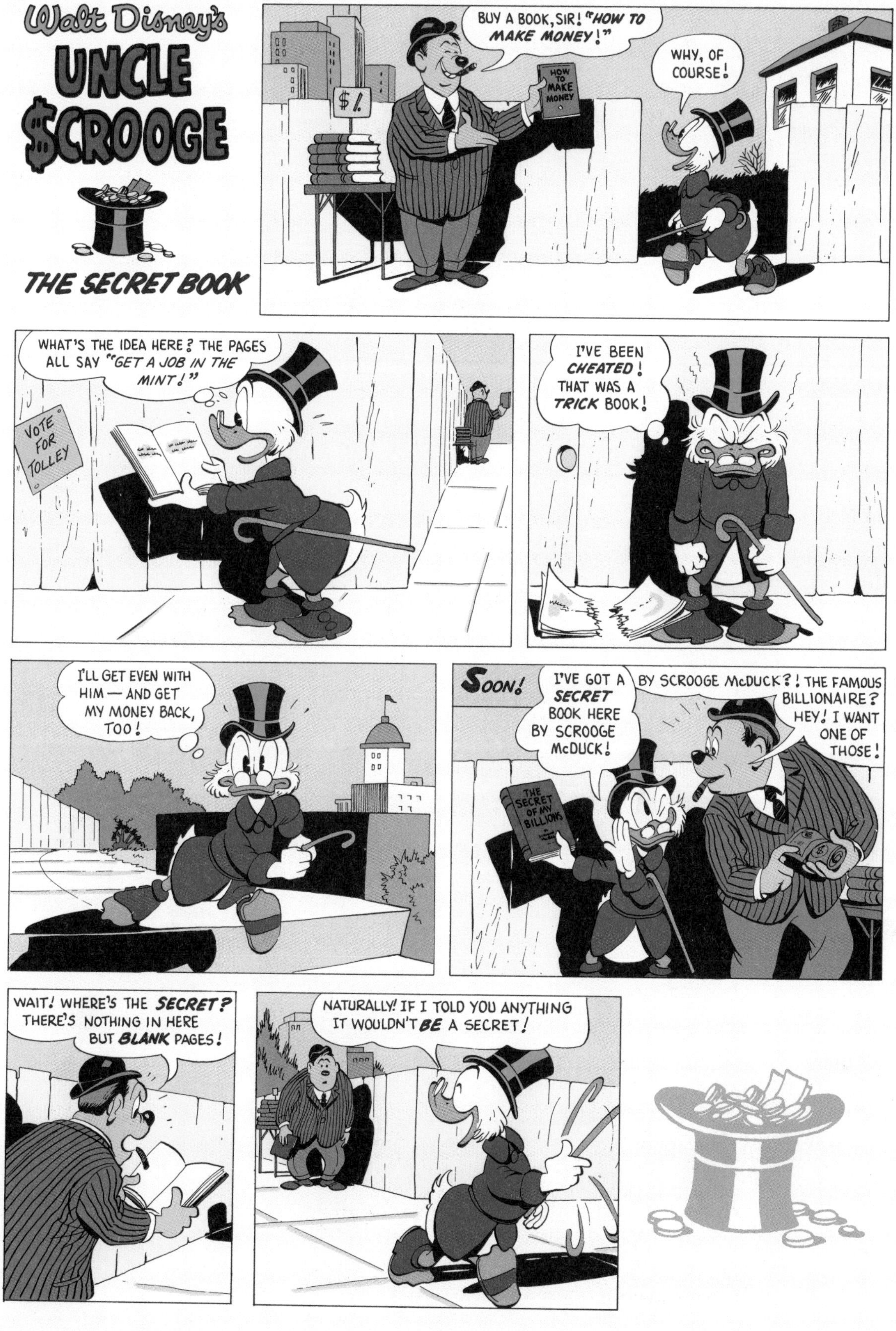
Walt Disney's
UNCLE $CROOGE
THE SECRET BOOK
BUY A BOOK, SIR! "HOW TO MAKE MONEY!"
$1.
HOW TO MAKE MONEY
WHY, OF COURSE!
WHAT'S THE IDEA HERE? THE PAGES ALL SAY "GET A JOB IN THE MINT!"
VOTE FOR TOLLEY
I'VE BEEN CHEATED! THAT WAS A TRICK BOOK!
I'LL GET EVEN WITH HIM — AND GET MY MONEY BACK, TOO!
SOON!
I'VE GOT A SECRET BOOK HERE BY SCROOGE McDUCK!
BY SCROOGE McDUCK?! THE FAMOUS BILLIONAIRE? HEY! I WANT ONE OF THOSE!
THE SECRET OF MY BILLIONS
WAIT! WHERE'S THE SECRET? THERE'S NOTHING IN HERE BUT BLANK PAGES!
NATURALLY! IF I TOLD YOU ANYTHING IT WOULDN'T BE A SECRET!

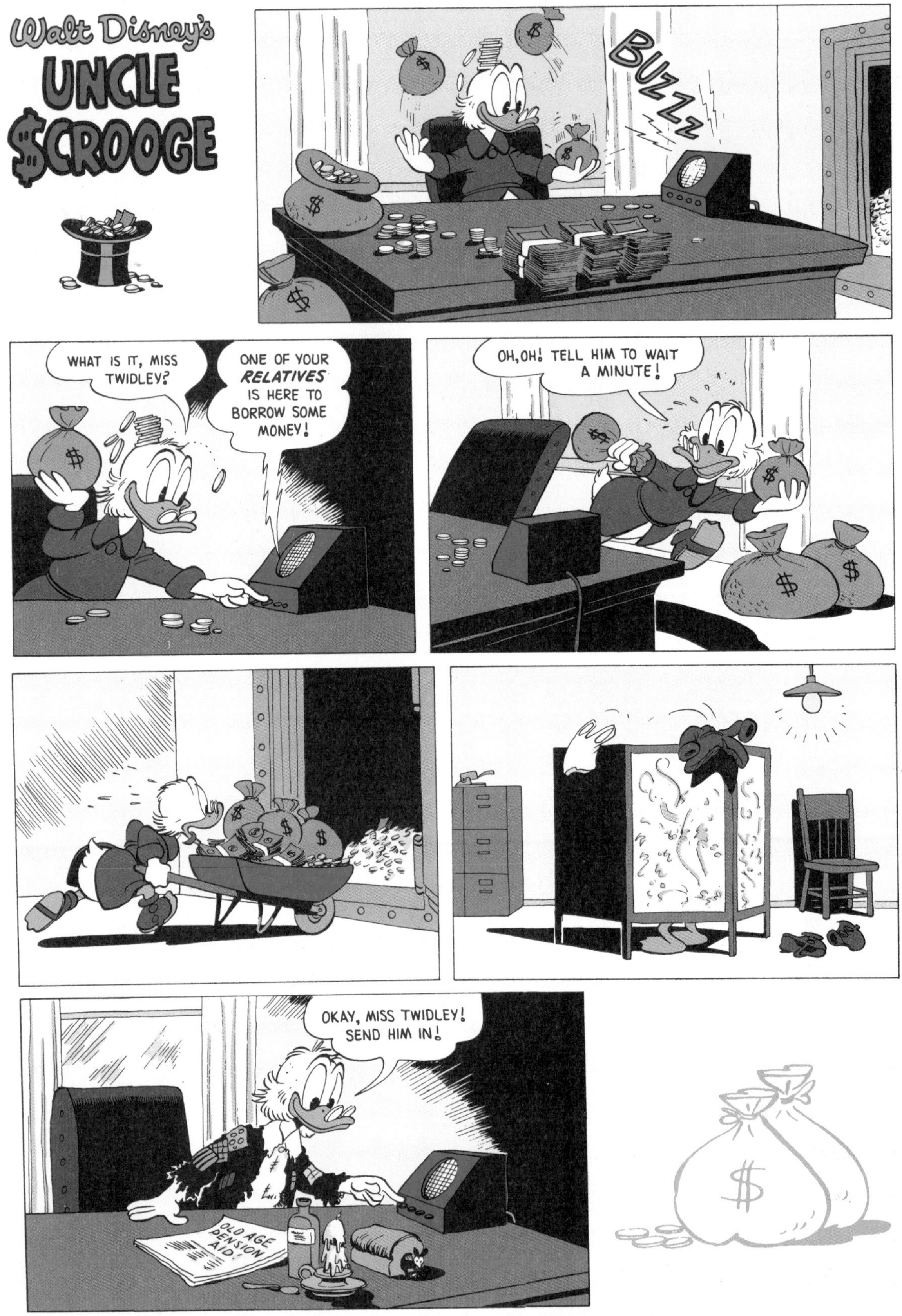
Walt Disney's
UNCLE $CROOGE
BUZZZ
WHAT IS IT, MISS TWIDLEY?
ONE OF YOUR RELATIVES IS HERE TO BORROW SOME MONEY!
OH,OH! TELL HIM TO WAIT A MINUTE!
OKAY, MISS TWIDLEY! SEND HIM IN!
OLD AGE PENSION AID!

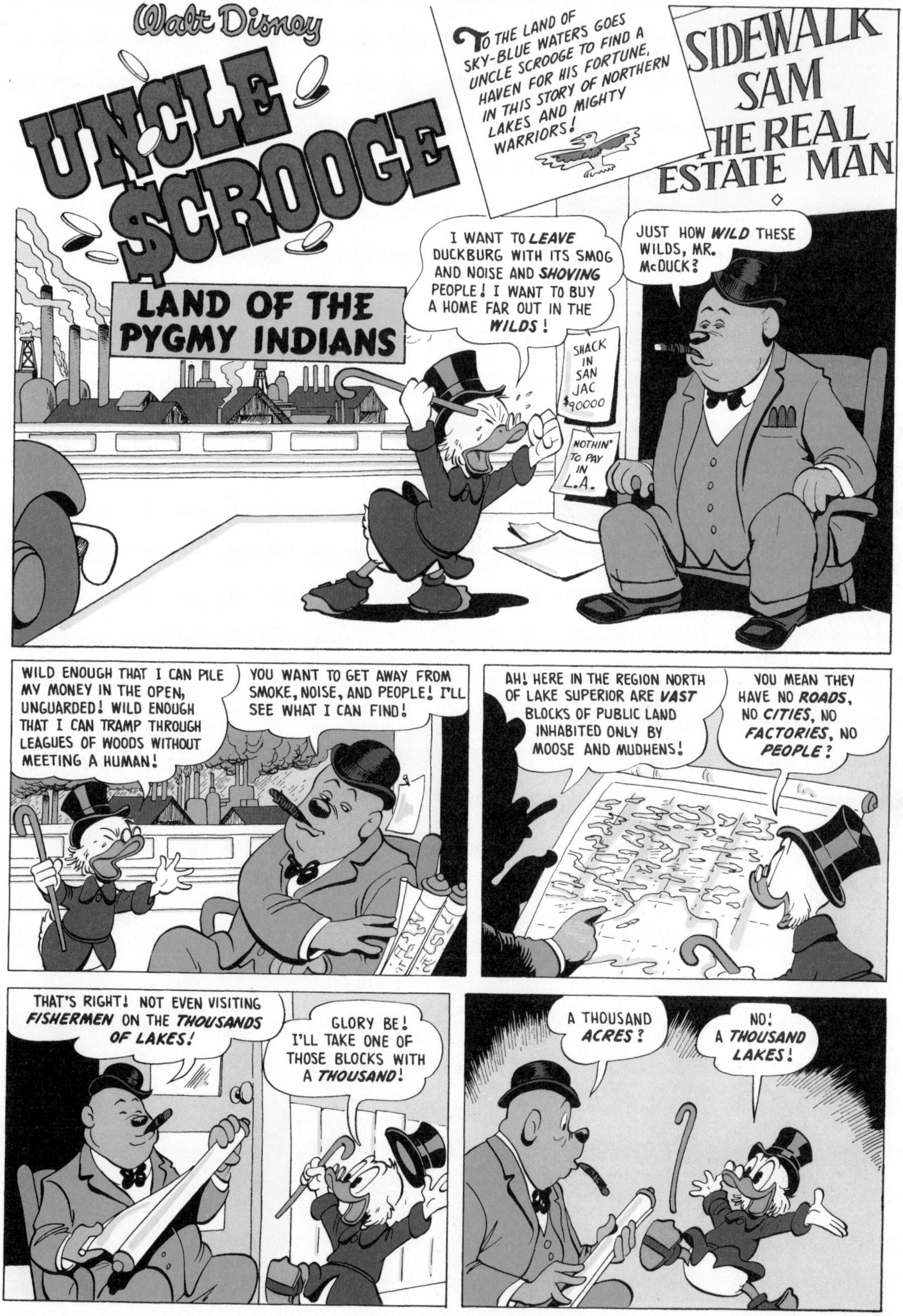
Walt Disney
UNCLE $CROOGE
LAND OF THE PYGMY INDIANS
TO THE LAND OF SKY-BLUE WATERS GOES UNCLE SCROOGE TO FIND A HAVEN FOR HIS FORTUNE, IN THIS STORY OF NORTHERN LAKES AND MIGHTY WARRIORS!
SIDEWALK SAM THE REAL ESTATE MAN
I WANT TO LEAVE DUCKBURG WITH ITS SMOG AND NOISE AND SHOVING PEOPLE! I WANT TO BUY A HOME FAR OUT IN THE WILDS!
JUST HOW WILD THESE WILDS, MR. McDUCK?
SHACK IN SAN JAC $90000
NOTHIN' TO PAY IN L.A.
WILD ENOUGH THAT I CAN PILE MY MONEY IN THE OPEN, UNGUARDED! WILD ENOUGH THAT I CAN TRAMP THROUGH LEAGUES OF WOODS WITHOUT MEETING A HUMAN!
YOU WANT TO GET AWAY FROM SMOKE, NOISE, AND PEOPLE! I'LL SEE WHAT I CAN FIND!
AH! HERE IN THE REGION NORTH OF LAKE SUPERIOR ARE VAST BLOCKS OF PUBLIC LAND INHABITED ONLY BY MOOSE AND MUDHENS!
YOU MEAN THEY HAVE NO ROADS, NO CITIES, NO FACTORIES, NO PEOPLE?
THAT'S RIGHT! NOT EVEN VISITING FISHERMEN ON THE THOUSANDS OF LAKES!
GLORY BE! I'LL TAKE ONE OF THOSE BLOCKS WITH A THOUSAND!
A THOUSAND ACRES?
NO! A THOUSAND LAKES!

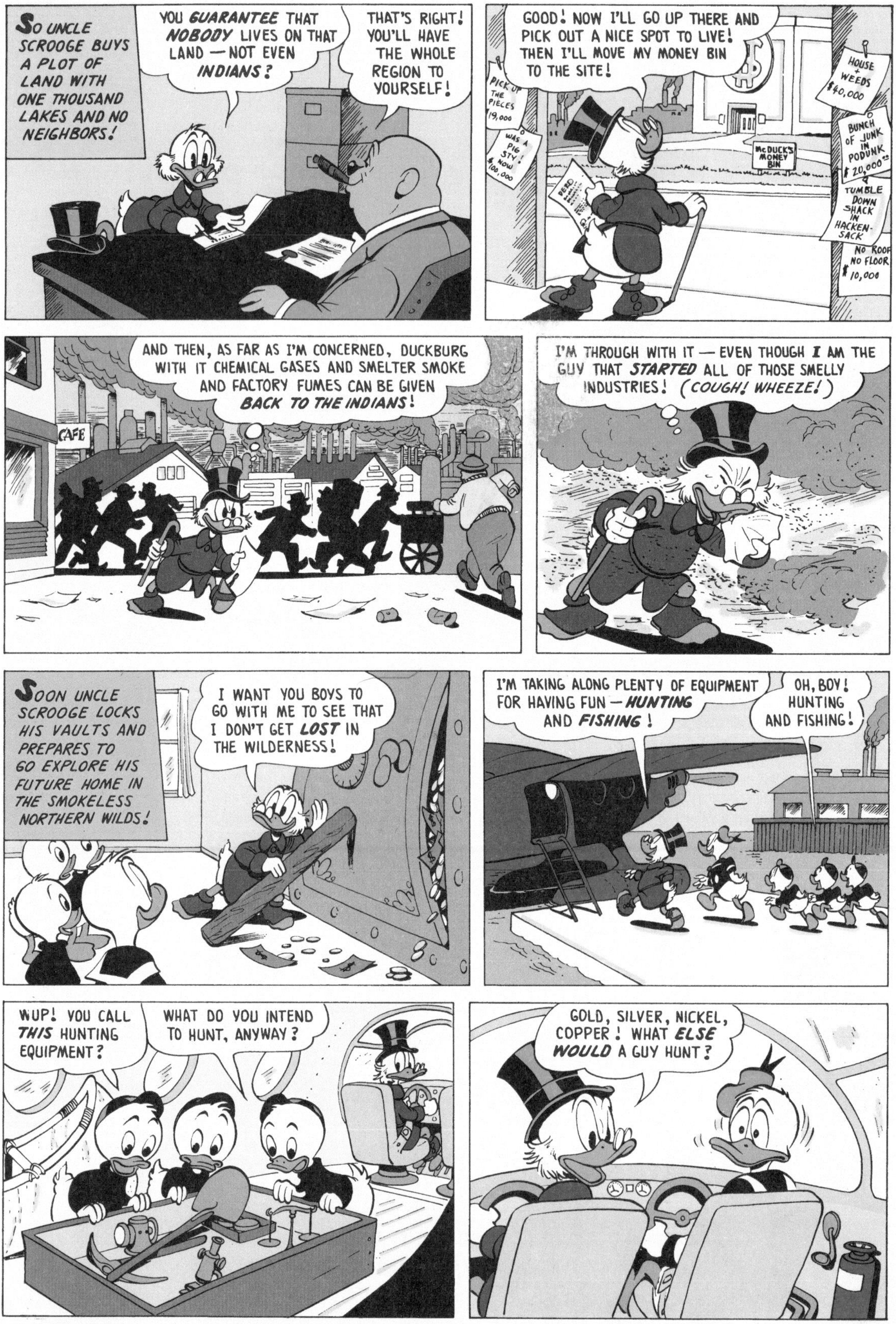
SO UNCLE SCROOGE BUYS A PLOT OF LAND WITH ONE THOUSAND LAKES AND NO NEIGHBORS!
YOU GUARANTEE THAT NOBODY LIVES ON THAT LAND — NOT EVEN INDIANS?
THAT'S RIGHT! YOU'LL HAVE THE WHOLE REGION TO YOURSELF!
GOOD! NOW I'LL GO UP THERE AND PICK OUT A NICE SPOT TO LIVE! THEN I'LL MOVE MY MONEY BIN TO THE SITE!
PICK UP THE PIECES 19,000
WAS A PIG STY! NOW $100,000
McDUCK'S MONEY BIN
HOUSE + WEEDS $40,000
BUNCH OF JUNK IN PODUNK $20,000
TUMBLE DOWN SHACK IN HACKEN-SACK NO ROOF NO FLOOR $10,000
AND THEN, AS FAR AS I'M CONCERNED, DUCKBURG WITH IT CHEMICAL GASES AND SMELTER SMOKE AND FACTORY FUMES CAN BE GIVEN BACK TO THE INDIANS!
CAFE
I'M THROUGH WITH IT — EVEN THOUGH I AM THE GUY THAT STARTED ALL OF THOSE SMELLY INDUSTRIES! (COUGH! WHEEZE!)
SOON UNCLE SCROOGE LOCKS HIS VAULTS AND PREPARES TO GO EXPLORE HIS FUTURE HOME IN THE SMOKELESS NORTHERN WILDS!
I WANT YOU BOYS TO GO WITH ME TO SEE THAT I DON'T GET LOST IN THE WILDERNESS!
I'M TAKING ALONG PLENTY OF EQUIPMENT FOR HAVING FUN — HUNTING AND FISHING!
OH, BOY! HUNTING AND FISHING!
WUP! YOU CALL THIS HUNTING EQUIPMENT?
WHAT DO YOU INTEND TO HUNT, ANYWAY?
GOLD, SILVER, NICKEL, COPPER! WHAT ELSE WOULD A GUY HUNT?

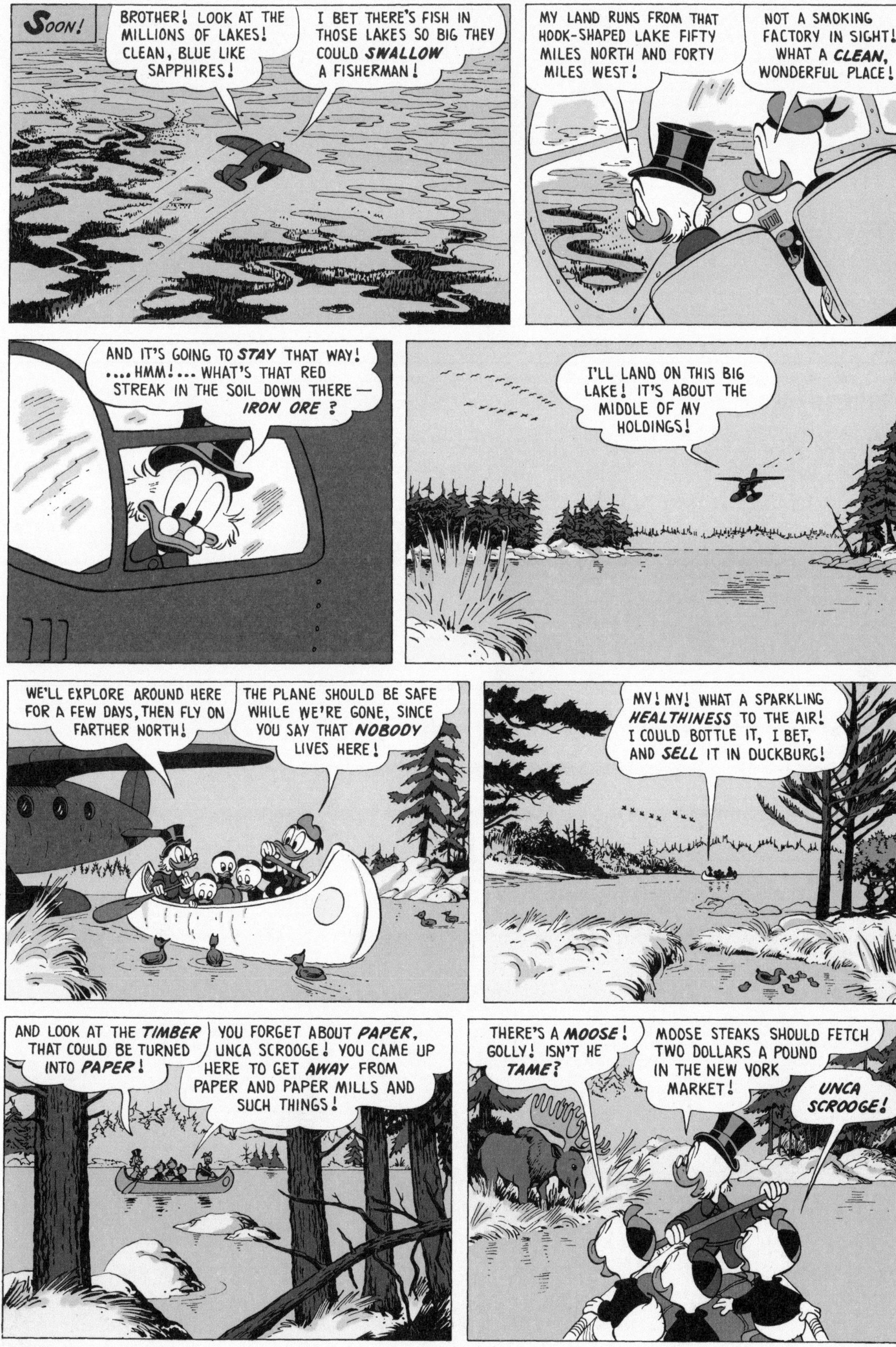
SOON!
BROTHER! LOOK AT THE MILLIONS OF LAKES! CLEAN, BLUE LIKE SAPPHIRES!
I BET THERE'S FISH IN THOSE LAKES SO BIG THEY COULD SWALLOW A FISHERMAN!
MY LAND RUNS FROM THAT HOOK-SHAPED LAKE FIFTY MILES NORTH AND FORTY MILES WEST!
NOT A SMOKING FACTORY IN SIGHT! WHAT A CLEAN, WONDERFUL PLACE!
AND IT'S GOING TO STAY THAT WAY! ....HMM!... WHAT'S THAT RED STREAK IN THE SOIL DOWN THERE— IRON ORE?
I'LL LAND ON THIS BIG LAKE! IT'S ABOUT THE MIDDLE OF MY HOLDINGS!
WE'LL EXPLORE AROUND HERE FOR A FEW DAYS, THEN FLY ON FARTHER NORTH!
THE PLANE SHOULD BE SAFE WHILE WE'RE GONE, SINCE YOU SAY THAT NOBODY LIVES HERE!
MY! MY! WHAT A SPARKLING HEALTHINESS TO THE AIR! I COULD BOTTLE IT, I BET, AND SELL IT IN DUCKBURG!
AND LOOK AT THE TIMBER THAT COULD BE TURNED INTO PAPER!
YOU FORGET ABOUT PAPER, UNCA SCROOGE! YOU CAME UP HERE TO GET AWAY FROM PAPER AND PAPER MILLS AND SUCH THINGS!
THERE'S A MOOSE! GOLLY! ISN'T HE TAME?
MOOSE STEAKS SHOULD FETCH TWO DOLLARS A POUND IN THE NEW YORK MARKET!
UNCA SCROOGE!

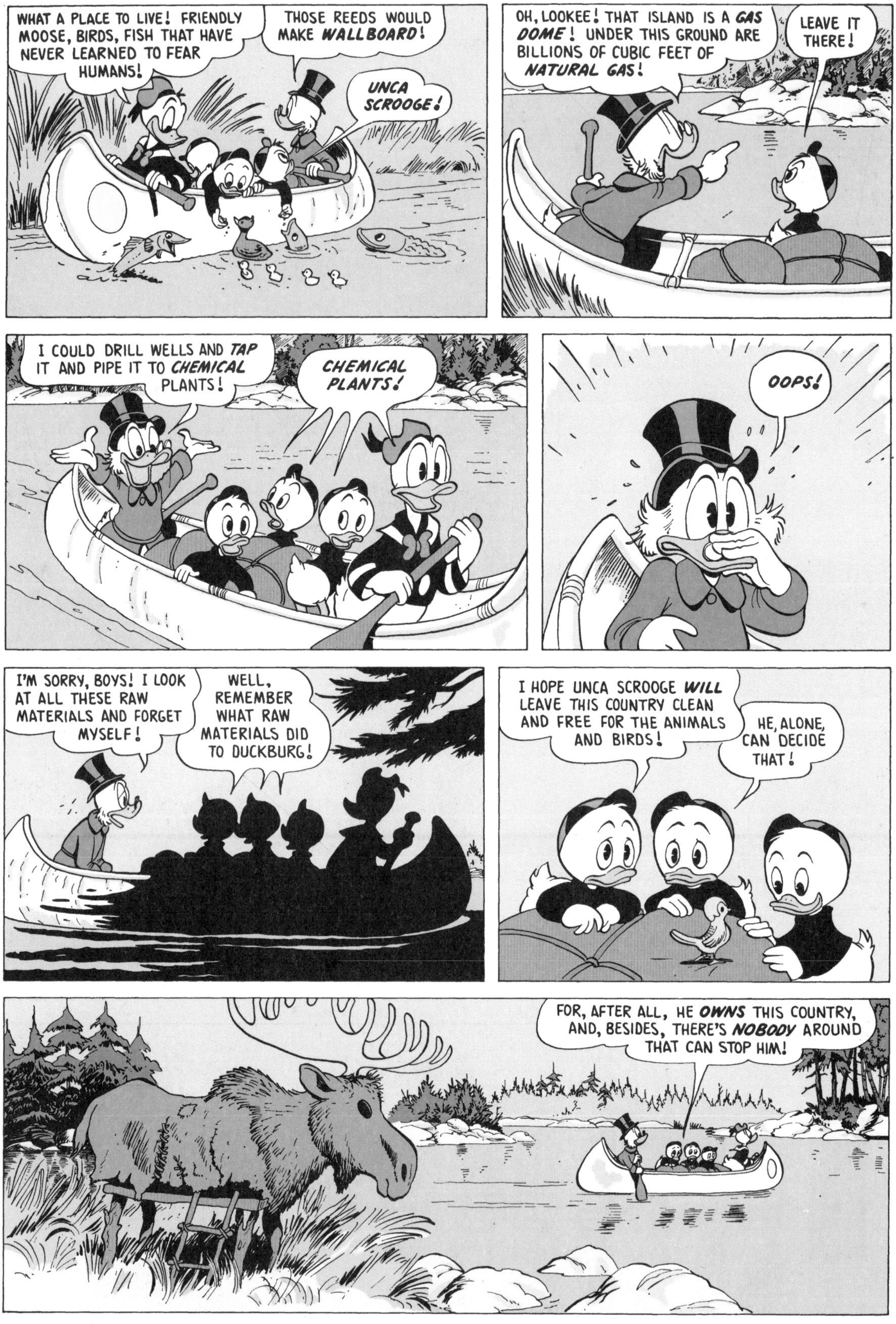
WHAT A PLACE TO LIVE! FRIENDLY MOOSE, BIRDS, FISH THAT HAVE NEVER LEARNED TO FEAR HUMANS!
THOSE REEDS WOULD MAKE WALLBOARD!
UNCA SCROOGE!
OH, LOOKEE! THAT ISLAND IS A GAS DOME! UNDER THIS GROUND ARE BILLIONS OF CUBIC FEET OF NATURAL GAS!
LEAVE IT THERE!
I COULD DRILL WELLS AND TAP IT AND PIPE IT TO CHEMICAL PLANTS!
CHEMICAL PLANTS!
OOPS!
I'M SORRY, BOYS! I LOOK AT ALL THESE RAW MATERIALS AND FORGET MYSELF!
WELL, REMEMBER WHAT RAW MATERIALS DID TO DUCKBURG!
I HOPE UNCA SCROOGE WILL LEAVE THIS COUNTRY CLEAN AND FREE FOR THE ANIMALS AND BIRDS!
HE, ALONE, CAN DECIDE THAT!
FOR, AFTER ALL, HE OWNS THIS COUNTRY, AND, BESIDES, THERE'S NOBODY AROUND THAT CAN STOP HIM!

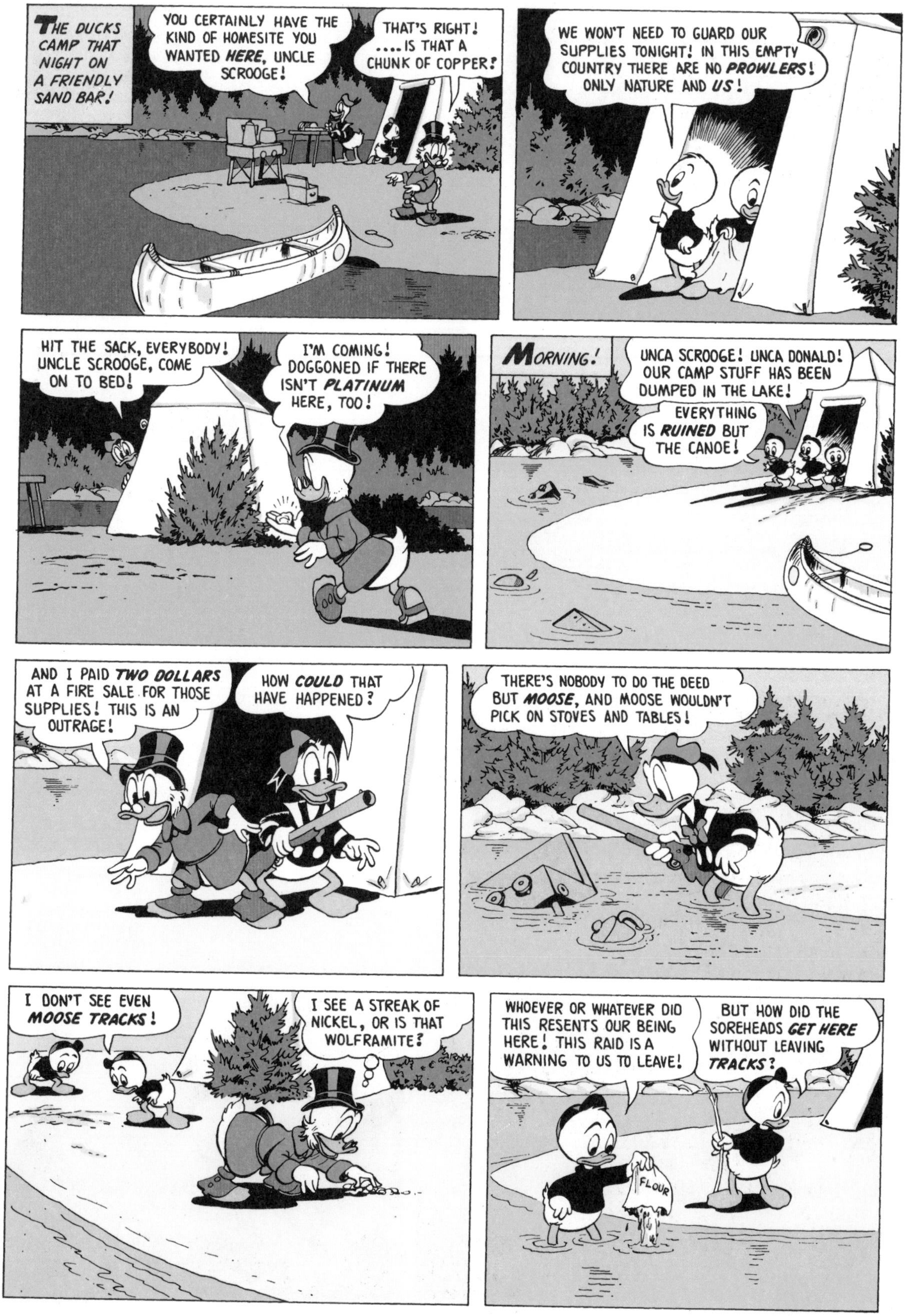
THE DUCKS CAMP THAT NIGHT ON A FRIENDLY SAND BAR!
YOU CERTAINLY HAVE THE KIND OF HOMESITE YOU WANTED HERE, UNCLE SCROOGE!
THAT'S RIGHT! ....IS THAT A CHUNK OF COPPER?
WE WON'T NEED TO GUARD OUR SUPPLIES TONIGHT! IN THIS EMPTY COUNTRY THERE ARE NO PROWLERS! ONLY NATURE AND US!
HIT THE SACK, EVERYBODY! UNCLE SCROOGE, COME ON TO BED!
I'M COMING! DOGGONED IF THERE ISN'T PLATINUM HERE, TOO!
MORNING!
UNCA SCROOGE! UNCA DONALD! OUR CAMP STUFF HAS BEEN DUMPED IN THE LAKE!
EVERYTHING IS RUINED BUT THE CANOE!
AND I PAID TWO DOLLARS AT A FIRE SALE FOR THOSE SUPPLIES! THIS IS AN OUTRAGE!
HOW COULD THAT HAVE HAPPENED?
THERE'S NOBODY TO DO THE DEED BUT MOOSE, AND MOOSE WOULDN'T PICK ON STOVES AND TABLES!
I DON'T SEE EVEN MOOSE TRACKS!
I SEE A STREAK OF NICKEL, OR IS THAT WOLFRAMITE?
WHOEVER OR WHATEVER DID THIS RESENTS OUR BEING HERE! THIS RAID IS A WARNING TO US TO LEAVE!
BUT HOW DID THE SOREHEADS GET HERE WITHOUT LEAVING TRACKS?
FLOUR

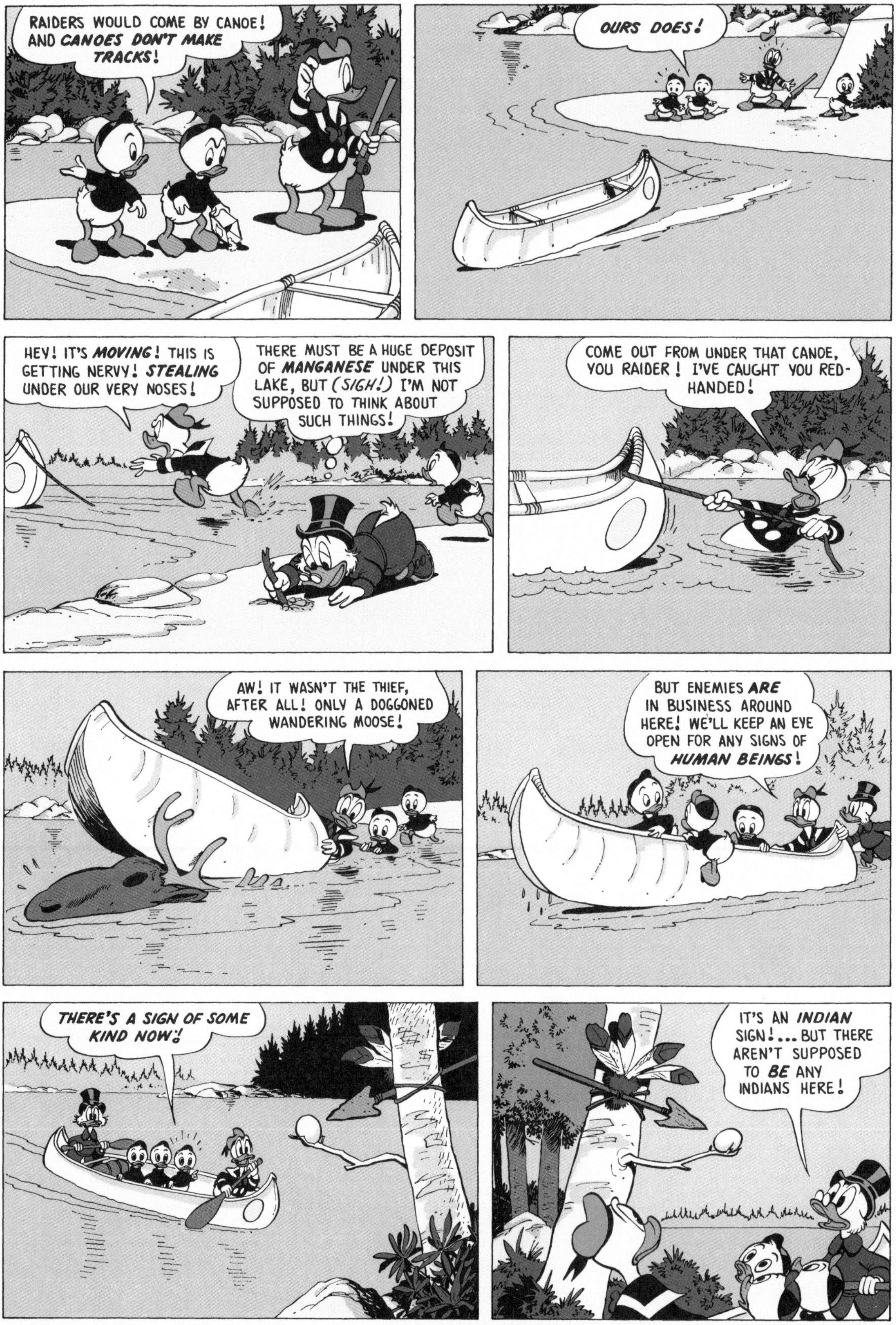
RAIDERS WOULD COME BY CANOE! AND CANOES DON'T MAKE TRACKS!
OURS DOES!
HEY! IT'S MOVING! THIS IS GETTING NERVY! STEALING UNDER OUR VERY NOSES!
THERE MUST BE A HUGE DEPOSIT OF MANGANESE UNDER THIS LAKE, BUT (SIGH!) I'M NOT SUPPOSED TO THINK ABOUT SUCH THINGS!
COME OUT FROM UNDER THAT CANOE, YOU RAIDER! I'VE CAUGHT YOU RED-HANDED!
AW! IT WASN'T THE THIEF, AFTER ALL! ONLY A DOGGONED WANDERING MOOSE!
BUT ENEMIES ARE IN BUSINESS AROUND HERE! WE'LL KEEP AN EYE OPEN FOR ANY SIGNS OF HUMAN BEINGS!
THERE'S A SIGN OF SOME KIND NOW!
IT'S AN INDIAN SIGN!... BUT THERE AREN'T SUPPOSED TO BE ANY INDIANS HERE!

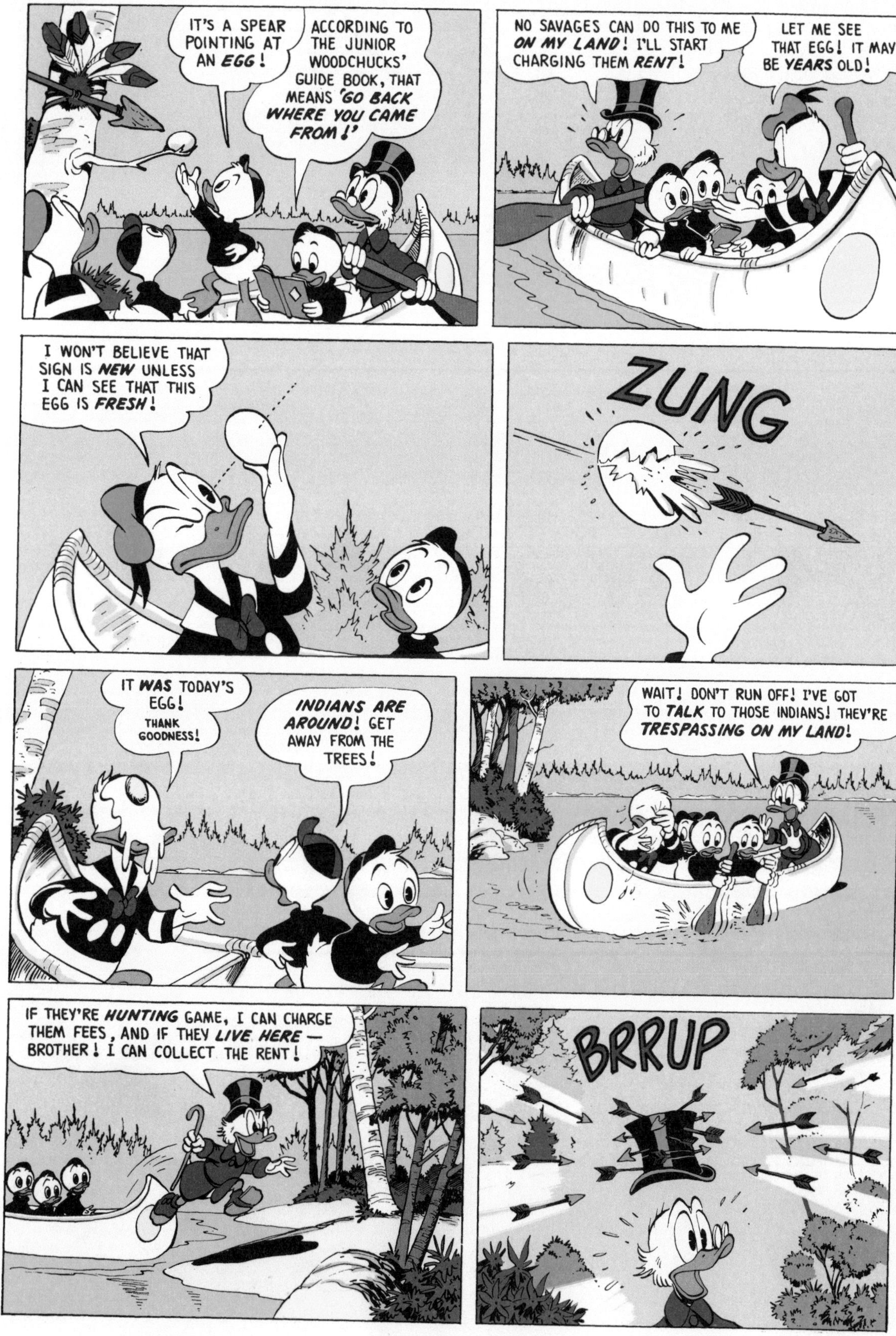
IT'S A SPEAR POINTING AT AN EGG!
ACCORDING TO THE JUNIOR WOODCHUCKS' GUIDE BOOK, THAT MEANS 'GO BACK WHERE YOU CAME FROM!'
NO SAVAGES CAN DO THIS TO ME ON MY LAND! I'LL START CHARGING THEM RENT!
LET ME SEE THAT EGG! IT MAY BE YEARS OLD!
I WON'T BELIEVE THAT SIGN IS NEW UNLESS I CAN SEE THAT THIS EGG IS FRESH!
ZUNG
IT WAS TODAY'S EGG! THANK GOODNESS!
INDIANS ARE AROUND! GET AWAY FROM THE TREES!
WAIT! DON'T RUN OFF! I'VE GOT TO TALK TO THOSE INDIANS! THEY'RE TRESPASSING ON MY LAND!
IF THEY'RE HUNTING GAME, I CAN CHARGE THEM FEES, AND IF THEY LIVE HERE — BROTHER! I CAN COLLECT THE RENT!
BRRUP

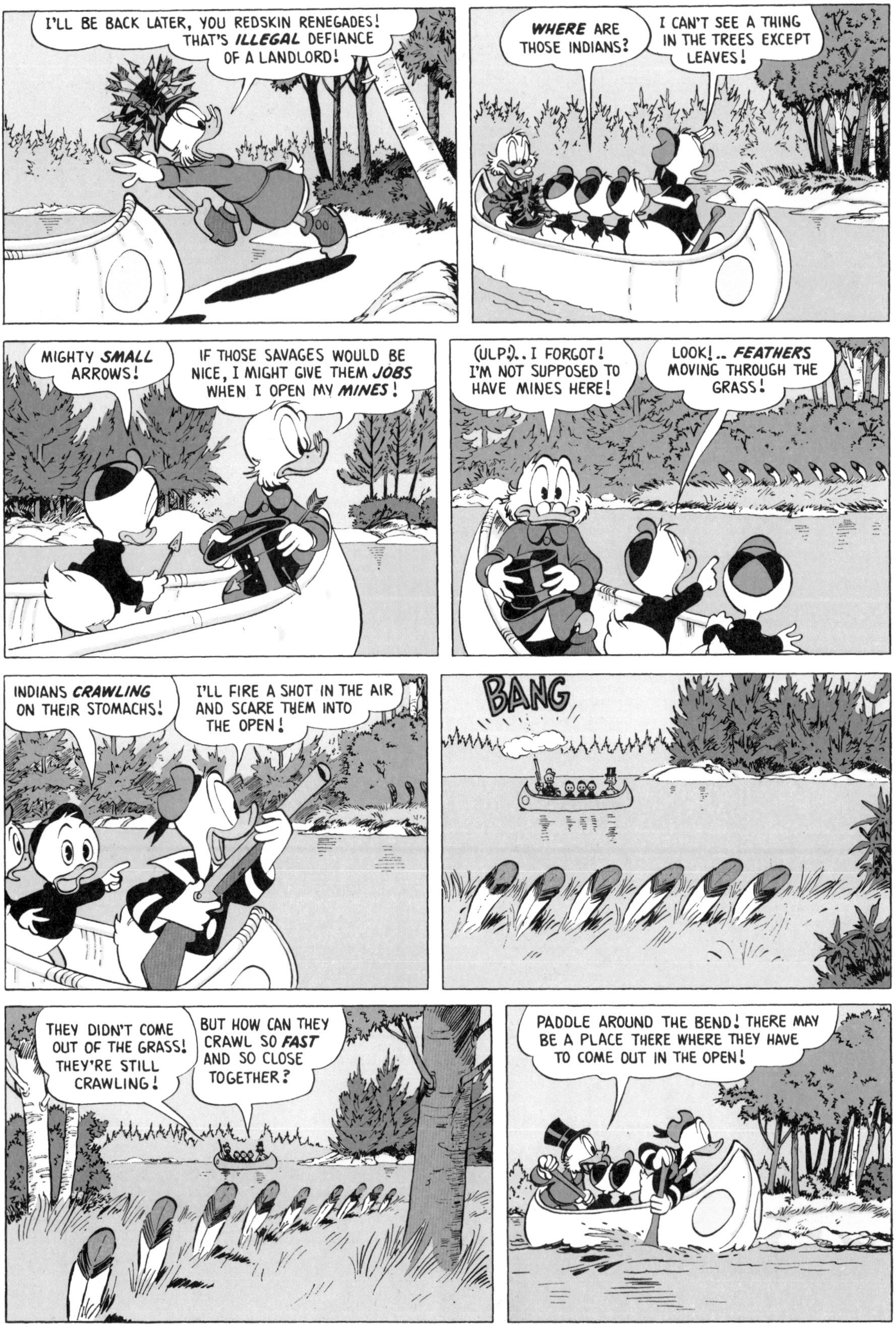

I'LL BE BACK LATER, YOU REDSKIN RENEGADES! THAT'S *ILLEGAL* DEFIANCE OF A LANDLORD!
WHERE ARE THOSE INDIANS?
I CAN'T SEE A THING IN THE TREES EXCEPT LEAVES!
MIGHTY *SMALL* ARROWS!
IF THOSE SAVAGES WOULD BE NICE, I MIGHT GIVE THEM *JOBS* WHEN I OPEN MY *MINES*!
(ULP!).. I FORGOT! I'M NOT SUPPOSED TO HAVE MINES HERE!
LOOK!.. *FEATHERS* MOVING THROUGH THE GRASS!
INDIANS *CRAWLING* ON THEIR STOMACHS!
I'LL FIRE A SHOT IN THE AIR AND SCARE THEM INTO THE OPEN!
BANG
THEY DIDN'T COME OUT OF THE GRASS! THEY'RE STILL CRAWLING!
BUT HOW CAN THEY CRAWL SO *FAST* AND SO CLOSE TOGETHER?
PADDLE AROUND THE BEND! THERE MAY BE A PLACE THERE WHERE THEY HAVE TO COME OUT IN THE OPEN!

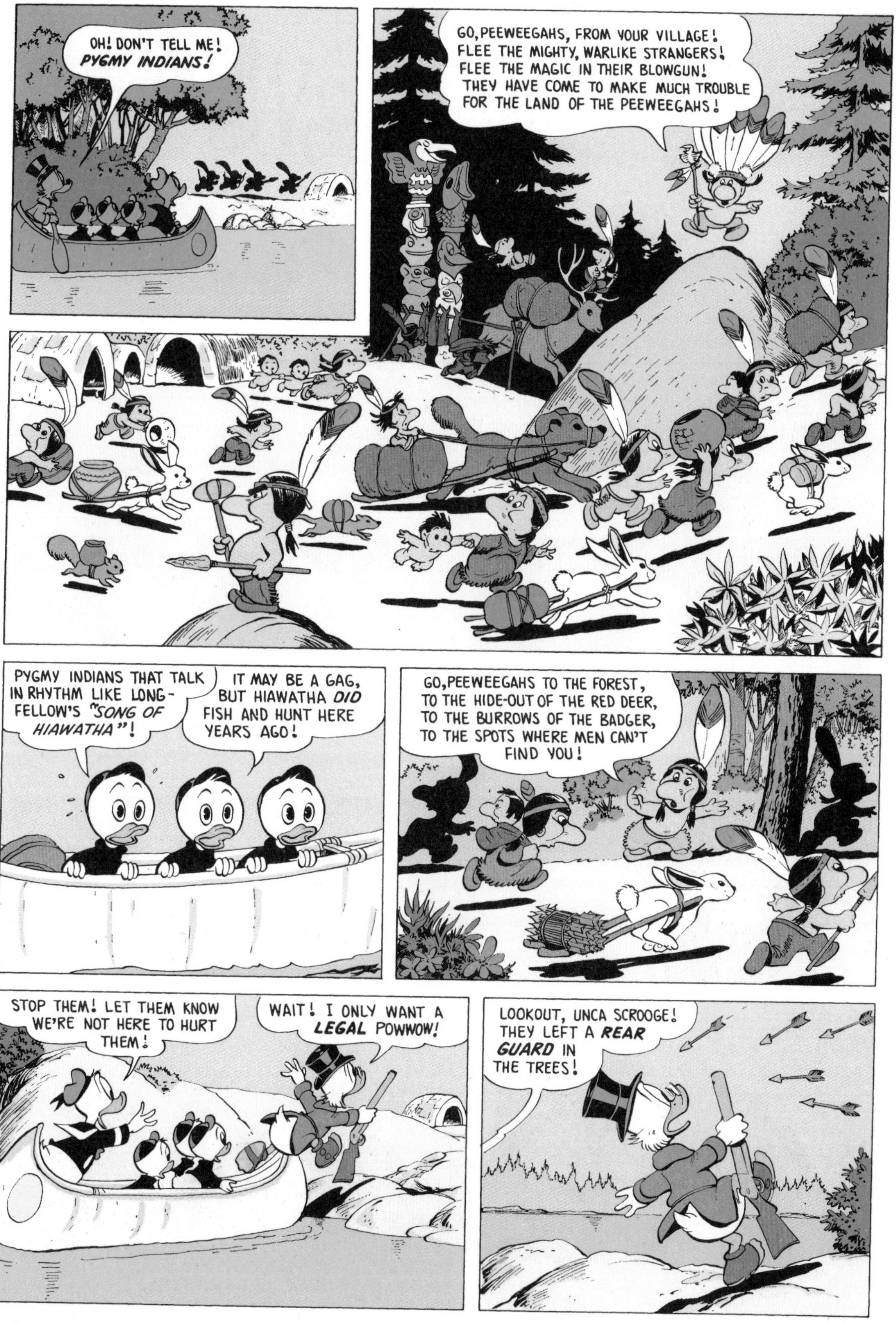
OH! DON'T TELL ME! PYGMY INDIANS!
GO, PEEWEEGAHS, FROM YOUR VILLAGE! FLEE THE MIGHTY, WARLIKE STRANGERS! FLEE THE MAGIC IN THEIR BLOWGUN! THEY HAVE COME TO MAKE MUCH TROUBLE FOR THE LAND OF THE PEEWEEGAHS!
PYGMY INDIANS THAT TALK IN RHYTHM LIKE LONG-FELLOW'S "SONG OF HIAWATHA"!
IT MAY BE A GAG, BUT HIAWATHA DID FISH AND HUNT HERE YEARS AGO!
GO, PEEWEEGAHS TO THE FOREST, TO THE HIDE-OUT OF THE RED DEER, TO THE BURROWS OF THE BADGER, TO THE SPOTS WHERE MEN CAN'T FIND YOU!
STOP THEM! LET THEM KNOW WE'RE NOT HERE TO HURT THEM!
WAIT! I ONLY WANT A LEGAL POWWOW!
LOOKOUT, UNCA SCROOGE! THEY LEFT A REAR GUARD IN THE TREES!

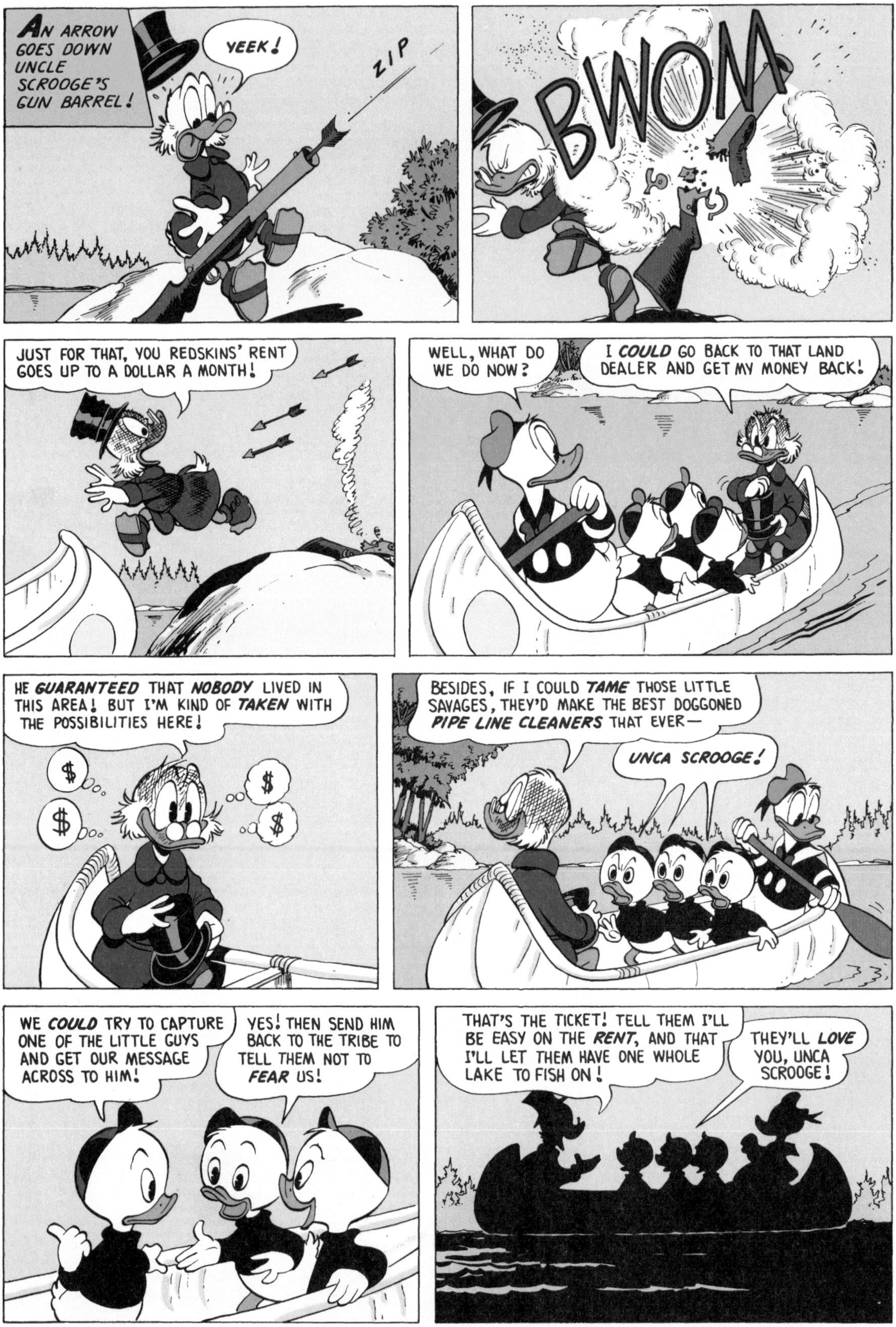
AN ARROW GOES DOWN UNCLE SCROOGE'S GUN BARREL!
YEEK!
ZIP
BWOM
JUST FOR THAT, YOU REDSKINS' RENT GOES UP TO A DOLLAR A MONTH!
WELL, WHAT DO WE DO NOW?
I COULD GO BACK TO THAT LAND DEALER AND GET MY MONEY BACK!
HE GUARANTEED THAT NOBODY LIVED IN THIS AREA! BUT I'M KIND OF TAKEN WITH THE POSSIBILITIES HERE!
$
$
$
$
BESIDES, IF I COULD TAME THOSE LITTLE SAVAGES, THEY'D MAKE THE BEST DOGGONED PIPE LINE CLEANERS THAT EVER—
UNCA SCROOGE!
WE COULD TRY TO CAPTURE ONE OF THE LITTLE GUYS AND GET OUR MESSAGE ACROSS TO HIM!
YES! THEN SEND HIM BACK TO THE TRIBE TO TELL THEM NOT TO FEAR US!
THAT'S THE TICKET! TELL THEM I'LL BE EASY ON THE RENT, AND THAT I'LL LET THEM HAVE ONE WHOLE LAKE TO FISH ON!
THEY'LL LOVE YOU, UNCA SCROOGE!

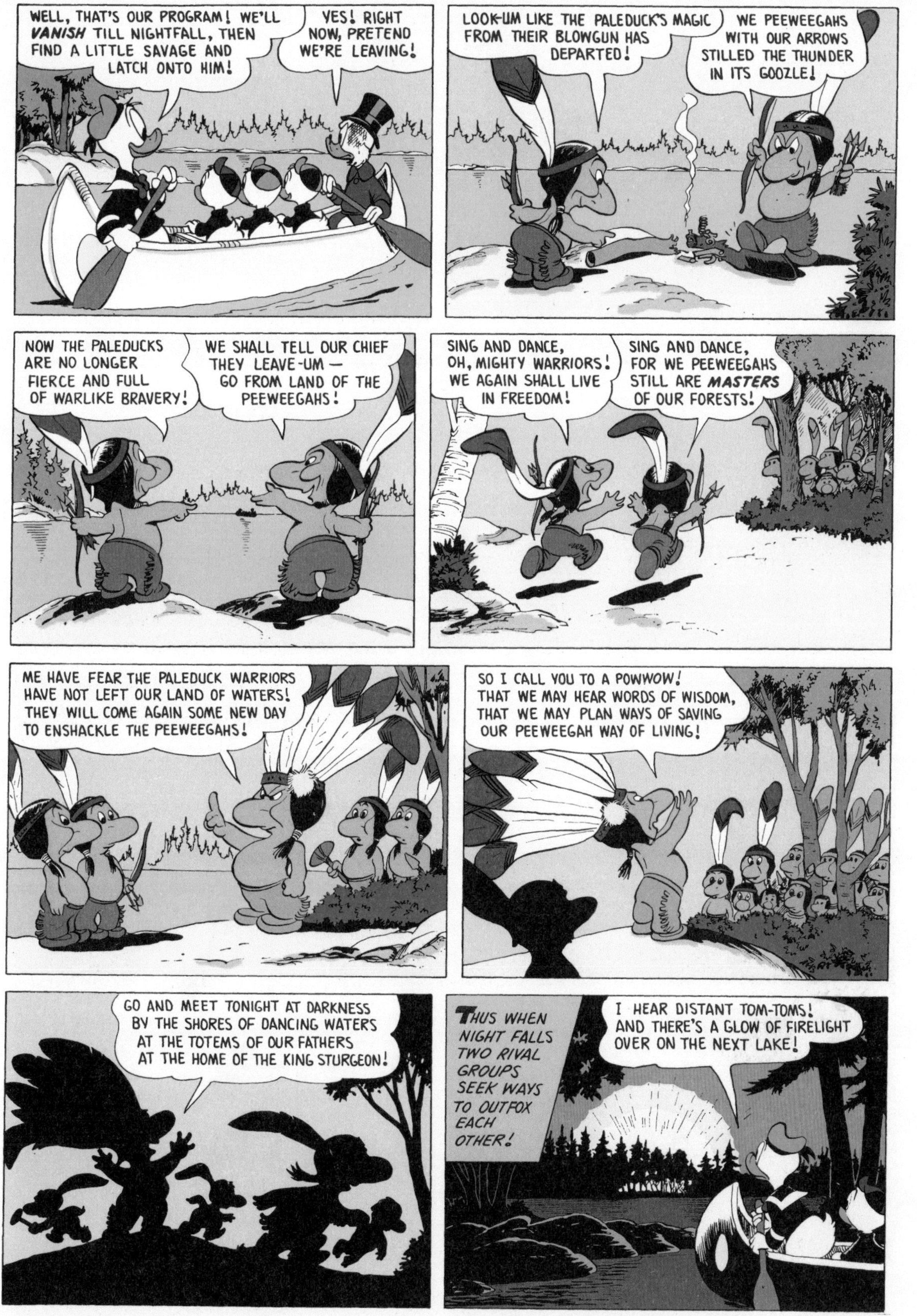
WELL, THAT'S OUR PROGRAM! WE'LL VANISH TILL NIGHTFALL, THEN FIND A LITTLE SAVAGE AND LATCH ONTO HIM!
YES! RIGHT NOW, PRETEND WE'RE LEAVING!
LOOK-UM LIKE THE PALEDUCK'S MAGIC FROM THEIR BLOWGUN HAS DEPARTED!
WE PEEWEEGAHS WITH OUR ARROWS STILLED THE THUNDER IN ITS GOOZLE!
NOW THE PALEDUCKS ARE NO LONGER FIERCE AND FULL OF WARLIKE BRAVERY!
WE SHALL TELL OUR CHIEF THEY LEAVE-UM — GO FROM LAND OF THE PEEWEEGAHS!
SING AND DANCE, OH, MIGHTY WARRIORS! WE AGAIN SHALL LIVE IN FREEDOM!
SING AND DANCE, FOR WE PEEWEEGAHS STILL ARE MASTERS OF OUR FORESTS!
ME HAVE FEAR THE PALEDUCK WARRIORS HAVE NOT LEFT OUR LAND OF WATERS! THEY WILL COME AGAIN SOME NEW DAY TO ENSHACKLE THE PEEWEEGAHS!
SO I CALL YOU TO A POWWOW! THAT WE MAY HEAR WORDS OF WISDOM, THAT WE MAY PLAN WAYS OF SAVING OUR PEEWEEGAH WAY OF LIVING!
GO AND MEET TONIGHT AT DARKNESS BY THE SHORES OF DANCING WATERS AT THE TOTEMS OF OUR FATHERS AT THE HOME OF THE KING STURGEON!
THUS WHEN NIGHT FALLS TWO RIVAL GROUPS SEEK WAYS TO OUTFOX EACH OTHER!
I HEAR DISTANT TOM-TOMS! AND THERE'S A GLOW OF FIRELIGHT OVER ON THE NEXT LAKE!

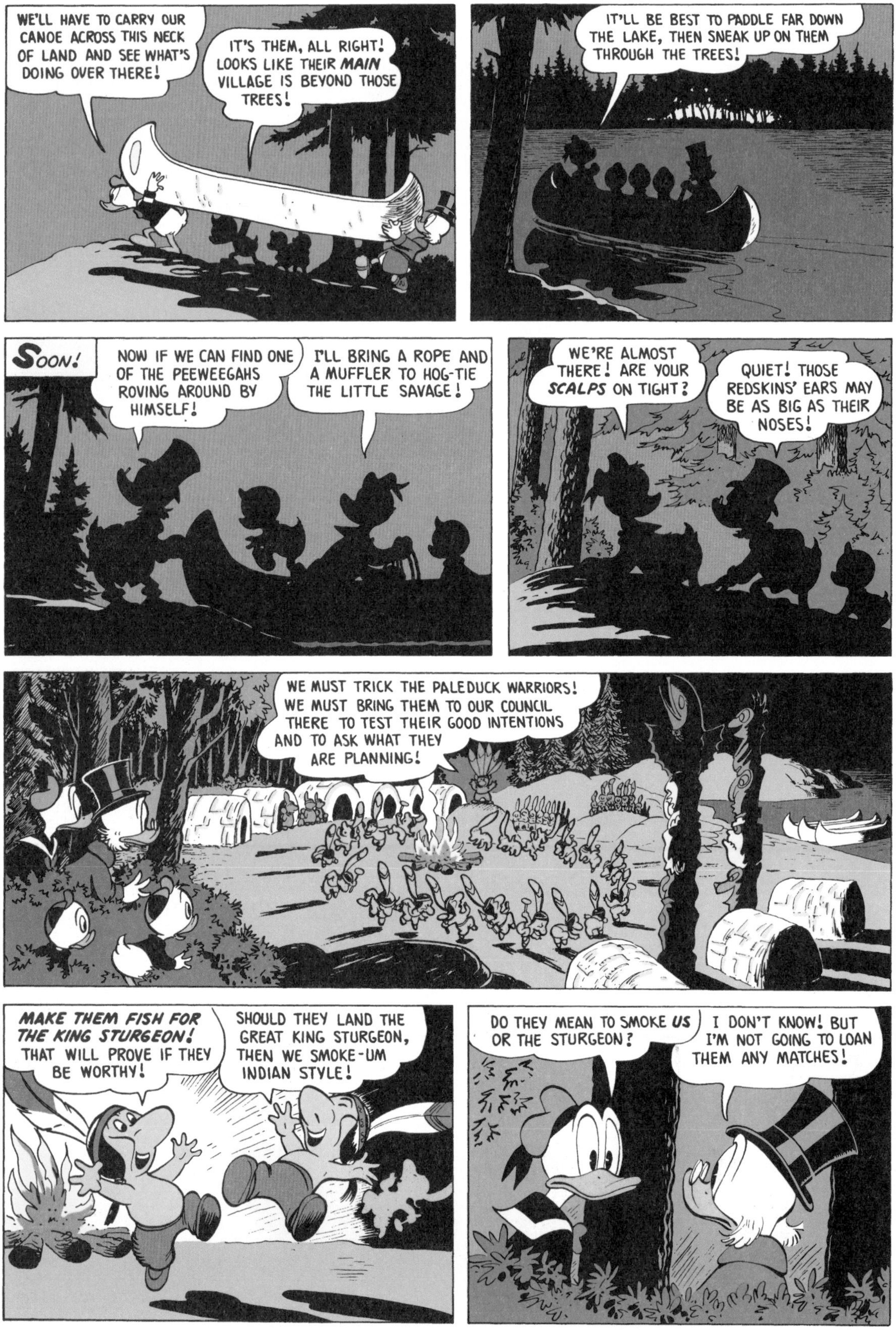
WE'LL HAVE TO CARRY OUR CANOE ACROSS THIS NECK OF LAND AND SEE WHAT'S DOING OVER THERE!
IT'S THEM, ALL RIGHT! LOOKS LIKE THEIR MAIN VILLAGE IS BEYOND THOSE TREES!
IT'LL BE BEST TO PADDLE FAR DOWN THE LAKE, THEN SNEAK UP ON THEM THROUGH THE TREES!
SOON!
NOW IF WE CAN FIND ONE OF THE PEEWEEGAHS ROVING AROUND BY HIMSELF!
I'LL BRING A ROPE AND A MUFFLER TO HOG-TIE THE LITTLE SAVAGE!
WE'RE ALMOST THERE! ARE YOUR SCALPS ON TIGHT?
QUIET! THOSE REDSKINS' EARS MAY BE AS BIG AS THEIR NOSES!
WE MUST TRICK THE PALEDUCK WARRIORS! WE MUST BRING THEM TO OUR COUNCIL THERE TO TEST THEIR GOOD INTENTIONS AND TO ASK WHAT THEY ARE PLANNING!
MAKE THEM FISH FOR THE KING STURGEON! THAT WILL PROVE IF THEY BE WORTHY!
SHOULD THEY LAND THE GREAT KING STURGEON, THEN WE SMOKE-UM INDIAN STYLE!
DO THEY MEAN TO SMOKE US OR THE STURGEON?
I DON'T KNOW! BUT I'M NOT GOING TO LOAN THEM ANY MATCHES!

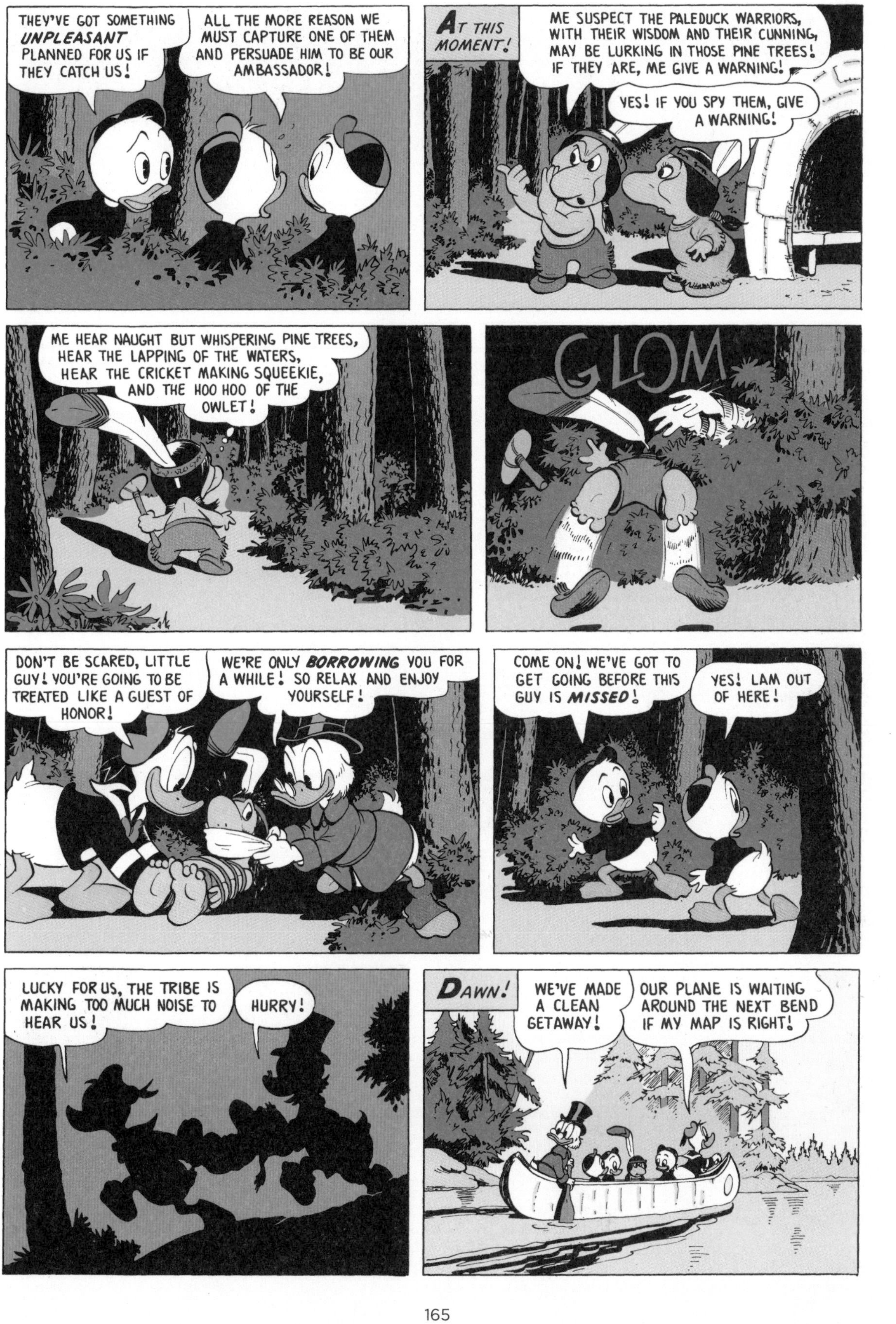
THEY'VE GOT SOMETHING UNPLEASANT PLANNED FOR US IF THEY CATCH US!
ALL THE MORE REASON WE MUST CAPTURE ONE OF THEM AND PERSUADE HIM TO BE OUR AMBASSADOR!
AT THIS MOMENT!
ME SUSPECT THE PALEDUCK WARRIORS, WITH THEIR WISDOM AND THEIR CUNNING, MAY BE LURKING IN THOSE PINE TREES! IF THEY ARE, ME GIVE A WARNING!
YES! IF YOU SPY THEM, GIVE A WARNING!
ME HEAR NAUGHT BUT WHISPERING PINE TREES, HEAR THE LAPPING OF THE WATERS, HEAR THE CRICKET MAKING SQUEEKIE, AND THE HOO HOO OF THE OWLET!
GLOM
DON'T BE SCARED, LITTLE GUY! YOU'RE GOING TO BE TREATED LIKE A GUEST OF HONOR!
WE'RE ONLY BORROWING YOU FOR A WHILE! SO RELAX AND ENJOY YOURSELF!
COME ON! WE'VE GOT TO GET GOING BEFORE THIS GUY IS MISSED!
YES! LAM OUT OF HERE!
LUCKY FOR US, THE TRIBE IS MAKING TOO MUCH NOISE TO HEAR US!
HURRY!
DAWN!
WE'VE MADE A CLEAN GETAWAY!
OUR PLANE IS WAITING AROUND THE NEXT BEND IF MY MAP IS RIGHT!

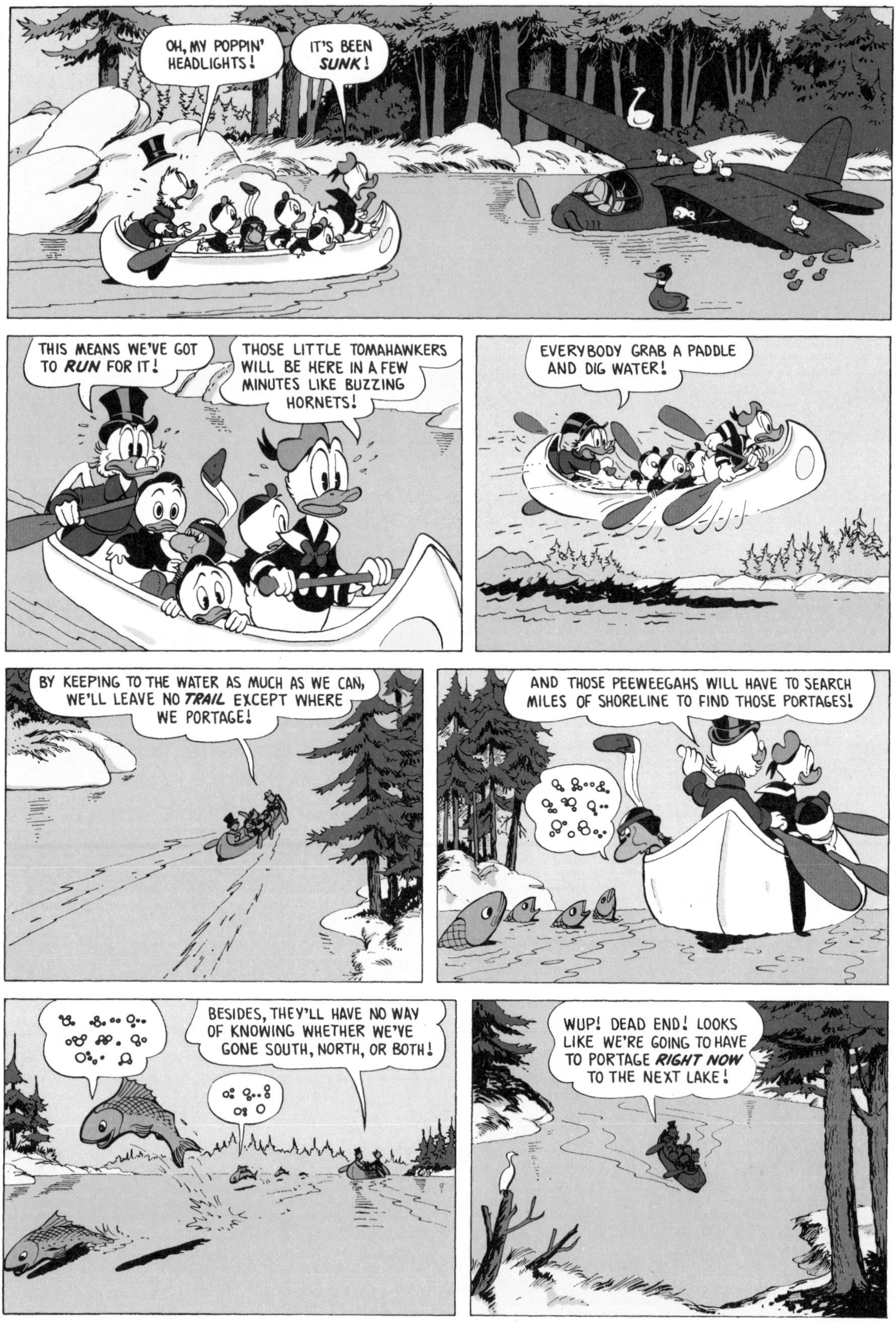
OH, MY POPPIN' HEADLIGHTS!
IT'S BEEN **SUNK**!
THIS MEANS WE'VE GOT TO **RUN** FOR IT!
THOSE LITTLE TOMAHAWKERS WILL BE HERE IN A FEW MINUTES LIKE BUZZING HORNETS!
EVERYBODY GRAB A PADDLE AND DIG WATER!
BY KEEPING TO THE WATER AS MUCH AS WE CAN, WE'LL LEAVE NO **TRAIL** EXCEPT WHERE WE PORTAGE!
AND THOSE PEEWEEGAHS WILL HAVE TO SEARCH MILES OF SHORELINE TO FIND THOSE PORTAGES!
BESIDES, THEY'LL HAVE NO WAY OF KNOWING WHETHER WE'VE GONE SOUTH, NORTH, OR BOTH!
WUP! DEAD END! LOOKS LIKE WE'RE GOING TO HAVE TO PORTAGE **RIGHT NOW** TO THE NEXT LAKE!

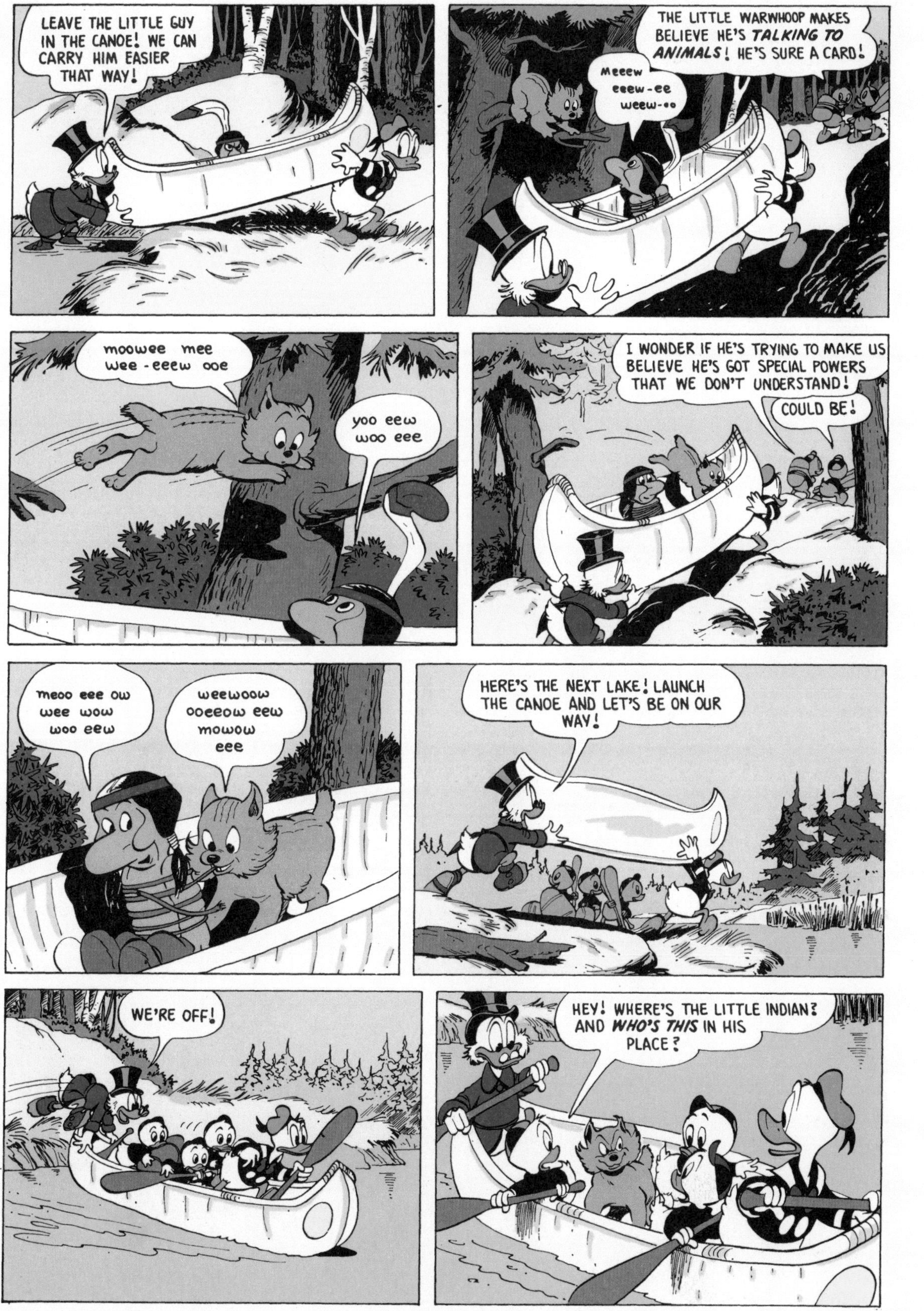
LEAVE THE LITTLE GUY IN THE CANOE! WE CAN CARRY HIM EASIER THAT WAY!
THE LITTLE WARWHOOP MAKES BELIEVE HE'S TALKING TO ANIMALS! HE'S SURE A CARD!
Meeew eeew-ee weew-oo
moowee mee wee-eeew ooe
yoo eew woo eee
I WONDER IF HE'S TRYING TO MAKE US BELIEVE HE'S GOT SPECIAL POWERS THAT WE DON'T UNDERSTAND!
COULD BE!
meoo eee ow wee wow woo eew
weewoow ooeeow eew mowow eee
HERE'S THE NEXT LAKE! LAUNCH THE CANOE AND LET'S BE ON OUR WAY!
WE'RE OFF!
HEY! WHERE'S THE LITTLE INDIAN? AND WHO'S THIS IN HIS PLACE?

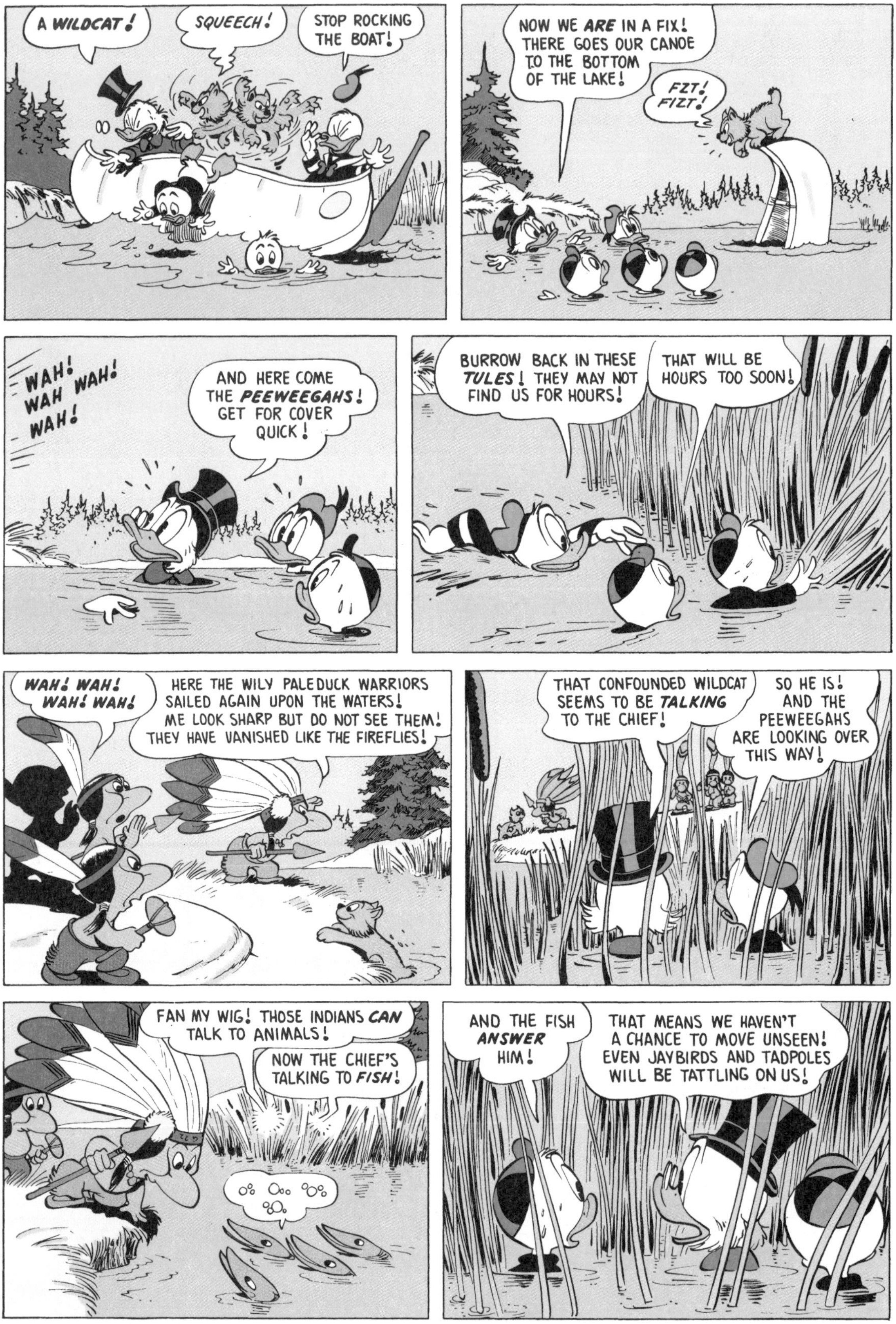
A WILDCAT!
SQUEECH!
STOP ROCKING THE BOAT!
NOW WE ARE IN A FIX! THERE GOES OUR CANOE TO THE BOTTOM OF THE LAKE!
FZT! FIZT!
WAH! WAH WAH! WAH!
AND HERE COME THE PEEWEEGAHS! GET FOR COVER QUICK!
BURROW BACK IN THESE TULES! THEY MAY NOT FIND US FOR HOURS!
THAT WILL BE HOURS TOO SOON!
WAH! WAH! WAH! WAH!
HERE THE WILY PALEDUCK WARRIORS SAILED AGAIN UPON THE WATERS! ME LOOK SHARP BUT DO NOT SEE THEM! THEY HAVE VANISHED LIKE THE FIREFLIES!
THAT CONFOUNDED WILDCAT SEEMS TO BE TALKING TO THE CHIEF!
SO HE IS! AND THE PEEWEEGAHS ARE LOOKING OVER THIS WAY!
FAN MY WIG! THOSE INDIANS CAN TALK TO ANIMALS!
NOW THE CHIEF'S TALKING TO FISH!
AND THE FISH ANSWER HIM!
THAT MEANS WE HAVEN'T A CHANCE TO MOVE UNSEEN! EVEN JAYBIRDS AND TADPOLES WILL BE TATTLING ON US!

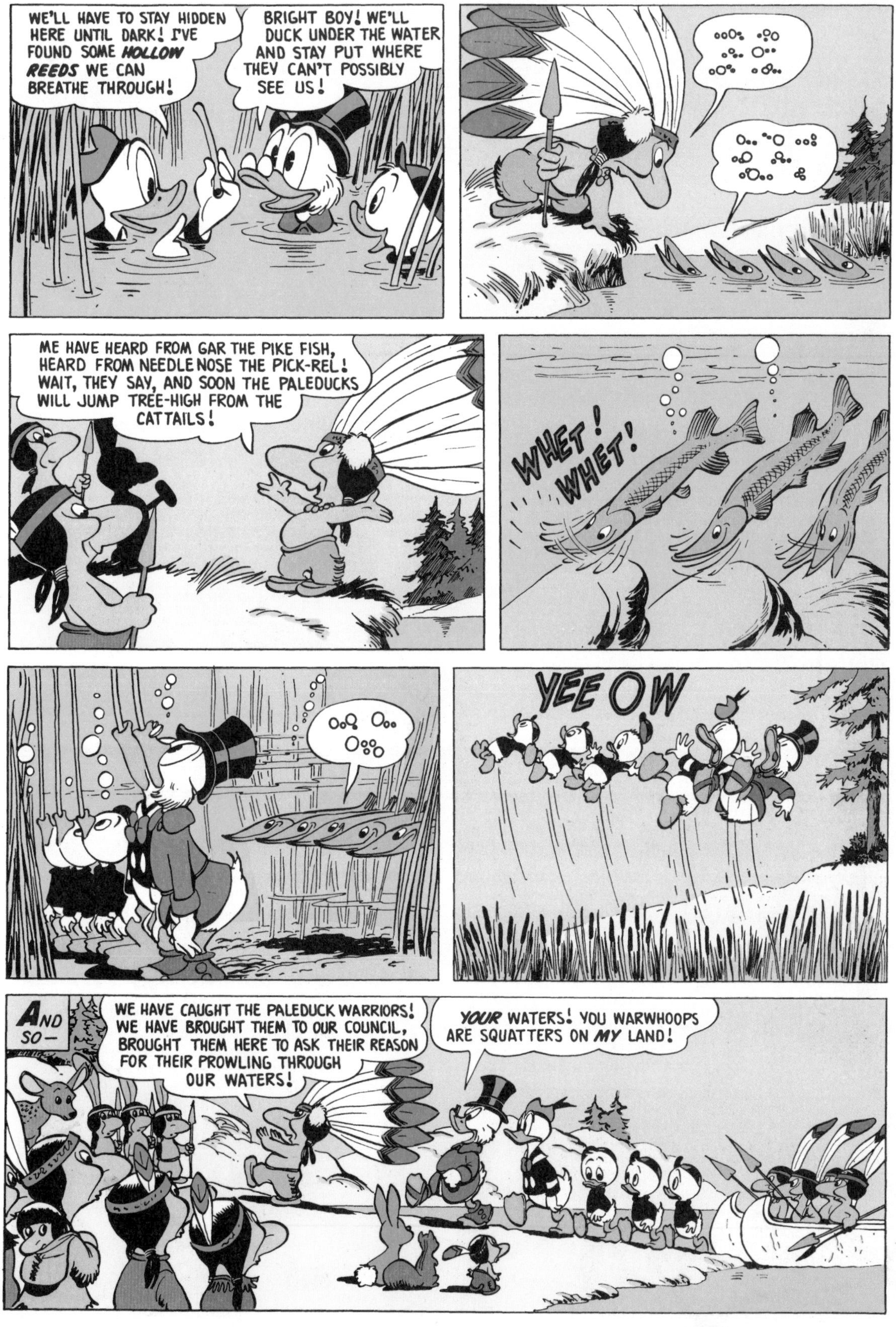

WE'LL HAVE TO STAY HIDDEN HERE UNTIL DARK! I'VE FOUND SOME HOLLOW REEDS WE CAN BREATHE THROUGH!
BRIGHT BOY! WE'LL DUCK UNDER THE WATER AND STAY PUT WHERE THEY CAN'T POSSIBLY SEE US!
ME HAVE HEARD FROM GAR THE PIKE FISH, HEARD FROM NEEDLE NOSE THE PICK-REL! WAIT, THEY SAY, AND SOON THE PALEDUCKS WILL JUMP TREE-HIGH FROM THE CATTAILS!
WHET! WHET!
YEEOW
AND SO—
WE HAVE CAUGHT THE PALEDUCK WARRIORS! WE HAVE BROUGHT THEM TO OUR COUNCIL, BROUGHT THEM HERE TO ASK THEIR REASON FOR THEIR PROWLING THROUGH OUR WATERS!
YOUR WATERS! YOU WARWHOOPS ARE SQUATTERS ON MY LAND!

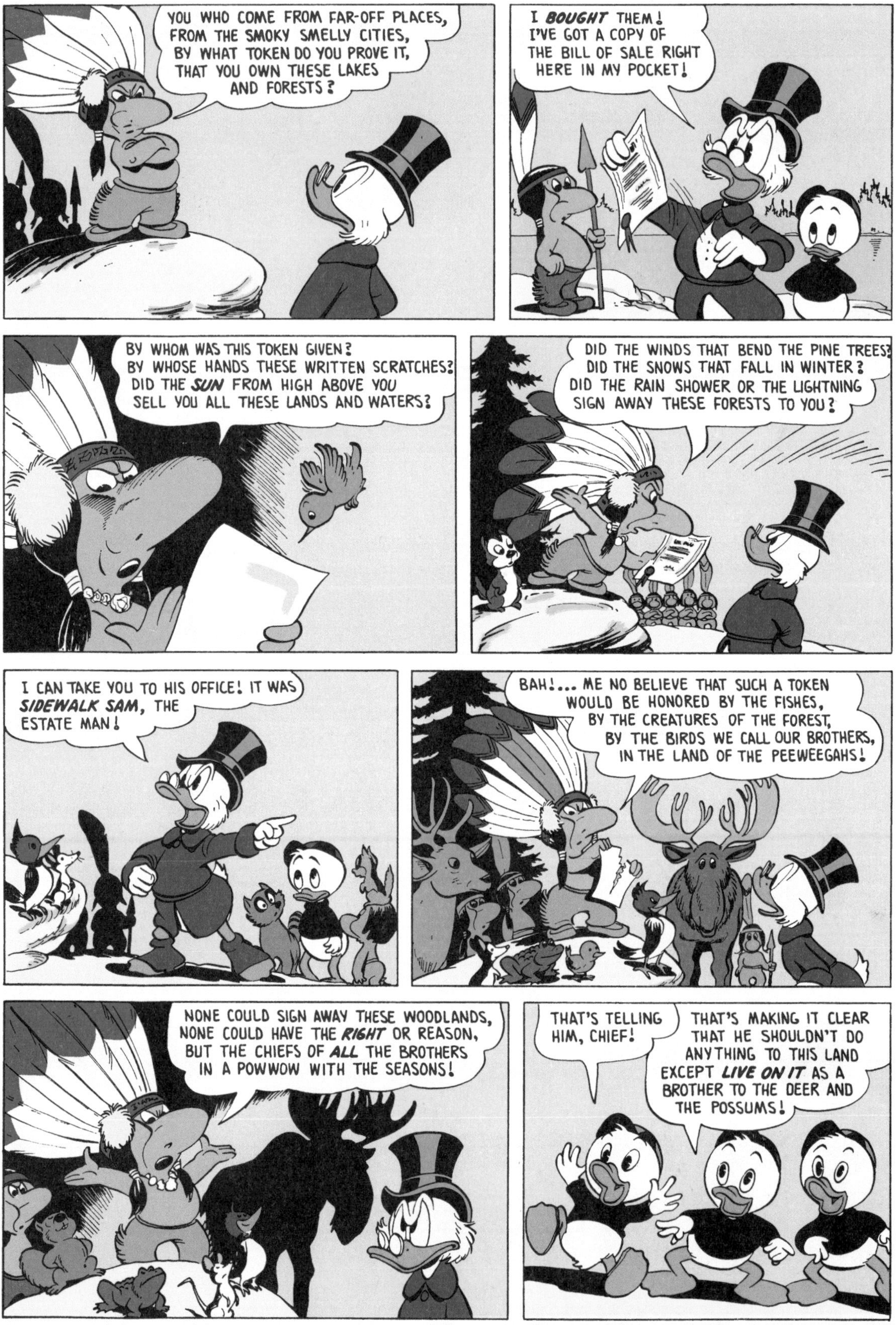
YOU WHO COME FROM FAR-OFF PLACES, FROM THE SMOKY SMELLY CITIES, BY WHAT TOKEN DO YOU PROVE IT, THAT YOU OWN THESE LAKES AND FORESTS?
I BOUGHT THEM! I'VE GOT A COPY OF THE BILL OF SALE RIGHT HERE IN MY POCKET!
BY WHOM WAS THIS TOKEN GIVEN? BY WHOSE HANDS THESE WRITTEN SCRATCHES? DID THE SUN FROM HIGH ABOVE YOU SELL YOU ALL THESE LANDS AND WATERS?
DID THE WINDS THAT BEND THE PINE TREES? DID THE SNOWS THAT FALL IN WINTER? DID THE RAIN SHOWER OR THE LIGHTNING SIGN AWAY THESE FORESTS TO YOU?
I CAN TAKE YOU TO HIS OFFICE! IT WAS SIDEWALK SAM, THE ESTATE MAN!
BAH!... ME NO BELIEVE THAT SUCH A TOKEN WOULD BE HONORED BY THE FISHES, BY THE CREATURES OF THE FOREST, BY THE BIRDS WE CALL OUR BROTHERS, IN THE LAND OF THE PEEWEEGAHS!
NONE COULD SIGN AWAY THESE WOODLANDS, NONE COULD HAVE THE RIGHT OR REASON, BUT THE CHIEFS OF ALL THE BROTHERS IN A POWWOW WITH THE SEASONS!
THAT'S TELLING HIM, CHIEF!
THAT'S MAKING IT CLEAR THAT HE SHOULDN'T DO ANYTHING TO THIS LAND EXCEPT LIVE ON IT AS A BROTHER TO THE DEER AND THE POSSUMS!

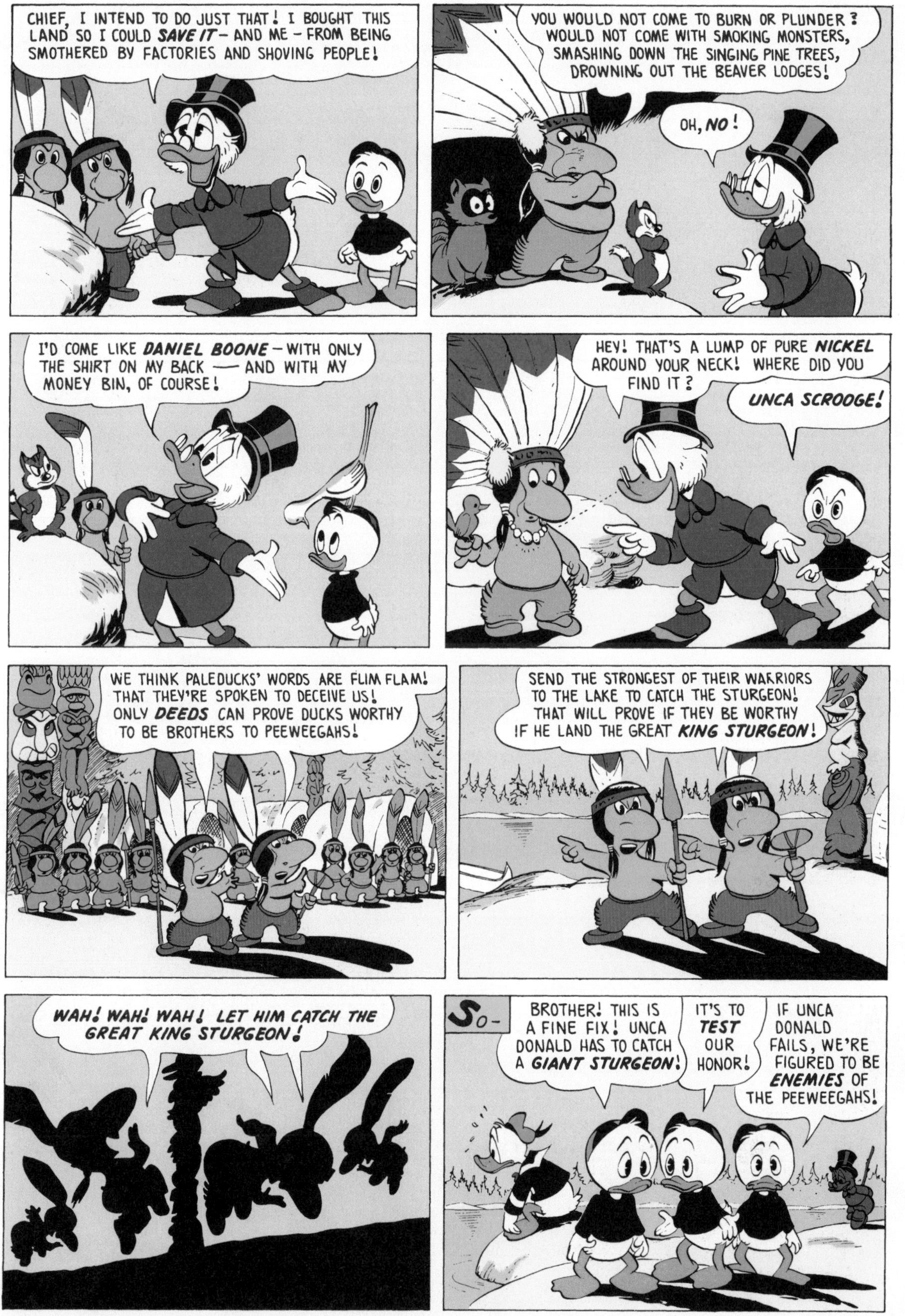
CHIEF, I INTEND TO DO JUST THAT! I BOUGHT THIS LAND SO I COULD SAVE IT – AND ME – FROM BEING SMOTHERED BY FACTORIES AND SHOVING PEOPLE!
YOU WOULD NOT COME TO BURN OR PLUNDER? WOULD NOT COME WITH SMOKING MONSTERS, SMASHING DOWN THE SINGING PINE TREES, DROWNING OUT THE BEAVER LODGES!
OH, NO!
I'D COME LIKE DANIEL BOONE – WITH ONLY THE SHIRT ON MY BACK — AND WITH MY MONEY BIN, OF COURSE!
HEY! THAT'S A LUMP OF PURE NICKEL AROUND YOUR NECK! WHERE DID YOU FIND IT?
UNCA SCROOGE!
WE THINK PALEDUCKS' WORDS ARE FLIM FLAM! THAT THEY'RE SPOKEN TO DECEIVE US! ONLY DEEDS CAN PROVE DUCKS WORTHY TO BE BROTHERS TO PEEWEEGAHS!
SEND THE STRONGEST OF THEIR WARRIORS TO THE LAKE TO CATCH THE STURGEON! THAT WILL PROVE IF THEY BE WORTHY IF HE LAND THE GREAT KING STURGEON!
WAH! WAH! WAH! LET HIM CATCH THE GREAT KING STURGEON!
SO-
BROTHER! THIS IS A FINE FIX! UNCA DONALD HAS TO CATCH A GIANT STURGEON!
IT'S TO TEST OUR HONOR!
IF UNCA DONALD FAILS, WE'RE FIGURED TO BE ENEMIES OF THE PEEWEEGAHS!

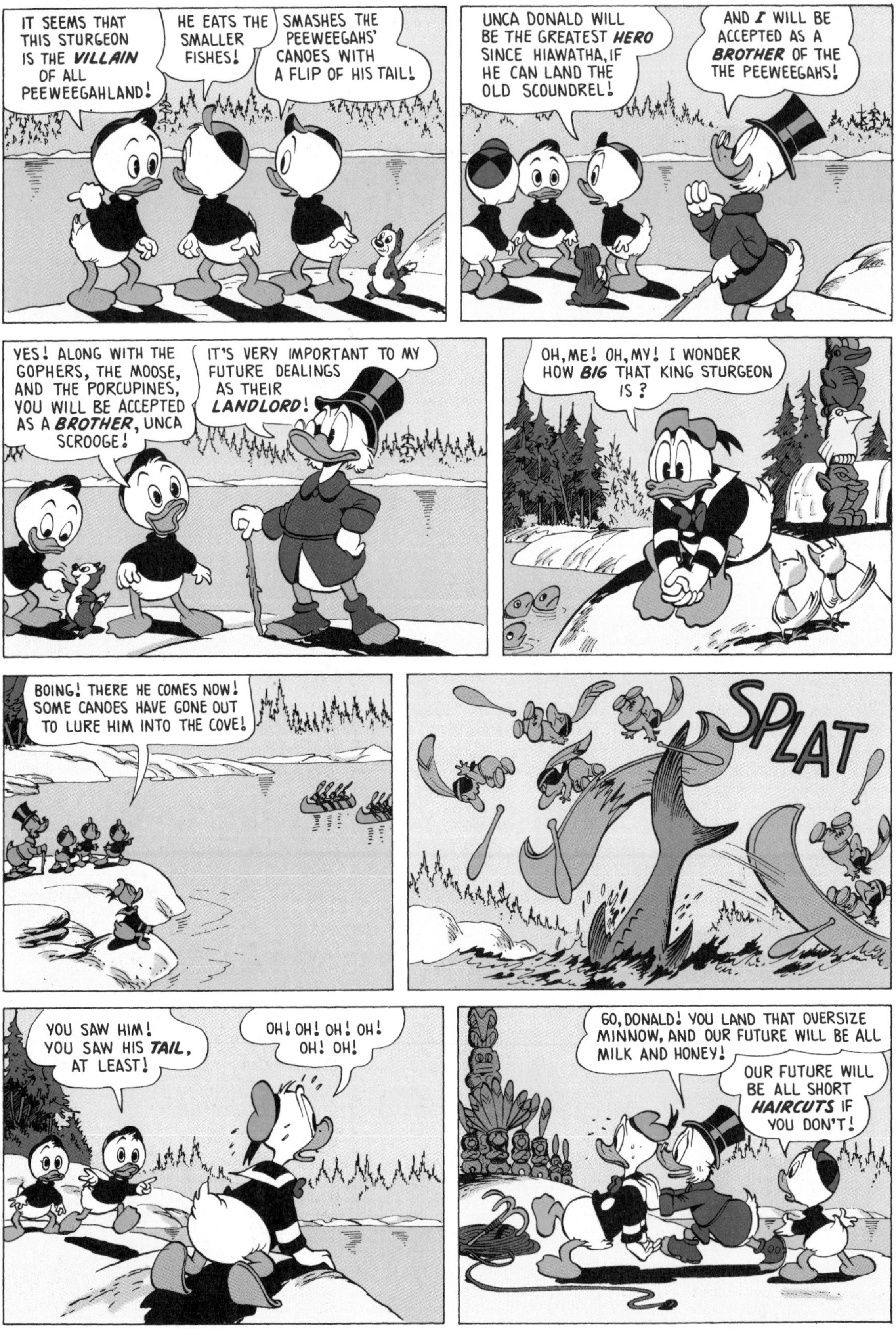
IT SEEMS THAT THIS STURGEON IS THE VILLAIN OF ALL PEEWEEGAHLAND!
HE EATS THE SMALLER FISHES!
SMASHES THE PEEWEEGAHS' CANOES WITH A FLIP OF HIS TAIL!
UNCA DONALD WILL BE THE GREATEST HERO SINCE HIAWATHA, IF HE CAN LAND THE OLD SCOUNDREL!
AND I WILL BE ACCEPTED AS A BROTHER OF THE THE PEEWEEGAHS!
YES! ALONG WITH THE GOPHERS, THE MOOSE, AND THE PORCUPINES, YOU WILL BE ACCEPTED AS A BROTHER, UNCA SCROOGE!
IT'S VERY IMPORTANT TO MY FUTURE DEALINGS AS THEIR LANDLORD!
OH, ME! OH, MY! I WONDER HOW BIG THAT KING STURGEON IS?
BOING! THERE HE COMES NOW! SOME CANOES HAVE GONE OUT TO LURE HIM INTO THE COVE!
SPLAT
YOU SAW HIM! YOU SAW HIS TAIL, AT LEAST!
OH! OH! OH! OH! OH! OH!
GO, DONALD! YOU LAND THAT OVERSIZE MINNOW, AND OUR FUTURE WILL BE ALL MILK AND HONEY!
OUR FUTURE WILL BE ALL SHORT HAIRCUTS IF YOU DON'T!

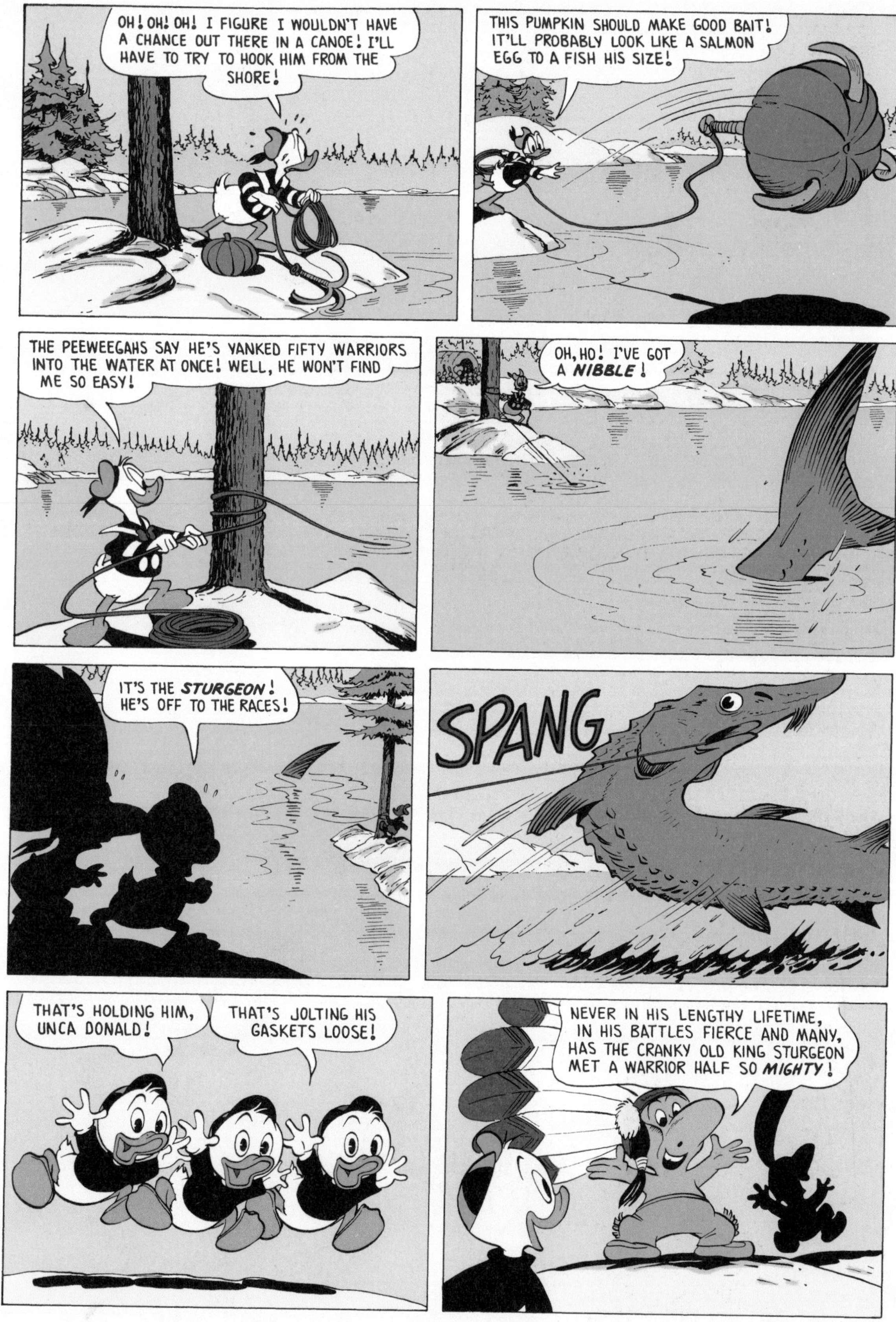
OH! OH! OH! I FIGURE I WOULDN'T HAVE A CHANCE OUT THERE IN A CANOE! I'LL HAVE TO TRY TO HOOK HIM FROM THE SHORE!
THIS PUMPKIN SHOULD MAKE GOOD BAIT! IT'LL PROBABLY LOOK LIKE A SALMON EGG TO A FISH HIS SIZE!
THE PEEWEEGAHS SAY HE'S YANKED FIFTY WARRIORS INTO THE WATER AT ONCE! WELL, HE WON'T FIND ME SO EASY!
OH, HO! I'VE GOT A NIBBLE!
IT'S THE STURGEON! HE'S OFF TO THE RACES!
SPANG
THAT'S HOLDING HIM, UNCA DONALD!
THAT'S JOLTING HIS GASKETS LOOSE!
NEVER IN HIS LENGTHY LIFETIME, IN HIS BATTLES FIERCE AND MANY, HAS THE CRANKY OLD KING STURGEON MET A WARRIOR HALF SO MIGHTY!

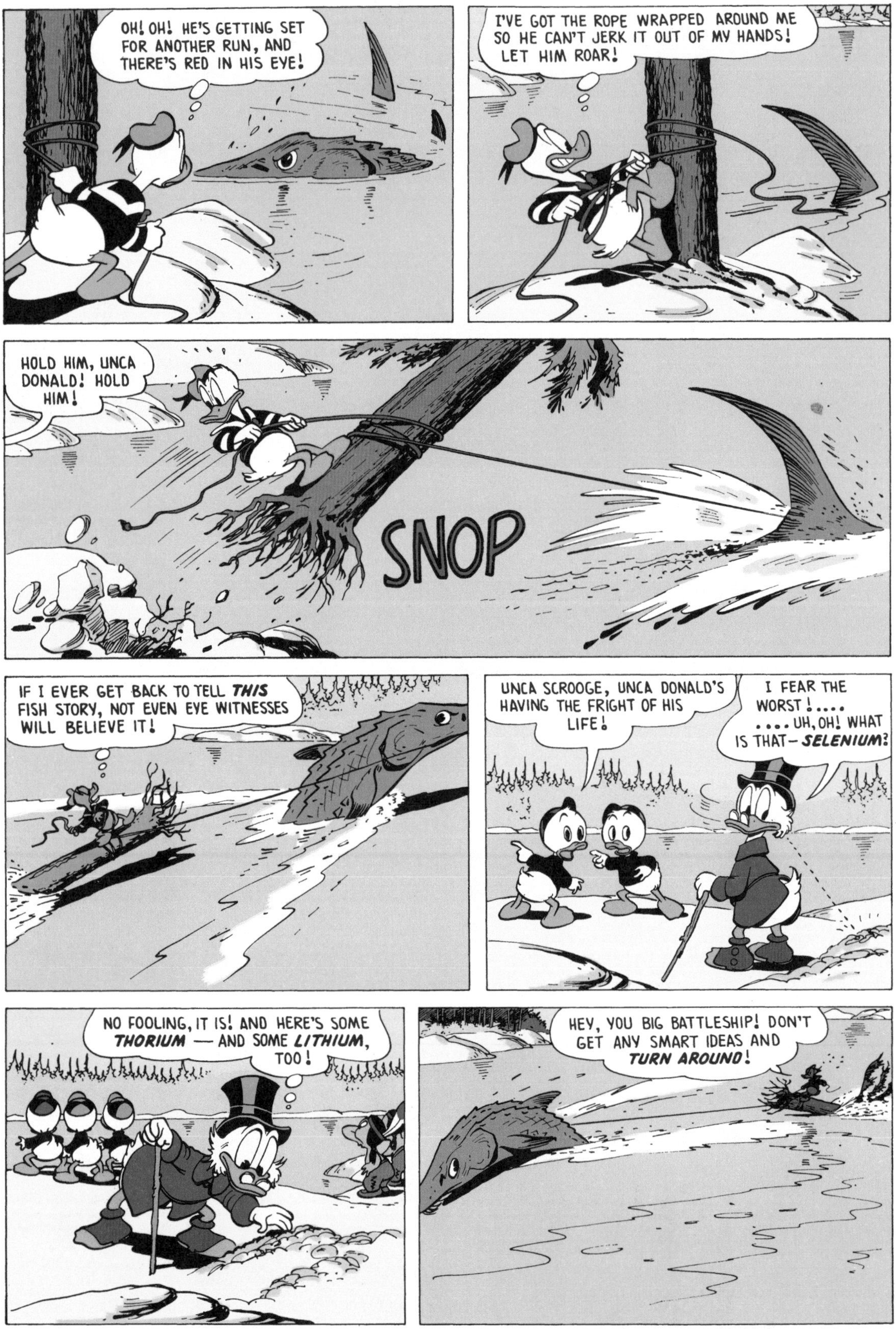
OH! OH! HE'S GETTING SET FOR ANOTHER RUN, AND THERE'S RED IN HIS EYE!
I'VE GOT THE ROPE WRAPPED AROUND ME SO HE CAN'T JERK IT OUT OF MY HANDS! LET HIM ROAR!
HOLD HIM, UNCA DONALD! HOLD HIM!
SNOP
IF I EVER GET BACK TO TELL *THIS* FISH STORY, NOT EVEN EYE WITNESSES WILL BELIEVE IT!
UNCA SCROOGE, UNCA DONALD'S HAVING THE FRIGHT OF HIS LIFE!
I FEAR THE WORST!.... ....UH, OH! WHAT IS THAT— *SELENIUM*?
NO FOOLING, IT IS! AND HERE'S SOME *THORIUM* — AND SOME *LITHIUM*, TOO!
HEY, YOU BIG BATTLESHIP! DON'T GET ANY SMART IDEAS AND *TURN AROUND*!

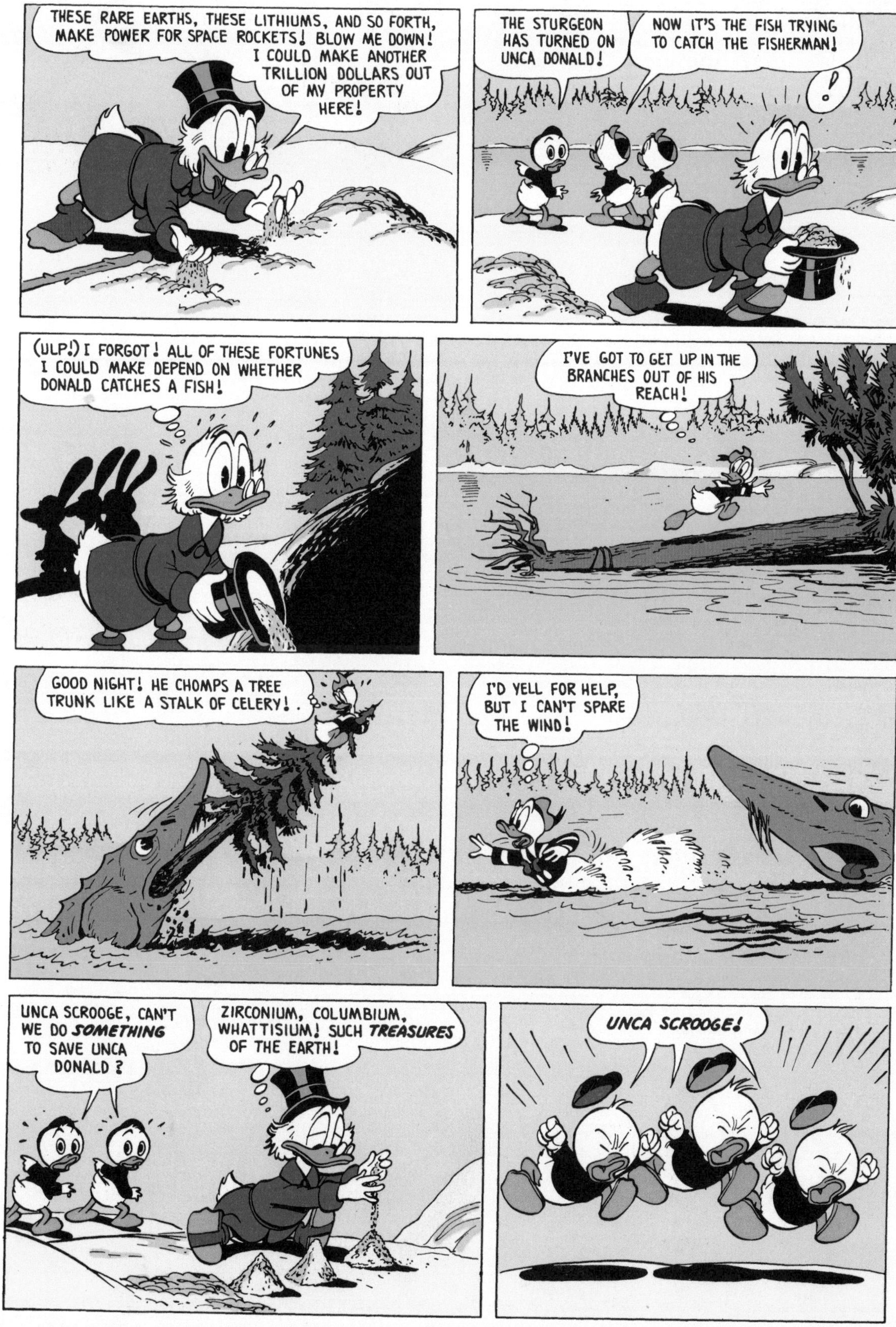
THESE RARE EARTHS, THESE LITHIUMS, AND SO FORTH, MAKE POWER FOR SPACE ROCKETS! BLOW ME DOWN! I COULD MAKE ANOTHER TRILLION DOLLARS OUT OF MY PROPERTY HERE!
THE STURGEON HAS TURNED ON UNCA DONALD!
NOW IT'S THE FISH TRYING TO CATCH THE FISHERMAN!
!
(ULP!) I FORGOT! ALL OF THESE FORTUNES I COULD MAKE DEPEND ON WHETHER DONALD CATCHES A FISH!
I'VE GOT TO GET UP IN THE BRANCHES OUT OF HIS REACH!
GOOD NIGHT! HE CHOMPS A TREE TRUNK LIKE A STALK OF CELERY!
I'D YELL FOR HELP, BUT I CAN'T SPARE THE WIND!
UNCA SCROOGE, CAN'T WE DO SOMETHING TO SAVE UNCA DONALD?
ZIRCONIUM, COLUMBIUM, WHATTISIUM! SUCH TREASURES OF THE EARTH!
UNCA SCROOGE!

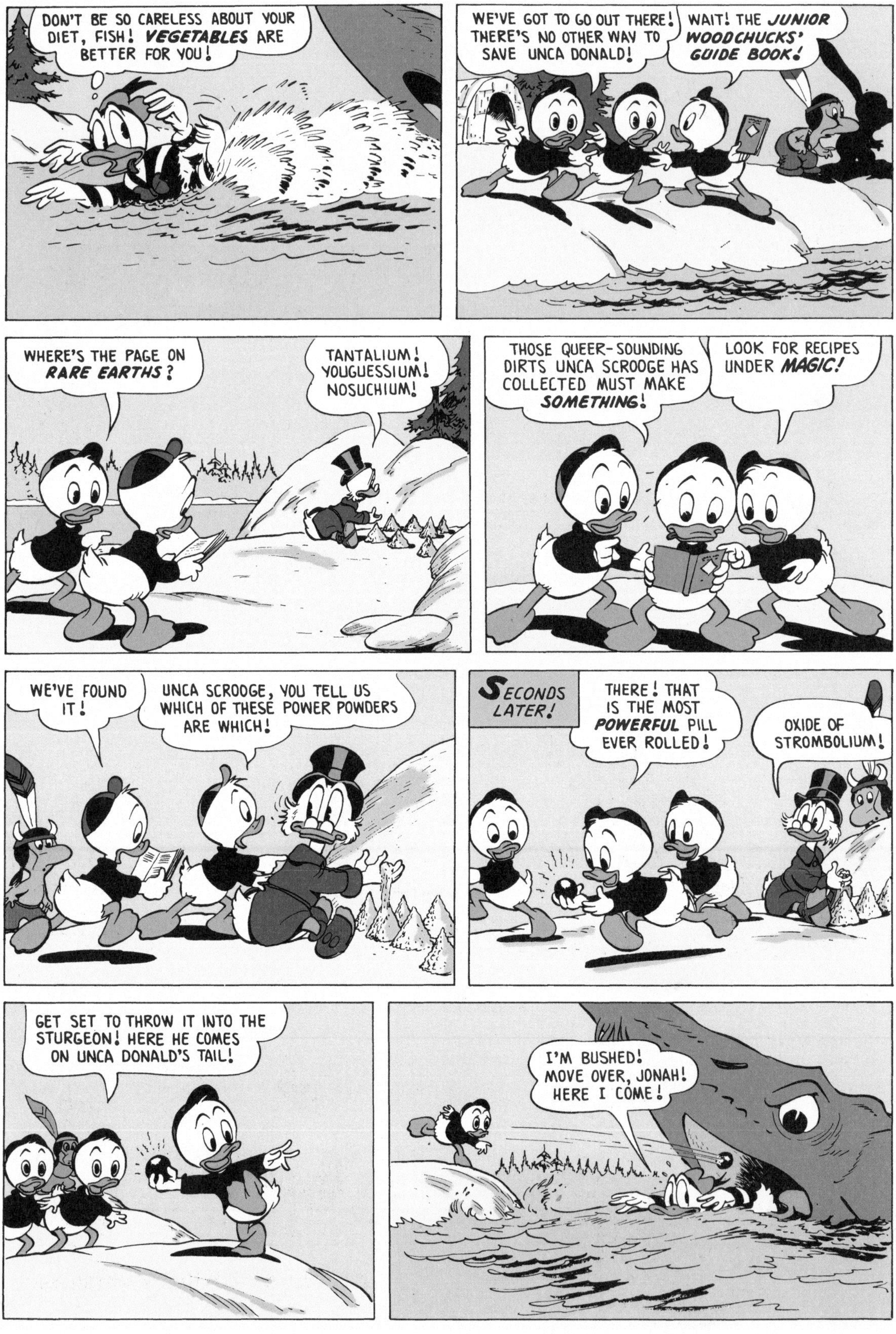
DON'T BE SO CARELESS ABOUT YOUR DIET, FISH! VEGETABLES ARE BETTER FOR YOU!
WE'VE GOT TO GO OUT THERE! THERE'S NO OTHER WAY TO SAVE UNCA DONALD!
WAIT! THE JUNIOR WOODCHUCKS' GUIDE BOOK!
WHERE'S THE PAGE ON RARE EARTHS?
TANTALIUM! YOUGUESSIUM! NOSUCHIUM!
THOSE QUEER-SOUNDING DIRTS UNCA SCROOGE HAS COLLECTED MUST MAKE SOMETHING!
LOOK FOR RECIPES UNDER MAGIC!
WE'VE FOUND IT!
UNCA SCROOGE, YOU TELL US WHICH OF THESE POWER POWDERS ARE WHICH!
SECONDS LATER!
THERE! THAT IS THE MOST POWERFUL PILL EVER ROLLED!
OXIDE OF STROMBOLIUM!
GET SET TO THROW IT INTO THE STURGEON! HERE HE COMES ON UNCA DONALD'S TAIL!
I'M BUSHED! MOVE OVER, JONAH! HERE I COME!

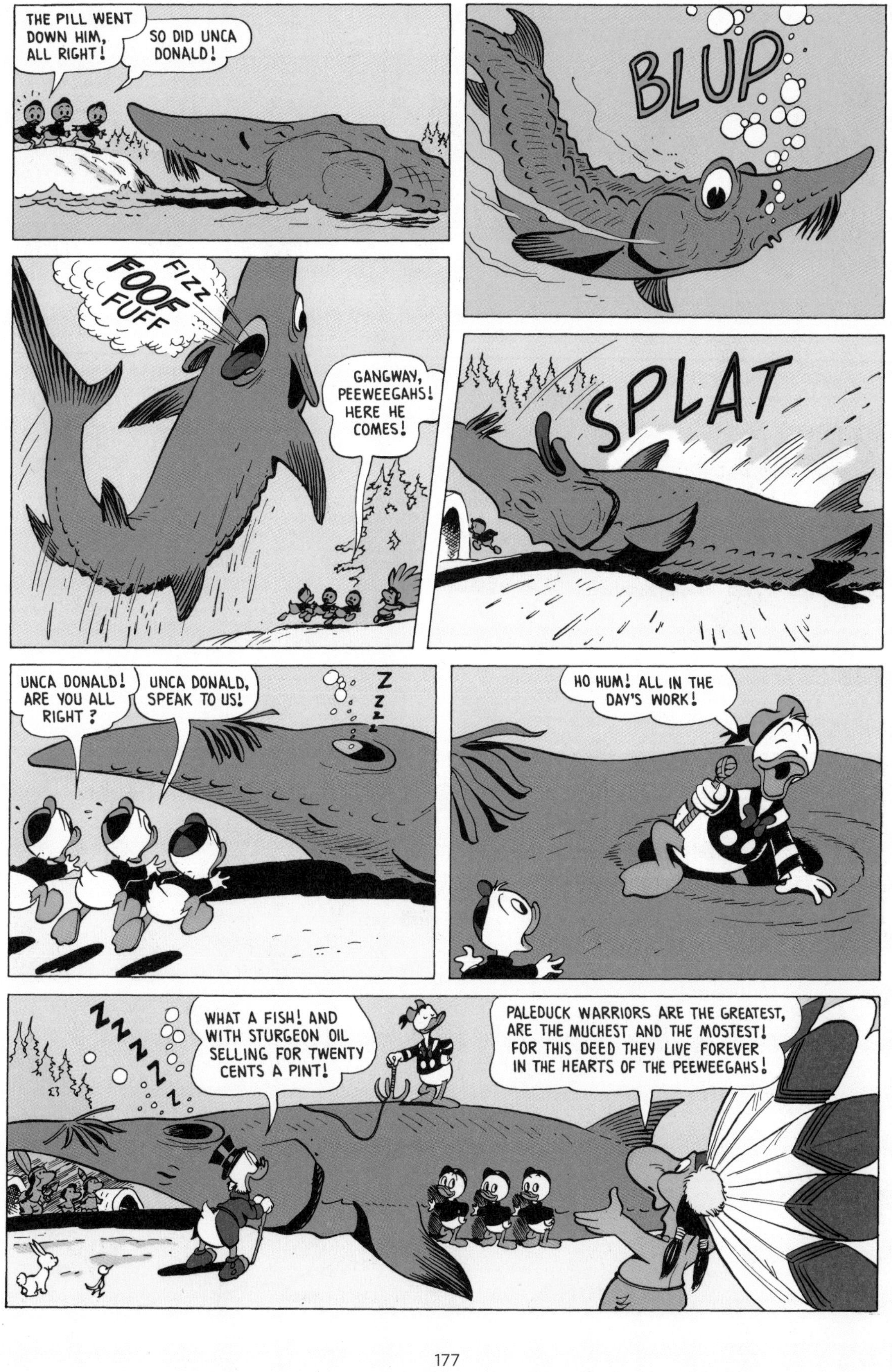
THE PILL WENT DOWN HIM, ALL RIGHT!
SO DID UNCA DONALD!
BLUP
FIZZ
FOOF
FUFF
GANGWAY, PEEWEEGAHS! HERE HE COMES!
SPLAT
UNCA DONALD! ARE YOU ALL RIGHT?
UNCA DONALD, SPEAK TO US!
Z Z Z
HO HUM! ALL IN THE DAY'S WORK!
Z Z Z Z Z Z
WHAT A FISH! AND WITH STURGEON OIL SELLING FOR TWENTY CENTS A PINT!
PALEDUCK WARRIORS ARE THE GREATEST, ARE THE MUCHEST AND THE MOSTEST! FOR THIS DEED THEY LIVE FOREVER IN THE HEARTS OF THE PEEWEEGAHS!

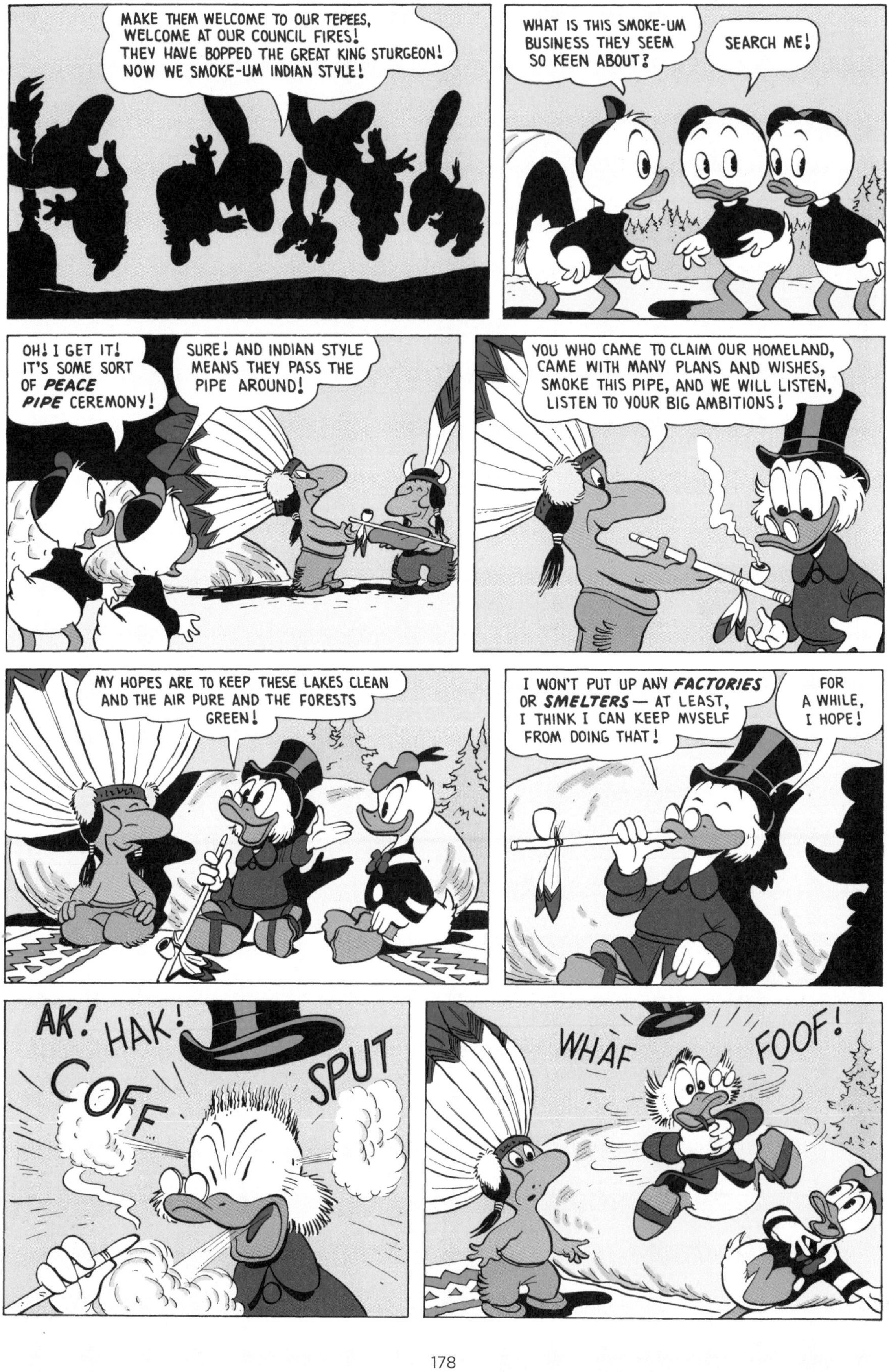
MAKE THEM WELCOME TO OUR TEPEES, WELCOME AT OUR COUNCIL FIRES! THEY HAVE BOPPED THE GREAT KING STURGEON! NOW WE SMOKE-UM INDIAN STYLE!
WHAT IS THIS SMOKE-UM BUSINESS THEY SEEM SO KEEN ABOUT?
SEARCH ME!
OH! I GET IT! IT'S SOME SORT OF PEACE PIPE CEREMONY!
SURE! AND INDIAN STYLE MEANS THEY PASS THE PIPE AROUND!
YOU WHO CAME TO CLAIM OUR HOMELAND, CAME WITH MANY PLANS AND WISHES, SMOKE THIS PIPE, AND WE WILL LISTEN, LISTEN TO YOUR BIG AMBITIONS!
MY HOPES ARE TO KEEP THESE LAKES CLEAN AND THE AIR PURE AND THE FORESTS GREEN!
I WON'T PUT UP ANY FACTORIES OR SMELTERS — AT LEAST, I THINK I CAN KEEP MYSELF FROM DOING THAT!
FOR A WHILE, I HOPE!
AK! HAK! COFF SPUT
WHAF FOOF!

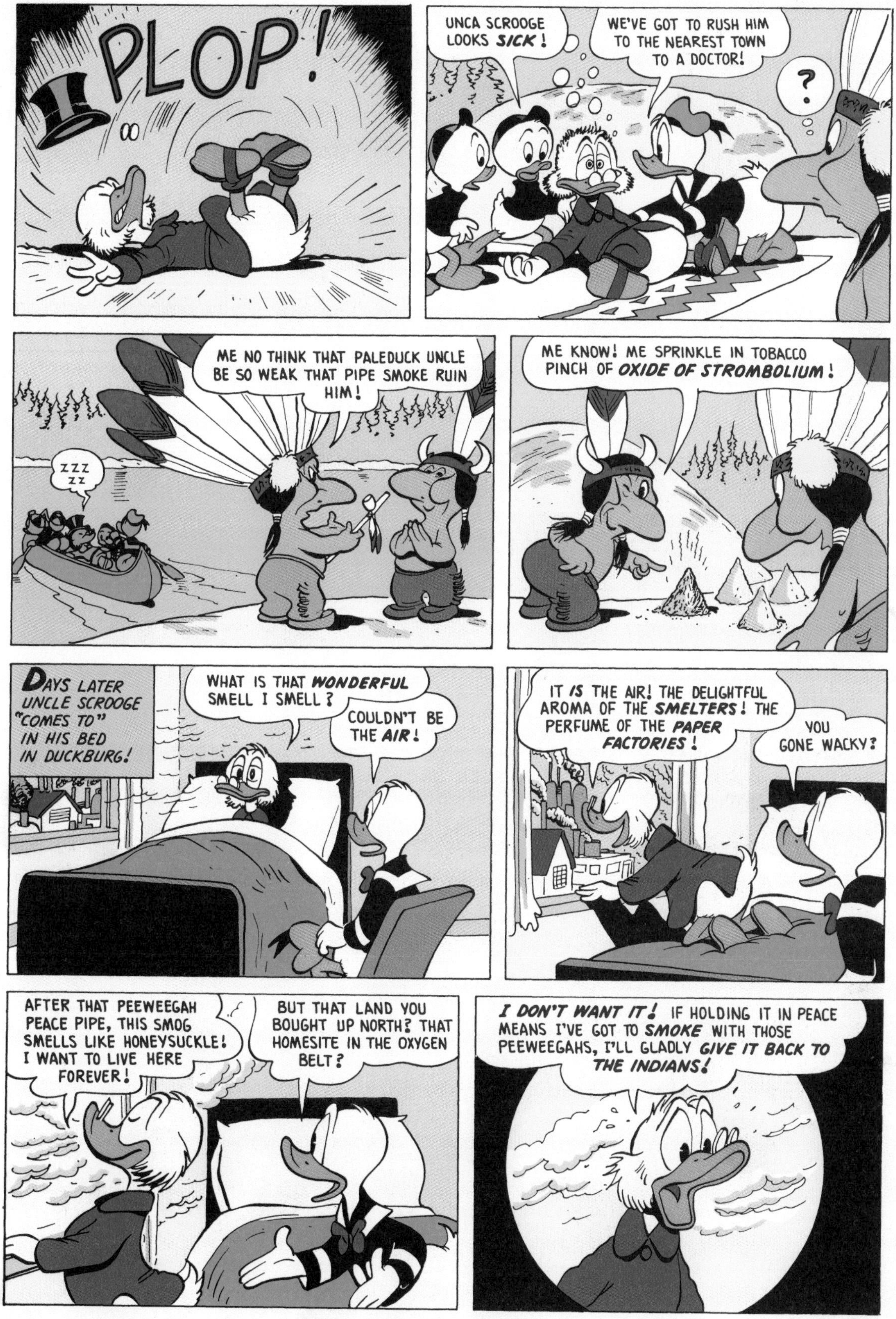
PLOP!
UNCA SCROOGE LOOKS SICK!
WE'VE GOT TO RUSH HIM TO THE NEAREST TOWN TO A DOCTOR!
?
ME NO THINK THAT PALEDUCK UNCLE BE SO WEAK THAT PIPE SMOKE RUIN HIM!
ZZZ ZZ
ME KNOW! ME SPRINKLE IN TOBACCO PINCH OF OXIDE OF STROMBOLIUM!
DAYS LATER UNCLE SCROOGE "COMES TO" IN HIS BED IN DUCKBURG!
WHAT IS THAT WONDERFUL SMELL I SMELL?
COULDN'T BE THE AIR!
IT IS THE AIR! THE DELIGHTFUL AROMA OF THE SMELTERS! THE PERFUME OF THE PAPER FACTORIES!
YOU GONE WACKY?
AFTER THAT PEEWEEGAH PEACE PIPE, THIS SMOG SMELLS LIKE HONEYSUCKLE! I WANT TO LIVE HERE FOREVER!
BUT THAT LAND YOU BOUGHT UP NORTH? THAT HOMESITE IN THE OXYGEN BELT?
I DON'T WANT IT! IF HOLDING IT IN PEACE MEANS I'VE GOT TO SMOKE WITH THOSE PEEWEEGAHS, I'LL GLADLY GIVE IT BACK TO THE INDIANS!

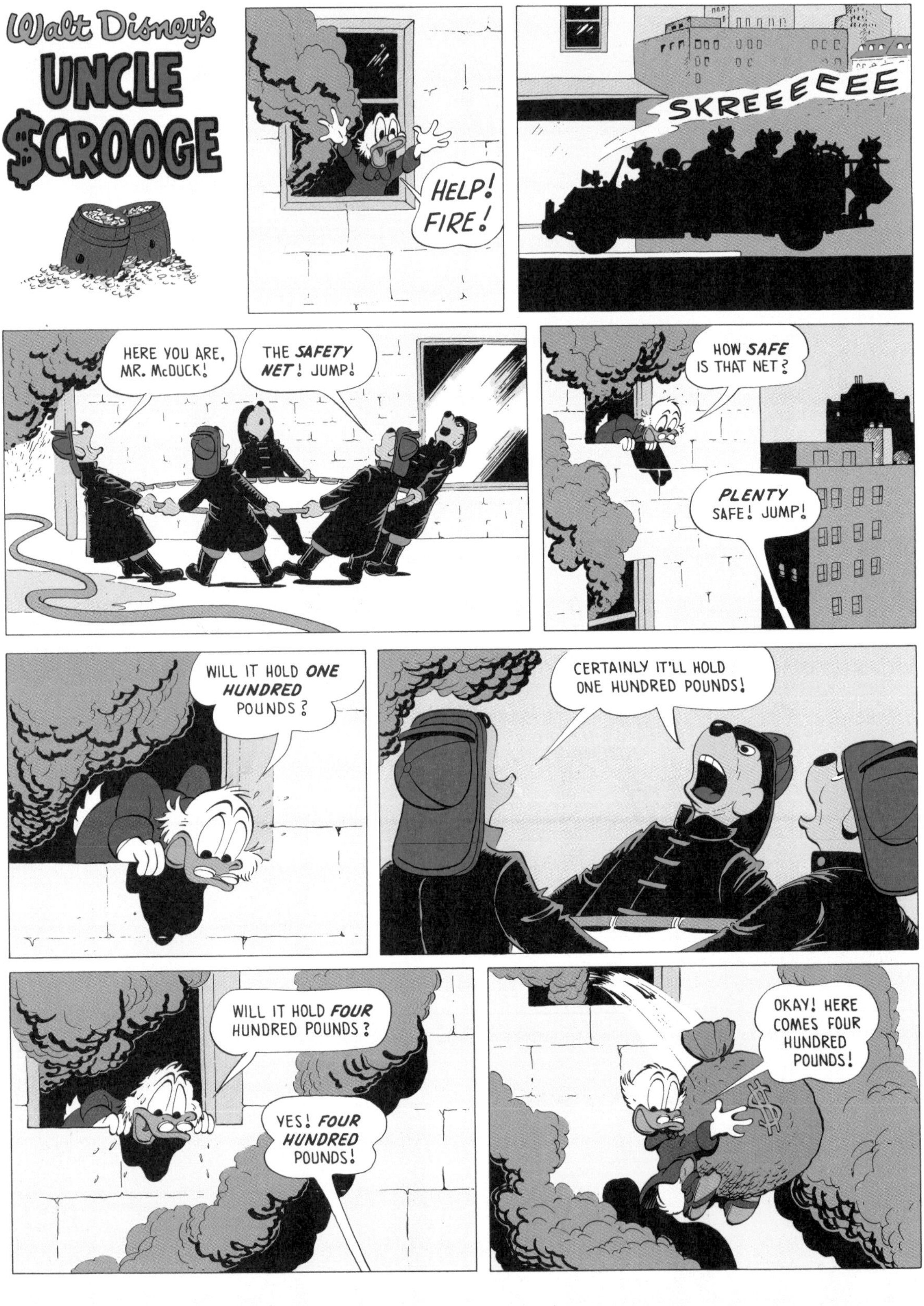
Walt Disney's
UNCLE $CROOGE
HELP! FIRE!
SKREEEEEEE
HERE YOU ARE, MR. McDUCK!
THE SAFETY NET! JUMP!
HOW SAFE IS THAT NET?
PLENTY SAFE! JUMP!
WILL IT HOLD ONE HUNDRED POUNDS?
CERTAINLY IT'LL HOLD ONE HUNDRED POUNDS!
WILL IT HOLD FOUR HUNDRED POUNDS?
YES! FOUR HUNDRED POUNDS!
OKAY! HERE COMES FOUR HUNDRED POUNDS!

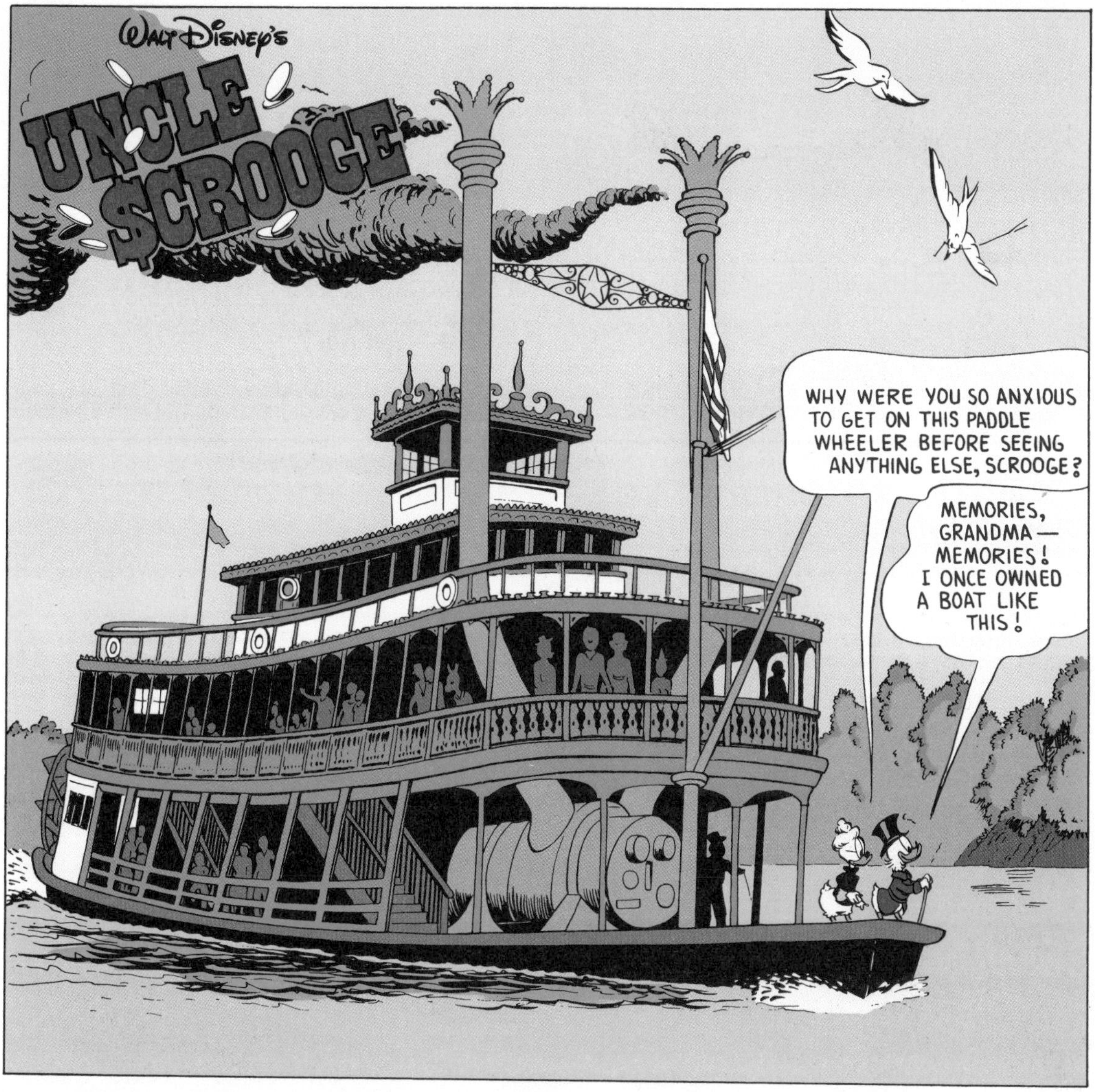
WALT DISNEY'S
UNCLE $CROOGE
WHY WERE YOU SO ANXIOUS TO GET ON THIS PADDLE WHEELER BEFORE SEEING ANYTHING ELSE, SCROOGE?
MEMORIES, GRANDMA— MEMORIES! I ONCE OWNED A BOAT LIKE THIS!

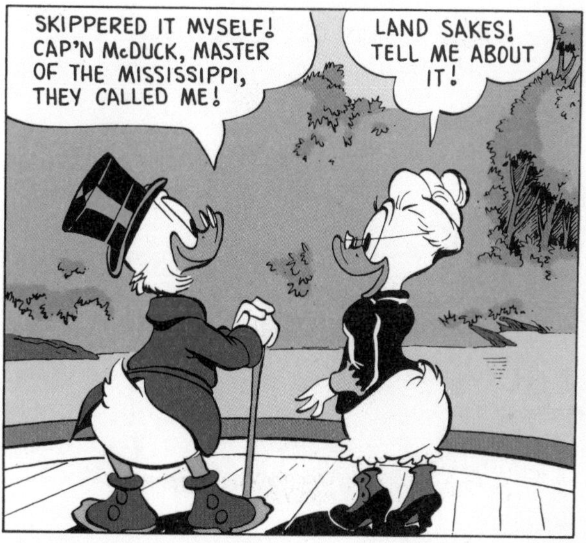
SKIPPERED IT MYSELF! CAP'N McDUCK, MASTER OF THE MISSISSIPPI, THEY CALLED ME!
LAND SAKES! TELL ME ABOUT IT!

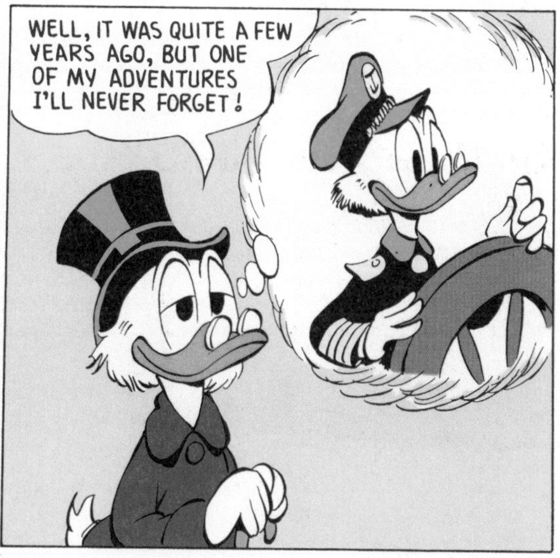
WELL, IT WAS QUITE A FEW YEARS AGO, BUT ONE OF MY ADVENTURES I'LL NEVER FORGET!

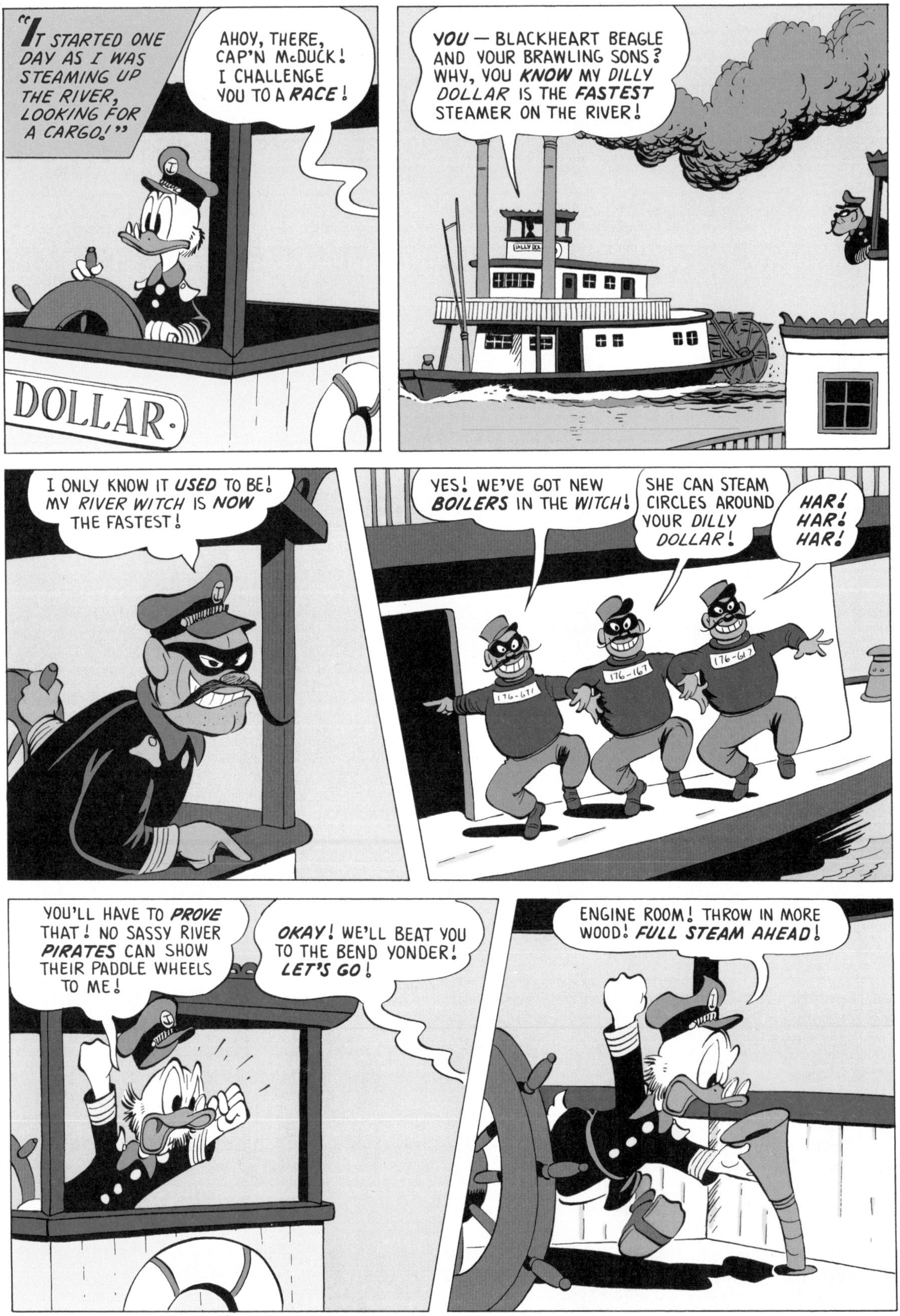
"IT STARTED ONE DAY AS I WAS STEAMING UP THE RIVER, LOOKING FOR A CARGO!"
AHOY, THERE, CAP'N McDUCK! I CHALLENGE YOU TO A RACE!
DOLLAR
YOU — BLACKHEART BEAGLE AND YOUR BRAWLING SONS? WHY, YOU KNOW MY DILLY DOLLAR IS THE FASTEST STEAMER ON THE RIVER!
I ONLY KNOW IT USED TO BE! MY RIVER WITCH IS NOW THE FASTEST!
YES! WE'VE GOT NEW BOILERS IN THE WITCH!
SHE CAN STEAM CIRCLES AROUND YOUR DILLY DOLLAR!
HAR! HAR! HAR!
YOU'LL HAVE TO PROVE THAT! NO SASSY RIVER PIRATES CAN SHOW THEIR PADDLE WHEELS TO ME!
OKAY! WE'LL BEAT YOU TO THE BEND YONDER! LET'S GO!
ENGINE ROOM! THROW IN MORE WOOD! FULL STEAM AHEAD!

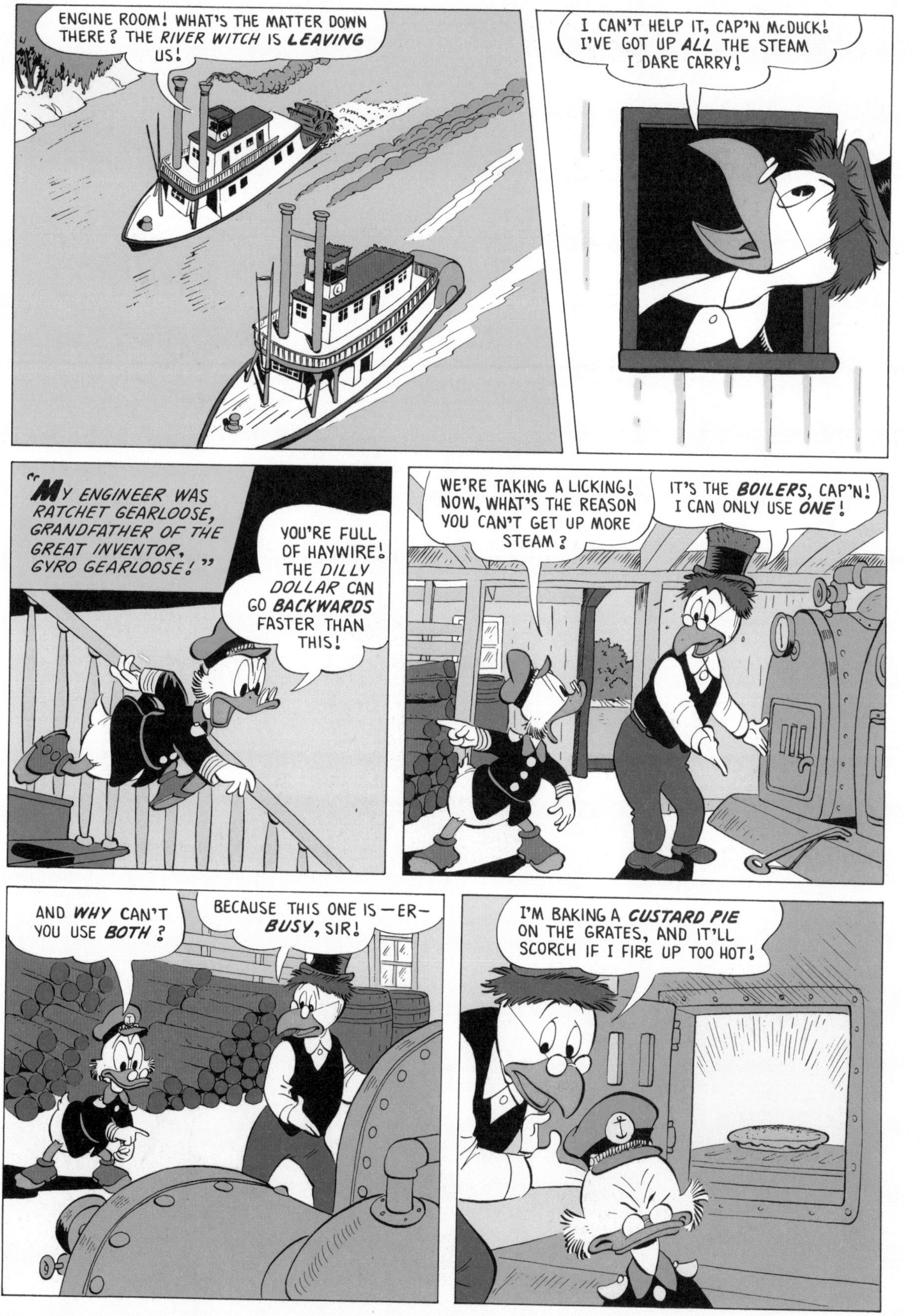
ENGINE ROOM! WHAT'S THE MATTER DOWN THERE? THE RIVER WITCH IS LEAVING US!
I CAN'T HELP IT, CAP'N McDUCK! I'VE GOT UP ALL THE STEAM I DARE CARRY!
"MY ENGINEER WAS RATCHET GEARLOOSE, GRANDFATHER OF THE GREAT INVENTOR, GYRO GEARLOOSE!"
YOU'RE FULL OF HAYWIRE! THE DILLY DOLLAR CAN GO BACKWARDS FASTER THAN THIS!
WE'RE TAKING A LICKING! NOW, WHAT'S THE REASON YOU CAN'T GET UP MORE STEAM?
IT'S THE BOILERS, CAP'N! I CAN ONLY USE ONE!
AND WHY CAN'T YOU USE BOTH?
BECAUSE THIS ONE IS—ER—BUSY, SIR!
I'M BAKING A CUSTARD PIE ON THE GRATES, AND IT'LL SCORCH IF I FIRE UP TOO HOT!

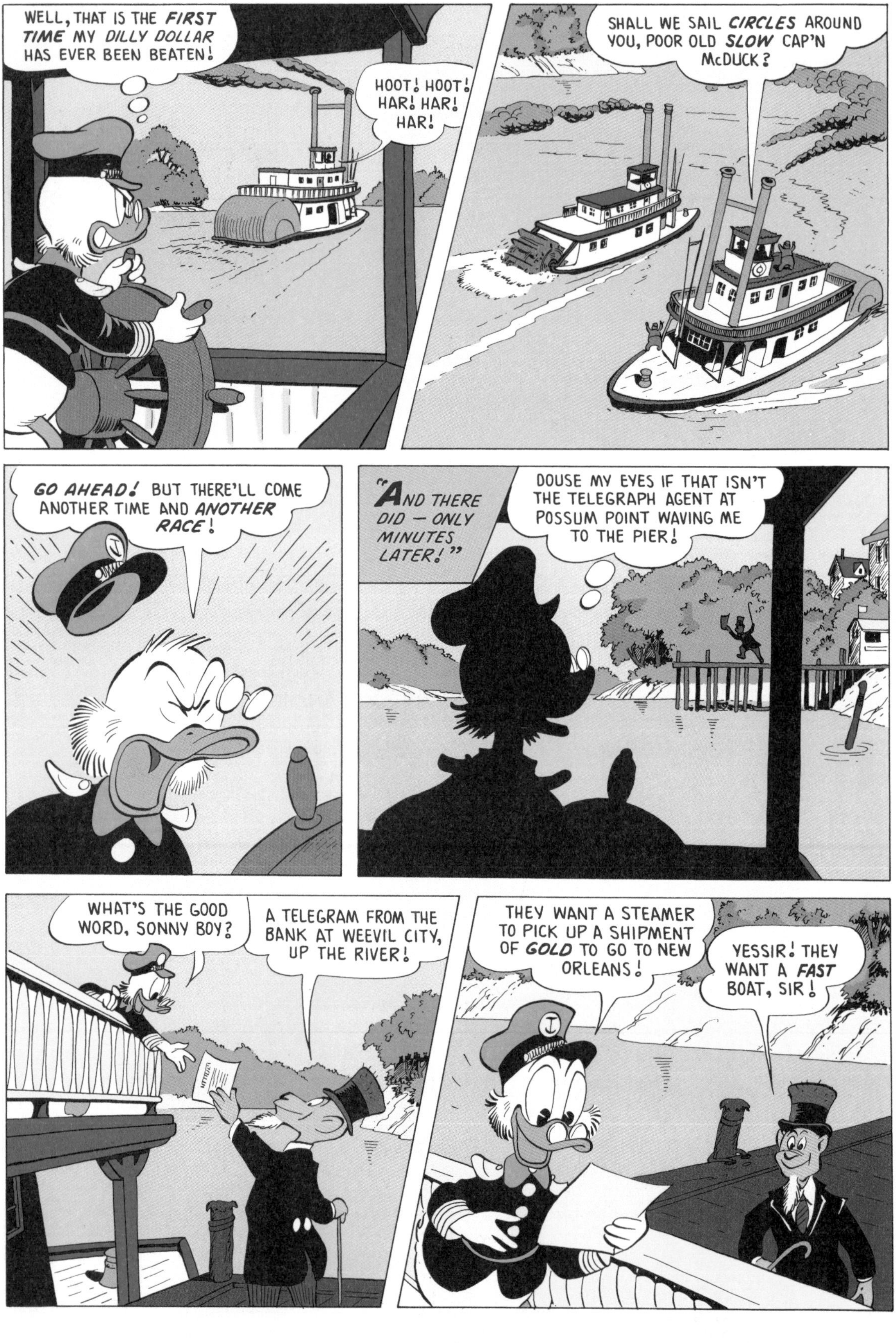
WELL, THAT IS THE FIRST TIME MY DILLY DOLLAR HAS EVER BEEN BEATEN!
HOOT! HOOT! HAR! HAR! HAR!
SHALL WE SAIL CIRCLES AROUND YOU, POOR OLD SLOW CAP'N McDUCK?
GO AHEAD! BUT THERE'LL COME ANOTHER TIME AND ANOTHER RACE!
"AND THERE DID — ONLY MINUTES LATER!"
DOUSE MY EYES IF THAT ISN'T THE TELEGRAPH AGENT AT POSSUM POINT WAVING ME TO THE PIER!
WHAT'S THE GOOD WORD, SONNY BOY?
A TELEGRAM FROM THE BANK AT WEEVIL CITY, UP THE RIVER!
THEY WANT A STEAMER TO PICK UP A SHIPMENT OF GOLD TO GO TO NEW ORLEANS!
YESSIR! THEY WANT A FAST BOAT, SIR!

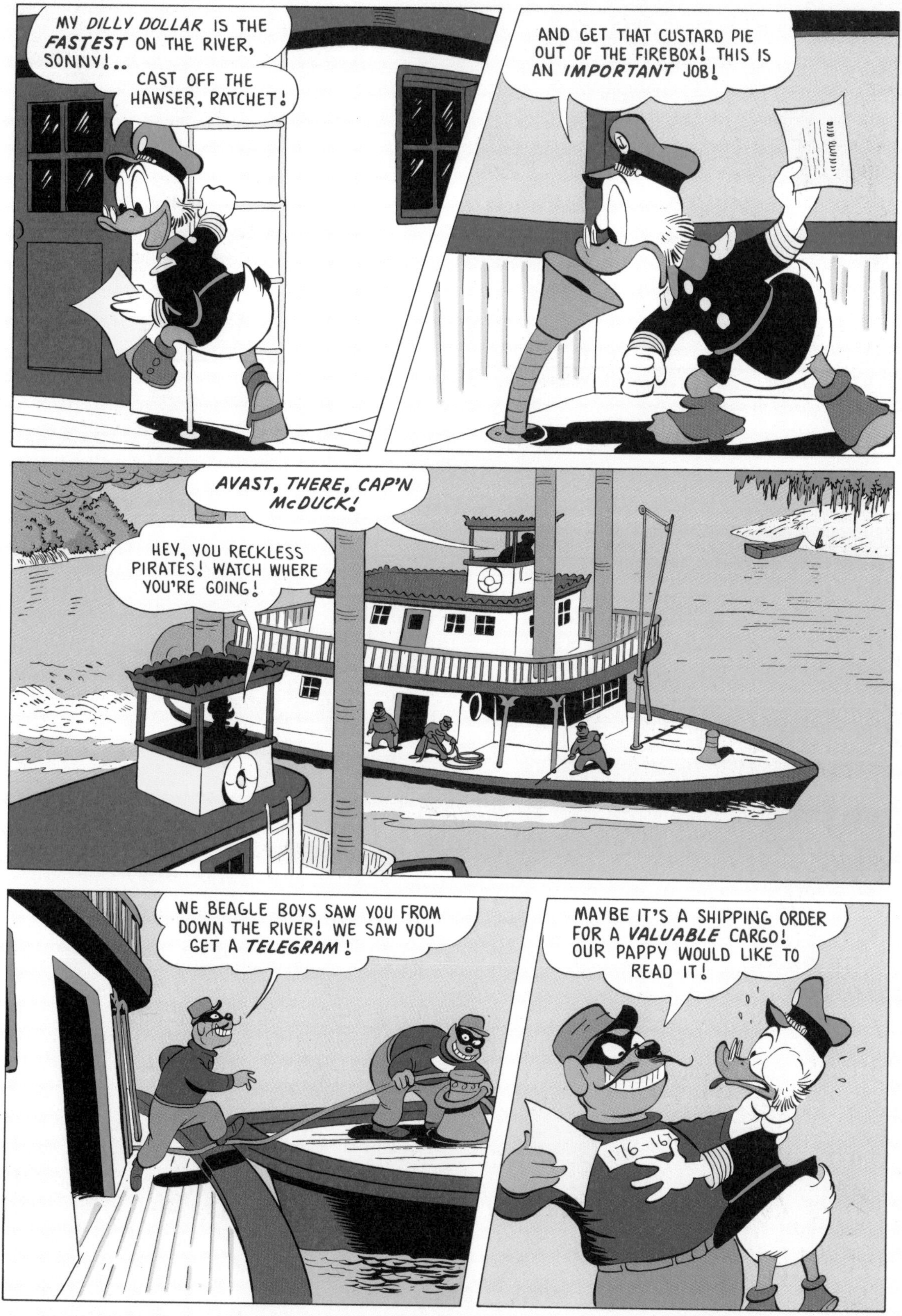
MY DILLY DOLLAR IS THE FASTEST ON THE RIVER, SONNY!..
CAST OFF THE HAWSER, RATCHET!
AND GET THAT CUSTARD PIE OUT OF THE FIREBOX! THIS IS AN IMPORTANT JOB!
AVAST, THERE, CAP'N McDUCK!
HEY, YOU RECKLESS PIRATES! WATCH WHERE YOU'RE GOING!
WE BEAGLE BOYS SAW YOU FROM DOWN THE RIVER! WE SAW YOU GET A TELEGRAM!
MAYBE IT'S A SHIPPING ORDER FOR A VALUABLE CARGO! OUR PAPPY WOULD LIKE TO READ IT!
176-167

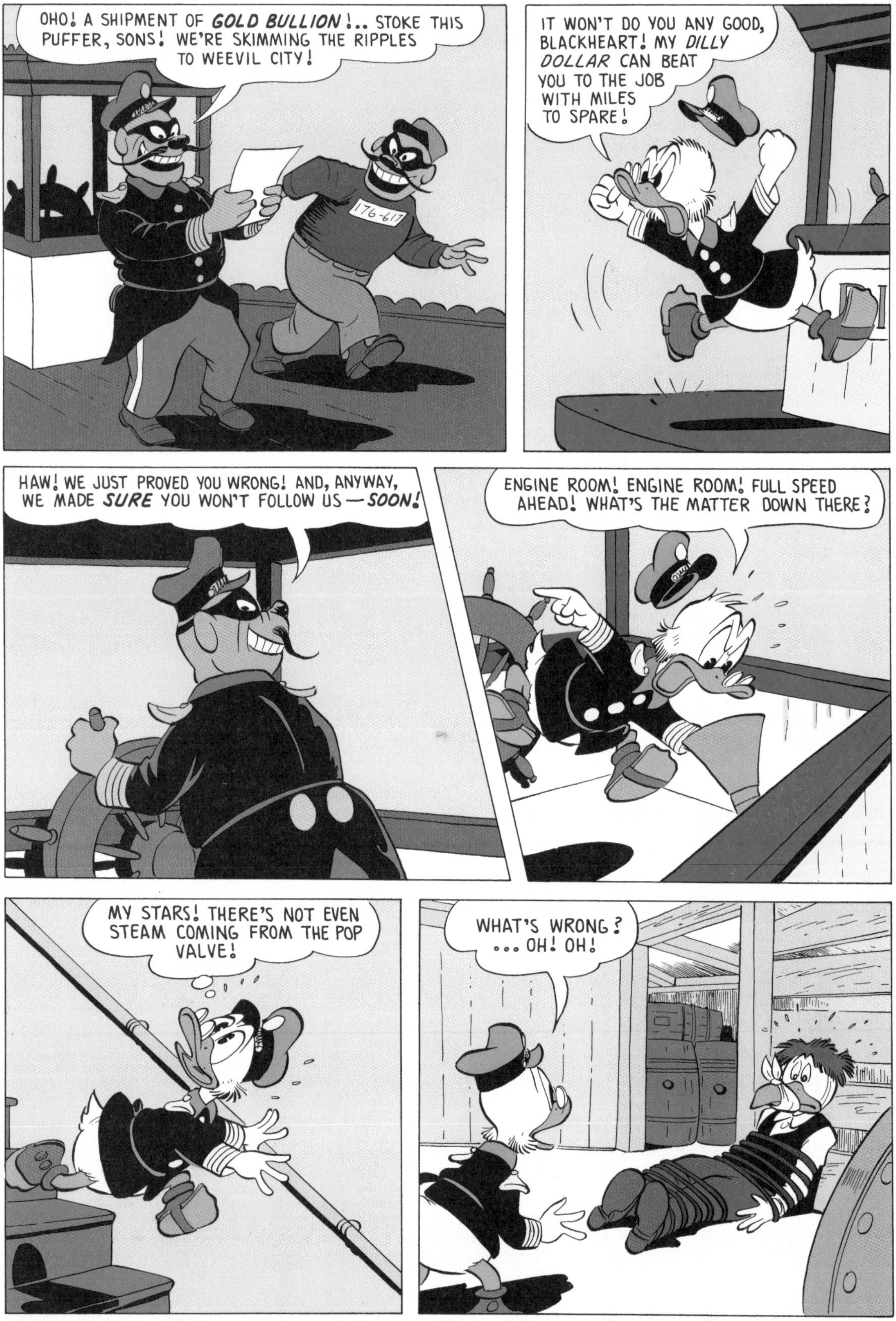
OHO! A SHIPMENT OF GOLD BULLION!.. STOKE THIS PUFFER, SONS! WE'RE SKIMMING THE RIPPLES TO WEEVIL CITY!
176-617
IT WON'T DO YOU ANY GOOD, BLACKHEART! MY DILLY DOLLAR CAN BEAT YOU TO THE JOB WITH MILES TO SPARE!
HAW! WE JUST PROVED YOU WRONG! AND, ANYWAY, WE MADE SURE YOU WON'T FOLLOW US—SOON!
ENGINE ROOM! ENGINE ROOM! FULL SPEED AHEAD! WHAT'S THE MATTER DOWN THERE?
MY STARS! THERE'S NOT EVEN STEAM COMING FROM THE POP VALVE!
WHAT'S WRONG? ... OH! OH!

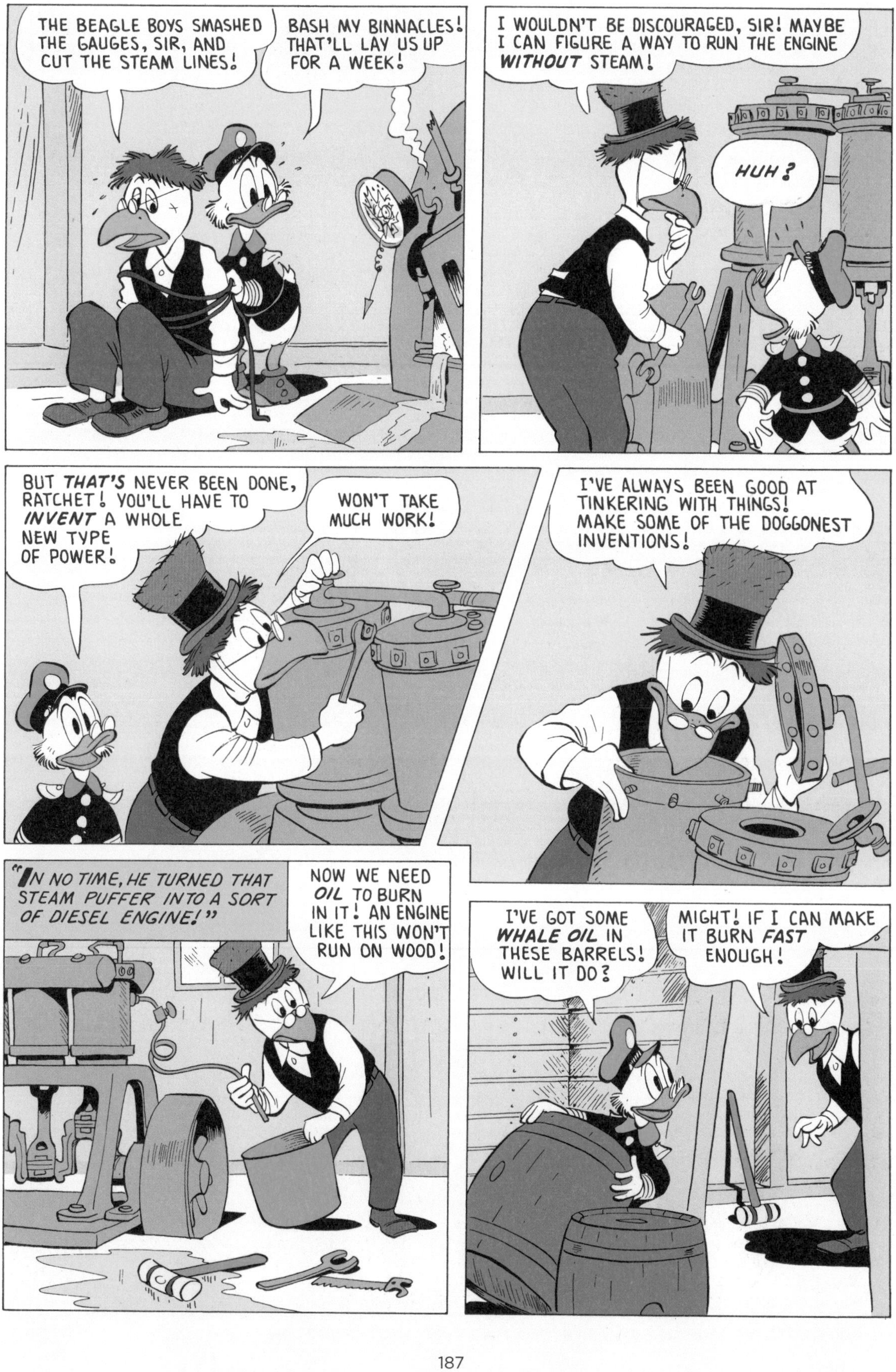
THE BEAGLE BOYS SMASHED THE GAUGES, SIR, AND CUT THE STEAM LINES!
BASH MY BINNACLES! THAT'LL LAY US UP FOR A WEEK!
I WOULDN'T BE DISCOURAGED, SIR! MAYBE I CAN FIGURE A WAY TO RUN THE ENGINE WITHOUT STEAM!
HUH?
BUT THAT'S NEVER BEEN DONE, RATCHET! YOU'LL HAVE TO INVENT A WHOLE NEW TYPE OF POWER!
WON'T TAKE MUCH WORK!
I'VE ALWAYS BEEN GOOD AT TINKERING WITH THINGS! MAKE SOME OF THE DOGGONEST INVENTIONS!
"IN NO TIME, HE TURNED THAT STEAM PUFFER INTO A SORT OF DIESEL ENGINE!"
NOW WE NEED OIL TO BURN IN IT! AN ENGINE LIKE THIS WON'T RUN ON WOOD!
I'VE GOT SOME WHALE OIL IN THESE BARRELS! WILL IT DO?
MIGHT! IF I CAN MAKE IT BURN FAST ENOUGH!

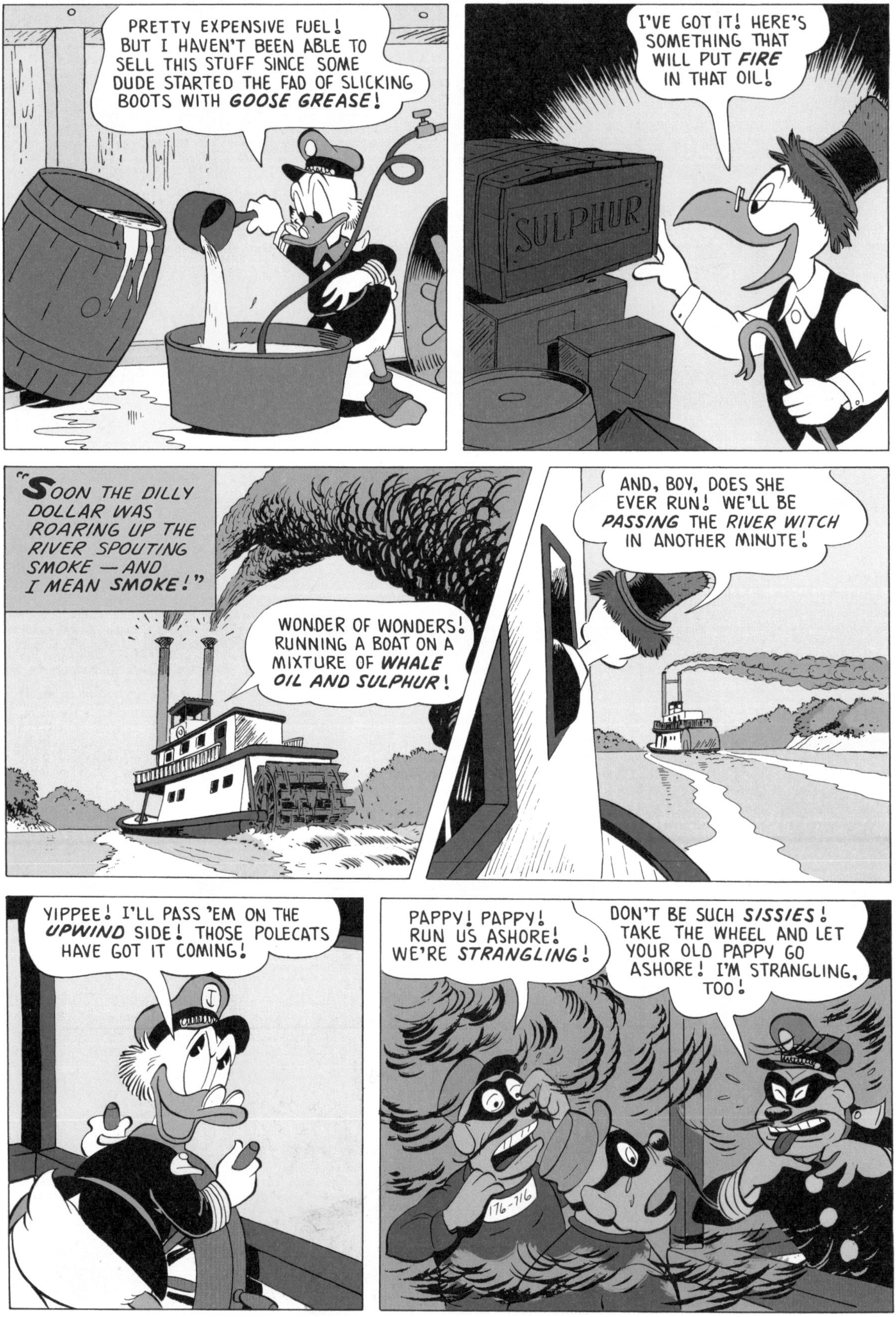

PRETTY EXPENSIVE FUEL! BUT I HAVEN'T BEEN ABLE TO SELL THIS STUFF SINCE SOME DUDE STARTED THE FAD OF SLICKING BOOTS WITH GOOSE GREASE!
I'VE GOT IT! HERE'S SOMETHING THAT WILL PUT FIRE IN THAT OIL!
SULPHUR
"SOON THE DILLY DOLLAR WAS ROARING UP THE RIVER SPOUTING SMOKE — AND I MEAN SMOKE!"
WONDER OF WONDERS! RUNNING A BOAT ON A MIXTURE OF WHALE OIL AND SULPHUR!
AND, BOY, DOES SHE EVER RUN! WE'LL BE PASSING THE RIVER WITCH IN ANOTHER MINUTE!
YIPPEE! I'LL PASS 'EM ON THE UPWIND SIDE! THOSE POLECATS HAVE GOT IT COMING!
PAPPY! PAPPY! RUN US ASHORE! WE'RE STRANGLING!
DON'T BE SUCH SISSIES! TAKE THE WHEEL AND LET YOUR OLD PAPPY GO ASHORE! I'M STRANGLING, TOO!
176-716

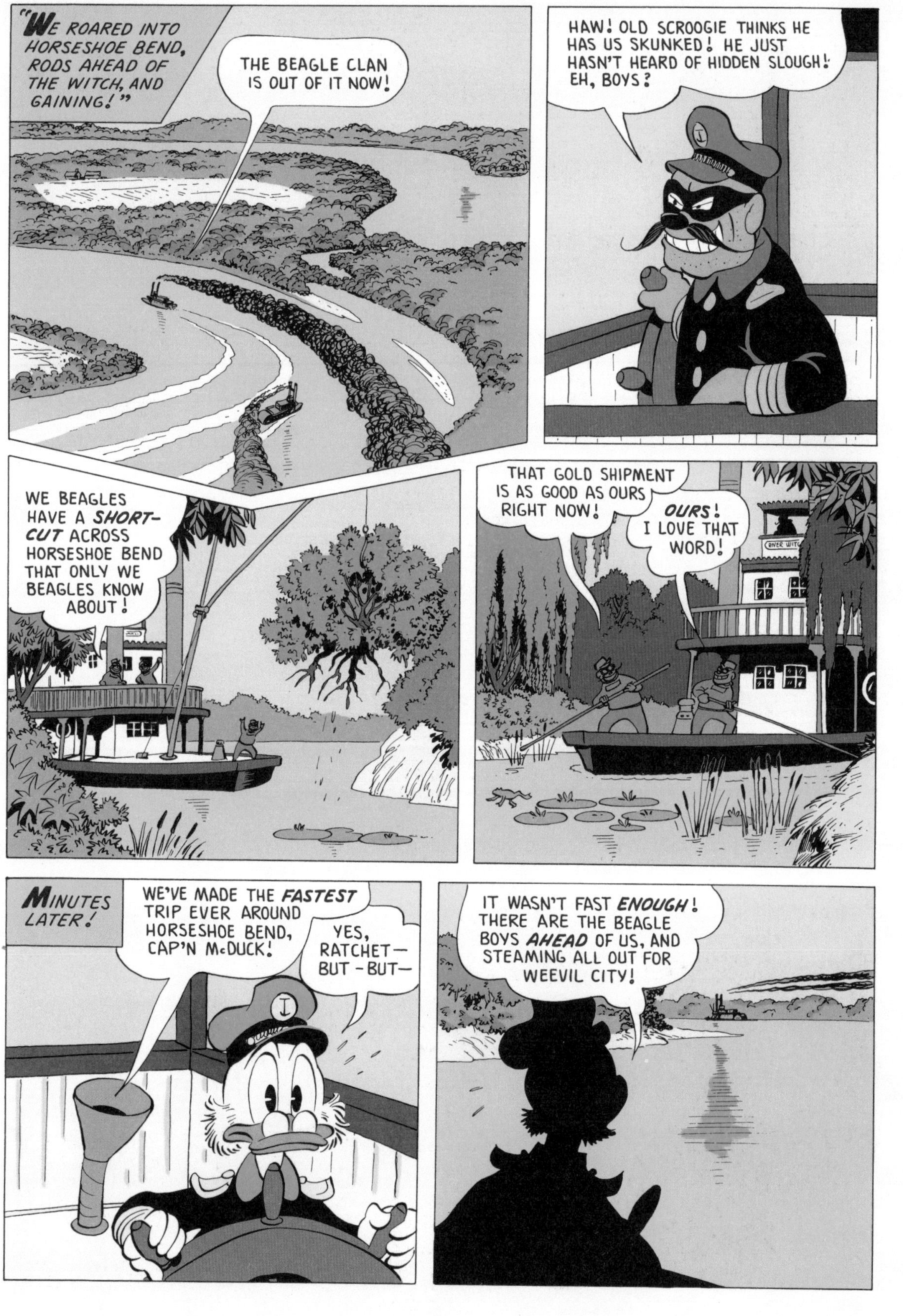
"WE ROARED INTO HORSESHOE BEND, RODS AHEAD OF THE WITCH, AND GAINING!"
THE BEAGLE CLAN IS OUT OF IT NOW!
HAW! OLD SCROOGIE THINKS HE HAS US SKUNKED! HE JUST HASN'T HEARD OF HIDDEN SLOUGH! EH, BOYS?
WE BEAGLES HAVE A SHORT-CUT ACROSS HORSESHOE BEND THAT ONLY WE BEAGLES KNOW ABOUT!
THAT GOLD SHIPMENT IS AS GOOD AS OURS RIGHT NOW!
OURS! I LOVE THAT WORD!
MINUTES LATER!
WE'VE MADE THE FASTEST TRIP EVER AROUND HORSESHOE BEND, CAP'N McDUCK!
YES, RATCHET— BUT -BUT—
IT WASN'T FAST ENOUGH! THERE ARE THE BEAGLE BOYS AHEAD OF US, AND STEAMING ALL OUT FOR WEEVIL CITY!

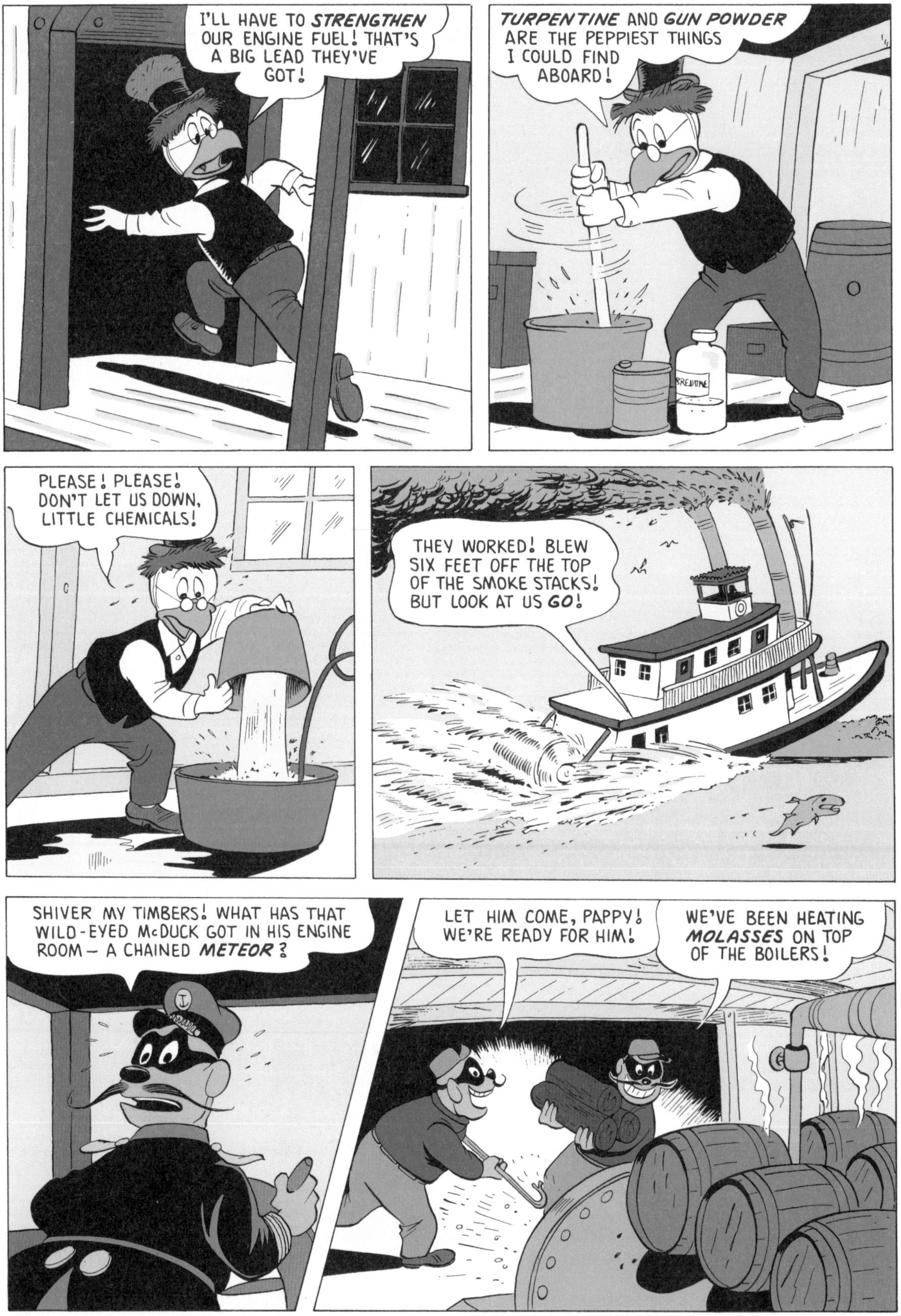
I'LL HAVE TO STRENGTHEN OUR ENGINE FUEL! THAT'S A BIG LEAD THEY'VE GOT!
TURPENTINE AND GUN POWDER ARE THE PEPPIEST THINGS I COULD FIND ABOARD!
PLEASE! PLEASE! DON'T LET US DOWN, LITTLE CHEMICALS!
THEY WORKED! BLEW SIX FEET OFF THE TOP OF THE SMOKE STACKS! BUT LOOK AT US GO!
SHIVER MY TIMBERS! WHAT HAS THAT WILD-EYED McDUCK GOT IN HIS ENGINE ROOM – A CHAINED METEOR?
LET HIM COME, PAPPY! WE'RE READY FOR HIM!
WE'VE BEEN HEATING MOLASSES ON TOP OF THE BOILERS!

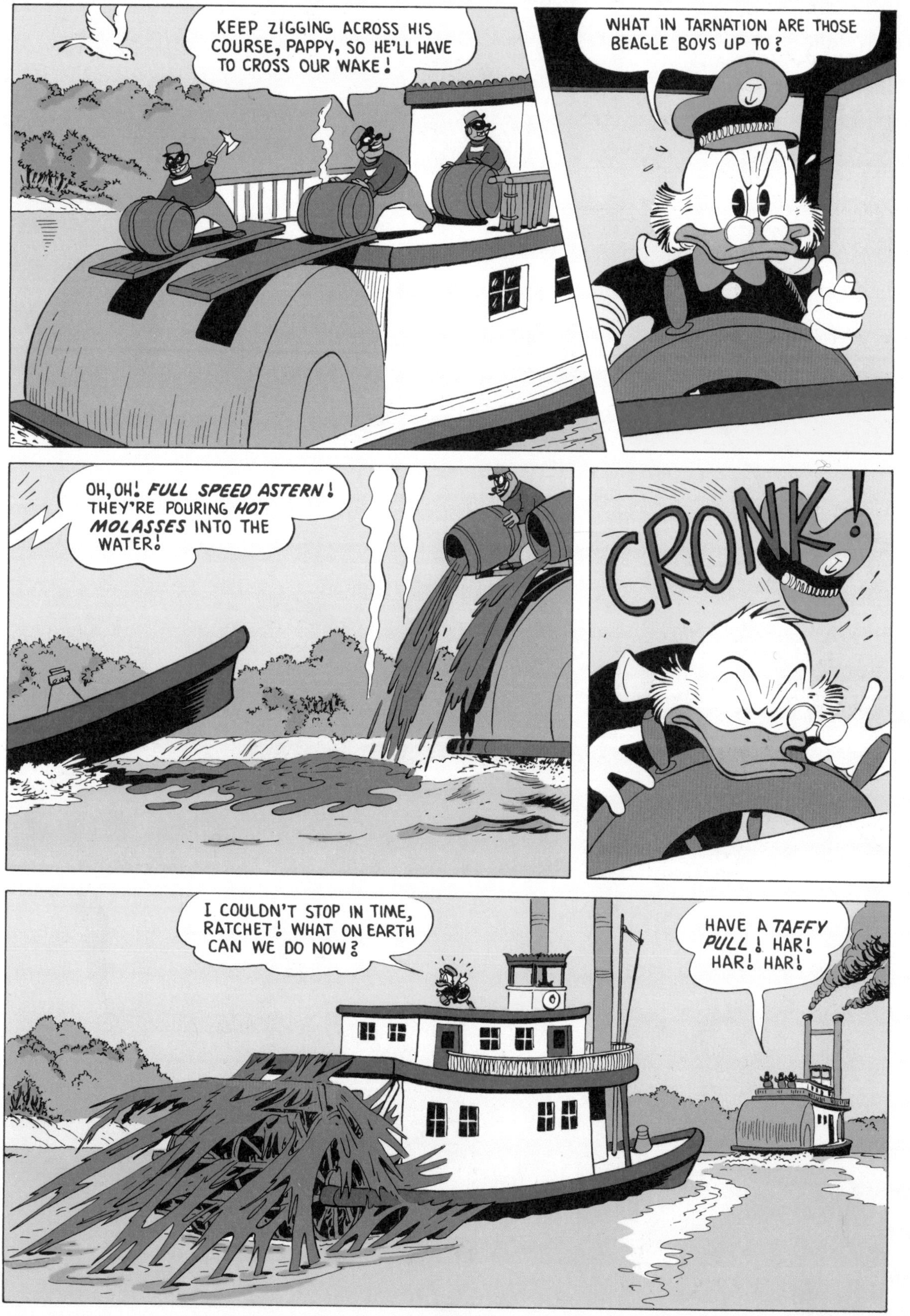
KEEP ZIGGING ACROSS HIS COURSE, PAPPY, SO HE'LL HAVE TO CROSS OUR WAKE!
WHAT IN TARNATION ARE THOSE BEAGLE BOYS UP TO?
OH, OH! FULL SPEED ASTERN! THEY'RE POURING HOT MOLASSES INTO THE WATER!
CRONK!
I COULDN'T STOP IN TIME, RATCHET! WHAT ON EARTH CAN WE DO NOW?
HAVE A TAFFY PULL! HAR! HAR! HAR!

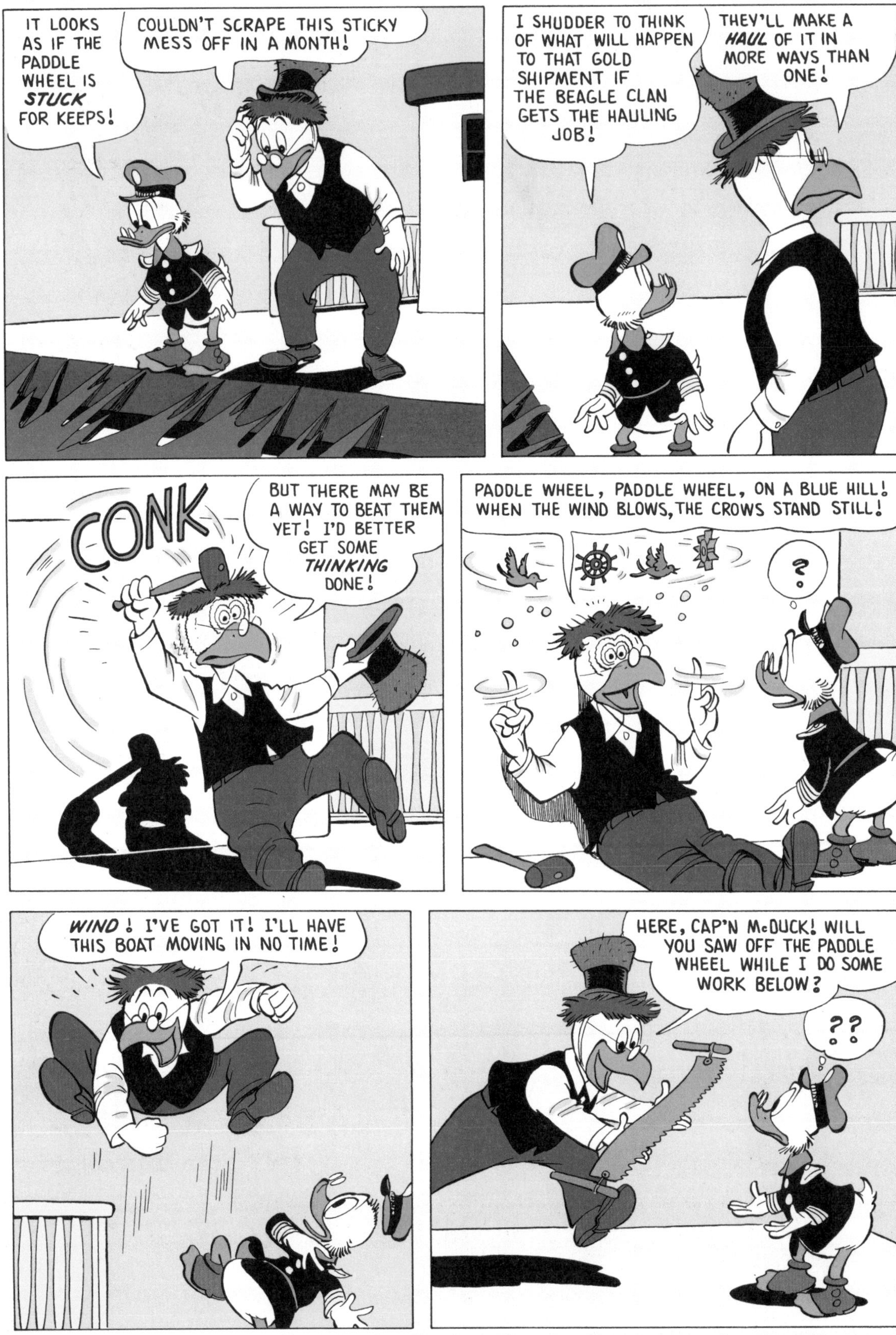
IT LOOKS AS IF THE PADDLE WHEEL IS STUCK FOR KEEPS!
COULDN'T SCRAPE THIS STICKY MESS OFF IN A MONTH!
I SHUDDER TO THINK OF WHAT WILL HAPPEN TO THAT GOLD SHIPMENT IF THE BEAGLE CLAN GETS THE HAULING JOB!
THEY'LL MAKE A HAUL OF IT IN MORE WAYS THAN ONE!
CONK
BUT THERE MAY BE A WAY TO BEAT THEM YET! I'D BETTER GET SOME THINKING DONE!
PADDLE WHEEL, PADDLE WHEEL, ON A BLUE HILL! WHEN THE WIND BLOWS, THE CROWS STAND STILL!
?
WIND! I'VE GOT IT! I'LL HAVE THIS BOAT MOVING IN NO TIME!
HERE, CAP'N McDUCK! WILL YOU SAW OFF THE PADDLE WHEEL WHILE I DO SOME WORK BELOW?
??

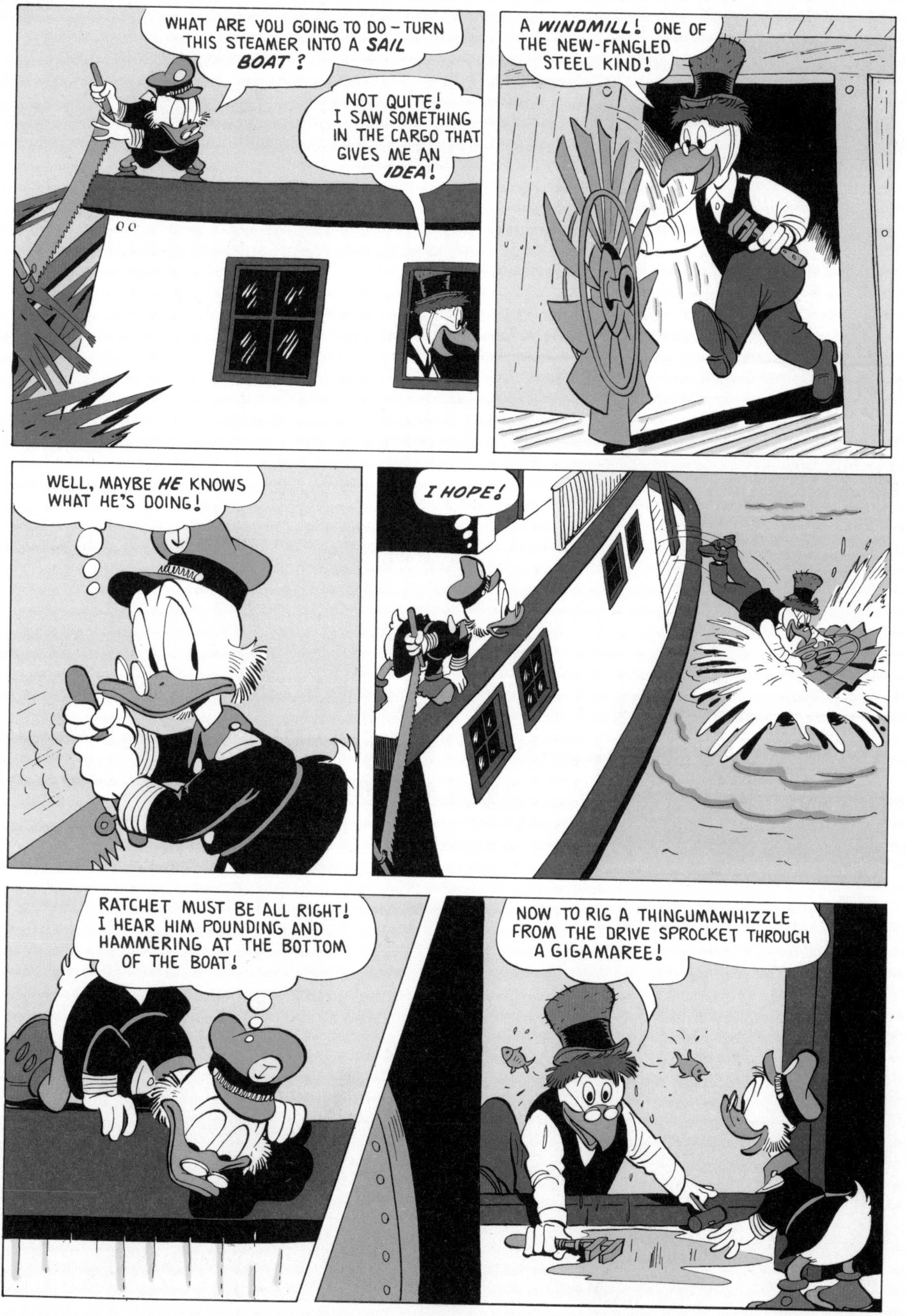
WHAT ARE YOU GOING TO DO – TURN THIS STEAMER INTO A *SAIL BOAT* ?
NOT QUITE! I SAW SOMETHING IN THE CARGO THAT GIVES ME AN *IDEA*!
A *WINDMILL*! ONE OF THE NEW-FANGLED STEEL KIND!
WELL, MAYBE *HE* KNOWS WHAT HE'S DOING!
I HOPE!
RATCHET MUST BE ALL RIGHT! I HEAR HIM POUNDING AND HAMMERING AT THE BOTTOM OF THE BOAT!
NOW TO RIG A THINGUMAWHIZZLE FROM THE DRIVE SPROCKET THROUGH A GIGAMAREE!

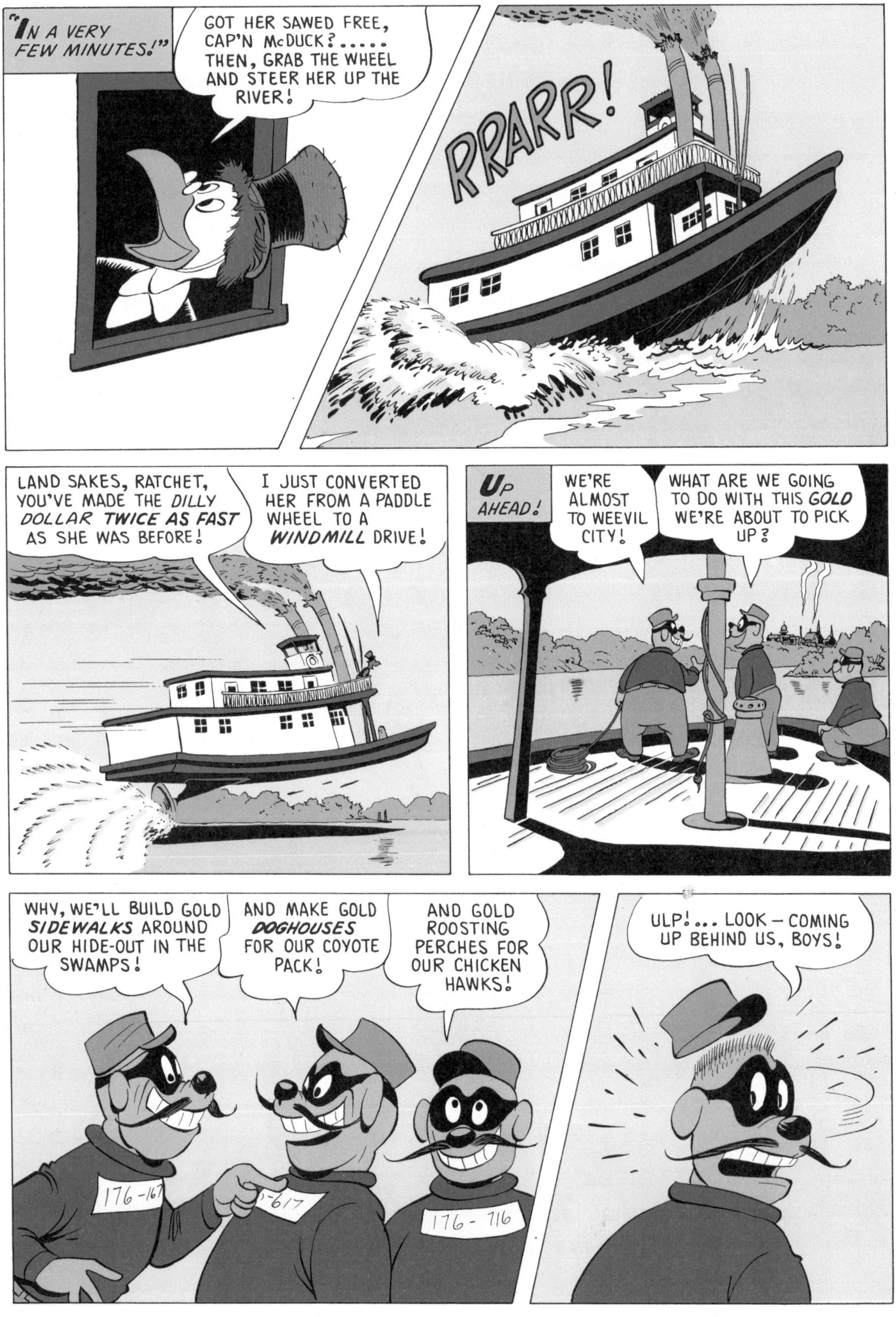
"IN A VERY FEW MINUTES!"
GOT HER SAWED FREE, CAP'N McDUCK? ..... THEN, GRAB THE WHEEL AND STEER HER UP THE RIVER!
RRARR!
LAND SAKES, RATCHET, YOU'VE MADE THE DILLY DOLLAR TWICE AS FAST AS SHE WAS BEFORE!
I JUST CONVERTED HER FROM A PADDLE WHEEL TO A WINDMILL DRIVE!
UP AHEAD!
WE'RE ALMOST TO WEEVIL CITY!
WHAT ARE WE GOING TO DO WITH THIS GOLD WE'RE ABOUT TO PICK UP?
WHY, WE'LL BUILD GOLD SIDEWALKS AROUND OUR HIDE-OUT IN THE SWAMPS!
AND MAKE GOLD DOGHOUSES FOR OUR COYOTE PACK!
AND GOLD ROOSTING PERCHES FOR OUR CHICKEN HAWKS!
176-167
176-716
ULP! ... LOOK — COMING UP BEHIND US, BOYS!

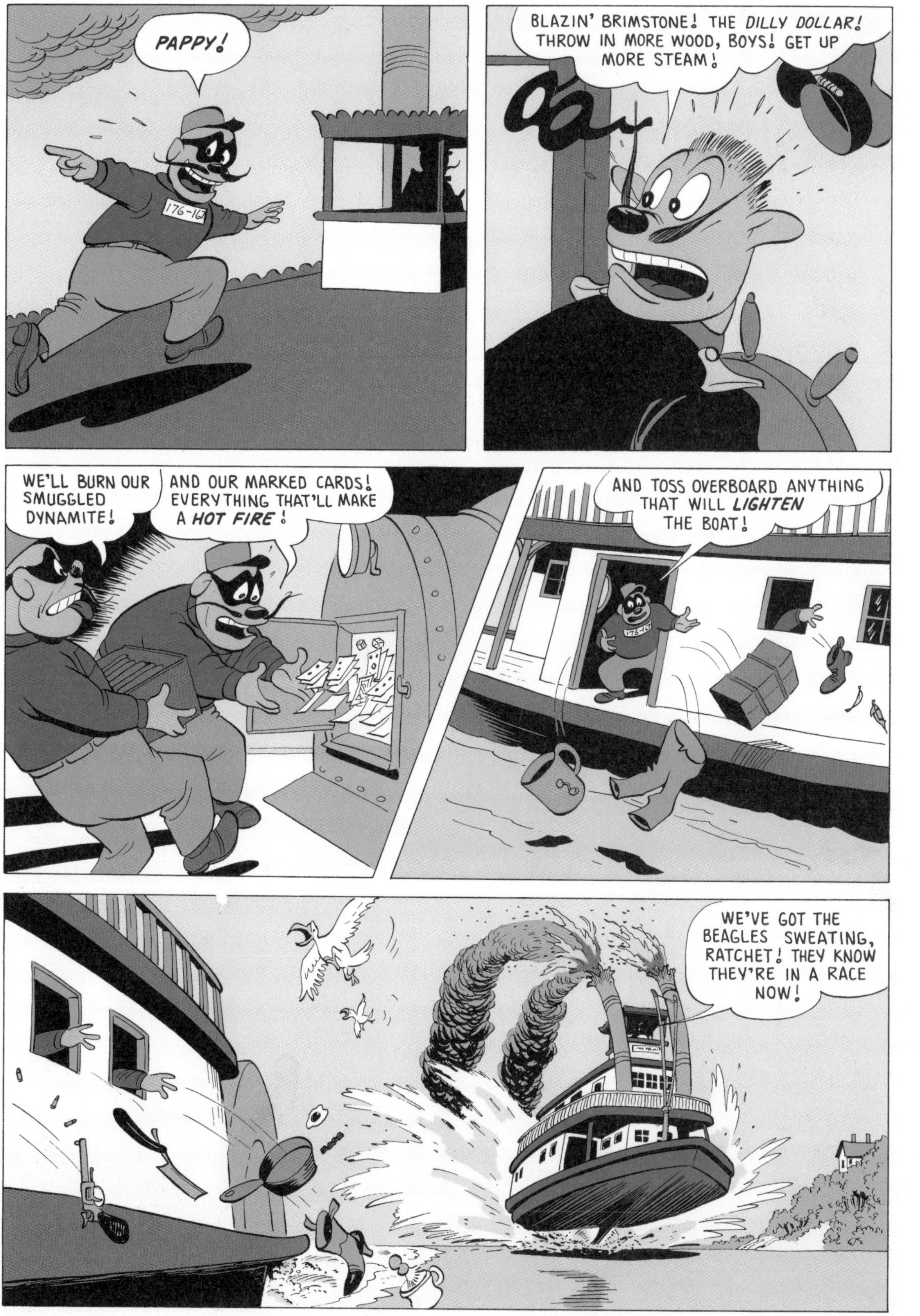
PAPPY!
BLAZIN' BRIMSTONE! THE DILLY DOLLAR! THROW IN MORE WOOD, BOYS! GET UP MORE STEAM!
WE'LL BURN OUR SMUGGLED DYNAMITE!
AND OUR MARKED CARDS! EVERYTHING THAT'LL MAKE A HOT FIRE!
AND TOSS OVERBOARD ANYTHING THAT WILL LIGHTEN THE BOAT!
WE'VE GOT THE BEAGLES SWEATING, RATCHET! THEY KNOW THEY'RE IN A RACE NOW!

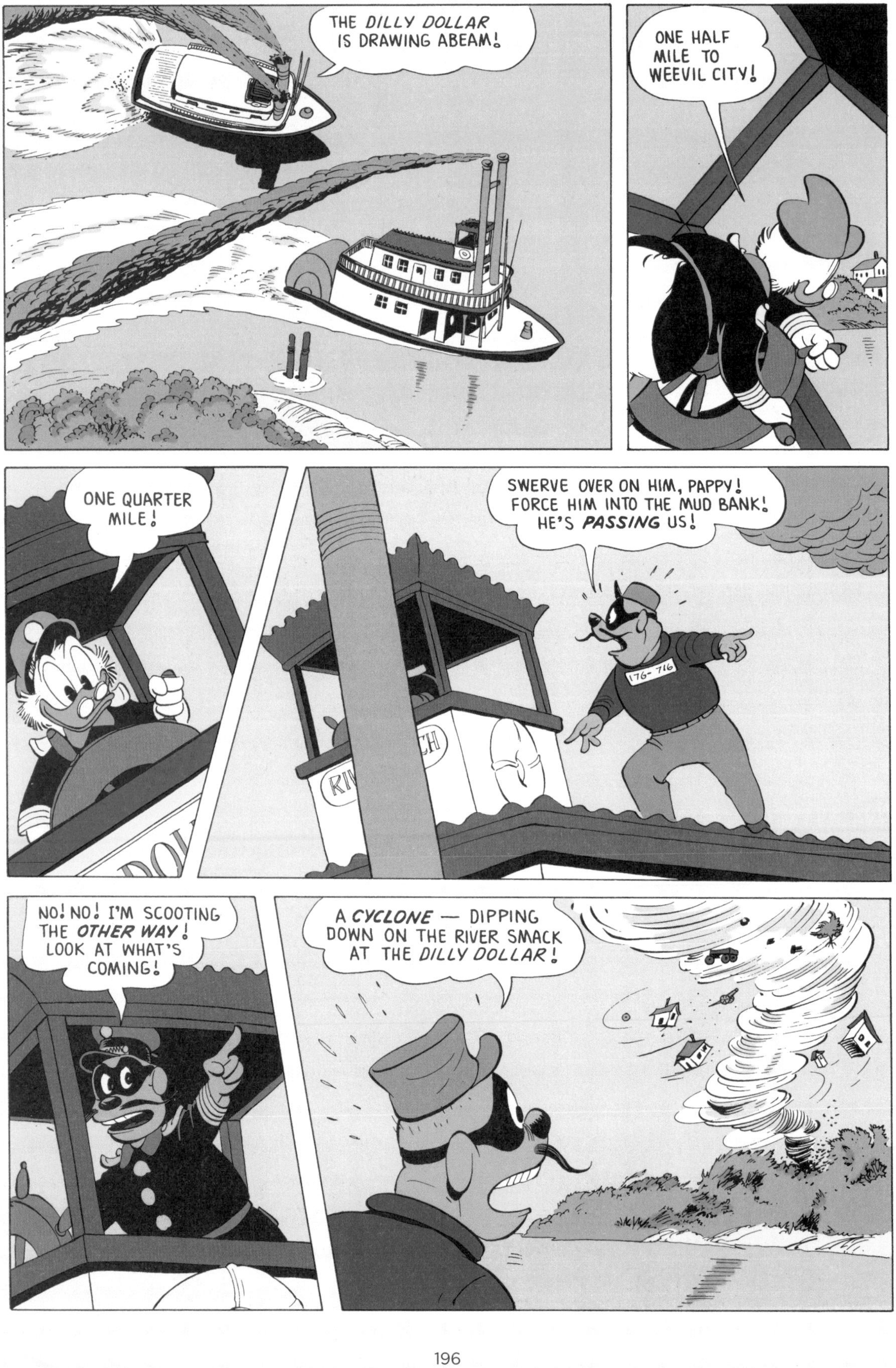
THE DILLY DOLLAR IS DRAWING ABEAM!
ONE HALF MILE TO WEEVIL CITY!
ONE QUARTER MILE!
SWERVE OVER ON HIM, PAPPY! FORCE HIM INTO THE MUD BANK! HE'S PASSING US!
176-716
NO! NO! I'M SCOOTING THE OTHER WAY! LOOK AT WHAT'S COMING!
A CYCLONE — DIPPING DOWN ON THE RIVER SMACK AT THE DILLY DOLLAR!

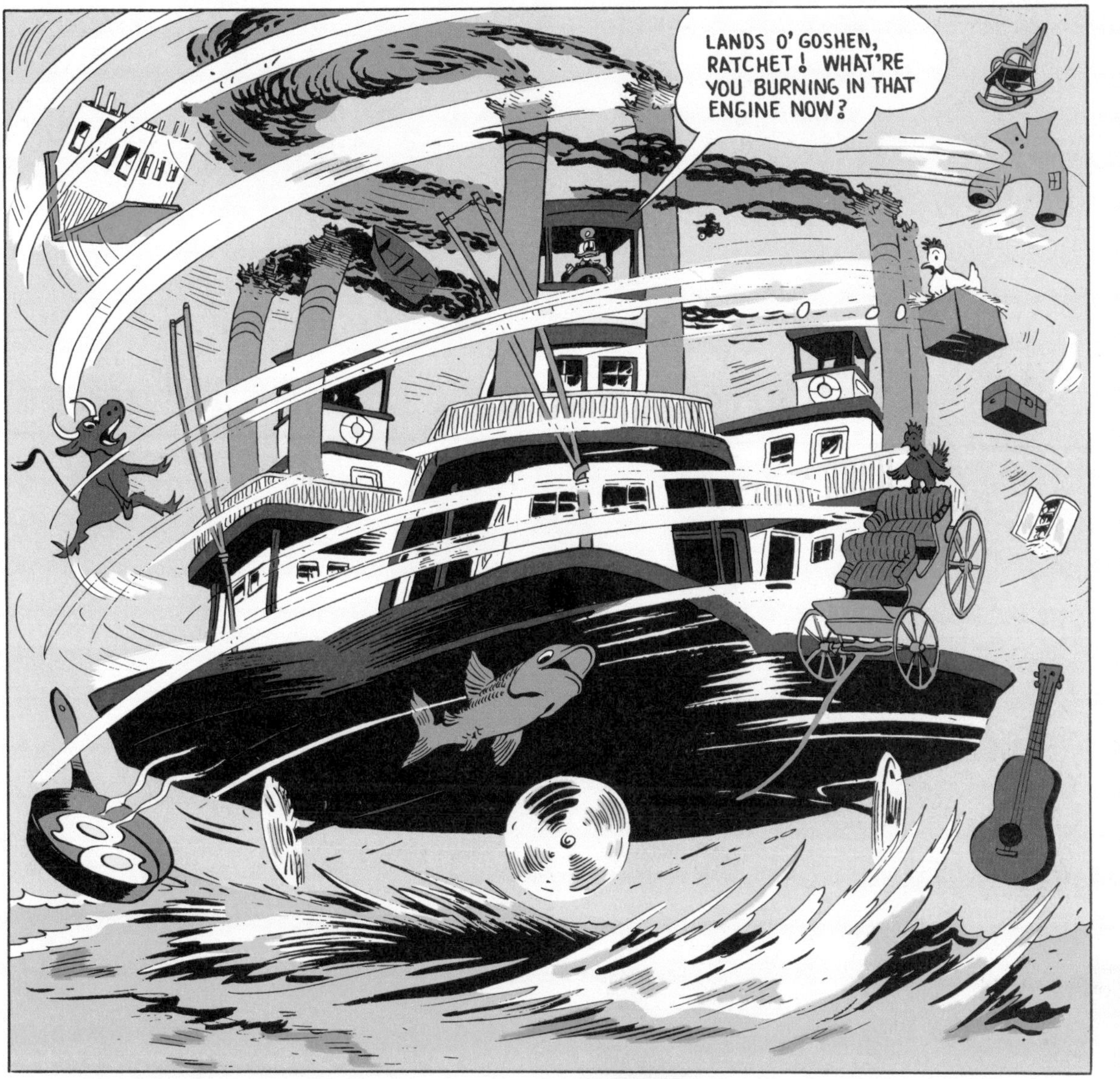
LANDS O' GOSHEN, RATCHET! WHAT'RE YOU BURNING IN THAT ENGINE NOW?

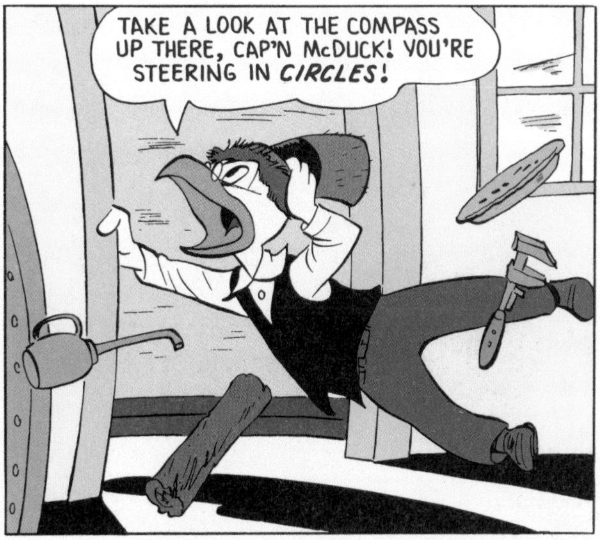
TAKE A LOOK AT THE COMPASS UP THERE, CAP'N McDUCK! YOU'RE STEERING IN *CIRCLES*!

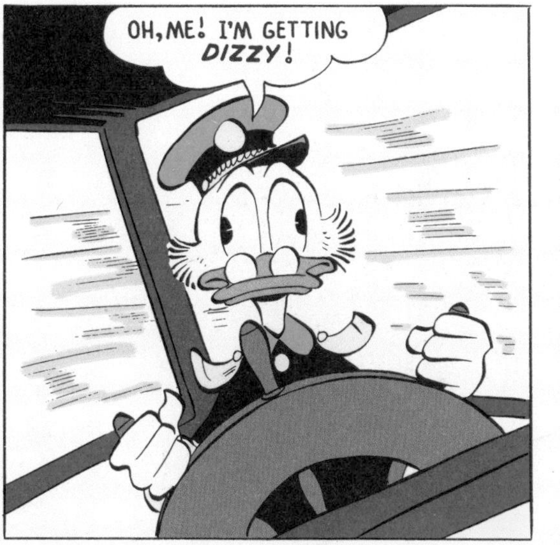
OH, ME! I'M GETTING *DIZZY*!

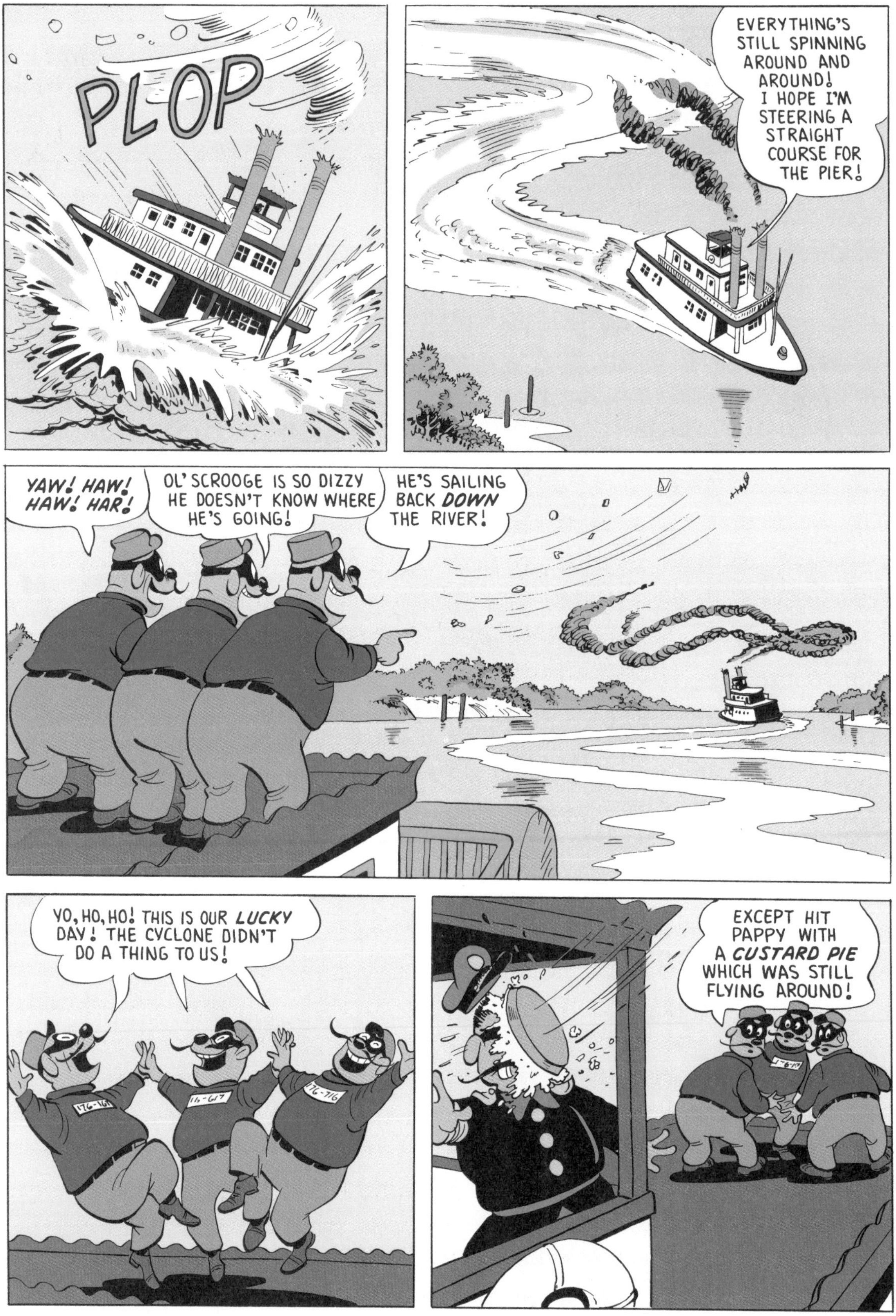
PLOP
EVERYTHING'S STILL SPINNING AROUND AND AROUND! I HOPE I'M STEERING A STRAIGHT COURSE FOR THE PIER!
YAW! HAW! HAW! HAR!
OL' SCROOGE IS SO DIZZY HE DOESN'T KNOW WHERE HE'S GOING!
HE'S SAILING BACK DOWN THE RIVER!
YO, HO, HO! THIS IS OUR LUCKY DAY! THE CYCLONE DIDN'T DO A THING TO US!
EXCEPT HIT PAPPY WITH A CUSTARD PIE WHICH WAS STILL FLYING AROUND!

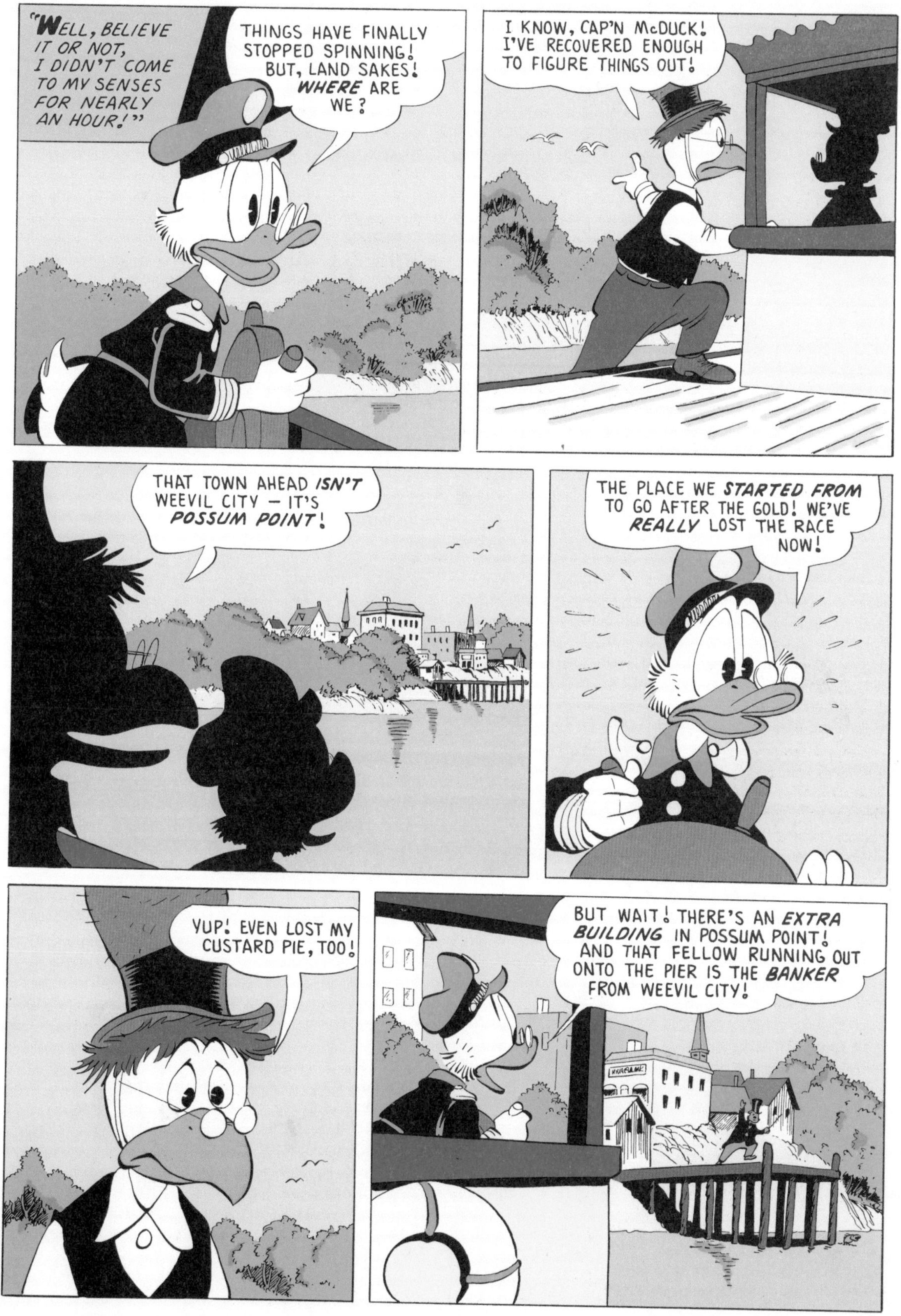
"WELL, BELIEVE IT OR NOT, I DIDN'T COME TO MY SENSES FOR NEARLY AN HOUR!"
THINGS HAVE FINALLY STOPPED SPINNING! BUT, LAND SAKES! WHERE ARE WE?
I KNOW, CAP'N McDUCK! I'VE RECOVERED ENOUGH TO FIGURE THINGS OUT!
THAT TOWN AHEAD ISN'T WEEVIL CITY — IT'S POSSUM POINT!
THE PLACE WE STARTED FROM TO GO AFTER THE GOLD! WE'VE REALLY LOST THE RACE NOW!
YUP! EVEN LOST MY CUSTARD PIE, TOO!
BUT WAIT! THERE'S AN EXTRA BUILDING IN POSSUM POINT! AND THAT FELLOW RUNNING OUT ONTO THE PIER IS THE BANKER FROM WEEVIL CITY!

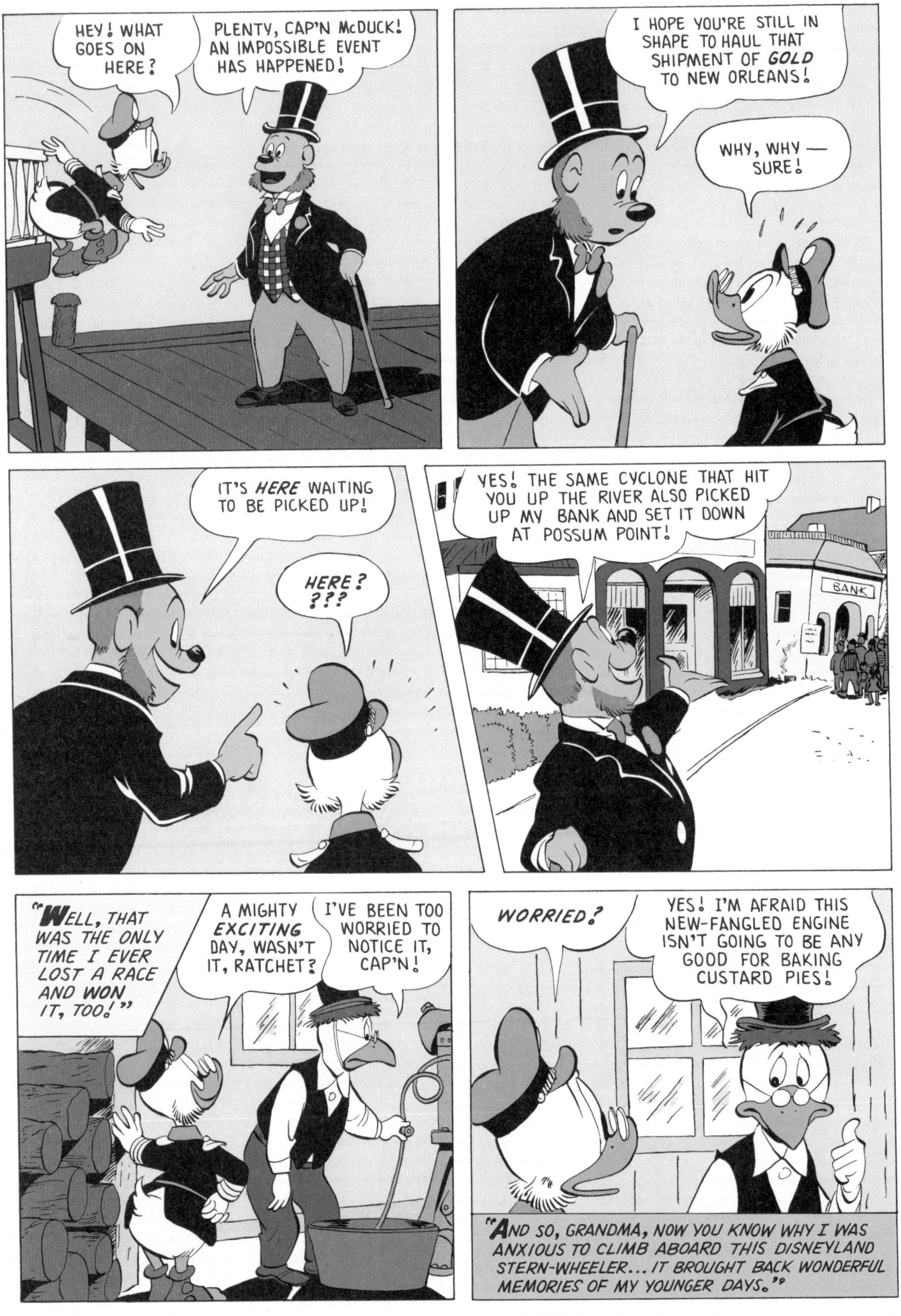
HEY! WHAT GOES ON HERE?
PLENTY, CAP'N McDUCK! AN IMPOSSIBLE EVENT HAS HAPPENED!
I HOPE YOU'RE STILL IN SHAPE TO HAUL THAT SHIPMENT OF GOLD TO NEW ORLEANS!
WHY, WHY — SURE!
IT'S HERE WAITING TO BE PICKED UP!
HERE? ???
YES! THE SAME CYCLONE THAT HIT YOU UP THE RIVER ALSO PICKED UP MY BANK AND SET IT DOWN AT POSSUM POINT!
BANK
"WELL, THAT WAS THE ONLY TIME I EVER LOST A RACE AND WON IT, TOO!"
A MIGHTY EXCITING DAY, WASN'T IT, RATCHET?
I'VE BEEN TOO WORRIED TO NOTICE IT, CAP'N!
WORRIED?
YES! I'M AFRAID THIS NEW-FANGLED ENGINE ISN'T GOING TO BE ANY GOOD FOR BAKING CUSTARD PIES!
"AND SO, GRANDMA, NOW YOU KNOW WHY I WAS ANXIOUS TO CLIMB ABOARD THIS DISNEYLAND STERN-WHEELER... IT BROUGHT BACK WONDERFUL MEMORIES OF MY YOUNGER DAYS."

Walt Disney
presents
Donald Duck
YOU SHOULD LET ME SELL YOU ONE OF THESE COMFORTABLE HOMBURGS, UNCLE SCROOGE!
THE HAT I'VE GOT IS JUST AS COMFORTABLE!
DUBS HATS
THIS OLD TOPPER IS THE MOST COMFORTABLE HAT EVER INVENTED! IT HELPS WARM ME IN WINTER AND COOL ME IN SUMMER!
LIKE THIS!
IN SUMMER THIS IS FILLED WITH ICE WATER!

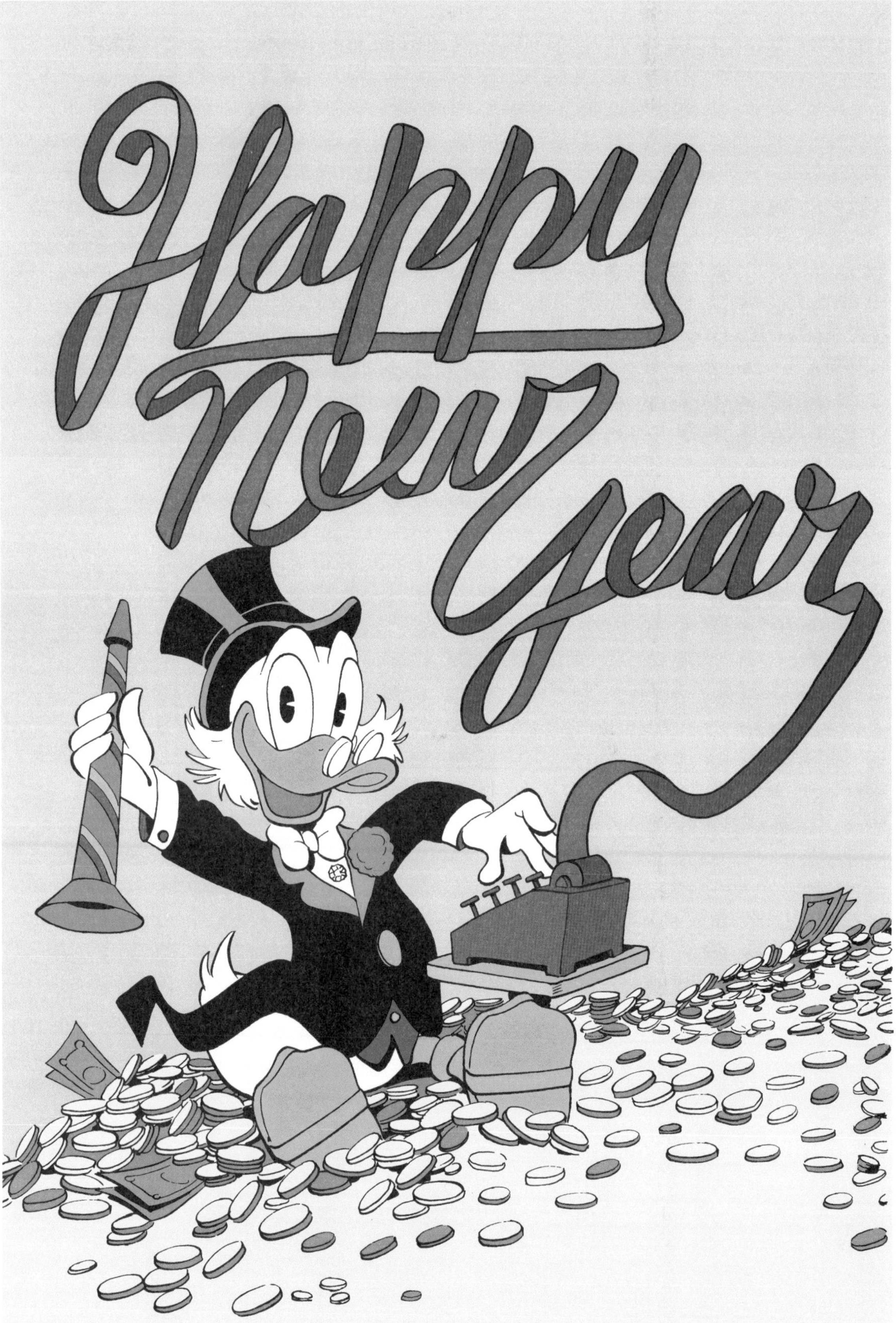
Happy New Year

Story Notes

THE LOST CROWN OF GENGHIS KHAN! *p. 1*

Build the legend, downplay the myth. That sentence could summarize almost all of Carl Barks's stories: he builds up the legend of the Ducks (especially his creation, Uncle Scrooge McDuck), but he always approaches existing myths with a down-to-earth practicality.

We can see that in this story, where Uncle Scrooge, Donald, and the nephews trek through the Himalayas (a range of mountains that includes the world's highest peak, Mt. Everest) to regain the lost crown of Genghis Khan, which was stolen from Scrooge's men by the Abominable Snowman — also called Yeti.

The Abominable Snowman — an ape-like entity who supposedly roams the Himalayan region and stands taller than an average human — was quite a topic in popular media when this story was first published. In 1954, Britain's *Daily Mail* printed an article that described a Himalayan expedition team obtaining hair specimens from what was alleged to be a Yeti scalp found in a monastery in

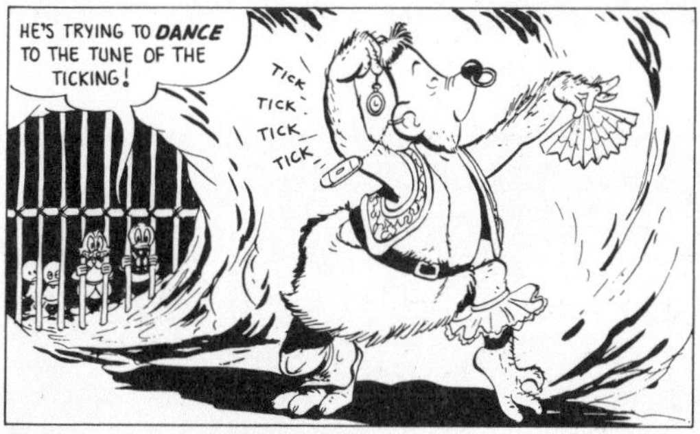
HE'S TRYING TO **DANCE** TO THE TUNE OF THE TICKING!
TICK TICK TICK TICK

Nepal. In 1953, award-winning science fiction writer Isaac Asimov published his short story "Everest," in which the Yeti were revealed to be Martians, living in the Himalayas because of the low-density atmosphere, very close to the conditions on Mars.

But here, the real Abominable (or Abdominal, as Donald calls him) is quite different from the creature of myth — he's a sort of giant child, fascinated by the ticking of Scrooge's classic watch. The old miser, always a good businessman, exchanges the watch for Genghis Khan's crown.

"The fierce, cunning Snowman! The legendary terror of the topless peaks!" says a disappointed Donald sarcastically. Barks downplayed the myth, as he had done in the past and would do in the future (with Greek and Norse gods in "Mythic Mystery," *Uncle Scrooge* #34, 1961, for example).

The watch itself, appearing in the first panel and proving crucial to the story, is a typical example of a Barksian narrative gimmick. At another point in this adventure, Scrooge has to use a trick to make the nephews follow him, though we can see that it looks more like a sort of role-playing game. "You've shanghaied us for nothing, Uncle Scrooge!" says Donald, after the trick is revealed. "We won't take the job!"

But in the end they do, and not only because they don't want their old relative going to Himalaya alone (after all, Scrooge is very resourceful), but because they like adventure, too.

The story, even if comparatively short (19 pages, in contrast to earlier 32-pagers) is a minor classic in its own right, but it grew in significance in later years when cartoonist Don Rosa paired it with another Barks classic, "Tralla La" (*Walt Disney's Uncle Scrooge: "Only a Poor Old Man"*; Volume 12 in this series) and made a combined sequel of sorts.

In "Return to Xanadu" (*Walt Disney Uncle Scrooge and Donald Duck: "Treasure Under Glass,"* The Don Rosa Library Vol. 3), Rosa sends the Ducks back to the valley of Tralla La to search for the rest of Genghis Khan's treasure. Rosa said he quotes Samuel Taylor Coleridge's famous poem "Kubla Khan" in the story because it "describ[es] Barks's valley of Tralla La in detail."

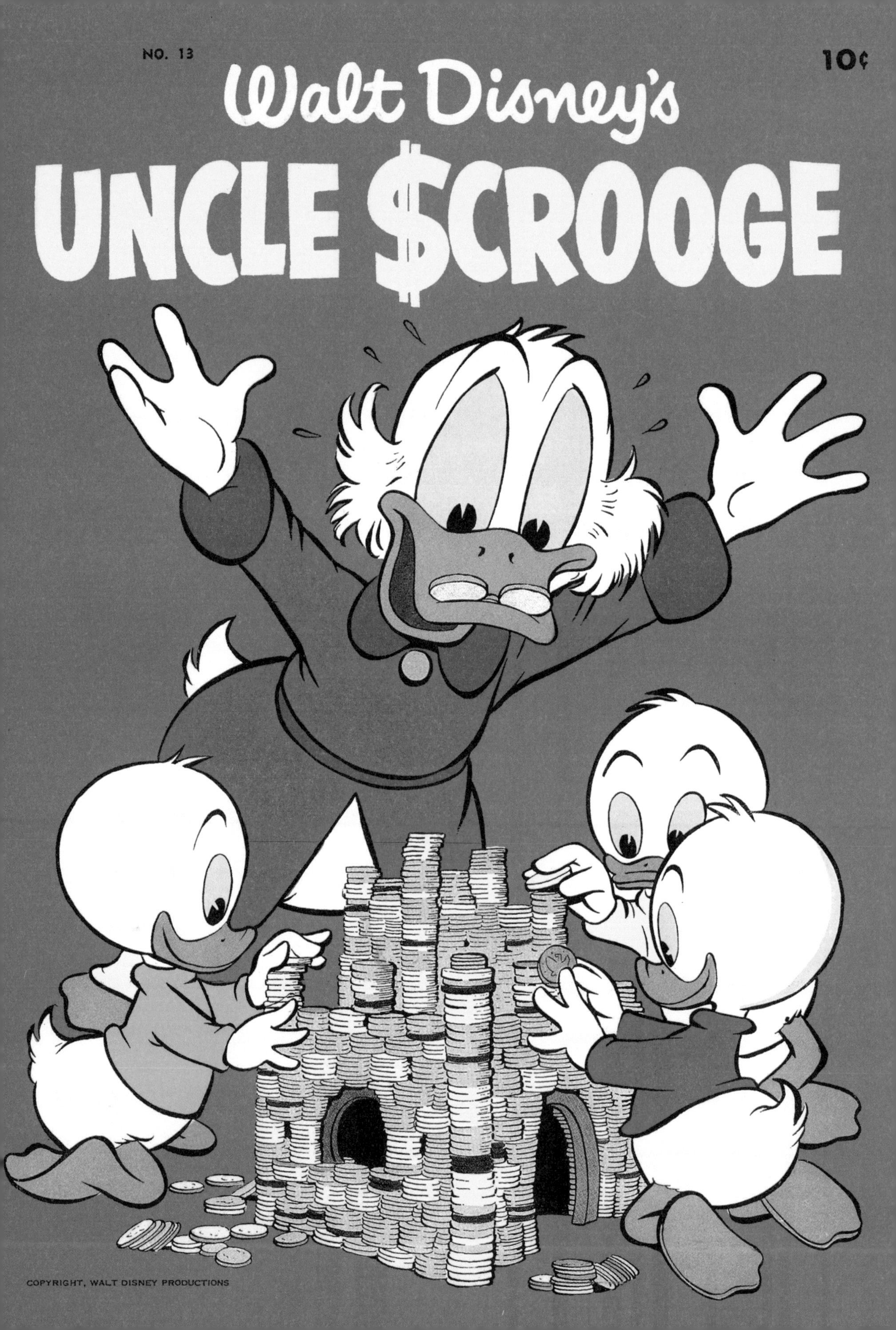
NO. 13
10¢
Walt Disney's
UNCLE $CROOGE
COPYRIGHT, WALT DISNEY PRODUCTIONS

"Return to Xanadu" is probably the first story where Don Rosa proves his ability to become another Duck Maestro, following in the webbed footprints of Carl Barks.

— STEFANO PRIARONE

LAND BENEATH THE GROUND! *p. 21*

Unlike most Barksian globetrotting farces, the cavernous corker "Land Beneath the Ground!" delves, quite literally, into the very bedrock of Duckburg.

We find Scrooge in the midst of another nerve-bursting anxiety attack over potential threats to his beloved lucre. Barks emphasizes the constant "caging" burden of McDuck's "fantasticatrillions" through subtle graphic matches on the Worry Room's padded walls, the dollar-dotted draperies, and even the sharp spikes of his *Citizen Kane*-esque wrought-iron security fence.

The most prescient opening gag, however, concerns the three ledgers recording the tycoon's oil interests. Note that the *Oil Wells Drilling* and *Oil Wells Flowing* volumes are both thicker and taller than the *Oil Wells Kaput* volume, which is dismally draped in mourning. Here we see the first, sly reference to the drilling, digging, and mining mischief to come. The exterior conversations with Donald that follow are filled with clear blue skies and well-appointed parks, providing comedic counterpoints for the as-yet undiscovered chasms and canyons of Terry Fermy.

Soon the action shifts into carnival mode with runaway mine cars (à la *Indiana Jones and the Temple of Doom*, but this scene was initially absent from the story; see p. 221), roller-coaster loop-the-loops, and funhouse moss slides that whisk the Ducks into the heart of Barks's screwball Wonderland.

Once in Terry Fermy, the Ducks discover phosphorus deposits that illuminate the land like "the sun room of the mad March Hare" and "slabs of germanium" that receive radio broadcasts. The spheroid-shaped natives of this exotic underworld gladly style their speech, fashions, education, and careers around the get-along mentality of fraternity-house athletics.

In this way, Terry Fermy's destructive Olympics indict the ego-driven mid-century Male. There is a good deal of *Mad Men's* Don Draper and John Updike's Harry "Rabbit" Angstrom — and, perhaps by association, a little bit of Scott Adams's Dilbert, too — in the macho motivations and manic cheers of cracking Fermies and slamming Terries.

Like Barks's other allegorical personifications of postmodern personality, they converse in goofy hipster lingo like the "straight cornpone" of Plain Awfullers from "Lost in the Andes" (*Walt Disney's Donald Duck: "Lost in the Andes"*), and they "dig" contemporary media messages via strange contraptions like the eel-powered jukeboxes of "The Secret of Atlantis" (*Walt Disney's Uncle Scrooge: "Only a Poor Old Man"*). Their entire global underground culture is built around an earthquake championship that bestows bragging rights for competitive destruction.

Yet the strangest aspect of Terry Fermy is its completely male population. There are no suggestions of family, home, or feminine influences of any kind — just groups, troops, and teams. Barks's Duck tales sometimes eschew

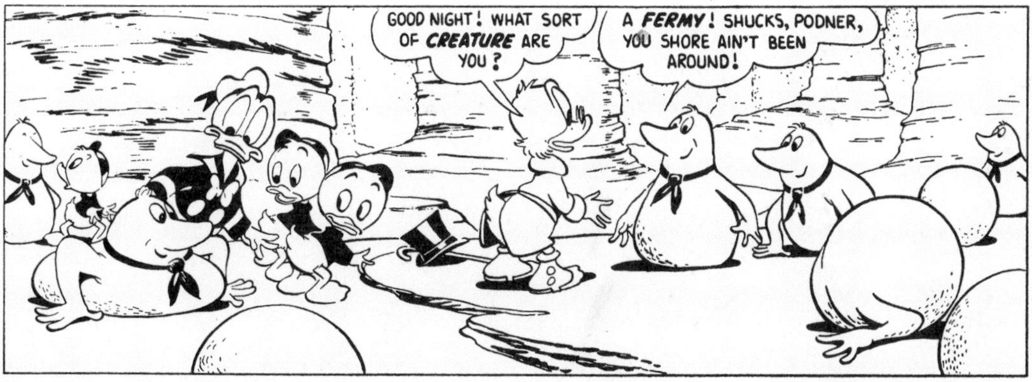
GOOD NIGHT! WHAT SORT OF CREATURE ARE YOU?
A FERMY! SHUCKS, PODNER, YOU SHORE AIN'T BEEN AROUND!

gender themes, but in this case he unveils an entirely masculine, homosocial world of brightly colored bowling-ball men who serve as sly metaphors for the codes of conformity, control, and conflict that defined Cold War America.

Placing competitive drive above all else, including Scrooge's billions, the boasting ballers of Terry Fermy ultimately choose ignorance and isolation and seal off their netherworld forever (not unlike the decision taken by their underground cousins in *Superman and the Mole Men*, the 1951 movie later repackaged and retitled as "The Unknown People" for *The Adventures of Superman* TV show in 1953 — three years before this story saw print).

Their final action makes room for what is perhaps the story's primary satire: the self-satisfied arrogance of science itself. From the beginning, Donald warns that professors "could only make guesses" about predicting earthquakes, and the conclusion's theory-spouting egghead "from the university" clearly lacks the Ducks' real-world wisdom.

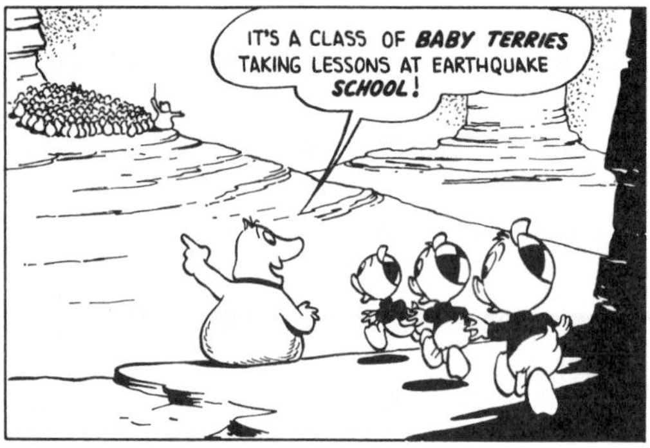
IT'S A CLASS OF BABY TERRIES TAKING LESSONS AT EARTHQUAKE SCHOOL!

Barks's skeptical anti-intellectualism drives many of his best works, but here the message is particularly strong. Hypothetical theories and tenacious teamwork may dictate life in metropolitan Duckburg and in the "Land Beneath the Ground!," but in Barks's view, crafty cunning, savvy subterfuge, and the practical application of the *Junior Woodchucks Guidebook* win the day.

An international favorite, "Land Beneath the Ground!" stands among Carl Barks's tightest satires and has been savored by generations, alongside swashduckling yarns like "The Secret of Atlantis" (*Walt Disney's Uncle Scrooge: "Only a Poor Old Man"*) and "The Lemming With the Locket" (*Walt Disney's Uncle Scrooge: "The Seven Cities of Gold"*).

Several pages were omitted from its initial publication (to make room for other stories in the issue in which it first appeared and thus qualify for a lower mailing cost to subscribers). It appears here in its restored, expanded form.

— DANIEL F. YEZBICK

FAULTY FORTUNE *p. 53*

In their critical treatise *How to Read Donald Duck* (1971), Ariel Dorfman and Armand Mattelart argue that colonialism is at the center of the Disney Duck comics, but in a metaphorical form: the rapaciousness of global capitalism becomes the smaller-scale conflict of an adventure story, in which the reader identifies with Uncle Scrooge or Donald Duck as they bilk natives out of natural resources or swindle customers in business deals.

Although this narrative is common in Carl Barks's stories, other critics have challenged Dorfman and Mattelart's argument. Thomas Andrae notes, for instance, that while it's possible to read some Barks tales as allegories of economic exploitation — and perhaps as commentaries on Barks's own feeling that the Disney corporation was exploiting *him* and his anonymous labor — there are other stories that don't follow, or actively undermine, the colonialist metaphor. "Faulty Fortune" is in the latter camp.

If colonialism is the wholesale, untrammeled exploitation of another country, then the Scrooge McDuck of "Faulty Fortune" is a poor, ineffectual colonialist who allows his fortune-seeking to be hampered by extant laws. In a box of Canny Brannies cereal, he legally wins a deed to "one square inch in Cowhide County." Everyone but Uncle Scrooge quickly realizes that the land is worthless — a barren desert terrain that (according to an odd sight gag on page 54, panel 6) a few thirsty trees share with lunchpail-toting vultures. The clerk at the county land office points out that none of the other landowners has ever bothered to see their properties. No one would care if Uncle Scrooge colonized this land, but he instead hires a surveyor to determine which plot is his. Later in the story, when Scrooge believes that the land is rich with oil, he

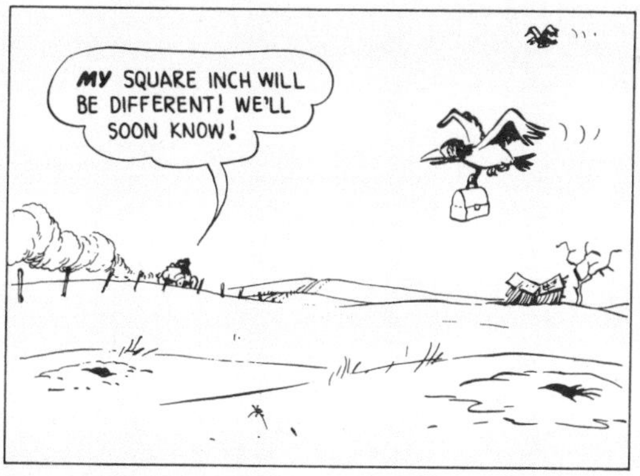

MY SQUARE INCH WILL BE DIFFERENT! WE'LL SOON KNOW!

establishes legal ownership over a bigger plot by sending Donald and the nephews to buy all available boxes of Canny Brannies and secure deeds in bulk. Uncle Scrooge follows the rules. He's not a robber baron who rewrites laws to accommodate his thirst for profit.

Unlike successful colonizers and capitalists, though, the Uncle Scrooge of "Faulty Fortune" is very bad at identifying moneymaking opportunities. Coffee bubbles convince him that the Canny Brannies' land is

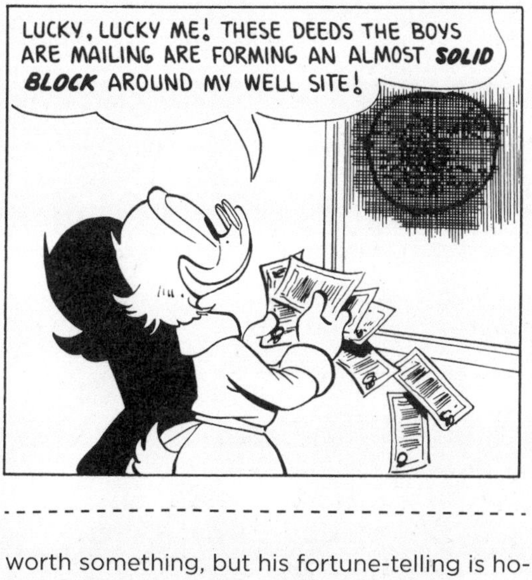

LUCKY, LUCKY ME! THESE DEEDS THE BOYS ARE MAILING ARE FORMING AN ALMOST SOLID BLOCK AROUND MY WELL SITE!

worth something, but his fortune-telling is hokum. (The end of "Faulty Fortune" returns to this point, as Donald teases Uncle Scrooge by saying, "If you go *broke*, you can always make a living *telling fortunes with coffee bubbles*!")

Scrooge discovers a prairie dog's feet are covered in oil and jumps to the conclusion that there's an ocean of oil beneath the arid land. On page 57, Scrooge consults a chart of his progress buying up deeds around his original plot, and the "solid block" looks like a puddle of oil, reinforcing his mistaken assumption about the exploitable resources at the site.

Finally, he wastes a million dollars drilling for oil without doing the basic land excavation that would've turned up the buried tractor. At every turn, Scrooge is wrong. Because he consistently misreads situations, he loses an enormous amount of money, and "Faulty Fortune" is more a cautionary tale about the risks of capitalism than a celebration of colonialism.

— CRAIG FISCHER

THE SECOND-RICHEST DUCK *p. 63*

Folk wisdom has it that everyone has a doppelganger. And that certainly turns out to be true for Uncle Scrooge, as we discover in "The Second-Richest Duck." Flintheart Glomgold, a multimillionaire Duck, lives in the Limpopo Valley, South Africa, in a money bin that, except for the pound logo on its façade, mirrors Scrooge's. If it weren't for his thick hair, beard, and his soft hat topped by a pompom, Glomgold would be a perfect Scrooge lookalike. More importantly, their respective fortunes also mirror each other, at exactly "one multiplujillion, nine obsquatumatillion, six hundred and twenty-three dollars and sixty-two cents."

So what is it that makes them different? As Scrooge, for the first time, confronts someone who is as rich as he is, Barks leads us to realize that Glomgold is not only meaner

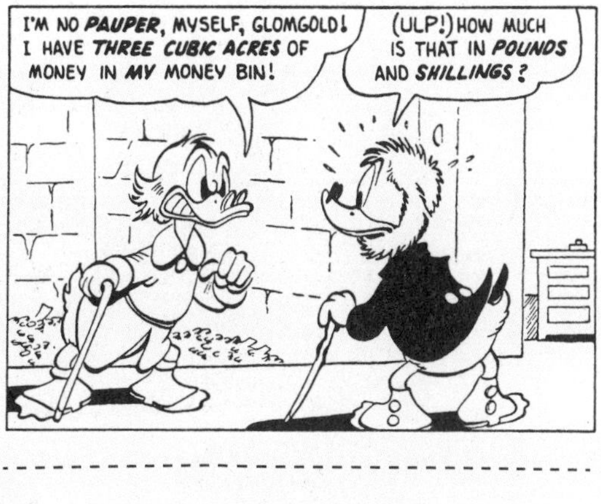

I'M NO PAUPER, MYSELF, GLOMGOLD! I HAVE THREE CUBIC ACRES OF MONEY IN MY MONEY BIN!
(ULP!) HOW MUCH IS THAT IN POUNDS AND SHILLINGS?

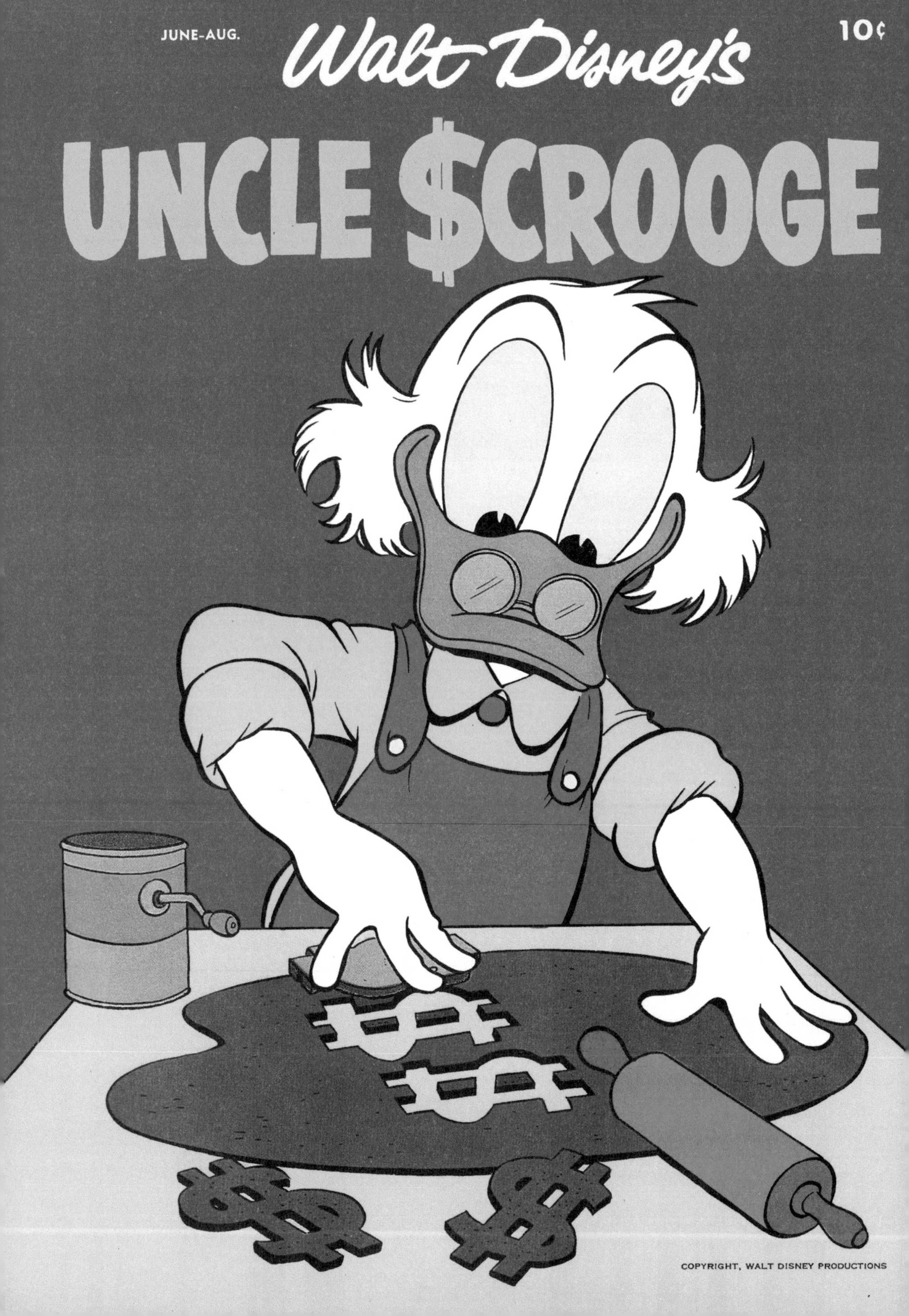
JUNE-AUG.
Walt Disney's
10¢
UNCLE $CROOGE
COPYRIGHT, WALT DISNEY PRODUCTIONS

than Scrooge, but dishonest, too. Further, Glomgold appears to be an isolated misanthropist (misavianist?), whereas Scrooge can count on his family's help and affection.

This tale is often referred to as the "Ball of String Story," as string is the thread that binds the whole yarn together. Barks had the string idea early on, remembering that,

THE LOCUST HORDE MOVES ON!
I'M RUINED! THEY ATE AT LEAST FIFTEEN HUNDRED MILES OF MY STRING!
POOR FELLOW!

years before, "saving tinfoil and string used to be quite a thing. [...] We always accumulated string around the house. We didn't have Scotch tape, so we used string for holding things together. Some people carried it to the point of seeing how big a ball of string they could accumulate." (*Uncle Scrooge McDuck: His Life & Times*, Celestial Arts, 1981)

Barks would use Glomgold twice more, in "The Money Champ" (*Uncle Scrooge* #27, September 1959) and "So Far and No Safari" (*Uncle Scrooge* #61, January 1966), linking the three adventures in what was to him a perfect triptych of stories.

Flintheart Glomgold would appear more than 240 more times (and counting) in comics produced both in the U.S. and other countries around the world. Where Barks had suggested that Glomgold might have British ancestry, when the character was featured in the *DuckTales* animated TV series (1987–1990), he was given a definite Scottish look, thus further reinforcing the "doppelganger" notion. And he remained the same self-centered villain he'd been 30 years before, incapable of giving anybody anything — with no strings attached.

— ALBERTO BECATTINI

MIGRATING MILLIONS *p. 85*

If you live long enough you will become convinced, as Carl Barks was, that All Change is for the Worse. In his quest to keep things as they are, Uncle Scrooge encounters a force he is helpless against: Eminent Domain. Like Superman in a keg of Kryptonite, Scrooge is deprived of his power to outbid and outcompete — the government has no competitors and is more inexorable than any Beagle Boy.

Change is a malign force that exists for the sake of changing and will change things for you wherever you hide. Though Barks does not see fit to make use of the concept, we see here that financial acumen emanates from Scrooge the way luck emanates from Gladstone Gander. No matter how remote, every place Scrooge seeks to plant his money bin becomes invaluable, and by the end, he has been paid three times for his property rights. Ultimately, Scrooge triumphs because

WE'RE LAYING OUT THE ROUTE OF THE NEW SUPER TURNPIKE! IT'S TO GO THROUGH YOUR TEN ACRES!
RIGHT THROUGH THE MONEY BIN!
OH, IS IT?

the material world as such means nothing to him — all that matters is the pure lucre, the representation of wealth itself.

His vulnerability is that for him, that representation must be tangible. With no regard for real property, all he need do is make his wealth mobile so that it may always be one step ahead of the land grabbers. Now his wealth can follow him wherever he goes. He should have thought of this years ago.

— R. FIORE

BACK TO LONG AGO! *p. 93*

Hypnosis is a playful plot device in a few of Carl Barks's early Duck tales. For example, in "Adventure Down Under" (*Walt Disney's Donald Duck: "Christmas on Bear Mountain"*), Donald is hypnotized into believing he is a kangaroo and sets off for Australia. By 1956, however, when Barks sat down to work on "Back to Long Ago!," hypnosis in America had become very serious business.

The immediate cause of the newfound obsession with hypnosis can be traced to an amateur hypnotist named Morey Bernstein who claimed to have uncovered a "past life" of one of his subjects — a Colorado housewife who, under hypnosis, began to speak in a brogue and identify herself as Bridey Murphy, a 19th-century Irishwoman. Early in 1956, Bernstein published *The Search for Bridey Murphy*, which quickly became a bestseller and sparked a hypnotism fad that grew to include movies, songs, a popular dance, and a cocktail (The Reincarnation).

Interest in hypnotism had been growing for a while. It had long been associated in the popular imagination with mesmerism and the occult, but pop psychology's rise in the postwar period rebranded hypnotism as a tool for unlocking hidden powers of the human mind. By the early 1950s, hypnotism was promising success in love and business.

The dark side of hypnotism was there as well, especially after reports that American soldiers in Korea were hypnotized by Chinese scientists and forced to turn against their country. The new concept of "brainwashing" was popularized in the 1956 book *The Rape of the Mind* and in Richard Condon's 1959 novel *The Manchurian Candidate* (made into a movie starring Frank Sinatra in 1962). If popular psychology fantasized hypnosis as unlocking superpowers in the mind, brainwashing portrayed the mind as capable of being reprogrammed and turned against the individual.

The case of Bridey Murphy promised to tip the scales once and for all. The human mind envisioned by Bernstein was powerful and immortal. Episodes of past-life regression were proof of the "unique creative forces which transcend the space-time-mass relations of matter," he enthused. For Bernstein, this unfettered human mind was a weapon against both the dehumanization of Fascism and the de-individualization of Communism. And for postwar Americans eager to see themselves at the center of a universe, nothing could be more attractive.

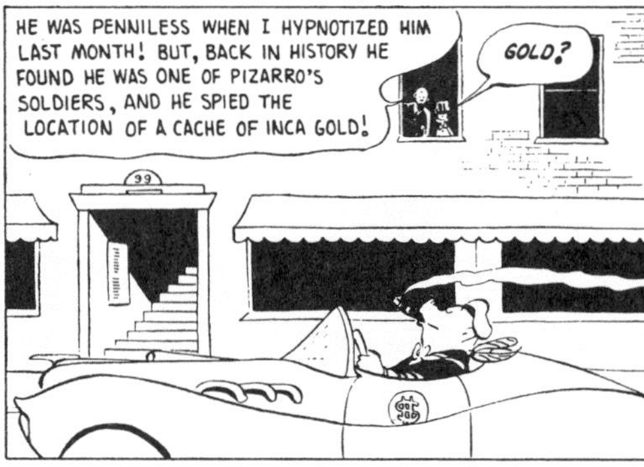

HE WAS PENNILESS WHEN I HYPNOTIZED HIM LAST MONTH! BUT, BACK IN HISTORY HE FOUND HE WAS ONE OF PIZARRO'S SOLDIERS, AND HE SPIED THE LOCATION OF A CACHE OF INCA GOLD!
GOLD?
99

For Barks, hypnosis was another absurd American fad. In "Back to Long Ago!," the hypnotist is unable to pay Scrooge's rent because so many competitors have jumped into the game, and his office is littered with titles — *The Search for Murphy's Bridie*, *Paging Gracie Macy* — that satirize the book that started it all. Perhaps more delightful for Barks was the opportunity to poke fun at the narcissism and materialism that underlies most fads — in this case the fantasy of "inheriting" hidden wealth that a past self had conveniently buried.

However, even as Barks pokes fun at the obsession with past-lives regression, he also embraces it as a narrative device, a powerful engine with which to expand the McDuck genealogy while connecting those ancestors ever more intimately to his modern-day Ducks. Here we are introduced to a new member of the clan: Malcolm "Matey" McDuck, a 16th-century sailor in the service of Queen Elizabeth I. Even Donald gets a past life in the form of Pintail Duck, Matey's companion in arms.

Past-life regression turned out to be a fad that was short-lived. But for the many lives of Barks's Ducks, the fun was just getting started.

— JARED GARDNER

THE COLOSSALEST SURPRISE QUIZ SHOW *p. 117*

There's not a plot to be found in this volume more straightforward than that of "The Colossalest Surprise Quiz Show." And although Barks has streamlined his narrative, this remains far from a facile or simplistic story.

Uncle Scrooge visually commands the stage to an unusual degree. He appears in every panel save for a consecutive trio, and even there he is very much "present," if invisible. During the final third of the tale, Barks refreshes the look of his protagonist by alternating his "live" color embodiment with that of a televised black-and-white image, often in a much-reduced scale.

But as far as changes go, Scrooge's appearance is the least of his alterations. On a majority of pages, Scrooge will undergo at least one major, highly animated, mood swing.

As for those three successive panels in which Scrooge is not seen, Barks pulls off an effect now more readily associated with film: that of "garden pathing" a viewer's focus in order to guide inferences to faulty conclusions. We see Scrooge at the bottom of the first page of the story set his alarm clock for the following day, all of ten minutes before the appointed hour. The next panel, the first without Scrooge, cuts immediately to the following morning, changing location and mood radically. We snake through the assembled throng from far away from the exterior of the TV studio, through the entrance, right up to the program chief's shuttered door — and quickly realize Scrooge's wholly insufficient preparation to arrive at the audition in time.

Oh we of little faith.

Thematically, several significant moral issues arise within the story, especially if read with an inquisitive, interactive youngster. Central, certainly, is the discomfort and inutility in pretending to be dumber than one really is. But there's also the inviolate, sacrosanct nature of a promise — that of Scrooge to attend the quiz show. Adults may tremble at the astonishing progressive-tax burden Scrooge faces while — hopefully — children will remain oblivious to the foolish strategy of skirting unpleasantries through self-destructive practices, regardless of whether they end up landing in a cart full of soft pillows or not.

— RICH KREINER

A COLD BARGAIN *p. 123*

When the auctioneer offers for sale a frozen ball of "the rarest element known to man," bankers and tycoons outbid each other in a frenzy to obtain the coveted bombastium. To Scrooge's amazement, the bids quickly escalate from one, to ten, to a hundred, to a thousand million dollars. Before he even has time to figure out what the mystery material is good for, the bids have already surpassed a hundred billion dollars.

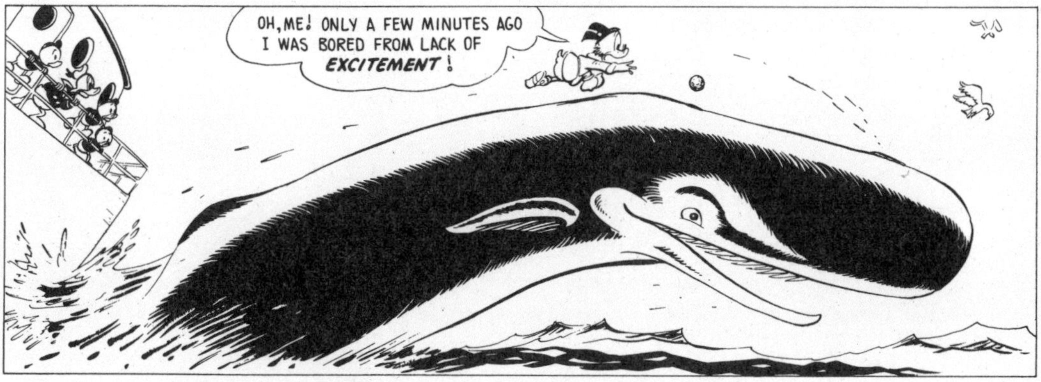
OH, ME! ONLY A FEW MINUTES AGO I WAS BORED FROM LACK OF EXCITEMENT!

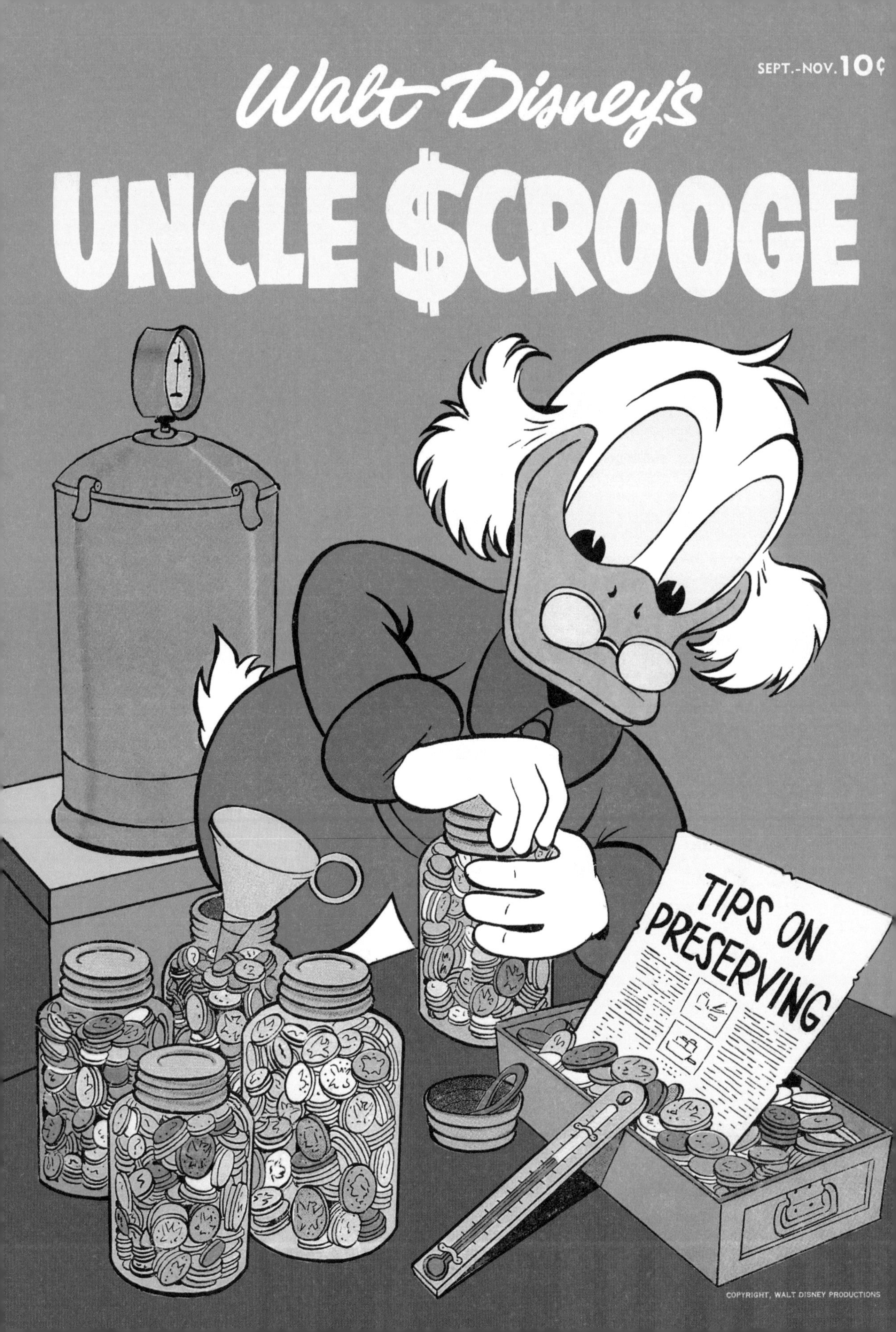
SEPT.-NOV. 10¢
Walt Disney's
UNCLE $CROOGE
TIPS ON PRESERVING
COPYRIGHT, WALT DISNEY PRODUCTIONS

Never to be outdone, Scrooge joins in, bidding a clean trillion. Here is Barks having fun at the expense of his most beloved creature: despite being the world's richest Duck and a seasoned financier, Scrooge is drawn into the bidding frenzy like the most gullible of impulse buyers, and he readily sinks truckloads of money into beating his competitor without even really knowing what he is buying in the first place.

This little gem of a story is 27 pages, but it has the rhythm and the atmosphere of a 10-pager. Despite the opening comment in the first panel of the story, this isn't adventure. It's not Tralla La or Cibola (*Walt Disney's Uncle Scrooge: "Only a Poor Old Man"* and *Walt Disney's Uncle Scrooge: "The Seven Cities of Gold"*): it's scene after scene of pure slapstick comedy. In one of the most memorable gags of the story, the antagonist tops Scrooge's trillion-dollar bid by all of the kitchen sinks of the happy people of Brutopia — only to be outbid again by our hero who, suddenly parsimonious, offers just one more kitchen sink.

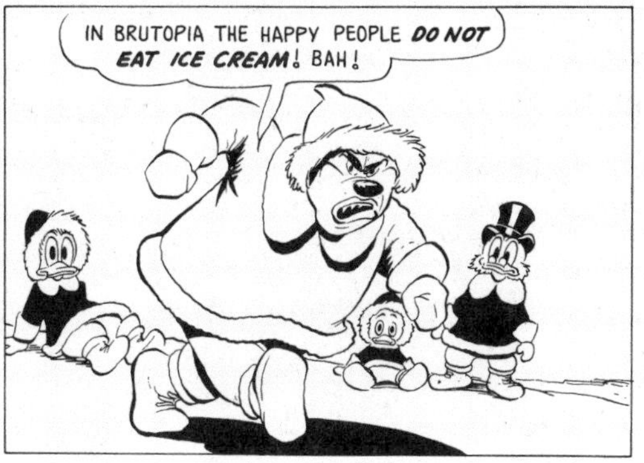
IN BRUTOPIA THE HAPPY PEOPLE DO NOT EAT ICE CREAM! BAH!

The belligerent Brutopia, claiming to be a happy paradise, is clearly the Soviet Union, and the bulky, menacing Brutopian representative with the thick eyebrows is obviously a Cold War–era caricature. (Do bear in mind the historical context. Nowadays, such ethnic stereotyping is inappropriate. In previous reprints of this story, some of Barks's artwork and dialogue was altered for that reason. Here, Fantagraphics has restored it to the way Barks originally wrote and drew it.)

But despite the politically charged meanings that some commentators ascribe to it, this tale is not about the U.S. vs. the U.S.S.R. — it's just some mindless unreal fun, from the exaggerated evaluation of the useless bombastium to the ease with which the frozen ball of wealth could end up being destroyed.

Barks, meanwhile, always enjoys depicting the beauty and innocence of nature: the majestic sperm whales jump and bounce in the water, oblivious to the plight of ducks and men, and a certain penguin is on the lookout for a certain round thing, because (appropriately) it is worth more than all the money in the world ...

— LEONARDO GORI and FRANCESCO STAJANO

LAND OF THE PYGMY INDIANS *p. 153*

Barks's earlier Uncle Scrooge stories provided him new opportunities for examining ideas that mattered to him in more concrete terms than he had been able to with Donald alone. Scrooge, Barks's greatest creation, is a character in perpetual conflict with himself. His desires clash with his principles and stories happen.

"Pygmy Indians" is a particularly rich example, offering in just 27 pages a rollicking American epic, subverting myth and addressing reality. Barks returns to tread terrain that he first explored in the imaginative if somewhat incoherent Donald Duck adventure "Mystery of the Swamp" (*Four Color #62*, January 1945). But this time he invests that story's basic structure with greater symbolic potency while simultaneously improving upon its gags — the wildcat in the canoe and the sharp-billed pikes are but two examples of inspired upgrades.

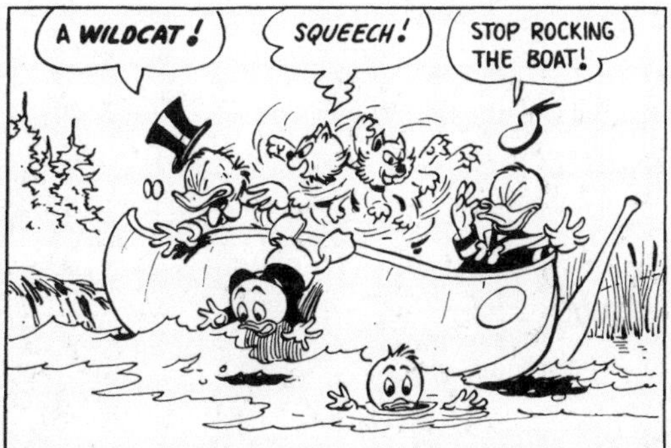
A WILDCAT!
SQUEECH!
STOP ROCKING THE BOAT!

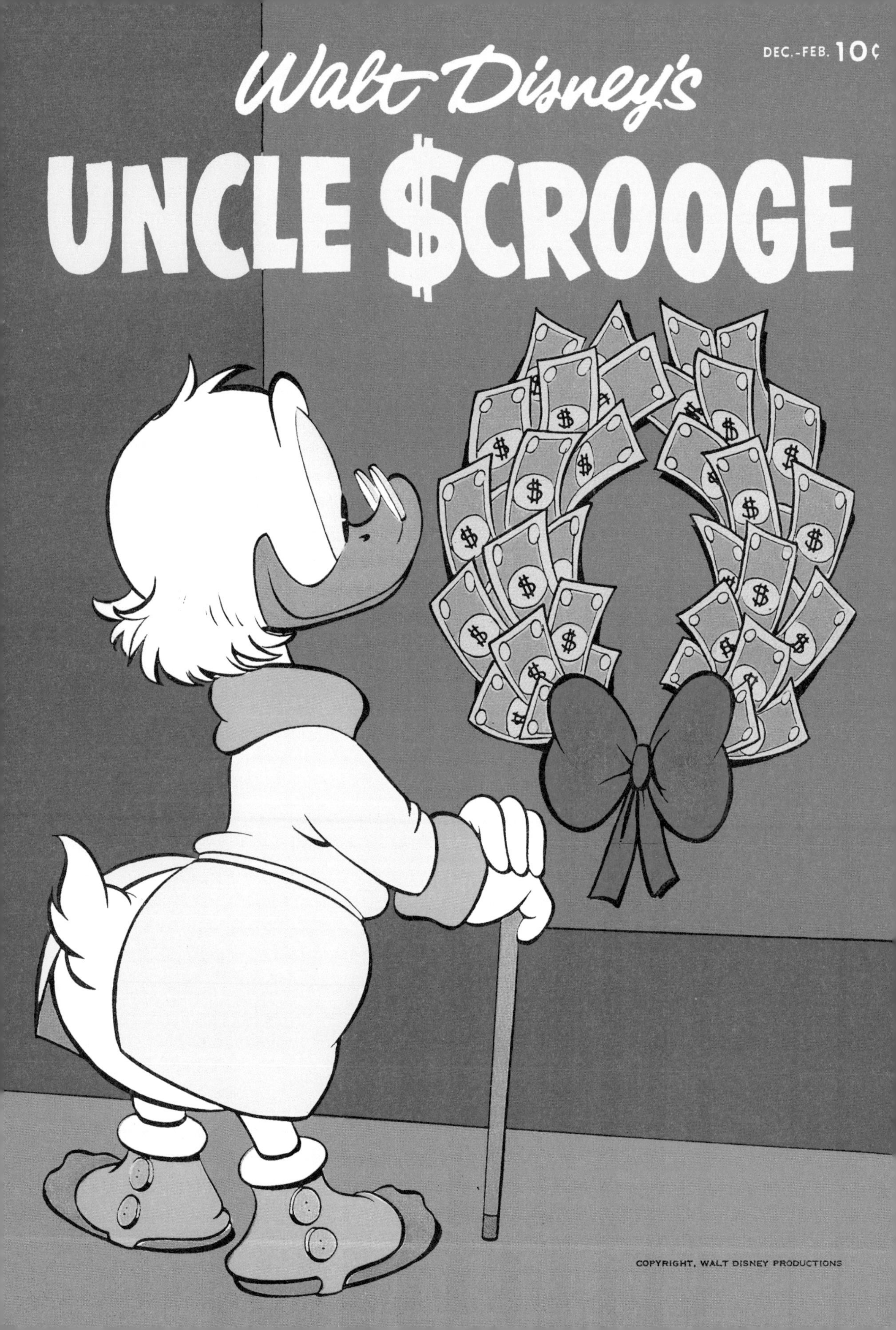
DEC.-FEB. 10¢
Walt Disney's
UNCLE $CROOGE
COPYRIGHT, WALT DISNEY PRODUCTIONS

At the same time, it adds considerable nuance to Barks's earlier, often one-dimensional treatments of American Indians in stories such as "Land of the Totem Poles" (*Walt Disney's Donald Duck: "Trail of the Unicorn"*).

Scrooge, suffocating in the world he made, craves the simple life. Sidewalk Sam, real estate huckster, offers him his very own Walden Pond — or, rather, a thousand of them. Vibrantly rendered by Barks (probably with his wife, the landscape painter Garé Barks, who also lettered the story), this new territory is a bona fide American pastoral, brimming with fat fish and friendly game.

Readers — along with Huey, Dewey, and Louie — of Longfellow's "Song of Hiawatha" will immediately recognize that Lake Superior is Indian country, and the Peeweegahs indeed speak in imitation of his purple trochaic tetrameter (while Scrooge hilariously rolls his eyes). Living as "brother[s] to the deer and the possums" — being able, even, to speak to them — they are the "noble savages" of colonial romanticism.

Scrooge, for his part, is an invader, unable to stay his desire to exploit the precious natural resources of 'his' new property. The Peeweegahs' diminutive size accentuates their vulnerability, while Scrooge's and Donald's blinkered language — "redskins," "savages," "tomahawkers" — emphasizes their chauvinism. Barks, characteristically, is more charitable to the younger generation who were his primary readers, but he was rarely one for facile contrasts, and even the three nephews — who idealize the Peeweegahs — are implicated in what follows.

Hiawatha's greatest conquest, the King Sturgeon, makes a comeback here redolent of Moby-Dick — the panel of his canoe-crushing tail is derived from Rockwell Kent's most famous illustration of the White Whale. It takes the ingenuity of modern science — concentrated oxide of strombolium! — to defeat this destructive natural force, threat to Peeweegah and Duck alike. And while the brave but ultimately inadequate Donald is hailed by the Indians as their savior in white, as per colonialist cliché, they simultaneously exploit their newfound scientific knowledge to get rid of their antagonists by rigging one of their presumably inviolable rituals, the peace pipe.

Thus, ultimately, native and colonizer are united in a humanity that is inevitably at odds with nature, and which stands ready to compromise on principles. A committed environmentalist, Barks's sympathy was with those living most harmoniously with the natural world, but he harbored few illusions about man's inherent destructiveness. His pessimism is starkly written in Scrooge's terrorized face as the story closes with noxious fumes surrounding him.

— MATTHIAS WIVEL

FANTASTIC RIVER RACE *p. 181*

It's a silly story, but the care Carl Barks put into "Fantastic River Race" shows he took his job as a storyteller seriously, and that he truly believed in the rich history he had created for his characters. (But not *too* seriously, since baking custard pies in a riverboat boiler and using whale oil and sulphur for fuel are the oddball quirks of the day.)

As Scrooge races the Beagle Boys up the Mississippi River to pick up a shipment of gold bullion to deliver to New Orleans, we never truly get the sense that McDuck is in actual danger. Yet there's real atmosphere, and it's not just due to the fantastic riverboat scenery.

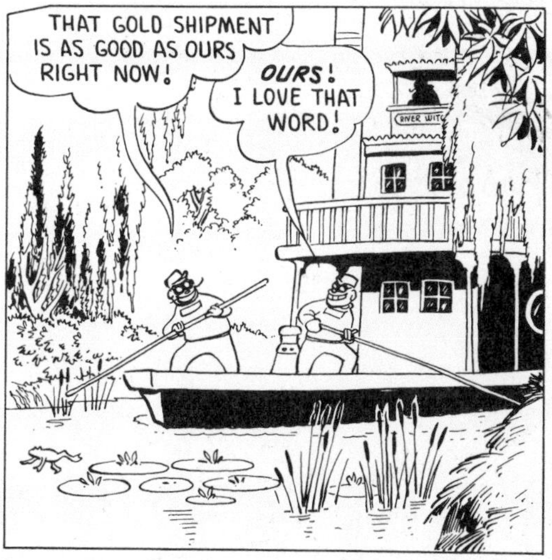
THAT GOLD SHIPMENT IS AS GOOD AS OURS RIGHT NOW!
OURS! I LOVE THAT WORD!

Barks portrays our cast as Mark Twain-period characters with great authenticity, and the time capsule element allows him to have some fun with the continuity he has been working to establish. Turns out the McDuck vs. the Beagle Boys rivalry spans generations,

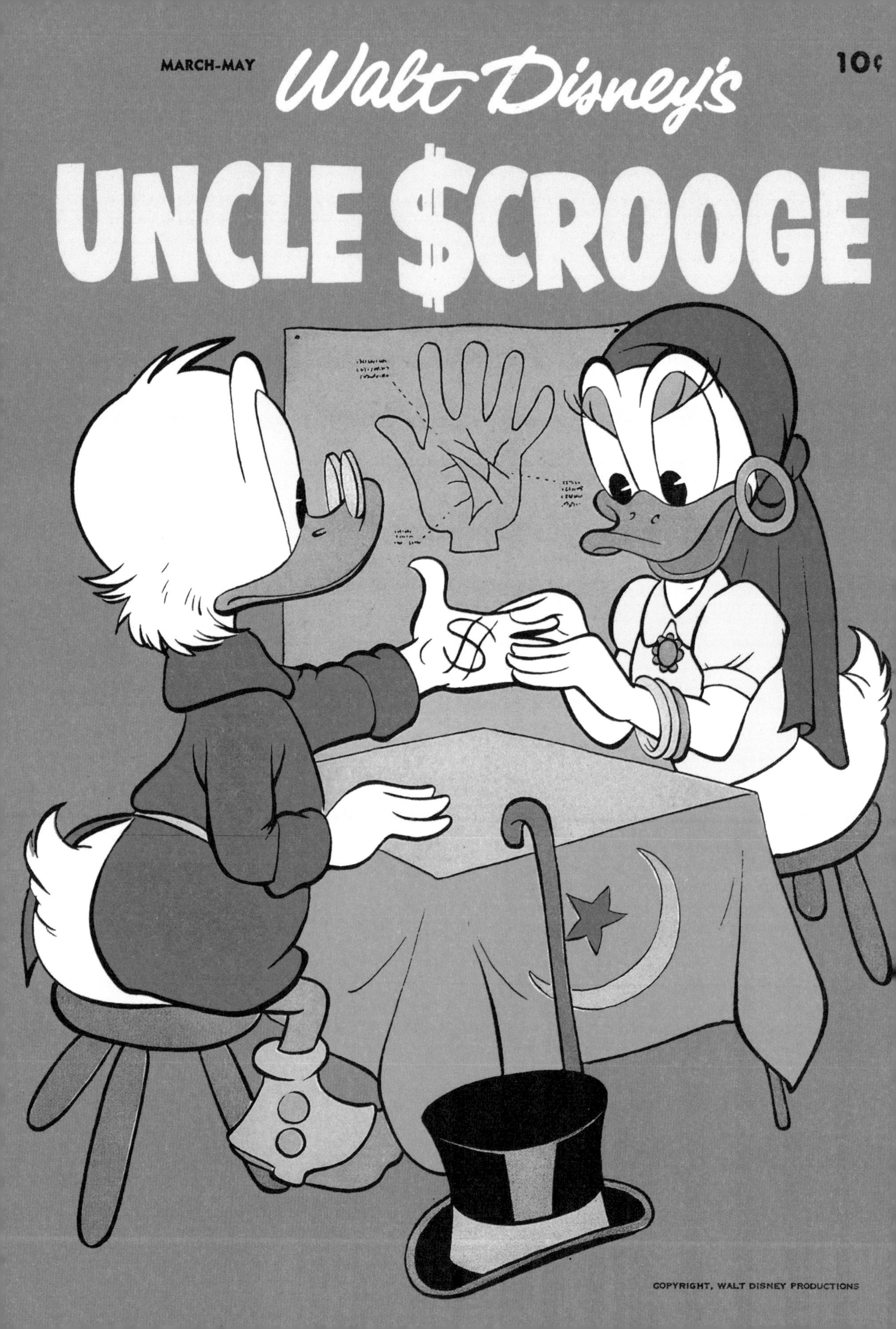
MARCH-MAY
Walt Disney's
10¢
UNCLE $CROOGE
COPYRIGHT, WALT DISNEY PRODUCTIONS

and Gyro inherited his kookier eccentricities from his grandfather, Ratchet Gearloose.

There's some debate over whether Blackheart Beagle is the same character as Grandpa Beagle, who first appeared in Scrooge's present day in "The Money Well" (*Uncle Scrooge* #21, scheduled for the next Uncle Scrooge volume in this series) and was shortly thereafter revived by Italian Disney writers as a crotchety ringleader for the Beagle Boys.

Don Rosa certainly believes they are the same character, as exemplified in his "Life and Times of Scrooge McDuck" stories (*Walt Disney Uncle Scrooge and Donald Duck: "The Last of the Clan McDuck,"* and *Walt Disney Uncle Scrooge and Donald Duck: "The Richest Duck in the World,"* The Don Rosa Library Vols. 4-5), as do other modern Disney writers. Barks never said they *weren't* the same, either, and given that he made "Fantastic River Race" and "The Money Well" the same year, it's unlikely he'd have concocted two wholly different Beagle coots. Even if Blackheart/Grandpa doesn't recognize Scrooge in "The Money Well," well — he's no spring chicken himself, so he might've been a little fuzzy in the wuzzy on that occasion.

— THAD KOMOROWSKI

THE UNCLE SCROOGE ONE-PAGERS

Carl Barks usually worked backwards, according to his wife, Garé, a fine artist in her own right. That is, he'd get an idea for a finale or punch line — the gag — and then figure out what was needed to achieve it. In his longer stories, Barks delighted in introducing numerous twists and turns, plots and subplots, and gags within gags, but in his six-to-eight-panel one-pagers he delivered the goods immediately.

According to Barks's records, the one-pagers in this volume were all written and drawn around the same time as the longer stories. But because of editorial reshufflings, some didn't see print until later. Let's take a look.

Nervous about burglars coming through your window on a dark night but don't want to spend a lot of your money feeding a guard dog? Paint an image of a growling police officer on your bedroom window — and

peacefully catch your zzzz's. That's Scrooge's solution in "The Art of Security" (p. 20).

In "Fashion Forecast" (p. 50), Scrooge visits the Duckburg Weather Bureau to ask the experts if the air that feels, looks, and smells like spring means that spring has finally arrived. Is the snow really gone until the next winter? Assured by the experts, Scrooge returns to his office, opens his petty cash safe, doffs the coonskin cap he's worn all winter, and eagerly takes out his top hat — secure in the knowledge that it's safe from kids throwing snowballs.

Mush begins "Mush! (p. 51) and mush ends "Mush!" Uncle Scrooge, in Alaska, has to mush with his trusty sled dogs through four panels of snow, storm, and aurora borealis before he arrives in Dawson. He takes a seat at a counter in a diner, but darn if the cheapest thing on the menu isn't — mush!

An idyllic day at the beach and Donald chides Uncle Scrooge for panning for gold while people laugh at him. But, eureka! A gold nugget turns up in Scrooge's pan! Who's laughing now? The next panel shows, in silhouette, "mere seconds later," the "Gold Rush" (p. 52) Scrooge's discovery inspires as the crowd runs about with shovels and gold pans. Donald gets snookered too, as he returns wielding shovel and pan. Where did all

Carl Barks's preliminary sketch for the cover shown opposite. Note the switch from the beagle-nosed palm reader to Daisy Duck instead.

this equipment come from? Scrooge stops by his hardware store on his way home where the manager informs him that he's sold all the pans that have been cluttering Scrooge's shelves for 50 years. Scrooge walks off, jauntily tossing and catching the nugget he found in '98 (1898, that is).

We know Barks got many of his stories and gags from books he read. "Fireflies Are Free" (p. 61) begins with Uncle Scrooge reading a book. The action picks up as Scrooge collects glowworms in the second panel, and, in reverse silhouette against the night sky, fireflies in the third. The final panel shows Scrooge triumphant, as usual, reading about rising

electric rates — by the bright (unmetered!) glow of his improvised insect-powered lamp.

In "Early to Build" (p. 62), Scrooge asks the city planning commissioner to recommend a low-cost style for the office building he wants to construct on his vacant lot. The commissioner recommends "Early American," so Scrooge decides to put up the earliest American-style structure he can think of — a tepee!

Scrooge would dearly love to have a bust of himself in his office waiting room, so Donald suggests his uncle visit Buffo, the great chiseler of busts ("Buffo or Bust," p. 83). But when Buffo meets Scrooge — the greatest of all chiselers — Buffo takes offense at the old miser's offer of one dollar to make a bust and tosses Scrooge headfirst into a puddle of thick mud. Unruffled, Scrooge pours a dime's worth of plaster into the impression of his face in the mud and ends up with a perfect bust of himself — made possible by Buffo.

In an about-face, Donald comes out on top in "Pound for Sound" (p. 84). He and

Scrooge figure out a way to sneak in to attend a concert, which Scrooge is "doggoned if [he] will pay five dollars to hear." Donald enjoys the concert from the wings after hiding in the viol case. Scrooge emerges in the final panels, still shaking violently — from his hiding place inside a kettledrum!

"China Shop Shakeup" (p. 92) is a soundless seven-panel pantomime. Pondering the sale price of a fine china cup from which to sip his afternoon tea, Uncle Scrooge accidentally drops and breaks the cup. The irate store manager hands Scrooge a bill for five bucks, in keeping with the sign proclaiming, "If you break it, you've bought it!" Scrooge, irate at the price he has to pay, slams his fist onto the display table, sending the remainder of the porcelain flying. In the final panel, the well-chastened Mr. McDuck is seen lugging a basket of shattered fine china shards out of the store. Perhaps he will glue them back together and peddle them to nephew Donald as antique seconds.

In "Fertile Assets" (p. 114), Scrooge's garden plants have been watered and fertilized but still look puny. The county plant expert tells him that he needs to supplement the soil with minerals. What kind of minerals? Scrooge wonders. Iron? Zinc? Aluminum? Brass? Tin? A week later he calls the expert to come look at his garden again. Amazed at the improvement, the expert asks, "What kind of minerals did you use?" "Old stuff I had in stock," replies McDuck, tossing in another shovelful of "gold droopees," "copper ha'pennies," and "silver dollars."

It's that chilly time of year, and Scrooge is running his heater on the least amount of oil possible, outraged at fuel costs — even though oil wells are everywhere in Duckburg. Suddenly realizing that "everywhere" includes his own backyard, he cobbles together a miniature oil derrick from Erector Set parts, powers it with a tiny motorized drill, and *Ka-Bing!* The old Duck soon has a "Backyard Bonanza" (p. 115) pumping out enough oil to keep his barrel filled. He can now luxuriate by the stove without concern for the rising price of fuel. (This was an era when comic book cartooning didn't generate much in the way of income, so we can easily imagine Barks imagining how Scrooge would handle the matter. Too bad Barks didn't live in Duckburg.)

In "The Eyes Have It" (p. 116), the rocky peak three miles away has tourists bragging about how good their eyesight is. One can see rock climbers, another can see a lunch box, a third can see a pop bottle. Peering over his pince-nez glasses, sharp-eyed Uncle Scrooge sees something but isn't telling the others what it is. He races across the valley and climbs the hill, only to discover that his eyesight must be failing him. From where he'd spied it, he'd thought that dime he's just picked was a quarter!

Barks didn't often add a title to his one-pagers, but for "Tree Trick" (p. 150) and "The Secret Book" (below), he did. Once again, the Beagle Boys are on the prowl, waiting for an unguarded moment from Uncle Scrooge to give them an opportunity to steal some of his money. Once again, Uncle Scrooge outsmarts them with a fake tree. In the final panel, we see that the bag of potting soil is really a bag of coins. No wonder Uncle Scrooge holds on to his money.

In "The Secret Book" (p. 151), Uncle Scrooge gets hoodwinked by a sidewalk shyster selling a book, *How To Make Money*. When the book's advice turns out to be "Get a job in the mint," Uncle Scrooge decides to get even and creates his own book, "The Secret of My Billions." The book hustler, unaware of who he's dealing with, gets taken in turn when it turns out that Scrooge's book has only blank pages. Uncle Scrooge, delighted in his trick, struts off, twirling his cane and explaining, "If I told you anything it wouldn't be a secret."

In "Relative Reaction" (p. 152), Scrooge is enjoying his money, juggling bags of coins and piling them on his head. Oh, the delight! But Miss Twidley interrupts, announcing over the intercom that a relative who wants to borrow money is here to see him. Quickly, Scrooge hides his hoard and changes clothes behind a folding screen. Telling Miss Twidley to "Send him in!" Uncle Scrooge appears in the last panel as only a poor old man in tattered clothes. Hey, is that little mouse peering out of the loaf of bread an ode to Mickey?

Scrooge dawdles in the window of his building, in spite of the smoke billowing out. "Will it hold 100 pounds?" "Certainly!" Will it hold 400 pounds?" "Yes!" the firemen assure him. It takes seven panels before he finally ascertains the "Net Worth" (p. 180) of the firemen's safety net and takes his leap. Finally, down he comes clutching a sack of money and altogether weighing — you guessed it — 400 pounds.

Donald wants to sell his uncle a comfortable hat, but Scrooge declares there's no more comfortable topper than the "All-Season Hat" (p. 201) he already owns — beneath which he balances a thermos of hot coffee on his head in winter and a thermos of ice water in summer. Donald does a slow burn. The sign on the counter, "Dubs Hats," indicates a brand or style of fitted hat.

Despite its Donald Duck logo, this story, according to Barks's records, was originally an Uncle Scrooge one-pager. It was pared down to a half-page and published in an issue of *Donald Duck*.

"Happy New Year" (p. 202), Uncle Scrooge proclaims from the uncurled tape of his adding machine. When originally published, this cheerful greeting was marred by one of those unsightly Dell pledge boxes, which obscured Scrooge's left foot. The original art is long gone, so for this book, Scrooge's left foot has been restored from Barks's own drawing of the right foot and by duplicating a few coins as well. Barks purists, take note: this restoration is pure Barks, and is as close as anyone is ever likely to get to its original state.

Barks gives us a treat in every one of his gags. Not just with the main gag, but with the richness of his backgrounds and the little jokes he throws in, just waiting to be discovered by alert readers.

— JOSEPH ROBERT COWLES

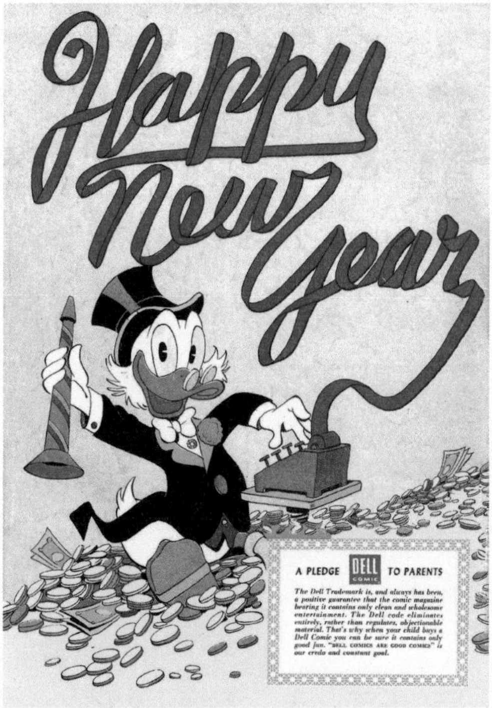
Happy New Year
A PLEDGE DELL COMIC TO PARENTS
The Dell Trademark is, and always has been, a positive guarantee that the comic magazine bearing it contains only clean and wholesome entertainment. The Dell code eliminates entirely, rather than regulates, objectionable material. That's why when your child buys a Dell Comic you can be sure it contains only good fun. "DELL COMICS ARE GOOD COMICS" is our credo and constant goal.

JUNE-AUG.

Walt Disney's

10¢

UNCLE $CROOGE

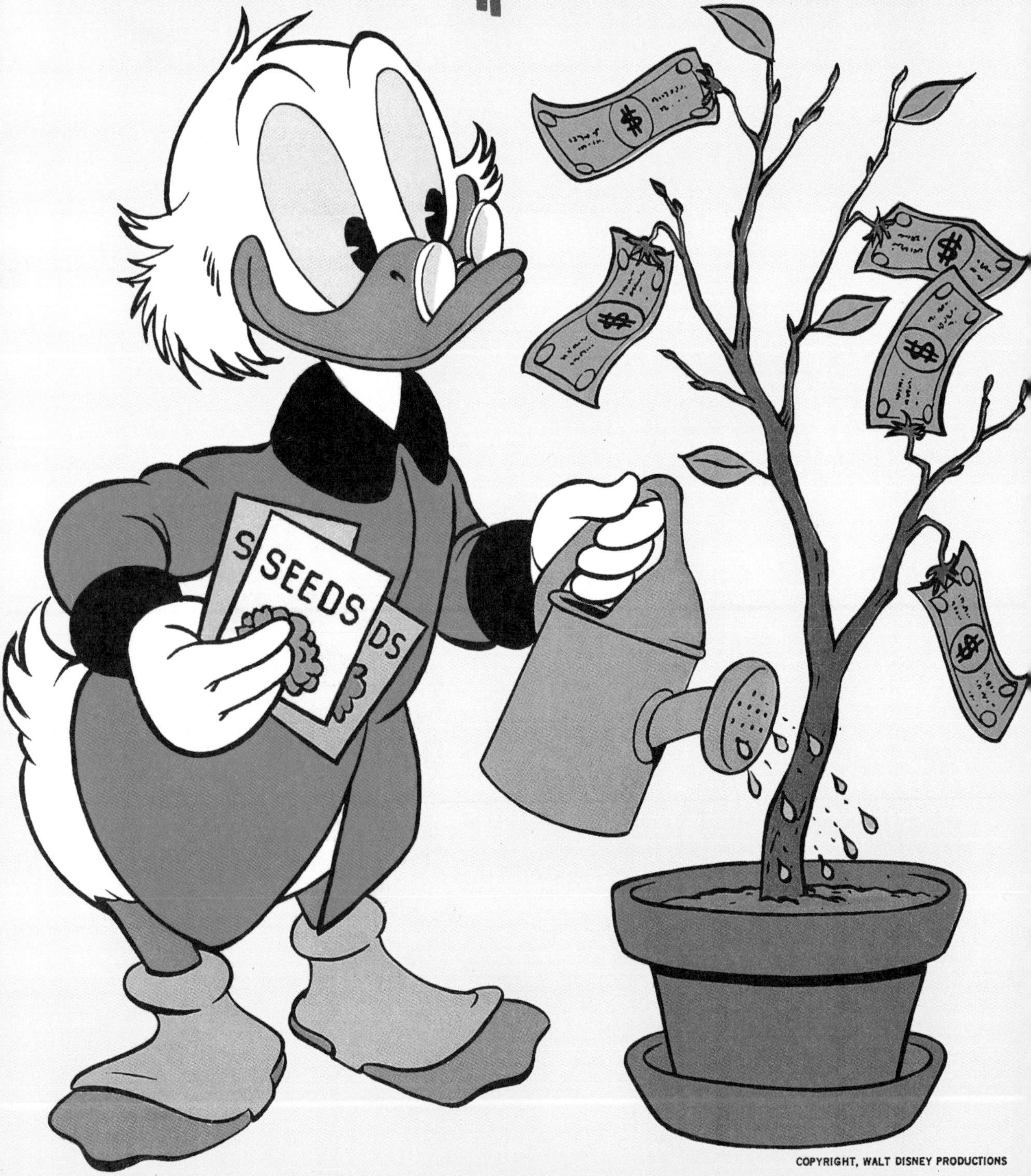
SEEDS

Back to What Should Have Been

There's a new surprise in this volume for Barks fans familiar with earlier printings of "Back to Long Ago." Film writer Pedro Peirano Olate recalled reading the story as a child in his native Chile, and, when he read it again years later in English, he realized that a sight gag (literally, in this case, a gag involving sight) was missing. Señor Olate was kind enough to share a scan of the story from the beat-up coverless comic book he had saved all these years, and from that we were able to restore the panel to the way Carl Barks intended it to be seen. (This story was first published in Chile in 1965, although it appeared in most European countries several years prior to that.)

TE PARECES A UN MARINERO QUE CONOCÍ... ¿CÓMO TE VERÍAS CON UN PARCHE EN EL OJO?
TENGO UNA EXTRAÑA SENSACIÓN RESPECTO A TI, TÍO RICO.

Not only were the dotted sight lines removed from the panel, but so were poor Donald's nostrils, along with a few lines in the brickwork in the background. While the U.S. version of the story was missing those details, the South American version was not, and so, with this edition, we present them for the first time to North American readers.

A much bigger job of recovery was done some years ago, when rescued pages of "Land Beneath the Ground," missing from its original publication, were restored. We have used that expanded version of the story here. Not all of the missing pages from this story have been found, and consequently there is a two-panel sequence that can't be fit back in without disrupting the present version's page flow. The two panels, which would fall between the second and third rows on page 43, are shown below. They're not essential to the flow of the story, so you can see why, when Barks was told he had to shorten things, he omitted them.

Another change in the restoration of "Land Beneath the Ground" was the addition of a new caption to bridge some material that remains missing. Compare the version of the

MORE SPEED! IT'S GROWING PITCH DARK UP HERE! WE CAN'T BE FAR FROM THE SHAFT!
PUSH, YOU FERMIES! RAH! RAH! RAH!
ROLL, YOU TERRIES! CHA! CHA! CHA!

panel shown below with the same panel on page 24.

Also, when Barks chose to cut the mine car roller coaster sequence (p. 29), he substituted it with a single panel showing Donald and Scrooge emerging from an underground lake. It only appeared in the truncated version of the story, following immediately after panel 1 on page 29, which then flows into the sequence that begins on page 30, panel 3. That "continuity patch" panel is shown at right.

In all, Barks had to remove five pages of his original version of "Land Beneath the Ground." That allowed the addition of other material to the issue, which then qualified it for a lower mailing cost to subscribers. This restoration brings the page count of "Land Beneath the Ground" up from the truncated 27-page version to a more satisfying 29 pages, but still shy of the full 32 that Barks originally drew. Hope remains that some day the missing pages will re-emerge. In the meantime, we can still enjoy this ripping good yarn in its present form.

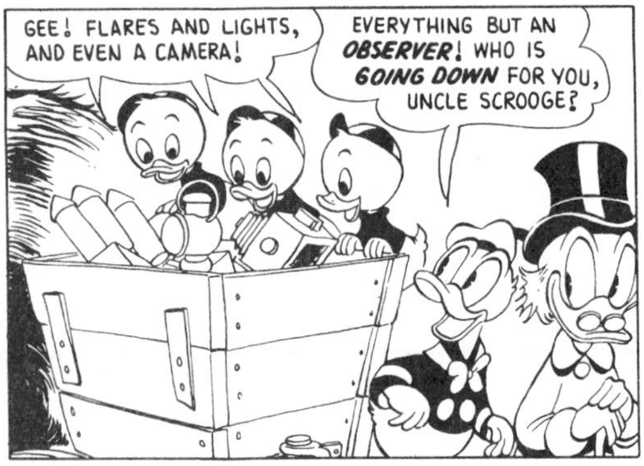
GEE! FLARES AND LIGHTS, AND EVEN A CAMERA!
EVERYTHING BUT AN OBSERVER! WHO IS GOING DOWN FOR YOU, UNCLE SCROOGE?

For "A Cold Bargain," we have gone back to Barks's depictions of the Brutopians as originally published. In earlier reprints of this story, Barks's work was "cleaned up" to lessen the ethnic stereotyping, and some words were changed. But we felt an obligation to present Barks's work as he originally intended, warts and all, with the understanding that attitudes have changed since the Cold War standoff between the U.S. and the U.S.S.R., and this remains a story from that time.

Quite a few of the stories in this volume were produced during a period when Dell Comics — which declined to join the Comics

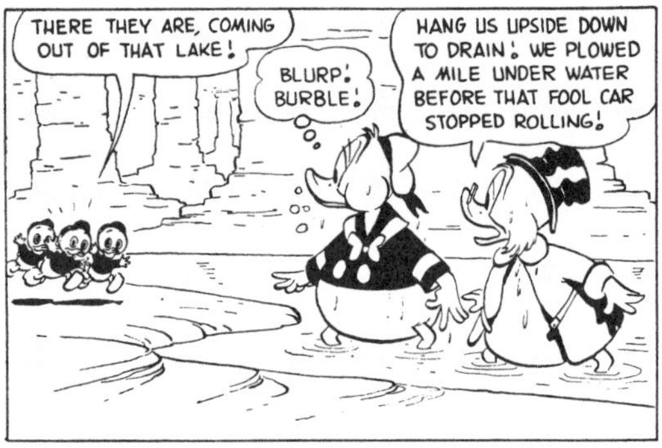
THERE THEY ARE, COMING OUT OF THAT LAKE!
BLURP! BURBLE!
HANG US UPSIDE DOWN TO DRAIN! WE PLOWED A MILE UNDER WATER BEFORE THAT FOOL CAR STOPPED ROLLING!

Code Authority — was keen on reinforcing the idea in the public mind that their comics were "clean and wholesome." The main way they did this was by clumsily inserting a "Dell Comic Pledge to Parents" into their stories. Literally — one or two panels would routinely be stripped out of a story to shoehorn in the publisher's promise. For the one-page gags, it was usually just one panel.

In some cases, the artists were informed in advance and instructed to allow room for the intrusion, but in other cases the decision of what to cut was made by the editors after the story had been submitted. You will see evidence of the Dell pledge scattered throughout this volume, where we have elected to excise those blocks of ugly text.

— J. MICHAEL CATRON

Carl Barks

LIFE AMONG THE DUCKS

by DONALD AULT

ABOVE: *Carl Barks at the 1982 San Diego Comic-Con. Photo by Alan Light.*

"I was a real misfit," Carl Barks said, thinking back over an early life of hard labor — as a farmer, a logger, a mule-skinner, a rivet heater, and a printing press feeder — before he was hired as a full-time cartoonist for an obscure risqué magazine in 1931.

Barks was born in 1901 and (mostly) raised in Merrill, Oregon. He had always wanted to be a cartoonist, but everything that happened to him in his early years seemed to stand in his way. He suffered a significant hearing loss after a bout with the measles. His mother died. He had to leave school after the eighth grade. His

father suffered a mental breakdown. His older brother was whisked off to World War I.

His first marriage, in 1921, was to a woman who was unsympathetic to his dreams and who ultimately bore two children "by accident," as Barks phrased it. The two divorced in 1930.

In 1931, he pulled up stakes from Merrill and headed to Minnesota, leaving his mother-in-law, whom he trusted more than his wife, in charge of his children.

Arriving in Minneapolis, he went to work for the *Calgary Eye-Opener*, that risqué magazine. He thought he would finally be drawing cartoons full time, but the editor and most of the staff were alcoholics, so Barks ended up running the whole show.

In 1935 he took "a great gamble" and, on the strength of some cartoons he'd submitted in response to an advertisement from the Disney Studio, he moved to California and entered an animation trial period. He was soon promoted to "story man" in Disney's Donald Duck animation unit, where he made significant contributions to 36 Donald cartoon shorts between 1936 and 1942, including helping to create Huey, Dewey, and Louie for "Donald's Nephews" in 1938. Ultimately, though, he grew dissatisfied. The production of animated cartoons "by committee," as he described it, stifled his imagination.

For that and other reasons, in 1942 he left Disney to run a chicken farm. But when he was offered a chance by Western Publishing to write and illustrate a new series of Donald Duck comic book stories, he jumped at it. The comic book format suited him, and the quality of his work persuaded the editors to grant him a freedom and autonomy he'd never known and that few others were ever granted. He would go on to write and draw more than 6,000 pages in over 500 stories and uncounted hundreds of covers between 1942 and 1966 for Western's Dell and Gold Key imprints.

Barks had almost no formal art training. He had taught himself how to draw by imitating his early favorite artists — Winsor McCay (*Little Nemo*), Frederick Opper (*Happy Hooligan*), Elzie Segar (*Popeye*), and Floyd Gottfredson (*Mickey Mouse*).

He taught himself how to write well by going back to the grammar books he had shunned in school, making up jingles and rhymes, and inventing other linguistic exercises to get a natural feel for the rhythm and dialogue of sequential narrative.

Barks married again in 1938, but that union ended disastrously in divorce in 1951. In 1954, Barks married Margaret Wynnfred Williams, known as Garé, who soon began assisting him by lettering and inking backgrounds on his comic book work. They remained happily together until her death in 1993.

He did his work in the California desert and often mailed his stories into the office. He worked his stories over and over "backward and forward." Barks was not a vain man but he had confidence in his talent. He knew what hard work was, and he knew that he'd put his best efforts into every story he produced.

On those occasions when he did go into Western's offices he would "just dare anybody to see if they could improve on it." His confidence was justified. His work was largely responsible for some of the best-selling comic books in the world — *Walt Disney's Comics and Stories* and *Uncle Scrooge*.

Because Western's policy was to keep their writers and artists anonymous, readers never knew the name of the "good duck artist" — but they could spot the superiority of his work. When fans determined to solve the mystery of his anonymity finally tracked him down (not unlike an adventure Huey, Dewey, and Louie might embark upon), Barks was quite happy to correspond and otherwise communicate with his legion of aficionados.

Given all the obstacles of his early years and the dark days that haunted him off and on for the rest of his life, it's remarkable that he laughed so easily and loved to make others laugh.

In the process of expanding Donald Duck's character far beyond the hot-tempered Donald of animation, Barks created a moveable locale (Duckburg) and a cast of dynamic characters: Scrooge McDuck, the Beagle Boys, Gladstone Gander, Gyro Gearloose, the Junior Woodchucks. And there were hundreds of others who made only one memorable appearance in the engaging, imaginative, and unpredictable comedy-adventures that he wrote and drew from scratch for nearly a quarter of a century.

Among many other honors, Carl Barks was one of the three initial inductees into the Will Eisner Comic Book Hall of Fame for comic book creators in 1987. (The other two were Jack Kirby and Will Eisner.) In 1991, Barks became the only Disney comic book artist to be recognized as a "Disney Legend," a special award created by Disney "to acknowledge and honor the many individuals whose imagination, talents, and dreams have created the Disney magic."

As Roy Disney said on Barks's passing in 2000 at age 99, "He challenged our imaginations and took us on some of the greatest adventures we have ever known. His prolific comic book creations entertained many generations of devoted fans and influenced countless artists over the years.... His timeless tales will stand as a legacy to his originality and brilliant artistic vision."

Contributors

Donald Ault is Professor of English at the University of Florida, founder and editor of *ImageTexT: Interdisciplinary Comics Studies*, editor of *Carl Barks: Conversations*, and executive producer of the video *The Duck Man: An Interview with Carl Barks*.

Alberto Becattini has taught high school English since 1983. Since 1978, he has written essays for Italian and U.S. publications about comics, specializing in Disney characters and American comics generally. Since 1992 he has been a freelance writer and consultant for The Walt Disney Company-Italy.

Joseph Robert Cowles writes for the quarterly newsletter of the Carl Barks Fan Club, contributed materials and commentary to Egmont's *Carl Barks Collection*, and is the author of *Recalling Carl*, a pictorial dissertation contending that Disney should be making feature films of Barks's stories. His Carl Barks website is TheGoodArtist.com.

R. Fiore, he explains, makes his way in life working Square John jobs, when they let him, not far from Historic Duckburg. This marginal existence has even from time to time led onto the grounds of the Walt Disney Company, which is an interesting place. In his spare time he's been writing about comic strips and animation longer than you've been alive, my child.

Craig Fischer is Associate Professor of English at Appalachian State University. His Monsters Eat Critics column, about comics' multifarious genres, runs at *The Comics Journal* website (tcj.com).

Jared Gardner studies and teaches comics at the Ohio State University. He is the author of three books and is a contributing writer to *The Comics Journal*.

Leonardo Gori is a comics scholar and collector, especially of syndicated newspaper strips of the '30s and Italian Disney authors. He wrote, with Frank Stajano and others, many books on Italian "fumetti" and American comics in Italy.

Thad Komorowski is an animation historian with a longstanding professional relationship with Disney comics. He is a regular contributor to Fantagraphics's Carl Barks and Floyd Gottfredson archival collections.

Rich Kreiner is a longtime writer for *The Comics Journal* and a longertime reader of Carl Barks. He lives with wife and cat in Maine.

Stefano Priarone writes about popular culture in many Italian newspapers and magazines.

Francesco ("Frank") Stajano has written on Disney comics, particularly with Leonardo Gori, and had the privilege of visiting Carl Barks at his home in Oregon in 1998. In real life he is an associate professor at the University of Cambridge in England.

Matthias Wivel is Curator of Sixteenth-Century Italian Painting at the National Gallery, London. He has written widely about comics for a decade and a half.

Daniel F. Yezbick teaches comics, film studies, and writing at Forest Park College. His essays on Barks and Disney comics have appeared in a variety of anthologies. He is the author of *Perfect Nonsense: The Chaotic Comics and Goofy Games of George Carlson* from Fantagraphics.

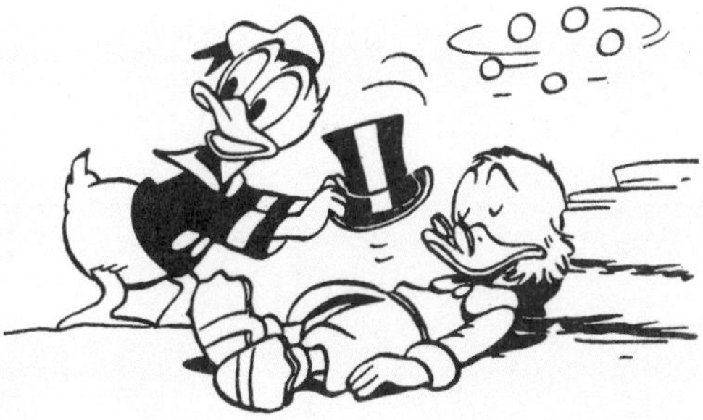

Where did these Duck stories first appear?

The Complete Carl Barks Disney Library collects Donald Duck and Uncle Scrooge stories by Carl Barks that were originally published in the traditional American four-color comic book format. Barks's first Duck story appeared in October 1942. The volumes in this project are numbered chronologically but are being released in a different order. This is volume 16.

Stories within a volume may or may not follow the publication sequence of the original comic books. We may take the liberty of rearranging the sequence of the stories within a volume for editorial or presentation purposes.

The original comic books were published under the Dell logo and some appeared in the so-called **Four Color** series — a name that appeared nowhere inside the comic book itself, but is generally agreed upon by historians to refer to the series of "one-shot"

comic books published by Dell that have sequential numbering. The **Four Color** issues are also sometimes referred to as "One Shots."

Some of the stories in this volume were originally published without a title. Some stories were retroactively assigned a title when they were reprinted in later years. Some stories were given titles by Barks in correspondence or interviews. (Sometimes Barks referred to the same story with different titles.) Some stories were never given an official title but have been informally assigned one by fans and indexers. For the untitled stories in this volume, we have used the title that seems most appropriate. The unofficial titles appear below with an asterisk enclosed in parentheses (*).

The following is the order in which the stories in this volume were originally published.

Uncle Scrooge #13
(March–May 1956)
>   Cover
>   The Art of Security (*)
>   Land Beneath the Ground!
>   Fashion Forecast (*)
>   Mush! (*)

Uncle Scrooge #14
(June–August 1956)
>   Cover
>   The Lost Crown of
>   Genghis Khan!
>   Faulty Fortune (*)
>   Gold Rush (*)
>   Fireflies Are Free (*)

Uncle Scrooge #15
(September–November 1956)
>   Cover
>   Buffo or Bust (*)
>   The Second-Richest Duck
>   Migrating Millions (*)
>   Pound for Sound (*)

Uncle Scrooge #16
(December 1956–February 1957)
>   Cover
>   Fertile Assets (*)
>   Back to Long Ago!
>   The Colossalest Surprise
>   Quiz Show (*)
>   Backyard Bonanza (*)
>   Happy New Year

Donald Duck #51
(January–February 1957)
>   All-Season Hat (*)

Uncle Scrooge #17
(March–May 1957)
>   Cover
>   Early to Build (*)
>   A Cold Bargain
>   The Eyes Have It (*)
>   China Shop Shakeup (*)

Uncle Scrooge #18
(June–August 1957)
>   Cover
>   Net Worth (*)
>   Land of the Pygmy Indians
>   Relative Reaction (*)

Uncle Scrooge Goes To Disneyland #1 (August 1957)
>   Fantastic River Race (*)

Uncle Scrooge #31
(September–November 1960)
>   The Secret Book

Uncle Scrooge #33
(March–May 1961)
>   Tree Trick